Washington's War on Nicaragua

Holly Sklar

South End Press   **Boston, MA**

10 9 8 7 6 5 4 3 2

Typesetting, design and layout by the South End Press collective
Cover by Lydia Sargent
Manufactured in the USA

Library of Congress Cataloging-in-Publication Data

Sklar, Holly, 1955-
Washington's War on Nicaragua, Holly Sklar.
p.   cm.
Bibliography: p.
Includes index.
ISBN 0-89608-296-2 : $40.00. ISBN 0-89608-295-4 (pbk.) : $15.00
1. United States--Foreign relations--Nicaragua. 2. Nicaragua--Foreign relations
--United States. 3. Nicaragua--Politics and government--1979- 4. United States
--Foreign relations--1977-1981. 5. United States--Foreign relations--1981-
I. Title.
E183.8.N5S55 1988
327.7307285--dc19   88-10160 CIP

South End Press, 116 St. Botolph St., Boston, MA 02115

Contents

Acknowledgements

My special thanks to Fernando Menendez for translating and transcribing numerous taped interviews; Ros Everdell, William LeoGrande, Betsy Cohn, Louis Wolf and Chip Berlet for critiquing the manuscript; David Brooks for research and interviews in Mexico; Amanda Lorio and Stephen Grun for their hospitality and insight; Lydia Sargent for the cover; and Todd Jailer and South End Press for their patience as I reworked the book to cover major new developments and their production speed once the manuscript was completed. Thanks also to Judy Appelbaum; Deborah Barry, Coordinadora Regional de Investigaciones Economicas y Sociales, Managua; Central American Historical Institute, Washington, DC; Data Center, Oakland; Susan Dorfman; Xabier Gorostiaga, Instituto Nacional de Investigaciones Economicas y Sociales, Managua; Luz Guerra, Central America Resource Center, Austin; Laura Henze; Instituto Historico Centroamericano, Managua; Peter Kornbluh, National Security Archive, Washington, DC; MADRE, New York; Maya Miller; North American Congress on Latin America, New York; Cory Paulsen; Michael Prokosch; Dan Siegel, Christic Institute, Washington, DC; and all those who agreed to be interviewed for this book.

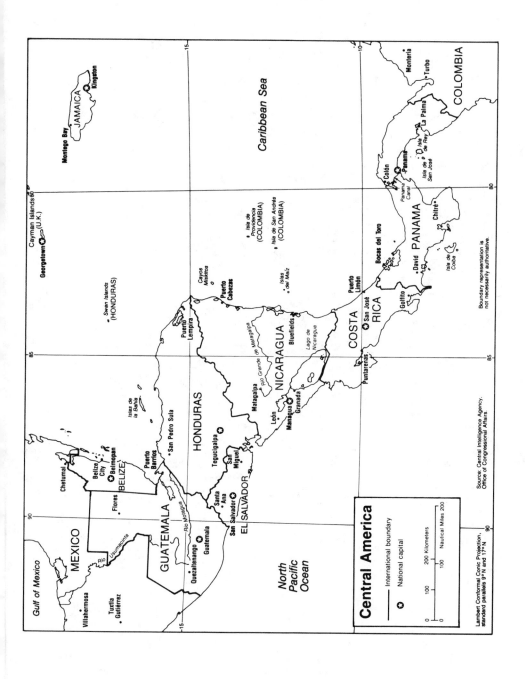

Central America

- — International boundary
- ⊛ National capital

| 0 | 100 | 200 Kilometers |
| 0 | 100 | Nautical Miles 200 |

Lambert Conformal Conic Projection,
standard parallels 9°N and 17°N

Source: Central Intelligence Agency,
Office of Congressional Affairs.

Boundary representation is
not necessarily authoritative.

MEXICO

Gulf of Mexico

Villahermosa

Tuxtla
Gutiérrez

Chetumal

Rio Usumacinta

Rio Motagua

Flores

GUATEMALA

Quezaltenango

Guatemala ⊛

Santa
Ana

San Salvador ⊛

EL SALVADOR

San
Miguel

Belize
City

BELIZE

Belmopan ⊛

Puerto
Barrios

San Pedro Sula

Islas de
la Bahía

HONDURAS

Tegucigalpa ⊛

Puerto
Lempira

Swan Islands
(HONDURAS)

Matagalpa

Rio Grande de Matagalpa

León

Managua ⊛

Granada

NICARAGUA

Lago de
Nicaragua

Bluefields

Puerto
Cabezas

Cayos
Miskitos

Islas
del Maíz

Isla de
Providencia
(COLOMBIA)

Isla de San Andrés
(COLOMBIA)

North
Pacific
Ocean

Puntarenas

San José ⊛

**COSTA
RICA**

Puerto
Limón

Golfito

Bocas del Toro

David

Isla de
Coiba

Chitré

PANAMA

Panama
Canal

Colón

Panamá ⊛

Isla de
San José

Isla del
Rey

La Palma

Montería

Turbo

COLOMBIA

Caribbean Sea

Cayman Islands
(U.K.)

Georgetown ⊛

Montego Bay

JAMAICA

Kingston

15

10

90

85

80

15

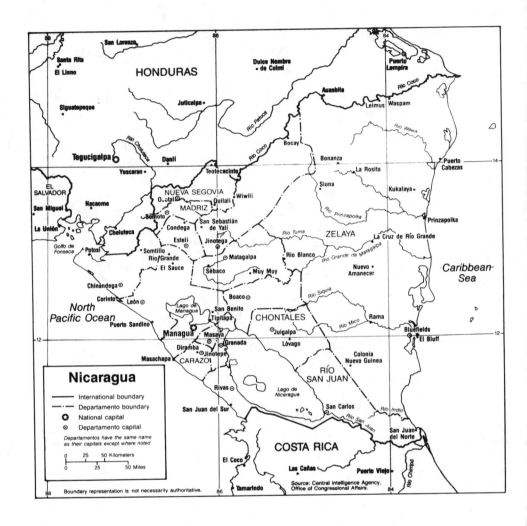

Nicaragua

———	International boundary
—·—·—	Departamento boundary
⊙	National capital
⊙	Departamento capital

Departamentos have the same name as their capitals except where noted

0	25	50 Kilometers
0	25	50 Miles

Boundary representation is not necessarily authoritative.

Source: Central Intelligence Agency, Office of Congressional Affairs.

Introduction

By their very nature, covert activities, or special activities, are a lie. There's great deceit—deception—practiced in the conduct of covert operations. They are at essence a lie.

Oliver North, Iran-Contra Hearings, July 7, 1987.

General Smedley Butler led American marines into Nicaragua eight years before the Russian revolution of 1917. He died before Oliver North was born.

Butler is a Marine Corps legend. He earned an extraordinary two Congressional Medals of Honor, the nation's highest military award for bravery. As a civilian, Butler was also a legend. He exposed a fascist conspiracy to stage a coup against Franklin D. Roosevelt and criticized the congressional committee that investigated the plot: "Like most committees, it has slaughtered the little and allowed the big to escape."[1] Butler unmasked the "war-mongers, dollar-patriots, war profiteers and military chiselers." He warned of "the evils of provocative militarism" and called for restructuring U.S. armed forces to serve a truly defensive mission. "As a soldier," said Butler, "I long suspected that war was a racket; not until I retired to civil life did I fully realize it."[2]

Reflecting on the notion of war as a racket, Butler wrote in 1935: "It may seem odd for me, a military man, to adopt such a comparison. Truthfulness compels me to. I spent 33 years and 4 months in active service as a member of our country's most agile military force—the Marine Corps...And during that period I spent most of my time being a high-class muscle man for Big Business, for Wall Street and for the bankers. In short, I was a racketeer for capitalism...

"Thus I helped make Mexico...safe for American oil interests in 1914. I helped make Haiti and Cuba a decent place for the National City Bank boys to collect revenues in. I helped in the raping of half a dozen Central American republics for

1

the benefit of Wall Street. The record of racketeering is long. I helped purify Nicaragua for the international banking house of Brown Brothers in 1909-12. I brought light to the Dominican Republic for American sugar interests in 1916. I helped make Honduras 'right' for American fruit companies in 1903. In China in 1927 I helped see to it that Standard Oil went its way unmolested.

"During those years, I had, as the boys in the back room would say, a swell racket. I was rewarded with honors, medals, promotion. Looking back on it, I feel I might have given Al Capone a few hints. The best *he* could do was to operate his racket in three city districts. We Marines operated on three *continents.*"[3]

Such candor would be enlightening today. The blunt truth is that blaming Nicaragua for provoking U.S. intervention is like blaming women for rape: They flaunt their independence. They hang out too much on the wrong block. They practice promiscuous nonaligned relations. They say no to the contras, but they mean yes. Somehow, Nicaragua has asked for it. What passes for debate in Washington is largely an argument over how much Nicaragua has asked for it, and what's the best way to give it to them. In Washington's war on Nicaragua, lies are as necessary as guns.

"Purifying" Nicaragua

U.S. marines have intervened in Nicaragua numerous times since the 1850s when they policed the country for Cornelius Vanderbilt and other patrons of Manifest Destiny.[4] Take Smedley Butler's experience. In 1909, General Juan Estrada, the governor for Nicaragua's Atlantic Coast, led a revolt against Liberal President Jose Santos Zelaya, a nationalist modernizer. Backed by U.S. investors and Conservative Party leaders Emiliano Chamorro and Adolfo Diaz, Estrada established a provisional government at the port of Bluefields.

New Orleans was Estrada's base of supply for arms and recruits. American mercenaries, such as Captain Godfrey Fowler of the Texas National Guard, instructed the rebels in the use of machine guns and commanded troops in combat. The Taft administration turned up the heat by breaking relations with the Zelaya government. Hoping to preserve Nicaraguan sovereignty, Zelaya resigned the presidency in December 1909 in favor of Jose Madriz. The U.S.-backed rebellion fared poorly. By May 1910, Nicaraguan government forces recaptured El Bluff, at the entrance to Bluefields Harbor.[5]

The U.S. Navy declared Bluefields a "neutral zone" and landed marines to deter Madriz from retaking the port. Smedley Butler provided this first-hand account: "Near Bluefields was the property of a large American gold mine, whose stock was owned mainly by Pittsburgh financiers and partly by the then Secretary of State, Philander C. Knox. President Madriz refused to recognize the validity of the gold mining concession and 225 Marines immediately were dispatched to Bluefields to 'protect American lives and property.' I commanded those Marines and in order to be sure that there was an American life to protect in Bluefields I made certain the local consul was on the job. There wasn't another American in miles. The technique of raping this country for American financiers demanded that the revolutionists have the true cause of patriotism on their side. Consequently, we marines soon developed the puppet revolutionary candidate for President, Juan J. Estrada, into another George Washington...

"The Marines bluffed the government forces out of Bluefields and with 367 revolutionists held the town. The government forces outside the city wanted to attack. I called upon the government generals to forbid them to shoot at the city. American lives would be endangered...

"Naturally the government forces gave up in disgust and retired to the town of Rama some miles down the trail from Bluefields. But the State Department representative who wanted the revolution run on the level, demanded that Estrada, Diaz and Chamorro go after the government forces and defeat them. This they were loath to do.

"They wanted to set up their own government right there and start levying taxes at once. But the State Department's orders were that the revolutionists must win the revolution. Else how would American interests be safe?

"Finally the revolutionists were convinced that they should attack Rama and defeat the government forces. We sent an American beachcomber on ahead to Rama to be sure there would be another American life to protect and then re-enacted the farce of Bluefields. The government forces were bluffed out of the town, the revolutionists entered. We forbade shooting by the government forces and they finally melted away, convinced of the hopelessness of opposing the revolutionists backed by the marines. The revolution ended then and there."

Madriz fled the country. "Everybody was happy," wrote Butler. "The gold mines and fruit companies operated unmolested, and canal schemes were plotted all over the country for years."[6]

Butler again led marines to Nicaragua in 1912. This time they went to battle to save the puppet government headed by Adolfo Diaz. One rebel leader refused to surrender: Benjamin Zeledon, the former Zelaya general whose Liberal Party forces held Masaya, a town near Managua. When Masaya fell, Major Butler wired Admiral Southerland, the commander-in-chief of the U.S. forces which included eight warships: "Government forces have captured Zeledon and have asked me if we want him...If you direct I can have Zeledon sent back here under guard or protected by my men in Masaya. Personally [I] would suggest that through some inaction on our part some one might hang him." Apparently wounded during capture, Zeledon died under mysterious circumstances. His body was paraded through the streets on the back of a horse.[7]

The intended lesson was fear. But in Augusto Cesar Sandino, the event inspired a nationalist spirit. Sandino later wrote: "At that time I was a kid of seventeen and I witnessed the crushing of Nicaraguans in Masaya and other parts of the Republic by North American filibusters. I saw Zeledon's body buried in Catarina, a town near my own. His death gave me the key to our country's plight in face of North American piracy; so we see our war as a continuation of his."[8]

President Taft portrayed the 1912 invasion in the rhetoric of "Dollar Diplomacy." He told Congress:

> In Central America the aim has been to help such countries as Nicaragua and Honduras to help themselves...It is obvious that the Monroe doctrine is more vital in the neighborhood of the Panama Canal and the zone of the Caribbean than anywhere else...It is therefore essential that the countries within that sphere shall be removed from the jeopardy involved by heavy foreign debt and chaotic national finances and from the ever present danger of international complications due to disorder at home. Hence, the United States has been glad to encourage and support American bankers who were willing to lend a helping hand to the financial rehabilitation of such countries because this financial rehabilitation and the protection of their customhouses from being the prey of would-be dictators would remove at one stroke the menace of foreign creditors and the menace of revolutionary disorder...
>
> During this last revolution in Nicaragua, the government of that republic having admitted its inability to protect American life and property against acts of sheer lawlessness on the part of the malcontents, and having requested this government to assume that office, it became necessary to land over 2,000 Marines and Bluejackets...
>
> Since the reestablishment of peace and order, elections have been held amid conditions of quiet and tranquillity. Nearly all the American Marines have now been withdrawn. The country should soon be on the road to recovery.[9]

The United States self-righteously exempted itself from the label "foreign." Smedley Butler rigged the 1912 elections to return Diaz to power, writing his wife Ethel, "Today, Nicaragua has enjoyed a fine 'free election,' with only one candidate being allowed to run—President Adolfo Diaz—who was unanimously elected. In order that this happy event might be pulled off without hitch and to the entire satisfaction of our State Department, we patrolled all the towns to prevent disorders..."[10] Some one hundred Marines remained in Nicaragua for the next thirteen years to ensure "peace and order." The revolving Diaz and Chamorro governments obediently followed the dictates of U.S. proconsuls, Customs collectors and bankers who induced Nicaragua to go into debt to pay for projects controlled by Americans. "Dollar Diplomacy" was loansharking writ large.

Sandino to Somoza

In 1926, rebellion again rocked Nicaragua. This time, it was Sandino who refused to surrender to marines sent by President Coolidge.

Coolidge's occupation of Nicaragua was not a popular one. In January 1927, Senator Burton Wheeler, a Montana Democrat, introduced a resolution calling for U.S. forces to withdraw. He told a New York rally sponsored by the Non-Intervention Citizens' Committee that "'protection of life and property' is the classic mask worn by dollar diplomacy when it turns its face toward the American people...The State Department has literally gutted the sovereignty of Nicaragua. At this moment it has the little republic hog-tied...Every strategic post, fiscal and military, is in the hands of the appointees of the State Department."[11]

The prior pretext for U.S. intervention—the "menace of foreign creditors"—was passe. The Coolidge administration tried out a new one: the menace of communism. Mexico was accused of plotting with the Russians to establish a hostile "Bolshevist regime" in Nicaragua—"a Bolshevist wedge between continental United States and the Panama Canal." That early Red scare produced more ridicule than fear. Many suspected Washington of setting up Mexico for war because of its threat to nationalize the holdings of U.S. oil companies.[12] (In 1914, Butler's marines went to Mexico to make it "safe for American oil interests.")

Butler described the military's role in producing Red scares as part of the effort "to make the common people military minded."[13] He unveiled the "domestic brand" of military intelligence as "mainly unadulterated Redhunting. Hence intelligence officers cooperate more or less openly with such bulwarks of home defense as William Randolph Hearst, Ralph Easley, Harry Jung of Chicago and such organizations as the National Security League, the American Vigilantes and the Order of '76 [racist, anti-Semitic and anti-union forerunners to rightwing groups discussed in later chapters].

"The intelligence men further justify their jobs by spy work on radical gatherings, by attending public forums in an attempt to detect political or economic heresy, by keeping tabs on various suspects, and by smelling out what they consider to be subversive activities everywhere." Butler called on military intelligence to be concerned with "the true domestic enemies of our nation—hunger, injustice and exploitation" and "not the subversive shadows of their own creation."[14]

Sandino's six-year guerrilla war against U.S. marines was the Vietnam War of its day. In 1933, the Hoover administration pulled out the troops, leaving behind a powerful National Guard headed by Anastasio Somoza Garcia.* Somoza was nicknamed "El Yanqui" for his Philadelphia-bred English and his pro-American opportunism.[15] He declared, "I'll give this country peace, if I have to shoot every other man in Nicaragua to get it."[16]

Having won the withdrawal of U.S. troops, Sandino signed a peace treaty with President Juan Sacasa and disarmed most of his followers. They received land to develop an agricultural cooperative in the Coco River valley. In February 1934, national guardsmen began taking up positions around Sandino's Wiwili encampment. Sandino went to Managua to insist that the *Guardia* comply with the peace agreement and respect the constitution. On February 21, after dining with President Sacasa, Sandino was picked up by guardsmen and executed. The Guard then assaulted Sandino's followers at Wiwili, slaughtering some 300 men, women and children.[17]

In June 1936, Somoza staged a coup and founded a dictatorship that passed from father to son to brother. The elder Somoza was shot in 1956 by a poet named Rigoberto Lopez Perez who was killed at the scene. Thousands of Nicaraguans were arrested and tortured in the post-assassination roundup, among them *La Prensa* publisher Pedro Joaquin Chamorro.

"Chamorro was lucky," explained author John Booth, "for he escaped the even more diabolical tortures suffered by his companions: electrical shocks...repeated near-drowning, lifting or dragging by a cord tied around the genitals, imprisonment

---

*Nicaraguans use the mother's family name as a second surname.

in a coffin-sized cell, or time in the Somoza family's private zoo. This last method incarcerated prisoners, for months in some cases, in barred cages open to the weather, next to lions and panthers, in the garden of the presidential residence." Held in a cell at the end of the garden, Chamorro observed how "in front of these animal cages often strolled the current president of the dynasty, Luis Somoza, and his brother Anastasio, with their wives, relatives, and children...carrying their dolls and toys."[18]

The Somoza dictatorship lasted 43 years, until the heirs to Sandino set Nicaragua on a different course.

1

Carter Strikes Out

Somoza believes that God has given him Nicaragua for a *hacienda* and its citizens as its peasants.

Venezuelan ambassador to the Organization of American States, 1978.[1]

Over a period of years, we sent over fourteen thousand men through various military training programs in the United States...Due to our close association with the U.S., Nicaragua was often referred to as "the little U.S.A." of Central America.

Anastasio Somoza.[2]

Obviously the Carter administration did not want the United States to lose control over the political, social and economic destiny of Nicaragua. And when they began to realize that, in fact, Somoza was no longer viable they began to worry about the possibility that the baby could be thrown out with the bathwater.

Nicaraguan Foreign Minister Miguel D'Escoto, May 9, 1986 interview with author.

From the memoirs of former President Jimmy Carter and his top two foreign policy advisers, you would barely know that during their tenure Nicaragua had a revolution. Carter discussed Nicaragua only briefly on 5 out of 596 pages in *Keeping Faith;* former Secretary of State Cyrus Vance and former National Security Adviser Zbigniew Brzezinski each gave Nicaragua a cursory mention on two pages in their respective memoirs. You would never know that Carter officials worked vigorously to derail the Nicaraguan revolution and, having failed in that, tried desperately to substitute the revolution's caboose, Somoza's conservative opposition, for its Sandinista locomotive.

As Brzezinski noted, Carter's views on foreign affairs had largely "been formed during his time with the Trilateral Commission."[3] Top State, Treasury and Defense officials were drawn from trilateralist ranks. Made up of political and business elites from North America, Western Europe and Japan, the commission works to strengthen the cohesion and dominance of the Western alliance in a changing world.[4] For two decades following World War II, the United States possessed overwhelming global economic and military supremacy. This *Pax Americana* was cut short by a revitalized Europe and Japan, a Soviet Union with superpower status and Third World movements seeking self-determination.

Trilateralism counseled accommodation with the Third World instead of relentless confrontation to restore the status quo. In Brzezinski's words, the Carter administration was "not trying to build dams against the forces of history but rather to channel these forces in a positive direction."[5] Accommodation is a form of intervention that relies on reform and selective repression to keep leftists out of power and employs cooptation and selective pressure to manage and weaken leftists once in power. Accommodationists assume the West can beat the Soviet Union through economic competition relying on trade, aid and investment—provided the United States does not default. Initial policy toward Latin America was guided by the recommendations of the Commission on United States-Latin American Relations chaired by trilateralist Sol Linowitz. A former chairman of the Xerox Corporation and ambassador to the Organization of American States, Linowitz served Carter as a negotiator for the Panama Canal treaty, Carter's first priority in Latin American relations.[6]

Carter policy toward Nicaragua reflected the trilateralist principle: "a minimum of social justice and reform will be necessary for stability in the long run."[7] In response to Sandinista revolution, Carter officials tried to find that minimum of reform. They found out that a minimum was not enough.

Revolutionary Tremors

General Anastasio "Tacho" Somoza Debayle was the third Somoza to rule Nicaragua as a family franchise in the U.S. orbit. Schooled in the United States since childhood, married to an American and more comfortable speaking English than Spanish, Somoza once remarked, "I know the U.S. better than my country."[8]

A year and a half before Somoza's ouster, the *Wall Street Journal* observed: "'Tacho,' a West Point graduate who took control of the country in the mid-1960s after the death of his older brother Luis, always has stressed his strong ties to the U.S. and his fierce opposition to communism. He and Luis allowed the U.S. to launch its ill-fated Cuban Bay of Pigs invasion from here, and he even offered to send troops to Vietnam. (At times, the U.S. presence here has lacked subtlety: A picture of recent U.S. Ambassador Turner Shelton, for example, adorns the Nicaraguan equivalent of a $3 bill.)"[9]

Relations were especially cozy during the Nixon administration. Somoza reportedly sent his mother to Washington with $1 million for Nixon's reelection campaign.[10] Turner Shelton, above-mentioned ambassador to Nicaragua from 1970 to 1975, was an associate of Nixon's close friend Bebe Rebozo and billionaire Howard Hughes. Hughes was living at the top of Managua's pyramid-shaped Intercontinental Hotel when the great earthquake sent him fleeing.[11]

The 1972 earthquake devastated Managua; the Intercontinental Hotel was one of only a few buildings left intact in the downtown area. Somoza siphoned off relief money and profiteered off grossly inadequate reconstruction. "The earth opened," recalled American nun Mary Hartman, and "peoples' eyes opened to the complete corruption of the government." Residents who received none of the relief goods donated from abroad saw the National Guard selling them later.[12]

The Sandinista National Liberation Front (FSLN), named for Nicaraguan hero Augusto Cesar Sandino, was founded in 1961. The Sandinistas catapulted into world attention in 1974, raiding a Christmas party honoring Ambassador Shelton. Shelton had already left, but Somoza's brother-in-law, who served as ambassador to the United States, was one of many prominent hostages. After three days, the FSLN won $1 million in ransom, the first national broadcast of Sandinista views and the release of fourteen political prisoners, including Daniel Ortega, freed after seven years in Somoza's jails.

Somoza imposed a state of siege and waged an intensive counterinsurgency campaign with support from the United States and CONDECA, the Central American Defense Council made up of Nicaragua, El Salvador, Guatemala and Honduras. A death squad named the Anti-Communist League of Nicaragua helped with Somoza's dirty work.[13]

In June 1976, a more human rights-conscious U.S. Congress heard testimony about widespread torture, rape, killings, mass arrests and disappearances. Liberal politicians wanted to cut off aid to Somoza. The Ford administration's ambassador to Nicaragua, James Theberge, began meeting with opposition leaders such as *La Prensa* publisher Pedro Joaquin Chamorro, a leader of the new Democratic Liberation Union (UDEL). But Somoza's days were not yet seen as numbered.

A year later, the *Wall Street Journal* (May 31, 1977) ran a two-page advertisement headed, "Nicaragua: An Investor's Dream Come True." Nicaragua was sold as "a Country Where Foreign Capital is Nurtured; 'Yanquis' Feel at Home." The "good investment climate" offered freedom of remittance on profits and capital, freedom from capital gains and dividend tax, and "low-cost abundant labor" which "takes pride in its task." The U.S. Department of Commerce predicted that "Nicaragua will continue to enjoy political stability and a bright economic future."[14]

In Somoza's investor's dream, one baby in eight died before their first birthday. In a country with abundant arable land two out of three children were undernourished and two out of three peasant farmers were completely landless or had plots too small for subsistence. Export crops soaked up 90 percent of all agricultural credit and used 22 times more arable land than that for growing basic food crops for domestic consumption. The paltry per capita income of about $830 was many times that earned by those on the lower levels of the economic pyramid. The poorest half of the population received 15 percent of the national income; the poorest fifth received about 3 percent. The richest 5 percent enjoyed 30 percent of the income and a higher share of the wealth, education and access to health care. In Somoza's investor's dream six out of ten deaths were caused by preventable and curable diseases. Over half the population was illiterate.[15]

While on a visit to Costa Rica, Anastasio Somoza Sr. heard his hosts boast of the schools they were building. "I don't want educated people," he retorted. "I want oxen."[16] His sons carried on in his footsteps.

"Democratization"

Somoza's state of siege took its toll. Many FSLN leaders, including founder Carlos Fonseca, were killed and many others were forced into exile. "When they felt that we were hard hit, scattered and divided, they [the United States and Somoza] decided it was time for a democratization plan," said Sandinista leader Humberto Ortega, now minister of defense.[17]

With the FSLN apparently wiped out, the Carter administration announced in June 1977 that it would not sign a new military aid agreement with Nicaragua unless there was "an improvement in the human rights situation."[18] On July 28, the 51-year-old Somoza suffered a heart attack and was flown to the Miami Heart Institute for treatment; Luis Somoza had died of a heart attack at the age of 44. The dictator and his dynasty looked strikingly vulnerable. Carter's new ambassador, Cuban-born sociology professor Mauricio Solaun, arrived in Nicaragua in August and extended U.S. efforts to reach out to non-Sandinista opposition leaders.

Somoza returned home on September 10 and lifted martial law nine days later. As recounted by Robert Pastor, Carter's director of Latin American and Caribbean Affairs for the National Security Council (NSC), a debate ensued in the Inter-Agency Group on Human Rights and Foreign Assistance—chaired by Deputy Secretary of State Warren Christopher—the central forum for Nicaragua policy at that time. The State Department Bureau of Human Rights, headed by Patricia Derian, opposed releasing aid to Nicaragua while the Bureau of Inter-American Affairs favored aid as a "carrot." Christopher "decided that having achieved the U.S. objective of getting Somoza to end the state of siege, the United States could not disapprove aid to Nicaragua. On the other hand, the Administration did not want to approve aid and lose important leverage to try to obtain free elections. Christopher chose to keep the options open: the United States would neither approve nor disapprove aid. The United States announced it would not provide any military aid *until* further progress was made in human rights; however, the law required the Administration to sign the 1977 military aid agreement [worth $2.5 million] before the end of the fiscal year [September 30], or the money would revert to the treasury and future leverage would be lost. There were no similar constraints built into the economic aid laws, so the Administration merely postponed that decision."[19]

Washington wanted Somoza to agree to step down at the end of his official presidential term in May 1981. With the Sandinistas out of the picture, the elections would result predictably in a successor government led by business elites aligned with the United States. Ambassador Solaun "felt that it was impossible to create a political center in Nicaragua without retaining part of the large Somoza political apparatus in public life, but he thought it was possible to remove Somoza and his closest family members and associates. He acknowledged that it would be *somocismo sin Somoza*—the same system, but without Somoza—at least for a transitional period."[20] (In mid 1978, the Carter administration oversaw just such a system-preserving succession in the Dominican Republic, when then-dictator Joaquin Balaguer was forced to concede electoral defeat to reformist leader Antonio Guzman.)

The Sandinistas, however, had not been eliminated. With the lifting of martial law, popular protest multiplied. In October 1977, the FSLN launched a military offensive, attacking National Guard posts in several towns including Masaya, about fifteen miles from the capital. The Guard barracks of San Carlos, on the southern end of Lake Nicaragua near the Costa Rican border, was the target of Sandinistas from the Solentiname island religious community led by Nicaraguan poet and priest Ernesto Cardenal.

"Three of us who took part in the assault on San Carlos were women," a combatant recalled, "and when the news broke I think it inspired other women to believe that they could join in the revolutionary struggle. We were also Christians, which had a great impact on Nicaraguans. It added a fresh dimension to people's idea of the Frente Sandinista."[21]

Somoza received another blow on October 18. A group of respected Nicaraguan priests, businessmen, academics and other professionals issued a statement insisting that the FSLN must be part of any solution to Nicaragua's problems. The group, based in San Jose, Costa Rica, became known as *Los Doce*, the Group of Twelve. Its members were (post-Somoza government positions appear in parentheses): Sergio Ramirez, lawyer and novelist (government junta member, elected vice president in 1984); Miguel D'Escoto, Maryknoll priest, director of social communications for the New York-based Maryknoll Society from 1970 to 1979 (foreign minister); Fernando Cardenal, younger brother of Ernesto Cardenal, Jesuit priest, founder of the Revolutionary Christian Movement (director of the 1980 Literacy Crusade and the Sandinista Youth Organization before becoming minister of education); Carlos Tunnermann, lawyer and former president of Nicaragua's National University (education minister, then ambassador to the United States); Ernesto Castillo, lawyer (minister of justice); Ricardo Colonel, cattle rancher (vice-minister of agricultural development); Enrique Boltodano, large coffee producer (comptroller-general); Joaquin Cuadra, investment lawyer (minister of finance, then president of the Central Bank); Casimiro Sotelo, architect (ambassador to Canada); Carlos Gutierrez, a dentist who maintained his practice in Mexico; Felipe Mantica, a businessman who dropped out of the Twelve before Somoza's overthrow; and Arturo Cruz, officer of the Inter-American Development Bank in Washington (Central Bank president, July 1979-May 1980; government junta member, May 1980-March 1981; ambassador to the United States, March-November 1981). Cruz left the government and was a contra leader until 1987. Three other people joined the Twelve before Somoza's overthrow: Roberto Arguello Hurtado, lawyer (president of the Supreme Court, then ambassador to France); Edgar Parrales, priest (ambassador to the Organization of American States); and Reinaldo Antonio Tefel, academic (minister of social welfare).[22]

The Group of Twelve, explained Carlos Tunnermann, "undertook the international work, to visit governments and international organizations, to make known that" the Sandinistas "were not terrorists, that they had taken up arms because it was necessary and that the terrorist was the government and the *somocista* system."[23]

Another group, more conservative than the Twelve, also formed. Headed by Archbishop Miguel Obando y Bravo, the Commission to Promote a National Dialogue included, among others, Monsignor Pablo Antonio Vega and Alfonso Robelo, president of the business group then called the Superior Council of Private Initiative (COSIP). As described by *New York Times* reporter Shirley Christian, the Dialogue's supporters "were people who wanted, or were willing to accept, a phased change that would not disrupt the economy and other aspects of Nicaraguan life. They talked about reaching some kind of agreement with Somoza whereby he would agree not to run again when his term as president ended in 1981 or would step aside sooner in favor of someone else from his party or the National Guard, with a guarantee of free elections at the end of 1980."[24] (Christian's place as Washington's favored chronicler of the Nicaraguan revolution was reinforced when the U.S. Information Agency gave out hundreds of free copies of her book at the 1987 International Book Fair in Managua, which was open to the Nicaraguan public and publishers from around the world, including official organs of the U.S. Government.)[25]

Wealthy Nicaraguans hedged their bets on Nicaragua's future, setting up secret bank accounts in the Cayman Islands to transfer millions of dollars outside the country. The contra network would later use the same Cayman Islands Bank, Banco de America Central (BAC), and the same system of Miami "pass through" accounts and Panamanian shell companies.[26]

Pressure Building

Events quickly outpaced Washington and the Dialogue. On the morning of January 10, 1978, Managua was jolted by the assassination of *La Prensa* editor Pedro Joaquin Chamorro. Thousands turned out for the funeral and later that month COSIP threw its support behind a three-week national strike; in February, COSIP expanded and changed its name to the Superior Council of Private Enterprise, COSEP. On February 2, the FSLN briefly captured Rivas and Granada as well as the counterinsurgency camp in Santa Clara, Nueva Segovia.

While the Sandinista movement gained momentum, the Dialogue's meeting with Somoza, planned for February, fell apart. "In addition to their outrage," wrote Christian, "a strong sense of fear swept businessmen, politicians, and trade unionists as they realized that what had happened to Chamorro could happen to them. They had always known, or suspected, that the National Guard treated the poor in a repressive manner...but they had felt themselves reasonably secure to carry out peaceful opposition. They had known they could be thrown into jail for a few weeks but had never expected to be killed...But Pedro Joaquin Chamorro was not a peasant. He had been one of them...Even those who were politically ambivalent now thought that Somoza should go because he could no longer provide the one thing that made strongmen attractive: public order...Above all, they now hoped the United States would step in and play its traditional role as arbiter of power struggles in Nicaragua."[27]

That traditional arbitration had never promoted the interests of the poor, who had suffered and died in the Somoza yoke. It would be no different this time around.

The Carter administration was divided over how fast and far to push Somoza. Assistant Secretary of State for Inter-American Affairs Terence Todman provided a conservative counterweight to Ambassador Solaun's Somocismo without Somoza. On February 16, Deputy Assistant Secretary of State Sally Shelton inadvertently exposed the shallowness of human rights policy in testimony to Congress: "Although problems remain, it is our opinion that marked progress has been manifested since early 1977." The National Guard behaved "in a generally restrained manner" following Chamorro's assassination and had a "duty," she said, "to protect the population from terrorism and acts of violence." Continued U.S. assistance for the Guard was necessary because it helped provide a "sense of security which is important for social, economic and political developments." Miguel D'Escoto challenged the U.S. view, testifying that at least twenty people had recently been killed; women demonstrating peacefully were beaten with chains wrapped in newspapers.[28]

The first mass insurrection took place at the end of February in Masaya's Indian community, Monimbo (about 20,000 residents). Somoza sent his son, Anastasio Somoza Portocarrero, known as *El Chiguin* (the Kid), to reimpose control. El Chiguin, educated at Harvard and trained at the U.S. Army Command and General Staff College at Fort Leavenworth, Kansas, commanded the elite troops of the misnamed Basic Infantry Training School (EEBI) modeled on the U.S. Special Forces.

"The *Guardia* entered the *barrio*," recalled one Monimbo resident, "and attacked us with tanks, armoured cars, helicopters and heavy machine-guns. People defended themselves with machetes, contact bombs [homemade bombs made up of such items as sulphur, gasoline, nails and pebbles], sticks and whatever else they could lay their hands on."[29] In Humberto Ortega's words, the Monimbo uprising "was the soul of the masses on a nationwide scale and became the heart of the insurrection that was to take place throughout the country."[30]

Somoza told a loyalist rally on February 26 that he would retire as chief of the Armed Forces and turn over the presidency to an elected successor on May 1, 1981. But elections had come and gone throughout the four decades of Somoza rule and, in Nicaragua at least, few expected the next election to bring an end to the Somoza dynasty. In March, Alfonso Robelo established the Nicaraguan Democratic Movement (MDN), a party of reformist businesspeople and professionals. In May, UDEL and the MDN formed a new coalition, the Broad Opposition Front (FAO).

The administration, meanwhile, released $160,000 in military credits to cover the purchase of equipment for a Nicaraguan military hospital and made the economic aid decision it had postponed the previous September. Most of a $12 million aid package was released in the form of loans for rural nutrition and educational development with the rationale that it was aid for the needy and not for Somoza. Representative Charles Wilson (D-TX), an influential conservative member of the House Appropriations Committee and a leading member of the so-called Nicaragua Lobby, had threatened to block action on other administration foreign aid requests if Nicaragua aid was not approved. Former NSC aide Robert Pastor explained: "Although the response by the Guard to the riots [sic] represented a serious concern, Somoza did not reimpose martial law or censorship of the press" and "the United States had made such loans to countries with worse human rights records."[31]

The People United

Three tendencies had emerged within the FSLN in the 1970s, with different approaches to revolutionary strategy. The Prolonged Popular War (GPP) tendency saw the revolutionary struggle as a long war of attrition led by a guerrilla army in the countryside. The Proletarian tendency stressed a prolonged struggle centered around urban workers and the poor. The *Terceristas* (Third Force or Insurrectionists) thought a prolonged struggle was unnecessary; a series of armed strikes could spark a popular insurrection. They advocated building a broad-based coalition, led by the FSLN, among all anti-Somoza forces, including those in the business class. In June 1978, the three tendencies reached preliminary agreement on strategic unity.

In July, student groups, the women's association (AMPRONAC), unions, professional associations and traditional left parties joined with the FSLN to form the United Peoples Movement (MPU). Among them was the Nicaraguan Socialist Party (PSN), the major communist party, which had earlier opposed armed struggle and allied with UDEL and the FAO. As a study commissioned by the Reagan State Department observed (contrary to Reaganaut rhetoric), "The Moscow-line Socialist Party had judged that the situation was not ripe for revolution, and had consequently condemned the Sandinistas' insurrectionary strategy as adventurist."[32]

The MPU program outlined radical political, economic and social change. It called for "a government with the representative participation of all political, economic, labor and cultural forces committed to raising the country from the stagnation, dependency and underdevelopment imposed by the dictatorship and its allies." It sketched an economic program "that corresponds to the social necessities of all Nicaraguans." The new "government will begin negotiations to obtain foreign aid from any country, regardless of ideology" and develop a comprehensive Agrarian Reform program "to put an end to the formation of *latifundios* and to institute, with the lands expropriated from the Somoza family, a program of cooperatives and state enterprises." Women "will be incorporated on a large scale into all economic, political, social and cultural tasks (establishing the principle of equal work for equal pay)."

Measures will be taken immediately "to end illiteracy...Programs of teacher training and school construction will be increased so that there will be no valley or district without access to education." The new unity government "will initiate health and hygiene programs...and will eradicate the diseases which now ravage children and affect great sectors of the population, such as malaria, gastroenteritis...as well as those diseases caused by malnutrition and hunger." A national army will be created "which will watch over the national interests of the people and the defense of the nation. It will cease to be an instrument of repression..."[33]

Leading members of the Group of Twelve returned from exile; a huge crowd greeted them at the airport. Trying to stanch his loss of international support, Somoza did not arrest the returnees. In mid July, he received a letter from President Carter, which was supported by Brzezinski and sent over the objections of State Department officials. The letter, dated June 30, applauded Somoza for his human rights and democratic initiatives at a time when the State Department was receiving reports of increased human rights violations by the National Guard.[34]

When Ambassador Solaun delivered the letter in mid July he advised Somoza to keep it confidential. In an account of his overthrow, Somoza noted that the letter "came at a time when I needed encouragement, and particularly from the United States." Its "contents...if publicly known, could assist me greatly in warding off my other enemies. I was not interested in a collector's item." Somoza later came to see the letter as a ploy, "designed to give us a false sense of security."[35]

> Dear Mr. President:
> I read your statements to the press on June 19 with great interest and appreciation. The steps toward respecting human rights that you are considering are important and heartening signs; and, as they are translated into actions, will mark a major advance for your nation in answering some of the criticisms recently aimed at the Nicaraguan government.
> I am pleased to learn of your willingness to cooperate with the Inter-American Commission on Human Rights...
> The Commission will be favorably impressed by your decision to allow the members of the so-called "Group of Twelve" to return to peaceful lives in Nicaragua. The freedoms of movement and of expression that are at stake in this case are among the central human rights that the Commission seeks to protect.
> You have spoken about a possible amnesty for Nicaraguans being held in jail for political reasons. I urge you to take the promising steps you have suggested; they would serve to improve the image abroad of the human rights situation in Nicaragua.
> I was also encouraged to hear your suggestions for a reform of the electoral system in order to ensure fair and free elections in which all political parties could compete fairly. This step is essential to the functioning of a democracy...
> I look forward to hearing of the implementation of your decisions and appreciate very much your announcement of these constructive actions. I hope that you will continue to communicate fully with my Ambassador, Mauricio Solaun, who enjoys my complete confidence.
> Sincerely,
> JIMMY CARTER

According to Pastor, the letter was a watershed for U.S. policy. It "impelled Brzezinski and Carter to focus on Nicaragua for the first time." After the letter—and the subsequent takeover of the National Palace—Nicaragua was seen "as a political-security crisis, and the Human Rights Bureau was excluded from the central deliberations, although it continued to play a role in defining the State Department position." A "mini" NSC Special Coordination Committee (SCC) met frequently to define Nicaragua policy; principals included Pastor and Assistant Secretary of State for Inter-American Affairs Viron "Pete" Vaky and, above them, Deputy National Security Adviser David Aaron, Deputy Secretary of State Warren Christopher and their bosses Brzezinski and Vance.[36]

Another Kind of Palace Coup

The FAO released its program on August 21, calling for a national unity government to succeed Somoza; it did not envision the radical restructuring of the economy endorsed by the MPU. The next day, the FSLN seized the National Palace with a small squad of guerrillas dressed in National Guard uniforms. The National Palace housed Nicaragua's congress and key government agencies such as the Ministries of Interior and Finance. The Sandinistas captured over 1,500 people including Somoza's cousin, Luis Pallais, vice president of the congress and director of the government newspaper, *Novedades*, and Somoza's nephew, the son of National Guard chief Jose Somoza, Somoza's half-brother.

Eden Pastora, who rejoined the FSLN in fall 1977 after spending four years as a fisherman in Costa Rica, was a leader of the palace raid. Dora Maria Tellez, now minister of health, conducted the negotiations for the Sandinistas. Archbishop Obando y Bravo served as one of the church mediators. Immediately after the takeover, Major Mike Echanis, an American mercenary advising the National Guard, urged Somoza to storm the Palace. Somoza refused to risk the death of so many supporters. "Mike the Merc" Echanis, who died shortly after in an airplane explosion, was a Vietnam veteran and martial arts director for *Soldier of Fortune*, a mercenary magazine and organization which would later support the contras.[37]

When the Palace action ended on the morning of August 24, the Sandinistas had won the release of 59 political prisoners, including Tomas Borge, the FSLN's only living founder, now minister of the interior, and Doris Tijerino, one of the first women to join the FSLN, now head of the National Police. Both had suffered severe torture.

Thousands of Nicaraguans lined the highway to the airport where two planes, provided by President Carlos Andres Perez of Venezuela and General Omar Torrijos of Panama, waited to take the guerrillas and freed prisoners out of the country. Anyone could see now that the Sandinistas had become national heroes. An FSLN communique, printed in *Novedades* as part of the settlement, warned of Somocismo without Somoza and called on the population to prepare for the final offensive.

As Humberto Ortega put it, the FSLN moved to "harness the avalanche" of rising popular resistance.[38]

The raid was timed to upset a planned National Guard coup against Somoza. On August 28, Somoza arrested 85 alleged conspirators.[39]

September Uprising

When insurrection broke out in September 1978, Somoza tried to shoot his way to peace with "one of the most barbaric military attacks ever perpetrated against a civilian population in the history of the Americas...When it was over, four out of seven of Nicaragua's largest cities lay partially or entirely in ruins."[40] An estimated 5,000 people were killed.

One by one, ending with Esteli, the Guard laid siege to the rebellious cities, cutting off food and utilities, and bombing and strafing by air. Guardsmen then carried out "Operation Clean-Up." The Inter-American Commission on Human Rights reported that "many persons were executed in a summary and collective fashion for the mere reason of living in neighborhoods where there had been activity by the FSLN; young people and defenseless children were killed." It was "a crime to be a male between the ages of 12 and 30," said one refugee.[41]

In Matagalpa, reported Amnesty International, guardsmen castrated the owner of the Hotel Soza before machinegunning him and his whole family. "In some areas," said Amnesty, "all males over fourteen years old were reportedly shot dead." A *Newsweek* reporter described how "after retaking Leon, Guardsmen executed five teenagers—three boys and two girls—in the street. The victims were forced to kneel and were summarily shot."[42]

Before Somoza's forces reoccupied the cities, the FSLN led a strategic retreat, minimizing guerrilla losses. Sandinista columns were swelled by young men and women fleeing the wrath of the Guard and new supporters emerged in the cities. Questioned later about the great loss of life and destruction in the September uprising, Humberto Ortega replied, "[It] was the only way to win...We simply paid the price of freedom. Had there been a less costly means, we would have used it."[43]

Mediation

The September insurrection prompted the Carter administration to take more aggressive action. Assistant Secretary of State Vaky believed that "only the United States could solve the problem of Somoza, and that it should use whatever force necessary—barring assassination—to remove him...He argued that the United States needed to get in front of events and assemble a coalition government," lest the situation polarize further and lead to a Sandinista victory.

Pastor and Anthony Lake, the State Department director of policy planning, argued that the United States should not go to Somoza or any chief of state and ask them to step down. Pastor "doubted that Somoza would step down just because the United States asked him. I suspected that he might be taping his official conversations (which he confirmed in his memoir), and that hours after our representative 'talked turkey' to him, we would all be hearing it on the evening news. The President's Press Secretary would then be questioned the next day: 'If President Carter is committed to the principle of nonintervention, why is he trying to overthrow Somoza?'...Carter would look foolish and impotent. Somoza would have a good laugh. In my mind, these were all powerful reasons for not being too explicit in seeking Somoza's departure. Vaky believed that if we were clear and tough enough with Somoza, he would not try something like that, and would simply leave...Vaky also discounted the domestic political fallout, believing that could be managed."

Carter, Vance and Christopher opted for a less forceful and more multilateral approach: mediation. Deputy National Security Adviser David Aaron suggested that the administration "look into the idea of a peace-keeping force during a post-Somoza period to reassure the National Guard and to keep the situation from being dominated by the Sandinistas."[44]

On September 23, the Organization of American States (OAS) approved a U.S.-led mediation initiative taking the form of a so-called International Commission of Friendly Cooperation and Conciliation. U.S. envoy William Jorden, former ambassador to Panama, met with Somoza and urged him to cooperate with the mediation, an effort which, he acknowledged, might lead to Somoza's resignation. Somoza secretly taped this and many other conversations with U.S. officials, reproducing the transcripts in his book, *Nicaragua Betrayed,* which was published by the John Birch Society press, Western Islands.

Jorden warned Somoza that Nicaragua was "gradually becoming dangerously polarized...I am not talking about the Sandinistas where there is obviously a polarization, but other elements in the society, political and [economic]. We are terribly concerned that everything you have built up, and your brother before you, is in danger of being destroyed. And that means the political structure, institutions. The economic prospects don't look to us to be very good...Obviously the opposition to your government is widespread...If it were only the Sandinistas, the situation would be manageable, but it has developed into something quite different...The actions that you have taken have ended the violence for the moment, but we are persuaded it is a temporary thing. I have very good reason to know that the Sandinistas are active. They are getting support, they are recruiting people, and it is only a matter of time before they start again...

"It is our judgement that we are in something of a downward spiral. There will be moments when it looks better, but I think it will go downward again and the situation will just gradually get to the point where perhaps total chaos could occur."

Jorden told Somoza, "The possibility of your departure from office before 1981 is one of the possibilities that has to be considered. I am not saying it has to be done, I am saying it has to be considered...We would like to work towards a solution that is dignified and smooth, as graceful as possible."

Jorden made clear that Washington was worried about the whole region, arguing, as the Reagan administration would later, "unless something is done to correct the situation and work towards a solution, I think that it does clearly play into the hands of Communists and Castro. I think that they are hoping that this will be a situation that they can use and establish a base in the mainland and go from there."

Somoza told Jorden at one point, "You will excuse me for saying this, it is painful for me to say it, but I don't trust the United States anymore." However, Somoza said later, "I want you to know that I'm doing my utmost to accommodate the United States without losing my pants."[45]

Playing for time, Somoza accepted the mediation. The United States, Guatemala and the Dominican Republic formed the Commission of Friendly Cooperation and Conciliation. William Bowdler, then director of the State Department Bureau of Intelligence and Research, represented the United States. "No one seemed to notice," wrote author Karl Bermann, "the curious (but apparently accidental) coincidence that both OAS mediators represented countries in which the United States had intervened to thwart revolutions in prior decades. The choice of Bowdler, however, was definitely not accidental—a former National Security Council member, he had helped set up the new government in the Dominican Republic during the intervention by US troops in 1965."[46] Somoza had contributed troops to that invasion.

Bowdler's general instructions were to promote and assist negotiations between Somoza and the FAO and to preserve the National Guard.[47] The FAO was represented in the mediation effort by Sergio Ramirez of the Group of Twelve, Alfonso Robelo of COSEP and Rafael Cordova Rivas, president of UDEL and a prominent lawyer.

Ramirez recalled the mediation effort as an attempt to "preserve the core of the system—National Guard, the economic establishment, the links of the system with the United States...with the goal of isolating the Sandinista Front." But, "this first attempt of the Carter administration to change the course of history in Nicaragua failed."[48]

The Group of Twelve split with the FAO in late October over the FAO's willingness to accept a continued role for Somoza's Nationalist Liberal Party and the National Guard. Other reformist groups such as the Independent Liberal Party (PLI) and the Popular Social Christian Party (PPSC) followed the Twelve out of the FAO. Members of the Twelve went back into exile. Arturo Cruz, still working in Washington for the Inter-American Development Bank, disagreed with the decision to split with the FAO.

The United States pursued negotiations with the depleted FAO and put some pressure on Somoza by influencing the International Monetary Fund (IMF) to postpone a decision on $20 million in credit for Nicaragua. "American officials are known to believe that a political solution to the Nicaraguan conflict can be reached within several weeks," the *Washington Post* reported.[49]

Plebiscite Ploy

Somoza would not resign. Instead he proposed a plebiscite, the outcome of which he could determine as the dynasty had determined elections before. Washington would only push Somoza so far so fast. In mid November, the administration decided not to block Israel from supplying arms to Somoza, believing that without new weapons and ammunition, the National Guard might be routed quickly by the Sandinistas: "If Somoza goes, we would prefer him to go peacefully. We would not like to see him toppled in an armed revolt."[50]

On November 13, the administration held what Pastor called "its first high-level intense discussion on Nicaragua"; the setting was the NSC Policy Review Committee. Vaky and Bowdler advocated finessing the plebiscite idea and applying sanctions to force Somoza to negotiate his departure in accordance with the FAO plan. Brzezinski, Vance and Christopher recommended transforming the plebiscite into a fair vote on Somoza's staying in power or stepping down, and Carter approved.[51]

"Moderate and leftist opposition leaders," observed *New York Times* reporter Alan Riding, "are distressed by their growing conviction that Washington believes the country's deep crisis can be resolved by replacing the Somoza dictatorship with an equally conservative, though less brutal, successor. They think Washington, fearing 'another Cuba,' is searching for stability rather than for social and economic change or even human rights—repeating, as they see it, American policy during its occupation of Nicaragua between 1912 and 1933, and its subsequent support for the Somoza family."[52]

Bowdler led the mediation effort to fashion a final plebiscite proposal on December 20, which the FAO accepted. If Somoza lost an internationally-supervised plebiscite scheduled for February 1979, he would resign and leave the country. An interim president approved by the Somocista congress would serve until an FAO-dominated "national unity" government, excluding the Sandinistas, selected another interim president to serve until an elected president was inaugurated in May 1981, at which time Somoza could return to Nicaragua. The National Guard would be reorganized. If Somoza won the plebiscite, the FAO would become a "peaceful opposition."

General Dennis McAuliffe, the head of the U.S. Army Southern Command based in Panama, joined Bowdler on December 21 in urging Somoza to accept the compromise plebiscite plan. "We on the military side of the United States," said McAuliffe, "recognize that we have had strong and very effective friendship with the military officers of this country and with you in particular. We do not want to throw that over, so to speak...But we do recognize...that the situation has changed. Speaking very frankly, Mr. President, it is our view that peace will not come to Nicaragua until you have removed yourself from the presidency and the scene...I'm just telling you that from the way we look at the situation, your presence in Nicaragua is a symbolic thing and as long as you remain in Nicaragua, you will attract terrorists and violence...If you follow the plan suggested by the United States, the leftists and communists will not take over and we will have a moderate government. What I'm saying Mr. President, is that we [will] have a moderate government that does not have the name Somoza."

McAuliffe assured Somoza of the continued importance of the National Guard: "We think the Guardia has the capability, certainly the officers are very well trained, and their attitudes are excellent. They will be able to assure peace and tranquility in the country."[53]

The day after Christmas, Vance convened a Policy Review Committee meeting with McAuliffe, Secretary of Defense Harold Brown, General Smith of the Joint Chiefs of Staff, Aaron, Pastor, Vaky, Bowdler and Solaun. They discussed how to pressure Somoza to accept a plebiscite plan he didn't control. Carter approved a phased array of sanctions to be implemented if Somoza's response was negative. After further mediation, during which Somoza tried to modify the plebiscite plan to make it more susceptible to manipulation, the FAO broke off talks on January 19, 1979.

At a Policy Review Committee meeting on January 26, CIA Director Stansfield Turner argued that Somoza had built up the National Guard during the mediation, the FSLN had lost support and were refocused on a longer-term armed struggle, and the moderate opposition was also weak. He "judged that the chances of Somoza remaining in power until 1981 were better than even." But the consensus position was summarized by Brown: "the longer Somoza stayed in power, the higher the chances were of a radical takeover. The only question was when the Sandinistas would assume power."[54] There was agreement to go ahead with sanctions.

The administration announced on February 8 that it was withdrawing the U.S. Military Group, terminating military aid (it had been suspended), withdrawing Peace Corps volunteers and cutting the embassy staff from 82 to 37; no new aid would be considered. These actions were largely symbolic. By then, Israel was the National Guard's chief supplier. Other current and future arms sources included Argentina, Guatemala, El Salvador, Honduras, Chile, Brazil, Taiwan, Portugal, Spain and South Africa.[55] Critics outside the administration urged, unsuccessfully, that Carter support an international arms boycott, investigate U.S. mercenary activity and cut Nicaragua's beef and sugar import quotas.

The Carter administration appeared to forget Jorden's warning about a downward spiral. As the National Guard waxed in control over the country after the September insurrection and negotiations collapsed, U.S. involvement waned. U.S. intelligence predicted that the Guard could defeat any new Sandinista military offensive.[56] Ambassador Solaun resigned after being recalled to Washington in late February, and the post went unfilled for many months.

With the failure of the mediation effort, President Perez of Venezuela attempted, with support from Panamanian leader Torrijos, to have Somoza's cousin Luis Pallais lead a coup. The coup, contemplating Somoza's consent, would install a national unity government with the participation of Eden Pastora. Pallais refused to approach Somoza with the idea and he denied it publicly when Torrijos leaked the plot.[57] When the more conservative Luis Herrera Campins succeeded Perez as president in March 1979 he reduced, but did not discontinue, Venezuela's secret supply of arms to the Sandinistas.[58]

Contrapreneurs at Somoza's Service

Years before the Iran-contra scandal brought him notoriety as an arms dealer associate of Richard Secord, CIA officer Thomas Clines offered private security and intelligence services to Somoza—apparently without the knowledge of CIA Director Stansfield Turner.[59] Clines asked Edwin Wilson, the former CIA agent later convicted of selling arms to Libya, to meet with Somoza. At the time, said Wilson, "everybody in the agency wants to help Somoza, but they want to do it covertly…[They] were willing to help Somoza behind the scenes."[60]

Documents obtained by *U.S. News & World Report* show that Wilson and Clines, on separate occasions in 1978, offered Somoza a $650,000 security and intelligence operation; Somoza found it too expensive.[61] Rep. Charles Wilson arranged and attended Edwin Wilson's (no relation) meeting with Somoza in Miami in early 1979. Rep. Wilson "said he had been socially acquainted with [Edwin] Wilson…and considered him to have 'a good track record.'" Although no agreement resulted from that meeting, associates of Clines did arrange a subsequent deal with Somoza.[62] According to one account, Somoza agreed in early 1979 to a contract with Clines to provide intelligence and assassination services and supply weapons, ammunition, aircraft and explosives beginning in March.[63] (The Clines-Wilson-Secord connection is discussed further in chapter 11.)

An undisclosed number of U.S. mercenaries, such as Mike Echanis, assisted Somoza. According to U.S. government and military sources, four former Green Berets and Navy unconventional warfare specialists living in Fayetteville, North Carolina, near Fort Bragg, were recruited to work for Somoza in "counterterrorist" operations, including the infiltration and sabotage of opposition groups and assassination of Somoza opponents. One of the four, Chuck Sanders, told friends that the CIA had "made arrangements" to work with them. The four men were killed in a plane crash in late 1978.[64]

As of June 1979, at least five Miami-based Cuban exiles were serving as top-level officers of the National Guard, according to a Somoza government source. One of those was Anselmo Aliegro, half-brother of then Florida Democratic Party Chairman Alfredo Duran. Some 25 other Cuban exiles were reportedly engaged in combat for Somoza.[65] After interviewing Nicaraguan refugees on the Costa Rican border, Venezuelan Foreign Minister Alberto Consalvi reported that U.S. mercenaries had committed a number of atrocities.[66]

Patriotic Front

In February 1979, the Group of Twelve and United Peoples Movement created the National Patriotic Front; the Popular Social Christian Party and the Independent Liberal Party joined. The Patriotic Front united around a statement of principles emphasizing national sovereignty, democracy, justice and social progress. As a precondition for "effective democracy," it demanded "the overthrow of the Somoza dictatorship and eradication of all its vestiges, rejecting all maneuvers that imply the continuation of the system of *Somocismo* without Somoza."[67]

The Patriotic Front led mass protests and organized for the final offensive. The MPU had developed a system of parallel power—peoples' power—inside Nicaragua, defending against and challenging the dictatorship with a strong grassroots base of Civil Defense Committees (CDCs), Christian base communities and popular organizations. CDCs, organized by block and neighborhood with democratically elected zonal steering committees, ensured that the population would be better prepared in future confrontations with the Guard.

> The CDCs collected medicines and first aid supplies, and trained older men and women in rudimentary first aid skills to tend the wounded. Basic foodstuffs were stored up, and reserve water supplies located. "Sandinista dining rooms" were organized where the combatants could come for nourishment during the fighting. "Security houses" were designated where key FSLN leadership could meet.
>
> Every person accepted a task. Some watched and reported on National Guard movement. Others reported the activities of Somoza's spies. Older persons and young children acted as messengers between the Committees in different blocks and neighborhoods, maintaining constant communication between the CDCs and the FSLN. The Popular Brigades—combatants who had not formally joined the FSLN—took responsibility for being ready at a moment's notice to dig street trenches and take up the street bricks to build barricades. Stores of home made weapons, such as molotov cocktails and "contact bombs" were made. Students built arsenals of arms and munitions seized in temporary take-overs of National Guard command posts.
>
> Because the National Guard entered any private home at will, and often resorted to aerial bombardment or setting fire to whole neighborhoods in order to force people into the streets, the CDCs established evacuation passageways by connecting each house, through hidden wall openings and tunnels.[68]

On March 7, the Sandinistas announced "the irreversible and unbreakable unity of the FSLN" and the appointment of a nine-person National Directorate with three representatives from each tendency: Daniel Ortega, Humberto Ortega and Victor Tirado of the Terceristas; Jaime Wheelock, Luis Carrion and Carlos Nuñez of the Proletarians; and Tomas Borge, Bayardo Arce and Henry Ruiz of the GPP.[69]

Fighting mounted and so did Somoza's increasingly desperate repression. Still, the Carter administration envisioned a Nicaraguan future without the Sandinistas. In April, Sergio Ramirez traveled to the United States to attend the Latin American Studies Association annual conference: "We stopped in Washington" to try and meet with U.S. government officials. "Nobody wanted to talk to us."[70]

Panama Canal Connection

In mid May the United States handed Somoza a carrot more hefty than earlier sticks: approval of a $65.6 million IMF loan over the objections of Senator Edward Kennedy (D-MA) and others. On May 20, Mexican President Jose Lopez Portillo broke relations with Nicaragua and encouraged other governments to do so, decrying the "horrendous acts of genocide" committed by the Guard.[71] (Costa Rica had broken relations with Somoza in late 1978 over border disputes.)

The Carter administration was less concerned with alienating the liberal Democrats in Congress who opposed aid to Somoza than with alienating the conservatives who supported aid to Somoza and opposed the Panama Canal treaty. Their rallying cry was raised by candidate Ronald Reagan in the 1976 primaries: "We built it, we paid for it, it's ours and we should tell Torrijos and company that we are going to keep it."

Carter saw the lack of a new Canal treaty as "something of a diplomatic cancer, which was poisoning our relations with Panama" and hurting the U.S. image throughout Latin America. It took a bruising political battle to win Senate ratification by a razor thin margin in March 1978. Ahead lay more battles to pass House and Senate legislation to implement the treaty. "Some members of the House," wrote Carter, "saw a chance to trade Panama treaty votes for support for [Somoza's] faltering regime."[72]

Nicaragua Lobby leader Rep. Charles Wilson threatened the administration with "rough treatment" on the treaty bill.[73] Even more important was Rep. John Murphy (D-NY), chairman of the House Merchant Marine and Fisheries Committee with jurisdiction in Canal matters. Murphy was a childhood friend of Somoza's since their days together at La Salle Military Academy in Oakdale, New York, and then West Point.

"Tacho was a man's man," remarked Murphy, "the kind of a man you like to have a drink with, to go fishing with, and the type of person everyone respected, not only for his strong personality but also for a very keen intellect."[74] (Murphy was indicted on June 18, 1980 on conspiracy and bribery charges resulting from the FBI's ABSCAM investigation. He was convicted and served sixteen months in federal prison.)[75]

House opponents, said Carter, "tried to block the treaties by claiming that Panama was giving aid to the opponents of Anastasio Somoza in Nicaragua, whom they tried to picture as agents of communist powers. To hear the 'evidence,' the House of Representatives held its first secret session in a hundred and fifty years, but it seemed that no new information was presented."[76] In May 1979, Carter reportedly told Panamanian President Aristedes Royo that because of the Nicaragua-Panama link, "the administration could not do anything about Nicaragua until the canal treaties cleared the House. U.S. sources, while conceding that had been an inhibiting factor, said that Carter was speaking at a time when the internal Nicaragua situation was quiet."[77]

The House approved an administration-Murphy compromise Canal treaty bill on June 21, but more battles loomed as the House and Senate enabling legislation was reconciled. Carter did not sign the final Canal legislation into law until September 27, two months after the Sandinista victory.

Final Offensives

The FSLN launched the final offensive on May 29, 1979 with a series of coordinated attacks followed by the call for a national insurrection and general strike. "From September until we launched the offensive in May," explained Humberto Ortega, "the brunt of military activity was borne by the guerrilla columns of the Northern Front and the ones in Nueva Guinea, in rural and mountainous areas...From a strategic standpoint, as of May Somoza had already lost the war. It was only a question of time."[78]

Until April, the U.S. Embassy was telling Washington that Somoza could probably survive militarily, but that month the defense attache, Lt. Colonel James McCoy, provided a more pessimistic assessment based on "the repudiation of Somoza by the entire population."[79] According to Pastor, the administration did not recognize that it was truly the final offensive until mid June. The CIA's initial assessment was that the fighting could conceivably develop into a second insurrection on the level of the September crisis, but it would not be adequate to displace Somoza.[80]

Leon, the second largest city, was liberated on June 4 under the command of Dora Maria Tellez, head of the FSLN's Rigoberto Lopez Perez western front. Women then made up an unprecedented 30 percent of the guerrilla force. Like Nicaraguans elsewhere, Leon's residents often fought with machetes and homemade bombs. There weren't enough guns to go around.

The day Leon fell, Pastor and U.S. Ambassador to Panama Ambler Moss met with Torrijos and tried to dissuade him from taking further action against Somoza "in order to ensure passage of the Canal legislation" and persuade him to stop sending arms to the Sandinistas. "It's too bad the United States is always so slow to recognize new realities, and that you didn't have the foresight to buy a share of Sandinista stock when I was first offering it," Torrijos told them.

"General," said Pastor, "we have not come to buy Sandinista stock, but to try to get you to sell yours." Torrijos tried to explain that the offensive would succeed.[81]

Somoza declared his last state of siege on June 6. At a Carter Policy Review Committee meeting on June 11, the general view was that the war was a standoff, the Guard would probably survive the current round of fighting, but Somoza would probably not be able to serve out his term. Brzezinski proposed that the United States issue a statement calling for "self-determination for Nicaragua and an end to the violence"; issue forceful private and public warnings to cease the arms flow to both sides; and "begin quietly exploring with other Latin governments the idea of an inter-American peace force that would only act in conjunction with Somoza's departure." The Pentagon was asked to look into military contingencies with the understanding that the United States would assume most of the responsibility for such a force.[82]

The CIA concluded on June 12 that the Guard was weaker and the Sandinistas stronger than was thought previously. Time was running out. The next day, the U.S. Embassy began evacuating Americans. On June 14, at U.S. request, an Israeli ship loaded with arms for Nicaragua turned back.[83]

The Provisional Government Junta of National Reconstruction was announced in San Jose, Costa Rica on June 16. Its five members were Daniel Ortega of the FSLN, Sergio Ramirez of the Twelve, Alfonso Robelo of the FAO, Violeta Barrios de Chamorro, a director of *La Prensa* and widow of the slain publisher, and Moises Hassan, MPU leader and former dean of the National Autonomous University of Nicaragua. Andean Pact countries—Colombia, Venezuela, Peru, Ecuador and Bolivia—announced that the FSLN guerrillas were "legitimate combatants," a form of tacit recognition. On June 18, the junta issued its first proclamation, spelling out an extensive program of political, economic and social reconstruction. By then, many Somocista politicians and officials had moved into the safer quarters of the Intercontinental Hotel adjacent to Somoza's headquarters, known as "the Bunker."

Washington desperately launched its own final offensive to block a Sandinista victory. The new ambassador to Nicaragua, Lawrence Pezzullo (previously based in Uruguay), called on Luis Pallais in Washington on June 18 to tell him the new U.S. strategy. According to Pallais, the United States "wanted Somoza to resign in a 'statesmanlike' manner after helping to arrange for a national reconstruction government that would include representation from the Nationalist Liberal Party, the Conservatives, other members of the FAO, and the FSLN. Individuals mentioned...included Alfonso Robelo; Adolfo Calero [director of the Nicaragua Coca-Cola Company]; Archbishop Obando y Bravo; and Eden Pastora—but none of the more radical Sandinistas." Elections would be organized within a "prudential" time with the help of the OAS. The National Guard would continue under new leadership.[84]

Somoza responded the next day. He would resign under the conditions of an orderly transition overseen by the OAS and exile without threat of extradition in the United States. Again, events outpaced Washington. On June 20, ABC television reporter Bill Stewart was murdered in cold blood at a National Guard checkpoint. Stewart's crew filmed as he was ordered to his knees, then to lie face down on the ground where he was suddenly shot in the head. The footage shown on American television reached millions who had not seen, or been moved by, earlier evidence of the Guard's brutality. Telegrams and phone calls from outraged Americans poured into the White House. "One consequence of the tragedy," observed Pastor, "was that it quieted the thunder from the right in the United States."[85] Today there is a monument to Bill Stewart in Managua.

The CIA predicted on June 19 that Somoza would last a week or more; it would repeat that assessment four more times at approximately weekly intervals. At a Special Coordination Committee meeting that day, Brzezinski, Vance, Christopher, Vaky, Pastor, Turner, Pezzullo and General David Jones, the chairman of the Joint Chiefs, discussed Nicaragua. Brzezinski, explained Pastor, asserted that "events in Nicaragua would impact on U.S.-Soviet relations and on the President's domestic political standing, particularly in the South and the West. Then he crisply defined the objective for U.S. policy—to move Somoza out and create in his place a viable government of national reconciliation. The question was how to accomplish this goal."

They debated the proposal the administration would bring before a special session of the OAS on June 21. Vance said the chances of gaining approval for a peacekeeping force were "slim." Christopher and Vaky suggested that after Somoza left, a government of national reconciliation could invite help from the United States. Brzezinski questioned whether the Guard or the government would hold together long enough to preclude a peacekeeping force. Brown and Brzezinski, said Pastor, "proposed that the President be informed that the discussion introduced two unattractive but possible alternatives—a Sandinista victory or U.S. intervention."

The State Department drafted Vance's speech for the OAS, omitting any reference to Cuban involvement in Nicaragua or the "peace force." After consulting with Brzezinski, Carter "wrote both points into the text."[86]

As Vance presented it to the OAS on June 21, the U.S. proposal called for: "formation of an interim government of national reconciliation acceptable to all major elements of the society; a cessation of arms shipments; a cease-fire; an O.A.S. peacekeeping presence to help establish a climate of peace and security; and a major international relief and reconstruction effort."

Vance's speech referred to "mounting evidence of involvement by Cuba and others in the internal problems of Nicaragua." But in testimony before a House subcommittee shortly after, Vaky admitted that Cuba was "not the only or even the most important" FSLN supporter.[87]

The U.S. plan generated heat, not support. Mexican Foreign Minister Jorge Castaneda declared, "It is not up to the OAS or anyone else to tell them how they should constitute their government once they knock down a dictator." Provisional government representative Miguel D'Escoto, given a seat in Panama's delegation, denounced the plan as "an attempt to violate the rights of Nicaraguans who have almost succeeded in throwing off the Somoza yoke."[88]

"For the first time since its origins in 1948," observed historian Walter LeFeber, "the OAS had rejected a U.S. proposal to intervene in an American state...The ghosts of past U.S. interventions could not be laid to rest; if North Americans had poor memories the Latin Americans did not." Viron Vaky "accurately observed that the OAS rejection 'reflected how deeply the American states were sensitized by the Dominican intervention of 1965, and how deeply they fear physical intervention.'"[89]

"I returned from the OAS meeting to the White House to brief Brzezinski and found him in a very different world, contemplating military intervention," recalled Pastor. At a meeting with Carter and others on June 22, Brzezinski forcefully presented the case for military intervention, spelling out "the major domestic and international implications of a Castroite take-over in Nicaragua. [The United States] would be considered as being incapable of dealing with problems in our own backyard and impotent in the face of Cuban intervention. This will have devastating domestic implications, including for SALT [Strategic Arms Limitation Treaty]."[90]

Vance spoke of the negative response in the OAS to the peacekeeping force and Carter rejected the idea of unilateral U.S. intervention. At a meeting the next day, Secretary of Defense Brown joined Vance in opposing unilateral intervention. Instead, the Special Coordination Committee agreed that the United States would continue to seek a negotiated transition in Nicaragua and that "after a new government was installed, the United States could help to support it while it opened negotiations with the [Sandinista-backed] junta."[91]

The OAS adopted a resolution on June 23 asserting "that the people of Nicaragua are suffering...the horrors of a bloody struggle against the armed forces" and calling for "immediate and definite replacement of the Somocista regime; installation...of a democratic government that involves...the representatives of the major groups opposed to the Somoza regime that reflect the free will of the people of Nicaragua; full guarantee of Human Rights for all the Nicaraguan people without exception; carrying out free elections as early as possible that lead to the establishment of a true democratic government that will guarantee peace, freedom and justice." It urged the "member states to carry out all the steps within their power to expedite a durable and peaceful solution to the Nicaraguan problem upon the said bases, respecting scrupulously the no intervention principle."

Seventeen countries, including the United States, supported the resolution. Only Nicaragua and Paraguay voted against it; Chile, El Salvador, Guatemala and Honduras abstained. The Carter administration transformed the language it had inserted about member states taking steps to facilitate a peaceful solution into a license to, in Pastor's words, "negotiate a transition in Nicaragua legitimately."[92]

Carter recognized the Canal treaty as a symbol of a new era in relations, but somehow he expected that Latin America would continue to sanction the U.S. intervention from which it suffered. Brzezinski too realized the symbolic importance of the treaty, writing in his memoirs: "Ratifying the treaty was seen by us as a necessary precondition for a more mature and historically more just relationship with Central America, a region which we had never understood too well and which we occasionally [sic] dominated the way that the Soviets have dominated Eastern Europe. It was a new beginning."

Brzezinski said he wanted "to develop an approach to the Central American problem that would combine genuine commitment to social reform and more effective impediments to Cuban penetration."[93] Expressing this two-track approach on a global scale in March 1980, Brzezinski argued that the United States was trying "to do two things," firstly, "to make the United States historically more relevant to a world of genuinely profound change; and secondly, to improve the United States' position in the geo-strategic balance with the Soviet Union."[94] These "two things" often conflict.

Brzezinski's earlier works revealed an accommodationist policy thinker who advocated that the United States "move to abandon the Monroe Doctrine"; have "a less anxious preoccupation with the Soviet Union"; and recognize that change in Latin America is likely to combine "a more socially responsible Catholicism with nationalism," producing "a highly differentiated pattern of change," whose radical manifestations even, "are not likely to be modeled on communist countries."[95]

Brzezinski turned out to be a dogmatic policy maker, letting his staunch anti-Sovietism become a myopic guide to policy in the Third World.

In his memoirs, Brzezinski wrote: "when a choice between the two had to be made, between projecting U.S. power or enhancing human rights (as, for example, in Iran), I felt that power had to come first. Without credible American power, we would simply not be able either to protect our interests or to advance more humane goals."[96] Brzezinski prevailed in making U.S. power the centerpiece of the OAS proposal. The Latin Americans broke new ground by rejecting it, seeking another way to protect regional interests and advance genuinely more humane goals.

"Let's Do It With Grace"

From June 9 to June 27, insurrection raged in Managua. Somoza's planes bombarded rebellious neighborhoods and opposition-owned factories. On the evening of June 27, the FSLN led a tactical retreat to Masaya, leaving snipers behind while some 6,000 guerrillas and supporters marched for two days, mainly across open country. They reached Masaya with few casualties. "If we can do that," said one participant, "we can do anything."[97]

By June 25, the administration had decided on a two-pronged strategy of beginning talks to try and influence the composition of the provisional junta while "quietly" trying to negotiate the establishment of a "third force," a so-called Executive Committee that could become an alternative governing structure. Administration officials judged the chances of success at about 50-50.[98]

Ambassador Pezzullo arrived in Managua on June 27 with the goals of obtaining Somoza's resignation, preserving the National Guard and forming an Executive Committee. By then, Somoza saw "the ball game was over. My chief concern was the welfare of those dedicated and loyal members of the Guardia Nacional and the members of the Liberal Party."[99]

Meanwhile, according to Shirley Christian, Pastora had sent a message to Washington: "if it wanted to prevent a victory by radicals, it should convince Somoza to pull the National Guard back from the south and give him a chance to get to Managua with his troops." Pastora thought "that because of his popularity and fame the FSLN would be forced to concede him more power in the new regime if he got there first."[100] The United States was not yet ready to support Pastora.

Beginning on June 27, Pezzullo and Somoza held a series of meetings to arrange Somoza's departure. Somoza introduced himself as "a Latin from Manhattan." Rep. Murphy was present at some meetings, acting as Somoza's adviser. Pezzullo reiterated the proposal he had made earlier to Pallais: Somoza would resign, turning over power to the congress who would then appoint a constitutional successor "which would immediately bring a ceasefire, a beginning of a political dialogue, which would give an opportunity for the forces in this country to seek a total solution and hopefully preserve as many institutions as are preservable."

By then, however, Somoza had little power to turn over, having lost control of much of the country outside Managua. Somoza suggested he could leave the next day, taking Pezzullo aback. "I don't want you to leave tomorrow," said Pezzullo. "I've just got to get organized a little bit...Please don't move too precipitously...Let's do it with grace."

The next day, Pezzullo told Somoza, "When you go, there is a chance to put something viable in its place quickly, and get into a transition government that we can get international support for, and put in the kind of resources that prevent going to the Left. Your Liberal Party will survive, your Guardia will survive—under a different name probably...If we let the damn thing go further, I think we are all out of business."[101]

Pezzullo met with Archbishop Obando y Bravo and Ismael Reyes, the president of the Nicaraguan Red Cross, to pursue the idea of an Executive Committee. Arturo Cruz, meanwhile, told the State Department "that a broadened junta was not the answer since the question was who had the guns? Cruz supported the idea of a neutral force [to] stand temporarily between the National Guard and the Sandinistas." He believed "that a compromise can possibly be found [with the FSLN] providing a role for the less-tainted elements of the present Guard."[102]

On June 29, Pezzullo stressed to Somoza his role in holding the Guard together behind a transition arrangement. The "Guardia will survive, not in the same form, but it will survive. If we all play our cards well." Pezzullo appeared confident the Sandinistas could be marginalized: "Once these extremists are put in a situation where there are other forces of [sic] play they are going to be the minority. They won't represent more than five or six percent."[103]

Pezzullo cabled Washington on June 30, observing that with "careful orchestration we have a better than even chance of preserving enough of the GN [Guardia Nacional] to maintain order and hold the FSLN in check after Somoza resigns."[104]

Somoza wrote out his resignation letter and carried it around for seventeen days awaiting Washington's final plan. Miguel D'Escoto recalled how U.S. officials "tried to say to us, in fact it wasn't so much the Nicaraguan people that were going to throw Somoza out. They were the ones who had his resignation in their pocket and they would only pull it out if we went ahead and did a couple of things," namely, preserve the National Guard and expand the junta.

Bowdler had met in Panama City on June 26 with D'Escoto and four junta members. It was the first official U.S. contact with Sandinista leaders. Bowdler's fundamental objective," D'Escoto told me, "was to get us to accept an augmentation of the junta—to increase it by five, that was the initial idea. Then it was by three, and then by maybe even two only, but to augment it. And also to take steps to ensure that the National Guard would only be 'cleansed,' but not totally destroyed, because the National Guard, said Bowdler, was going to be the guarantee for order...He was saying to me inevitably after the revolution, after the overthrow of Somoza, people would want to take justice in their hands and there would be all kinds of summary executions and [firing squads] and this kind of thing. And that it was indispensable to keep the National Guard as the only ones capable of maintaining order.

"And when we argued against that, and showed the lack of logic and coherence in his arguments and...in the American demand that the number of people in the junta be augmented, the only thing, the only argument that he could have...was 'Well, this is what the United States wants and it is important to please the United States,' and that's it. It's important to please the United States.

"But, another argument later on that made a little bit more sense was that President Carter had refused to...recognize the junta that had been named, and that he would lose credibility if all of a sudden, without any change, he went ahead and accepted it...It would make him look as if he was defeated somehow and this would enhance the possibility of Reagan coming to power. And, certainly, that wouldn't be in our best interests. So, we should get involved in the American electoral situation—that's practically what he was saying—and prevent the worst imaginable thing. We should go ahead and engage in this face-saving move.

"And I remember I would say, 'I could understand the difficulties in the United States, but that Nicaragua, you know, was an independent nation. We had our own problems and we have to act on the basis of our interest.'"[105]

Washington's plan for reconstituting the provisional government was not only rejected by the junta, it was rejected by those who were seen as the alternatives. On June 29, the FAO and COSEP reiterated their support for the Sandinista-backed junta and said they would not participate in a competing administration.[106]

The next day, Vaky cabled Pezzullo, telling him "what follows after Somoza's departure is too uncertain as yet...Hence Somoza should stay in place until this is determined."[107]

The administration moved away from the two-track strategy on July 2 to focus on reshaping the provisional junta and securing the survival of a modified National Guard that would be legitimized by countries such as Panama, Venezuela and Costa Rica. CIA Director Turner suggested that the United States could support the Guard indirectly through Israel. But Carter was prepared to provide direct and overt support for the Guard if it had some national and international legitimacy. The administration attempted to recruit an acceptable new Guard commander and secure a slot for him on the junta.[108]

On July 6, Somoza publicly acknowledged that he was ready to resign, but the timing was in U.S. hands.[109] Hopeful that Somoza could transfer power to a fellow Liberal Party member who would then carry out a cease-fire and new elections, Pezzullo cabled Washington: "Even though this successor government would smack somewhat of Somocismo sin Somoza, it would be a bold strike and a break with the past. Somoza would be gone. We would be viewed as the instrument which brought about his departure and ended the bloodletting."[110]

"The United States has always intervened when we Nicaraguans have tried to define our own future," said a wealthy young businessman. "Now it is willing to see Nicaragua bombed back to the Stone Age in order to maintain its system of domination."[111]

The businessman could not know how right he was. In a cable to Secretary of State Vance, Pezzullo recommended against pressuring Somoza to stop the bombardments: "I believe it is ill-advised to go to Somoza and ask for a bombing halt."

He explained, "Air power is the only effective force the GN has to combat the FSLN Force which is capturing more towns daily and clearly has the momentum."[112]

At this point, recalled Ramirez, "when the insurrection was already working and we were able to establish our own parallel government in Costa Rica," Bowdler "was not trying to save all the pieces of the machine of the Somoza system…The only thing Mr. Bowdler was trying to save was the National Guard. Of course, the National Guard was the central piece of this machine."[113]

As *Washington Post* reporter Karen DeYoung described it, "U.S. policy calls for breaking up the Sandinista army after the war and integrating some 'moderate' guerrillas into a future armed force dominated by the National Guard."[114]

On July 10, knowing that it was being held responsible for the continued bloodbath, given Somoza's readiness to resign, and fearing a complete collapse of the Guard, the administration "decided to bring the crisis to a head." Meeting in Costa Rica, Bowdler presented the junta with an ultimatum to expand its membership, accept a new Guard commander and agree to a cease-fire and elections or, as Pastor described it, "the United States would consider alternative approaches to facilitate a transition. The administration had no idea what alternatives were available, but threats made in desperation are not generally inhibited by the absence of rational alternatives."[115]

The junta called Washington's bluff. It released a "Plan to Achieve Peace" on July 11: Somoza was to resign to congress which in turn would cede power to the junta. The junta would dissolve the Somocista congress and carry out a cease-fire; guardsmen who immediately ceased fighting would be eligible to join a new Nicaraguan army (with a Sandinista core). Guardsmen and others guilty of serious crimes would be tried. In a letter presenting the plan to OAS Secretary General Alejandro Orfila, the junta stated that "those collaborators with the regime that may wish to leave the country and that are not responsible for the genocide we have suffered or for other serious crimes that demand trial by the civil courts, may do so with all the necessary guarantees, which the government of national reconstruction authorizes as of now." And it announced "the plan to call the first free elections our country has known in this century, so that Nicaraguans can elect their representatives to the city councils and to a constituent assembly, and later elect the country's highest authorities."[116]

Somoza informed Francisco Urcuyo, president of the Chamber of Deputies of the Nicaraguan congress, that he should be ready to serve as interim president following Somoza's imminent resignation.

Sandinista Triumph

On July 12, the FSLN's Radio Sandino announced that Leon, Esteli, Chinandega, Matagalpa and Masaya were all liberated territory.

The next day, Washington added a new element to its continued attempt to shape post-Somoza Nicaragua. Because "Pastora was considered more independent than the Directorate a meeting with him was authorized to explore future possibilities for cooperation." Torrijos and President Carazo of Costa Rica had been trying to arrange a meeting between Pastora and U.S. officials for about eight months, but the administration had refused. According to Pastor, the administration discovered "that Pastora was much more suspicious of the United States than the United States was of him. The initial discussions were difficult and not satisfactory."[117]

On July 14, the junta announced the names of twelve members of the new Nicaraguan cabinet, including Miguel D'Escoto as foreign minister, Arturo Cruz as president of the Central Bank, Carlos Tunnermann as minister of education, Tomas Borge as interior minister and Bernardino Larios, a National Guard colonel who had defected the year before, as minister of defense.

Pezzullo, meeting with Somoza, and Bowdler, meeting with the junta, negotiated a plan for Somoza's resignation and transfer of power. The gist of it was that Somoza, his family and most of the Guard's top officers would fly to the United States. An interim president (Urcuyo) appointed by the Nicaraguan congress would meet at the airport with a delegation of representatives from the junta, the FSLN directorate, Bowdler and Archbishop Obando. The interim president would announce an immediate cease-fire and, with the new commander of the National Guard, would arrange a rapid transfer of power to the junta.

On July 15, Archbishop Obando, Red Cross President Ismail Reyes, Jose Esteban Gonzales of the Permanent Commission on Human Rights and other anti-Sandinistas traveled to Venezuela to meet with President Luis Herrera Campins in a last-ditch effort to expand the junta. That same day, Pezzullo submitted the names of six candidates to Somoza for the position of chief of the National Guard, including Colonel Enrique Bermudez, who would later head the major contra force. Somoza selected Colonel Federico Mejia for the double post of director of the National Guard and chief of staff. According to Luis Pallais, Mejia "was going to offer one of the posts to Eden Pastora in the negotiations that were expected to follow Somoza's departure."[118] According to Pezzullo, Mejia would be Guardia chief of staff and Humberto Ortega would be chief of staff of the FSLN.[119]

The FSLN delayed their Managua offensive on July 16, pending Somoza's expected resignation the next morning. Meeting at the Intercontinental Hotel at about 1:00 A.M. on July 17, the Nicaraguan congress promptly accepted Somoza's resignation and Urcuyo became acting president. Somoza, his family and his closest associates left for Florida close to the prearranged hour of 4 A.M. Somoza took the caskets of his father and brother with him into exile.

That was the beginning and the end of the orderly transfer of power. In a nationwide address, Urcuyo called on the guerrillas to lay down their arms and asked all "national democratic organizations" to join him in a dialogue to create a new government. As it appeared that Urcuyo was prepared to serve out Somoza's term, the negotiated transition process dissolved into chaos. One military analyst commented, "Washington's whole game plan is to avert a Sandinista triumph. It can't let things fall apart now."[120] But Pezzullo called Vaky to tell him "the whole thing is coming apart." Pezzullo couldn't put it back together.[121]

As Sandinista forces closed in on Managua, the National Guard disintegrated. Junta members flew to Leon on July 18 and declared it the provisional capital. Pezzullo and most of the embassy staff left Nicaragua to show they did not support Urcuyo; Deputy Secretary of State Warren Christopher called Somoza in Miami Beach and threatened to cut short his stay if Urcuyo did not get back on track. Somoza secured Urcuyo's agreement to resign, but by then events had passed them by. By evening, Urcuyo and other Somocistas left Nicaragua on Guatemalan Air Force planes. Colonel Mejia left early the next morning, joining a frantic migration of guardsmen and mercenaries. The junta called for the Guard to surrender. About 2,000 guardsmen fled over the border to Honduras. Another 1,000 on the southern front commandeered boats at the port of San Juan del Sur and took off for El Salvador.

During the last days of fighting, the Carter administration arranged to airlift food into Nicaragua where supplies were running low. U.S. military planes were ruled out to avoid the appearance of intervention. So the Agency for International Development awarded the delivery contract to a private firm, Southern Air Transport. "Oh, my God," said one official when informed that Southern Air Transport, a well-known CIA proprietary (officially sold in 1973), had the contract. Another official remarked, "Who else are you going to get to fly stuff to a country where there's a war going on?"[122]

July 19 was the day of victory. Wary of U.S. anger over the collapse of the transition plan, Somoza spent the day moving his exile to the Bahamas; two weeks later, he moved to Paraguay, where he lived until his murder on September 17, 1980. On July 20, the junta and Sandinista directorate left Leon and entered Managua to the triumphant celebrating of hundreds of thousands of Nicaraguans.

Meanwhile, an American named "Bill" landed in Managua on July 19 in a DC-8 with phony Red Cross insignia. His mission, explained journalist Christopher Dickey, "was to rescue Colonel Justiniano Perez, the second in command of the EEBI." Bill found "Tino" Perez in the crowd at the Guatemalan Embassy and took him out dressed in Red Cross guise. "Over the next few days, Bill went about the business of pulling together remnants of the Guardia officer corps and their families from Guatemala and El Salvador. By the time the DC-8 set down in Miami again there were about 130 people on board. Survivors of the old Guardia, they had the potential, they hoped, to build a new one with a little help from friends like Bill and Congressman Murphy."[123]

2

Fleeting Coexistence

We don't want to be a second Cuba. We want to establish a first Nicaragua. We want a Nicaraguan revolution.

Father Ernesto Cardenal, *New York Times*, June 30, 1979.

As Dr. Hans Morgenthau once wrote: "The real issue facing American foreign policy...is not how to preserve stability in the face of revolution, but how to create stability out of revolution."

Assistant Secretary of State Viron Vaky,
testimony before the House Foreign Affairs Committee, September 1979.

The Sandinistas reciprocated the suspicions that U.S. policy makers had of them, but their mistrust was related to the asymmetry in power: the Sandinistas had to be much more suspicious because the capacity of the United States to undermine their revolution was infinitely greater than their capacity to affect U.S. interests.

Robert Pastor, former NSC director of Latin American and Caribbean Affairs.[1]

"Year of Liberation." That's how 1979 is recorded in the annals of the new Nicaragua. "Since July 19, we are no longer a banana republic, we are no longer anyone's backyard," said Sandinista leader Bayardo Arce. "We aren't part of any bloc," but rather "part of humanity," struggling "to transform relations of dependency and submission into relations of friendship and solidarity, of mutual respect and cooperation."[2]

The old Nicaragua was in ruins. Up to 50,000 Nicaraguans died in the last five years of struggle leading to Somoza's overthrow, most in the closing two years of insurrection. That represented 2 percent of the Nicaraguan population, then numbering about 2.5 million. The U.S equivalent would be over 4.5 million dead.

Human cost was compounded by economic devastation. Cities spared by the earthquake were wrecked by Somoza's bombs. There was over $480 million dollars in direct economic damage. More than $500 million disappeared in capital flight—to the Caymans, Miami and other money sanctuaries. To top it off, the Somozas looted the national treasury and left behind a foreign debt of $1.6 billion.[3] A classified U.S. intelligence report put the Somoza family wealth at $900 million, more than half the national debt.[4]

The ruins of war rested on a foundation of poverty. The UN Economic Commission for Latin America (ECLA) estimated that 62.5 percent of the prerevolutionary Nicaraguan population lived in a state of critical poverty. Two out of three Nicaraguans did not have enough income to cover their most basic needs. More than one out of three Nicaraguans lived in "extreme poverty." They "did not even have sufficient income to cover the value of the minimum shopping basket of food considered necessary in order to meet their biological nutritional needs."[5]

Infant mortality was 121 per 1,000 live births. Less than 20 percent of pregnant women and children under five received any health care. In rural areas, where nearly half the population lived, 93 percent of the homes had no safe drinking water. Less than one in ten rural children were able to finish primary school.[6] More than half the Nicaraguan population is under sixteen years old. The revolution promised a better future.

The new government was called the Government of National Reconstruction. Even with enduring peace, reconstruction would have been difficult. The World Bank reported in 1981: "the negative consequences of the war are far from over. Per capita income levels of 1977 will not be attained, in the best of circumstances, until the late 1980s."[7] The goal of the new government was not to reconstruct the poverty of the past, but to combine development with equity.

In the words of Agriculture Minister Jaime Wheelock, "On July 19th we won our political independence; now we confront the even more difficult task of winning our economic independence."[8]

Logic of the Majority

"People would dream 'maybe Somoza will fall this year,' " recalled Dora Maria Tellez. "We realized that the problem was Somocismo and...that this country had never been truly independent. Here the companies would take the gold and the Nicaraguan miners kept the tuberculosis. Wood was taken away and the misery remained here. All the natural riches would leave...We produced sugar because the United States decided we should grow sugar, and bananas because the United States needed bananas...We [didn't] grow corn or beans in an efficient amount because no one outside the country decided we should grow them...

"Somocismo had carried corruption to all levels. Such basic things as patriotism, that was a word that lacked all meaning in this country. Sovereignty, that was a forgotten phrase. Dignity, no one knew what it was. Somoza used to say that every man had his price. Everyone could be bought. So we also had to make a moral revolution."[9]

The new Nicaragua was guided by the "logic of the majority"—the poor majority who had known tyranny of the minority and never before had a chance to exercise the democratic principle of majority rule. "It was the poor who dug trenches, built roadblocks and held off the guards with homemade bombs, pistols and hunting rifles, and, in the main, it was the poor who died," wrote Alan Riding. "In reality, the insurrection and the victory belonged to them."[10] The rights of the wealthy minority would be protected, but not their privileges.

In the view of Nicaraguan elites and the U.S. government, it was not the poor who made the revolution, but the middle and upper classes who turned on Somoza after the assassination of Pedro Joaquin Chamorro. As Shirley Christian put it, "it was not the masses, but the economic and political elites who made it possible for the Sandinistas to march triumphantly into Managua."[11]

For the elites the revolution culminated on July 19 with the fall of the dictatorship. A transitional government would bring forth procedural democracy in the political system, but the socio-economic system would be little changed. Years later, such a "revolution" occurred in the Philippines with the 1986 ouster of Ferdinand Marcos. There, the euphoria of Corazon Aquino's "people power" gave way to indignation among peasants, workers and students as promises of social and economic reform appeared more and more shallow.

In Nicaragua the opposite occurred. For the Sandinistas, July 19 is the date of the "triumph" in the war of national liberation. The revolution, the war against poverty and exploitation, was just beginning. As the promises of radical social and economic change were translated into practice, Nicaraguan elites protested that the Sandinistas were "betraying the revolution."

As Bayardo Arce put it, "The bourgeoisie thought we were a bunch of brave, dedicated boys who would fight to the death to overthrow Somoza and then say, 'here you are. Now give me a scholarship to finish my degree.' Now they're surprised we have a political project."[12]

The Sandinista project promised political pluralism, participatory democracy, nonalignment and a mixed economy composed of a private sector, with both individual and cooperative ownership, and a state sector. In *Sandinismo*, political pluralism is tied to the economic pluralism of a mixed economy. In Arce's words, "We don't see the possibility of creating true political pluralism without true economic pluralism, in the sense that both processes correspond with a better distribution of national resources."[13]

Sergio Ramirez would later dismiss claims that the Sandinistas "stole" or "betrayed" the revolution: "The fundamental promises were made to the poorest of our country…And the original program continues, growing and multiplying for them, in cooperatives, in schools, in health-care centers, in land, in dignity, in national sovereignty." Those who speak of betrayal of the revolution are speaking of a "program in which the winds of revolution did not so much as rustle their privileges of so many decades...It would have been impossible to make a revolution with such sacrifice, at the expense of so much blood, and cut it to such a pattern—a pattern that is egoistic, hardly Christian, and certainly not altruistic. This idea of a revolution without consequences, we have genuinely betrayed."[14]

Seven years into the revolution and six years into the contra war, I asked a U.S. ambassador in Central America whether, in his view, the Nicaraguan government had done anything positive for the people. He remarked that the Sandinistas have "tried to extend social services and economic opportunities geographically, into the capillaries...to the smallest villages." He mentioned increased educational opportunities. That wasn't all. He said, "They've also greatly enhanced a sense of national identity, of pride...This doesn't work particularly for American concerns in Central America, but you have to admire it. It's inspiring."[15]

A rural woman active in AMNLAE, the Nicaraguan Women's Association, said simply, "I personally feel as if I was born again."[16]

Fall-Back Strategy

The Carter administration believed that confrontation would be counterproductive and increase the prospect of "another Cuba" in Nicaragua. In Carter's words, "We were trying to maintain our ties with Nicaragua, to keep it from turning to Cuba and the Soviet Union."[17]

Nicaraguan officials were well aware of debate in the United States over policy toward their country. In August 1979, Rep. Murphy had presented Colonel Enrique Bermudez, Tino Perez and other ex-Guard officers in a Washington press conference. Miguel D'Escoto recalled the debate as turning "around the issue of whether Nicaragua had been definitively lost or whether it was still redeemable...I think it was Cyrus Vance and President Carter [who] were of the opinion that maybe it's lost, but maybe it wasn't. If it wasn't, and one acted as if it was, then for sure it would be. So let's give it a chance and try to work along with it in a plan to bring...[it] back."[18]

Of course, the Nicaraguans didn't see themselves as lost. They were establishing their own identity and they resented being seen as something to be "lost" by the United States and found by the Soviet Union—as if independence was not a possibility, much less a right, for small Third World countries. The Soviet Union did not even establish diplomatic relations with the new Nicaraguan government until October 18, three months after Somoza's overthrow.

Having failed to prevent the Sandinista revolution, the Carter administration now tried to mold it. "Our use of aid is pure behavior modification," explained a U.S. diplomat in Central America. "U.S. dollars are rewarded like lumps of sugar to good little countries and withheld for shock value from stubborn, naughty countries."[19]

Washington wanted to limit the pace and scope of economic reform. Washington's agents were the business and agricultural elites represented in COSEP, who profited from an economic system dependent upon the United States. By the logic of that minority, the needs of the poor majority would remain subordinate.

In international affairs, the administration expected Nicaragua to politically reciprocate the solidarity that Salvadoran revolutionaries had shown the FSLN. But it also expected Nicaragua to restrain its material assistance in the interest of good relations with the United States. Given Cuba's history of support for the FSLN, the administration expected Nicaragua and Cuba to have friendly relations. But it expected those relations to be counterbalanced by ties to other Latin American countries such as Mexico, Venezuela, Panama and Costa Rica. And, of course, Washington wanted Nicaragua to limit relations, especially military relations, with the Soviet Union.

In testimony before Congress in September 1979, Ambassador Pezzullo insisted that the revolution "is very much a Nicaraguan phenomenon...Sandinismo...is a Nicaraguan home-grown movement. Sandino predates Castro... The nature of this thing is such that you have to see it take its own form and then identify that form, rather than make prejudgements about it...

"They are attracted to Castro for some things. They are attracted to Castro because Castro was the first real leader that emerged in the last couple of decades who defied U.S. dominance of the area, even Latins who are not pro-Castro sympathized with Castro on that count.

"Second, a lot of these fellows went there to train. The reality of the world is if you want to overthrow a tyrant you don't go to Boston for training. You can go to Havana. So, there is that solidarity. They feel this. But that does not mean they are going to follow a Cuban model or even try to impose that kind of system."[20]

Policymakers were concerned about creating a self-fulfilling prophecy in Nicaragua. They "consciously set out to avoid repeating the errors of 1959 and 1960, when U.S. hostility drove the Cuban revolution into the arms of the Soviet Union."[21] This time, the administration would be more "patient and openminded," judging the Sandinistas "not by what they've said in the past but by what they do in the future."[22]

Six weeks after Somoza's ouster, one former Carter official wrote: "Administration experts are surprised and pleased. Perhaps never has so much civil war been followed by so much peace. It is clear so far that the junta is trying to prevent executions and arbitrary retribution...And despite Washington's long support for the repulsive Somoza regime...the junta is working with the United States."[23]

Public sentiment for punishing those responsible for crimes under Somoza was widespread and the junta moved quickly to channel the mass outcry for retribution into an orderly legal process. Special Tribunals and Special Appellate Courts functioned from December 1979 until February 1981 to try military personnel, civilian employees and public officials of the Somoza regime who were accused of crimes. Capital punishment was outlawed; the maximum sentence was 30 years. Out of a total of 4,250 defendants, 267 were acquitted and 30 had their charges dropped. Of those convicted, approximately 38 percent received sentences of from 1 to 5 years, 6 percent from 6 to 10 years, 27 percent from 11 to 20 years and 29 percent from

20 to 30 years. Clemency procedures established in October 1981 resulted in pardons or commuted sentences for hundreds of prisoners.[24]

Assistant Secretary Vaky told Congress in September 1979 that the Nicaraguan government "has shown generally moderate pluralistic tendencies in its initial policies. It is not distinguishably Marxist in orientation, although Marxist figures are present in key positions. It has restrained reprisals, promulgated a decree guaranteeing individual rights, and has permitted an independent press and radio. It has promised free elections." In foreign affairs, Nicaragua "has indicated a desire for friendly relations with all countries, including their northern neighbors. Nicaraguan leaders have denied any intention of exporting revolution...

"Nicaragua's future internal policies and relationships with the outside world will, in fact, be determined by those Nicaraguans who best define and meet the country's needs during the reconstruction period...

"The course of the Nicaraguan revolution can thus be affected in no small way by how the U.S. perceives it and relates to it. We might write it off as already radicalized and beyond redemption, but that would not only be untrue at this moment, it would also surely drive the revolution into radicalization."[25] (Vaky resigned in December 1979 and was replaced as assistant secretary by William Bowdler.)

Military Scrap

Just as the United States was testing Nicaragua, Nicaragua was testing the United States. The Nicaraguan government wanted good relations with Washington, based upon pragmatic and flexible policies on both sides. But would the United States give up control over Nicaraguan destiny? How far would the Carter administration go in its attempt at "behavior modification"?

Nicaragua's mistrust of the United States was far less paranoid than U.S. fears of the Sandinistas. The United States had sent marines against Sandino. The Sandinistas could not assume that the United States would not fight his heirs. Washington tried to impose "peacekeeping forces" in Nicaragua to preempt a Sandinista victory and had destroyed most reformist and revolutionary governments in Latin America—such as Arbenz in Guatemala (1954) and Allende in Chile (1973).

Before July 1979 was over, Minister of the Interior Tomas Borge raised unofficially the issue of U.S. military aid for Nicaragua in a meeting with Ambassador Pezzullo. At a press conference announcing formation of the new Sandinista Army, Luis Carrion, a member of the general command, made clear that Nicaragua expected to have to defend itself against counterrevolutionary attacks; he cited efforts in Miami and Honduras to organize Somocista forces.[26]

Deputy Interior Minister Eden Pastora claimed on August 11 that Nicaragua would seek arms "from the socialist bloc or elsewhere" if U.S. arms were not forthcoming. At the same time, he angrily rejected a call by Nicaraguan bishops to grant amnesty to imprisoned ex-guardsmen: "How can we let out those who are murderers? If you had seen the unscrupulous people who—without batting an eye—

led us to common graves with 50 bodies and said they had killed them...before they died they mutilated them—cut off their genitals, their arms or legs and bled them to death. Don't come to us and ask amnesty for those criminals."[27]

The following day, Borge said that Pastora's remarks on armaments did not represent official government policy. Borge did not rule out the purchase of arms from socialist countries, but he characterized it as a step of last resort. Nicaragua, he said, did not want to give "pretext to feelings that we are aligning ourselves with them politically."[28] In late August, Defense Minister Larios extended Nicaragua's search for arms, with visits to Belgium, West Germany, Spain, Mexico, Brazil and Cuba.[29]

Washington was well aware of Nicaragua's military vulnerability. The Pentagon and State Department reported: "To an even greater degree than other elements of government, the Nicaraguan defense establishment was swept away. Nothing remains except for some small arms and the scattered remnants of other equipment, all of it battlescarred and most of it fit for little more than salvage. The armed forces of Nicaragua must be entirely rebuilt, both its personnel and equipment."[30]

A visitor to Managua could walk through a graveyard of armored vehicles. They had gone to battle against the Nicaraguan people, but could not be put to their defense.

Within the Carter administration, proponents of selling arms to Nicaragua argued it would be a positive sign of friendship and "if we don't, the Cubans will."[31] But the prevailing view was that, whatever the pros and cons of providing arms to Nicaragua, the political reality in the United States virtually precluded it. Carter would have enough trouble winning congressional approval of economic aid.

When the administration proposed to train some Nicaraguan military personnel at the U.S. Army School of the Americas, the Nicaraguan government rejected it. Nicaraguans had enough experience with U.S. training of the National Guard. The $2.5 million in military aid still in the pipeline from Somoza's final year was cancelled. Nicaragua received $3,000 for binoculars and compasses and $20,000 for six Sandinista Army officers to tour Forts Stewart, Benning and Jackson in November.[32] By then, cross-border attacks were increasing; Nicaragua lost twenty militia in an October ambush.

$75 Million

U.S. government economists estimated that Nicaragua would need at least $800 million in outside assistance through 1980 and $200 to $250 million yearly for several years after that to restore the economy.[33] Since July 17, the United States had provided $8 million in disaster aid and had approved another $39 million for various projects.[34] In November, Carter submitted an urgent request for $75 million in economic aid for Nicaragua. It was designed primarily to provide direct support of the private sector and finance the purchase of U.S. goods and services. Of the $75 million, $70 million was a loan. Only $5 million was a grant—for scholarships, technical assistance and support for private voluntary agencies. Pezzullo urged congressional approval, arguing "the moderates need our support too badly for us to be sitting on the side of the road waiting for things to happen."[35]

Nicaragua became the most controversial country on the administration's proposed list of foreign aid recipients for 1980. The Senate passed the aid request on January 29, 1980 by a comfortable margin. On February 25, the House held another rare secret session to examine classified data on Soviet involvement in Nicaragua. On February 27, after heated debate, the aid legislation passed narrowly in the House by five votes, but was saddled with numerous conditions. The administration hoped these restrictive provisions would be removed in a House-Senate conference committee, but congressional critics of aid, then led by Rep. Robert Bauman (R-MD), blocked the bill from going to conference. The stalemate was broken only when the Senate voted on May 19 to accept the House version.

As signed into law, the bill required that at least 60 percent of the aid be used to assist the private sector. It required the president to certify that the "Government of Nicaragua has not cooperated with or harbors any international terrorist organization, or is aiding, abetting, or supporting acts of violence or terrorism in other countries." It required termination of aid if the government engaged in a "consistent pattern of gross violations of internationally recognized human rights"; engaged in a "consistent pattern of violations of the right to organize and operate labor unions free from political oppression"; or engaged in "systematic violations of free speech and press." And it required termination of aid if the president determined that Soviet, Cuban or other foreign combat forces were stationed in Nicaragua and that their presence there "constitutes a threat to the national security of the United States or to any other Latin American ally of the United States."[36]

Congress finally appropriated the $75 million on July 2 in the supplemental assistance bill for fiscal 1980 (October 1, 1979-September 30, 1980). That month, Ambassador Pezzullo declared Nicaragua to be "an acceptable model" of revolution.[37] However, the required presidential certification that Nicaragua did not support terrorism was mired in controversy. Carter finally signed the aid certification on September 12—relying on the State Department Bureau of Intelligence and Research—over the continued objections of congressional critics.[38] Disbursement of the funds could finally begin on October 1, 1980.

Year of Literacy

As the U.S. Congress debated whether Nicaragua was a "second Cuba," the new Nicaragua took shape. The FSLN's political program promised "a massive campaign to immediately wipe out illiteracy." A national literacy crusade was launched under the direction of former Group of Twelve member, Father Fernando Cardenal. Mass organizations such as the Sandinista Youth Organization, National Association of Nicaraguan Educators, Rural Workers' Association, AMNLAE (the women's association) and Sandinista Defense Committees were instrumental in carrying out the campaign. For five months beginning in March 1980, some 60,000 young *brigadis-tas*, a majority of them female, went into the countryside to teach—and to learn.

One peasant farmer wrote to the mother of his literacy teacher: "Do you know I'm not ignorant anymore? I know how to read now. Not perfectly, you understand, but I know how. And do you know, your son isn't ignorant anymore either? Now he knows how we live...He knows the life of the mountains. Your son, ma'am, has learned to read from our book."[39]

Nicaragua's literacy crusade earned UNESCO's 1980 first prize for literacy. The illiteracy rate was reduced from over 50 percent to 13 percent. A special campaign was organized for the Atlantic Coast to teach literacy in Miskito, English and Sumu as well as Spanish. In the last phase of the crusade, local coordinators were trained to lead continuing adult education in popular education collectives (CEPs). By 1983, there were 17,377 CEPs throughout the country.[40] In the formal education sector there was a massive expansion from preschool to graduate studies. The total school population more than doubled between 1979 and 1984.

The literacy crusade was the first mass project based on the logic of the majority. Consciously political as well as pedagogical, it was seen as a "second war of liberation." In the words of Sergio Ramirez, it was part of the process of preparing the poor, peasants and workers "both politically and technically to become the genuine authors of development."[41] Carlos Fernando Chamorro, the son of Violeta Chamorro and longtime editor of the Sandinista newspaper, *Barricada*, described the literacy crusade as "the first revolutionary measure taken in favor of press freedom," in that it developed "peoples' rights of access to culture, to be able to read and write."[42]

To its detractors, the literacy campaign was communist brainwashing. Junta member Alfonso Robelo complained that the literacy crusade "was being organized in such a way as to manipulate the poor and the ignorant for ideological or partisan political ends. This, he said, was immoral."[43]

The second war of liberation had its casualties. Newscasts announced the first one on May 19, 1980: "Eight ex-National Guardsmen crossed the border from Honduras yesterday and murdered the literacy teacher Georgino Andrade."[44] Pedro Rafael Pavon, one of Andrade's killers, received the maximum sentence of 30 years. He told the court that Andrade was killed "because he was a communist."[45] Six other literacy workers were murdered in the course of the campaign.

Conflicting Logic

In April, the junta announced the expansion of the Council of State, a legislative body to be inaugurated in May. Under the Plan of Government drawn up in June 1979, the Council was to have had 33 members representing the FSLN, diverse political parties, labor, private enterprise, and religious, professional and mass organizations. The expanded Council would have 47 seats (later increased to 51), meaning less strength for COSEP-affiliated forces in relation to the Sandinistas, but a still higher proportion than determined by the actual size of their constituency. The total number of large property owners—agricultural, commercial and industrial—was approximately 2,000 persons in 1980; the total for medium-sized property owners was about 40,000.[46] Of these, many were allied with COSEP; but others were allied with the FSLN or the less conservative opposition. COSEP's membership was later put at 35,000.[47]

The Sandinistas argued that new grassroots organizations had formed since the triumph and others had expanded (notably, the trade unions and the Sandinista Defense Committees, which reached 520,000 to 600,000 members by 1984). By the logic of participatory democracy, they should be adequately represented on the Council. In discussing the experience of his union with me later, Sandinista Workers' Federation (CST) Secretary General Lucio Jimenez stressed political power as a "fundamental gain...[With] the triumph of the revolution, as the working class, we felt there was no barrier between us and our aspirations. Before the barriers were the Somocista Guard, the Somocista dictatorship. We could now say that we were masters of our aspirations."[48]

In July 1979, there were 133 trade unions with 27,020 members. By December 1983, there were 1,103 unions with 233,032 members, the overwhelming majority of them Sandinista-affiliated. The CST had 504 unions with 111,498 members and the Rural Workers' Association (ATC) had 480 unions with 40,000 members. In contrast, the labor federations associated with the conservative opposition, the Nicaraguan Workers' Federation (CTN) and Council of Trade Union Unification (CUS), had then a combined total of 38 unions, representing 4,404 members. Over four-and-a-half times as many workers were represented by labor federations affiliated with three non-Sandinista leftwing parties: the General Confederation of Labor-Independent (CGTI), Federation of Trade Union Action and Unity (CAUS) and Workers' Front (FO) had a combined total of over 34 unions representing 19,961 members.

The Sandinista-affiliated National Union of Farmers and Ranchers (UNAG) was formed in 1981 by small- and medium-scale producers originally associated with the ATC. UNAG producers supplied 78 percent of basic agricultural products and 41 percent of all export crops, according to a 1982 report. By 1984, UNAG included 75,000 individual producers and cooperative members.[49]

Alfonso Robelo and Violeta Chamorro opposed expanding the Council of State. Chamorro resigned from the junta on April 19, 1980, citing only health reasons. On April 23, Robelo resigned, expressing great dissatisfaction with the direction of the government.

Washington expressed alarm at the resignations and Pezzullo played a mediating role between COSEP and the FSLN. Some COSEP leaders such as Jose Francisco Cardenal, president of the Chamber of Construction, insisted that the Council of State be limited to 33 members. But after the junta agreed to lift the state of emergency (in effect since the insurrection), establish safeguards against illegal property confiscations and announce a timetable for elections, COSEP agreed to take its seats on the Council. On May 4, Cardenal was elected as a vice president of the

Council. It was a post he didn't want. Days later, angry at COSEP as well as the FSLN, Cardenal went into exile and joined the counterrevolution.[50]

The Robelo and Chamorro resignations did not result in a junta shift to the left. They were replaced by two non-Sandinista conservatives: Arturo Cruz, then head of the Central Bank, and Rafael Cordova Rivas, leader of the Conservative Party. "Political pluralism has been maintained," said Cordova Rivas. "It has never ceased to exist. A clear example of it is the Council of State, in which political parties of different ideologies are represented."[51]

The government pursued its program of a mixed economy. With widespread support, the junta had expropriated the extensive properties of Somoza and Somocistas who had gone into exile. This gave the state control of 20 percent of agricultural production and 41 percent of overall production of goods and services by 1980, up from 15 percent under Somoza.[52] Under the mixed economy, private property rights are guaranteed. But following the government's commitment to meet society's basic needs, private property also carries a responsibility: to use productive assets and not let them sit idle. Moreover, unlike the Somoza era, laws regulating wages, health and safety and working conditions were enforced. The open question was whether large producers would invest under a system that sanctioned private profit, but which they did not control politically.

The new government offered private agricultural producers a package of incentives "unprecedented" even under Somoza, according to analyst Joseph Collins. Among the incentives were enough credit, at below-inflation interest rates, to cover all working costs; guaranteed prices, ensuring a profit, for export crops to be renegotiated yearly with the producers' associations; and a government promise to absorb any drop in international commodity prices and to share with producers any unexpected price gains.

While some producers reinvested their profits back into new production, others did not. Instead, they decapitalized, transferring profits to bank accounts outside the country. As decapitalization increased, the government-business partnership became more precarious. Still, in the first two years, "the government did not take over additional land," observed Collins, "even if it were lying idle or being run down; the ministry [of agriculture] had all the land it could handle. The only exceptions were farms where campesinos or farmworkers put tremendous pressure on the ministry."

"A vicious circle of self-fulfilling prophecies was at work," said Collins. "The more landowners decapitalized, the more they were denounced by workers and by the government, and the more insecure all landowners felt (and were). Thus the circle starts again."[53]

One young executive admitted he had sent $80,000 out of the country since the revolution. "Why shouldn't I?...The government gives us economic incentives, but what we want is a climate of political confidence."[54]

In May, as the Council of State was being inaugurated, the Catholic hierarchy called for the resignation of priests holding government positions, arguing that "the exceptional circumstances" that necessitated their participation had passed. The four priests affected were Foreign Minister Miguel D'Escoto, Culture Minister Ernesto Cardenal, Literacy Campaign Director Fernando Cardenal and Minister of Social Welfare Edgar Parrales. The priests refused to resign, insisting that the government needed them and that the people, active in Christian base communities, supported them. This initial dispute was not resolved until July 1981, when the bishops agreed to let the priests remain in the government on the condition that they not administer the sacraments in public or private.[55]

The prominent role of Christian clergy and laity in the Sandinista revolution set an example that both Washington and the Vatican wanted erased. As Sister Luz Beatriz Arellano of the Ecumenical Valdivieso Center put it, "The integration of Christianity and revolution scares the Church hierarchy, the elite and Washington because they always [before] had the excuse that revolution was communism was atheism."[56]

Growing disputes at the national level were mirrored in the powerful Chamorro family. The day after Violeta Chamorro resigned from the junta, Pedro Joaquin Chamorro's brother Xavier was removed as editor of *La Prensa*. Xavier had supported the workers' union demands for formal representation on the paper's editorial council and was deemed too pro-government by the family. In support of Xavier, the staff went on strike. A subsequent settlement provided Xavier with resources to start an independent paper, *El Nuevo Diario*.

Most of *La Prensa's* employees went with Xavier Chamorro to *Nuevo Diario*, but the reconstituted *La Prensa* retained the respect of its name. Violeta's son Pedro Joaquin Jr. became the new editor of *La Prensa*. Younger son Carlos Fernando was editor of the official Sandinista paper, *Barricada*. Their sister Cristiana later became assistant director of *La Prensa*. Sister Claudia is a Sandinista who became ambassador to Costa Rica, the country where Pedro Joaquin Jr. would later choose exile.

La Prensa became an international symbol. For opponents of the Sandinistas, it is a symbol of dissent. For Sandinista supporters, it is a symbol of U.S.-backed counterrevolution.

Foiled Plot

The Sandinista-COSEP truce didn't last long. The November 1980 election of Ronald Reagan as president of the United States signaled a turn from mediation to heightened polarization. There were parties to celebrate Reagan's victory among Nicaraguan elites. "They still think politics are determined in the USA," said junta member Moises Hassan. "They believe Reagan will get rid of the 'Sandinista communists.'"[57]

COSEP walked out of the Council of State on November 12 along with the most rightwing parties and unions (the major opposition parties, including the Independent Liberal Party and the Democratic Conservative Party, remained in the Council). A week later they had a martyr: Jorge Salazar, vice president of COSEP and president of its affiliated National Union of Agricultural Producers (UPANIC).

By the summer of 1980, Salazar was engaged in an armed plot to overthrow the government. At the time, Nicaragua faced sporadic cross-border raids by Honduran-based ex-National Guardsmen and attacks by the Somocista Anti-Communist Armed Forces (FARAC), financed largely by members of the Livestock Federation of Nicaragua. FARAC's largest armed action was the five-hour seizure of San Jose de los Remates in the central province of Boaco in May 1980. The government also had to deal with an ultraleft workers' paramilitary organization, the Milpas, who thought the Sandinistas were too pro-capitalist.[58]

Salazar began plotting secretly with Jose Francisco "Chicano" Cardenal even before the Council of State dispute in April. According to Cardenal, Salazar was looking to Washington as early as February for funds to start a clandestine radio station.[59] Salazar traveled outside Nicaragua to meet with Cardenal, then the exile leader of the Nicaraguan Democratic Union (UDN), as well as Col. Enrique Bermudez, who had organized Guardia forces into the Fifteenth of September Legion. Cardenal joined Bermudez in forming the Nicaraguan Revolutionary Democratic Alliance (ADREN). Leonardo Somarriba, vice president of the Chamber of Commerce, joined Salazar's conspiracy in early September. According to former contra spokesman Edgar Chamorro, Somarriba was working for the CIA as well as Salvadoran Foreign Minister Fidel Chavez Mena while still in Nicaragua.[60]

Cardenal went to El Salvador to assist Salazar in acquiring arms. Cardenal and Raul Arana, a former Managua builder active in ADREN, arranged a meeting with the commander of the Salvadoran Army, Colonel Jaime Gutierrez, with the aid of Foreign Minister Chavez Mena. Cardenal wanted Gutierrez to provide arms for Salazar and training facilities for ex-guardsmen. Before Cardenal had secured any commitment from Gutierrez, Somarriba and Salazar made their own trip to El Salvador, again through the offices of Chavez Mena, to meet with Gutierrez. According to Somarriba, Gutierrez made no commitments to aid Salazar; according to Cardenal and Arana he did.[61] "The Salvadorans," said Cardenal, "were going to give us territory for training and arms, and they were going to give us money, too."[62]

According to former National Security Council aide Robert Pastor, the U.S. Embassy in Managua first learned of the Salazar conspiracy in October: "The Ambassador was informed; he was not asked for help." That statement rings rather hollow in light of Cardenal's report of an earlier approach to the United States and debate in the administration over whether to help. As Pastor described it, the conspiracy "was a high-risk temptation" for the administration. "Some in the Administration were prepared to pay the price of again being labeled 'interventionistic' if the coup succeeded, but if it failed, not only would the Carter Administration be blamed for ineptness [as the presidential elections were fast approaching], but its strategy of trying to moderate the Sandinistas would be finished. On the other hand, if this conspiracy was actually just a sophisticated way to entrap moderates, then the United States should discourage them, or alternatively, keep its distance...Those who were most pessimistic and suspicious of the Sandinistas tended to be in favor of supporting a coup, and those who were less pessimistic both about what had happened in Nicaragua and what could be expected in the future were more inclined to resist the temptation."

Ambassador Pezzullo was one of those "less pessimistic" about Nicaragua. He was also increasingly convinced that the Sandinistas not only knew of the conspiracy but were entrapping Salazar. Both Pezzullo and Eden Pastora warned Salazar.[63]

The charges of entrapment are not supported by the evidence regarding the development of the plot, but Sandinista intelligence did infiltrate the conspiracy— no thanks to the U.S. Embassy. On November 18, Salazar was killed while on his way to evaluate a farm's suitability for storing arms. According to the Nicaraguan government, the unarmed Salazar was killed in a shoot-out between his accomplice and security police who were trying to capture them. Eight Nicaraguans, most of them active in COSEP, including Somarriba, were found guilty of plotting to overthrow the government. They were released by order of the Nicaraguan Supreme Court after having served less than one year.

After spending several weeks in jail, Somarriba left Nicaragua for Miami. According to Edgar Chamorro, Somarriba helped Chavez Mena channel CIA funds to the campaign of Jose Napoleon Duarte during the 1984 Salvadoran elections. Somarriba continued working with the CIA and the contras.[64]

"Exporting Revolution"

When the U.S. Congress linked Nicaragua and El Salvador, it wasn't referring to Salvadoran support for the export of counterrevolution to Nicaragua, but to an alleged Nicaraguan role in the "export of revolution" to El Salvador.

In a speech to the University of Amsterdam in October 1983, Tomas Borge remarked, "We can export coffee and cotton, poetry, and even our example, but we could never export revolutions, because they originate in the inferno of each country."[65]

El Salvador's inferno was described by Jose Napoleon Duarte in a 1980 interview with then *New York Times* reporter Raymond Bonner. Bonner asked Duarte "why the guerrillas were in the hills."

"Fifty years of lies, fifty years of injustice, fifty years of frustration," responded Duarte. "This is a history of people starving to death, living in misery. For fifty years the same people had all the power, all the money, all the jobs, all the education, all the opportunities."

The response surprised Bonner who had not expected Duarte to suggest any justification for the revolution. What surprised Bonner more, however, "was what he had not said. He had said nothing about Castro or Cuba. He had not mentioned the Sandinistas or Nicaragua. There was no talk of the cold war and the Soviet Union. (Duarte was to raise those themes later, when they reflected the views of the Reagan administration in Washington.) What Duarte was saying was that the revolution had been caused and fueled by the conditions in El Salvador."[66]

Those conditions were described by one Salvadoran this way: "I used to work on the hacienda...My job was to take care of the [owner's] dogs. I gave them meat and bowls of milk, food that I couldn't give to my own family. When the dogs were sick, I took them to the veterinarian...When my children were sick, the [owner] gave me his sympathy, but no medicine as they died. To watch your children die of sickness and hunger while you can do nothing is a violence to the spirit. We have suffered that silently for too many years."[67]

El Salvador's last fifty years of lies, injustice and frustration began with a 1932 massacre, *La Matanza*. Having recently grabbed power in a coup, General Maximiliano Hernandez Martinez crushed a peasant rebellion and slaughtered 30,000 Salvadorans. "It is a greater crime to kill an ant than a man," Hernandez Martinez once said, "for when a man dies he becomes reincarnated, while an ant dies forever."[68]

El Salvador's contemporary death squads are heirs to the Hernandez Martinez legacy. Indeed, Jeane Kirkpatrick praised Hernandez Martinez as a "hero" in a 1981 paper for the American Enterprise Institute: "It is said that 30,000 persons lost their lives...To many Salvadoreans the violence of this repression seems less important than the fact of restored order and the thirteen years of civil peace that ensued." Kirkpatrick continued, "The traditionalist death squads that pursue revolutionary activists and leaders in contemporary El Salvador call themselves Hernandez Martinez Brigades, seeking thereby to place themselves in El Salvador's political tradition and communicate their purposes."[69]

Salvadoran rebels take their name from a different hero, the revolutionary Agustin Farabundo Marti, executed in 1932. For a time, he fought with Sandino against the U.S. marines. By Washington's logic, one could argue that El Salvador has exported revolution to Nicaragua.

In the words of Sergio Ramirez, "Revolutions throughout history have always been 'exportable,' if we wish to use this somewhat mercantile term when discussing the dynamic by which ideas circulate beyond borders...The revolution that gave birth to the United States as a nation was the most exported revolution of modern history...The constitution of the new United States and the explosive ideas that inspired it were carried by muleback throughout all Central America, like a smuggled item. That emerging republic, led by wild-eyed radicals...represented a threat to the internal security and strategic interests of Spain in the New World; the great imperial power began to crack."[70] In 1775, Patrick Henry declared "Give me liberty or give me death." In Nicaragua the revolutionaries cried "patria libre o morir," free homeland or death.

Revolutionary ideas circulate beyond borders, and so does material aid. But revolution is not a product of outside aid or outside ideas. The American revolution received aid from the French, but the French did not "export revolution" to the then British colonies. The Sandinista revolution received aid from Costa Rica, Venezuela, Panama and Cuba, but those countries did not "export revolution" to Nicaragua. And as the Duarte passage above makes clear, the Salvadoran revolution is a product of Salvadoran experience, not an export of Nicaragua, whatever level of material aid can in fact be traced to Nicaragua.

The "exporting revolution" charge has served to pin the blame for deteriorating relations between Nicaragua and the United States on the Sandinistas. It has been used to delegitimize revolutions both in Nicaragua and El Salvador, and to legitimize an increasingly militaristic U.S. policy of counterrevolution.

Salvador Refrain

The Carter administration tried to learn from its too little, too late approach in Nicaragua and defuse growing popular revolution in El Salvador by backing the reformist military coup of October 15, 1979. That same month, in an effort to deflect criticism from the right (rightwingers blamed Carter for "losing" not only Nicaragua, but also Grenada and Iran, and were trying to block ratification of the SALT II nuclear weapons treaty with the Soviet Union) as well as to establish the traditional rationale for an increased military commitment, the Carter administration upped the East-West ante in Central America.

On the pretext of the August "discovery" of a brigade of Soviet troops in Cuba, which had been there for seventeen years with Washington's knowledge, Carter announced the formation of a permanent Caribbean military task force and expanded military maneuvers. In a televised address, Carter also pledged increased economic assistance "to insure the ability of troubled peoples to resist social turmoil and possible communist domination."[71]

The administration announced it was sending $5.7 million in military assistance to El Salvador, a large amount when compared to past military aid to that country. In January 1980, the new Salvadoran government junta collapsed when civilians Guillermo Ungo, Ramon Mayorga and Mario Antonio Andino resigned, along with most ministers and deputy ministers. The Christian Democrats climbed aboard the military-driven train as it headed to the right.

The junta reformers had tried to sway the reactionaries, arguing "if the massacres didn't stop and if the reforms weren't implemented, there was going to be a terrible bloodbath." National Guard Commander Colonel Vides Casanova rebuffed them. The country had survived the killing of 30,000 peasants in 1932, he said. "Today, the armed forces are prepared to kill 200,000-300,000, if that's what it takes to stop a Communist takeover."[72] At least 40,000 civilians were killed between October 1979 and January 1984.

Salvadoran Archbishop Oscar Arnulfo Romero wrote to Carter in February 1980 to plead that U.S. aid be withheld. He advised Carter that "neither the [civilian-military] junta nor the Christian Democrats govern the country. Political power is in the hands of the armed forces...They know only how to repress the people and defend the interests of the Salvadoran oligarchy." And he told Carter, "It would be totally wrong and deplorable if the Salvadoran people were to be frustrated, repressed, or in any way impeded from deciding for itself the economic and political future of our country by intervention on the part of a foreign power."[73]

As Bonner explained, Archbishop Romero's "unceasing condemnations of the government repression and, directly or indirectly, the U.S. policy of backing the junta caused serious problems for the Carter administration." Romero was respected internationally; in 1978, he was nominated for the Nobel Peace Prize by members of the British Parliament.

Robert Wagner, a former mayor of New York, was twice sent by Carter to the Vatican "in an effort to mute Romero's criticisms of the junta and to gain his backing of the U.S. policy." In Wagner's words, "there was a fear [in the administration] that he [Archbishop Romero] was a little too far over to the left."

Pope John Paul II was sympathetic. He passed on U.S. concerns in a private audience with Romero. The pope cautioned Romero "to be careful of ideologies that can seep into the defense of human rights and in the long run produce dictatorships and violations of human rights."

"But Holy Father," Romero replied, "in my country it is very dangerous to speak of anti-Communism, because anti-Communism is what the right preaches, not out of love for Christian sentiments but out of a selfish concern to preserve its own interests."[74]

Romero called on Christian Democrats to resign from the junta on February 17: "Your presence is covering the repressive character of this government, especially abroad. You are an important political force. It is urgent that you question how best you can use that force in favor of the poor: as isolated and impotent members of a government controlled by the repressive military, or as one more force that incorporates itself into a broad project of popular government."[75] Christian Democrat Hector Dada resigned from the junta on March 3. Jose Napoleon Duarte took his place in a third reorganization of the junta. Romero concluded his sermon on March 23 with an impassioned appeal to members of the army, the National Guard and the police: "Brothers, you are part of our people. You kill your own peasant brothers and sisters...In the name of God, and in the name of this suffering people whose laments rise to heaven each day more tumultuous, I beg you, I ask you, I order you in the name of God: Stop the repression!"

Romero was gunned down while saying mass the following day. Shortly after, Carter's request for military aid to El Salvador was approved. By most accounts, Salvadoran rightist Roberto D'Aubuisson directed Romero's assassination; President Duarte publicly accused D'Aubuisson in late 1987.[76] Ricardo "Chino" Lau, chief of intelligence operations for Somoza and a founding contra officer, was reportedly contracted to arrange the hit.[77] Wealthy Salvadorans contributed $120,000 to pay for the murder.[78]

As repression in El Salvador intensified and frustrated reformers joined the opposition, Washington continued with the same propaganda refrain: moderate centrist government battling the extremes of left and right. In April 1980, opposition groups united in the Democratic Revolutionary Front (FDR). On November 27, the top five leaders of the FDR were dragged by security forces from a Jesuit high school where they were preparing a press conference. They were tortured, murdered and mutilated. Among the five was FDR President Enrique Alvarez, who had served as minister of agriculture until January 1980. Former junta member Guillermo Ungo—Duarte's running mate in El Salvador's aborted 1972 elections—succeeded Alvarez as FDR president.

In a December 7, 1980 *New York Times* roundtable on Central America, Jeane Kirkpatrick asserted, "I think that the degree of commitment to moderation and democratic institutions within the Salvadoran military is very frequently underestimated in this country. And I think it's a terrible injustice to the Government and the military when you suggest that they were somehow responsible for terrorism and assassination."

She added: "May I say a final word about the tragic, because murder is always tragic, assassinations of the leaders of the far left [the five FDR leaders]. That it was the Government who accepted the Catholic church's offers for negotiation and it was precisely those leaders of the far left who rejected that offer [sic]. I must say that I found myself thinking that it's a reminder that people who choose to live by the sword can expect to die by it."

The Maximiliano Hernandez Martinez Anti-Communist Brigade took credit for the FDR killings. In a communique, the Brigade warned "the priests who have an affinity for the terrorist Marxist bands that they will have the same fate if they insist in their sermons on poisoning the minds of Salvadoran youth."

The Brigade's claim was a cover. As even a CIA report noted, the executions "were the work of the security forces."[79] Often, the "death squads" served this cover purpose. They were not simply rightwing vigilantes; they were the auxiliary arm of the counterinsurgency forces built up over two decades by the United States.

As journalist Allan Nairn explained, beginning with the Kennedy administration, officials of the State Department, CIA and U.S. military "conceived and organized ORDEN, the rural paramilitary and intelligence network described by Amnesty International as a movement designed 'to use clandestine terror against government opponents.' Out of ORDEN grew the notorious *Mano Blanco*, the White Hand, which a former U.S. ambassador to El Salvador, Raul H. Castro, has called 'nothing less than the birth of the Death Squads'; conceived and organized ANSESAL, the elite presidential intelligence service that gathered files on Salvadoran dissidents and, in the words of one U.S. official, relied on Death Squads as 'the operative arms of intelligence gathering'; enlisted General Jose Alberto 'Chele' Medrano, the founder of ORDEN and ANSESAL, as a CIA agent...[and] provided American technical and intelligence advisors who often worked directly with ANSESAL, the security forces, and the general staff with electronic, photographic, and personal surveillance of individuals who were later assassinated by Death Squads."

Chele Medrano, a graduate of the U.S. Office of Public Safety program for training foreign police officers (abolished in 1974 but reincarnated by Reagan under a lower profile), received a medal from President Johnson in 1968 "in recognition of exceptionally meritorious service." Years later, when the Reagan administration publicly condemned the death squads, the CIA continued "to provide training, support, and intelligence to security forces directly involved in Death Squad activity."[80] For example, Colonel Nicolas Carranza, the head of the Treasury Police, was paid $90,000 a year as a CIA informant while Treasury agents carried out torture and murder.[81] As one U.S. official in El Salvador put it, referring to D'Aubuisson's death squad activities, "The C.I.A. didn't mind what was going on so long as they were killing communists."[82]

Four more bodies were found in El Salvador on December 4, 1980—the bodies of four American churchwomen. Sisters Ita Ford, Maura Clarke and Dorothy Kazel and lay missionary Jean Donovan were driving home from El Salvador's international airport when National Guardsmen abducted them. They were raped before being murdered. Jeane Kirkpatrick opined, they "were not just nuns...They were political activists on behalf of the Frente [FMLN]."

The Carter administration quickly announced the suspension of all economic and military aid to El Salvador. But according to Bonner, what most bothered policy makers (outside the Bureau of Human Rights headed by Patricia Derian) "was not the loss of the women's lives but that their assassinations would make it more difficult for the United States to continue backing the Duarte government."[83] Duarte had become president of the junta on December 13.

From a diary entry reproduced in his memoirs, it is clear that Carter knew of the slaughter in El Salvador: *"they are going through a blood bath down there...They don't have anybody in the jails. They're all dead. It's their accepted way of enforcing the so-called law.*—DIARY, DECEMBER 11, 1980." (Carter's italics.)

He wrote: "I was determined that the murderers of the nuns be brought to justice, that elections be scheduled, that some equitable system of justice be established and that promised land reforms be carried out. We had to convince the Salvadorans that brutal persecution of their own people was the major obstacle to their economic and political stability. Their top priority was to obtain more military weapons, but we held firm to our policy."[84]

This, the last reference in Carter's memoirs to his administration's actions in Central America, left out critical policy shifts during the last month in office. In mid December, the administration resumed economic aid, citing the Salvadoran government's supposed "commitment to a thorough, professional and expeditious investigation of the killings" of the churchwomen. The administration knew this was untrue.[85]

On January 2, 1981, the State Department sent a secret cable instructing the U.S. Embassy "to advise the Salvadoran government that the United States was prepared to send military equipment 'on [an] expedited basis,' and would immediately 'deploy to San Salvador' two groups of advisors—one for helicopter maintenance; the other 'to deal with guerrilla warfare.'" Assistant Secretary of State for Human Rights Patricia Derian expressed her "profound disappointment."[86]

Two more Americans were killed on January 4. Land reform advisers Michael Hammer and Mark Pearlman were blasted with submachineguns while eating dinner with Land Reform Agency head Jose Rodolfo Viera, also killed, in San Salvador's Sheraton Hotel. Economic aid went forward.

The FMLN began a "final offensive" on January 10 in an attempt to present President-elect Reagan with a *fait accompli*. By the next day, the Salvadoran government was pronouncing the offensive a failure; that was more clear on January 12. Aware that the Salvadoran government did not need new U.S. aid to repulse the offensive, the administration used it as an excuse to publicly announce on January 14 that it was resuming military assistance.

Carter announced on January 17 that $5 million in emergency combat aid would be sent to El Salvador along with U.S. advisers. "Unable to say that the military aid was necessary to defeat the guerrillas," wrote Bonner, "the administration needed another pretext. It found one—perhaps concocted it." The pretext was Nicaraguan arms.

Fonseca Gulf Incident

"I believe reports that a group of approximately 100 men landed from Nicaragua about 4:00 P.M. yesterday," Ambassador Robert White told reporters on January 14. He said Soviet- and Chinese-made weapons had been captured in recent days. "This changes the nature of the insurgency movement here, and makes it clear that it is dependent on outside sources...We cannot stand idly by and watch the guerrillas receive outside assistance."

In their own press conference, Duarte and other Salvadoran government officials said that five boats landed at El Cuco, a small village in the eastern part of the country on the Gulf of Fonseca; 53 guerrillas were supposedly killed. When reporters asked for proof that the boats came from Nicaragua, the defense minister said "they were made of wood not native to El Salvador." A prominent businessman who saw the televised press conference said, "I had to laugh. It was better than watching a comedy."[87]

Unfortunately, the U.S. media didn't treat the story as comedy. The Gulf of Fonseca incident was as contrived as the Gulf of Tonkin incident of 1964. Both propaganda events had their intended impact.

An American diplomat in El Salvador concluded the boat landing was "staged." Referring to Soviet-made grenades found near the landing site, he said, "It looks as if they were planted. I can't quite picture how people would—if they were attacked—drop grenades along the way—like Hansel and Gretel. It just seemed all too pat."[88]

State Department claims went beyond the boat landing to "intelligence reports" supposedly showing significant military support from a number of countries. A senior Carter administration official with access to all intelligence traffic rebutted this: "Our impression was that the guerrillas got most of their arms on the international black market, primarily in Miami."[89]

Most observers agree that some arms were shipped via Nicaragua to the FMLN, mainly between November 1980 and January 1981. Until that point, as Robert Pastor acknowledged, the Sandinistas had avoided supplying arms to the FMLN in the interest of maintaining non-hostile relations with the United States.[90] The Sandinistas expected the incoming Reagan administration to be hostile, whatever Nicaragua's behavior.

The World Court concluded, in its 1986 judgement finding the United States in violation of international law in attacking Nicaragua: "the Court is satisfied that, between July 1979...and the early months of 1981, an intermittent flow of arms was routed via the territory of Nicaragua to the armed opposition in El Salvador. On the other hand, the evidence is insufficient to satisfy the Court that, since the early months of 1981, assistance has continued to reach the Salvadorian armed opposition from the territory of Nicaragua on any significant scale, or that the Government of Nicaragua was responsible for any flow of arms at either period."[91]

Suspension

In mid January, just before leaving office, Carter suspended aid to Nicaragua, pending an investigation into Nicaragua's alleged role in supplying arms to the FMLN. Carter officials argued that was the only option, short of terminating aid, under the conditions of the aid legislation.[92] Carter also cancelled authorization of negotiations for the renewal of Public Law 480 long-term, low-interest loans for the sale of wheat and cooking oil.[93]

Candidate Ronald Reagan had opposed aid to Nicaragua: "I disagree with...the aid that we have provided...I think we are seeing the application of the domino theory...and I think it's time the people of the United States realize...that we're the last domino."[94] President Reagan would transform the "export of revolution" charge into a mantra.

Reagan inherited more than an aid suspension from Carter. He inherited a presidential "finding" that had authorized covert action in Nicaragua since 1978. Secret CIA assistance first went to Nicaraguan "moderates"—in political parties, business organizations, the press and labor unions—in the hope they could replace Somoza. It continued after Somoza was deposed to bolster opposition to the Sandinistas.[95] (See "The CIA's Blueprint for Nicaragua," appendix A.)

Even as Carter was taking action against Nicaragua for its alleged support of "terrorism," the U.S. government was providing safe haven for contra leaders and tolerating the existence of contra training camps on U.S. soil. Under Reagan, official U.S. policy would evolve from apparent non-interference with exile efforts aimed at overthrowing the Nicaraguan government to organizing those efforts.

Looking back on the Carter administration, Miguel D'Escoto told me: "At first they tried to buy us out...Every time we went somewhere, [the U.S. ambassador and other officials] would come, as they used to do before in Nicaragua, to give all the points that the United States wanted to make in any international forum, in a meeting of the United Nations or the Nonaligned countries, or the Organization of American States, or what have you. They always had a position and they wanted to impress on us the need to be carriers of American concerns.

"Always, of course, they would say, 'Nicaragua is a sovereign country, but if you don't do this, it would be very difficult to obtain these things.' It was a very clear, crude invitation for political prostitution.

"And when that failed, they began to use threats...threats of economic and political isolation. They wanted to get Nicaragua to cry uncle in the least expensive way. And they were not obviously initially interested in military means to achieve that goal. It's impossible for us to say whether President Carter would have been willing. I don't know. But certainly...the military option only becomes a reality with the advent of the Reagan administration."[96]

After leaving office, Viron Vaky observed: "The premise of U.S. policy to date has been that the die has not been cast in Nicaragua, and that if non-Marxist elements in that society remain viable, there is a good chance that the internal process can evolve toward a Mexican rather than a Cuban model...It is essential to supply aid to keep the monetary/economic system viable and enmeshed in the international economy, and to support the private sector." A few Reagan policy thinkers "have argued that the United States should not only stop providing aid to Nicaragua but should destabilize the Sandinista government as well. No course could be better calculated to inflame the whole isthmus, raise tensions in the Hemisphere and create the potential for a Spanish civil-war situation."[97]

3

Reagan Strikes Back

Nicaragua has committed a grave sin, that of national dignity in the face of the empire. And the empire does not permit that, as Rome did not permit it of Carthage and Israel. How could the United States allow this flea to tickle? It must be punished.

Rafael Cordova Rivas, Democratic Conservative Party leader,
April 30, 1986 interview with author.

The biggest lesson I learned from Vietnam is not to trust government statements...They fit the facts to fit the policy. We made a great mistake in Vietnam and are making another one in Central America.

J. William Fulbright, former Senate Foreign Relations Committee chairman,
New York Times, April 30, 1985.

Ronald Reagan twisted the facts on Nicaragua long before moving into the White House. Somoza's Nicaragua "has been getting a bad press," candidate Reagan told his radio audience on January 2, 1978. "It has never been known as a major violator of human rights."[1]

In a March 1979 radio broadcast, Reagan seconded Idaho Rep. Steve Symms' concern that "the Caribbean is rapidly becoming a Communist lake in what should be an American pond." Reagan added: "The troubles in Nicaragua bear a Cuban label also. While there are people in that troubled land who probably have justified grievances against the Somoza regime, there is no question but that most of the rebels are Cuban-trained, Cuban-armed, and dedicated to creating another Communist country in this hemisphere."[2]

Behind the Cubans are the Soviets. As Reagan told the *Wall Street Journal* in 1980: "The Soviet Union underlies all the unrest that is going on. If they weren't engaged in this game of dominos, there wouldn't be any hotspots in the world." Reagan wanted to recommit the United States to a policy of "rollback" of the "Soviet empire."

Santa Fe Tales

"Open the southern front!" Lewis Tambs was happy to carry out those National Security Council instructions when he became ambassador to Costa Rica in the summer of 1985. They fit a policy blueprint he had helped create as editor of the 1980 Committee of Santa Fe report, *A New Inter-American Policy for the Eighties.* Other committee members included Roger Fontaine, who served Reagan as NSC adviser for Latin America affairs before becoming a columnist with the Moonie-owned *Washington Times;* retired Lt. General Gordon Sumner, special adviser to Reagan's first assistant secretary of state for Inter-American affairs; David C. Jordan of the U.S. Strategic Institute; and L. Francis "Lynn" Bouchey, president of the Council for Inter-American Security, a major vehicle for far right propaganda about the "Soviet threat" in the Western hemisphere.

The Santa Fe report blasted the Carter administration for a policy of "anxious accommodation." It declared: "War, not peace, is the norm in international affairs...Survival demands a new U.S. foreign policy. America must seize the initiative or perish. For World War III is almost over. The Soviet Union, operating under the cover of increasing nuclear superiority, is strangling the Western industrialized nations by interdicting their oil and ore supplies and is encircling the People's Republic of China." (Note that China, a communist country once supposedly poised to seize Southeast Asian dominos beginning with Vietnam, has been transformed from "Red threat" to Red target.) After the first two phases of "World War III," containment and detente, the Soviets lead on the Santa Fe scoreboard. Latin America and Southern Asia are the "scenes of strife" in the third phase.

> America is everywhere in retreat. The impending loss of the petroleum of the Middle East and potential interdiction of the sea routes spanning the Indian Ocean, along with the Soviet satellization of the mineral zone of Southern Africa, foreshadow the Findlandization of Western Europe and the alienation of Japan.
> Even the Caribbean, America's maritime crossroad and petroleum refining center, is becoming a Marxist-Leninist lake. Never before has the Republic been in such jeopardy from its exposed southern flank. Never before has American foreign policy abused, abandoned and betrayed its allies to the south in Latin America.
> ...It is time to sound a clarion call for freedom, dignity and national self-interest which will echo the spirit of the American people. Either a *Pax Sovietica* or a worldwide counter-projection of American power is in the offing. The hour of decision can no longer be postponed.[3]

In war, declared the Committee of Santa Fe, "there is no substitute for victory." The United States must "reaffirm the core principle of the Monroe Doctrine: namely, no hostile foreign power will be allowed bases or military and *political allies* in the region." (Italics added.) Under the Monroe-Reagan Doctrine, the internal politics of foreign countries are indeed subject to U.S. control. Cuba must be brought back into the U.S. sphere. If punitive measures and propaganda fail (the report advocated a Radio Free Cuba, later inaugurated as Radio Marti), "a war of national liberation against Castro must be launched."

Religion is a battleground in Santa Fe's World War III: "U.S. foreign policy must begin to counter (not react against) liberation theology." Marxist-Leninist forces have infiltrated the religious community "with ideas that are less Christian than Communist." (Perhaps the best known idea of liberation theology is the "preferential option for the poor.")

The Santa Fe Committee called for the United States to abandon "human rights, which is a culturally and politically relative concept that the [Carter] Administration has used for intervention for political change in countries of this hemisphere, adversely affecting the peace, stability and security of the region." It must be replaced with "a non-interventionist policy of political and ethical realism."[4]

Reality Check

Santa Fe "political and ethical realism" should not be confused with reality. In reality, "Soviet world influence was at its height in the 1950s and there has been no significant positive Soviet geopolitical momentum for many years." That's the sober assessment of the Center for Defense Information, led by retired U.S. military officers.[5]

Noting that with decolonization the number of independent nations rose from about 70 in 1945 to 165 in 1987, the Center reports that "the percentage of Soviet-influenced countries in the world was 10% in 1945 in the aftermath of World War II, rose to nearly 15% in the late 1950s, declined to 9% in the mid-1960s, and finally rose back to over 12% in the mid-1970s. It has remained at 11%" since 1980. "Considering that nearly all the new countries in the past 40 years have been former colonies of Western powers, the degree of Soviet success in exercising significant influence in these numerous anti-colonial countries is less than one might have expected."

A U.S. Army War College conference on the Soviet Union and the Third World concluded "that Soviet influence in the Third World remains limited, in part by the strong impulses toward autonomy and national self-determination of the Third World countries themselves. Many of Moscow's biggest 'victories' have resulted from events over which it had little or no control."[6]

A study by CIA analysts agreed: "Reduced Western influence in Third World countries has not necessarily led to a corresponding rise in Soviet influence. New governments often have translated anticolonialist positions into strong nationalist policies jealous of any foreign influence. Despite the commitment of some [Third World countries] to a 'Socialist' system, they usually have wanted their own brand of socialism, and have not been attracted to Soviet Communist ideology, either by economic or military aid."[7]

According to the Center for Defense Information, the eighteen countries with significant Soviet influence (i.e. "high levels of involvement and presence accompanied by a close and cooperative relationship," not necessarily approaching control) are: Afghanistan, Angola, Bulgaria, Cambodia, Cuba, Czechoslovakia, Ethiopia, East Germany, Hungary, Laos, Libya, Mongolia, Mozambique, Poland, Romania, Syria, Vietnam and South Yemen. Nicaragua is not on the list.

As one CIA analyst in the Office of Soviet Analysis put it, "In reviewing Soviet policy toward Nicaragua since 1979, one is struck by the general caution with which Moscow has proceeded."[8]

"I don't think the Soviets give a shit about what happens here," a U.S. ambassador in Central America told me in 1986. "Nicaragua is a little present that arrived on their doorstep, and they are slowly unwrapping it to see what's inside. They like the fact that it makes Ronald Reagan so mad."[9]

Reality is not a zero-sum game. A U.S. "loss" need not mean a Soviet "gain" and vice-versa. Similarly, a U.S. gain may not be a Soviet "loss," because it wasn't a Soviet proxy to begin with. Chile and Grenada are good examples; they were "rescued" from nothing but their own nationalism.

Stand By Your Dictator

Preceding the Santa Fe report was an article by Jeane Kirkpatrick, then a professor of political science at Georgetown University and a member of the Cold Warriors' council known as the Committee on the Present Danger. In "Dictatorships and Double Standards," Kirkpatrick elaborated her now-famous ideologically-biased distinction between moderate autocracies (authoritarian) and revolutionary autocracies (totalitarian). (In 1949, the chairman of the New York Council on Foreign Relations differentiated "autocratic" from "totalitarian" rule in an attempt to justify support for Somoza I.)[10] Kirkpatrick's formulation is rightwing doublespeak designed to mask brutality in the name of "anti-communism."

Kirkpatrick derided a Carter policy "whose crowning achievement has been to lay the groundwork for a transfer of the Panama Canal from the United States to a swaggering Latin dictator of Castroite bent." She spun the myth that the Carterites "not only failed to prevent" the fall of Somoza (and the Shah of Iran), but "actively collaborated in the replacement of moderate autocrats friendly to American interests with less friendly autocrats of extremist persuasion."[11]

Tom Farer, former president of the Inter-American Commission on Human Rights, was one of the few establishment commentators to critique Kirkpatrick without paying homage to her budding intellectual mystique. Her thesis, he said, "rests on an almost demented parody of Latin American political realities...On the most elementary facts Kirkpatrick is misinformed."[12]

According to Kirkpatrick, "Generally speaking, traditional autocrats tolerate social inequities, brutality, and poverty while revolutionary autocracies create them.

"Traditional autocrats leave in place existing allocations of wealth, power, status, and other resources which in most traditional societies favor an affluent few and maintain masses in poverty. But they worship traditional gods and observe traditional taboos. They do not disturb the habitual rhythms of work and leisure, habitual places of residence, habitual patterns of family and personal relations. Because the miseries of traditional life are familiar, they are bearable to ordinary people who, growing up in the society, learn to cope, as children born to untouchables in India acquire the skills and attitudes necessary for survival in the miserable roles they are destined to fill. Such societies create no refugees."[13]

Kirkpatrick regularly twists facts to fit her racist and anti-democratic views. The hundreds of thousands of political exiles from Somoza's Nicaragua, the Shah's Iran, Marcos' Philippines and other "moderate autocrats" are erased. Or they are cast as "economic migrants," like Salvadorans treated by the Reagan administration as surplus seekers of fortune, not sanctuary.

In a rejoinder to Kirkpatrick, Mexican novelist and former diplomat Carlos Fuentes asked, "Can't she hear the thousands of innocent dead in El Salvador answering her that they are not 'moderately dead'?" In the Reaganaut universe, communists kill innocents; those killed by anti-communists are generally not the truly innocent. Remember Kirkpatrick's characterization of the four murdered churchwomen: they "were not just nuns…They were political activists on behalf of the Frente."

In an August 1979 radio broadcast titled "Common Sense from a Neighbor," Reagan told his listeners this about Argentina, then under military dictatorship: "Today, Argentina is at peace, the terrorist threat nearly eliminated…In the process of bringing stability to a terrorized nation of 25 million, a small number were caught in the crossfire, among them a few innocents…If you ask the average Argentine-in-the-street what he thinks about the state of his country's economy, chances are you'll find him pleased, not seething, about the way things are going."[14]

At least 9,000 and as many as 30,000 Argentinians were "disappeared" in the military dictatorship's "dirty war." A U.S. equivalent would be 79,000 to 264,000; taking the lower figure, that's more than one and a half times the number of American deaths in the Vietnam War.

Reagan's reflections on Argentina were no aberration. He gave this account of events in Chile: "Allende was a Marxist and took Chile down the road to socialism…Journalists who have made an honest effort to talk with the Chilean man-in-the-street report that there would have been a people's revolt if the military overthrow of the Allende regime had not taken place." General Pinochet "promised to restore democratic rule also and to allow elections. True, they haven't taken place as yet, but there is reason to believe that if and when they do the general might just be the favorite candidate if he chooses to run." Reagan doesn't tell us why the Chilean people gave Allende's party even more support in the 1973 mid-term congressional elections, the last elections before Chilean democracy was crushed by the military in a U.S.-backed coup.

By the time of Reagan's comments in 1979, tens of thousands of Chileans had been disappeared or driven into exile (where Kirkpatrick disappeared them with the stroke of a pen). During the first five months of 1980, according to Amnesty International, 2,000 people were arrested on political charges and most of them were tortured.[15]

Self-Fulfilling Prophets

The Reagan-Bush team's intent to demonize and destabilize the Nicaraguan government was clear from the beginning. The July 1980 Republican platform stated: "We deplore the Marxist Sandinista takeover of Nicaragua and the attempts to destabilize El Salvador, Guatemala, and Honduras...We oppose the Carter Administration aid program for the government of Nicaragua. However, we will support the efforts of the Nicaraguan people to establish a free and independent government...We will return to the fundamental principle of treating a friend as a friend and self-proclaimed enemies as enemies, without apology."

In the name of freedom, "friends" are granted absolution for breaking democratic promises the "enemies" are accused of betraying.

Shortly after the Republican convention, Business International Corporation's Latin American Forecasting Study reported on Nicaragua as seen without red-colored lenses: the Nicaraguan government "seems to be gravitating toward a relatively moderate course...The private sector still has an audible voice, although clearly not a dominant one. There are several functioning political parties in the country, but none are expected to have the force or popularity of a Sandinist party with a good grassroots organization. It is thought by most observers that the Sandinist Party would likely win any election held."

The report gave the Nicaraguan government "equal odds for moving right or left"; that would depend on many factors, including the government's ability "to solve the country's economic and social problems, some of which are potentially explosive." Among the potential pitfalls were: "labor unrest prodded by high unemployment," inflation and "foreign exchange constraint, relief from which will depend largely on the largesse of outside governments and institutions."

The report predicted that reconstruction from the revolutionary war would "necessarily run through 1983 at least, if not beyond." The 1980 economic reactivation plan was "having positive effects, but it is falling short of its goals...Assuming that the political formula remains workable and the government can instill the private sector with enough confidence to keep tilling the land and production lines active, GDP [Gross Domestic Product] could make another major gain next year, followed by more moderate rises in subsequent years." Regarding agriculture, the report noted that "the government is trying to stimulate this priority sector through production bonuses given to private growers. If commodity prices hold up in the next few years and the private growers reinvest, the outlook for this sector is for good to moderate growth throughout the forecast period." The outlook for industry was "only fair, principally because the levels of destruction were greater and the investment necessary to reactivate industry is far more than required for agriculture." The report also noted that "future repayment of the burdensome $1.6 billion foreign debt [acquired under Somoza] will cloud the foreign exchange outlook for years to come."[16]

Nicaragua wasn't playing its Reagan-supporting role as a totalitarian threat. Most observers thought the Sandinistas would win elections. The private sector was being offered incentives to invest and Sandinista "mismanagement" wasn't the cause of the country's economic problems.

The economy was Nicaragua's Achilles heel and a number of pressure points were evident from the Business International report: the economy would hurt for many years due to wartime losses, high reconstruction costs, foreign debt and worsening terms of trade (declining prices for exports such as coffee and rising prices for imports such as tractors). Economic crisis could be blamed on Sandinista mismanagement and compounded by capital flight and a new war. The United States could "make the economy scream"—as Nixon did with Chile—by cutting off aid and pressuring other countries and international agencies to do so.[17]

In an October 1980 Heritage Foundation *Backgrounder*, Cleto DiGiovanni, a high-level CIA clandestine operative until late 1978, advocated economic warfare as part of a comprehensive strategy for destabilizing Nicaragua (following the CIA blueprint predicted earlier by ex-agent Philip Agee and excerpted in appendix A): "In a well orchestrated program targeted against the Marxist Sandinista government, we should use our limited resources to support the free labor unions, the Church, the private sector, the independent political parties, the free press, and those who truly defend human rights [sic]...We should not abandon the Nicaraguan people, but we must abandon the Sandinista government...Despite its show of arms, [the Nicaraguan] government is still weak and could be dislodged through a determined, coordinated, and targeted effort."

DiGiovanni sketched one route of attack: "Nicaraguan workers continue to have an emotional attachment to the revolutionary movement. This attachment can be expected to weaken as the economy deteriorates...There are some indications of growing broadly based support to take to arms to overthrow the Sandinista government, and this support could increase as further economic problems develop."[18]

Economic warfare would contribute to the Reagan administration's self-fulfilling prophecy of Sandinista gloom and doom. As seen in the chart below, Nicaragua actually did better economically than its neighbors until 1983, when the economy began reeling under the strain of war, decapitalization and regional economic crisis.

No Business as Usual

The Nicaraguan government had responded to news of Reagan's election by reiterating, "we want friendly relations with the United States and any other country that respects our sovereignty and independence." Said Sandinista leader Bayardo

Central America: Economic and Social Comparisons, 1979-1985

	Population (millions)	Gross Domestic Product (GDP) Per Capita $U.S.			GDP Real Growth Per Capita (%)	GDP Real Growth	GDP Change Per Capita
	1985	1980	1983	1985	1979-83	1979-83	1983-85
Costa Rica	2.5	1910	1648	1708			4
El Salvador	4.8	923	770	771			--
Guatemala	7.9	1488	1292	1216			-6
Honduras	4.4	810	726	719			-1
Nicaragua	3.3	954	941	845	7.67	22.5	-10
Central America					-14.71	-5.7	

	Socioeconomic Ranking* (141) countries (142)		Adult Literacy Rate %		Public Expenditures Education Per Capita $U.S.		Infant Mortality Rate Deaths under one year per 1000 live births		Public Expenditures Health Per Capita $U.S.	
	1979	1983	1979	1983	1979	1983	1979	1983	1979	1983
Costa Rica	52	65	93	93	92	58	22	20	19	24
El Salvador	82	89	63	66	24	28	53	71	9	11
Guatemala	86	90	50	54	19	20	69	64	9	16
Honduras	92	93	60	62	20	28	103	81	10	11
Nicaragua	86	75	50	88	19	40	122	75	10	40

*Average ranks of Gross National Product, Health and Education per capita (lower number means higher rank.)

Research assistance by Laura Henze.

Sources: Ruth Leger Sivard, *World Military and Social Expenditures 1982 and 1986* (Washington, DC: World Priorities); Inter-American Development Bank, *Economic and Social Progress in Latin America 1986 Report*; Michael E. Conroy, "Economic Legacy and Policies," Table 10.2, in Walker, ed. *Nicaragua*, p. 224.

Arce, "We know the new Government's announced platform would involve chan-ges in the policies of President Carter, but we must see what parts of its program it carries out in practice."[19]

The new secretary of state was General Alexander Haig. He rose rapidly through military and political ranks to become Nixon's chief of staff and supreme commander of NATO before passing through the revolving door to the presidency of United Technologies Corporation, a top military contractor. As secretary of state, Haig wasted no time in putting changes in Nicaragua policy into practice.

As Haig told the story in his memoirs, "I encountered Rita Delia Casco, the fiery young ambassador of the Sandinista regime, at a Washington soiree...The am-bassador expressed confidence that there would be no change in U.S.-Nicaraguan relations as a result of the election. I stated bluntly that this confidence was misplaced. While the Sandinistas betrayed their neighbors, there would be no busi-ness as usual. America was prepared not only to cut off all aid, but to do other things as well."[20]

As Rita Delia Casco recalled it, she met Haig at an inaugural reception and it was he who was fiery. "He told me right there in front of everybody, 'You tell your government to stop sending aid to the Salvadoran rebels or we'll go to the source.' I don't remember the exact words now, but it was very threatening."

During the Carter administration, she explained, Nicaraguan diplomats had close contact and open channels of communication with officials in the State Depart-ment and the National Security Council. This "completely changed from the mo-ment the Reagan administration took over...There was a complete blackout...There was no way of communicating." Reagan officials expressed their "hostile at-titude...even in very simple details...as trying to embarrass me in a social oc-casion...We really got into their guts...It was a very irrational feeling."[21]

"By small gestures and large we maintained our position," said Haig. "On my recommendation, President Reagan froze economic aid to Nicaragua two days after taking office, and indefinitely suspended all aid to the Nicaraguan government...on April 1." The administration also suspended a $9.6 million sale of wheat in February and cancelled it completely in March.

Some U.S. officials thought American citizens should be evacuated from Nicaragua before the aid cutoff was announced. "Instead," said Haig, "we had taken certain precautions, including the formation of a military rescue force, to be sure that there would be no repetition of the disgrace of Teheran."[22] As planning for a so-called rescue force went forward it quickly evolved into a full-scale invasion force. In the words of a former Joint Chiefs of Staff operations officer, "the White House was looking for a way to justify an invasion force that could topple the regime."[23]

The Nicaraguans, of course, took no hostages, and to this day the only American citizens in Nicaragua to be harmed have been those kidnapped or killed by the contras, or those flying and fighting on the contra side.

Government junta member Arturo Cruz had argued against the cutoff: "A sup-pression of U.S. aid would be very negative and counterproductive...The economic crisis would be translated into a real radicalization and Nicaragua would have to look to other blocs for funds."

In its request for foreign assistance for fiscal year 1982, the Reagan administration had included $35 million for Nicaragua, pending the outcome of events. John Bushnell, acting assistant secretary of state for Inter-American affairs, told Congress that stringent conditions on aid would be maintained, but "failure to budget for the outcome we desire in Nicaragua would be defeatism of the first order."[24]

The April aid cutoff exempted a fiscal year 1981 grant of $7.5 million (successor to the fiscal 1980 $5 million grant) for an Agency for International Development (AID) program of support for private sector organizations. Distributed through the U.S. Embassy in Managua, grant recipients included COSEP and its member organizations; the Social Action Committee of the Moravian Church on the Atlantic Coast; the Archdiocese of Managua and the American Institute for Free Labor Development (AIFLD), an organization with longstanding ties to the CIA. A grant of $5.1 million was appropriated for 1982.

In August 1982, the Nicaraguan government rejected the continuing private sector aid, arguing in a letter to AID "that the agreements have political motivations designed to promote resistance and destabilize the revolutionary government." Nicaragua indicated its willingness to discuss other types of economic assistance. Most of the grants actually ended up being expended, a portion after Nicaragua moved to block the funding.[25]

Some COSEP leaders were indeed involved in armed plots against the government, as discussed in the previous chapter. A clergyman arrested in late 1980 for aiding Miskito and Somocista insurgents testified to receiving money for arms and supplies from the Moravian Social Action Committee. In late 1981, an AIFLD representative in Nicaragua was identified as a "conscious CIA agent" by Richard Martinez, who had himself organized workers in preparation for the 1964 coup in Brazil. He found the activities of AIFLD and the unions it sponsored in Nicaragua to be similar to those in Brazil.[26] On February 25, 1982, *Diario Las Americas*, a conservative daily in Miami, reported that the AIFLD-supported Council of Trade Union Unification (CUS) had formed an exile branch. The exile leader, CUS Assistant Secretary General Frank Jimenez, pledged the loyalty of CUS to the contra organization UDN and its military arm, the Nicaraguan Revolutionary Armed Forces (FARN).[27]

Ambassador Pezzullo was surprised by the administration decision to cut off aid to Nicaragua. He had told Daniel Ortega and Sergio Ramirez in mid February 1981 that Nicaragua had a month to halt any arms traffic to El Salvador or face termination of aid. He was assured that Nicaraguan territory would not be used for transshipping arms to El Salvador. U.S. intelligence found that arms traffic had stopped.[28] When the administration announced the aid cutoff in April, State Department spokesperson William Dyess acknowledged that the United States had "no hard evidence of arms movements through Nicaragua during the past few weeks" and said that Nicaragua's response to U.S. demands for a halt in assistance to the FMLN had been "positive."[29]

When Nicaragua moved vigorously to halt arms shipments across its territory, the Reagan administration parried by escalating its demands—insisting, for example, that Nicaragua cut political ties with the FMLN—and taking more aggressive action. It was a pattern that would be repeated in coming years as the administration translated "no business as usual" into undeclared war.

White Paper

"International terrorism will take the place of human rights in our concern," declared Haig on January 28, 1981. The administration moved quickly to define "international terrorism" as Soviet-sponsored subversion. Fed by administration leaks, the *New York Times* ran a front-page February 6 story reporting a Soviet-El Salvador arms pipeline supposedly exposed in secret documents captured from Salvadoran rebels. On February 20, the *New York Times* informed us again on the front page that the State Department provided U.S. allies with a memorandum asserting that "the insurgency in El Salvador has been progressively transformed into a textbook case of indirect armed aggression by Communist powers."[30] Nicaragua was central to the plot.

UN Ambassador Jeane Kirkpatrick turned up the rhetorical volume, declaring: "Our position in the Western Hemisphere has deteriorated to the point where we must now defend ourselves against a ring of Soviet bases being established on and around our borders." White House Counselor Ed Meese declared that the United States "will take the necessary steps to keep the peace any place in the world, and that includes El Salvador." He wouldn't specify what those steps might be: "The President has said many times he would like potential or real adversaries to go to bed every night wondering what we will do the next day. I don't think we would rule out anything."[31]

The State Department released the White Paper, *Communist Interference in El Salvador,* on February 23. "The White Paper was swallowed whole and regurgitated in a fashion not equalled since the Johnson Administration's White Paper on Vietnam 15 years ago," said Hodding Carter, press secretary to Jimmy Carter.[32] In the case of Vietnam, the Big Lie of the United States defending South Vietnam against North Vietnamese (Chinese) aggression endured even as the *Pentagon Papers* were exposed and the country turned against the war. So would the Big Lie of the United States defending Central American countries against Nicaraguan aggression.

The day the Reagan White Paper was released, Assistant Secretary Bushnell told reporters, "There is some evidence that the [arms] flow [through Nicaragua] may have stopped in the last couple of weeks."[33] A week later, the administration sent twenty more military "advisers" to El Salvador and announced plans to supply $25 million more in military aid.

The White Paper was gradually exposed in the media as a textbook case of U.S. government disinformation. Nevertheless, the administration achieved its central objective: it set the agenda, placing El Salvador and Nicaragua in a Cold War context, ensuring that mainstream debate would be restricted to the means to be used in achieving the shared goal of stopping "communist aggression."

Reagan media strategists, explained Jack Nelson of the *Los Angeles Times*, "realize that the first impressions are lasting impressions, that's part of their public relations genius." He cited Grenada as the perfect example: "There are still people who think that place was crawling with armed Cubans. It doesn't matter how often you go back and say that the fact is there were only 500 or 600 Cubans, that you got the truth out of Havana and lies out of Washington, people just say, 'Aw, that's just the press.'"[34]

The official spin-controllers know they have the advantage. As George Bush's press secretary, Peter Teeley, told reporters following the 1984 vice-presidential debate: "You can say anything you want in a debate, and 80 million people hear it. If reporters then document that a candidate spoke untruthfully, so what? Maybe 200 people read it, or 2,000 or 20,000."[35]

The mainstream media compounds the problem by repeating official lines, long after they are proven false, and by rehabilitating, even glorifying, official liars.* It's bad enough that standard operating procedure is to act as a megaphone for the official line—thereby protecting continued access to official leaks—under the guise of objective news reporting, generally following up, if at all, with delayed and buried rebuttals. Big Media further condones deceit by granting lifelong tenure as respected commentators to such notorious liars as Henry Kissinger. His accountability-resistant Teflon coating is even stronger than Ronald Reagan's, withstanding everything from wiretapping the phones of prominent journalists to destroying Chilean democracy to the secret bombing of Cambodia.[36]

As a United Fruit Company public relations specialist said of their success in using the press to create a favorable climate of opinion for the CIA-orchestrated Guatemalan coup of 1954: "It is difficult to make a convincing case for manipulation of the press when the victims proved so eager for the experience."[37]

The White Paper was exposed as a "political frameup" about a month after publication: James Petras wrote in *The Nation*, "its evidence is flimsy, circumstantial or nonexistent; the reasoning and logic is slipshod and internally inconsistent; it assumes what needs to be proven; and, finally, what facts are presented refute the very case the State Department is attempting to demonstrate."[38]

The *Wall Street Journal* weighed in on June 8—after dissection elsewhere of the actual documents behind the White Paper by reporter John Dinges—with this double-edged front-page headline: "Apparent Errors Cloud U.S. 'White Paper' on Reds in El Salvador." Jonathan Kwitny reported that Jon D. Glassman, a principal engineer of the White Paper, acknowledged there were "mistakes" and "guessing" and parts were possibly "misleading" and "over-embellished."[39]

Two days later, the *New York Times* backtracked with a page six story titled "U.S. Officials Concede Flaws in Salvador White Paper but Defend Its Conclusion." The article replayed an earlier piece of disinformation which was resurrected in the

---

* Bob Woodward's *Veil*, for example, is laced with recycled disinformation regarding Nicaragua, El Salvador and Grenada, credentialed by Woodward's reputation as an investigative journalist. Woodward's portrayal of the late CIA Director William Casey is more like a covertly authorized biography than an expose.

White Paper: "The result was an ambitious report in which the strongest case for an international Communist conspiracy to 'take over' a Central American country was presented on the basis of limited evidence...Even Robert F. White, the former United States Ambassador to El Salvador, who was removed by Mr. Haig and who has criticized increased military assistance to the Salvadorans has not questioned the basic conclusion. While still Ambassador, Mr. White said during the January guerrilla offensive that at least 100 insurgents had entered El Salvador by sea from Nicaragua to join the uprising. 'We can't stand idly by and watch the guerrilla movement receive outside aid,' said Mr. White, who recommended that limited military aid be restored to the Salvadoran armed forces."[40]

The *Times* used White's past comments to revalidate an already disproven charge (the Fonseca Gulf incident) while implicitly discrediting his current opposition to military aid for El Salvador. The article concluded by taking at face value other "evidence" of arms deliveries "following procedures and routes described in the documents."

Kwitny summed up the case in his book, *Endless Enemies:* the White Paper "says that a unified, Soviet-run international communist network took over the El Salvador rebellion to such an extent that the uprising constitutes a foreign, armed aggression rather than a legitimate civil war. In fact, so far as we can rely on the documents at all, they show the opposite: a disorganized, ragtag rebellion. Some of its participants have gone around begging for help from the most likely sources, and have been consistently stalled off and sent home empty-handed, or with much less than they asked for. Not only do the documents not prove the thesis, the thesis simply isn't true."[41]

Regarding the authenticity of the documents themselves, former CIA officer Philip Agee concluded that the "most sensational of [the White Paper] documents show indications of having been falsified...The CIA could have fabricated all 19 of these documents, perhaps working with Salvadoran security officials, and then arranged for them to be inserted among documents that actually had been captured. Such an operation would not be the first time."[42]

As Raymond Bonner noted, "Administration officials, including Glassman, have offered conflicting versions of how they came into possession of the documents: whether they were supplied by the Salvadorans or whether Glassman himself found them." Some of the documents were reportedly provided by Roberto D'Aubuisson, who had them in his possession in Guatemala.[43]

In late 1980, a Reagan adviser, retired General Daniel O. Graham, former head of the Defense Intelligence Agency, met with D'Aubuisson in Miami. "During the conversation, a number of Salvadorans present remembered Graham asking D'Aubuisson if he could find proof that the Salvadoran guerrillas were being manipulated by outside forces, because the incoming Reagan Administration believed proof of such manipulation was what was needed to 'influence American public opinion...to increase military and economic support for El Salvador.'"[44]

Writing about the White Paper in his memoirs, Haig called it "a sober, even a pedestrian treatment of the available information." He insisted it ran up against "the will to disbelieve—to reject, as a matter of automatic faith, anything that what is now called the establishment said and to suspect everything that it did as a trick to delude or defraud the common people."[45]

Haig's analysis of U.S. society was no more accurate than his analysis of Central America. The mainstream media is possessed of a strong will to believe the "truth" as defined by the establishment of which it is a part. Accusing the press of being leftish, or even leftist, is one more form of pressure to ensure that press "objectivity" means reporting the news to fit the government's agenda; the relatively few exceptions to the rule are used to deny the rule. To the Reaganites, anything less than airtight privilege is reverse discrimination.

Haig discussed the media quite differently earlier in his book: "the White House wizards understood the great intangible power that the government holds over the press…Information is power; manifestly the press cannot live without information. It has no information of its own; it follows, then, that it must rely on others to manufacture the stuff.

"The government is the great smithy of information. Appreciating this, Reagan's men exercised their intangible power. They opened the doors to the workshop and escorted reporters inside in a way hitherto unknown in Washington. They literally told them everything. For the first time in living memory, you could actually believe almost everything you read…[The press] had never had sources like this. And, of course, it could not risk losing these sources by offending them, so it wrote what it was given."[46] And the public, of course, is expected to believe the "truth" it gets from the media as manufactured by the government.

Nicaragua responded to arms trafficking accusations by calling for joint border patrols with Honduras—the only land bridge between Nicaragua and El Salvador, which do not share a common border. The media ignored this and the Reagan administration made sure it never happened. Border patrols would undermine Washington's propaganda as well as Honduras' role as the contras' staging area.

The "export of revolution" charge would be rejuvenated again and again in the campaign to paint Nicaragua as the aggressor, the United States as the righteous defender.

"Revolution Beyond Our Borders" Revisited

On July 19, 1981, the second anniversary of the Nicaraguan revolution, Tomas Borge declared: "We are proud to be Nicaraguans. This revolution transcends national boundaries." To stop there in quoting Borge, as the administration does, is to consciously distort Borge's meaning, for here is what immediately followed:

> Our revolution has always been internationalist, ever since Sandino fought in the Segovias. There were internationalists from all over the world who fought alongside Sandino, men from Venezuela, Mexico, Peru. Another who fought alongside Sandino was the great hero of the Salvadoran people named Farabundo Marti.
>
> It is not strange that we are internationalists, because this is something we got from Sandino. All the revolutionaries and all the peoples of Latin America especially know that

our people's heart is with them, beats alongside theirs. Our heart goes out to Latin America, and we also know that Latin America's heart goes out to the Nicaraguan revolution. *This does not mean that we export our revolution. It is enough—and we couldn't do otherwise— for us to export our example, the example of the courage, sensitivity, and determination of our people.*

How could we not be upset about the injustices that are committed in different parts of the world? But we know that it is the people themselves of these countries who must make their revolutions, and we know that by advancing our revolution we are also helping our brothers and sisters in the rest of Latin America. We know what is resting on our revolution—not only the aspirations of our people, but also the hopes of all the dispossessed of Latin America. This carries with it enormous responsibility, because as we have said before and repeat today, our internationalism is primarily expressed in consolidating our own revolution, working selflessly day in and day out and training ourselves militarily to defend our homeland.[47] (Italics added.)

This was not a call to arms for El Salvador, but a call to Nicaraguans to defend *their* revolution with internationalist spirit and nationalist deeds.

In Washington's Ministry of Truth, Borge's words would be turned on their head. Borge, it was claimed, said Nicaragua's revolution "goes beyond our borders." The phrase would be repeated in various forms by U.S. officials and enshrined in a September 1985 State Department report on Nicaragua, *Revolution Beyond Our Borders,* months after a State Department official acknowledged, regarding this and other phrases attributed to Sandinista leaders, "that people have been quoting some of these things from 1981 on, and some of them have become distorted."[48]

No slander is too much. Secretary of State George Shultz, Haig's successor, told the Senate Foreign Relations Committee that in calling for a "revolution without frontiers," the Sandinistas had revealed their true intentions just as Hitler had spelled out his goals in *Mein Kampf.*[49]

Finding I

Three weeks before the administration publicly cut off economic aid to Nicaragua, it secretly authorized the covert war. A March 9, 1981 presidential finding determined that secret operations in Central America were important to U.S. national security. It authorized a $19.5 million program of expanded CIA activity in the region, including assistance to Sandinista opponents inside Nicaragua and efforts to interdict arms headed to Salvadoran guerrillas.

Arms interdiction was the first pretext for supporting the contras. When CIA Director William Casey presented the finding to the House and Senate Intelligence Committees he emphasized protection of the Salvadoran government from "communist-supported insurgency."[50]

Haig accused the Soviet Union of having "a hit list" for the domination of Central America. On March 18, he told the House Foreign Affairs Committee that the insurgency in El Salvador was part of a four-phased operation, beginning with "the seizure of Nicaragua." Next comes El Salvador, to be followed by Honduras and Guatemala. Asked whether this was "a Caribbean domino theory," Haig replied, "I wouldn't call it necessarily a domino theory. I would call it a priority target list—a hit list, if you will—for the ultimate takeover of Central America."

Central America was only one of many supposed target areas: "Soviet adventurism in the Horn of Africa, in South Asia, in the Persian Gulf, and in South-West Africa appears to conform to a basic and ominous objective: to strike at countries on or near the vital resource lines of the Western world."[51] Since virtually all countries are "on or near" vital resource lines (by Washington's elastic definition), this provided a blanket warrant for global U.S. police actions.

Haig—who served as secretary of state until resigning on June 25, 1982—didn't mention the March 1981 finding in his memoirs, or any aspect of the covert war against Nicaragua, aside from a vague reference to "certain covert measures" in discussing options for El Salvador.[52] Haig described the early policy debate, not its outcome. He wanted more than the covert war he got. Haig saw Central America as a strategic choke point (one of many) and favored "a high level of intensity at the beginning, with all the risk that this entails."

In Haig's view, there actually wasn't much risk since "Castro had fallen between two superpowers." In a remarkable passage contradicting his whole hit list thesis (Haig didn't seem to notice), Haig revealed that conversations with Soviet Ambassador Dobrynin "convinced me that Cuban activities in the Western Hemisphere were a matter between the United States and Cuba."

Haig said he never contemplated direct military action against Cuba, "but it was obvious that Cuba, an island nation of 11 million people lying 100 miles off the coast of a United States with a population of 230 million, simply could not stand up to the geostrategic assets available to the larger country." As Haig told it, "a carrier group, or two, maneuvering between Cuba and the Central American mainland would have been a useful reminder of the…ability to blockade Cuba if that became necessary."

In fact, Haig repeatedly advocated a naval blockade of Cuba and Nicaragua, and suggested more direct military action, including invasion. Never mind that, in Haig's view, "The flow of arms into Nicaragua and thence into El Salvador slackened, a signal from Havana and Moscow that they had received and understood the American message."[52] That assessment didn't get in the way of the hit list rhetoric or arms-interdiction charade.

Reagan's advisers were divided into two camps: Haig's high-intensity/go-to-the-source minority vs. the incrementalist majority. Reagan's White House troika of Ed Meese, Michael Deaver and James Baker did not want to squander political capital needed for Reagan's domestic program (especially the Reaganomics tax cut) by rapidly escalating the war in Central America. Secretary of Defense Caspar Weinberger sided with those in the Pentagon who didn't want to spread their ostensibly inadequate forces even thinner, nor undermine public support for Reagan's military buildup by fueling fears of a new Vietnam War. "You want an effective presence there," said a senior officer, "not just a silhouette on the horizon."[53] The Pentagon brass wanted to be prepared to win the next war—politically and militarily. In Haig's account, the March 9 finding doesn't exist and the debate continued through March: "On March 23, I told Ed Meese that whatever we were going to do in Central America, we must get it started in ten days."[54]

While Reagan was sympathetic, there was little support in the administration for Haig's proposal to "go to the source" against Cuba. There was broad agreement, however, on destabilizing Nicaragua and increasing military support for El Salvador, Honduras and Guatemala. Assistant Secretary of State for Inter-American Affairs Thomas Enders pressed for development of the contras as a central tool of U.S. policy. Haig was opposed initially, thinking "the contras were a sideshow that could detract attention from the main event, which was Cuba, and that they could never win."[55]

Enders didn't think the contras could win either, but they could help destabilize Nicaragua and serve as a bargaining chip for concessions in any negotiations. Enders, a "soft-liner" by Reaganite standards, spoke of the need to "get rid of the Sandinistas" in administration meetings.[56]

The debate was between two types of rollback: slower and faster. Soon, everyone had a stake in the contras.

A U.S. diplomat in Honduras described the contras as a no-lose instrument of pressure: "Some people around here and in Washington really thought—and still do, I guess—that they could incite an insurrection and overthrow the Sandinistas. I always thought that was a lot of crap. But in any event, the theory was that we couldn't lose. If they took Managua, wonderful. If not, the idea was that the Sandinistas would react one of two ways. Either they'd liberalize and stop exporting revolution, which is fine and dandy, or they'd tighten up, alienate their own people, their international support and their backers in the United States, in the long run making themselves much more vulnerable. In a way, that one was even better—or so the idea went."[57]

4

The Avengers

You know there's no revolution without counterrevolution...The American revolution also had its counterrevolution—[its] Torries...They try to tell people that because there are some who are against the revolution that the revolution is no good [but] the previous order had to depend on some base...There must be some remnants of this support.

Miguel D'Escoto, May 9, 1986 interview with author.

Come the counterrevolution, there will be a massacre in Nicaragua. We have a lot of scores to settle. There will be bodies from the border to Managua.

Contra officer, Newsweek, November 8, 1982.

We got contras because the CIA put together Somocistas, Argentinians and the CIA...You cannot expect too much democracy from that.

Edgar Chamorro, former contra spokesman,
November 24, 1986 interview with author.

Nicaragua formed a popular militia to defend the revolution against attacks by ex-National Guardsmen and threats from the United States. "The cost of defense is high," said government junta member Moises Hassan. "But we won't be caught off guard." Speaking of the importance of the popular militias, he said, "We have no fear of an armed people."[1]

In March 1981, the U.S. media published their first accounts of contra training in the United States. *Parade* photographer Eddie Adams visited one camp, located about twenty minutes by car from Miami's international airport. Clad in battle fatigues, the recruits trained with automatic weapons and said they were "armed to

the teeth with an arsenal of weapons that even includes amphibious assault boats."
Florida hosted at least ten paramilitary organizations composed of Cuban and
Nicaraguan exiles, including the Cuban terrorist group, Alpha 66. Some advertised
for recruits over Spanish-language Miami radio stations and spoke freely about their
goal of "liberating" Nicaragua and Cuba.

Parade interviewed a contra known as Max Vargas: "They confiscated my
family's trucking company...I was successful. I made money, a million dollars a
month...I want Nicaragua to be the way I remember it. We're training people not
only here in Florida, but in Guatemala, Honduras, El Salvador and Costa Rica. We
have training camps in California too." ("Max Vargas" is reportedly an alias for Cuban
exile Felipe Vidal, a key operative for the contra southern front discussed later.)[2]

Asked about U.S. assistance, a State Department spokesperson commented,
"The new Administration is not going to turn back the clock 21 years in Cuba or 17
months in Nicaragua and support any exile groups. It's illegal. It's a breach of international law. It's also stupid."[3] The spokesperson was right about it being illegal
and stupid.

The *New York Times* followed *Parade*, visiting the "Cuba" camp, located "in
the brush and swamplands of Miami, just beyond new housing developments and
a trash dump." Camp commander Jorge Gonzales, known as "Bombillo" (Light Bulb),
said most members of the paramilitary group, including their top officer, a Vietnam
veteran, were in Central America on a mission. All the Nicaraguans at "Cuba" were
ex-National Guard.

"The hour of our return is approaching," declared a Nicaraguan with Guardia
insignia on his beret, "but we can't say when." He said some 600 Nicaraguans were
training in the United States. Bombillo remarked, "The principal aid we've received
has been the declarations of the President. It's not weapons we need, but freedom
of action."[4] They got both.

"Max Vargas," later identified by the Justice Department as a CIA operative,
bought two rifles at the Costa Gun Shop in Miami on August 6 and sent them to
UDN-FARN leader Fernando "El Negro" Chamorro in Honduras. Chamorro's agent
in Miami, Raul Arana, later revealed that in 1981 he sent several large shipments of
arms from Miami to Honduras.[5]

Former CIA officer Thomas Clines followed up his support of Somoza by assisting the guardsmen in exile. He reportedly worked with two Cuban exile CIA
veterans who would later play critical roles in the contra supply operation managed
by Richard Secord: Rafael Quintero and Felix Rodriguez.[6]

Contra camp trainees traveled to Central America to fight with such groups as
the UDN-FARN and the National Liberation Army (ELN), composed of ex-guardsmen
and led by former Somoza business partner Pedro Ortega ("Juan Carlos"). In mid
August, the FBI insisted that "no laws are being violated as long as the commandos
train on private property with registered weapons and refrain from using the United
States as a jumping off point for an invasion."[7]

Nicaragua lodged official protests, seeking to have the U.S. government enforce the Neutrality Act. First enacted by Congress in 1794, the Neutrality Act makes
it a crime to organize, finance, participate in or launch a paramilitary expedition

against a country with which the United States is not (formally) at war. The U.S. government chose instead to condone violations of the law. Later in 1981, U.S. officials would reinterpret the law to better justify the training camps.

September 15th Legion

In the fall of 1980, a group of former guardsmen trained at a Guatemalan farm called Detachment 101. These "soldiers" of the September 15th Legion "were becoming just another bunch of hired guns in Guatemala's bloody underworld of politics and crime."[8] They were called on for "special operations": robbery, extortion, kidnapping and assassination. The orders came through Ricardo Lau, the killer Roberto D'Aubuisson reportedly contracted to arrange the assassination of Salvadoran Archbishop Romero.

Major Ricardo "El Chino" Lau served with the Security Police and later as Somoza's chief of intelligence operations. A top CIA officer called him a Somoza "hatchet man." He was "a torturer," said a guardsman who had worked with him. "He operated where they put on the hood and the 220 current." Lau plied his torture trade during the insurrection as head of the infamous Model Jail in Managua. He reportedly ran "a checkpoint near the airport where young men were stopped and their knees checked for scrapes and bruises. Those who had them were assumed to have been behind the barricades and were shot."[9]

Lau was right-hand man to contra commander Enrique Bermudez, who arrived in Guatemala in mid 1980. Colonel Bermudez, Somoza's last military attache in Washington, organized the Legion with funds from Somoza's cousin Luis Pallais.[10] Under Somoza, Bermudez served as Nicaragua's representative to the Inter-American Defense Board and commanded the National Guard contingent sent to help the United States occupy the Dominican Republic in 1965. Among his contacts in the United States was retired Lt. General Gordon Sumner, coauthor of the Santa Fe report, chairman of the Council for Inter-American Security and former chairman of the Inter-American Defense Board.

The Legion's chief patron in Guatemala was Mario Sandoval, godfather of the Latin American death squads. His National Liberation Movement was created in 1954 by the CIA in preparation for the overthrow of the democratically elected government of Jacobo Arbenz.[11] Since 1972, Sandoval has headed the Guatemalan chapter of the World Anti-Communist League. Andres Nazario Sargen, secretary general of Alpha 66, is a longstanding League member. So was Anastasio Somoza.

World Anti-Communist League

While researching their book on the World Anti-Communist League (WACL), journalists Scott Anderson and Jon Lee Anderson received a letter from a former League member: "In considering the World Anti-Communist League you have entered a world of ideological fanaticism, racialism, ignorance and fear which is almost beyond the comprehension of the average American...Your subject matter is a collection of oriental fascists, militarists, rightwing terrorists who put bombs in civilian aircraft, death squads, assassins, criminals and many people who are as much opposed to democracy as they are communism."[12]

With chapters now in over 90 countries on six continents, WACL was founded in 1966 by two dictatorships, South Korea and Taiwan, and the Anti-Bolshevik Bloc of Nations (ABN), which united East European fascists who were valued for their anti-communism and resettled in the West with the aid of the Vatican and U.S. and British intelligence. Formed with U.S. government funds, the ABN is described as "the largest and most important umbrella for Nazi collaborators in the world."[13]

The late Yaroslav Stetsko, chairman of the ABN and a longtime WACL leader, met with President Reagan in the White House in 1983. The Ukranian Stetsko assisted in the 1941 Nazi invasion of the Soviet Union and led the occupation of Lvov. "During the period in which Stetsko was in Lvov and, by his own claim, in charge of the city, an estimated seven thousand residents, mostly Jews, were murdered."[14]

Latter-day fascist Roberto D'Aubuisson, a League member, once told German reporters that he admired Hitler because, "you Europeans had the right idea. You saw the Jews were behind communism and you started to kill them."[15]

The World Anti-Communist League is an outgrowth of the Asian Peoples Anti-Communist League, formed in 1954, also with U.S. government support, by the South Korean Central Intelligence Agency (KCIA) and Chiang Kai-Shek's Kuomintang (KMT). In 1947, before losing to Mao on the Chinese mainland, Chiang's forces crushed an independence movement on occupied Formosa (Taiwan) with a massacre of some 20,000 people.

Taiwan became a laboratory for "total and unconventional warfare." It established a Political Warfare Cadres Academy—D'Aubuisson is a graduate—with the assistance of WACL associate Ray Cline, who was CIA station chief in Taiwan from 1958 to 1962, then CIA deputy director for intelligence, State Department director of intelligence and founder of the U.S. Global Strategy Council. U.S. military personnel taught at the academy, drawn largely from the U.S. Military Group stationed in Taiwan.[16]

In Latin America, WACL's affiliates formed the Latin American Anti-Communist Confederation (CAL). In 1974, CAL introduced a resolution at WACL's annual conference seeking the overthrow of the U.S. government, which was considered soft on communism, and installation of a military junta. CAL was organized by the Mexican Tecos, whose leaders were the principal authors of the 1962 *Complot Contra La Iglesia* (Conspiracy Against the Church). A response to the liberalism of Vatican Council II, the *Complot* has been called "one of the most scathingly anti-semitic and unabashedly pro-Nazi tracts ever written."[17]

Liberation theology has been a prime CAL target. In 1975, Bolivia formulated the Banzer Plan (named after then dictator Hugo Banzer) which, as journalist Penny Lernoux explains, aimed "to smear, arrest, expel, or murder any dissident priest or bishop in the Bolivian Church." The CIA assisted Bolivia by providing personal data, names of friends, addresses, writings, contacts abroad and other intelligence on certain priests. Between 1975 and 1978, twelve foreign missionaries were arrested in Bolivia and half of them deported. Iowan missionary Father Raymond Herman was murdered in his parish rectory in October 1976. In El Salvador death squads killed Fathers Rutilio Grande and Alfonso Navarro in 1977. The "White Warriors' Union" took responsibility for Navarro's murder and issued the slogan: "Be a patriot! Kill a priest!"[18]

The attack on liberation theology was regionalized when ten countries backed the Banzer Plan at the 1977 CAL conference in Paraguay. WACL adopted a "priest tracking" resolution in 1978. Between 1964 (the year of the military coup in Brazil) and 1978, at least 79 priests, bishops, religious (members of religious orders) and well known Christian lay leaders were killed in Latin America, many of them between 1975 and 1977. Argentina, El Salvador and Honduras led the murders in that period. The killing has continued.[19]

The chairman of WACL and head of the U.S. chapter during the late 1970s was Roger Pearson, a well-connected white supremacist, eugenicist and neo-Nazi, who reportedly "once bragged to an associate about his alleged role in hiding Nazi doctor Josef Mengele."[20] As editor of the Liberty Lobby magazine, *Western Destiny*, Pearson wrote in 1965: "Our Race can only survive if we can prevent them [Jews and blacks] from capturing the minds, morals and souls of our children." By the mid 1970s, he was serving on the editorial boards of the Heritage Foundation and the American Security Council.

Under Pearson's guidance WACL added Western European chapters composed of Nazi collaborators, neo-Nazis and rightwing terrorists—from the racist British League of Rights to Giorgio Almirante's Italian Social Movement, whose members included Pino Rauti, founder of the outlawed *Ordine Nuovo*. Rauti's former deputy, Elio Massagrande, attended WACL's 1979 conference in Paraguay while "high on Interpol's list of wanted fugitives."[21] As tensions rose with the non-fascist European chapters, Pearson was asked to resign in 1980. The American chapter was then headed briefly by Elmore D. Greaves, organizer of Mississippi's segregationist Citizens Council during the 1960s.

In April 1982, Pea. son received a letter from President Reagan, which he used to solicit donations and subscriptions to his magazines. "Your substantial contributions to promoting and upholding those ideals and principles that we value at home and abroad are greatly appreciated," Reagan wrote. The letter was not repudiated even after White House officials were informed of Pearson's background.[22]

Moonstruck

WACL provided a strong base for the Reverend Sun Myung Moon's Unification Church, which is closely tied to the KCIA. Known for its totalitarian indoctrination of young people (in 1982, Moon arranged 2,000 couples at random for marriage in a mass ceremony at Madison Square Garden), in the 1940s Moon's first church practiced the ritual of "blood separation": female church members "were required to have sexual relations with Moon, to clear themselves of 'the taint of Satan.' "[23]

The Unification Church supposedly left WACL in 1975 when Moon denounced it as fascist after a frustrated takeover attempt. But Moon continued to be represented by the powerful Japanese Unification Church through its front group, *Shokyo Rengo* (Victory Over Communism), founded by such men as the late Yoshio Kodama, leader of the Japanese organized crime syndicate, the *Yakuza,* and Ryoichi Sasakawa, who has described himself as the "world's wealthiest fascist."[24]

WACL members work with the Unification Church in support of the contras through Moonie affiliates like CAUSA and the Moon-owned *Washington Times,* established in 1982. CAUSA (Confederation of Associations for the Unity [originally Unification] of the Societies of America) was founded in 1980 by Colonel Bo Hi Pak, the former KCIA operative who is Moon's top deputy, and Kim Sang In, former KCIA station chief in Mexico City. CAUSA's first executive director was Warren Richardson, formerly general counsel to the Liberty Lobby.

Moonie connections with the U.S. right and the Reagan administration are extensive. For example, retired Major General Daniel Graham, a member of CAUSA USA's advisory board, heads the Star Wars lobby group, High Frontier. F. Lynn Bouchey, president of the Council for Inter-American Security and member of the Committee of Santa Fe, helped organize two CAUSA conferences. *Washington Times* editor Arnaud de Borchgrave serves on Ray Cline's U.S. Global Strategy Council, a Reagan advisory group. The Strategy Council's executive director is retired General E. David Woellner, president of CAUSA World Services. *Washington Times* columnists include Ray Cline's son-in-law Roger Fontaine, a Committee of Santa Fe member and former Reagan Latin America adviser, and Jeremiah O'Leary, formerly special assistant to National Security Adviser William Clark.[25]

Moon money has become a major source of nourishment for New Right leaders and organizations. The Unification Church contributed $775,000 in 1984 to the Conservative Alliance (CALL), a non-profit lobbying group headed by the late John "Terry" Dolan who also led the National Conservative Political Action Committee (NCPAC) and served on CAUSA USA's advisory board.[26] Direct mail fundraiser Richard Viguerie was bailed out of debt in 1987 when Bo Hi Pak's U.S. Property Development Corporation purchased Viguerie's Virginia headquarters. Viguerie has served on the board of the Moon-dominated American Freedom Coalition (AFC) which was his biggest new direct-mail client as of December 1987.[27]

Moon's quest for global theocracy is no secret. In 1978, a House subcommittee tracing the Unification Church's connections with South Korean security and intelligence forces quoted Moon: "If we manipulate seven nations at least...the U.S., England, France, Germany, Soviet Russia and maybe Korea and Japan...then we can get a hold of the whole world."

By the time Moon was released from a U.S. prison in the summer of 1985 after serving a year-long sentence for perjury and falsification of documents, his image had been dramatically rehabilitated. His supporters claimed he was unjustly imprisoned for "tax evasion" and people of diverse political backgrounds saw him as a persecuted religious leader. Rightwing Senator Orrin Hatch (R-UT) lauded Moon for providing American youth with "a religious alternative to Communism."[28]

In a January 1987 "God's Day" speech, Moon showed his image may have mellowed, but not his views: "Without knowing it, even President Reagan is guided by Father [Moon]. History will make the position of [Reverend] Moon clear and his enemies, the American population and government will bow down to him. That is Father's tactic, the natural subjugation of the American government and population."[29]

Reagan administration-Moonie ties are extensive enough that an analyst for the Pentagon-funded Institute of Defense Analysis warned of the effects their exposure could have on the 1984 elections: "Current Moonie involvement with government officials, contractors and grantees...could create a major scandal...If efforts are not taken to stop their growing influence and weed out current Moonie involvement in government, the President stands a good chance of being portrayed in the media as a poor, naive incompetent."[30] As it turned out, Mooniegate was just one more scandal Reagan avoided in the years preceding the Iran-contra revelations.

Singlaub's WACL Warriors

Retired Major General John Singlaub organized the current American WACL chapter, the United States Council for World Freedom (USCWF), in 1981 with a loan of nearly $20,000 from Taiwan. Based in Phoenix, Arizona, it received tax-exempt status in 1982. Daniel Graham became USCWF vice chairman and advisory board members have included General Lewis Walt, former commander of Marine Corps forces in Vietnam; John Fisher, former president of the American Security Council; Howard Phillips, chairman of the Conservative Caucus; Andy Messing, head of the National Defense Council; and lawyer Fred Schlafly, husband of longtime rightwing activist Phyllis Schlafly.[31]

Singlaub served from 1983 to 1986 as chairman of the World Anti-Communist League. (He was succeeded by former Belgian Defense Minister Jose Desmarets, who has warned against the "subtle forms" of communism: "ecology, pacifism and neutralism.")[32] Singlaub remains chairman óf the USCWF. Under Singlaub's leadership WACL became more action oriented. Committees were formed to support counterrevolution in eight countries: Nicaragua, Angola, Mozambique, Ethiopia, Afghanistan, Laos, Cambodia and Vietnam. In 1987, Singlaub became increasingly involved in counterinsurgency in the Philippines, where CAUSA is also active.[33]

"Jack" Singlaub has a long history of involvement in covert operations, beginning with the World War II Office of Strategic Services (OSS). He served as CIA desk officer for China in 1949 and deputy station chief in South Korea during the Korean War. During the Vietnam War he commanded the Special Operations Group—Military Assistance Command, Vietnam - Studies and Observation Group (MACVSOG)—which carried out the Phoenix operation responsible for the assassination of 20,000 to 41,000 Vietnamese.[34] In 1976, Singlaub became head of the U.S. command in South Korea. He was removed by President Carter in 1978, when he publicly opposed Carter's plans to withdraw most U.S. troops, and retired from the military in 1980. In 1984, Singlaub chaired a special Pentagon panel on the war in El Salvador and also became a key player in the contra supply network.

Anderson and Anderson describe WACL as "the international fraternity of the practitioners of unconventional war, old and new"—from the Nazis to South Africa to Latin America. As defined by Singlaub, "The term 'unconventional war' includes, in addition to terrorism, subversion and guerrilla warfare, such covert and non-military activities as sabotage, economic warfare, support to resistance groups, black and gray psychological operations, disinformation activities, and political warfare." Singlaub would help make sure the United States did not "lack the capability and will to exercise [this] third option for our own defense, to take pressure off any ally, or to exploit to our advantage the many vulnerabilities that now exist in the Soviet Empire."[35]

The unconventional warriors practice their trade inside the United States as well, carrying on the political spying and militaristic propaganda that General Smedley Butler confronted decades ago (discussed further in chapter 15). Singlaub served until 1984 on the advisory board of Western Goals, founded in 1979 by the late Rep. Larry McDonald (D-GA), board member and then chairman of the John Birch Society. As investigative journalist Chip Berlet explains, Western Goals "was essentially a cover for the continued domestic political spying of the John Birch Society. Its chief spymaster was John Rees."[36] The late Roy Cohn, Joe McCarthy's right-hand lawyer, served on the Western Goals advisory board, along with retired military officers such as General Lewis Walt and Admiral Thomas Moorer. The Western Goals data bank included files accessed by McDonald as head of the now-defunct House Un-American Activities Committee (HUAC) as well as from police "red squads." After McDonald's death in September 1983 (on Korean Airlines flight 007), Linda Guell took over and Rees left with his file collection. As Berlet explains, Western Goals was "pretty much a shell" when Carl "Spitz" Channell became its president and used it as a fundraising vehicle for the contras.[37]

Singlaub served as cochairman, with Graham, of the American Security Council's Coalition for Peace Through Strength (it includes such Nazi-led WACL affiliates as the Bulgarian National Front). The American Security Council (ASC) was established during the 1950s by corporations wanting background checks done on employees. Its file archives include the files collected by Harry Jung's American Vigilante Intelligence Federation founded in 1927 as an anti-union spy group and fueled by anti-Semitism. The ASC Task Force on Central America, formed after Somoza's overthrow, included Singlaub, Graham, Haig and Reps. Larry McDonald, John Murphy and Charles Wilson, among others.[38] Singlaub also serves as an adviser to the Council for Inter-American Security led by Lynn Bouchey, which also combined global militarism with surveillance of the U.S. left.

In December 1979, Singlaub and Graham, who served on Reagan's defense advisory committee, led a supportive American Security Council delegation to Guatemala. In a later interview with Allan Nairn, Singlaub—who served as honorary chairman of the 1980 Reagan Campaign in Colorado—said that he was "terribly impressed" at how the regime of General Romeo Lucas Garcia was "desperately trying to promote human rights." He urged sympathetic understanding of the death squads, arguing that the Carter administration's unwillingness to back the Guatemalan regime in eliminating its enemies was "prompting those who are dedicated to retaining the free enterprise system and to continuing progress toward political and economic development to take matters in their own hands."

The message from Singlaub and Graham was clear, according to one high Guatemalan official: "Mr. Reagan recognizes that a good deal of dirty work has to be done." Gordon Sumner of the Council for Inter-American Security and the ASC Task Force on Central America also defended the death squads to Nairn, arguing that while regrettable, "there is really no other choice."[39]

In February 1981, Amnesty International released a report entitled, *Guatemala, a Government Program of Political Murder.* The report described how death squad victims were targeted for murder in an annex of the National Palace under the direction of President Lucas Garcia. It concluded that "nearly 5,000 Guatemalans have been seized without warrant and killed since General Lucas Garcia became President of Guatemala in 1978. The bodies of the victims have been found piled up in ravines, dumped at roadsides or buried in mass graves. Thousands bore the scars of torture, and death had come to most by strangling with a garrotte, by being suffocated in rubber hoods or by being shot in the head."[40]

Deaver and Hannaford, the public relations firm then headed by Reagan aides Peter Hannaford and Michael Deaver, represented the rightwing Guatemalan group, *Amigos del Pais* (Friends of the Country). *Amigos* leader Roberto Alejos provided the ranch used as a training camp by the CIA for the 1961 Bay of Pigs invasion force. In late 1979, Reagan had private talks with Alejos and with Manuel Ayau, "chief ideologue and theorist of the Guatemalan right" and member of Mario Sandoval's National Liberation Movement.

The Reagan presidential campaign reportedly received millions of dollars from Guatemalans and U.S. businessmen living in Guatemala. The campaign did not disclose these contributions to the Federal Election Commission, with one exception: the wife of John Trotter, manager of Guatemala's Coca-Cola bottling plant where five union leaders were murdered, was listed for $750. According to one businessman solicited by the Reagan campaign, there were explicit instructions: "Do not give to Mr. Reagan's campaign directly." Contributions were directed to an undisclosed committee in California. As for the Guatemalan contributors, "one government official tells of a meeting in the National Palace...where Guatemalan businessmen and government members boasted of funneling money to Reagan but cautioned all listening that the connection was to be kept confidential."[41]

Death squad godfather Mario Sandoval attended Reagan's 1981 inaugural ball. So did Adolfo Cuellar, chairman of El Salvador's WACL chapter until his murder later that year. Cuellar is remembered by former Salvadoran army officers "as a man who used to appear at interrogation centers and beg for permission to torture the prisoners."[42]

Singlaub claimed that in 1983 there was a purge of violent elements in the Latin chapters: "The people in WACL from Latin American [sic] now are good, respectable anti-communists."[43] Although CAL was replaced in 1984 by the Federation of Latin American Democratic Entities (FEDAL), not much changed besides the name. According to Anderson and Anderson, only the Mexican Tecos were purged.

When President Reagan sent "warm greetings" to the 1984 WACL conference in San Diego, Mario Sandoval was there. So was contra leader Adolfo Calero, along with assorted racists and fascists from around the world. Said Reagan, "The World Anti-Communist League has long played a leadership role in drawing attention to the gallant struggle now being waged by the true freedom fighters of our day. Nancy and I send you our best wishes for every future success."[44]

"If I have to get rid of half of Guatemala, so the other half can live in peace, I'll do it," declared Mario Sandoval during his failed 1985 bid for the Guatemalan presidency.[45] He attended the September 1985 WACL conference in Dallas, along with contra leaders Adolfo Calero and Enrique Bermudez and contra donor Ellen Garwood of Texas. Tom Posey's Civilian Military Assistance mercenaries provided security.[46]

WACL members called for support of the South African government in its "defense against Moscow-Peking [sic] insurgency." On September 11, the third day of the conference, Chairman Singlaub proclaimed: "We commemorate today...the date that the first country was liberated from communism: the military overthrow of the Allende regime in Chile...We send a salute to General Augusto Pinochet in Chile, and to Juan Ramon Chaves, president of [Paraguay's] Colorado Party [also founded on September 11], offering our congratulations." The Colorado Party of dictator General Alfredo Stroessner has ruled Paraguay for over 30 years. The contra leaders promised that the 1986 WACL convention would be held in Managua.[47]

The Argentine Axis

The Reagan administration "looked to the Argentinians as the people who could clean up Central America of communists," former contra spokesman Edgar Chamorro told me.[48] Clean up meant dirty war.

The Argentine military fancied itself on the frontlines of World War III. It took over the government in a 1976 coup and was proud of victory in the "dirty war" against "subversion," targeting the *Montonero* movement and anyone deemed a sympathizer. The term "subversive," stated a 1977 Argentine government report, "is used as a synonym for 'terrorist.'" The labels were hard to avoid. According to the report, lobbying by university students for student cafeterias was a clear sign of potential terrorism.[49] Between 9,000 and 30,000 "subversives" in universities, labor unions, churches, journalism, etc. were rounded up, tortured and disappeared.[50]

There were many Argentinians among the 64,000 Latin American soldiers and officers—including 170 heads of state, ministers, commanding officers and directors of intelligence—trained between 1950 and 1973 at the U.S. Army School of the

Americas in the Panama Canal Zone. Course 0-47 on urban counterinsurgency operations taught how to detect the presence of communist guerrillas: "The refusal of peasants to pay rents, taxes, or agricultural loans or any difficulty in collecting these will indicate the existence of an active insurrection that has succeeded in convincing the peasants of the injustices of the present system, and is directing or instigating them to disobey its precepts…Hostility on the part of the local population to the government forces, in contrast to their amiable or neutral attitude in the past. This can indicate a change of loyalty or of behavior inspired by fear, often manifested by children refusing to fraternize with members of the internal-security forces…Short, unjustified, and unusual absences from work on the part of government employees."

As taught by the U.S. military, subversion was a product of foreign, communist influences. It could take the form of nonviolent action, including consciousness-raising work (promoted by Christian base communities), demonstrations, strikes, "compromised" social sciences and other activities that "attract the discontented among the populace, although those who protest are not the people themselves but an atomized group of malcontents and adventurers."

At the U.S. Army Institute for Military Assistance at Fort Bragg, North Carolina, Latin Americans were taught "Population Protection and Resources Management," utilizing such techniques as a national identity card system, search operations, checkpoints, curfews and block controls to monitor the movement of people and goods. "The semester concluded with a discussion of the role of the mass media and propaganda in building support for the government, 'since by their nature most [of these] measures are rather harsh…[and] they should be coordinated with an intense PSYOPS [psychological operations] campaign to convince the population that these harsh methods are for their own good.'"[51]

Under the Latin American Doctrine of National Security all dissidents are enemies of the state and all opposition is communist subversion. But the National Security States were not always doctrinaire. For most of their rule from 1976 to 1983, the Argentine generals did not direct their World War III on subversion against the Soviet Union. They maintained a foreign policy of "ideological pluralism," driven by economic pragmatism, which led to increasingly profitable relations with the Soviet Union. When President Carter declared a grain embargo against the Soviet Union in 1980, Argentina's wheat sales to the Soviet Union skyrocketed. By the end of 1980, the Soviet Union was the largest importer of Argentine exports, including grain, meat and wool, and Argentina was the Soviet Union's second largest trading partner after India.[52]

In an effort to institutionalize the National Security Doctrine of stamping out the "subversive" threat in whatever country it arose, the Chilean secret police, then known as DINA, initiated Operation Condor in 1976. "It now seems likely," wrote Anderson and Anderson, "that the car-bomb killing of Chilean dissident Orlando Letelier [along with his U.S. associate Ronni Karpen Moffitt] in Washington in 1976 (orchestrated by an American contract agent of the Chilean secret police and conducted by anti-Castro Cuban exiles) and the attempted murder of [Chilean Christian

Democrat] Bernardo Leighton (shot by an Italian fascist on orders from Chile, with the 'credit' taken by Cuban exiles) are examples of the work of Condor."

While officially dismantled after exposure in the late 1970s, Condor "has simply changed form," with Latin American governments often contracting out assignments to groups such as CAL.[53] From his exile in Paraguay, Somoza reportedly helped finance CAL-connected anti-Communist terrorist groups, including Croatian terrorists wanted in Yugoslavia.[54]

In September 1980, WACL members gathered in Buenos Aires for CAL's annual meeting. They were hosted by the military junta and the Argentine Anti-Communist Alliance (AAA) death squad. Among those attending were Senator Jesse Helms' (R-NC) aide-at-large John Carbaugh, Mario Sandoval, Roberto D'Aubuisson and Italian terrorist Stefano Delle Chiaie, who was wanted for a string of murders and bombings in Europe, including the August 1980 Bologna, Italy railway station bombing killing 85 people. Delle Chiaie journeyed to the CAL conference from Bolivia, where he was in a cocaine and terror partnership with Nazi Klaus Barbie (alias Klaus Altmann).[55]

The July 1980 coup that put General Luis Garcia Meza in the Bolivian presidency was a product of multinational intrigue and repression involving Bolivian military and cocaine lords, the Argentine military, WACL's Bolivia chapter, Barbie's Nazi network and CAUSA. After visiting the newly installed dictator in La Paz, Colonel Bo Hi Pak proclaimed, "I have erected a throne for Father Moon in the world's highest city."[56] The cocaine kings could not long sustain their rule. Barbie, the Nazi "Butcher of Lyons," who first escaped justice by working for U.S. intelligence, was deported to France in 1982 to stand trial for war crimes after Bolivia returned to elected government. (Delle Chiaie was captured in Venezuela in 1987 and extradited to Italy.)

At the 1980 CAL meeting, Argentina agreed to help wage dirty war in El Salvador, and within two months sent at least 50 Argentine unconventional warfare advisers. Argentine advisers also operated in Honduras (discussed further in chapter 6).[57] In defense of "ideological frontiers," the Argentine military also assisted the former guardsmen of Somoza's regime, providing training in Argentina, Honduras and Costa Rica.

Details of the Argentine program were disclosed in December 1982 by Hector Frances, a defecting officer from Argentine Army Intelligence Battalion 601.[58] According to both Hector Frances and Enrique Bermudez, ex-guardsmen began training in Argentina in late 1980.[59]

Frances was a military adviser to the contras in Costa Rica, earning $2,500 to $3,000 a month. According to Frances, the contras ran a Basic Infantry Training School in Costa Rica where they received arms provided by Somoza's son, El Chiguin. "The arms arrived in t.v. boxes by Costa Rican airlines. That equipment was to arm 100 men who had plans to infiltrate Nicaragua and attempt the assassination of the Nicaraguan revolutionary leadership."[60]

The contras collaborated with the ultraright *Costa Rica Libre* (Free Costa Rica Movement) in plotting the overthrow of the Nicaraguan government and creating hospitable conditions under President Monge. Costa Rica Libre chief Bernal Urbana Pinto heads Costa Rica's WACL chapter and has served as vice president of FEDAL.

A founding member of Costa Rica Libre, Benjamin Piza Carranza, became minister of public security in 1984; he disavowed continuing links with the group.[61]

La Tripartita

The early contra war relied on a three-sided arrangement, "La Tripartita": the United States supplied direction and money; Argentina provided training and cover; and Honduras was the main base of operations.

Following the March 1981 presidential finding on Central America, State Department Ambassador-At-Large Vernon "Dick" Walters (later UN Ambassador) was dispatched to negotiate arrangements with the contras and the Argentinians. Walters, a retired lieutenant general who speaks eight languages including Spanish, has a long career in covert operations involving him in such affairs as the 1953 overthrow of the Mossadegh government in Iran, the 1964 overthrow of the Goulart government in Brazil and the 1973 overthrow of the Allende government in Chile.[62] From 1972 until 1976, Walters served as deputy director of Central Intelligence.

In March 1981, the Reagan administration asked Congress to repeal the 1978 ban on military sales and assistance to Argentina, stating that "the prohibitions have acted to frustrate serious dialogue with the Argentinians regarding mutual strategic concerns." The Reaganites had broader concerns than Central America. They had ill-fated dreams of a political-military pact, the South Atlantic Treaty Organization (SATO), linking South America's Southern Cone countries (Argentina, Chile, Bolivia, Uruguay, Paraguay) with Brazil, the United States and South Africa. SATO was promoted as "protection" for the sea lanes of the Cape Route from the Persian Gulf around South Africa's Cape of Good Hope and past the tip of South America on the way to the United States and Europe.[63]

On April 2, 1981, the day after Washington cut off aid to Nicaragua, the *New York Times*' Alan Riding reported on contra activities in Honduras under the headline, "Rightist Exiles Plan Invasion of Nicaragua." Nicaraguan "exile leaders asserted that a 600-man 'freedom force' stationed in Honduras near the Nicaraguan border would soon be joined by thousands of sympathizers from Guatemala and Miami." Said UDN leader Jose Francisco Cardenal, "Nicaragua cannot be liberated only by Nicaraguans, just as Somoza was not overthrown only by Nicaraguans…The green light has to come soon from the United States." Asked about Pentagon and CIA involvement, Cardenal replied, "No comment."

Edgar Chamorro, who worked with Cardenal in the UDN during 1980 and 1981, described the U.S. role in organizing the contras in testimony to the World Court. During the first half of 1981, Cardenal was contacted by representatives of the CIA "and began to have frequent meetings with them in Washington and in Miami. He also began to receive monetary payments…He was told that the United States Government was prepared to help us remove the F.S.L.N. from power in Nicaragua, but that, as a condition for receiving this help, we had to join forces with the ex-National Guardsmen who had fled to Honduras when the Somoza Government fell and had been conducting sporadic raids on Nicaraguan border positions ever since. Cardenal was taken to Honduras by his C.I.A. contacts on several occasions to meet with these Guardsmen."

According to Chamorro, Cardenal and the UDN "initially opposed any linkage with the Guardsmen. The C.I.A. and high-ranking United States Government officials insisted that we merge with the Guardsmen. Lt. General Vernon Walters...met with Cardenal to encourage him to accept the C.I.A.'s proposal. We were well aware of the crimes the Guardsmen had committed against the Nicaraguan people while in the service of President Somoza, and we wanted nothing to do with them. However, we recognized that without help from the United States Government we had no chance of removing the Sandinistas from power, so we eventually acceded to the C.I.A.'s and General Walters' insistence that we join forces with the Guardsmen...Cardenal and I and others believed the C.I.A.'s assurances that we, the civilians, would control the Guardsmen in the new organization that was to be created.

"At that time, the ex-National Guardsmen were divided into several small bands operating along the Nicaragua-Honduras border. The largest of the bands...[was] the 15th of September Legion. The bands were poorly armed and equipped, and thoroughly disorganized. They were not an effective military force and represented no more than a minor irritant to the Nicaraguan Government. Prior to the U.D.N.'s merger with these people, General Walters himself arranged for all of the bands to be incorporated within the 15th of September Legion, and for the military government of Argentina to send several army officers to serve as advisers and trainers."

Chamorro described the merger of the September 15th Legion and the UDN on August 10, 1981. It "was accomplished...at a meeting in Guatemala City, Guatemala, where formal documents were signed. The meeting was arranged and the documents were prepared by the C.I.A. The new organization was called the *Fuerza Democratica Nicaragüense* ('Nicaraguan Democratic Force') or, by its Spanish acronym, F.D.N. It was to be headed by a political junta, consisting of Cardenal, Aristides Sanchez (a politician loyal to General Somoza and closely associated with Bermudez) and Mariano Mendoza, formerly a labor leader in Nicaragua; the political junta soon established itself in Tegucigalpa, Honduras, taking up residence in a house rented for it by the C.I.A. Bermudez was assigned to head the military general staff, and it, too, was based in Honduras. The name of the organization, the members of the political junta, and the members of the general staff were all chosen or approved by the C.I.A.

"Soon after the merger, the F.D.N. began to receive a substantial and steady flow of financial, military and other assistance from the C.I.A. Former National Guardsmen who had sought exile in El Salvador, Guatemala and the United States...were recruited to enlarge the military component of the organization. They were offered regular salaries, the funds for which were supplied by the C.I.A. Training was provided by Argentinian military officers, two of whom—Col. Oswaldo Ribeiro and Col. Santiago Villejas [sic]—I got to know quite well; the Argentinians were also paid by the C.I.A. A special unit was created for sabotage, especially demolitions; it was trained directly by C.I.A. personnel at Lepaterique, near Tegucigalpa. Arms, ammunition, equipment and food were supplied by the C.I.A. Our first combat units were sent into Nicaraguan territory in December 1981."[64]

Colonel Osvaldo "Balita" (Little Bullet) Riveiro headed Argentine contra operations in Honduras. Santiago Villegas served as chief of logistics and military operations. When Villegas met Cardenal in Miami in August he "claimed the Americans had promised equipment for ten thousand men" by the end of 1981.[65] The Argentinians worked closely with Colonel Gustavo Alvarez, then head of Honduran Public Security forces and a graduate of the Argentine military academy, class of 1961.

The contras were commanded by Enrique Bermudez and former Guardia Major Emilio "Fiero" (Fierce) Echaverry, the son-in-law of an Argentine officer and graduate of the Argentine military academy along with Alvarez. Ricardo Lau was in charge of counterintelligence and special operations. In September 1981, six mid-level officers asked for the removal of Bermudez and Lau on the grounds of misuse of funds, negligence of duty, lying and lack of patriotic spirit. Bermudez was accused of embezzling $50,000 in funds provided to the contras by the Argentinians at CIA behest. The Argentinians stood behind Bermudez and forced out the founding September 15th Legion officers who had brought the charges.[66]

The RIG and the Proconsul

In August 1981, CIA Director William Casey picked Duane "Dewey" Clarridge (alias Dewey Maroni) to head the CIA's Latin America division. He replaced Nestor Sanchez, who moved over to the Defense Department as deputy assistant secretary for international security affairs. Clarridge, formerly the Rome station chief, had impressed Casey as "a real doer, a real take-charge guy."[67] Clarridge had also served the CIA in Nepal, India and Turkey. Like many on Reagan's Latin America team, he came to his post with no prior experience in the region.

The man picked to run the war on the ground from Honduras, the northern front, was John Negroponte. More proconsul than ambassador, Negroponte was a diplomatic veteran of the Vietnam War, having served in the U.S. embassy in Saigon and then on Kissinger's NSC staff as a Vietnam expert. He told rightwingers wary of his ties to the "liberal" Kissinger that he had opposed Kissinger's "sellout" of Vietnam at the Paris Peace talks. Before taking up his Honduras post in November 1981, Negroponte served in Ecuador and Greece.[68]

Assistant Secretary of State for Inter-American Affairs Thomas Enders chaired the Special Interagency Group (or Core Group), which was later called the Restricted Interdepartmental Group (RIG). Members included Dewey Clarridge from CIA, Nestor Sanchez from Defense, General Paul Gorman representing the Joint Chiefs of Staff (until he became chief of the Southern Command and Vice Admiral Arthur Morreau took his place) and, beginning in early 1983, Marine officer Oliver North of the NSC (substituting for and then replacing Roger Fontaine). "Often, it was not what it seemed," said a RIG member. "When it got too big there would be a steering group."

Nicaragua wasn't Enders' first secret war. In late 1971, he became deputy chief of the U.S. Embassy in Cambodia. He was considered, wrote William Shawcross in *Sideshow*, a "can-do sort of guy." He understood the administration line, that Cambodia was "secondary to the main problem," Vietnam. "When investigators from Congressional committees or Congress' General Accounting Office appeared, Enders did what he could to block their inquiries. He was openly hostile to and contemptuous of the press (the feeling was reciprocated), and he made a considerable effort to have the Cambodians expel one of the most dogged of the American journalists in Phnom Penh, Sylvana Foa of UPI and *Newsweek*."[69]

Enders "soon became Haig's favorite diplomat in the embassy, and Kissinger was equally impressed." In 1973, Enders chaired a secret embassy panel overseeing the illegal U.S. bombing strikes in Cambodia. Supposedly targeting North Vietnamese lines of communication into South Vietnam, "maps from one secret history of the B-52 campaign" in 1973 "show that many of the bombs were falling on the most heavily populated areas of Cambodia."[70] When Haig picked Enders to be his top aide for Latin America, he, like Haig, had no Latin America experience. Enders' director of Central American and Panamanian affairs, L. Craig Johnstone, was CIA Director William Colby's director of evaluations in Vietnam.[71]

"I never knew very much about Cambodia," said John Negroponte. "I don't think anyone did. I am a Vietnam expert, and I always thought of Cambodia as just an adjunct to the whole damn thing. I knew what I had to know, but I didn't get involved in the gory details."[72] Six years after wreaking havoc in Southeast Asia, the "can-do guys" had a new war to run in Central America.

"There was," said one RIG member, "a kind of tendency to want to prove your manhood."[73]

Enders' Dead End

August 1981 was a busy month. While Vernon Walters and the CIA organized the FDN, Enders took a trip to Managua. The Nicaraguans had wanted a meeting with Haig to improve U.S.-Nicaragua relations. Instead, Ambassador Pezzullo, who was resigning his post, convinced Enders to hold talks, "to retain the relationship."[74]

Enders met with junta Coordinator Daniel Ortega, Foreign Minister D'Escoto and other officials on August 11 and 12. In Pezzullo's view, Enders "made a good-faith effort" to negotiate, but "the circumstances required a quick victory. There was no way that it could happen." Rather than a good faith effort, the negotiations seemed designed to fail because Enders presented non-negotiable demands, more like an ultimatum for surrender. "I was flabbergasted by the demands," said Arturo Cruz, then Nicaragua's ambassador to Washington. "I told them this sounds like the conditions of a victorious power."

"We all have to sound like Attila the diplomat," said one U.S. official.[75] At 6 feet, 8 inches, Enders looked the part of Attila the diplomat. Michael Barnes, former chairman of the House Subcommittee on Western Hemisphere Affairs, summed up the Nicaraguans' impression: "They said this arrogant guy came down here, 11 feet tall and said, 'You're going to do A, B and C or we're going to blow you off the face of the Earth.' "[76]

As D'Escoto recalled it, the essence of Enders' "message was this: we are going along a path that can only lead to greater and greater confrontation and the time has come to stop and to see if we cannot take this other road."[77] The major issue was Nicaragua's alleged export of revolution. For the Nicaraguans, it appeared to be a no-win issue. They had closed down a clandestine FMLN radio station and curtailed the transshipment of weapons across Nicaraguan territory. The U.S. government acknowledged this, but terminated aid anyway.

There had been no verified reports of arms shipments from Nicaragua to El Salvador since April, according to David MacMichael, a CIA intelligence analyst from 1981 to 1983.[78] Yet, in a July 16 speech on El Salvador, Enders asserted, "After their arms trafficking was exposed, Cuba and Nicaragua reduced the flow in March and early April. Recently, however, an ominous upswing has occurred, not to the volume reached this winter, but to levels that enable the guerrillas to sustain military operations despite their inability to generate fresh support." Washington would never admit that the FMLN-FDR had broad *internal* support. Enders insisted that a halt to the alleged arms flow was a precondition to any negotiated agreement, including a renewal of aid, refusing to acknowledge that such a precondition had already been met.

"I cannot assure you," D'Escoto told Enders, "no one can assure you, that there is not one weapon or a very insignificant amount of weapons any more than you can assure me that they are not coming from the States. A little amount can filter from any country without the authorities knowing. But I can assure you that no important amount of arms trafficking is taking place from here."

Enders remained insistent and D'Escoto tried to break the impasse by asking him to explain how the alleged arms flow was taking place. "The greatest bulk," said Enders, "is going through your common land border with Honduras."

"What is this greatest bulk?" D'Escoto asked. "What 90 percent?...'Yeah, about 90 percent is going through your common land border with Honduras.' And then, I said, 'and the rest?' And he says...'through new routes that have been opened...on the Atlantic.' So that apparently they would go by boat to another beach, to some beach in Honduras and then cross the whole Honduran territory [El Salvador is on the Pacific side]." Some arms, said Enders, would pass "through this new route and then others through the Gulf of Fonseca." D'Escoto said, "Well, I can assure you...that none of this is happening in any significant amount because we would know about it.

"And then he [Enders] says, 'Well, what right do you have to claim, why do you claim to have the right to govern a country when you don't even know what is happening in your own territory?' And I said to him..you have just told me that all of this, in fact, is going through Honduran territory...I would like to know if you believe that the Hondurans are accomplices with us, or, if they don't know that this is happening?...Obviously, I said, you don't believe that they are accomplices, so they must not know. So have you ever told them by what right did they have to govern if they don't know what is happening in their own territory? And he said that he hadn't...

"And I said...why don't you give us tips as to how this is happening so that we can investigate. And he...quoted some saying that a government that doesn't guard its sources will burn them...He said that, besides, we did not have the degree of intimacy in the relations between both our countries for him to be able to tell me such delicate information. I responded...that he wouldn't burn any sources. I wasn't asking for any sources. I was asking for information. And besides that...he already said that it was U-2 photographs and satellite photographs and that we had no bows and arrows that we can hide. I said, so what are you burning?...

"I lamented that we don't have the type of relationship that permits you to give us information, but certainly you have that relationship with Honduras. I said I'm not in the habit of suggesting to other governments what to do, but since you're always suggesting to us, I think I can afford to tell you something. I said, you can kill two birds with one stone by preventing these arms from getting to El Salvador and, at the same time, having the proof that you have to present to the world to demonstrate your charges...Why don't you help the Hondurans...and give them the information that you have so that they can catch us there?...

" 'Father,' he says, 'you have been in politics long enough to, by this time, to come to realize that not everything that sounds in theory possible is actually feasible.' And then I said that there was another way, that we had already had a meeting between the head of state of Honduras and Comandante Ortega...that in that meeting we had in principle agreed to a joint patrol operation along our common border, and that the Hondurans were dragging their feet in arranging for the meetings that they were committed to have in order to concretize this. And could they [the U.S. government] not exert some influence on Honduras to carry out what they have already committed to. And there was no response to that.

"About a week after that, or two weeks after that, in a press conference in Washington...somebody asked [Enders] about this [border patrol proposal] because I had made it public, and he said that this was not a practical thing. Of course, it was important for the United States not to have this border operation because they were planning this whole use of Honduras as a base for aggression against Nicaragua."

After the argument seesawed back and forth a while, Enders stood up. "He's very tall," said D'Escoto. He stood up shaking his finger, "and he says, 'Father, you must remember, the United States is exactly 100 times larger than you are.' In other words shape up...And, of course, I said not 100 times. That's not true. I said thousands and thousands of times more powerful economically and militarily, which is what matters. But, yes, 100 times larger territorially, which is the least important. But, nonetheless, we were not about to cry uncle as President Reagan would later demand."[79]

An exchange of correspondence followed the August meetings. In September, Washington offered to enforce the neutrality laws as regards Nicaraguan exiles and sign a joint nonaggression declaration, whereby the United States would not intervene against Nicaragua if Nicaragua did not intervene against its neighbors. From the Nicaraguan point of view, enforcement of neutrality laws was something the U.S. government was already responsible for. And nonintervention was a requirement of all signatories to the Rio treaty and the United Nations charter. The United States did not have the right to act as prosecutor, judge and jury on the matter of nonintervention.

As reported by Roy Gutman, the United States never formally presented Nicaragua with its security demands: "The substance of the U.S. position was shown to Cruz, but a few hours later he was told to forget he had seen it." A summary provided to Gutman "makes it easy to understand why. Nicaragua was to freeze acquisition of heavy weapons—armed or unarmed helicopters and planes, armored personnel carriers, horwitzers, and armed vehicles. Replacements would be allowed. But Nicaragua would have to get rid of systems not possessed by other countries. 'They were to be re-exported,' a State Department official said. The weapons were not to be resold to third countries, or dumped at sea, but recrated and shipped back to countries of origin." Craig Johnstone, who drafted all the U.S. papers, viewed the document as a "very reasonable proposal."[80]

The security draft also demanded that Nicaragua limit its army to 15,000 to 17,000 soldiers, and eventually reduce it to less than 10,000. Presumably, neither the United States nor its Central American allies were required to make any reductions. Though Nicaragua would have to get rid of weapons systems its neighbors didn't have, it would be prohibited from acquiring systems its neighbors did have, such as advanced fighter aircraft.

According to Gutman, the negotiations fell apart when Cruz reacted negatively to the security draft which Johnstone quickly told him to forget. That was in late September or early October. On October 7, the United States began joint naval maneuvers with Honduras—*Halcon Vista* 81—and Ortega denounced them as a rehearsal for attacking Nicaragua in a speech to the United Nations. U.S. officials took Ortega's speech as a violation of a tacit agreement to lower the level of rhetoric. Nicaragua, on the other hand, was supposed to accept as routine the maneuvers with Honduras, as well as the earlier Ocean Venture exercises in the Caribbean. Meanwhile, on August 28, Haig had accused the Salvadoran rebels of engaging in "straight terrorism" fed by external assistance and said that the United States was considering ways of confronting Cuba. It was "premature," he said, to reveal them.[81] Nicaragua knew that Washington considered it an accomplice of Cuba.

Nicaraguan Deputy Foreign Minister Victor Hugo Tinoco sent a letter on October 31 that reviewed Nicaragua's complaints about the maneuvers and lack of economic aid, and said "progress depended on concrete U.S. actions to close the exile training camps." He said Nicaragua was open to further talks, but Enders saw the letter as ending the discussions.[82]

"You can't negotiate when you always take the most extreme position," observed Pezzullo. "You leave the other guy no opportunity." He told Gutman his experience "leads me to the conclusion that this administration can't negotiate."[83] The Reagan administration would take seven months just to fill the ambassador's slot after Pezzullo left on August 18.

In the Core Group's view, Nicaragua gets all the blame. "Few people thought that the Sandinistas would talk to us seriously. But we had to try," said one official. The reason was domestic politics. When asked to take new action against Nicaragua, Congress would want to know whether diplomatic means had been tried. Now the administration had their answer: "They haven't worked."[84]

"When you throw yourself into a revolution, there are no quick answers," said Pezzullo before leaving Nicaragua. "The questions are easy—Where is it going? Who are the new leaders? and so—but answers are impossible." One problem, said Pezzullo, "is that if you get too specific in your answers, you lose the capacity to understand the movement...because the moment you pigeonhole someone, you start building your argument to fit your conclusions. My basic feeling about a revolutionary movement is that you better move with it and live with it. And if you're going to exert influence, exert it in the process of living with it."[85]

Taking the War to Nicaragua

The Reagan administration had no intention of living with the Nicaraguan revolution. In the summer of 1981, General Haig ordered Marine Colonel Robert "Bud" McFarlane, a former officer in Vietnam then serving Haig as State Department counselor, to prepare a report. Titled "Taking the War to Nicaragua," it covered options for military action against Cuba and Nicaragua. A U.S. invasion of Nicaragua was reportedly imminent enough in 1981 that, as one military officer recalled, he received $400,000 in Defense Department funds, which the CIA converted into local currency, to cover costs in Nicaragua.[86]

On November 1, CIA Director Casey met in Washington with Argentina's army chief of staff, General Leopoldo Galtieri, to polish their mutual projects. Days later, the annual Conference of American Armies brought together U.S., Latin and Caribbean military and intelligence officers at Washington's Fort McNair to discuss "countering terrorism, subversion and armed insurrection." In his keynote address, Secretary of Defense Weinberger stressed the need for solidarity against the threat of Cuban and Nicaraguan influence and insurgency in Central America and the Caribbean.[87]

Days later, it was reported that Haig "has been pressing the Pentagon to examine a series of options for possible military action in El Salvador and against Cuba and Nicaragua." The Pentagon was asked to show what U.S. forces could do if there was a decision to blockade Nicaragua or launch specific operations against Cuba including a show of airpower, large naval exercises, a quarantine on arms shipments to the island, a general blockade as an act of war, or an invasion by U.S. and possibly Latin American forces. Latin American governments were asked if they might join in any kind of military operations. Meanwhile, CIA specialists said there was no strong evidence to support the view "that Cuba is still directly involved in the supply of men and arms" for El Salvador. The Defense Intelligence Agency said there was.[88]

Lt. General Wallace Nutting, head of the U.S. Southern Command (Southcom) embracing Central and South America, put some of his views on the record on November 14. "Someone," he said, "is going to have to rethink" regulations preventing U.S. advisers from going into the field if the "fragile" situation in El Salvador worsened. Washington must make it clear to the guerrillas that " 'you're not going to get El Salvador' and make them believe it." White House Counselor Ed Meese talked of a possible future naval blockade of Nicaragua.[89]

Haig, said one RIG member, "had this real hard-on for Castro." He wanted to knock him off.[90] So did Reagan. Reagan "understood that the Soviet Union—the empire of evil, in his eyes—lay beyond his reach. But as the men in his innermost circle knew, he had to be dissuaded from the private fantasy that Cuba might by liberated by force of arms; the appraisal of the CIA was that the Fidelistas would simply take to the hills again and turn the island into a front-porch Vietnam."[91]

The consensus aim of administration policy would be to "draw the line" in El Salvador, and re-draw it in Nicaragua. In testimony before the House Foreign Affairs Committee on November 12, Haig described the situation in Nicaragua as "very, very disturbing...I think we cannot delude ourselves as Americans about that and then wonder—perhaps six months or a year from now—what happened when we have another Cuba in this hemisphere and perhaps the expansion of this disease throughout Central America."

Rep. Gerry Studds (D-MA) asked Haig, "Can you provide this committee and this Congress with an assurance that the United States is not and will not participate in or encourage in any way direct or indirect efforts to overthrow or destabilize the current government in Nicaragua?"

"No," Haig replied, "I would not give you such an assurance." He said Studds "should be concerned instead about mounting evidence of the totalitarian character of the Sandinista regime."

"Are you prepared to say that we are not planning a military blockade?" asked Rep. Barnes.

"I'm not prepared to give reassurances of any kind," said Haig. "If you are trying to reassure regimes that are moving toward totalitarian government, I question if that is a sound course." Haig would only repeat President Reagan's statement that the United States had "no plans for putting Americans in combat anyplace in the world."

"Based on your responses," Barnes told Haig, "if I were a Nicaraguan, I'd be building a bomb shelter this afternoon."[92]

5

Semi-Secret War

It was hubris. We were going to knock off these little brown people on
the cheap.

Anonymous U.S. official.[1]

For us, invasion is not a theoretical possibility but a historical fact. People
forget that under U.S. Marine occupation 50 years ago, we were the first
country in the world to be dive-bombed.

Miguel D'Escoto.[2]

November 1981 was a time of heated administration rhetoric. Mexican President Jose Lopez Portillo accused Washington of conducting "verbal terrorism" and warned that a U.S. attack on Nicaragua would be "a gigantic historical error."[3]

It was also a time of secret escalation. The *Boston Globe* caught wind of the covert war on December 4.[4] Two months later, fueled by administration leaks, the *Washington Post* made the operation front-page news. By then contra forces had launched and lost an offensive on the Atlantic Coast, but the *Post* (and the *New York Times*) showcased supposed blueprints for new operations while largely missing the war that was already underway.

"President Reagan has authorized a broad program of U.S. planning and action in war-torn Central America, including the encouragement of political and paramilitary operations by other governments against the Cuban presence in Nicaragua, informed sources said yesterday."[5] That *Washington Post* lead and the story that followed parrotted the administration line that Nicaragua was a platform for Cuban subversion in Central America.

Three weeks later, the *Post* reported: "President Reagan has authorized covert operations against the Central American nation of Nicaragua, which, administration officials have charged, is serving as the military command center and supply line to guerrillas in El Salvador."

"According to informed administration officials," the article continued, "the president has ruled out the use of U.S. military forces in direct anti-Nicaraguan operations. But the authorized covert plan directs the CIA to begin to build and fund a paramilitary force of up to 500 Latin Americans, who are to operate out of commando camps spread along the Nicaraguan-Honduran border...The officials stressed that it will take months for the paramilitary force to be recruited, trained and positioned to begin operations...As part of this plan, the commandos eventually would attempt to destroy vital Nicaraguan targets, such as power plants and bridges [two bridges were blown four days later], in an effort to disrupt the economy and divert the attention and the resources of the government. CIA strategists believe these covert operations inside Nicaragua will slow the flow of arms to El Salvador and disrupt what they claim is a Soviet- and Cuban-controlled government in Nicaragua...CIA forces would be supplemented by another Latin American commando force of up to 1,000 men—some of whom currently are undergoing training by Argentine military officials."

The *Post* went on to report administration alarm at "convincing intelligence reports that one Soviet-Cuban goal in the region is the development of an active insurgency to destabilize Mexico during this decade."[6]

The *New York Times* supplemented accounts of the covert operation in a March 14 piece containing more disinformation than the others about a supposed agreement with Argentina that "no support would be given to followers of General Somoza."[7] Washington, we were told, was supporting only political "moderates." By this time, the Guardia-dominated FDN, formed after months of U.S. support for the contras, was seven months old. None of these prominent accounts in the newspapers of record managed to note that Argentina was not a bastion of democracy, but a military dictatorship.

A week earlier, *The Nation* had put the lie to the "no Somocistas" line, reporting that members of the House and Senate Intelligence Committees were briefed "that the aim of the C.I.A.'s covert action is to incite unrest in Nicaragua using former Somoza guardsmen, dissident elements and ethnic minorities in Nicaragua and exile groups in the United States." Differing from mainstream accounts that treated Nicaragua and the covert war as an abstraction, *The Nation* described ongoing attacks. As Nicaraguan officials saw it, "the former guardsmen's attacks are intended to provoke retaliatory measures by the Nicaraguan Army, thus creating a pretext for foreign military intervention."[8]

Finding II

The secret course for the war on Nicaragua was affirmed at an NSC meeting on November 16, 1981. The CIA-run contras were to spearhead the Sandinista overthrow.

Then CIA analyst David MacMichael attended a meeting of the CIA's Latin American Affairs office in which the Nicaragua plan was discussed: "a covert force of approximately 1,500 men was to be organized to carry out military and paramilitary actions...In general the appreciation at that time was that the Nicaraguan Government leadership was immature, impulsive, possessed, in the phrase used, of a 'guerrilla' mentality and it was presumed that in response to the actions of this covert force that in all likelihood the Nicaraguan Government would engage in hot pursuit of this covert paramilitary force, across international boundaries within Central America, it was assumed that in response to the state of emergency generated by these attacks that the Nicaraguan Government would clamp down and eliminate civil liberties, to exile or confine its political opponents, and finally that diplomatic relations between the United States and Nicaragua would probably be exacerbated and that United States diplomatic personnel within Nicaragua could expect to be harassed or otherwise restricted or affected...

"It would serve to demonstrate what was believed, which was that the Nicaraguan Government was inherently aggressive and a danger to its neighbours in the region and that such crossing of territorial boundaries would demonstrate this and possibly allow for the use of sanctions or other actions under the Organization of American States' charter...

"It was assumed that the Nicaraguan Government...had rather successfully portrayed itself as an open and democratic society and thus gained a good deal of support in world public opinion and that by causing its true nature as a repressive and totalitarian government to be displayed it would lose this support."

Regarding the expected harassment of U.S. diplomats, MacMichael thought that "the purpose here was to be able to demonstrate the essential hostility of the Nicaraguan Government toward the United States and thus help to justify in United States public opinion actions which the United States might take against Nicaragua."[9]

CIA Director William Casey, Reagan's good friend and 1980 campaign manager, and the first CIA director to hold presidential Cabinet rank, was enthusiastic about the Nicaragua project. "Casey wanted a rollback of communism," a U.S. official observed. "But you know, he could never even pronounce the word 'Nicaragua'—he always said something like 'Nicarga' or 'Nigara.' The place itself didn't seem to matter to him."[10]

Casey earned his reputation as a spymaster during World War II service as chief of intelligence for the OSS European Theater. He kept up his ties to the "intelligence community," serving, for example, on the advisory board of the National Intelligence Study Center and on President Ford's Foreign Intelligence Advisory Board.[11] Like most members of the Reagan Cabinet, Casey was a millionaire. He made his fortune in venture capital and tax law, and authored such books as *Tax Sheltered Investments*. In 1961, Casey was sued for plagiarizing material in one of his books; a jury found against Casey and awarded the other party damages. When President Nixon appointed him in 1971 to head the Securities and Exchange Commission (SEC), Casey tried to mislead Senators about the plagiarism case during confirmation hearings.[12] In his first two years as CIA director, Casey—the ultimate insider—made millions playing the stock and bond markets before public outrage prompted him to put his investments in a blind trust. Reagan's trust in Casey never wavered.

U.S. News & World Report profiled Casey in 1984 as the "Intelligence Chief With Nine Lives": "Nearly every committee that has checked his qualifications for public office—first as chief of the SEC, then as under secretary of state, head of the Export-Import bank and director of the CIA—has complained of misstatements, lapses of memory and reluctant disclosures of assets and clients."[13] These talents would be standard operating procedure in the Nicaragua project.

Reagan signed National Security Decision Directive (NSDD) 17 on November 23, 1981 authorizing the CIA to "work with foreign governments as appropriate" to conduct political and "paramilitary" operations "against [the] Cuban presence and Cuban-Sandinista support infrastructure in Nicaragua and elsewhere in Central America."[14] Specifically, the CIA was allocated $19.95 million to build a 500-man force. It was understood that "more funds and manpower will be needed." The CIA force would complement a 1,000-man force being trained by Argentina. Washington reportedly paid Argentina $50 million to provide the training.[15]

A document accompanying NSDD 17 pretended that covert activities would "build popular support in Central America and Nicaragua for an opposition front that would be nationalistic, anti-Cuban and anti-Somoza." It acknowledged that "in some instances CIA might (possibly using U.S. personnel) take unilateral paramilitary action against special Cuban targets [*sic*]."

Reagan signed the congressionally-mandated presidential intelligence finding on December 1. Presenting the finding to the Intelligence Committees, administration officials emphasized arms interdiction. Casey said the United States was "buying in" to an existing Argentine operation to train Nicaraguan exiles. By one account, "the impression left with some members of the Intelligence committees was of crack teams of commandos hitting arms caches, ammunition dumps, Cuban military patrols and a couple of key bridges along the arms supply route in the dead of night and withdrawing unseen from Nicaragua to their Honduran bases."[16]

The arms flow from Miami to the contras, meanwhile, went unimpeded. "Two Nicaraguan exiles said one CIA official in Miami gave them general advice in late 1981 on how to smuggle weapons out of Miami, where the contras buy virtually all their weapons…[The official] counseled them to ship the guns in parts to avoid detection by U.S. Customs officials."[17]

The arms interdiction rationale gave the congressional committees an excuse to exercise oversight as overlook. It was irrational to think that Somoza guardsmen were risking their lives, not to avenge their defeat and attempt to retake power, but simply to serve as arms traffic cops for the United States and El Salvador. As one contra source said, "If that's what the CIA told Congress, they forgot to tell us."[18]

When the CIA told the House Intelligence Committee in February 1982 that it was not trying to overthrow any government, one committee member asserted, "We didn't believe them."[19] Congressional oversight was marked by the willing suspension of disbelief. Unfortunately, most Americans weren't in on the act.

The overseers overlooked it when the first major contra action took place in November 1981 on the eastern side of Nicaragua—far from El Salvador.

Miskito Front

The Atlantic Coast of Nicaragua presented Washington with familiar targets of opportunity: ethnic minorities. Two decades earlier, Washington exploited Hmong tribespeople (called "Meo," a historical derogatory term, by foreigners) in its effort to control Laos, another "sideshow" to the war in Vietnam. Prohibited from using U.S. military personnel by a 1962 agreement recognizing Laotian neutrality, Washington intervened covertly via the CIA.[20]

The United States built a clandestine Hmong army led by Vang Pao, an opium dealer and former French mercenary. The secret war's secret air arm was the CIA proprietary, Air America.[21] By the time the 1973 Paris Peace accords brought a U.S. withdrawal from Indochina, a third of the Hmong population had died. Thousands ended up in Thai refugee camps. Thousands more have resettled in the United States, including Vang Pao.

Many alumni from the Laos campaign reunited in the war on Nicaragua. Operating out of Udorn Air Force Base in Thailand, Richard Secord directed the Air Wing of the joint Pentagon-CIA Special Operations Group. Before taking charge of the air operation himself, Secord served as deputy to Harry "Heinie" Aderholt, who now heads the Air Commando Association, a private group aiding the contras. Ted Shackley was the CIA station chief in Vientiane, Laos and then Saigon. Shackley's deputy Tom Clines was the CIA chief at Vang Pao's Long Tieng base which served as the CIA headquarters for northern Laos as well as an opium and heroin trafficking center.[22] Donald Gregg, national security adviser to Vice President George Bush and before that head of the NSC Intelligence Directorate, served under Shackley in Vietnam. Felix Rodriguez, a manager of the contra supply operation in El Salvador, worked for Shackley and Gregg in Vietnam. Eugene Hasenfus was a cargo kicker for Air America years before his fateful hitch with Southern Air Transport. John Singlaub oversaw secret missions in Laos as commander of the joint Special Operations Group. Then Lieutenant Oliver North reportedly served under Singlaub's command, running paramilitary operations with the Hmong.[23]

Air America transported the CIA and Hmong officers who "offered the [Hmong] villagers guns, rice and money in exchange for recruits" and kept the secret army and loyal villagers supplied. "The millions of AID dollars that Congress thought it was appropriating for civilian help were mostly being used for support of the secret army, although tens of thousands of refugees were also fed. Deceiving the U.S. Congress was considered a legitimate tactic of the secret war; of course, the enemy knew exactly what was going on, but the CIA was determined that the American public should not share this knowledge. Air America spoke openly of its humanitarian drops of rice, blankets, and medicine, but did not mention what the men called 'hard' rice drops—ammunition, grenades, bombs, and weapons to the secret army."[24] In the contra war, AID's "soft rice"—food, clothing, boots, etc.—is also known as "humanitarian" aid.

Nicaragua's Atlantic Coast does not share the history or culture of the rest of the country. The once British-dominated Atlantic Coast, home to about 10 percent of the Nicaraguan population, maintains strong Indian and Afro-Caribbean traditions, conservatism fostered by the influential Protestant Moravian Church and deep-rooted hostility to the "Spaniard" majority. The largely rural Miskito Indians (about 67,000 people) dominate Northern Zelaya (renamed Atlantico Norte in 1987)—part of the Mosquitia extending into Honduras. The English-speaking Creole Blacks (about 26,000 people) reside mainly in and around the port towns of Southern Zelaya (renamed Atlantico Sur). There are smaller Sumu, Garifuna and Rama Indian communities. The majority of people on the Atlantic Coast are Mestizos of mixed Indian and Hispanic origin (over 182,000 people).

In 1980, a new indigenous mass organization, MISURASATA (Unity of the Miskito, Sumu, Rama and Sandinistas), took a seat in the Council of State. With the political opening provided by the revolution, MISURASATA launched an increasingly ambitious campaign for Atlantic Coast autonomy. Brooklyn Rivera, an anti-Sandinista Miskito leader, later observed, "The fervor of the revolutionary triumph injected into the soul, heart and atmosphere that everybody could express themselves and participate. Before there was no incentive."[25] There had been almost no revolutionary action on the Atlantic Coast and few residents belonged to the FSLN. While the Nicaraguan government was responsive to demands for bilingual education and open to the granting of communal land titles following Indian tradition, it was alarmed by MISURASATA's claim to 38 percent of the national territory based on a study of native land titles.

In late February 1981, 33 MISURASATA leaders were detained and accused of fomenting a separatist uprising. All except Steadman Fagoth were released within two weeks. Nicaraguan officials said that Fagoth was conducting subversive activities to destabilize the government under a counterrevolutionary plot known as Plan 81 and made public evidence that Fagoth had infiltrated the student movement as an informer for Somoza.

Tensions exploded when four Miskitos and four Sandinista soldiers were killed as soldiers attempted to arrest MISURASATA leaders in the community of Prinzapolka. As news of the arrests spread and rumors transformed the four Miskito deaths into mass assassinations, Miskitos began crossing the Rio Coco into Honduras. "Blood had been spilled," wrote one analyst, "and the Miskitu movement assumed a millenarian mystique; rumors abounded that the young Miskitu men were arming to return, and that the United States was going to recognize 'secret' nineteenth-century treaties between the Miskitu king and the British Crown guaranteeing nationhood for the Moskitia."[26]

In an effort to promote dialogue and conciliation, the Nicaraguan government granted the popular Steadman Fagoth a conditional release in May to accept a scholarship for study abroad. Instead Fagoth went into exile, linking up with the September 15th Legion in Honduras. Some 1,000 Miskitos joined him. Fagoth dropped the Sandinista part of MISURASATA, forming the MISURA guerrilla force. He allied MISURA with the FDN and broadcast over the September 15th radio, calling on Miskitos to participate in a holy war against the "Sandino-communists."

The "Red Christmas" offensive began in November 1981 with contra attacks in the Rio Coco area. According to the Nicaraguan government, the plan was to capture territory on the Atlantic Coast and establish a provisional government that would be supported militarily by the United States. On December 20, seven government soldiers in San Carlos were tortured, killed and mutilated. Some 60 or more people, including civilians, died during the two-month offensive.[27]

Mirna Cunningham, Nicaragua's only Miskito doctor, and Regina Lewis, a Miskito nurse, were kidnapped on December 28 outside the hospital in Bilwaskarma by about twenty contras; the hospital was ransacked and had to be closed. Mirna Cunningham recounted multiple gang rapes beginning after they were taken to a house on the Rio Coco: "they had us there for seven hours. During those hours we were raped for the first time. While they were raping us, they were chanting slogans like, 'Christ yesterday, Christ today, Christ tomorrow.'"

Cunningham and Lewis were taken across the river to a training camp in Honduras where their captors, Miskitos and former members of Somoza's elite EEBI unit, boasted of their support from the United States. They "said that they had Americans who came in and trained them for these camps that were deeper in Honduras. They said that they received help from the Honduran army. That they would come and help them transport their things. They were very proud of the help that they were receiving from the U.S. Government. They offered us Camel cigarettes, for example, as a proof that they were smoking good cigarettes. And they said they were getting canned food, good clothes and things like that, as a way to tell us why they were fighting."

After two or three hours in the camp, recalled Cunningham, "They told us that they were going to kill us, but they wanted to kill us in Nicaragua to leave our bodies as an example to the other people who work with the Nicaraguan government...On our way back we were raped again, by all the ones who were taking us to the village."

Inside Nicaragua, Cunningham and Lewis were released, but the contras told them to leave the Atlantic Coast because they did not want doctors there.[28] In 1984, Mirna Cunningham became government minister for Northern Zelaya.

In January 1982, the Nicaraguan government responded to the military threat in a controversial move designed both to protect the civilian population and deny FDN-MISURA fighters a civilian base of support. It relocated 8,500 Miskitos and Sumus from the Rio Coco region 50 miles south to a resettlement camp called Tasba Pri (Free Land). The ill-chosen name was a sign that the government had a long way to go in distinguishing between just Indian grievances and pro-contra secessionism. Sandinista soldiers burned structures and crops in the evacuated area to deny them to the contras. Another 10,000 people crossed the river into Honduras.

The U.S. government seized on the relocation to accuse Nicaragua of genocide. Haig dramatically produced a photo he said showed Miskito bodies being burned by Sandinista troops. The French magazine *Le Figaro*, source of the photo, corrected him, explaining it showed the Red Cross burning corpses of people killed by Somoza's National Guard on the Pacific Coast in 1978.

Appearing on Public Television's MacNeil-Lehrer show with Miguel D'Escoto, Jeane Kirkpatrick asserted that "some 250,000 Mestizo Indians [*sic*—are being so badly repressed that concentration camps have been built on the coast of Nicaragua in the effort to try to imprison them, to eliminate their opposition."

"I don't know what country she is talking about," responded D'Escoto, denying her allegations.[29]

The human rights organization Americas Watch found Steadman Fagoth's charges of nearly 300 Miskito deaths and thousands of disappearances during the relocation to be baseless.[30] The Inter-American Commission on Human Rights (IACHR) found only one incident of noncombatant killing by Sandinista forces. On December 23, between fourteen and seventeen Miskito prisoners were shot in Leimus in retaliation for the San Carlos killings. Americas Watch substantiated one subsequent case: in Walpa Siksa in 1982, seven Miskito youths were killed by Sandinista soldiers "who were later severely punished by their officers."[31] Over the next two years the government significantly altered the training and composition of the Atlantic Coast security forces; by 1984, 70 percent were from the Coast.[32]

The relocation of citizens during wartime has an infamous precedent in the United States. In February 1942, President Franklin Roosevelt signed an executive order giving the army the power to arrest all Japanese-American men, women and children on the West Coast. Without warrants or court hearings, 120,000 people were forcibly taken from their homes to detention camps where they were imprisoned for three to four years. Many permanently lost their homes and property. Over four decades later during debate leading to passage of a bill to apologize and partially compensate detention camp survivors, Senator Spark Matsunaga of Hawaii emotionally recalled how an elderly Japanese man playing with his grandson was machinegunned to death by a guard when he went to retrieve a ball between the camp fences.[33] Racism was apparent in that Japanese-Americans were suspected *en masse* as spies and saboteurs, while German-Americans were not rounded up. In fact, there was not a single case of Japanese-American espionage or sabotage.

While Pearl Harbor was an exceptional attack on U.S. territory (Hawaii, located about 2,400 miles southwest of San Francisco, did not become a state until 1959), Red Christmas was just the first of many assaults aimed at taking territory on Nicaragua's mainland and overthrowing the Nicaraguan government. Though it criticized the conduct of the Atlantic Coast relocation, Americas Watch found that it was not unreasonable for the Nicaraguan government to relocate civilians away from a border area to facilitate the defense of the country's territorial integrity. The IACHR concurred. Over the next two years, conditions improved and the Tasba Pri settlements were transformed into villages with substantial housing, education, health care and employment opportunities. Three churches were built in the main village of Sumubila: Moravian, Catholic and another Protestant denomination. Some Miskitos left Tasba Pri for Managua, Puerto Cabezas or other villages on the Atlantic Coast. Remaining residents were granted title to their houses and small plots of land, and other land was farmed collectively.[34]

Whatever the actual conditions of the relocation, it was a traumatic event that exacerbated Atlantic Coast hostilities. On December 1, 1983, the government signaled a concerted effort to recognize past wrongdoing and improve relations by declaring a general amnesty for Miskito prisoners and fighters. Washington has consistently attempted to sabotage the process of negotiating peace and autonomy for the Atlantic Coast.

Rigging Human Rights

Americas Watch charged the Reagan administration with degrading the human rights cause by using "human rights criticism of Nicaragua as an instrument of warfare." This is especially apparent in regard to the Miskitos. In a May 9, 1984 speech, Reagan repeated charges that had been thoroughly discredited: "There has been an attempt to wipe out an entire culture, the Miskito Indians, thousands of whom have been slaughtered or herded into detention camps where they have been starved and abused."

America's Watch reported: "Unlike several other Latin American governments that have come under harsh criticism (though not from this administration), the [Nicaraguan government] has responded to human rights organizations with efforts to improve the situation. Equally as significant as the administration's strident complaints against Nicaragua is its silence regarding these improvements. In early 1984, for example, the [Nicaraguan government] conducted several investigations of abuses in remote areas, which resulted in the prosecution and appropriate punishment of members of the security forces. In the most important of these cases, forty-four security agents and civilians were prosecuted for several cases of murder, rape, theft, and other abuses that had taken place in a border region of Matagalpa and Jinotega. Thirteen of them received heavy sentences...In April 1984, an Army sub-lieutenant was sentenced to eighteen years in prison for raping a Miskito woman in the village of Lapan. In regard to the Miskito minority, there has been a clear effort to improve relations and resolve past conflicts."[35]

Reagan's use of human rights as an instrument of warfare has meant portraying Nicaragua as the worst violator of human rights in Central America, when, even at its low point on the Atlantic Coast in 1982, the Nicaraguan human rights situation has been far better than in El Salvador (discussed earlier) and Guatemala. Guatemalan state terrorism under General Romeo Lucas Garcia was discussed in the previous chapter. During the dictatorial reign of General Efrain Rios Montt, from March 1982 to August 1983, thousands more Indians were massacred (Indians make up a majority of the Guatemalan population). Even the conservative Guatemalan newspaper, *El Grafico*, denounced the "genocidal annihilation that is taking place in the Indian zones of the country."

Rios Montt spoke openly of his murderous policies, announcing on Guatemalan television that he had "declared a state of siege so that we could kill legally." On December 5, 1982, following a meeting with Reagan, Rios Montt told reporters, "We have no scorched-earth policy. We have a policy of scorched Communists."

Reagan officials stooped to new lows of disinformation in their appeals for military and economic aid for Guatemala. Contrary to all evidence, Ambassador

Frederick Chapin told members of Congress that "most of the killings in the rural areas have been done by insurgents." When asked about reports of massacres of peasants, he insisted "those incidents simply haven't taken place." He compared the civil patrol system—where Indian men and boys are forcibly conscripted into unpaid service in the army's pacification campaign—to "the American frontier, with armed citizens defending themselves."

After meeting Rios Montt on December 4, 1982, Reagan called him "a man of great personal integrity and commitment" who "wants to improve the quality of life for all Guatemalans and to promote social justice" and is "totally dedicated to democracy." As for human rights criticism, Reagan said Rios Montt was getting a "bum rap."

When Rios Montt was deposed by General Humberto Mejia Victores in August 1983, the Reagan administration belatedly acknowledged some past abuses—but only to make the case that under Mejia human rights conditions were improving.[36] Orwell would be impressed with the Reagan administration's ongoing rewrites of history.

Tightening the Screws

In a speech to the OAS on December 4, 1981, Haig accused Nicaragua of militarization and interventionism, and said the United States would take action to prevent any nation in Central America from becoming a "platform for terror and war." But, he claimed, "We do not close the doors to the search for proper relations." In Managua, Daniel Ortega responded that the door Haig left open was "so small that in order to pass through it we would have to do so on our knees."[37]

Hector Fabian, a Cuban exile leader training contras in the Florida Everglades, predicted later in December that "within three months the situation in Nicaragua will blow up." He said that at least 100 trainees had infiltrated into Nicaragua. "Under the Carter and Nixon Administrations, what we were doing was a crime," explained Fabian, the former New York director of operations for Cuban exile terrorist leader Orlando Bosch. "With the Reagan Administration, no one has bothered us for 10 months."

"As long as they don't hurt anybody and as long as they don't actually conspire to invade in a specific way," the exiles are not breaking the law, said Assistant Secretary of State Enders. "If you attack a country or assist in an attack on a country, or conspire to do this, all these things are illegal. However, it is not illegal to have military exercises, guys running around the fields with guns, or to say 'Uncle Sam, we're ready when you're ready—wink, wink—and here we go.' "[38]

Nicaragua protested U.S. aggression to Washington and international forums. It also sought defensive armaments from abroad. On January 8, 1982, France announced that it would sell $15.8 million in nonoffensive military equipment to Nicaragua and train ten Nicaraguan naval officers and pilots. The small arms package included two coastal patrol boats, two helicopters, rocket launchers and rocket rounds, and a fleet of transport trucks.

The nominally socialist Mitterand government was vehemently anti-Soviet. French officials said they wanted to offer Nicaragua an alternative to Cuban and Soviet military aid. "When a country such as Nicaragua applies to France for aid," explained a French foreign ministry official, "it is often because it is seeking to escape dependency on one of the superpowers." U.S. policy was "the worst possible—designed to push the junta right into the arms of Moscow."[39]

The U.S. response was harsh. "The French are pulling the rug out from under us," said one Pentagon official.[40] Haig told French Foreign Minister Claude Cheysson that the deal was "a stab in the back."[41]

Relentless U.S. pressure brought results. The first deliveries of French military equipment were stalled until July.[42] There would be no new arms sales. Wrote one analyst: "France, with the world's third largest arms export industry, a popular new left-wing government and a history of relative independence from Washington, proved unable to fulfill Nicaragua's hopes of Western arms supplies. For the Sandinistas, the lesson was clear. Henceforth, Nicaraguan diplomacy, trade and aid initiatives would have to factor in the Soviet bloc's exclusive role as supplier of Nicaragua's defense needs—which escalated rapidly as Washington's preference for a military solution became ever more apparent."[43] The only other defense agreement with a Western European country was a $5.5 million 1983 contract with Holland to improve port defenses at Corinto.[44]

In January 1982, Nicaraguan security captured UDN member William Baltodano and thwarted a conspiracy to blow up the national oil refinery and cement factory and attack Sandinista leaders. In his confession, Baltodano implicated the CIA, the Argentine military, Honduran special security forces, the Venezuelan Embassy in Nicaragua, the Salvadoran Embassy in Costa Rica and Jose Esteban Gonzales, who was head of the Nicaraguan Permanent Commission on Human Rights until he went into exile the previous September. Arms were purchased in Miami.[45]

The United States finally applied the Neutrality Act on January 18, but not against the contras. A small group of Haitian refugees, conspiring against the Duvalier dictatorship, were charged with violating the act in a Miami Court. The next day, the *New York Times* editorialized: "What is illegal for Haitian refugees is no less illegal for Nicaraguan exiles…The letter and spirit of the Neutrality Act are offended by adventurers who boast that hundreds of recruits have already been airdropped into Nicaragua to fight against the left-wing Sandinista government. By comparison, the prosecuted Haitians are hapless romantics. Their leaking boat was seized just before it sank; their revolutionary arsenal consisted of 6 guns and 20 pipe bombs."

That same month a State Department spokeswoman confirmed that the Reagan administration would oppose any Nicaraguan credit or aid request before any international lending institution.[46] Already the United States had blocked a World Bank loan to replace fishing boats taken from Nicaragua by fleeing Somocistas. On January 14, the World Bank approved a $16 million loan to Nicaragua for municipal reconstruction—assisting improvements in storm drainage, street paving and lighting in low-income neighborhoods—over U.S. objection. Over the next year, World Bank loans were shut off completely.[47]

While administration ideology dictated an economic blockade of Nicaragua, ideology dictated economic largesse for El Salvador. Criteria changed accordingly. Testifying before the House Subcommittee on Inter-American Affairs on February 2, Enders defended the administration's decision to certify El Salvador as eligible for aid despite "a troubled" human rights situation. Nicaragua again became the excuse for state terror in El Salvador—and the decoy for denying that the Salvadoran guerrillas had widespread popular support.

"There is no mistaking that the decisive battle for Central America is underway in El Salvador," claimed Enders. "If after Nicaragua, El Salvador is captured by a violent minority, who in Central America would not live in fear? How long would it be before major strategic United States interests—the Panama Canal, sea lanes, oil supplies—were at risk?"[48]

Two days later, Enders told the Senate Foreign Relations Committee that "the clandestine infiltration of arms and munitions into El Salvador is again approaching the high levels recorded before last year's final offensive." The made-in-Washington charge was contradicted by the absence of evidence on the ground. The Honduran Army had no evidence of arms shipments through Honduras.[49] Faced with doubts about the overland route, the administration said arms were coming by sea or air. As Raymond Bonner observed, "even the intelligence agencies couldn't agree. While the CIA would be reporting that there was an increase in the flow by air, another agency would be saying no, there is a decrease in the air traffic, but an increase in arms coming by sea. 'It was just ludicrous,' said a source" with access to the intelligence reports of the CIA, Defense Intelligence Agency (DIA) and National Security Agency (NSA).

As Bonner explained, the United States "has the most sophisticated surveillance equipment and methods in the world, including earth-orbiting satellites that can read the license plate of a moving car. From its communications center at Fort Meade, Maryland, NSA spies eavesdrop on conversations between tank commanders in the Iranian desert. In El Salvador the Reagan administration has unleashed a massive intelligence-gathering operation, spending at least $50 million during just the first two years. More than 150 CIA operatives roamed through the tiny country, infiltrating peasant organizations and guerrilla groups. Even the Defense Department's highly secret Intelligence Support Activity (ISA) has agents there." In addition, the contras were deployed along the Nicaraguan-Honduran border, the CIA "financed Honduran gunboats to operate in the Gulf of Fonseca in order to halt the arms flow" and "a sophisticated eavesdropping post was established on a small island in the gulf."

With all that what was the evidence? "Two or three small planes crashed in El Salvador in late 1980 and early 1981, and a semitrailer with a false roof, in which 100 automatic rifles were secreted, was seized on the Honduran-Salvadoran border." The truck was cited often as evidence of arms shipments from Nicaragua; the White Paper contained a photograph of it. But according to the Honduran government, the truck had originated in Costa Rica, not Nicaragua. There wasn't much else, said Bonner. "The reason, quite simply, was that 'you're just hearing bullshit; the intelligence just doesn't support the charges,' as one intelligence source put it."[50]

Shortly after Enders' testimony to Congress, Haig—in finest Haigspeak— refused to rule out the use of military force in Central America: "There are no current plans for the use of American forces. On the other hand and as a matter of principle, the sterility of drawing lines around America's potential options constitutes the promulgation of roadways for those who are seeking to move against America's vital interests."[51]

A bomb exploded at Managua's international airport on February 21, killing four baggage handlers and seriously wounding three others. That same day on a visit to Managua, Mexican President Lopez Portillo launched an effort to stimulate negotiations over the three "knots" of tension: El Salvador, Nicaragua and U.S. relations with Cuba. The Nicaraguan and Cuban governments and the Salvadoran rebels all responded positively. Daniel Ortega announced a five-point peace plan including negotiations with Washington, nonaggression pacts with Central American countries and joint border patrols with Honduras and Costa Rica.[52]

Three weeks later, Lopez Portillo lamented that the Caribbean Basin had been converted into a "frontier" between the United States and the Soviet Union. "The security of the United States will not be resolved in Central America," he said, "but rather by reaching a negotiated understanding with the Soviet Union." He said that Nicaragua was building up its armed forces "because it is afraid" of its neighbors and of the United States. "The people of the United States have a right to security, but the peoples of small poor countries also have their rights. Why not recognize them?"[53]

The Reagan administration did not even pay lip service to the Mexican initiative until Congress forced its hand; 106 House members sent Reagan a letter urging him to accept the Mexican offer for negotiations. As one U.S. official explained, "We were cool to the initiative from the beginning, but we were effectively ambushed by Congress and public opinion. We had to agree to negotiate or appear unreasonable."[54]

In April, the administration showed its disdain for serious negotiations by conditioning talks on Nicaragua making internal political changes. "At that point," said Deputy Assistant Secretary Craig Johnstone, "we elevated democratic pluralism [sic] in Nicaragua to be the sine qua non of restoring relations."[55] U.S.-Nicaragua contacts sputtered along, explained analyst William LeoGrande, "with Nicaragua constantly urging that negotiations be started and the United States refusing. Finally, in August the administration abandoned even this pretext; Nicaragua's diplomatic note of August never received a reply."[56]

Slide Show

The March 10, 1982 *Washington Post* and *New York Times* front-page headlines were similar: "U.S. Shows Photos To Back Charge of Nicaragua Buildup" (*Post*);

"U.S. Offers Photos of Bases to Prove Nicaragua Threat" (*Times*). The accompanying photo was the same: it showed Defense Intelligence Agency Deputy Director John Hughes pointing to a slide of a reconnaissance photo of a Nicaraguan military base. Hughes' presence added to the drama; he had conducted the briefings during the 1962 Cuban missile crisis. The slide was highlighted with such labels as "Soviet-Style Physical Training Area" and "Soviet-Style Obstacle Course." The *New York Times* ran two full pages of transcript from the briefing.

The front pages were different in one respect. The *Washington Post* ran a related story with a much smaller headline: "U.S. Approves Covert Plan in Nicaragua." The next day's *New York Times* headline gave the official story: "U.S. Reportedly Sending Millions to Foster Moderates in Nicaragua."

At the slide briefing, CIA Deputy Director Bobby Inman declared, "It's time to get some concern in this country about their [Nicaragua's] military buildup. It's vastly beyond any defensive need."[57] Not surprisingly, the Nicaraguans didn't see it that way. As Sergio Ramirez put it, "When Mr. Haig is saying every day that they are going to bomb us and attack us and blockade us, how can they turn around and ask us not to defend ourselves?"[58] The slide show was evidence of detailed U.S. aerial surveillance; the destroyers off Nicaragua's Pacific Coast showed the blockade threat was not shallow.

The briefing made a number of specific charges, down to the most comical details. Pointing to one slide, Hughes remarked, "There's the Soviet physical...training area, situated here, with chin-bars and other types of equipment to exercise the forces, and a running track." Pointing to slides of tanks, he said, "Here is the T-54/55 tank here, with a hundred-millimeter gun, in the open...If you look closely you can see the gun turret, tubes in the turret."

The briefing also included slides showing Rio Coco villages before and after the relocation, alleging that "many Indian villages along the northeast border have been demolished by the Sandinistas' security forces. And 23,000 are now homeless." One slide was marked "Destroyed Church."

In response to reporters' questions about the destruction of Miskito villages, Inman concocted a Nicaraguan-Cuban military plot: "You saw the pictures of the expansion of the airfields, over in that coast, the area near the Indian area. If they've got any plans for movement of Cuban troops, Cuban support, supplies, or even simply additional support forces for any involvement outside Nicaragua over into that area, that's clearly the staging area that they would want to use." He insisted there was "no confirming evidence" that cross-border raids from Honduras had been conducted in that area. "I wouldn't discount that there had been one or more small raids, but certainly we would have found evidence of the large-scale engagements that were put out in the press."

Asked about reported covert action against Nicaragua, Inman replied "I would suggest to you that $19 million or $29 million isn't going to buy you much of any kind these days, and certainly not against that kind of a military force." Left unspoken was the White House wish that the military buildup provoked by its covert war would prompt Congress to support increased military aid for Central American allies and the contras.

Like the February 1981 White Paper, the slide briefing was a disinformation exercise designed to drum up public support for administration policy. Slides were shown of airfields near Managua, Puerto Cabezas and Bluefields allegedly being improved to accommodate Soviet aircraft. Nicaraguan Agriculture Minister Jaime Wheelock, who was in the United States at the time, refuted the portrayal of airstrip improvements as proof of Soviet-Cuban designs on Central America. He explained that the feasibility study for lengthening the airstrips was prepared under Somoza in 1976 by a U.S. company.[59]

Retired Marine Lt. Colonel John Buchanan made extended tours of Central America between April and August 1982. He testified to Congress "that a smokescreen is being laid and a military debacle is in the offing." Referring to the March briefing, he said "that the capabilities of the Sandinistas have been deliberately exaggerated by the Reagan administration...As it is with the T-55 [tank], so it is with many other elements of the Sandinista arsenal. Many of the weapons are either ill-suited to the region, outmoded, or in a state of disrepair. This is particularly true of the logistical infrastructure needed to sustain a protracted war. There is only one oil refinery—highly vulnerable to attack."

Buchanan refuted the idea of a Nicaraguan tank invasion of Honduras, explaining the features of the tank and of the terrain which make such a scenario ludicrous. The tank is a mechanical disaster ill-suited for tropical combat. Given the rugged terrain, with steep mountains and narrow valleys, the only realistic route is the Pan American Highway (Choluteca corridor) where the tanks would be sitting ducks for Honduran (and U.S.) airpower.[60]

Senior U.S. intelligence officials for Central America also discredited possible scenarios for a Nicaraguan invasion of Honduras when they briefed reporter Allan Nairn. "There's no real good way to do it," said one official.[61] Nicaraguan statements and actions made clear that they didn't want "to do it," period. Managua tried repeatedly to set up joint patrols with Honduras to monitor the border.

Lt. Colonel Buchanan visited many of the "military installations" that were the subject of the slide briefing and pointed out numerous gaps between photo images and on-the-ground reality. For the record, he "saw little significant difference between a 'Soviet-style obstacle course' and the obstacle courses I ran as a young Marine." He sketched the few significant military targets in Nicaragua: "port facilities at Corinto, Puerto Cabezas and Bluefields; a couple of oil tanks at Corinto; one oil refinery near Managua; four airfields, only one of which is really significant, a tank park and 49 military garrisons," most of them tiny. "For example, the 'military garrison' near Somoto, where I stopped for lunch, was comprised of two small buildings and a one-vehicle lean-to maintenance shed." As for Managua, it "doesn't offer much of a target either; after the 1972 earthquake most of Managua already resembles a bombed-out city."

Buchanan explained that Nicaraguan and Honduran armed forces had different strengths and weaknesses; Nicaragua had a larger army, for example, and Honduras far superior air power. A "projected U.S.-financed arms buildup in Honduras could tip this balance, and would likely elicit a countervailing reaction from Nicaragua. In both cases, poor nations are being forced to divert scarce resources from social and economic development into costly and increasingly lethal military hardware." A war between Nicaragua and Honduras, Buchanan concluded, would be a "war without winners."[62]

Soviet military aid to Nicaragua increased gradually between 1979 and 1982 as the contra war intensified. The U.S. government's own intelligence figures substantiate this point, which the Reagan administration tries so hard to distort. In 1979, Nicaragua imported $5 million worth of Soviet-bloc military supplies, according to U.S. intelligence sources. During 1980 there was a small increase to 850 metric tons of material worth $6 to $7 million. In 1981, Soviet-bloc arms shipments rose to 900 tons, with a U.S.-estimated pricetag of $39 to $45 million. Most of the tonnage was accounted for by 25 or more secondhand Soviet T-54 and T-55 tanks from Algeria, weighing 32 metric tons each. In November 1981, the Nicaraguan Army stood at an estimated 25,000 soldiers—larger than the Honduran Army, but smaller than El Salvador's.

The first real jump in Soviet-bloc military imports came in 1982, amid intensifying contra attacks and U.S. threats, and after France and other Western countries closed their doors to Nicaraguan requests for military aid. In 1982, Soviet-bloc military imports totaled an estimated 6,700 metric tons worth $80 million, according to administration sources.[63]

The House Intelligence Committee discussed the March briefing and a classified followup in a September 1982 report. It concluded that the public briefing format, structured around evidence of increased offensive capability, "obscured DIA's analytic judgement on the difficult, but essential, questions about the significance of the build-up: what do Nicaragua's leaders intend to do with it, and what is the likelihood of Nicaragua's initiating various sorts of offensive operations against its neighbors? These issues were addressed directly in a separate, classified briefing, whose analytic judgements about Nicaragua's intentions were quite distinct from those that appeared implicit in the briefing on the build-up."[64] In other words, DIA admitted a defensive purpose to the buildup.

Even Southern Command chief General Wallace Nutting did not lend much credence to administration rhetoric about a Sandinista threat to Nicaragua's neighbors: "They are interested first, I think, in consolidating internal control and secondly upon (sic) defending their revolution and perhaps only thirdly in using it (their armed forces) in an aggressive way."[65]

The administration followed up the slide show on March 12 with what it thought would be first-hand confirmation of Cuban-Nicaraguan export of revolution. The State Department presented Orlando Jose Tardencillas, a Nicaraguan captured the previous year while fighting with the guerrillas in El Salvador. U.S. officials expected him to say he had been trained in Cuba and Ethiopia and sent to El Salvador by the Nicaraguan government.

At the press conference, Tardencillas shocked his handlers by saying, "An official of the U.S. Embassy told me that they needed to demonstrate the presence of Cubans in El Salvador." Physically and psychologically tortured in El Salvador before being brought to the United States, Tardencillas explained: "They gave me an option. They said I could come here or face certain death. All my previous statements about training in Ethiopia and Cuba were false." The Nicaraguan government neither sent him to El Salvador nor contacted him there. Instead, the nineteen-year-old self-described revolutionary joined the Salvadoran guerrillas on his own initiative in April 1980. He said he never saw another Nicaraguan—or Cuban—while in El Salvador.

The next day, Tardencillas was released to the Nicaraguan Embassy and returned home. "It was a disaster," said a senior U.S. official. "I don't know whether to laugh or cry."[66]

It wasn't the only public relations disaster. Days earlier, Haig had told Congress that a "Nicaraguan military man" had been captured in El Salvador. Mexico quickly discredited Haig's account, saying the man was a student in Mexico traveling home to Nicaragua overland through El Salvador. Another administration plan, to reveal the "sordid backgrounds" of Sandinista leaders, was shelved. "It turned out to be not such a hot idea," said one Reagan aide. "There wasn't any dirt."[67]

The week before the slide briefing, the *Washington Post* ran an unusually candid story titled, "U.S. Diplomats in Central America See Gap Between Policy, Facts." The "diplomats say they are particularly worried about what they perceive as a tendency of the senior decision-makers to force what is often inconclusive and possibly misleading information to match the policy rather than tailoring the policy to the facts." In the words of one diplomat, the United States is "making policy on the basis of our own propaganda."

Unfortunately, the slide briefing's propaganda success outweighed the PR failures. And inside Nicaragua a new stage of the war was beginning.

Blowup

On March 14, CIA trained saboteurs from Honduras blew up two key bridges in northern Nicaragua: the Rio Negro bridge, near the town of Somotillo in Chinandega Province and the Rico Coco bridge near Ocotal in Nueva Segovia.

"Who lives?" shouted one of the commandos seconds before the Rio Negro bridge exploded. "Somoza!" the others responded.[68]

The White House refused to confirm or deny Nicaragua's charges of CIA involvement. Appearing on ABC's "Good Morning America," Meese asserted, "The United States is not in the habit of engaging in sinister plots. Beyond that, however, it is our policy not to either confirm or deny such statements as that."[69]

In May, CIA officials confirmed U.S. involvement in the sinister plot. They told the House Intelligence Committee that the bridges were destroyed by a CIA trained and equipped demolition team. As recounted in the *Washington Post*, "This confirmation brought no objection from the committee because the bridges were seen as supporting illicit arms traffic from Nicaragua to guerrillas in El Salvador, according to House Committee members. 'We had to do that,' one member said."

Committee members reportedly "questioned the CIA officials at length about the arms they had interdicted by this time and about whether they had discovered any Cuban military patrols, which they expected to find in the Nicaraguan countryside. The CIA officials said they had not actually captured or blown up any caches of arms or ammunition but that the presence of the paramilitary teams in the arms-trafficking corridors was dramatically reducing the flow of arms to El Salvador." The CIA officials reported that the contra "force stood at about 1,100 men and that training was going well. No Cuban units, however, had been sighted."[70] The oversight charade continued.

Nicaragua didn't need CIA confirmation to recognize the bridge demolitions as salvos in an intensifying war. The government placed its armed forces on full alert and declared a state of emergency which mandated prior censorship of military information, restricted the right to strike and limited freedom of movement in the war zones. U.S. officials enthusiastically denounced the state of emergency they had consciously provoked as a sign of Nicaraguan totalitarianism. There were no such denunciations of the much harsher state of siege renewed regularly in El Salvador since 1980. There were no reminders that every government, no matter how democratic, has employed extraordinary measures in wartime, including the United States.

Whatever one thinks of the emergency measures Nicaragua has imposed, U.S. hypocrisy in denouncing them should be evident. Washington's goal is to have people judge Nicaragua not only with a double standard, but with a formula in which the war does not appear as a factor. Washington points to emergency measures in Nicaragua to justify support for the contras; then it wants you to forget the contra war in judging Nicaraguan behavior.

Projecting Paranoia

As word of mercenary recruitment for missions in Central America circulated at gun shows and other meeting grounds for soldiers of fortune, CBS Evening News reported on March 22 that a former Green Beret was approached by his ex-commanding officer "with an offer that he finally refused": a $50,000 contract for six months' employment, including six weeks of training in Central America followed by infiltration or air drops inside Nicaragua "to do the same kind of thing he did as a Green Beret during the Vietnam war." His family would receive lifetime benefits if he did not survive. The veteran's wife said that "some of the men involved are in the [military] service already." CBS "learned that they are being offered financial bonuses and may be pulled out of their current units to take part in the enterprise." The "mission, which is said to have White House approval, is scheduled to go forward beginning in April." Neither the CIA nor the Defense Department would comment on the report.

Daniel Ortega brought Nicaragua's case to the UN Security Council on March 25. "We are willing to improve the climate of relations with the United States on the basis of mutual respect and unconditional recognition of our right to self-determination," said Ortega. He reiterated Nicaragua's support for bilateral and regional peace negotiations and called on the United States to put a stop to using Honduras "as a base for armed aggressions and terrorist operations"; to counterrevolutionary training camps in U.S. territory; to "the traffic in arms and counterrevolutionaries between the territory of the United States and Honduras"; to U.S. participation in financing, training and organizing contra forces; to the presence of U.S. warships off Nicaragua's coasts; and to the "flights of spy planes that violate Nicaragua's airspace."[71]

UN Ambassador Jeane Kirkpatrick assumed the role of psychiatrist: "The government of Nicaragua has accused the United States of the kinds of political behavior of which *it* is guilty...These charges—as extravagant as they are baseless—are an interesting example of projection, a psychological operation in which one's own feelings and intentions are simultaneously denied and attributed—that is, projected—to someone else."

"Hostility," Kirkpatrick continued, "is the dominant emotion and projection the key mechanism of the paranoid style of politics which, much to our regret, has characterized the political behavior of the Sandinista leadership. The principal object of Sandinista hostility, I further regret to say, is the government and people of the United States." The U.S. government, she lied, "did not oppose the Sandinista rise to power. It has not attempted to prevent its consolidation. The U.S. government gave the Sandinistas moral and political support in the crucial phases of the civil war."[72]

Real world U.S. policy was elaborated in a secret April 1982 NSC document, "U.S. Policy in Central America and Cuba" through fiscal year 1984. Exposed in the press a year later, the document spelled out the goal of preventing the "proliferation of Cuba-model states" in Central America. "In Nicaragua, the Sandinistas are under increased pressure as a result of our covert efforts and because of the poor state of their economy." But, the NSC warned, "We continue to have serious difficulties with U.S. public and Congressional opinion, which jeopardizes our ability to stay the course. International opinion, particularly in Europe and Mexico, continues to work against our policies." The administration must "step up efforts to co-opt [the] negotiations issue to avoid Congressionally-mandated negotiations, which would work against our interests."[73] Opposition from Congress, the public and U.S. allies was just another obstacle to overcome. The goal of negotiations was better public relations, not improved relations with Nicaragua.

The news wasn't all bad for the administration on the public opinion front. At the annual Corporate Briefing Session sponsored by the Association of American Chambers of Commerce in Latin America (AACCLA) and the Council of the Americas, an association of U.S. corporations with investments in Latin America, R. Bruce Cuthbertson, AACCLA's regional vice president for Central America declared, "There is no future" in Nicaragua "unless the Sandinistas are thrown out." The entire future of Central America depended on it, he said.

The warm remarks for repressive governments throughout the region made clear that those assembled were concerned with corporate freedom, not political freedom. "I honestly believe," said Stanley Urban, president of the Haitian-American Chamber of Commerce and Industry, "that a dictatorship is the best form of government for these people [Haitians]. There are six million illiterates on that island. Think what the Ruskies could do there." He said, "there's more democracy for business in Haiti than for business in the United States." In Haiti labor was cheap and disciplined at a daily minimum wage of $2.64. "In other words," he exclaimed, "the whole country is virtually a free trade zone!"[74]

Transition

A secret July 1982 Defense Intelligence Agency report (leaked in 1983) examined events in Nicaragua. "Since 14 March 1982, insurgency has become increasingly more widespread," stated the DIA report without mentioning the U.S. role in supporting the contras. "Although the present level of activity does not pose a military threat to the Sandinista regime, it is likely to escalate in the months ahead as opposition to the present leadership grows." After noting that insurgent activity increased significantly at the end of December in the northern Atlantic Coast—contrary to Bobby Inman's assertions at the slide briefing—the report stated that a new wave of guerrilla activity was initiated with the sabotaging of the two bridges in March. "In response to these incidents and allegations that 'U.S.-backed forces' were planning to invade Nicaragua, the government decreed a 'state of national emergency'...In the 100-day period from 14 March to 21 June, at least 106 insurgent incidents occurred within Nicaragua."

Among the types of operations the DIA described were "attacks by small guerrilla bands on individual Sandinista soldiers, and the assassination of minor government officials and a Cuban adviser." Without skipping a beat, the report listed the next type of operation: "burning of a customs warehouse, buildings belonging to the Ministry of Construction, and crops." Assassination was not treated as anything out of the ordinary. The report did engage in a partial coverup, though, by apparently counting teachers (including a Cuban teacher), health workers and other victims as "minor government officials and a Cuban adviser."

Since the 1970s, presidential executive orders have prohibited assassination. President Reagan's order of December 4, 1981 states: "No person employed by or acting on behalf of the United States government shall engage in, or conspire to engage in assassination." The U.S.-backed contras were clearly engaging in assassination with the knowledge of U.S. intelligence.

The DIA characterized the FDN as "the largest, best organized, and most effective of the anti-government insurgent groups" and noted it was led by ex-Somoza National Guard officers. The report also described a non-FDN September 15th Legion faction led by Tino Perez and other ex-guardsmen as a "terrorist group." The Legion claimed credit for the December 1981 bombing of a Nicaraguan civilian airlines (AERONICA) Boeing 727 in Mexico City, the October 1981 hijacking of a Costa Rican airliner and the February 1982 explosion of a bomb unloaded from a Honduran aircraft at Managua's international airport.

The DIA report concluded: "There are no indications that any of these groups pose a serious military threat to the present Sandinista leadership or that there are any serious unification efforts underway. However the 15 April defection by such a popular and charismatic revolutionary hero as Eden Pastora could influence some members of these groups, particularly dissident Sandinistas, to join him in forming an umbrella group. Regardless, antigovernment insurgency is likely to continue to escalate in the months ahead. Whether it will succeed eventually in overthrowing the government will depend largely on successful unification efforts, the extent of popular support received both from within and outside Nicaragua, and the effectiveness of Sandinista counterinsurgency operations."[75] The DIA report never mentioned arms interdiction.

As former contra spokesman Edgar Chamorro explained to the World Court, "1982 was a year of transition for the FDN...From a collection of small, disorganized and ineffectual bands of ex-National guardsmen, the F.D.N. grew into a well-organized, well-armed, well-equipped and well-trained fighting force of approximately 4,000 men capable of inflicting great harm on Nicaragua. This was due entirely to the C.I.A. which organized, armed, equipped, trained and supplied us."

Chamorro said that "after the initial recruitment of ex-Guardsmen from throughout the region (to serve as officers or commanders of military units), efforts were made to recruit 'foot soldiers' for the force from inside Nicaragua. Some Nicaraguans joined the force voluntarily, either because of dissatisfaction with the Nicaraguan Government, family ties with leaders of the force, promises of food, clothing, boots and weapons, or a combination of these reasons. Many other members of the force were recruited forcibly. F.D.N. units would arrive at an undefended village, assemble all the residents in the town square and then proceed to kill—in full view of the others—all persons suspected of working for the Nicaraguan Government or the F.S.L.N., including police, local militia members, party members, health workers, teachers, and farmers from government-sponsored cooperatives. In this atmosphere, it was not difficult to persuade those able-bodied men left alive to return with the F.D.N. units to their base camps in Honduras and enlist in the force. This was, unfortunately, a widespread practice that accounted for many recruits."[76]

Chamorro told me he often heard stories about forced recruiting. In Jinotega, for example, there was a contra commander known as "El Tigrillo" (Little Tiger): "He had a reputation of being a rapist, recruiting people by force...a very abusive person. There were other commanders who had the reputation of intimidating people—'if you don't join, we kill you.' "

The intimidation and torment did not end once a Nicaraguan was "recruited." Chamorro explained how "the FDN used a lot of physical punishment on young recruits, to scare them...They used to tie people to trees, like you read about in cartoons. It's true...When I got there in January 1983, I heard a lot of stories like that. There was this crazy commander who used to tie people and intimidate people, or bury people alive up to their head. I mean all kinds of strange things, even mentally, psychologically abnormal characters, pathological things. And strange tortures I heard about. Slowly you hear. They tend to deny [this] to look like good people, but many are psychopaths or misfits of all kinds.

"How do I know that? Because I talked to people. Some of the leaders, they don't want to know what's going on. They just want to be in Washington or Miami, make short visits. They close their eyes, they don't want to find out. But I'm a fella who used to mix with people a lot...I used to spend more time at the bases...

"Some of these State Department propagandists have all the answers. They tend to say: 'Why don't they just run away?' Because it's hard to run away...You have to wait for a good night or a place where you feel safe, you're not afraid. So many people are killed...[They worry that the Sandinistas] might think he's a traitor...It's very complex and each person responds according to his fears or his beliefs. Most people, once they are caught, they tend to stay. It's hard to get out. There are many like that.

"How many? I can't be specific, or give a percentage, but in some areas they were saying that was the norm. There were people who also see an opportunity to get goods like boots, clothing, weapons that make them feel strong or powerful. So, they grab that, they feel good about it."

Besides the people recruited forcibly, or those who joined out of personal hostility towards the Sandinistas, or fear of the future, or because their relatives were with the contras, Chamorro described another group of recruits. They "are just adventurers, that join anything that goes by and promises a new, better life, or they believe the U.S. is going to give them more things later, or some are just bored with their life there. And they see an opportunity to leave their wife with children like they've done before."[77] The contras reportedly also recruited unemployed Hondurans.[78]

The Wrong War

On March 25, 1982, the U.S.-Argentine-Honduran "Tripartita" was shaken by a different kind of Argentine military operation, the effort to assert Argentine sovereignty over the Malvinas Islands known as the Falklands under British rule. As Southcom's General Nutting put it, the Argentine-British war was "the wrong war in the wrong place at the wrong time with the wrong participants."[79]

The U.S.-Argentine alliance in Central America was a casualty of the war. Argentine President Galtieri thought Washington would acquiesce to the Malvinas/Falklands takeover in the interest of their budding security relationship. Secretary Haig tried shuttle diplomacy to avert war between Buenos Aires and London, and when that failed, the United States sided with the British.

Kirkpatrick had argued against the administration siding openly with the British. Haig reportedly accused Kirkpatrick of being "mentally and emotionally incapable of thinking clearly on this issue because of her close links with the Latins." Kirkpatrick called Haig and his aides "Brits in American clothes" and derided Haig's "belief that 'eventually the Latins will come whoring after us because they are, for the most part, right-wing juntas, and right-wing juntas don't rest well in bed with communists.' "[80]

On May 29, the OAS voted to condemn the British attack, and urged that the United States halt aid to Britain and respect the principle of "inter-American continental solidarity" under the Rio treaty. Nicaragua was a staunch supporter of Argentine sovereignty and Cuban-Argentine relations warmed considerably as Argentina looked to other Third World nations for solidarity.

The war ended on June 14 with a British military victory. In the wake of that national disgrace, the Argentine military dictatorship gave way to an elected government. Top military leaders were tried and punished for crimes in the domestic dirty war. As the Mothers of the Disappeared declared during their regular vigil at the Plaza del Mayo in Buenos Aires, "The Malvinas are ours—and so are the disappeared."

"We've lost our proxy in Central America," a U.S. official lamented. "We've lost our spear carrier."[81] Before ceding power, the Argentine military began to withdraw their contra advisers. But Argentine support was not disbanded completely until civilian President Raul Alfonsin took office in December 1983. Meanwhile, Washington gained another spear carrier: Eden Pastora.

Pastora's Southern Front

In July 1981, Eden Pastora resigned his posts as national chief of the People's Militia and deputy minister of defense and went underground, explaining, "I am going to the trenches where the duty of being an internationalist fighter leads me." The Sandinista leadership did not condone Pastora's actions, but they did not expect him to resurface later with his guns pointed at the Nicaraguan government.

Pastora tried collaborating with the Guatemalan revolutionary movement, but the Guatemalans ended up rejecting him because of his "political and ideological inconsistency, and his lack of revolutionary commitment." By December, Pastora was in contact with U.S. officials. In the spring of 1982, a U.S. diplomat in Central America could say: "We're really pulling for Comandante Cero [Pastora's *nom de guerre*]. There's no doubt about it. I don't know if we're giving him money, but I wouldn't be surprised if we were. He's our boy."[82]

Pastora resurfaced in Costa Rica on April 15, 1982, denouncing the Sandinista leadership and vowing to overthrow them. Christopher Dickey, an admirer of Pastora, wrote then: "Pastora, 45, condemned the 'bourgeois' style of the nine powerful members of the ruling Sandinista Front's National Directorate, even though he was known for his own extravagant style in the first year after the revolution and today he wore a diamond ring and a gold watch."[83] Pastora accused the Sandinistas of dragging Nicaragua into the East-West conflict and portrayed himself not as an ally of the Somocista contras, but as the authentic voice of a betrayed Nicaraguan revolution.

For Nicaraguans, Pastora was the moral equivalent of Benedict Arnold, the American revolutionary war general who became a traitor serving the British. The FSLN directorate called Pastora a deserter, comparing him to past figures who "preferred to ally with the enemy invader with no concern for the national sovereignty of Nicaragua."[84] Two days after Pastora's San Jose press conference, several thousand demonstrators gathered in Managua to condemn "the traitor Pastora."

By July, Pastora's alliance with Alfonso Robelo and Arturo Cruz was widely known. Pastora dreamed of serving as president of Nicaragua. After the ouster of the Nicaraguan government, he expected to serve as head of state and commander in chief. After six months, Nicaraguans would elect a constituent assembly. General elections would take place one year later.[85] Pastora would presumably run.

The Revolutionary Democratic Alliance (ARDE) was formed in September by Pastora's Revolutionary Sandino Front, Robelo's MDN, Fernando "El Negro" Chamorro's UDN-FARN and Brooklyn Rivera's faction of MISURA, known by the old name MISURASATA. Rivera had been second-in-command to Steadman Fagoth until he split in 1982.

Describing himself as once "closer than a brother" to Fagoth, Rivera claimed that by 1982 Fagoth had become "psychopathic" and "totally blinded and sick with power and personal ambition." In 1984, Rivera accused Fagoth of allying with "the dirtiest, most assassinating right wing elements of the Honduran army...[choosing] the dirtiest Somozists expelled from the FDN for thievery and murder, as his protective godfathers."[86]

The chief of MISURA's military operations was quoted in September 1984 saying, "I love killing; I have been killing for the past seven years. There's nothing I like better. If I could, I'd kill several people a day."[87]

While its public image and documented record is better than MISURA's, Rivera's forces also committed atrocities. In the summer of 1983, they kidnapped Thomas Hunter, a Creole who headed a fishing cooperative in Southern Zelaya. "Rivera's troops took Hunter to their camp in nearby Punta Fusil and after protracted torture finally killed him, but not before cutting off his ears and forcing him to eat them."[88]

Pastora proclaimed independence from the United States even as he and ARDE grew more dependent upon CIA support. For CIA Latin America Division chief Dewey Clarridge, Pastora had been "a walking, breathing target of opportunity." Early in 1982, Clarridge put a proposition to Pastora. He would "help make Pastora the star of the second revolution as he had been the star of the first."[89]

Pastora's stage would be his old stomping grounds, the southern front and its Costa Rican sanctuary. He also had a diplomatic front: the social democratic governments of Europe and Latin America who Washington hoped would support Pastora over the Sandinistas.

In July 1982, Donald Gregg, then head of the NSC Intelligence Directorate responsible for all covert action projects, prepared a new draft presidential finding to cover the provision of financial and material support, training and arms for Pastora's forces which were clearly targeting the Nicaraguan government and not supposed Salvadoran arms supply routes. It was decided that the existing finding was broad enough.[90] To protect his anti-Somocista and nationalist image, Pastora's arrangement with Washington was as deniable as possible, for as long as possible.

Pastora's secret marriage of convenience with the FDN was always shaky. The Somocistas didn't like Pastora and his allies, Cruz and Robelo. Pastora didn't like the Somocistas. He wanted the former Guardia removed. They wanted him to be a puppet—or they wanted him dead. Bermudez and Lau used to talk "none too discreetly, about how they wanted to kill Pastora and Alfonso Robelo."[91] Washington counseled togetherness until Pastora came to be seen as a disappointing prima donna. Then more people wanted him dead.

6

Fire, Smoke and Mirrors

Compared to the statements and actions that are coming out of Washington, it seems they must be using our reports as toilet paper...We've pointed out the distortions time and time again and been totally ignored or told to shut up.

U.S. Embassy official in Nicaragua, April 1982.[1]

Everything you do to destroy a Marxist regime is moral.

General Gustavo Alvarez, chief of the Honduran Army until March 1984.[2]

The FDN amassed a long record of atrocities against Nicaraguan citizens and little public support inside or outside the country. Father James Feltz, a Milwaukee native, is a witness to contra atrocities. He was pastor of Bocana de Paiwas in the Matagalpa region when an FDN band invaded on March 3, 1982.

"We were meeting with the Catholic Action Committee when seven armed men walked in, pointed their guns at us, and intimidated the whole group of Christians there. They told us that if we had anything to do with the revolutionary process it'd go hard on us indeed. And after harassing, threatening, and intimidating everybody, they bragged that they had just killed the town judge. One of them had a great deal of blood on his shirt. The murdered judge's name was Emiliano Perez Obando, and was a Delegate of the Word of God [Church lay preacher] in the parish of Paiwas. They said they'd left him to die not far away, but that anyone who went to help him was under 'sentence of death'...

"[Feltz and another priest] found Emiliano wounded and dying. His body was still warm, but he was near death. We had hope that if we could get him to a doctor or a hospital we might be able to save his life. We borrowed a car and raced away...

"On the way to Rio Blanco, Emiliano died in my arms. He had ten kids and another on the way. It was terribly hard for me to have to go and tell his widow that this courageous person was dead...His murder was a very heavy blow for the whole population of the parish, the town, and all the villages of the region...He was admired by many people. This was my first close contact with the contras in all their savage brutality. I could see the contras didn't have any trace of humanity left. I saw how they boasted of having murdered this person, and how they enjoyed intimidating people. I saw how they'd enjoyed murdering Emiliano."[3]

In another case, on October 28 in the northern region of El Jicaro-Murra, "five armed men dressed in blue FDN uniforms broke down the door of the house where Maria Bustillo, 57, was living with her husband, Ricardo, a Delegate of the Word, and five of their children. The intruders ordered everyone to the floor, face down, and warned that whoever moved would be killed. After striking Ricardo and kicking the children, they tied them up two by two and led them away, telling Maria, 'Careful you old bitch, you're going to find out tomorrow.'

"When Maria went out the next morning to look for her family, she found her five children dead, about 50 yards from the house. 'They were all cut up. Their ears were pulled off, their noses and other parts were cut off.' Her husband Ricardo was found dead in a nearby town along with another man, Raul Moreno. 'They were also left broken up. He had false teeth and they took them, his arms were broken and his hands were cut up.'

"After the massacre, Maria took refuge in El Jicaro." El Jicaro would be attacked twice in 1983.[4]

A Nicaraguan businessman opposed to the Sandinistas observed, "You can give the guardsmen expensive American equipment and new uniforms, but they still behave like guardsmen. You ask people to choose between Sandinists and Somocists and they can't choose the guard."[5]

Target Jalapa

Edgar Chamorro testified to the World Court that by the end of 1982, the FDN was "ready to launch our first major military offensive designed to take and hold Nicaraguan territory, which the C.I.A. was urging us to do. Our principal objective was the town of Jalapa, in northern Nicaragua. More than 1,000 of our fighters were involved, and we used light artillery (mortars, supplied by the C.I.A.) in combat for the first time. Although we inflicted casualties on the Sandinistas and caused substantial destruction in Jalapa and other neighboring towns, our offensive was repulsed and we were forced to retreat to Honduras and regroup without having accomplished our objective."

The "beak of Jalapa" is an area of northwest Nicaragua surrounded on three sides by Honduras. It appeared an easy target for contra Plan C, described by captured FDN commander Pedro Javier "El Muerto" (The Dead Man) Nunez Cabezas: take Jalapa, "declare it a liberated zone and install a provisional government and ask for military aid from friendly governments such as the United States, Honduras and Argentina."

Small FDN bands had made prior assaults in the region. Before July 1982, there were 120 villages in the mountains and valleys outside the town of Jalapa. As contra attacks increased, peasants abandoned most of the surrounding villages and swelled Jalapa's population to more than double its normal 9,000 inhabitants. Crops of corn, beans, rice and coffee were lost, straining food supplies and cutting export revenues. Lisa Fitzgerald, a nun and former assistant attorney general in Massachusetts, lived in Jalapa during 1982 and 1983. She went to help teach Nicaraguans and ended up having to educate Americans about the war their government was waging.

By July 1982, said Fitzgerald, "incursions by 'contra' bands from Honduras began to make trips into the mountain areas very dangerous. We could no longer travel without an armed escort. After August of that year, travel was made impossible. Several months later, all of us, each nun and priest working in Jalapa, were named on the 'contra' radio station and threatened if we continued to participate in the national literacy program."

Contra attacks multiplied. On September 22, for example, a veterinarian and an accountant working for the Ministry of Agrarian Reform were ambushed on the road from Jalapa to Ocotal. Contras cut their throats. On October 15, contras dragged Cruz Urrutia from his home in Siuce where he was a farmer, Delegate of the Word, health worker and adult education promoter. His mutilated body was found a day later. On November 15, contras forcibly assembled the community of La Ceiba to watch as four farmers were tortured, shot and had their heads blown off by a grenade. During November and December an estimated 400 men, women and children were abducted to Honduras. In January, contras kidnapped an entire coffee-picking crew of 60 people.[6]

Defended mainly by border guard troops and local militia, Jalapa withstood the late 1982 offensive. Four other attempts to take the town between March and June 1983 also failed. But many more civilians were murdered or kidnapped. Lisa Fitzgerald recorded 337 abductions from January through June 1, 1983. "Of these, 37 persons escaped. I interviewed five of them; all were forced to carry equipment for the contras. They reported some of their friends were shot immediately after they were abducted and others were taken to Honduras."[7]

Base Country Honduras

There were more than 100 U.S. advisers in Honduras by March 1982. In April, the chief of the Honduran Army, General Gustavo Alvarez, said that his country would agree to U.S. intervention in Central America if it were the only way to "preserve peace."[8] At month's end, Honduras rejected Nicaragua's offer of a bilateral nonaggression treaty and denied that Honduran territory was harboring counter-revolutionary groups.[9]

As the contras escalated cross-border attacks during July and August, the United States and Honduras held military exercises and built a permanent military base at Durzuna, about 25 miles from the Nicaraguan border. U.S. troops left behind most of their equipment for the contras when the exercises ended. By the end of 1982, Honduras hosted more than 150 CIA agents.[10] A Honduran officer summed up his country's proxy role this way: "The U.S. will supply all the arms, equipment and body bags that we need and all we have to do is supply the bodies."[11]

Honduras was also a U.S. proxy in El Salvador's war. In March 1981, for example, Honduran soldiers blocked Salvadoran refugees from crossing the Lempa River into Honduras as they were being bombed by the Salvadoran Air Force. About 200 people, mostly women and children, were killed. In November and December, the Honduran Army allowed Salvadoran soldiers to raid refugee camps in La Virtud. In June 1982, Honduras and El Salvador launched a series of "hammer and anvil" operations along their border to trap Salvadoran guerrillas and would-be refugees.[12]

The Honduran Army played a crucial logistical role as contra operations expanded. It moved supplies to the border by truck where sometimes the contras "would pay individuals $10 a kilometer to carry them, sometimes loaded on mules, into Nicaragua."[13] At times the Honduran Army pounded Nicaragua with mortar fire to cover contra forces. Nicaragua accused the United States of trying to provoke war with Honduras as a pretext for overthrowing the Nicaraguan government.

In September 1982, Venezuela (in a policy shift) joined Mexico in urging that Nicaragua, Honduras and the United States take swift diplomatic action to prevent the outbreak of regional war. The U.S. Congress expressed interest and President Reagan paid the initiative the usual lip service. In October, United Nations members angered Washington by electing Nicaragua to one of the rotating seats on the Security Council.

On November 4, Nicaragua declared a military emergency zone in five northern border provinces experiencing daily attacks. Around the same time, *Newsweek* published a dramatic cover story: "America's Secret War—Target: Nicaragua." Some twenty Argentine advisers were still on the scene, but it was clearly Washington's war. CIA Director Casey personally inspected the operation. Ambassador Negroponte ran it. Contras called him "The Boss."

"Negroponte is the spearhead," declared a Washington insider. "He was sent down there by Haig and Enders to carry out the operation without any qualms of conscience." Honduras' first civilian president in many years, Roberto Suazo, elected in November 1981, was only the nominal head of state. Alvarez was the official commander in chief and de facto Honduran leader. He shared power with Negroponte, not Suazo. An aide to Alvarez said of Alvarez and Negroponte, "they both run the Army, although only one of them has the title for that job." As a member of the Honduran military command put it, Negroponte and Alvarez "discuss what should be done, and then Alvarez does what Negroponte tells him to."

The economy was also a joint venture. During President Suazo's January 1982 inauguration a messenger delivered a four-page letter from the U.S. Embassy. "Encouraging a prompt 'revitalization' of the ailing economy, the letter—using the imperative form of Spanish—directed the government of Honduras to take 11 specific actions, such as reducing taxes on mining companies and lifting some price controls. The government dutifully complied with many of the demands."[14]

In return for shares of its sovereignty, Honduras received increased U.S. military and economic assistance through 1985: $47.5 million in 1981, $112 million in 1982, $145.2 million in 1983, $171.5 million in 1984 and $282.6 million in 1985.[15] Second only to Haiti in hemispheric poverty, the Honduran people did not benefit as the country was transformed into a Bases and Banana Republic.

"We live in a formal democracy. We have the forms of a democratic system but we don't have a real, working democracy," said Christian Democratic leader Efrain Diaz. The "military has not diminished its influence. It has become stronger...Congress has become a rubber stamp...The country has lost all autonomy in foreign affairs. This country has become an occupied country...a base of military operations for the U.S." It is "increasingly difficult," he said, "to have a dissident view here." It means "being called Communist."[16]

Dissidents risked death. Alvarez "professionalized" the nascent Honduran death squad network—linked to the World Anti-Communist League affiliate CAL— with the help of Argentine advisers during 1980 and 1981. In the Honduran version of dirty war, students, professors, union leaders and other alleged subversives were tortured and murdered. A death squad member called "Ephron" explained one method of body disposal: "We got people, killed them, put their bodies aboard helicopters, and threw them in the Rio Sumpul [the river dividing part of Honduras and El Salvador and an area of intense fighting between the Salvadoran Army and the Salvadoran guerrillas] to make it look like the Salvadorans did it. Before dumping them, we would remove all ID and put Salvadoran coins in their pockets." Body dumps, like those in El Salvador, appeared for the first time in 1981 and human rights groups cited Honduras for gross abuses. "The so-called disappeared," retorted Alvarez, "are probably subversives who are in Cuba and Nicaragua training to come back and subvert the Fatherland."[17]

Dr. Ramon Custodio, president of the Committee for the Defense of Human Rights in Honduras (CODEH) and former president of the medical college in Tegucigalpa, scoffed at the idea the Reagan administration was defending democracy in Honduras. Asked why he put himself at personal risk leading the human rights organization, he said, "It's my duty to defend human rights...I'd hate to be living in this country and be silent and be in the position of the many German people when Hitler came to power."

Jorge Arturo Reina, a leader of the Honduran Liberal Peoples Alliance (ALIPO) and a former chancellor of the National University, saw the United States crushing the aspirations of Central Americans in its campaign to restore "the Pretorian Guard of Somoza." He observed, "From more war we will have more poverty, more destruction, more backwardness...Reagan calls it 'America's backyard.' It is a yard plagued by misery, hunger and poverty. It's not a garden. It's a desert that can be turned into a cemetery."[18]

Newsweek portrayed the contra operation as out of control, having "escalated far beyond Washington's original intentions" to interdict weapons and support

Nicaraguan moderates. It made Negroponte the fall guy for a potential Bay of Pigs. Despite its flaws, the *Newsweek* piece brought millions more Americans in on the increasingly open secret of Washington's war on Nicaragua. The growing public worry was not another Bay of Pigs but another Vietnam.

FDN Facelift

Edgar Chamorro was working as a commodities broker for Cargill Corporation and part-time staffer for the FDN's political junta when he was approached by CIA officer "Steve Davis" in November 1982. Davis asked him to join a new FDN political directorate. Over lunch near Chamorro's home in Key Biscayne, Florida, Davis told Chamorro that "he was speaking in the name of the President of the United States, who wants 'to get rid of the Sandinistas.' 'Davis' explained to me that the FDN had a bad image in the United States, and particularly among members of the Congress, because it was perceived as an organization of ex-National Guardsmen. He told me that in order to maintain the support of the Congress for the C.I.A.'s activities it was necessary to replace the political junta with a group of prominent Nicaraguan civilians who had no ties with the National Guard or the Somoza Government. 'Davis' left without asking me to make a commitment. He told me I would be contacted again in the near future.

"Later that month, 'Davis' telephoned me and asked me to have dinner with him in his hotel suite at the Holiday Inn in Miami. When I arrived, 'Davis' introduced me to another C.I.A. man, who used the name 'Tony Feldman.' 'Feldman' was introduced as 'Davis' ' superior from Washington...'Feldman' told me that the C.I.A. had decided on a seven-member political directorate for the F.D.N. because any larger group would be unmanageable. He said that I had been selected as one of the seven, and he asked me to accept. He told me that the United States Government was prepared to give its full backing to the F.D.N. so that, by the end of December 1983, we would be marching into Managua to take over the Nicaraguan Government."[19]

Chamorro agreed to join. On December 7, 1982, he met with U.S. officials and other directorate members at the Four Ambassadors Hotel in Miami to rehearse a press conference for the following day. Chamorro met FDN military chief Enrique Bermudez for the first time. Tony Feldman (also known as Philip Mason) was accompanied by CIA officer Joe Fernandez (alias Tomas Castillo).

As Chamorro described it, "Feldman introduced two lawyers from Washington who briefed us on the Neutrality Act...Feldman was worried we were going to tell the press that we were trying to overthrow the Sandinistas, which, of course, is exactly what we wanted to do. He emphasized that we should say instead that we were trying to 'create conditions for democracy.' "

Various questions were rehearsed. If asked about funding, Feldman advised, "Say your sources want to remain confidential." The CIA men agreed there was no way to finesse the question "Have you had any contact with U.S. government officials?" The contra leaders were told "to lie and say, 'No.' "[20]

The press conference was held at the Hilton Conference Center in Ft. Lauderdale to avoid the risk of antiwar demonstrations in Miami. Leonardo Somarriba, one of Jorge Salazar's coconspirators, worked with CIA officials in arranging the press conference and organizing the directorate.[21]

Chamorro read the FDN statement of principles and goals: "We the Directorate of the Nicaraguan Democratic Force commit ourselves to guide and support this effort of the Nicaraguan people to salvage our sacred patriotic honor, offering for this purpose all-out industry, dedication, and if necessary, our very lives."

The Nicaraguans hadn't written the final statement, including the part about offering up their lives. Chamorro explained that the draft he coauthored with other Nicaraguans "was mostly about the right to private property, and it was very anticommunist." Fernandez (Castillo) didn't like it. "Shit, who wrote this?" said Fernandez, "It sounds like all you want is to get back what you lost. You have to write something more progressive, more political. We'll get someone from Washington to help you."

That's when "George" was called in. George was John Mallett who served as deputy and then chief of the CIA station in Honduras. "The Americans, I began to realize," said Chamorro, "liked to make all the crucial decisions."[22]

The CIA's carefully-packaged new contra front still embraced Somocistas. Besides Chamorro the directorate included: ex-National Guard officer Enrique Bermudez; Alfonso Callejas, a vice president under Somoza and uncle of Alfonso Robelo, active in church affairs; Marcos Zeledon, a former leader of COSEP and manager of Quaker Oats of Nicaragua; Indalecio Rodriguez, a conservative intellectual and former rector of the Central America University; and Lucia Cardenal de Salazar, the widow of Jorge Salazar and sister-in-law of Alfonso Robelo. The CIA men, said Chamorro, "wanted at all costs to have a woman on the directorate." They thought that would improve the contras' human rights image.

Jose Francisco Cardenal was not selected. "It was clear," said Chamorro, "they didn't want Cardenal because he didn't get along with Bermudez." When he wasn't named, Cardenal quit contra politics and later took up selling life insurance in Miami.[23]

Chamorro told the World Court that in January 1983, at the direction of Joe Fernandez (whom he knew as Castillo), "we put out a 12-point 'peace initiative' drafted by the C.I.A., which essentially demanded the surrender of the Sandinista Government. I thought this was premature, but 'Castillo' insisted that it be done to get the F.D.N. favorable publicity."

Meanwhile, Adolfo Calero was added to the directorate. According to Chamorro, Calero "had been working for the C.I.A. in Nicaragua for a long time. He served as, among other things, a conduit of funds from the United States Embassy to various student and labor organizations. 'Feldman' had told me that the C.I.A. was bringing him out of Nicaragua...to serve on the F.D.N.'s political directorate."[24]

"Each of us in the directorate," Chamorro explained, "was tasked to act as a link between the CIA and the sector we were assigned to represent inside Nicaragua.

We were used as conduits of financial support from the CIA to groups in Nicaragua, such as private sector organizations and political parties, and as conduits of information from those sectors back to the CIA. The CIA wanted the FDN to be *the* official opposition group."[25]

Boland I: Flashing Yellow Light

The arms interdiction fiction had worn thin by the spring of 1982. Growing contra forces "were being outfitted with U.S.-financed equipment through Honduran military depots and were paid a subsistence fee of $23 per month, according to CIA officials."[26] More members of Congress questioned the program. A former lobbyist for administration policy acknowledged, "It was hard to spell out what we wanted to Congress. They wouldn't have gone for it then."[27]

Casey misled the Intelligence Committees, claiming that contra forces had swelled because Nicaraguans were "recruiting themselves" to fight the Sandinistas. Administration cover stories didn't jibe. Congress was also told the operation was forced to employ more ex-guardsmen than had been planned "because they were the only ones who wanted to fight."[28]

The administration rewrote the contra plot in July. It leaked a State Department policy paper advocating a major expansion of the contras and increased military aid to Honduras and Costa Rica on the grounds that Nicaragua was receiving massive arms shipments from the Soviet Union.

"We responded positively," recalled Michael Barnes, former chairman of the House Subcommittee on Inter-American Affairs. "There was some exaggeration, but there was a real threat. The Sandinistas said they were doing it because the United States wanted to overthrow them, and I told them, 'We aren't going to do that, you're just paranoid.' "[29]

In August, the Intelligence Committees attempted to leash the covert operation to its alleged goal of arms interdiction. The classified annex of the 1983 Intelligence Authorization Act prohibited U.S. aid "for the purpose of overthrowing the Government of Nicaragua or provoking a military exchange between Nicaragua and Honduras." It was not designed to cut off the covert war, but to control it.

In the fall, the administration fashioned a new cover for the war: harassing and punishing Nicaragua in order to convince the Sandinistas to stop "exporting revolution." This would later be changed to pressuring the Sandinistas to negotiate.

On December 8, FDN chief Enrique Bermudez repudiated the still-lingering arms interdiction rationale while paying lip service to the stated U.S. concern for democracy: "It is not acceptable to us to carry out missions to interdict Cuban and Russian supply lines to El Salvador. We are Nicaraguans and our objective is to overthrow the Communists and install a democratic government in our country."[30]

That same day, Congress debated an amendment offered by then Rep. Tom Harkin (D-IA) to prohibit U.S. assistance to any group involved in paramilitary actions against Nicaragua. House Intelligence Committee Chairman Edward Boland

(D-MA) offered the previously classified committee measure as a less-restrictive substitute. With the support of the Republican leadership, the Boland amendment passed unanimously. It was signed into law on December 21, remaining in effect until December 8, 1983:

> None of the funds provided in this Act may be used by the Central Intelligence Agency or the Department of Defense to furnish military equipment, military training or advice, or other support for military activities, to any group or individual, not part of a country's armed forces, for the purpose of overthrowing the Government of Nicaragua or provoking a military exchange between Nicaragua and Honduras.

Boland provided a vehicle for continuing covert operations against Nicaragua, and the administration gladly took him for a ride. "There were always two tracks," a CIA official explained, "the publicly stated CIA objective of interdicting weapons to Salvadorean guerrillas, and the overthrow of the Sandinista government."[31]

In answer to an inquiry by the General Accounting Office, the Department of Defense (DOD) General Counsel William H. Taft IV contended that Boland referred "to the purpose of U.S. Government agencies, not the purpose of the individuals and groups receiving assistance from these agencies...Therefore it is not legally relevant under the Boland Amendment whether the Government of Nicaragua is in fact eventually overthrown, or whether an exchange between Nicaragua and Honduras takes place. What is relevant is the immediate motive or purpose for which the assistance is provided, not the long-term intent of those who are assisted. Assistance provided to pressure Nicaragua to cease its intervention in El Salvador—even if it resulted in the fall of the present regime—would not contravene the Boland Amendment, while assistance given to overthrow that regime, even if totally ineffective or actually counterproductive, would violate this statute."

DOD argued that the letter and spirit of the law was being observed because if the House meant to cover the purposes of the groups receiving aid then it would not have rejected the Harkin amendment. "To suggest that the Harkin Amendment was somehow incorporated into the 'spirit' of the Boland Amendment is untenable."[32] The administration continued to officially deny its purpose was to overthrow the Nicaraguan government, and Congress didn't hold it accountable to off-the-record admissions of intent or for actions that clearly contradicted its denials.

Before the Boland amendment, said Edgar Chamorro, CIA agents "spoke openly and confidently about replacing the government in Managua. Thereafter...[if] any of us ever said anything publicly about overthrowing the Nicaraguan Government, we would be visited immediately by a C.I.A. official who would say, 'That's not the language we want you to use.' But our goal, and that of the C.I.A. as well (as we were repeatedly assured in private), was to overthrow the Government of Nicaragua...It was never our objective to stop the supposed flow of arms, of which we never saw any evidence in the first place. The public statements by United States Government officials about the arms flow, we were told by the C.I.A. agents with whom we worked, were necessary to maintain the support of the Congress and should not be taken seriously by us."[33]

U.S. "punishment" of Nicaragua translated into terrorism. On December 23, 1982, Nicaraguan Interior Minister Tomas Borge presented evidence of an aborted contra urban terror plan called "Bitter Christmas": C-4 plastic explosive packed into flashlights and children's lunch boxes for detonation in supermarkets, movie theaters and buses on Christmas Eve.[34]

As FDN forces continued their offensive in the Jalapa region, five MISURA columns of 125 men each crossed from Honduras into Nicaragua on December 30 on a mission to capture the strategic seaport of Puerto Cabezas. Another group sabotaged port installations. The plan was to capture the port and hold it until the U.S.-backed Honduran military airlifted in reinforcements and a provisional government was installed.[35] It failed when the Nicaraguan Army intercepted and scattered the main attack forces.

Buying Guns and Journalists

Edgar Chamorro worked full time for the FDN from January 1983 until June 1984. He remained on the political directorate until November 1984, when he was ousted for speaking too openly about contra human rights abuses.

Chamorro was put in charge of FDN public relations because of his background in the field and his relatively moderate credentials. "We wanted to set up highly visible headquarters in a shopping center or office building," he told the World Court, "but the C.I.A. did not like the idea. They said it would become a target for demonstrations or violence. They insisted that we take an elegant suite at the David Williams Hotel in Coral Gables, Florida which the C.I.A. paid for." At the end of January, the CIA instructed Chamorro to relocate to Tegucigalpa, Honduras to run the FDN's new communications office. The CIA station in Honduras "gave me money, in cash, to hire several writers, reporters, and technicians to prepare a monthly bulletin called 'Commandos,' to run a clandestine radio station, and to write press releases."

Bribing reporters was part of Chamorro's job: "I also received money from the C.I.A. to bribe Honduran journalists and broadcasters to write and speak favorably about the F.D.N. and to attack the Government of Nicaragua and call for its overthrow. Approximately 15 Honduran journalists and broadcasters were on the C.I.A.'s payroll, and our influence was thereby extended to every major Honduran newspaper and radio and television station." Chamorro learned from CIA colleagues "that the same tactic was employed in Costa Rica in an effort to turn the newspapers and radio and television stations of that country against the Nicaraguan Government."[36]

According to Carlos Morales, a professor of journalism and former president of the Costa Rican journalists' union, at least eight Costa Rican journalists, including three top editors, were receiving monthly CIA payments either directly or through contra groups as of 1987. "There may be more, but these I know for certain because most are former students of mine, and some have talked with me about it," he said.

The eight journalists cited by Morales received about 30,000 *colones* (about $500) a month—more than the monthly salary of about 20,000 colones earned by most Costa Rican journalists. "Their job," said Morales, "is to get into the press stories, commentaries, or editorials attacking Nicaragua and sympathetic to the contras."[37]

In Honduras, Chamorro worked closely with CIA Deputy Station Chief John Mallett (George). "Together with 'George,' and subject to his approval, I planned all the activities of my communications office and prepared a budget. The budget was reviewed by the C.I.A. station in Tegucigalpa and, if approved, sent to Washington to obtain the necessary funds, which were always provided to me in cash." Other CIA agents worked with FDN directorate member Indalecio Rodriguez in developing the budget for "civilian affairs," covering assistance for Nicaraguan refugees in Honduras or family members of contra combatants, and with Adolfo Calero and Enrique Bermudez on the military and logistics budget.

The FDN, explained Chamorro, "never received money to purchase arms, ammunition or military equipment. These were acquired for us and delivered directly to us by the C.I.A. One of the senior agents at the C.I.A.'s Tegucigalpa station, known to us as 'the Colonel,' was an expert in these matters...As long as I was in Honduras (until June 1984), the F.D.N. never acquired its own arms, ammunition or other military equipment. We were just the end receivers. The main items in the military and logistics budget that Calero and Bermudez worked on were things that could be acquired locally, such as food for our men, for which money had to be obtained from the C.I.A. Calero and Bermudez were our main links with the C.I.A. They met constantly with the C.I.A. station chief."[38]

The contras received Soviet weapons captured by the Israelis in Lebanon and by guerrillas in Afghanistan. According to FDN sources, "most of the best weaponry—RPG7 rocket launchers, 60 mm mortars, FAL and AK47 assault rifles—went to the FDN...The older weapons, including World War II-era MI carbines, went to the...Miskito Indians."[39]

Chamorro explained what U.S. intelligence was intercepting in Central America besides the famous arms flow to El Salvador: "The C.I.A. working with United States military personnel, operated various electronic interception stations in Honduras for the purpose of intercepting radio and telephonic communications among Nicaraguan Government military units. By means of these interception activities, and by breaking the Nicaraguan Government codes, the C.I.A. was able to determine—and to advise us of—the precise locations of all Nicaraguan Government military units. The information obtained by the C.I.A. in this manner was ordinarily corroborated by overflights of Nicaraguan territory by United States satellites and sophisticated surveillance aircraft. With this information, our own forces knew the areas in which they could safely operate free of government troops. If our units were instructed to do battle with the government troops, they knew where to set up ambushes, because the C.I.A. informed them of the precise routes the government troops would take. This type of intelligence was invaluable to us. Without it, our forces would not have been able to operate with any degree of effectiveness inside Nicaragua."

The CIA, said Chamorro, repeatedly ordered the FDN "to move our troops inside Nicaragua and to keep them there as long as possible. After our offensive at the end of 1982 was turned back, almost all of our troops were in Honduras and our own officers believed that they needed more training and more time before they would be ready to return to Nicaragua. The F.D.N. officers were overruled by the C.I.A., however. The agency told us that we had to move our men back into Nicaragua and keep fighting. We had no choice, but to obey."

"Death Swooping Down"

According to Chamorro, the CIA instructed the contras in 1983 "not to destroy farms or crops because that would be politically counterproductive. In 1984, however, we were instructed to destroy export crops (especially coffee and tobacco), and to attack farms and cooperatives."[40]

CIA instructions were apparently contradictory because the contras attacked farms throughout 1983 as well. It was part of their general war on social programs and the economy. With all their sophisticated intelligence on the Nicaraguan military, the contras were far more effective in terrorizing civilians than in fighting troops. Here are some examples:

On March 5, 1983, 80 contras seized the San Carlos farm near Muy-Muy, Matagalpa. They burned the farmhouse and kidnapped the farm manager. On March 12, a group of 150 contras assassinated five members of a popular education collective meeting in a school in the El Jicaro district. Near Rio Blanco in the Matagalpa region, contras kidnapped education administrator Maria Martinez Alvarez. "Her body was later found with her throat slit and her breasts cut off."

On March 26, 200 contras attacked the district of Rancho Grande with mortar fire. Pierre Grosjean, a French doctor, was killed along with two Nicaraguan civilians and two militia members; seventeen people were wounded, including seven children. On April 30, 100 FDN troops ambushed and assassinated fourteen people on the road near Wiwili in Jinotega province, including Albrecht Pflaum, a German doctor. Three women—two nurses and an employee of the National Development bank—were raped and murdered. Some of the men were also tortured before being killed.

In late April, an ARDE band assaulted people in three small villages near La Azucena, Rio San Juan. They tortured and murdered eleven peasants who worked in cooperatives, education and civil defense, and kidnapped ten others. More than twenty families were told they would be killed if they did not join ARDE's military operations.[41]

Father James Feltz experienced attacks in late August and early September by a 500-member contra force led by the ex-Guard Renato. Recalling them crossing the Rio Grande de Matagalpa and invading the area, Feltz said, "It's like death swooping down, it's like Attila's hordes."

Feltz described how the contras "headed for the region around El Guayabo. On the way they ran into a man named...'Chico' Sotelo. Chico had livestock and was not much for the revolution. Certainly he was no Sandinista. He had his money and his private property. But he made the mistake of pulling out his UNAG passbook. Well, all they had to do was see he belonged to the [National Union of Farmers and Ranchers] and they shot him on the spot, right there on the road...And they kept burning houses. The death march got as far as El Guayabo. There there's a little hamlet called San Francisco, and they killed several people there; they killed people if they were members of defense committees or shopkeepers or maybe members of the militia. But nobody was armed. They raped a fourteen-year-old girl. Then they slit her throat and cut off her head. They hung the head on a pole along the road...

"There was another special case of cruelty on that same contra operation. An eleven-year-old girl, Cristina Borge Diaz, was visiting her uncle. The uncle was on the contras' list, and they came and killed him. When they saw the little girl, they decided to have a little fun, so they used her for target practice. The first one took a shot at her from a galloping horse. He missed. 'Kill her,' he told a companion. And the other shot her in the back. The bullet came out her chest. Another bullet grazed her scalp, another hit her in the right hand, and another in the left hip. Then they left. The little girl lay there until a worker coming back from the fields found her that way, more dead than alive." Miraculously, said Feltz, she recovered after treatment in Managua. She told her story to a meeting of Nicaraguan-based U.S. missionaries and visiting U.S. bishops in February 1985.[42]

New Phase

In early February 1983, the United States held the first Big Pine military exercises with Honduras. Some 4,000 Hondurans and 1,600 U.S. troops maneuvered near Puerto Lempira in the Mosquitia region, operating less than ten miles from the Nicaraguan border. According to the Department of Defense, Big Pine's objectives were: "assisting Honduras in developing procedures to defend its territory, testing deployment techniques and exercising logistical support of a field force."[43]

Congress, meanwhile, was informed that contra ranks had reached 5,500. House and Senate fact-finding missions to the region concluded that the administration was violating the spirit of the Boland amendment, if not the letter. In April, even State Department officials raised questions about the legality of U.S. policy, contending that contra support operations had inadvertently gone beyond interdiction and "could be seen as intended to overthrow" the Nicaraguan government.[44] As Casey continued playing charades with the Intelligence Committees, the CIA spent an additional $11 million from a secret fund to support the war.[45]

Few in Congress took up the challenge of Representatives Berkely Bedell (D-IA) and Robert Torricelli (D-NJ) upon their return from Honduras and Nicaragua. Declared Bedell in a speech to the House, "If the American people could have talked with the common people of Nicaragua, whose women and children are being indiscriminately kidnapped, tortured and killed by terrorists financed by the American taxpayers, they would rise up in legitimate anger and demand that support for the criminal activity be ended at once."[46]

A new phase of the contra war opened with the development of large contra task forces (about 250 combatants) grouped under regional commandos (500 to 2,000 combatants). Virtually all the task force commanders, regional commanders and central staff of the FDN were ex-National Guard (see chapter 10). In some areas, where there was a history of recruitment for the National Guard (e.g. the San Francisco zone), where government programs were still scarce (e.g. the mountains of Matagalpa and Boaco), or where peasants were discontented with the form and pace of the agrarian reform, the contras were able to build a network of collaborators.[47]

Religious manipulation also played a role in contra recruiting. Anti-Sandinista clergy, politicians and the contras themselves demonized the Sandinistas, portraying them as atheist communists who would abolish private property and freedom of worship. Flor de Maria Monterrey, head of the Institute for the Study of Sandinismo, said peasants were told that the Sandinistas "will take away your chicken...and the radio you bought" and " 'They're going to take away your novenas and your Hail Marys.' To say they'll take that away from you is like taking away your life."[48]

Contra task forces launched a new drive on Jalapa under the March 1983 Plan Siembra (Harvest). Other contra units penetrated the interior provinces of Madriz, Jinotega and Esteli to divert Sandinista forces. The offensive was defeated in May. To meet the intensifying contra assaults and raise the costs of direct U.S. invasion, Nicaragua stepped up popular mobilization and expanded the army.

Under the slogan "All Arms to the People," thousands more Nicaraguans were organized into volunteer militias, reserve infantry battalions and self-defense agricultural cooperatives (where some farmers stood guard to protect others in the field). The army expanded to about 24,000 in 1983.[49]

On July 19, 1983, the fourth anniversary of the revolution, the government announced the Patriotic Military Service Law (SMP) under which a draft would begin in September. Army forces would grow to about 40,000 in 1984. Not surprisingly, the draft exacerbated tensions within the country. The Nicaraguan Bishops' Conference denounced the draft as service to an army that represented the FSLN, not the country, and advocated "conscientious objection" by those not allied ideologically with the Sandinistas.

The Bishops' August 29 statement opposing the draft was printed and debated in all three national newspapers—notwithstanding the state of emergency. *La Prensa's* September 1 headline read (in translation): "Episcopal Conference suggests: 'Conscientious Objection'—Nobody Can Be Obligated To Take Up Arms For A Party." *El Nuevo Diario's* headline read "Widespread Christian Support for SMP"; it featured remarks by a protestant minister.

Viewing the draft from another angle, the national women's organization AMNLAE argued in the Council of State that women should be included in the SMP. As AMNLAE Council of State delegate Magda Enriques argued, "The mandate from our grass roots was to struggle to the end to get equal status so we called two general assemblies in Managua to discuss the whole issue. We demanded scientific, not emotional, explanations for the exclusion of women. There was a national debate in the media. In the end, they agreed to accept women volunteers into active service, which was something of a victory."[50] Although women were not drafted along with men (ages 18 to 25), they continued to serve in the army and made up an estimated 45 percent of the popular militia (out of a total of about 50,000 members in 1984) as well as half the membership in the Sandinista Defense Committees.

Reagan Storms the Hill

With an eye to congressional concern over escalating U.S. involvement in Central America, Assistant Secretary Enders talked of exploring negotiations with the increasingly powerful Salvadoran guerrillas while continuing military aid to the Salvadoran regime. His "two-track strategy" was adamantly opposed by Casey, Kirkpatrick, Weinberger and National Security Adviser William Clark. Even the appearance of negotiations with the revolutionaries would award them too much legitimacy and detract from the campaign against Nicaragua.

"The feeling never was that we could negotiate an agreement on El Salvador or Nicaragua," said a high U.S. official. "Notwithstanding, we decided in February that we needed to move on the diplomatic side to deflect the perception of our only going for a military solution."

U.S. officials acknowledged "that the guerrillas are now getting most of their arms from within El Salvador—by capturing or buying them—but insist that the flow from Nicaragua is essential to the guerrillas' maintaining their current level of operations." Incredibly, U.S. officials said the "surveillance operation for Nicaragua is even greater than the one for the Soviet Union. 'We can hear a toilet flush in Managua,' an intelligence analyst said."[51] Asked about the lack of evidence to substantiate administration claims, officials gave the usual excuses about jeopardizing intelligence sources. These mysterious sources were evidently reporting on magic arms shipments that could be seen but not captured.

Of course, administration officials had to insist that the alleged arms flow from Nicaragua was essential lest they jeopardize support for U.S. intervention. They could not admit that, unlike the contras, El Salvador's FMLN-FDR was a militarily and politically effective, popularly supported revolutionary force. By late 1983, the revolutionaries controlled one-fourth of El Salvador's territory, governing liberated zones in Chalatenango, Morazan, San Vicente, Usulutan, Cuscatlan and San Miguel.

Reagan raised the political stakes on Central America in an April 27 speech to a joint session of Congress: "El Salvador is nearer to Texas than Texas is to Miami. Nicaragua is just as close to Miami, San Antonio, San Diego, and Tucson as those cities are to Washington where we are gathered tonight."

Nicaragua, claimed Reagan, "has rejected our repeated peace efforts. It has broken its promises to us, to the Organization of American States, and, most important of all, to the people of Nicaragua...The Sandinista revolution turned out to be just an exchange of one set of autocratic rulers for another...Even worse than its predecessor, it is helping Cuba and the Soviets to destabilize our hemisphere...Violence has been Nicaragua's most important export to the world."

Reagan continued with war-is-peace rhetoric: "We do not seek its overthrow...We have attempted to have a dialogue with the government of Nicaragua but it persists in its efforts to spread violence. We should not—and we will not—protect the Nicaraguan government from the anger of its own people. But we should, through diplomacy, offer an alternative. And, as Nicaragua ponders its options, we can and will—with all the resources of diplomacy—protect each country of Central America from the danger of war...Nicaragua's dictatorial junta...likes to pretend they are today being attacked by forces based in Honduras. The fact is, it is Nicaragua's government that threatens Honduras, not the reverse...

"Must we just accept the destabilization of an entire region from the Panama Canal to Mexico on our southern border? Must we sit by while independent nations of this hemisphere are integrated into the most aggressive empire the modern world has seen?...I do not believe there is a majority in the Congress or the country that counsels passivity, resignation, defeatism, in the face of this challenge to freedom and security in our hemisphere."

In early May, Reagan began referring to the contras as freedom fighters and publicly acknowledged U.S. support. At a May 5 White House press conference, Reagan said, "Now, if they [the Congress] want to tell us that we can give money and do the same things we've been doing—money, giving, providing subsistence and so forth to these people directly and making it overt instead of covert—that's all right with me." Questioned about his use of the term freedom fighters, Reagan said "I just used the word, I guess, 'freedom fighters' because the fact that we know that the thing that brought those people together is the desire, as I said, for the same revolutionary principles that they once fought [sic] and have been betrayed in."[52]

Reagan's scare tactics were damaging Nicaragua's image in the United States, but they weren't generating majority support for the contras. *Business Week*, which could hardly be accused of pro-communist sympathies, editorialized: "In Nicaragua, the Administration has launched the U.S. on a high-risk adventure—as House and Senate intelligence oversight committees belatedly realize—by financing, arming, and training an army of Nicaraguan exiles to invade the country from Honduras. The Administration's suggestion that such an attack will persuade Managua's Sandinist government to create a more democratic and pluralist society seems implausible: Wars often radicalize regimes and nations rather than induce them to moderate their policies. And if the objective is to topple the Sandinist government, which so far has managed to contain the invasion mainly with militia, the Administration may find itself facing the now-familiar dilemma of having to escalate the conflict or face a serious political defeat in the eyes of the American public and of the world...What the Administration must do, in fact, is to halt its support of such attacks before they trigger even wider conflicts and more serious destabilization in Central America."[53]

A companion piece questioned Reagan's portrayal of Nicaragua as having failed to fulfill the pledges of the revolution: "Actually, the Sandinists' performance on their pledges is mixed. *La Prensa*, the leading newspaper, has been strictly censored since March, 1982, when the government reacted to anti-Sandinist, or *contra*, assaults by imposing a state of emergency...Broadcasts of Radio Catolica, the station of the Managua archdiocese, are now censored for what the government considers political content...But the church, as a religious institution, is stronger than it was before the revolution, and there is no government interference with religious teaching in Roman Catholic schools—the country's best—in which 30% of Nicaraguan pupils are enrolled. Two priests serve as government ministers, and many priests, as well as large members of the faithful, continue to support the Sandinists. 'The conflicts between church and state are political, not religious,' says Enrique Alvarado, a supporter of the Sandinists who is vice-rector of the University of Central America, a Jesuit institution in Managua. 'The church hierarchy had its own idea of the revolution, which was a replacement of Somoza, leaving the institutions more or less intact.' "

On the economy, *Business Week* observed that "the Sandinists have also left 70% of the economy in private hands—including an Exxon refinery, product distribution networks of Texaco and Socal, and a General Mills joint venture that produces more than half of the country's flour...Private businessmen complain of price and currency controls, a government export monopoly, competition for small retailers from government-sponsored retail outlets, and other restrictions."

Regarding human rights, *Business Week* noted, "The number of political prisoners is estimated at around 200...And five people disappeared in March, believed to have been detained by government security forces. Bad as this is, it is 'equal to the best day in El Salvador in the last 18 months,' notes a Western diplomat."[54]

And, fortunately, it wasn't as bad as *Business Week* reported. According to Americas Watch, a total of 31 persons were reported disappeared by the CPDH (the anti-Sandinista Permanent Human Rights Commission) during 1983. But unlike El Salvador—with 535 disappearances and 5,143 known political killings of civilian noncombatants by the Salvadoran armed forces and associated paramilitary forces recorded by the Church human rights office, *Tutela Legal*, in 1983—"disappeared" is not a synonym for murdered.

In most Nicaraguan cases, disappeared means an unreported arrest. According to Americas Watch, "the establishment of a complaint office at the Ministry of the Interior, as well as procedures established within the DSGE [Security Police] had a positive effect, as arrests that take place in Managua and other large cities are accounted for almost immediately...Together with the high proportion of those who disappear who later reappear, this leads us to believe, as we stated in our two earlier reports, that the [Nicaraguan government] does not have a centrally directed policy of forced disappearances as the phenomenon has been defined in relation to events that have happened on a large scale in El Salvador, Guatemala, Chile and Argentina at different times since the early 1970s."

Americas Watch observed that "most of the hundreds of arrests that have taken place since the establishment of the state of emergency seem related to the violent activity displayed against the government by forces operating from outside Nicaragua and within the territory, with covert but undeniable support from the United States."

Americas Watch called on Nicaragua to improve its human rights record while noting areas where it had already done so. It pointed out that Nicaragua is visited frequently by human rights observers and that government human rights officials try to facilitate such inquiries. "Americas Watch is pleased to acknowledge that some of the recommendations contained in our earlier reports have been taken into account, particularly in the creation of a central registry of arrests. The [Nicaraguan government] is even more receptive to the work of intergovernmental organizations with which it is connected by treaty organizations. For example, Nicaragua is the only country that has made a full report to the UN Committee on Human Rights when its case has been discussed; all of the few other states that have accepted the jurisdiction of this office of the UN make cursory presentations to that body."

Looking at contra human rights abuses, Americas Watch observed that "in the Northwestern mountain areas, the FDN has engaged repeatedly in kidnappings, torture and murder of unarmed civilians, mostly in villages and farm cooperatives...There is also no case reported yet of the FDN taking prisoners among the members of the Sandinista Army or militias that they claim to encounter frequently." MISURA and MISURASATA "have engaged in forceful recruitment of refugees [in Honduras], through the use of relief assistance and by violent means, to the point where international voluntary agencies operating in the area have taken measures to avoid involvement in such practices."[55]

In his speech to Congress, Reagan accused the Sandinistas of breaking promises to the OAS. The charge would be repeated often in coming years. It refers specifically to a July 12, 1979 letter that the provisional junta sent to the OAS secretary general with its plan to achieve peace and establish the Government of National Reconstruction. The letter was not a formal commitment to the OAS and OAS officers have never treated it as such. It is certainly not a treaty that U.S. officials could legitimately point to as a test of Nicaragua's compliance with treaty agreements.

Leaving aside the question of legal standing, contrary to Reagan's charges, the new Nicaraguan government did fulfill its stated intentions to prevent extralegal punishment of National Guardsmen and Somocistas, to allow Nicaraguans not accused of crimes to leave the country and to hold elections (local elections in 1980, national elections in 1984).[56] Moreover, Nicaragua has been open to international human rights organizations as indicated above. The Reagan administration used the bogus OAS charge as one more tool to delegitimize the Nicaraguan government and divert attention from the real violation of OAS commitments: U.S. violation of the nonintervention articles of the OAS charter to which it is legally bound under U.S. and international law.

Sticks and Stones

An administration list of possible diplomatic and military moves was leaked to the press in April 1983 along with the idea that the United States was "building a case against the Sandinista government that eventually could enable the United States to declare Nicaragua a second Cuba and a threat to inter-American security." Administration officials talked of a possible second Cuban missile crisis, suggesting that Nicaragua was considering deploying Cuban troops and even basing Soviet nuclear missiles on Nicaraguan soil.

Among the "diplomatic" options were: denial of a visa for Interior Minister Tomas Borge; new economic sanctions, including a reduction or cutoff of Nicaragua's sugar quota; pressure on U.S. and other Western banks to deny new credits; a break in diplomatic relations or an indefinite delay in the appointment of Nicaragua's new ambassador to Washington; pressure on key Latin American countries such as Mexico and Brazil "to shift their positions on Nicaragua, along with reminders of U.S. aid last year when their economies began to crumble under the pressure of foreign debts"; an emergency session of the OAS to seek a vote to condemn Nicaragua or invoke the Rio treaty to sanction military action in case Cuban forces or Soviet jet fighters are discovered in Nicaragua; request for a UN Security Council session to declare an international crisis if Soviet missiles are detected in Nicaragua; and a new negotiations effort.

Military options included an open declaration of support for the contras; selective U.S. air strikes against Soviet- or Cuban-built military installations in Nicaragua if MIGs are acquired; a blockade of Nicaragua, and perhaps Cuba, and deployment of U.S. combat forces and jet fighters in Honduras if Soviet nuclear missiles are deployed.[57]

Asked about the possibility of allowing the Soviet Union to install nuclear missiles, Tomas Borge was unequivocal: "We made a revolution to liberate our country from foreign domination. Neither would we permit it, in the first place, nor has it ever been proposed by the Soviet Union. We have said repeatedly that there will be no foreign military bases in our country."[58]

Nicaragua made no moves to realize U.S. fantasies of a second Cuban missile crisis, but Washington carried out some of the above options in short order. Nicaragua's sugar quota was cut by 90 percent on May 10. Borge was denied a visa in mid May to take up speaking invitations at Harvard and Johns Hopkins Universities. Mexico and other Latin American countries were pressured. In June, the United States officially declared its opposition to all multilateral loans for Nicaragua when it vetoed a $2.2 million road-building loan from the Inter-American Development Bank (IDB) which the 42 other members had approved.[59] By then Washington had successfully shut off World Bank funding.

On June 5, Nicaragua expelled three employees of the U.S. Embassy in Managua, accusing them of being CIA agents working under diplomatic cover to destabilize the government. Nicaragua presented evidence of a plot to assassinate Foreign Minister D'Escoto with a poisoned bottle of Benedictine liquor. D'Escoto was reportedly targeted because his vocation as a priest gave the revolution too much respectability in international affairs. Nicaragua also accused the United States of sponsoring terrorist commando squads and working with conservative political parties, unions and media to destabilize the government.[60]

Using the expulsion of the three U.S. officials as an excuse, Washington closed down all six of Nicaragua's consulates in the United States and expelled 21 consular officials. The Nicaraguan government identified the move as part of an economic boycott because the consulates handled virtually all of Nicaragua's $300 million annual trade with the United States.[61]

On the diplomatic front, Special Envoy Richard Stone (serving until February 1984) went to Central America in June on what was widely seen as one in a series of diplomatic missions designed mainly for public relations. Stone, who was a registered lobbyist for the Guatemalan dictatorship after losing his Florida Senate seat in 1980, put "democracy" in Nicaragua at the top of the list of U.S. concerns, saying without it military agreements would "require minute verification." A State Department official acknowledged, "For some, to insist on democracy means not to accept a Marxist-Leninist government. Thus it is a code word for overthrow."[62]

D'Escoto recalled one of his last meetings with Richard Stone in Managua. At one point Stone asked, " 'Father, do you think that it really would be possible for both of our nations to normalize relations?' And I said, 'I think it not only could be, but should be. And all it takes is for both of us to want it. I assure you…that Nicaragua wants to normalize relations…I think that the place to begin is by committing both of our governments to respect in the most categorical way the principles established in the charters of the United Nations and the Organization of American States, both of which we have signed in our laws. That is to say, to regulate our relations with the…principles of international law.'

" 'Father, that is your problem,' he [Stone] says. 'It must be your background.' [They are] always emphasizing the fact that I'm not a professional politician…He says, 'But now you have been in politics long enough…to have come to realize that politics is made of concrete things…You talk about international law, Father. That is philosophy.' As if to say poetry, or something optional, I don't know. He says international law 'is philosophy.'

"He says, 'The contras,' and he looked me straight in the eye, 'the contras, they give you a lot of difficulty, don't they Father.' Exactly those words, I remember…And I said, 'They surely do, but they wouldn't for too long…if your government would stop financing them and arming them and directing them.' And he said, 'Well, I guess you are hopeless. There you go again, philosophy…The only reality is that they have been, that they are and that they will continue to receive aid…'

"And then he says to me, 'You seem to be an intelligent person.' Intelligent or rational…'And intelligent people,' he says, 'don't like to have difficulties. You have already acknowledged that the contras do give you a headache. And therefore presumably you…would prefer not to have this headache.' And, 'You should do as we say.' That crude, 'You should do as we say.' And then he says, 'You will see how almost by magic the problem will disappear.' And I could have almost imagined someone with a hat pulling out a rabbit…

"In other words, I could see the United States as this great big power telling us fall down on your knees and worship us, and say thy will be done Uncle Sam because you're big and powerful. You have a huge nuclear arsenal and therefore we accept to bow down on our knees and burn incense before the imperial idol. And for having refused to burn this incense our country is condemned to death."

The United States, D'Escoto told me, has "become accustomed to a modality of relationship with Latin America, a modality of relationship which not only does it regard as a God-given right to maintain, but what is more important, they find it difficult to envision how they can survive without this modality of relationship. This is the situation that we have had with...the former colonial powers...And the owners of slaves, it must be the same way...Those who inherited that system found it difficult to envision how they could live without it...When [the United States] acts the way it acts against Nicaragua it's not because of any particular hatred of Nicaragua, it's because of fear. People can do awful things in fear...

"And they feel that if Nicaragua is able to get away with it then other countries will follow suit. And in behaving the way they are...against Nicaragua, they're trying to send a clear message to Latin America. And the message is, 'Don't try to get loose from our control. It will be to no avail, because in the end, after much suffering, you will have to end up crying uncle.' This is the message. And Nicaragua's response, of course, and this is what angers them, is 'Patria libre o morir.' And this is no slogan...although Patrick Henry was an American, they don't really believe it. They think that's only from history books."[63]

Managua by Christmas?

In May 1983, Casey and Enders secretly told the Intelligence Committees that the contras had a good chance of overthrowing the Nicaraguan government by the end of the year. According to a Republican member of the Senate committee, "We were told that there are 7,000 rebels and their numbers are growing. The scenario they presented has the rebels picking up more and more popular support, which will produce desertions in the Nicaraguan military, all setting the stage for a drive on Managua that forces the Government out of power. They think it can work." A House committee member said, "They were telling us that, in effect, if we cut off assistance to the rebels now we would be responsible for aborting a great chance to reverse Communist gains in Central America." A senior national security official filled in more details. A pincer-type assault on Managua would involve an FDN drive from the north, an eastern front of Miskito forces and a southern front led by Pastora.[64] A 1982 internal CIA planning memo had set a Managua-by-Christmas timetable.[65]

Casey immediately denied predicting that the contras could overthrow the Nicaraguan government by year's end.[66] But Frank McNeil, then ambassador to Costa Rica, participated in a strategy session called by Casey in the spring of 1983, where the same assertion was made; McNeil rejected it as nonsense. When McNeil retired in February 1987 as deputy director of the State Department's Bureau of Intelligence and Research, he accused Assistant Secretary of State Elliott Abrams of "McCarthyism" in treating analytical differences, especially over contra effectiveness, as disloyalty. McNeil wrote that although in many respects Central America is different from Vietnam, in Washington "echoes of Vietnam abound. Then, as now, improper or illegal actions were committed in the name of national security and liberties taken with intelligence. Then, as now, those running the war, arguing that victory was around the corner, deceived themselves and the president. Four years ago this spring, I heard a senior CIA official in all seriousness assert that the contras would threaten Managua by Christmas of that year."[67]

The House Intelligence Committee voted on May 3, 1983 to cut off money for the covert operation. It recommended instead that Congress authorize $80 million in overt aid to Central American allies for the apparently immortal objective of arms interdiction. The Senate Intelligence Committee did not concur. It voted to continue funding the covert war until September, at which time the president would have to submit a new finding for approval.

The House Intelligence Committee published a report on May 13 stating, finally, that the contra program was aimed not at arms interdiction, but at overthrowing the Nicaraguan government. It asserted: "If there ever was a formula for U.S. policy failure in Central America, it would involve two elements: (1) acts that could be characterized as U.S. intervention in Nicaragua; and (2) an alliance with the followers of Somoza. Both characterizations can now be made."[68]

Still, the arms interdiction fiction persisted. U.S. Ambassador to Nicaragua Tony Quainton had told U.S. citizens in March that "massive [he amended that to substantial] amounts of arms are going by dugout canoes across the Gulf of Fonseca. These cannot be detected from satellite."[69] Despite declassified U.S. reconnaissance photos showing all sorts of wooden structures, from small sheds to "Soviet-style obstacle courses," the administration expected people to believe that dugout canoes represented the latest in stealth technology. As former CIA analyst David MacMichael put it, the purported arms flow is a "talisman…you must continue to insist on it even in the face of no evidence whatsoever."[70]

Besides infrared and other surveillance techniques, canoe hunters could use modern night-vision scopes and old-fashioned searchlights. The CIA sponsored a flotilla of radar-equipped armed speedboats—known as Piranhas—ostensibly to interdict arms shipments through the twenty-mile wide Gulf of Fonseca. According to their Honduran commander, Captain Gonzalez, the crews had not intercepted a single weapons shipment in almost a year of patrolling. "To be honest, I don't believe that Nicaraguan boats are crossing the gulf to El Salvador," he said. Gonzales added (with a nod to the talisman), "I think it's more probable that their boats are swinging out into the Pacific and moving toward land well past the gulf."[71]

At the end of May, Enders was ousted; he became ambassador to Spain. White House officials said privately that he was not tough enough.[72] Policy was being driven by hardest-liners Casey, Kirkpatrick and National Security Adviser William Clark, the former judge from California who had acted as the Reagan loyalists' watchdog in his previous post as Haig's deputy. With zero foreign policy experience,

Clark was motivated primarily, in *Time's* words, "by a nearly fanatic devotion to Reagan's interests and a visceral anti-communism." He saw Congress' role as one of ratifying presidential decisions.[73] Langhorne Motley, an Alaska developer serving as ambassador to Brazil, became the new assistant secretary of state for Inter-American Affairs. Also, General Paul Gorman replaced General Wallace Nutting as chief of the Southern Command.

FDN forces failed again to capture Jalapa, or any other city, town or village, and establish a provisional government to be recognized by the United States. Nicaragua dubbed 1983 "The Year of Struggle for Peace and Sovereignty." The contras would not be celebrating Christmas in Managua.

In late June 1983, intelligence analysts made a new prediction: in six months, contra forces would control almost one-third of the population in rural areas and more than half the national territory. But they would have difficulty holding large population centers and would not be able to overthrow the Nicaraguan government in "the foreseeable future."[74] They were right about the latter points.

There was a political advantage to the more pessimistic prediction. In a bizarre twist to the administration's contorted logic, contra supporters argued that the program complied with the Boland amendment because the contras were incapable of overthrowing the Nicaraguan government.

Trampling Democracy

"Support for democratic resistance within Nicaragua does not exist." That was the view of the Defense Department as stated in a leaked July 1983 NSC strategy paper.[75] An extensive analysis of the document in the *New York Times* did not even mention this assessment, much less attempt to explain its implications.[76] The only thing the contras were resisting was the will of the Nicaraguan people to carry the revolution forward.

Assessing the military situation in Nicaragua and El Salvador, the NSC document stated, "The situation in Central America is nearing a critical point." It "is still possible to accomplish U.S. objectives without the direct use of U.S. troops (although the credible threat of such use is needed to deter overt Soviet/Cuban intervention), *provided* that the U.S. takes timely and effective action." (NSC italics.)

Regarding Nicaragua specifically, the NSC stated, "No threat should be made [without] willingness to follow through [with] military force." It recommended "relaxation/nonrenewal of all legislative restrictions"; "a comprehensive diplomatic strategy" in Central America "with specific attention to the isolation of Nicaragua"; and pressing "Western European governments at the highest level to cease financial support for the Sandinistas."

The NSC document noted that "Honduras is pivotal to U.S. policy"; it "has openly aligned itself with the U.S." Actions to be taken included increased military assistance to Honduras and military exercises, including the construction and improvement of Honduran air and naval facilities and the possible prepositioning of

U.S. military stocks "to obviate diversion of critical U.S. airlift in an emergency." Israel and Venezuela were given as examples of countries to be enlisted in providing military assistance and aiding so-called civic action projects.

There was inter-agency agreement on the need for an "invigorated strategy" to build congressional support, specifically through the appointment of a bipartisan commission. Henry Kissinger was later chosen to lead it.

"Reagan Plans Rise In Military Moves in Latin America—Link to War Games, Plan Calls for Preparing a Possible Quarantine of the Nicaraguans" read the *New York Times* headline of July 23. A companion piece described Honduras' role in U.S. strategy. The lead article made clear that air, sea and land maneuvers beginning in August would lay the groundwork for an expanded U.S. military presence and a possible blockade. "The plan approved by Mr. Reagan does not envisage any immediate combat role for United States forces, but does call for making preparations so that American forces can be swiftly called into action if necessary."

The article ended on a seemingly innocuous note: "The officials said planning for the Navy called for some carrier training operations near Grenada, an island nation in the Caribbean, and off the coast of Suriname, a small South American country that was once a Dutch colony."[77] Two CIA plans to overthrow the government of Suriname were squashed by Congress in 1981 and 1982.[78] Grenada was another story (discussed in the next chapter).

On July 24, the *New York Times* ran a front-page story: "Efforts to Oust The Sandinistas Held Ineffective." The article said that "after more than a year of intense activity, the Honduran-based rebels...have failed to achieve significant military gains or to cause a serious political threat to the Government." While designed to proceed rapidly, based on the assumption that it would gain wide popular support, the contra war "instead was becoming more like a long but very limited war of attrition." The open question was whether the United States would intensify direct actions in an effort to achieve the objective of overthrowing the Nicaraguan government.[79]

These high-profile administration leaks fueled congressional fears of open-ended U.S. involvement. The House voted 228-195 on July 28 to cut off contra support by September 30, adopting legislation cosponsored by Edward Boland and Clement Zablocki (D-WI). The full bill authorized $80 million in overt aid for weapons interdiction, still endorsing the administration assumption that Nicaragua was "exporting revolution."

As Rep. Barnes put it, "People are trying to find a way to be on both sides of the issue." The more conservative Rep. Dan Mica (D-FL) said, "Many of us believe the President is acting illegally under United States laws, but we also think the Nicaragua thing will eventually become a major problem for this hemisphere."[80]

The administration still had the support of the Republican-controlled Senate and knew the House was vulnerable to aggressive lobbying. Right after losing the July vote, Reagan approved a CIA plan authorizing expansion of the contras to between 12,000 and 15,000. The plan emphasized the importance of destroying economic installations and would rely heavily on the direct involvement of U.S. personnel.

While counting on congressional acquiescence, the administration also pursued contra support outside the budget appropriations process. Israeli aid has already been mentioned, as has U.S. aid passing through Honduras under the cover of military maneuvers. In June, Reagan authorized "Operation Elephant Herd," another secret CIA-Pentagon plan to bypass congressional funding restrictions. Under the program, implemented in December, the Pentagon set aside $12 million worth of military equipment—including three Cessna 0-2 observation planes that were modified to carry rockets by Summit Aviation of Delaware—and declared it to be "surplus to requirements" of the military. "Surplus" material is considered to have no dollar value and thus could be transferred to the CIA for the contras without being counted as part of the $24 million in total military aid allowed by Congress for 1984.

Government officials said "Project Elephant Herd was not a unique operation. They say congressional restrictions on military aid—not just to contras, but to many countries and rebel groups—are frequently circumvented in this way." "Congress may occasionally get angry that Defense is imaginative," one official said. "They'd write a new law to try to tie us down, and within five minutes somebody would find a way to drive an elephant through it. That's been going on forever."[81]

Gunboast Diplomacy

Big Pine II maneuvers with Honduras—"probably the longest military exercise ever"—began August 5 and ended February 8, 1984.[82] From late July until September 1983, the United States conducted three major naval maneuvers off the Atlantic and Pacific Coasts of Central America, involving nineteen ships including the carrier USS Ranger with 70 aircraft aboard. Another "no notice" naval exercise began in early November. Newsweek heralded the naval maneuvers in a cover story: "Gunboat Diplomacy: Reagan Gets Tougher with Nicaragua." Time's cover story a week later was "Central America: The Big Stick Approach."[83]

At the peak of Big Pine II, which involved artillery and field training maneuvers, an amphibious assault landing and practice air strikes, there were 6,000 U.S. military personnel in Honduras. About 5,000 Honduran soldiers were trained. Construction was carried out without direct congressional appropriations, utilizing instead the Joint Chiefs' military exercise fund and operating and maintenance funds. At Aguacate, used as a contra supply base in central Honduras, U.S. Army Engineers lengthened a dirt and stone runway to 8,000 feet and built huts and a water system. At San Lorenzo, in southern Honduras, close to El Salvador and near the key land route into Nicaragua, they built a 4,000-foot dirt runway, water wells and wooden huts. At Trujillo on the northern Caribbean coast, near the major port of Puerto Castilla, Navy Seabees extended a concrete runway to 4,000 feet. About a mile away they built Camp Sea Eagle with enough huts to house 800 troops. In addition, the United States signed an agreement with Honduras providing for construction of and access to airfields at Golason Airfield at La Ceiba on the northern coast; La Mesa at

San Pedro Sula in northwest Honduras near the Guatemalan border; and Palmerola Air Base, near Comayagua in central Honduras.

When the maneuvers began in August, officials in El Salvador and Washington were saying that the flow of Salvadoran rebel military supplies from outside the country was only a trickle. Salvadoran officers did not dispute the FMLN's claim that they were capturing sufficient weapons to outfit their forces. And middlemen were reportedly selling the guerrillas arms from the major army and air force ammunition dump at Ilopango Air Base. Still, officials insisted that guerrilla success depended on outside supplies of ammunition, radio batteries and medicine. The shipments across the Gulf of Fonseca were history; now the supply was supposedly by light aircraft. Yet, with all the U.S. surveillance, "there has not been a single report of an aircraft originating in Nicaragua being shot down or even seen by Government forces here."[84]

It was reported in early August that "while reluctant to commit U.S. troops to combat in Central America, most Pentagon brass think they'd win in a walk once committed." In explaining why a Nicaragua invasion would be winnable while Vietnam was not, the Pentagon assumptions ranged from optimistic to racist: Nicaragua's neighbors "would side with the United States…'We can shut them off without a supply siphon like the Ho Chi Minh Trail.' " Any Soviet or Cuban "temptation to intervene would be daunted by the American naval forces required to support a U.S. invasion: two carrier battle groups each on the Caribbean and Pacific sides of Nicaragua." Nicaragua's "regular force of 22,000 without air support beyond old surplus U.S. trainers and with a navy limited to shore patrol craft, could not offer meaningful resistance to a simultaneous U.S. heliborne assault and amphibious landing. If spread out on alert in response to American exercises on the Caribbean and Pacific sides, plus ground exercises as planned in eastern and western Honduras, resistance would be even more feeble."

As for the threat of a regionalized war, "guerrilla forces in El Salvador, like Sandinista troops once their command posts and major concentrations are overwhelmed, will yield easily. 'Latin American troops don't have heart in any kind of war where there's a lot of killing; that's their history,' said a Marine colonel. 'They're not like the Asiatics.' "[85]

7

Shockwaves

At dawn on September 8, 1983, two small planes crossed Nicaraguan airspace and appeared over Managua. One dropped its bombs in a residential neighborhood, near the home of Foreign Minister Miguel D'Escoto, who happened to be away at a Contadora meeting. It escaped. The other plane attacked the international airport and adjacent air base with two jerry-rigged 150-pound bombs. Brought down by antiaircraft fire, it crashed into the control tower. Several people were wounded and part of the civilian passenger terminal was demolished. As *El Nuevo Diario* reported it, hundreds of waiting passengers, family and friends narrowly escaped a "frightful death."[1] I happened to be in Managua for an international education conference. The air strikes were a lesson in terrorism.

Eden Pastora's ARDE forces claimed responsibility for the attack. Although both pilots died in the crash, documents identified one as a Miami resident and former pilot for the Nicaraguan airline, AERONICA. The other was a deserter from the Nicaraguan Air Force. Their twin-engine, propeller-driven Cessna was registered to Investair Leasing Corporation of McLean, Virginia. Investair was managed by a former top official of Intermountain Aviation, a company once owned by the CIA, and its marketing director was formerly secretary-treasurer of the now-defunct CIA proprietary Air America.[2]

On September 19, President Reagan signed a new Nicaragua finding, authorizing the provision of "support, equipment and training assistance to Nicaraguan paramilitary resistance groups." To mollify Congress, the newly stated objectives were "inducing the Sandinista Government...to enter into negotiations with its neighbors" and "putting pressure on the Sandinistas and their allies to cease provision of arms, training, command and control facilities and sanctuary to leftist guerrillas in El Salvador."[3]

CIA Director Casey and Secretary of State Shultz presented the finding to the congressional Intelligence Committees on September 20, along with a request for $45 million in funding for 1984. Instead of talking about interdicting weapons, administration officials spoke of "pressuring" the Sandinistas to negotiate and stop "exporting revolution." With an eye to the Boland amendment, Congress was told there was "no thought of the administration backing the insurgents in trying to overthrow the Sandinista government."[4] Meanwhile, the CIA implemented plans to use U.S. agents and military personnel for direct attacks inside Nicaragua.

On October 3, the Nicaraguan Army shot down a DC-3 on a contra supply mission. Three men were captured. At a press conference, the pilot said he had flown nine supply missions in two months. The missions were directed from Tegucigalpa by CIA contra coordinator Raymond Doty (known as Colonel Raymond)—a former Army Special Forces lieutenant colonel who was a paramilitary trainer in the CIA war in Laos—in conjunction with "Major West" at the Aguacate Air Base.[5] It would be three more years before a downed contra supply plane drew the attention it deserved in the United States.

Trained Piranhas

CIA Latin America chief Dewey Clarridge met with FDN leaders in Tegucigalpa in July 1983. "As he sat among us," recalled Edgar Chamorro, "he reminded me of a proconsul come to tell his subjects what to do and how to do it. I have never witnessed such arrogance while working with a foreigner." The only time the CIA's subjects in the FDN directorate all met together in Honduras was when Clarridge came to town.[6]

The CIA was frustrated by the contras' poor showing on the battlefield and ready to take more direct action. As Chamorro testified to the World Court, "Clarridge told us that the C.I.A. had decided that something must be done to cut off Nicaragua's oil supplies, because without oil the Nicaraguan military would be immobilized and its capacity to resist our forces would be drastically reduced. Clarridge spoke of various alternatives. He said the Agency was considering a plan 'to sink ships' bringing oil to Nicaragua, but that one problem with this plan was that if a ship belonging to the Soviet Union were sunk it could trigger a serious international incident. Clarridge said that the C.I.A. was also considering an attack on Nicaragua's sole oil refinery, located near Managua. According to Clarridge, however, the refinery was located in a densely populated area, and the civilian casualties resulting from such an attack would be politically counterproductive. Finally, Clarridge said that the Agency had decided on a plan to attack the oil pipelines at Puerto Sandino, on Nicaragua's Pacific Coast, where the oil tankers delivering oil to Nicaragua discharge their cargo."[7]

In September, the contras began the Plan Marathon offensive against Ocotal and Somoto near the northwestern border with Honduras, supported by task force operations in the Jinotega and Matagalpa regions. On October 18, 300 FDN troops "devastated Pantasma, Jinotega, destroying the school, two peasant cooperatives, the bank, the Agrarian Reform office, a sawmill, the coffee warehouse, three foodstuffs dispensaries, and eight tractors. The contras murdered 40 citizens; seven of the town's 20 civilian defenders were killed trying to fend off the attack. Material losses came to 34 million cordobas." Adolfo Calero was quoted in the *Miami Herald* a few days later, promising, "There will be more Pantasmas."[8]

Like previous contra offensives, Operation Marathon ended in failure. It "underlined both the contras' incompetence and the Agency's misguided expectations," observed Christopher Dickey.[9] Before it was over, Washington began the direct actions promised in July.

The day of the airport bombing, September 8, the United States launched a series of assaults on oil installations by blowing up the pipeline at Puerto Sandino. "Although the F.D.N. had nothing whatsoever to do with this operation," said Chamorro, "we were instructed by the C.I.A. to publicly claim responsibility in order to cover the C.I.A.'s involvement. We did."[10]

The heavily-armed Piranha speedboats, which fared poorly against phantom arms shipments, proved effective in carrying out rocket attacks and transporting saboteurs from a secret U.S. "mother ship" anchored off the coast of Nicaragua. American covert agents worked with specially-trained Latin operatives known as "Unilaterally Controlled Latin Assets," or UCLAs. Recruited from El Salvador, Honduras, Argentina, Chile, Ecuador and Bolivia, the UCLAs were trained in unconventional warfare (e.g. underwater demolitions) by U.S. Special Forces in Panama, Honduras and the United States. "Our mission was to sabotage ports, refineries, boats, bridges," said one Honduran UCLA, "and try to make it appear that the contras had done it." He also said that one of their missions was to blow up a building in Managua in April 1984 during a meeting of Sandinista leaders, but it was aborted when explosives failed to reach the hit team.[11]

A Piranha rocket attack on October 10, 1983 put thousands of Nicaraguan civilians in mortal danger. The target was Corinto, Nicaragua's largest commercial port, on the northern Pacific coast. Five large oil and gasoline tanks were destroyed (including an Esso/Exxon tank), igniting over three million gallons of fuel. Tons of medical supplies and stores of export coffee and shrimp were also lost. Some 23,000 Corinto residents had to be evacuated. Over 100 people were injured. According to one of the Mexican engineers sent to help put out the fires, had more flammable products in the area been set ablaze, "not a soul would have survived." Nicaragua angrily protested to the U.S. government, saying "this type of terrorist act, which could not be carried off without advice and funding of the U.S. administration, constitutes one of the most violent forms of contempt for human life."[12] Exxon announced that it would no longer rent oil tankers for the transport of Mexican oil to Nicaragua.

Casey was "elated" with the Corinto attack and immediately showed reconnaissance photos to Reagan.[13] The FDN claimed responsibility as instructed, but within days administration officials confirmed, at least partially, the U.S. role for reporters. At an October 19 press conference, a reporter asked Reagan, "regarding the recent rebel attacks on a Nicaraguan oil depot, is it proper for the C.I.A. to be involved in planning such attacks and supplying equipment for air raids, and do the American people have a right to be informed about any C.I.A. role?"

"I think covert actions have been a part of government and a part of government's responsibilities for as long as there's been a government," replied Reagan. "I'm not going to comment on what, if any, connections such activities might have had with what has been going on or with some of the specific operations down there, but I do believe in the right of a country when it believes that its interests are best served to practice covert activity and then—while you people may have a right to know, you can't let your people know without letting the wrong people know—those that are in opposition to what you're doing."[14] The Nicaraguans, of course, already knew the United States was behind the attacks. It was the American people whose information was censored.

Pentagon Specials: Yellow Fruit and Night Stalkers

The CIA was not the only agency behind the sabotage missions. As Defense Secretary Weinberger stated in a secret 1983 memorandum to the president, the Pentagon would "provide a wide range of logistical support and manpower to assist CIA covert operations in Central America, including support of Nicaraguan rebels."[15] That support didn't end with the Boland amendment, and it went far beyond surveillance and contra support via military maneuvers. The Pentagon's Special Operations Division and Army Intelligence Support Activity (ISA) played critical roles.

The Special Operations Division, first headed by Colonel James Longhofer, operated "in the black," under strict cover within the office of the Army's deputy chief of staff for operations (DCSOPS). It was appropriated more than $325 million between 1981 and 1983. "By the fall of 1983," wrote Seymour Hersh, "the Army, working through Longhofer's unit had become an invaluable asset" in the covert war against Nicaragua. "The men in Special Operations were instrumental in ferrying Army Special Forces personnel under cover to Honduras, where they helped C.I.A. operatives train specially recruited Honduran troops for bloody hit-and-run operations into Nicaragua. They supplied Army rapid-firing cannons known as 'bushmasters' to the small boats used by the C.I.A. to mine harbors and destroy oil depots during a series of controversial raids on Nicaragua's east coast in the fall of 1983. One of Longhofer's helicopter mechanics was aboard the C.I.A. ship that directed the 1983 mining of harbors inside Nicaragua…The C.I.A.'s attacks caused a political uproar when they were disclosed to Congress the next spring. But the Army's role was known to only a few members of the Congressional intelligence subcommittees, who said nothing."[16]

The Army and the CIA established a special aviation company called Seaspray (later renamed Quasar Talent) in March 1981, headquartered at Fort Eustis, Virginia; another secret headquarters in Tampa, Florida supported Central America operations. Seaspray undertook direct attacks on Nicaraguan targets such as airfields.[17]

In April 1981, the Army established the 160th Special Operations Aviation Battalion, a secret helicopter training and support unit based at Fort Campbell, Kentucky, which became widely exposed after the invasion of Grenada. Longhofer said the purpose of the new 160th unit was "deception…We set it up so the media would think the 160th was the big secret unit and would dig up Fort Campbell looking for it." Seaspray, which was integrated into a CIA proprietary named Aviation Tech Services, remained secret until 1985.

According to Hersh, "Longhofer's most enduring accomplishment was an aerial intelligence operation in Central America…established in March 1982." Code named Queens Hunter, it set up a front civilian aerial photography operation in Honduras, staffed partly by specially assigned National Security communications experts, to monitor the Nicaraguan government and Salvadoran rebels.

In addition to the Special Operations Division, the Army established a separate covert entity known as the Intelligence Support Activity (ISA), headed by Colonel Jerry King until May 1984. ISA was also under the Army deputy chief of staff for operations, and relied on the Special Operations Division "for mission planning and operational support, including all the laundered cash deemed necessary. The men and officers assigned to the unit were issued no military weapons or clothing; they trained at civilian locations, flew in unmarked aircraft and were prepared to be disavowed by their Government if necessary."[18]

One of ISA's assignments in Nicaragua was to create "pathfinders," secretly marked routes and support facilities such as business fronts to provide cover for U.S. agents. Posing as third-country tourists or businesspeople, ISA agents set up safe houses, secret landing zones and other facilities to support U.S. military operations in Nicaragua including an invasion force. ISA agents reportedly entered Nicaragua using false credentials showing they were part of the embassy staff until 1984; then they relied on false passports from neighboring countries.[19]

By December 1983, in a relatively quiet precursor to the Iran-contra affair, the Special Operations Division's ultra secret unit code named Yellow Fruit—with its commercial cover company, Business Security International—was embroiled in financial and other scandals. Yellow Fruit was shut down and its director, Lt. Colonel Dale Duncan, who had publicly "retired" as part of his cover, was court-martialed and is serving a ten-year sentence (reduced to seven) at Fort Leavenworth, Kansas. Longhofer was allowed to remain on duty in an administrative job in Washington while appealing his court-martial and reduced one-year sentence. In Longhofer's view, he and the others who were convicted or reprimanded are scapegoats for higher-ups in the Pentagon. As for the Intelligence Support Activity, its morale may have suffered but its personnel grew to number 300.[20] Planning begun under Yellow Fruit for off-the-books contra support was picked up by the so-called private Enterprise (see chapter 11).

While Seaspray remained hidden the media spotlight was trained on Task Force 160 after the October 1983 Grenada invasion. Nicknamed Night Stalkers, the motto of Task Force 160 pilots is "Death waits in the dark." Relatives later told Knight-Ridder reporters that Task Force 160 members have "engaged in covert missions in hostile areas of Central America to aid pro-American forces. If downed or captured, the soldiers, who wore civilian clothes and flew at night were told to expect no U.S. government acknowledgement or intervention...Instead, they were instructed to blow up their CH-47 Chinook and UH-60 Black Hawk helicopters with preplaced explosive charges." Then they were expected to buy or fight their way out, "using bribe money made available by their superiors and privately purchased weapons of their own choosing."

William Donald Alvey of Morgantown, Kentucky, discussed several Nicaragua missions with his son, Don. "He was kind of vague about the missions," said Alvey. "He'd go somewhere and pick up a group of people in a clearing in the jungle—armed troops, speaking Spanish—and take them to another clearing in the jungle somewhere." They would usually be ferried between Honduras and Nicaragua. Alvey insisted they were not training exercises. "Don said one time you could tell damn well they had been in a fight because a lot of them were wounded." Alvey also recalled his son speaking of ferrying troops into Nicaragua from an offshore ship.

"Don told me," Alvey said, "that if he ever failed to return from one of those missions, the Army already had a story to make up for his and his crew's disappearance and nobody would ever know the difference." According to the Army, "Warrant Officer Donald R. Alvey, 26, was killed on March 20, 1983, when a Chinook helicopter he was piloting crashed 23 miles offshore of Norfolk, Va."

Whether Donald Alvey was actually killed as the Army reported, the U.S. military has a history of covering up deaths occuring during secret missions. As a former Army officer explained, the solution to the problem of military personnel killed working with the CIA in secret missions in Laos and Cambodia was "bodywashing...If a guy was killed on a mission, and if it was sensitive politically, we'd ship the body back home and have a jeep roll over on him at Fort Huachuca," an Army intelligence and covert operations base southeast of Tucson, Arizona. Or "we'd arrange a chopper crash, or wait until one happened and insert a body or two into the wreckage later. It's not that difficult."[21]

A Task Force 160 helicopter pilot, Captain Keith Lucas, was shot down on the morning of the Grenada invasion while supporting a covert Delta Force mission. Following the pattern of "laundering" special operations casualties, "Lucas's father was told by the military that his son's death would not be reported as having occurred in Grenada because he was on a secret operation." The military had to drop the cover when the father went public with his story.[22]

The Senate Intelligence Committee briefly investigated Task Force 160 following the news accounts in December 1984. It reportedly accepted the Pentagon's denial that the unit had participated in military missions into El Salvador, Honduras or Nicaragua.[23]

Target Grenada

Among the objectives listed in the Pentagon's classified 1982 Consolidated Defense Guidance was: "reverse communist gains in El Salvador, Nicaragua, Grenada and other areas of Latin America."[24] Days after 241 marines were killed in a suicide bombing attack in Beirut, U.S. military forces invaded the Caribbean island of Grenada. With a population of 110,000, Grenada, at 133 square miles, is about the size of Martha's Vineyard, Massachusetts.

The catalyst for the Grenada invasion was the murder of Prime Minister Maurice Bishop and other top government officials following their ouster by Deputy Prime Minister Bernard Coard and General Hudson Austin. The immediate pretexts were a call by other Caribbean nations for military intervention and the rescue of American medical students on the island. The larger pretext was stopping Cuban/Soviet expansionism in the Caribbean and defending U.S. national security. The overlooked background was years of U.S. hostility toward Grenada since Bishop's New Jewel Movement (Joint Endeavor for Welfare, Education and Liberation) overthrew the dictatorial Eric Gairy and his Mongoose Gang enforcers in a March 1979 coup costing only one life.

When the new government, fearing a Gairy countercoup, asked the United States for security assistance, the Carter administration refused and warned the socialist New Jewel Movement (NJM) not to develop close ties with Cuba. Gairy's legacy was an impoverished economy with an unemployment rate of nearly 50 percent and few health and education services. The NJM needed assistance. Unlike Washington, Cuba was prepared to help, as was Canada, Venezuela and the European Economic Community (EEC). In the NJM's first year in office, private sector investment increased by over 130 percent and the government embarked upon an ambitious program of public housing, public works, equal rights for women and free education and health care.

The Reagan administration conducted covert activities against Grenada, such as giving aid to opposition groups, after the Senate Intelligence Committee rejected a more extensive plan to destabilize the government. It also launched full-scale economic warfare.[25] "Not one penny for Grenada," Secretary of State Haig ordered U.S. officers in international financial institutions. In 1981, Washington tried to block an International Monetary Fund (IMF) loan for construction of Grenada's international airport at Point Salines. Because IMF decisions are supposed to be made on non-political grounds, the United States argued that the airport would worsen

Grenada's balance of payments problems. "IMF staff economists replied that a serviceable international airport would, on the contrary, improve Grenada's balance of payments by encouraging tourism." Nonetheless, the loan was cut by one-third under U.S. pressure.[26]

The airport became the focal point of U.S. polemics against Grenada. Reagan portrayed Cuban construction assistance as a sinister plot to make Grenada a base for subversion of the Caribbean and a threat to shipping. On March 10 and 23, 1983, Reagan displayed reconnaissance photos of the construction site marked with such headings as "10,000 Foot Runway" and "New Cuban Housing." The display did not show the many resident American students who jogged on the open construction site, nor reveal the non-threatening information that the airport was funded by a British government-backed loan and construction was managed by the Plessey Company, a British international contracting firm, which "stated that the airport was being built to civilian specifications and contained no standard military features such as hardened fueling facilities or bomb shelters for fighter aircraft...The Point Salines runway was actually shorter than other regional airports such as those in Trinidad, Jamaica, and nearby Barbados."[27]

Recalling Reagan's March 10 speech, former Ambassador Sally Shelton said, "I was absolutely staggered, because he was talking about a Grenada that didn't have much resemblance to the Grenada to which I had been accredited as ambassador." Francis McNeil, former deputy director of intelligence for the State Department, acknowledged, "we pretty much lived by the descriptions in our own rhetoric, rather than seeking the reality of the situation on the island...It was kind of 'I'll huff and I'll puff and I'll blow your Marxist house down' kind of thing."[28]

During the U.S.-led Ocean Venture naval maneuvers from August to October 1981, Grenada (and the Grenadines) was the thinly-veiled target of a mock invasion of "Amber and the Amberdines." In the exercise scenario, Amber was influenced by "Country Red" (Cuba) to "export terrorism" by supporting a guerrilla movement in "Country Azure." Azure invited the United States to neutralize the guerrillas and the United States invaded Amber to rescue American hostages. U.S. troops remained until a pro-U.S. Amber government was installed.

The Bishop government protested this dress rehearsal for invasion and responded by acquiring small arms and increasing the size of its minute army and civilian militia. Those defensive actions were then portrayed by Washington as signs of Grenada's aggressive intent. Grenada had already experienced real assaults: in June 1980, for example, a bomb exploded under the grandstand at Queen's Park just before a rally at which Bishop and other NJM leaders were to appear. Three young girls were killed and other spectators were injured.[29] In spring 1983, Bishop wrote Reagan in an effort to improve relations. The letter was answered coolly by a lower-level U.S. diplomat in Barbados. When Bishop went to Washington, Reagan refused to meet him. Instead of responding positively to Bishop's attempts to improve relations, the administration chose to exploit his death later in the year.

Shocked and angered by the October 19 murder of Bishop and his colleagues, most Grenadians had little will to resist the U.S. invasion. The widespread sentiment was: "No Bishop, No Work, No Revo." Indeed, after Bishop was arrested on October 14, the so-called Revolutionary Military Council had disarmed the civilian militia and deposited their largely antiquated weapons in half-full warehouses that the U.S. military would later photograph—selectively—as evidence of Grenada's "military buildup."

The Cuban government publicly denounced the coup and made clear amid signs of an imminent U.S. invasion that Cubans would fight only in self-defense. Castro sent the U.S. government an urgent message on October 22, suggesting that the United States and Cuba communicate "to avoid violence." Cuba received no reply until 90 minutes after the invasion began on October 25.

The invasion torpedoed a diplomatic initiative by the Caribbean Common Market (CARICOM) aiming to ensure safety on the island and restore civilian rule. Instead, Washington arranged for the smaller Organization of Eastern Caribbean States (OECS) to "invite" U.S. military intervention. The decision was not unanimous as required under the OECS charter and, even if unanimous, it would not have been legal under international law. It was later revealed that the OECS request was actually drafted in Washington. After Prime Minister Eugenia Charles of Dominica appeared with Reagan to announce the invasion, Rep. Gus Savage (D-IL) described her as "this puppet of our President [who] represents 'Aunt Jemimaism' in geopolitics."[30] At one point, the CIA passed $100,000 to her government for "a secret support operation"; a Senator on the Intelligence Committee called it a "payoff."[31]

Clues began to accumulate that the invasion was planned weeks in advance. According to a congressional source, the Pentagon admitted in a secret briefing that it knew of the coup against Bishop two weeks ahead of time. U.S. Ambassador to France Evan Galbraith said on French television on October 26 that the invasion was "an action which had begun two weeks ago." Later he said he had "misspoken." Also revealing were Ranger exercises reported in early November: "from September 23 to October 2, the 2nd Battalion of the 75th Rangers Division, stationed at Fort Lewis, Washington—one of two Ranger units which participated in the actual invasion—spent six days practicing taking over an airport, complete with parachute jumps onto runways, capturing airport buildings, taking captives, and liberating hostages. Although an Army spokesman referred to the exercises as occurring 'regularly' at Ephrata Municipal Airport—which happened to have a runway the same length as the Point Salines runway—an airport official told reporters, 'It would be pretty farfetched to say it's done on a regular basis. They've done it twice to my knowledge—in 1981 and this time.' "[32]

About 600 Americans attended St. George's medical school in Grenada. First-hand accounts indicated that coup leaders Bernard Coard and Hudson Austin were taking special measures to reassure the school and the U.S. government that the students were not in any danger. Peter Bourne, former health official in the Carter administration and a visiting professor at the medical school where his father, Dr. Geoffrey Bourne, was vice-chancellor, recounted these events in the *Los Angeles Times:*

> I contacted my father who assured me not only that there was no cause for alarm, but that Coard had guaranteed the safety of the medical school and students. We remained in contact over the next several days by telephone and through the medical school telex

link to its Bayshore office in New York...Despite a 24-hour curfew, Coard provided government vehicles so that students could get from one campus to another in safety.

On Wednesday 19 October, I received a call from a member of the board of trustees, a distinguished and conservative man [reportedly Senator Alfonse D'Amato (R-NY)] who said that the State Department was pressuring school officials in New York to say publicly that the students in Grenada were in danger so that Washington would have a pretext to invade the island. I urged that they not accede to such pressure...

Still concerned about the safety of the medical students in the event of a US invasion, my father convinced Austin to allow representatives of the US embassy in Barbados to come to the island the next morning, Saturday 22 October...US embassy officials met with Austin and other members of the military council and the medical students...

On Monday morning the airport was reopened as General Austin had promised, and any students who wanted to leave could do so. The only problem was that Barbados was already preparing with Washington to invade the next day and refused to let the commercial airline LIAT fly to the island. A few students left by charter plane as did British and Canadian citizens alarmed by the continuing rumors of imminent invasion.

That same morning I received a telegram from my father...which said, 'We are all still well and safe. News distorted and exaggerated'...[33]

The real danger to the students came when the main U.S. invasion force landed at Point Salines airport, located adjacent to one of the school's three campuses. The supposed U.S. rescue forces were surprised to learn from students of the other sites. It took four days to reach all the students. None were ever taken hostage or otherwise harmed by Grenadians (or Cubans). On October 26, many of the students were evacuated while fighting still raged at Grand Anse Bay. Not surprisingly, they were scared and happy to get off the island. Their well-publicized joy upon arrival in the United States was used to promote the "rescue" pretext.

The main U.S. invasion, code named "Urgent Fury," began at dawn on October 25, with a landing of 1,900 U.S. Army Rangers and Marines. Growing to 7,000, the invasion force was billed as multinational, but the Caribbean contingent of 300 men, mainly from Jamaica, engaged in police duty only after combat ceased. During the Point Salines assault the barracks housing Cuban construction workers were fired upon and they fought back; 24 Cubans were killed and 59 wounded during the invasion.

After the Cuban airport workers were captured, Washington played up the Cuban threat angle by claiming that 800 to 1,000 Cubans were resisting in the hills. When the smokescreen cleared, Cuba's official count of its citizens on the island proved accurate: 784 Cubans including airport workers as well as diplomats and their families.

The Reagan administration showed its respect for freedom of the press by censoring coverage of the invasion. Reporters were kept off Grenada for three days after which press restrictions remained in effect. Meanwhile, Washington's disinformation campaign left lasting impressions of an expansionist "terror island."

In his televised address of October 27, Reagan claimed: "We had to assume that several hundred Cubans working on the airport could be military reserves. As it turned out the number was much larger and they were a military force. Six hundred of them were taken prisoner and we have discovered a complete base with weapons and communications equipment which makes it clear a Cuban occupation of the island had been planned.

"Two hours ago we released the first photos from Grenada. They included pictures of a warehouse of military equipment, one of three we've uncovered so far. This warehouse contained weapons and ammunition stacked almost to the ceiling, enough to supply thousands of terrorists.

"Grenada, we were told, was a friendly island paradise for tourism. Well it wasn't. It was a Soviet-Cuban colony being readied as a major military bastion to export terror and undermine democracy. We got there just in time."[34]

When the UN Security Council approved a resolution "deeply deploring" the invasion as a "flagrant violation of international law," the United States cast the sole negative vote to veto it. Though the *New York Times* and *Washington Post* editorialized against the invasion—unlike such prominent liberal commentators as Bill Moyers, then with CBS News—their overall coverage largely reinforced the official line about the Cuban threat. When Bernard Coard was captured on October 30, the *New York Times* headline read "Pro-Cuban Seized," despite the fact that Cuba had denounced the coup.

On Grenada, Gairy's Mongoose Gang members were released from prison and NJM supporters and many others, including foreigners working on the island, were rounded up, arrested and interrogated without regard to due process. In one account demonstrating the broad sweep of the arrests and interrogations, Regina Fuchs, a West German nurse working at a clinic in Grenada, said "that she was kept in Richmond Hill jail for two days and interrogated relentlessly about whether she had ever demonstrated against the Vietnam War, whom she knew when she attended medical school, whether she had ever met [former CIA agent] Philip Agee in Germany, and the like. She was falsely accused of harboring fugitives by two Americans, one named Ed and the other named Frank Gonzales, who identified himself to her as CIA."[35]

Grenadian casualties were ignored or underestimated. Later Pentagon figures showed 67 Grenadians killed and 358 wounded—including 21 mental patients killed when U.S. aircraft bombed their hospital. According to military analyst Richard Gabriel, "even if the Pentagon's figures are accepted as accurate, the number of civilians killed and wounded is far too high for an operation of the size and intensity of Urgent Fury. Conversations with U.S. claims-settlement personnel on the island as well as with Grenadian civilians suggest that there was a good deal of indiscriminate shooting, mostly from the air, at targets that were not clearly identified. A favorite sport of helicopter gunship pilots in Grenada on 'roam and kill' missions seems to have been to machine-gun livestock from the air. In one instance, an old woman was killed from AC-130 gunship fire, and in another, an infant was machine-gunned in her crib by helicopter gunship fire."

The U.S. government played politics with American casualties as well. Of the nineteen deaths the Pentagon admitted to, more than two-thirds were killed by "friendly fire" or in helicopter crashes and other accidents. The official casualty numbers excluded special forces personnel. According to Gabriel, "If they are included, the death toll jumps from nineteen to twenty-nine, including the six Delta Force soldiers and the four [Navy] Seals killed [by drowning] before the invasion officially began." The Pentagon also tried to conceal the true number of wounded. "When it was later reported by the press that the number who received Purple Hearts was higher than the number listed as wounded, the [Joint Chiefs of Staff] again adjusted the number of wounded upward, to 152."

The invasion was, as Gabriel explained, a political and bureaucratic success, whatever its military shortcomings: "almost every unit and officer that took part (and even many who did not) was able to enhance his career by being awarded a medal…If the medals already awarded are added to those pending, the number approaches 19,600!"[36]

Grenada was remodeled under U.S. direction. U.S. psychological warfare (psyops) teams plastered the island with propaganda posters and pro-U.S. graffiti and transformed Radio Free Grenada into Spice Island Radio. In July 1987, *Newsweek* published a brief story on the station, "Grenada Fights the Calypso Menace," making light of censorship under the government of Prime Minister Herbert Blaize. The article said "politically sensitive" calypso music "will be banned from the island's only radio station, which is government owned." A government censor explained that "whenever a composer seems to be saying wrong things or lying directly, we can ban the song." *Newsweek* commented that the "censorship is probably more futile than repressive."[37] So much for concerns over peacetime censorship in U.S.-backed Grenada.

Secretary of State Shultz was an early visitor to "liberated" Grenada. "It's really a lovely place," he said in 1984. "The terrain is more rugged than I imagined, but it is certainly a lovely piece of real estate."[38]

The Point Salines airport was recognized for what it always was, an economic necessity. The United States "contracted with Morrison-[Knudsen], an Idaho construction company that was part of a consortium that built most of the roads, ports and bridges in Vietnam, to complete the airport for $21.8 million."[39]

As time passed, the rewriting of history to justify U.S. intervention was illustrated on the *New York Times* editorial pages. On December 10, 1984, the *Times* praised the election of Herbert Blaize as a "constructive sequel" to the invasion. His victory was hardly a surprise given that his legal challenger was the deposed ruler Eric Gairy and the CIA had allocated $675,000 (amounting to more than $6 for every Grenadian) from its political action funds to influence the election.[40] Although the *Times* was still skeptical about administration claims about the students and the invitation to intervene, it twisted reality to claim, "Lost somewhere in the long list of justifications was the most compelling reason for the action: the fear that Grenada had been led into the Soviet and Cuban orbit by Mr. Bishop and was to be sealed in by his murder."

In January 1985, the liberal *New York Times* columnist Tom Wicker found a silver lining to the invasion in the Blaize government: "Asked why his predecessors, Mr. Bishop and Sir Eric, had invested so little in the island's basic needs, Mr. Blaze [*sic*] laughed, not mirthfully, and replied: 'They had other priorities'—an outsize military force in Mr. Bishop's case, and what an American called 'squandermania' in Sir Eric's…[the Blaize] Government is evidence, even for Americans who opposed the intervention, that it worked: Grenada is peaceful again, and has a new chance for prosperity."[41]

Leaving aside Wicker's distortion of Bishop's record, Reaganomics brought no prosperity to Grenada. The official unemployment rate shot up from 12 percent in 1982 to 27 percent in 1985. The NJM's housing projects, free milk program and education programs were abolished.[42] One sign of the regression in women's status is the revival of prostitution.

Reagan visited Grenada in February 1986 and was hailed by Blaize as "our own national hero" and "our rescuer after God." Reagan likened events in Nicaragua to those that prompted the Grenada invasion. He would not be satisfied, he said, "until all the people of the Americas have joined us in the warm sunshine of liberty and justice."[43]

Nicaragua Next?

For many Americans the Grenada invasion was balm for the fresh wounds of Beirut and the scars of Teheran. Revenge went down easier in the guise of rescue. For some the revenge went deeper to the U.S. defeat in Vietnam. As a top CIA official put it, "this Administration came to power with the intention of punching someone in the nose."[44] Democratic Party leaders who had denounced the invasion as "gunboat diplomacy" (House Speaker Tip O'Neill's words) quickly tacked to the winds of public opinion and pronounced it "justified." The narrow majority in support of the invasion loomed even larger on the political horizon.

Grenada was an opportunity for the Reagan administration to show that the United States was no "paper tiger." As one senior official put it, "What good are maneuvers and shows of force, if you never use it?"[45] The obvious question was would Nicaragua be next? U.S. citizens living in Nicaragua began weekly protest vigils in front of the American Embassy, displaying the banner: "We Don't Want to be Rescued."

Fearing a Grenada-style invasion in Central America, U.S. peace activists undertook new initiatives. One effort led to the formation of the National Pledge of Resistance, a broad-based network of tens of thousands of U.S. citizens, each pledged to join in legal protest or nonviolent civil disobedience "if the United States invades, bombs, sends combat troops, or otherwise significantly escalates its intervention in Central America." The religious-based Witness for Peace began sending U.S. volunteers to maintain a nonviolent presence in Jalapa and other Nicaraguan war zones. These efforts were part of a diverse and dynamic movement to educate and organize people against the ongoing, many-sided U.S. invasion of Central America and compel a change in policy.

In Grenada, observed military analyst Richard Gabriel, "the ability of U.S. ground forces to move rapidly and boldly against the enemy and to demonstrate effective small-unit fire and maneuver was absent. Should U.S. ground forces ever engage in El Salvador or Nicaragua and use the same tactics, the war will be long—

and bloody."[46] In Nicaragua, U.S. forces would be resisted not only by a larger, battle-hardened army, but by an armed population.

Nicaragua's defense preparations were prudent, not paranoid. Nicaraguans were mobilized through the militias and Sandinista Defense Committees to improve their readiness for armed defense, medical care and emergency evacuation. Backyard bomb shelters were dug all over Managua. Nicaragua wanted to send a clear message to Washington: the costs of an invasion here will be far higher than Grenada.

Invasion talk circulated throughout Central America and in Washington. CONDECA, the Central American Defense Council once led by Somoza, was reactivated on October 1, 1983—just weeks before the Grenada invasion—by El Salvador, Honduras, Guatemala and Panama. General Paul Gorman, chief of the U.S. Southern Command, was in attendance. CONDECA military leaders met secretly in Tegucigalpa on October 22 and 23 and discussed the legality of joint military action "for the pacification of Nicaragua." They agreed that the contras "can establish a government somewhere in [Nicaraguan] territory, and, once recognized internationally, can ask for aid from CONDECA." At a press conference earlier in the month, the FDN had declared its strategy to establish a provisional government and call for multinational assistance. CONDECA leaders also agreed they could act to defend the "peace" in any country in Central America and call upon the United States for support. The consensus was that "a war situation is predictable."[47] General Alvarez of Honduras told U.S. officials that he intended to celebrate his next birthday—December 12—in Managua.[48]

U.S. officials denied plans to support CONDECA action against Nicaragua. But the Washington-based Council on Hemispheric Affairs warned of an invasion plan, code named Operation Pegasus, involving air strikes, a naval blockade and a land invasion by CONDECA troops. They cited an administration source who had leaked details of the Grenada invasion six days before it took place.[49]

For some U.S. officials, Grenada was a warning that consuming Nicaragua would not be easy. For others it was an appetizer, whetting their desire for the main course. A shared lesson was that U.S. forces and their Central America battlefield should be better prepared.

"Stepped Up Intensity"

Fresh from victory in Grenada, "the CIA and the administration generally were feeling a new potency in the fall of 1983," wrote Christopher Dickey. "Dewey [Clarridge] reportedly took to driving around with a bumper sticker that said 'Nicaragua Next.' Old acquaintances of his, bumping into him at an airport, remember him gushing about what was going on with 'my war.' "[50]

In the last three months of 1983, the Nicaraguan government undertook a series of measures to enhance political pluralism, demonstrate its commitment to negotiations and reduce tensions following the Grenada invasion. On October 20,

Foreign Minister Miguel D'Escoto presented Assistant Secretary of State Langhorne Motley with four draft treaty proposals—to be implemented under the auspices of the Contadora Group formed earlier in the year (discussed in chapter 13)—including bilateral treaties between Nicaragua and the United States and between Nicaragua and Honduras, and multilateral treaties regarding the war in El Salvador and regional peace and security. The State Department dismissed them all.

Also on October 20, the House of Representatives voted again to replace covert aid to Nicaragua with an overt $80 million "interdiction assistance" program. During the debate, Rep. Michael Barnes, back from a recent visit to Nicaragua, told fellow House members: "Myth would have it that the covert operations are designed to force the Nicaraguans to the negotiating table. But the trouble with that is that the Nicaraguans were already there. Nicaragua has been trying to have talks with the Reagan Administration all along. It is not Nicaragua that will not negotiate. It is us. Nicaragua has long since demonstrated its willingness to address our security concerns on the sole condition that we be prepared to address their security concerns.

"The one thing that the Nicaraguans will not negotiate about is their revolution. And here we get to the real purpose of the covert operations. They are designed to overthrow the Nicaraguan revolution."[51]

The Senate voted, as expected, to approve contra funding on November 3. In a "compromise" on November 18, Congress approved $24 million in contra aid. It was expected to last until June 1984.

In November, Nicaragua eased press censorship; the Salvadoran revolutionaries moved their Political and Diplomatic Commission out of Nicaragua; and about 2,000 Cuban teachers and technical advisers returned home. On November 30, Nicaragua presented three more treaty proposals, containing provisions for the exclusion of foreign military advisers and restrictions on arms. Motley dismissed these actions as "false signals."[52]

On December 1, Nicaragua freed Miskito prisoners and declared a general amnesty for insurgents in Northern Zelaya. The amnesty decree recognized a governmental commitment to ethnic minority rights. Three days later, Nicaragua announced an amnesty for counterrevolutionary exiles including those engaged in armed and illegal activities, excluding ex-National Guard officers and others in the contra leadership. It stipulated that returnees would have the option of participating in the land distribution program under the Agrarian Reform and that "in the case of agricultural proprietors who may have abandoned their lands, and which later may have been occupied, their lands shall be restored to them or adequate compensation made." Amnesty beneficiaries would have full rights to participate in coming elections. By December 15, more than 100 peasants had taken advantage of the amnesty and resettled in the departments of Ocotal and Esteli.[53]

The Nicaraguan government announced steps leading to commencement of the electoral process on January 31, 1984 for national elections then scheduled for 1985 (they were moved up to November 1984). In a full-page "Message to the People of the United States from the People of Nicaragua" appearing in the *New York Times* on December 11, 1983, Nicaragua published the amnesty and electoral decrees and reiterated Nicaragua's desire for a peaceful solution to the crisis in Central America with the "right to freely determine our own future in peace and security" without "interference or direction from *any* foreign power."

The prevailing mood in the Reagan administration was, in the words of one official, "the Sandinistas are on the ropes—keep the pressure on."[54] On December 20, the Special Interagency Working Group concluded: "Given the distinct possibility that we may be unable to obtain additional funding in FY [Fiscal Year]-84 or FY-85 our objective should be to bring the Nicaragua situation to a head in 1984." At a National Security Planning Group meeting on January 6, 1984, Reagan concurred in the recommendation to "proceed with stepped up intensity."[55]

An internal CIA memorandum reported on nineteen attacks involving helicopters and Piranha speedboats (called Q boats by the CIA) launched from CIA "mother ships" between January 1 and April 10, 1984. Army Intelligence Support Activity (ISA) and Task Force 160 personnel participated.

On January 4, for example, U.S. helicopters and speedboats rocketed the port of Potosi. "CIA crewed Merlin aircraft equipped with FLIR [Forward looking infrared radar] provided real time intelligence support." On March 7, speedboats attacked the San Juan del Sur oil and storage facility. When Nicaraguan forces responded, a U.S. "support helicopter laid down suppressing rocket fire which enabled 'Q' boats to withdraw safely."

By March 29, plans were made to support a Pastora attack on San Juan del Norte with the goal of installing a provisional government.[56] On April 9, U.S. helicopters provided fire support to the ARDE assault on San Juan del Norte. "ARDE was satisfied with the fire display," noted the CIA report.[57] But a Nicaraguan counteroffensive routed the ARDE forces and dashed U.S. plans to establish a provisional government on the Atlantic Coast.

In another incident, not contained in the CIA summary, a Honduran-based U.S. Army UH-1H helicopter was shot down over Nicaragua on January 11, while apparently providing logistical support for a contra assault force. U.S. pilot Chief Warrant Officer Jeffrey Schwab was killed.[58] By one account, Schwab's helicopter was inadvertently directed over Nicaragua while on its way from San Lorenzo to Aguacate, when a U.S. radio operator mistook it for a CIA reconnaissance and resupply mission.[59]

On March 24, 1984, as reported in the Costa Rican *La Prensa Libre*, a DC-3 crashed while supplying arms to the contras in Costa Rica. Eyewitnesses saw armed men take seven bodies from the wreckage, douse two with gasoline and burn them, remove other bodies and torch documents. Four of the seven dead men were said to be North Americans.[60]

The DC-3 crashed on a mountainside near the ranch of American John Hull, which served as a base for the contra supply operation. Eden Pastora and top aide Karol Prado said later that CIA station chief "Tomas Castillo" and a South American CIA agent, "Ivan Gomez," ordered them to remove teeth and jawbones and mutilate the bodies to destroy physical evidence. Unidentified helicopters removed some bodies from the scene before Costa Rican investigators arrived. Prado identified the DC-3's pilot as Renato Torrealba, who was married to an American and "recognized as Castillo's number one pilot."

Although it had Canadian serial markings, the DC-3 was owned by the U.S. government. Federal Aviation Administration (FAA) records listed the owner of the plane as one Robert Branch of Indianapolis who lost custody to the U.S. government in July 1983 because of the plane's alleged use in drug trafficking. According to FAA agent Edwin McDaniel, the plane was "released without the normal paperwork because it was 'slated for military use.' "[61]

Mining the Harbors

In January 1984, Washington began mining Nicaragua's harbors, an action considered the equivalent of a blockade and an act of war under international law. President Reagan approved the mining on the recommendation of National Security Adviser Robert McFarlane (Clarridge takes credit for the mining idea).[62] Indeed, Reagan was briefed on and approved even "relatively minor operational details," such as Ambassador Negroponte's November 1983 recommendation to increase by 3,000 the number of weapons supplied to the contras.[63]

Edgar Chamorro told the World Court how he was first informed of the mining on January 5: "at 2:00 a.m., the C.I.A. deputy station chief of Tegucigalpa, the agent I knew as 'George,' woke me up at my house in Tegucigalpa and handed me a press release in excellent Spanish. I was surprised to read that we—the F.D.N.—were taking credit for having mined several Nicaraguan harbors. 'George' [John Mallett] told me to rush to our clandestine radio station and read this announcement before the Sandinistas broke the news. [Nicaraguan radio had actually reported on the mining two days earlier.] The truth is that we played no role in the mining of the harbors. But we did as instructed and broadcast the communique...Ironically, approximately two months later, after a Soviet ship struck one of the mines, the same agent instructed us to deny that one of 'our' mines had damaged the ship to avoid an international incident."[64]

Mines were deployed in the ports of Corinto, Puerto Sandino and El Bluff (near Bluefields) from January through March 1984. A variety of mines were used, most reportedly products of the CIA Weapons Group in Langley, Virginia, assisted by the Mines Division of the U.S. Navy Surface Weapons Center in Silver Spring, Maryland. CIA weapons specialists in Honduras did the final assembly. The most sophisticated and damaging mines were ten-foot long cylinders filled with 300 pounds of C-4 plastic explosive. They had a magnetometer to detect disturbances when heavy steel ships passed overhead; at a certain threshold, a battery-charged jolt of electricity set off the mine. Floating mines, disguised with a rubberized cap to make them look like rocks, would be set off by the wake of a passing ship. Others responded to direct contact or had acoustic triggers.[65]

Mines damaged or destroyed nine ships and fishing vessels by the end of March, disrupting shipping during the key November to April harvest season for Nicaragua's principal export crops. Two Nicaraguan fishing boats were blown up in El Bluff on February 25. On March 1, a large Dutch dredger was hit in Corinto.

On March 7, a Panamanian ship carrying medicine, food and industrial supplies suffered severe damage. A Soviet tanker carrying 250,000 barrels of crude oil was
damaged by a mine in Puerto Sandino on March 20. On March 27, Corinto mines
destroyed a Nicaraguan shrimp boat and damaged a Liberian ship carrying molas-
ses. Two days later, a Nicaraguan fishing vessel was destroyed. On March 30, another
Nicaraguan shrimp boat was destroyed and a Japanese ship carrying bicycles, auto
spare parts, construction materials and cotton was damaged.[66] With no minesweepers, Nicaragua tried to clear the mines by dragging a deep sea fishing net between two fishing boats. A French offer to provide minesweepers in cooperation
with another European country never materialized.

The mines killed two Nicaraguans and injured fifteen sailors, including five on
the Soviet oil tanker.[67] Not to be outdone by the FDN, ARDE claimed credit on March
1 for the mines at Corinto and El Bluff, saying they were designed to cut off Soviet
military supplies. "The coasts of Nicaragua are a war zone," declared ARDE, "and
therefore we are not responsible for loss of civilian lives in this zone."[68]

As word of U.S. involvement leaked out, administration officials justified the
mining as a form of self-defense under international law. "If the country whose ports
are being mined is considered responsible for some kind of aggression, in this case
support for guerrillas in El Salvador, then mining is considered an act of self-defense
just like any other use of force," claimed one U.S. official. The official acknowledged
that according to international standards, naval mines should not be used to close
international waters or to interfere with the free passage of vessels from third
countries. But, he claimed, "in the case of Nicaragua, any ships entering Nicaraguan
waters give up their right to safe passage."[69]

France and Britain protested the mining along with countries whose ships were
hit. "If one accepts it in one part of the world," said French Foreign Minister Claude
Cheysson, "there is no reason not to accept it in the Strait of Hormuz as well."[70]
Those words came back to haunt the United States in July 1987, when a Kuwaiti oil
tanker under U.S. flag protection struck a mine in the Persian Gulf. The United States
recognized no right to self-defense on the part of Iran or Iraq to mine waterways in
their ongoing war. There, where it suited U.S. interests, Washington loudly
proclaimed the right of free passage on the seas and made sure that the evening
newscasts were full of pictures of damaged tankers and floating mines.

The mines, said Interior Minister Tomas Borge in a March 1984 interview, "are
not just Nicaragua's problem, but rather everyone's problem. Generally there are
certain rules that one respects. It's not difficult for anyone to mine a port, but no
one does it. The decision taken by the CIA to mine our ports opens up the opportunity for any [group] to take the decision to mine any port...Who is to say that
[Central American revolutionaries] wouldn't mine New York or Puerto Limon [Costa
Rica] or any other port they'd want. This means that they [the United States] have
started a risky game."

Borge described the mines as an irresponsible and terrorist response to the
failure of the contras inside Nicaragua. "They have realized that they cannot militarily overthrow Nicaragua. Therefore they've decided to sow destabilization and to

worsen the economic crisis, which is difficult enough already and has become worse due to the aggression...

"The outlook is more war. The outlook is more death. The [U.S.] government is making an effort to approve $20 million more designated for the so-called covert war. I don't know why they call it covert, because it hasn't even a fig leaf. The most serious thing about all of this is that it's accepted as a natural thing that a government decides to designate millions of dollars to assault another country—that resources coming from American [tax dollars] are designated to sow death in another country. And that the North American people don't realize that their money is being designated to murder citizens in another country—while they cut back social programs in the U.S...

"What would happen if we designated 50 million cordobas to place bombs in the White House? Everyone would say we were murderers and that we were crazy. Fine, why not say that of those who are sending millions of dollars to murder Nicaraguans...Would it be justified for us, who are partisans of totally eliminating racial discrimination worldwide to decide to send resources to punish those who discriminate against Blacks or Puerto Ricans or Latinos? We are enemies of discrimination, but we have no right to make decisions that involve an intervention in the internal matters of other countries."[71]

Nicaragua did not retaliate. Instead, it took its case to the United Nations and the World Court. It introduced a resolution in the UN Security Council on March 30, denouncing "the escalation of acts of military aggression brought against" Nicaragua by the United States. A majority supported the resolution; the United States vetoed it.

The mines brought the "Nicaragua situation to a head," but not in Nicaragua. They caused a political explosion in the United States. Senator Barry Goldwater (R-AZ), chairman of the Senate Intelligence Committee and a staunch administration supporter, lit the first fuse. "Dear Bill," Goldwater wrote Casey on April 9:

> All this past weekend, I've been trying to figure out how I can most easily tell you my feelings about the discovery of the President having approved mining some of the harbors of Central America. It gets down to one, little, simple phrase: I am pissed off!
>
> I understand you had briefed the House on this matter. I've heard that. Now, during the important debate we had all last week and the week before, on whether we would increase funds for the Nicaragua program, we were doing all right until a member of the committee charged that the President had approved the mining. I strongly denied that because I had never heard of it...
>
> Bill, this is no way to run a railroad...The President has asked us to back his foreign policy. Bill, how can we back his foreign policy when we don't know what the hell he is doing?...Mine the harbors in Nicaragua? This is an act violating international law. It is an act of war. For the life of me, I don't see how we are going to explain it.[72]

As Goldwater noted, the House Intelligence Committee was informed of the mining on January 31. Mining opponents, such as Boland, registered their concern with the CIA. Casey insisted that he had also informed the Senate committee in March. Some Senators defended Casey, but most did not. As one said, "Casey did mention mining but in the midst of a list of other actions the *contras* were taking.

At no time did he say the CIA was directly involved in mining or that President Reagan had authorized it."

Yet, as *Time* put it, "Since the mines were already exploding at the time of the briefings...it seems strange that the Senators did not question Casey persistently about them." In a cover story on the mining, *Time* ended up wanting it both ways, like the politicians, urging negotiations while advocating continued aid to the contras: "the *contras* are fighting for an ideal, and the U.S., after arming, training and encouraging them, cannot suddenly abandon them to their fates."[73]

The Senate had voted on April 5 to support the administration request for $21 million in supplemental contra aid. Senators expressed bipartisan pique with an April 10 vote protesting the mining. The non-binding resolution read: "It is the sense of Congress that no funds heretofore or hereafter appropriated in any act of Congress shall be obligated or expended for the purpose of planning, executing or supporting the mining of the ports or territorial waters of Nicaragua."[74] Among the twelve senators voting against the resolution were Barry Goldwater, Bob Dole (R-KS) and John Tower (R-TX).

The *New York Times* declared the mining, "Illegal, Deceptive and Dumb" and compared it to German U-boats torpedoing neutral shipping in 1917. "When challenged by a protest about damage to a Soviet freighter, the Administration condoned the practice, contending that neutrals should have known the waters were dangerous. That is actually the same argument invoked by the German Kaiser."[75]

When asked to justify his decision authorizing the mining, President Reagan insisted, "Those were homemade mines that couldn't sink a ship...I think that there was much ado about nothing." Assistant Secretary Motley called the minings a "legitimate form of self-defense" and explained that the "mining comes within the menu of pressures brought in order to modify Nicaraguan behavior."[76]

Fleeing the World Court

"Sometimes people ask me," Foreign Minister D'Escoto told me, " 'Father, what is the future of Nicaragua in this uneven struggle?' And I say, what would be the future of humanity if there were no countries like Nicaragua totally committed to stand up and be counted in the struggle against the...United States' [attempt] to replace the international legal order with the principle that might makes right. [Against] a government that is committed to the institutionalization of lynching, international lynching, as a method for resolving situations—a country committed to total lawlessness.

"Is this the kind of precedent that we want to allow to become established as the law? And, if it is, what's going to happen if everyone continues to bow down to President Reagan just because he is so strong? Just like David, we are so much smaller and weaker when compared to Goliath, we believe in another kind of power. We like to believe in justice. We like to believe in the possibility of those things that perhaps to some people are only meant for poems. That's why we took the United

States to the International Court of Justice, not only to defend Nicaragua, but to defend the international legal order."⁷⁷ (In 1960, the World Court had settled a border dispute between Nicaragua and Honduras when it determined the Rio Coco as the legal border between the two countries.)

The World Court "Case Concerning Military and Paramilitary Activities In and Against Nicaragua," filed on April 9, 1984, covered such actions as the presidential findings authorizing covert activities; U.S. military maneuvers in Honduras aimed at intimidating Nicaragua and supplying the contras; and attacks on civilian and economic targets, including mining the harbors. Nicaragua's legal team of Nicaraguan, American, French and British lawyers included Carlos Arguello, ambassador to the Netherlands and former minister of justice; Paul Reichler and Judy Appelbaum, whose Washington firm represents the Nicaraguan government on international legal matters; and Abram Chayes, Harvard Law School professor and former legal adviser to the Department of State under President Kennedy.

Nicaragua challenged U.S. claims of self-defense and charged that U.S. actions violated the charters of the United Nations and the OAS as well as the U.S. Constitution. Article 15 of the OAS charter, for example, reads: "No state or group of states has the right to intervene, directly or indirectly, for any reason whatsoever, in the internal or external affairs of any other state. The foregoing principle prohibits not only armed forces but also any other form of interference or attempted threat against the personality of the State or against its political, economic, and cultural elements."⁷⁸

Rushing to preempt Nicaragua's suit, the Reagan administration announced on April 6 that it would not recognize World Court jurisdiction in matters concerning Central America for a two-year period. The move was widely denounced as hypocritical, unwise and illegal. In the 1946 agreement (ratified by the U.S. Senate) accepting the Court's authority, the United States stipulated that six-months notice will be given if jurisdictional recognition is to be withdrawn. This provision was included specifically as "a renunciation of any intention to withdraw our obligation in the face of a threatened legal proceeding."

The American Society of International Law adopted a resolution deploring the administration's attempt to sidestep Nicaragua's legal challenge; this was reportedly the first vote condemning an action of the U.S. government in the Law Society's 78-year history. The vote followed a speech by UN Ambassador Jeane Kirkpatrick in which she again turned Orwell on his head, saying, "to portray Nicaragua as victim in the current situation is a complete, Orwellian inversion of what is actually happening in Central America."⁷⁹

Meanwhile, thirteen Democrats on the House Judiciary Committee called on Attorney General William French Smith to appoint a special prosecutor to determine whether President Reagan and his top aides committed federal crimes, such as violation of the Neutrality Act, in connection with the Nicaragua policy. Nothing happened.

The United States went to the World Court in 1980 with a case against Iran for holding U.S. hostages. Although Iran refused to accept the Court's jurisdiction, the United States received a favorable ruling. "When Iran refused to participate, the U.S. took the position that the court should go right ahead," observed D'Escoto. "When we take this step, it is regarded as improper and propaganda." Clearly in the wrong this time around, U.S. officials disparaged the Court's impartiality. Said Kirkpatrick, "It's a semilegal, semijuridical, semipolitical body, which nations sometimes accept and sometimes don't."[80]

Nicaragua had no reason to expect partiality from the Court. At the time it brought suit, the Court was comprised of fifteen judges mainly from countries friendly to the United States. In addition to a U.S. judge, there were judges from Britain, France, Italy, West Germany, Japan, India, Argentina, Brazil, Algeria, Senegal, Nigeria, Syria, Poland and the Soviet Union.

The World Court issued a preliminary restraining order on May 10, 1984, granting provisional measures of protection to Nicaragua. The Court ruled 15 to 0 that the United States should halt immediately any attempts to blockade or mine Nicaraguan ports. On a vote of 14 to 1 (with the U.S. judge dissenting), the Court ruled that Nicaragua's political independence and sovereignty "should be fully respected and should not be jeopardized by any military or paramilitary activities." State Department spokesman John Hughes claimed that "nothing contained in the measures indicated by the Court is inconsistent with current United States policy or activities with respect to Nicaragua."[81] In fact, only the mining had been suspended.

Seven months later, on November 26, the Court rejected U.S. arguments that it had no jurisdiction in the case and stated that the provisional measures issued in May should remain in effect pending resolution of the case. On January 18, 1985, the United States announced it would boycott the proceedings and attacked Nicaragua's "misuse of the Court for political purposes."[82]

D'Escoto blasted the U.S. withdrawal from the Court as a return to the "law of the jungle, which confirms the United States' warlike policies, based on the concept that brute force governs relations between the weak and powerful nations." He called on the United States to decide "if it is for or against international law."[83]

House Judiciary Chairman Peter Rodino issued a prophetic denunciation of the World Court boycott: "On the weekend that President Reagan vowed to uphold the Constitution for his second term in office, his administration decided to flout international law by walking out of the World Court proceedings in Nicaragua's suit...In the 39-year history of the World Court, only three other nations have ever walked out on a case...Iran, Iceland, and Albania...

"Only a [sic] eleven years ago, we prevented the unraveling of our system by a President who tried to place himself above the law. Let us hope that history will not record our withdrawal from the World Court as the first sign of a new arrogance of power."[84]

It wasn't the first sign, but the administration's actions certainly represented an arrogance of power—an arrogance of power that Congress never tamed in the few times it tried.

Kissinger and Other Maneuvers

The Reagan administration had hoped that 1984 would bring a bipartisan Central America policy. The Kissinger Commission was to have laid the foundation.

The January 1984 commission report took a hard line toward Nicaragua following the lead of Chairman Kissinger, who had earlier stated, "It escapes me why we have to apply the Brezhnev Doctrine in Central America and assert that any Communist government that has established itself can never be changed."[85]

"The triumph of hostile forces in what the Soviets call the 'strategic rear' of the United States would be read as a sign of U.S. impotence," declared the Kissinger Commission report. It urged a massive program of economic and military aid for the region and portrayed the consolidation of the Sandinista government as "constituting a permanent security threat." In keeping with the official Reagan line, the majority of individual commission members saw the contras as "one of the incentives working in favor of a negotiated settlement." The commission did not render a "collective judgement" on the contra issue; two commission members, Mayor Henry Cisneros of San Antonio and Professor Carlos F. Diaz-Alejandro of Yale University, explicitly dissented from the majority and registered their opposition to support for the contras.[86]

On a lightning visit to Nicaragua on October 15, 1983, Kissinger remarked, "we should not be asked to choose between peace and democracy."[87] Democracy, as stated earlier by a U.S. official, is a euphemism for the overthrow of the Sandinista-led government. Accompanying the Kissinger Commission, Oliver North delighted in introducing himself as the "advance man for the U.S. invasion."

The late Nora Astorga, Nicaragua's former UN ambassador and deputy foreign minister, said the Kissinger Commission "came with a preconceived idea and it wanted to confirm that idea." Commissioners spent less than a day in Nicaragua, much of it in meetings with opposition leaders. During the meeting with Daniel Ortega, recalled Astorga, someone whispered to Kissinger, "Let's not listen to this son of a bitch any longer."[88]

Kissinger's preference for delusion over reality was apparent in his displeasure with Ambassador Tony Quainton. Quainton, assigned to Nicaragua after heading the State Department's Office for Combatting Terrorism, reportedly "undercut" Kissinger Commission findings by reporting that the Nicaraguan government had some positive features.[89]

In a meeting with U.S. citizens in March 1984, just before leaving his post in Nicaragua, Quainton (later U.S. ambassador to Kuwait, where he had to deal with a different round of minings) defended U.S. concern over Nicaragua's military build-up, but he readily acknowledged positive Nicaraguan initiatives. The positives included education and literacy, which "brought people into contact with a whole new world of ideas they hadn't experienced before." He cited urban housing and public health, especially rural health, for reaching "those who had no health care before"; he noted that some health posts were staffed by Cuban medical personnel. Land reform, he said, has made the most profound impact after education. Ironically, he said the Nicaraguan land reform was not "as radical as in El Salvador" in terms of the privately-held property that could be affected, at least theoretically. Nicaragua, he explained, is not a land-poor country, and the yardstick for land reform is not size of holdings, but productivity. He said notwithstanding the problem "that it only takes a few cases of land confiscation perceived as politically-motivated to generate producer anxiety," Nicaragua's was "one of the most sensible land reforms in Latin America." He added that there was a lot of debate in Nicaragua; "these are a very open people."[90]

Kissinger's portrayal of Nicaragua was quite different. He characterized Sandinista Nicaragua as not only worse than under Somoza, but "as bad or worse than Nazi Germany." People who disagreed with him were in the enemy camp. As Kissinger reportedly said of Reverend Eugene Stockwell, a respected officer of the World Council of Churches, before his testimony to the commission about conditions in Nicaragua, "If that man [Eugene] Stockwell is not a KGB agent, they're getting his services for free."[91]

Mexican writer Carlos Fuentes challenged the Kissinger-Reagan view of Central America: "Clearly, the stage is being set for a confrontation meant to overthrow the Sandinista Government and demonstrate Washington's version of the Brezhnev doctrine—that no Central American country can ever leave the United States' sphere of influence...

"Everyone knows that if the rightist counterrevolutionaries fighting in the north of Nicaragua were to reach Managua, they would not create a democratic regime. They would first stage a bloodbath and then restore the former dictatorship. By then, no one in Washington would give a pound of sugar for the destiny of Nicaraguan democracy. The counterrevolutionaries would reverse the social and juridical changes wrought by the Sandinistas—such as the literacy campaign, health care programs and various provisions necessary for holding elections...Nicaragua would fall once again into the pit of world indifference and internal oppression of the Somoza years. Nicaragua would again be a model servant of the United States."[92]

To comply verbally with congressional guidelines, Reagan officials continued to argue that the United States was not trying to overthrow the Nicaraguan government because the contras could not win. Asked, "What chance do the *contras* have of overthrowing the Sandinista regime?" Casey replied: "I think there's no chance that they will be able to overthrow the government. In the resistance, you have, it is said, perhaps 15,000 men with rifles scattered around the open, unpopulated parts of the country, which is where the guerrillas can hide. They can't go into the cities, which the government is protecting with tanks and 75,000 men in the Army, the militia and the security forces. So they're not going to overthrow that government."[93] (Notice that even Casey admits the defensive role of the tanks and troops.)

On April 1, the United States launched a three-month military exercise with Honduras provocatively code named Grenadero I. U.S. Army engineers constructed airstrips at Cucuyagua near the Salvadoran border and Jamastran near the Nicaraguan border, capable of landing giant C-130s. U.S., Honduran and Salvadoran troops practiced airborne and helicopter assault operations. On April 13, U.S. and Honduran forces practiced a parachute drop near Aguacate during other exercises code named

Lightning II; the purpose was "to secure an operations base from which to stage an assault on an airfield." Ocean Venture '84 ran from April 20 to May 6. Involving 30,000 troops and hundreds of ships including the aircraft carrier *America*, the exercise included the evacuation of 300 people from the U.S. naval base at Guantanamo Bay, Cuba. King's Guard coastal surveillance exercises involving U.S., Honduran and Salvadoran forces ran from April 26 to May 7. In July and August, the United States and Honduras conducted counterinsurgency exercises under Operation Lempira, practicing rapid deployment tactics. During Crown Dragonfly exercises in September, U.S. and Honduran fighters practiced bombing runs. These are just some of the maneuvers that took place throughout 1984.[94]

The *New York Times* reported in April that senior administration officials were acknowledging privately that intervention by U.S. combat forces in Central America was a possibility and contingency plans were being drawn up, utilizing the provisions of the Rio treaty. According to U.S. officials, a presidential decision on sending troops would not be taken until 1985, 1986 or later, after the current program had been given a chance to work.[95]

Senior officials disparaged the possibility of a negotiated settlement with Nicaragua, claiming that the Sandinistas (and the Salvadoran FMLN-FDR) could not be trusted to keep agreements, and force is the only thing they understand. "There must be a change in personalities in the Nicaraguan Government," said one official, "before there can be serious negotiations."[96] Once again the message was clear: the only negotiations to move past the lip service stage would be a surrender by the Nicaraguan government.

Aftershock: Boland Cutoff

The Kissinger Commission strengthened a growing bipartisan consensus on supporting the Salvadoran regime. It could not keep contra aid afloat amid the shockwaves from mining Nicaragua's harbors.

President Reagan appealed on May 9 for public support of his Central America policy in a nationally televised litany of lies and disinformation: "If we continue to provide too little help, our choice will be a Communist Central America with additional Communist military bases on the mainland of this hemisphere and Communist subversion spreading southward and northward. This Communist subversion poses the threat that 100 million people from Panama to the open border on our south could come under the control of pro-Soviet regimes...There has been an attempt to wipe out an entire culture, the Miskito indians, thousands of whom have been slaughtered or herded into detention camps where they have been starved and abused...The Sandinista rule is a Communist reign of terror...But we Americans must understand and come to grips with the fact that the Sandinistas are not content to brutalize their own land. They seek to export their terror to every other country in the region...The Sandinista military buildup began two and a half years before the anti-Sandinista freedom fighters had taken up arms...They claim the buildup is because they are threatened by their neighbors. Well, that, too is a lie...The Sandinistas claim the buildup is in response to American aggression, and this is the most cynical lie of all. The truth is that they announced at their first anniversary, in July of 1980, that their revolution was going to spread beyond their own borders...When the Sandinistas were fighting the Somoza regime, the United States' policy was: Hands off. We did not attempt to prop up Somoza. The United States did everything to show its openness toward the Sandinistas, its friendliness...As soon as I took office, we attempted to show friendship to the Sandinistas and provided economic aid to Nicaragua. But it did no good. They kept on exporting terrorism."

Reagan made his rollback policy explicit: "Communist subversion is not an irreversible tide. We have seen it rolled back in Venezuela and, most recently, in Grenada...The tide of the future can be a freedom tide. All it takes is the will and resources to get the job done."

He also baited contra critics with the Nazi-Munich analogy: "There are those in this country who would yield to the temptation to do nothing. They are the new isolationists, very much like the isolationists of the late 1930's who knew what was happening in Europe but chose not to face the terrible challenge history had given them. They preferred a policy of wishful thinking that if they only gave up one more country, allowed just one more international transgression, then surely, sooner or later, the aggressor's appetite would be satisfied...Well, they didn't stop the aggressors—they emboldened them. They didn't prevent war—they assured it...Let us show the world that we want no hostile, Communist colonies here in the Americas: South, Central or North."[97]

Again Reagan's mud-slinging smeared Nicaragua's image in the United States. Yet, on May 24, emboldened by domestic and international outrage over the mining and by the World Court ruling, the House rejected the supplemental contra aid request which the Senate had approved. The administration then concentrated on winning congressional approval of $28 million in funding for fiscal year 1985.

On June 1, after visiting El Salvador, Secretary of State Shultz made a surprise stopover in Managua and agreed that the United States would hold exploratory talks. Later in the month, U.S. Special Envoy Harry Schlaudeman and Nicaraguan Deputy Foreign Minister Victor Hugo Tinoco began meeting in Manzanillo, Mexico. It was, unfortunately, another episode of Washington's diplomatic charades, this time with an eye to the 1984 presidential elections as well as renewed contra funding. U.S. troop levels in Honduras were reduced (temporarily), according to U.S. sources in Tegucigalpa, as part of an overall effort to deemphasize the Central America issue during the presidential campaign.[98] Washington broke off the Manzanillo talks at the beginning of 1985.

The morning of Shultz's June 1, 1984 visit, a contra force of 500 to 600 troops invaded Ocotal, northern Nicaragua's largest city with a population of about 21,000, in another failed effort to "liberate" territory leaving death and destruction in its wake. According to an American Maryknoll nun living in Ocotal, "The fighting started about 4:30, just as it was getting light. They went up to the door of Radio Segovia, the local radio station. When the man came to the door they shot him. They then spread gasoline all over, and he burned to death. So did another man inside. They burned down the radio station. Another group attacked the other end of town. They destroyed the machinery in the lumber yard, and injured the ears of the children who were nearby. There were more than 30 of them.

"They destroyed the grainery. They went in shooting, killed the men guarding the place, spread gasoline all over and burned up six silos. They deliberately burned the grain, the corn, the beans, the sorghum."[99]

The contras also burned the coffee plant and the electric company building. A nurse on duty at the Ocotal hospital during the attack reported that contras fired at the hospital and several bullets entered the nursery and women's ward. Fortunately, no one was injured. The contras retreated at about 11:00 A.M when the local militia was reinforced by a Nicaraguan spotter plane and two helicopters. The attack left 16 Nicaraguans dead and 27 wounded.[100]

On October 3, the Senate voted to approve the contra aid request of $28 million. Administration supporters belatedly acknowledged the arms interdiction pretense. Said Senate Intelligence Committee Chairman Malcolm Wallop (R-WY), "I would hope...that we do not give the erroneous impression that we have fostered the Nicaraguan assistance solely to interdict arms for the war in El Salvador. That would cheapen both our motives and those of the Nicaraguans freedom fighting. We would thereby say that they are mere little mercenaries of the United States, off doing business for El Salvador. That was never true."[101]

The House rejected the aid and agreed only to consider $14 million in new funding after February 28, 1985. This time there was no compromise splitting the difference between the House cutoff and Senate funding. As of October 12, 1984, the law banned all contra support:

> During fiscal year 1985, no funds available to the Central Intelligence Agency, the Department of Defense, or any other agency or entity of the United States involved in intelligence activities may be obligated or expended for the purpose or which would have the effect of supporting, directly or indirectly, military or paramilitary operations in Nicaragua by any nation, group, organization, movement or individual.

The Reagan administration treated the new Boland amendment as just another obstacle to hurdle in its relentless pursuit of war.

8

Terrorist Manuals

I believe it is irrefutable that a number of the Contras' actions have to be characterized as terrorism, as State-supported terrorism.

Stansfield Turner, former director of Central Intelligence, testimony before the House Subcommittee on Western Hemisphere Affairs, April 16, 1985.

It was Edgar Chamorro's job to improve the contras' image. "This was challenging," he told the World Court, "because it was standard F.D.N. practice to kill prisoners and suspected Sandinista collaborators. In talking with officers in the F.D.N. camps along the Honduran border, I frequently heard offhand remarks like, 'Oh, I cut his throat.' "

The CIA, said Chamorro, "did not discourage such tactics. To the contrary, the Agency severely criticized me when I admitted to the press that the F.D.N. had regularly kidnapped and executed agrarian reform workers and civilians. We were told that the only way to defeat the Sandinistas was to use the tactics the Agency attributed to 'Communist' insurgencies elsewhere: kill, kidnap, rob and torture." These tactics, said Chamorro, "were reflected in an operations manual prepared for our forces by a C.I.A. agent who used the name 'John Kirkpatrick.' "[1]

John Kirkpatrick was a U.S. Army counterinsurgency specialist, with experience in the Vietnam-era Phoenix program, working under contract to the CIA's International Activities Division. In October 1983, at Dewey Clarridge's direction, Kirkpatrick wrote the detailed contra manual, *Psychological Operations in Guerrilla Warfare*, under the pseudonym Tayacan; CIA contra coordinator Ray Doty was also involved in its planning and preparation.[2] Kirkpatrick's model was a 1968 manual used by the Army Special Warfare School at Fort Bragg, North Carolina. *Psychological Operations in Guerrilla Warfare* closely followed the Army manual's Lesson Plan No. 643, titled "Armed Psyop" and subtitled "Implicit and Explicit Terror."[3]

Like the "winning hearts and minds" approach employed in Vietnam, the CIA contra manual advocated a mix of political propaganda and terror to dominate the population. Assassination is standard operating procedure for the contras, just as it was in the Phoenix program, notwithstanding the fact that assassination violates U.S. law. As stated in the 1967 U.S. Army field manual, "Handbook on Aggressor Insurgent War," which advocated the "selective use of terror as opposed to mass terror": "The assassination of a government official will lead some people to refrain from seeking public office and this will weaken the enemy government. Likewise, the assassination of a village leader will make it difficult to obtain another leader enabling the insurgent movement to have more freedom of action. Such actions display the government's inability to protect its officials, causing the populace to lose respect for the government."[4] As in Vietnam, the contras' targets have not been restricted to "enemy" officials or community leaders.

The CIA contra manual counsels assassination in a section titled "Selective Use of Violence for Propagandistic Effects," stating: "It is possible to neutralize carefully selected and planned targets, such as court judges, [justices of the peace], police and State Security officials, CDS chiefs, etc."[5] A hit list that starts with court judges and ends with *etcetera* is a mighty broad license for murder.

Implicit and Explicit Terror

"Guerrilla warfare," states the contra manual's preface, "is essentially a political war…In effect, the human being should be considered the priority objective in a political war. And conceived as the military target of guerrilla war, the human being has his most critical point in his mind. Once his mind has been reached, the 'political animal' has been defeated, without necessarily receiving bullets." Notice how the phrase "defeated without necessarily receiving bullets" reinforces the contra view that civilians not tied to the contra cause are legitimate targets for elimination.

According to the manual, armed propaganda "includes all acts carried out by an armed force, whose results improve the attitude of the people toward this force, and it does not include forced indoctrination." The manual quickly contradicts the latter point, but first it suggests that "during the patrols and other operations around or in the midst of villages, each guerrilla should be respectful and courteous with the people. In addition he should move with care and always be well prepared to fight, if necessary. But he should not always see all the people as enemies, with suspicions or hostility. Even in war, it is possible to smile, laugh or greet people. Truly, the cause of our revolutionary base, the reason why we are struggling is our people."[6]

It is telling evidence of why the contras have no broad popular base that the CIA finds it necessary to implore that they "should not *always* see *all* the people as enemies." (Italics added.)

The manual suggests slogans to help people appreciate contra weapons. For example: "With weapons we can impose demands such as hospitals, schools, better roads, and social services for the people, for you." It doesn't say whether the contras shout that before or after they destroy the local "Sandinista" hospitals, schools, roads and social services. Here's another slogan: "With weapons we can change the Sandino-Communist regime and return to the people a true democracy so that we will all have economic opportunities." Given that the system before the revolution was Somoza dictatorship and nearly all top contra military commanders are ex-Guardia, it is hardly surprising that few Nicaraguans are inspired by the phrase "return to the people a true democracy."

The manual draws a fine line between "implicit and explicit terror," contradicting the statement that armed propaganda does not involve forced indoctrination: "A guerrilla force always involves implicit terror because the population, without saying it aloud, feels terror that the weapons may be used against them. However, if the terror does not become explicit, positive results can be expected."

"Implicit terror" is illustrated this way: "An armed guerrilla force can occupy an entire town or small city which is neutral or relatively passive in the conflict. In order to conduct the armed propaganda in an effective manner, the following should be carried out simultaneously: Destroy the military or police installations and remove the survivors to a 'public place.' Cut all the outside lines of communication: cables, radio, messengers. Set up ambushes, in order to delay the reinforcements in all the possible entry routes. Kidnap all officials or agents of the Sandinista government and replace them in 'public places' with military or civilian persons of trust to our movement." The contras are directed to gather the population for a public tribunal and "shame, ridicule and humiliate the 'personal symbols' of the government...and foster popular participation through guerrillas within the multitude, shouting slogans and jeers. Reduce the influence of individuals in tune with the regime, pointing out their weaknesses and taking them out of the town, without damaging them publicly."[7]

The manual reinforces explicitly the contra practice of kidnapping civilians, under the broad sweep of "officials or agents of the Sandinista government" or "individuals in tune with the regime," cautioning only that they should not be "damaging" them *publicly.*

The manual not only condones the kidnapping and killing of noncombatants, it explains how to rationalize the killings. In the case of shooting "a citizen who was trying to leave the town or city in which the guerrillas are carrying out armed propaganda or political proselytism," the manual suggests that the contras "explain that if that citizen had managed to escape, he would have alerted the enemy that is near the town or city, and they would carry out acts of reprisal such as rapes, pillage, destruction, captures, etc., in this way terrorizing the inhabitants of the place for having given attention and hospitalities to the guerrillas of the town." Using Jeane Kirkpatrick's lingo, the contras projected their own behavior onto the Sandinistas.

In the case of public executions, the manual recommends that the contras "gather together the population affected, so that they will be present, take part in the act, and formulate accusations against the oppressor."[8] In practice, the contras favored executions without the convention of kangaroo courts.

Fifth Columns

The manual describes how "armed propaganda team" cadres should infiltrate the population and serve as the "antennas" of the movement, finding and exploiting "the socio-political weaknesses in the target society." The model is "the Fifth Column which was used in the first part of the Second World War, and through infiltration and subversion tactics allowed the Germans to penetrate the target countries before the invasions."[9]

The manual explains how to develop and control "front organizations" in urban areas. The first recruitment section refers to *involuntary* recruitment through extortion and frame-ups: "The initial recruitment to the movement, if it is involuntary, will be carried out through several 'private' consultations with a cadre, (without his knowing that he is talking to a member of ours). Then, the recruit will be informed that he or she is already inside the movement, and he will be exposed to the police of the regime if he or she does not cooperate...The notification of the police, denouncing a target who does not want to join the guerrillas, can be carried out easily, when it becomes necessary, through a letter with false statements of citizens who are not implicated in the movement."

There is an unstated side benefit to these frame-up jobs: if the government arrests people because of these false allegations who are, in fact, innocent, it alienates the accused, their families and associates, and exposes itself to charges of human rights abuse and political harassment (because many of those targeted for recruitment are active in opposition parties or groups), even if those arrested are released after investigation or trial.

Trusted voluntary recruits are to target potential new recruits, finding out their "personal habits, preferences and aversions [and] weaknesses." Recruits such as doctors, lawyers, businesspeople, landholders, minor state officials, politicians, priests, missionaries, professors, teachers and workers would be "used for subjective internal control of groups and associations to which they belong or may belong."

Contra cadres in the target groups are to stress particular themes. For example, in economic interest groups the contra cadres would manipulate peoples' frustration over "taxes, import-export tariffs, transportation costs, etc." The assumption is that "for all the target groups...the hostility towards the obstacles to their aspirations will gradually become transferred to the current regime." Cadres are advised to maintain a low profile "so that the development of hostile feelings towards the false Sandinista regime seems to come spontaneously from the members of the group and not from suggestions of the cadre. This is internal subjective control."

"Anti-governmental hostility," states the manual, "should be generalized and not necessarily in our favor. If a group develops a feeling in our favor it can be utilized. But the main objective is to precondition the target groups for the fusion in mass organizations later in the operation, when other activities have been successfully undertaken."[10]

The manual describes the development of clandestine cells of "internal cadres" and the process of "fusion" leading to insurrection through mass front organizations. "The development and control of the 'cover' organizations...will give our movement the ability to create the 'whiplash' effect within the population, when the order for fusion is given." The aim will be "to shake up the Sandinista structure and replace it."

Through "preconditioning campaigns" aimed "at the political parties, professional organizations, students, laborers, the masses of the unemployed, the ethnic minorities and any other sector of society that is vulnerable or recruitable" the contras "create a negative 'image' of the common enemy," the Sandinistas. The mass media and public demonstrations and meetings play a critical role: "Our psychological war cadres will create compulsive obsessions of a temporary nature in places of public concentrations, constantly hammering away at the themes pointed out or desired, the same as in group gatherings; in informal conversations expressing discontent; in addition passing out brochures and flyers, and writing editorial articles both on the radio and in newspapers, focused on the intention of preparing the mind of the people for the decisive moment, which will erupt in general violence."[11]

There is also an unstated side benefit to this fifth column strategy. State of emergency restrictions on the media and public meetings, designed to frustrate the CIA-contra strategy, create resentment among legitimate opposition groups. Through its fifth column strategy, the contras are working not only to establish an internal base, but to blur the distinctions between non-contra opposition and pro-contra opposition so that security measures will be seen as political (religious, ethnic or economic) repression rather than, as the government argues, justifiable, extraordinary measures to protect the sovereignty of the country and the lives of its citizens.

Criminals and Martyrs

According to the manual, agitators should be "mobilized toward the areas where the hostile and criminal elements of the FSLN, CDS and others live, with an effort for them to be armed with clubs, iron rods, placards and if possible, small firearms, which they will carry hidden."

"If possible," states the manual, "professional criminals will be hired to carry out specific selective 'jobs.' " (In perhaps the most famous case of U.S. government reliance on professional criminals, the CIA contracted Mafia gangsters to assassinate Fidel Castro.) The manual also advises that the unemployed be hired for "unspecified 'jobs.' "

The nature of these "jobs" becomes clearer when the manual advocates the creation of martyrs: "Specific tasks will be assigned to others, in order to create a 'martyr' for the cause, taking the demonstrators to a confrontation with the authorities, in order to bring about uprisings or shootings, which will cause the death of one or more persons, who would become the martyrs, a situation that should be made use of immediately against the regime, in order to create greater conflicts."[12]

In a section on how to lead an uprising at mass meetings, the manual calls for guerrilla cadre to assume such roles as bodyguards for the demonstration leaders, messengers, carriers of banners and placards, agitators of rallying cries and applause, and shock troops. The shock troops "should be equipped with weapons (knives, razors, chains, clubs, bludgeons) and should march slightly behind the innocent and gullible participants. They should carry their weapons hidden. They will enter into action only as 'reinforcements,' if the guerrilla agitators are attacked by the police. They will enter the scene quickly, violently and by surprise, in order to distract the authorities, in this way making possible the withdrawal or rapid escape of the in-side commando."[13]

As we have seen above, the manual advocates provoking confrontations with the police in order to create martyrs. In the CIA school of contra ethics, contra terrorists are protected and whisked from the scene while "innocent and gullible participants" are set up for unwitting martyrdom.

"A Bullet is Sharper Than Words"

Edgar Chamorro assisted in translating the manual into Spanish. He told the World Court that before the manual was distributed, "I attempted to excise two passages that I thought were immoral and dangerous...One recommended hiring professional criminals. The other advocated killing some of our own colleagues to create martyrs for the cause. I did not particularly want to be 'martyred' by the C.I.A. So I locked up all the copies of the manual and hired two youths to cut out the offending pages and glue in expurgated pages. About 2,000 copies of the manual, with only those two passages changed, were then distributed to F.D.N. troops." At least 5,000 copies of the original manual were reportedly printed and distributed by the CIA, so thousands circulated without the changes made by Chamorro. A *Soldier of Fortune* affiliate printed and distributed another 500 copies.

"Upon reflection," said Chamorro, "I found many of the tactics advocated in the manual to be offensive, and I complained to the C.I.A. station chief in Tegucigalpa. The station chief defended 'Kirkpatrick' and the manual, and no action was ever taken in response to my complaints. In fact, the practices advocated in the manual were employed by F.D.N. troops. Many civilians were killed in cold blood. Many others were tortured, mutilated, raped, robbed or otherwise abused.

"As time went on, I became more and more troubled by the frequent reports I received of atrocities committed by our troops against civilians and against Sandinista prisoners. Calero and Bermudez refused to discuss the subject with me, so I went straight to our unit commanders as they returned from combat missions inside Nicaragua and asked them about their activities. I was saddened by what I was told. The atrocities I had heard about were not isolated incidents, but reflected a consistent pattern of behavior by our troops. There were unit commanders who openly bragged about their murders, mutilations, etc. When I questioned them about the propriety or wisdom of doing those things they told me it was the only way to win this war, that the best way to win the loyalty of the civilian population was to intimidate it and make it fearful of us."

Chamorro complained to the CIA, as well as to Calero and Bermudez, to no avail. He recalled a visit by Dewey Clarridge in June 1984: "Although he was well aware of the terrorist tactics the F.D.N. troops were employing he spoke warmly to Bermudez: 'Well done, Colonel,' I remember him saying. 'Keep it up. Your boys are doing fine.' "

Shortly after that, Chamorro acknowledged to a newspaper reporter that FDN troops had killed civilians and executed prisoners. "Calero told me I could no longer work in Honduras," said Chamorro, "and I was reassigned to the local F.D.N. committee in Miami. I was given nothing to do and I no longer had much interest in working for the F.D.N., or to be more accurate, for the C.I.A."[14] Chamorro broke with the FDN in November 1984.

While working in the FDN, Chamorro tried to have people trained in human rights. The commanders were hostile, he told me, and the people trained were "looked on in suspicion" and "labeled weak or wimps or human rightists." Some were killed in the field as "spies."

CIA officer Ray Doty shared Bermudez's approach. Doty said "a bullet is sharper than any words," Chamorro recalled. Doty was in the fire power school of thought: "You want to change a country you just do it with fire power...He laughed at the [political] training."

"Educating in democracy," observed Chamorro, "is not just making people march singing democratic songs. That's what Americans do—they come and they repeat slogans. But that doesn't transform a person into a democratic person."[15]

Freedom Fighters Manual

The CIA produced a second manual, the *Freedom Fighters Manual.* Written in comic book style, it billed itself as a "practical guide to liberate Nicaragua from oppression and misery by paralyzing the military-industrial complex of the traitorous Marxist state without having to use special tools and with minimal risk for the combatant." An introductory passage notes, "The following pages present a series of useful sabotage techniques, the majority of which can be done with simple household tools such as scissors, empty bottles, screwdrivers, matches, etc."

Ranging from petty acts to life-threatening violence, the "useful sabotage techniques" are as follows (in order of presentation): Don't do maintenance work on vehicles and machines. Hide and damage tools. Throw tools into sewers. Arrive late to work. Delay in completing tasks. Call in sick to work. Leave lights on. Leave water taps on. Plant flowers on state farms. Hoard and steal food from the government. Leave open the corral gates on state farms (a sign in the accompanying illustration says "FSLN Cooperative"). Spread rumors. Phone in false hotel reservations, etc. Spill liquids (an illustration has a man apparently at work spilling coffee on his papers). Drop typewriters. Steal, hide key documents. Threaten the boss by telephone. Phone in false alarms of fires and crimes. Break light bulbs and windows. Damage books. Cut telephone cables. Cut alarm system cables. Stop up toilets and drains. Paint anti-Sandinista slogans (the illustration shows "Long Live the Pope"). Break police station windows, street lights and traffic lights. Put nails on roads and highways. Put nails next to the tires of parked vehicles. Pour dirt into gas tanks. Pour water in gas tanks. Cut and perforate the upholstery of vehicles. Break windshield wipers and headlights of vehicles. Cut and puncture tires. Put dirt in the carburetor and distributor. Break the distributor coil. Cut the distributor coil cables. Steal the rotor cap. Take an ice pick or similar tool to the gas tank, tires and radiator. Perforate battery covers. Invert battery cable connections. Throw nails in battery cells. Cut down trees over highways. Put rocks on highways. Dig ditches in highways. The last set of illustrated directions shows how to bring down telephone lines; puncture tires with a homemade arrowhead; make a delayed fire using matches and a cigarette; make a molotov cocktail (the illustration shows a man throwing it at a police station); and puncture fuel tanks with an icepick and light the fuel with a molotov cocktail. The manual ends with an appeal to Nicaraguan soldiers and militia to join the contras, "with your weapons if possible."[16]

The manual gives away its non-Nicaraguan origin with non-Nicaraguan language and illustrations. For example, in Nicaragua one finds match boxes, but not match books. The tall hotel illustrated resembles none in Nicaragua (including the famous pyramid-shaped Intercontinental). The brick police station with plate glass windows is not Nicaraguan style. And while the easy chair is a familiar site to North Americans, a Nicaraguan would likely be found in a wooden rocking chair.

When the Washington-based Central American Historical Institute publicized the *Freedom Fighters Manual*—discovered following a June 1984 contra attack on Ocotal—there was little interest outside of an Associated Press story by Robert Parry.[17] The other CIA manual was a different story, when it finally appeared in the major media just weeks before the U.S. presidential election.[18]

Rogue Manual?

"A Central Intelligence Agency document that became public this week tells Nicaraguan rebels how to win popular support and gives advice on political assassination, blackmail and mob violence," reported the *New York Times'* Joel Brinkley on October 17, 1984. In the face of congressional inquiry and rising public condemnation, the administration first tried to pass the manual off as a draft, insisting it was later revised for distribution. Edgar Chamorro quickly refuted this, as did CIA officials.[19]

During an October 21 debate with Democratic presidential contender Walter Mondale, Reagan answered a question about the manual with this tall tale: "We have a gentleman down in Nicaragua who is on contract to the C.I.A. advising, supposedly, on military tactics, the contras. And he drew up this manual. It was turned over to the agency head of the C.I.A. in Nicaragua to be printed, and a number of pages were excised before it was printed. But some way or other, there were 12 of the original copies that got down there and were not submitted for this printing process by the C.I.A. Now those are the details as we have them, and as soon as we have an investigation and find out where any blame lies for the few that did not get excised or changed, we certainly are going to do something about that. We'll take the proper action at the proper time."[20]

The *New York Times* editorialized on October 25 about the "Bad Manual, Bad War." The editorial should have been titled "Bad Manual, Badly-run War, Bad Sandinistas." The manuals and minings, said the *Times,* revived "the spectacle of an agency running out of control. Its having to be stopped from illegal minings and murders can only destroy the painfully rebuilt consensus for prudent covert operations under reliable executive and legislative control...The bitter consequence of this wretched affair is that it drowns out a necessary debate over what can legitimately be demanded of the hostile Sandinistas. Indeed, it gives them a chance to blame Americans for the great damage they have done to their country. And it undercuts— you might say 'neutralizes'—the cause of freedom."

CIA Director Casey defended the manual, claiming its overall thrust was on political awareness, civic action and respect for human rights. Reagan insisted there was "nothing in that manual that talked of assassination at all." He asserted that "the real word was 'remove'—meaning remove from office. If you came into a village or town, remove from office representatives of the Sandinista government. When they translated it into the Spanish, they translated it 'neutralize' instead of remove." When asked by reporters "how would you go about doing that without violence and force?" Reagan responded, to laughter, that "You just say to the fellow that's sitting there in the office—you're not in the office anymore."[21] In the actual manual, the reference to neutralizing judges, etc., is in a section with "violence" in the very title.

Reagan promised during the presidential debate to take "the proper action at the proper time." "Whoever was involved ought to be fired," said National Security Adviser Robert McFarlane. However, after completion of a report by the CIA's inspector general and with the presidential election behind him, Reagan concluded that the manual was "much ado about nothing."[22]

Proper action turned out to be a warmup for the Iran-contra fall-guy plan. John Kirkpatrick resigned his contract with the CIA and some six mid-level employees were reprimanded. One of those reprimanded was the former station chief in Honduras, Donald Winters. He had left Honduras in June 1984 after being embarrassed by the sudden ouster of General Alvarez on March 31. Alvarez was close enough to the station chief to be named godfather when Winter and his wife adopted a Honduran girl.[23] But in carrying out his role as local godfather for the U.S. government, Alvarez had made too many enemies in the Honduran military.

The House Intelligence Committee concluded on December 5 that the manual violated the Boland amendment because it advised the contras on overthrowing the Nicaraguan government. In a preview of the Iran-contra hearings, Congress was a watchdog with blinders.

According to the House Intelligence Committee, "the manual has caused embarrassment to the United States and should never have been released in any of its various forms. Specific actions it describes are repugnant to American values." The committee accepted the administration line that "no one but its author paid much attention to the manual," and said that some CIA officers did not know of the executive order's ban on assassination. "The incident of the manual illustrates once again to a majority of the Committee that the CIA did not have adequate command and control of the entire Nicaraguan covert action...CIA officials up the chain of command either never read the manual or were never made aware of it. Negligence, not intent to violate the law, marked the manual's history."[24]

The real problem was not careless management but state terrorism with impunity. In late 1983, Dewey Clarridge had secretly briefed the Intelligence Committees on the kind of contra murders advocated in the manual. He told the committees that the contras had killed "civilians and Sandinista officials in the provinces, as well as heads of cooperatives, nurses, doctors and judges." But he claimed that this didn't violate the presidential order prohibiting assassinations: "These events don't constitute assassinations because as far as we are concerned assassinations are only those of heads of state."[25]

Dewey Clarridge was rewarded, not reprimanded. He reportedly received an award for his service in Latin America and the highest bonus of the year. He was promoted to European division chief and then head of the CIA Counterterrorism Unit (he became embroiled in the Iran-contra affair). Ray Doty was not disciplined. Oliver North helped arrange a job on the NSC staff for the head of the CIA's Nicaragua task force, Vincent Cannistraro. North also helped find a job (undisclosed) for the manual's author, John Kirkpatrick. Joe Fernandez (alias Tomas Castillo), the CIA's main liaison with the contras when the manual was produced, carried on as CIA station chief in Costa Rica.[26]

Outlaw State

The manual, like the larger war on Nicaragua, violated U.S. and international law. The World Court found that in producing and disseminating *Psychological Operations in Guerrilla Warfare* to contra forces, the United States "encouraged the commission by them of acts contrary to general principles of humanitarian law." These principles include Article 3 of the 1949 Geneva Conventions, which covers noncombatants including "members of armed forces who have laid down their arms and those placed *hors de combat* by sickness, wounds, detention, or any other cause." The World Court cited the prohibitions of "violence to life and person, in particular murder of all kinds [mutilation, cruel treatment and torture]" and "the passing of sentences and the carrying out of executions without previous judgement pronounced by a regularly constituted court, affording all the judicial guarantees which are recognized as indispensable by civilized peoples."[27] Other provisions of Article 3 include prohibitions against the "taking of hostages" and "outrages upon personal dignity, in particular humiliating and degrading treatment."

Americas Watch found in a March 1985 study that "the contra forces have systematically violated the applicable laws of war throughout the conflict. They have attacked civilians indiscriminately; they have tortured and mutilated prisoners; they have murdered those placed *hors de combat* by their wounds; they have taken hostages; and they have committed outrages against personal dignity." By "publishing and distributing" the CIA manual, "the United States has directly solicited the contras to engage in violations of the laws of war."

In regard to the Nicaraguan government, Americas Watch observed: "The evidence that we have gathered shows a sharp decline in violations of the laws of war by the Nicaraguan government following 1982…The most serious abuse [of the laws of war] currently attributable to the Nicaraguan government that we have found is its continuing failure to account publicly for what happened to victims of abuses in 1981 and 1982 and to provide redress to victims and their families."[28]

A follow-up Americas Watch report reaffirmed its findings of systematic violations of the laws of war by the contras and found further that the contras, particularly the FDN, "practice terror as a deliberate policy." The report added, "We have detected no improvement in the practices of the contras subsequent to the publication of our March report, though we do note that, shortly after that report was published, the FDN announced that it had taken two prisoners and had offered to turn them over to the International Committee of the Red Cross. This is the first and only instance that we know of in which the FDN took prisoners."[29] As noted earlier, FDN forces have systematically killed prisoners.

Congressional investigation of the CIA contra manual obscured more than it illuminated. Most importantly, Congress covered up the role of the U.S. government in sponsoring "terror as a deliberate policy."

Journalist William Greider perceptively described the "drama of collective denial" played out over the manual—a drama often in revival: "One of the least attractive qualities about us Americans is our stubborn belief that we are the innocents of the world. America plays fair. America is generous and aboveboard in its actions toward others. Yet in spite of these good intentions, we are constantly bombarded with hostile invectives and attacked by fanatics using devious tactics.

"From time to time, when we are confronted by incontrovertible evidence that America plays dirty too, most citizens instinctively seem to deny its meaning. It must be a mistake…We Americans are for democracy and fair play; we are opposed to terrorism and deceit. Any deviation from our high moral standards must be a temporary aberration."[30] Or so U.S. leaders and history books would have us believe.

9

Ballots, Bullets and MIGs

I don't see why we need to stand by and watch a country go communist due to the irresponsibility of its own people.

Henry Kissinger, referring to Chile, June 27, 1970.[1]

The Marines, now in Nicaragua, are there to protect American lives and property and to aid in carrying out an agreement whereby we have undertaken to do what we can to restore and maintain order and insure a fair and free election.

Republican Platform, 1928.

Just as we assert the right of self-government, it follows that all people throughout the world should enjoy that same human right...We support continued assistance to the democratic freedom fighters in Nicaragua. Nicaragua cannot be allowed to remain a Communist sanctuary.

Republican Platform, 1984.

The "drama of collective denial" over the CIA manuals was one act in the national drama of Ronald Reagan's reelection. As *Newsweek* explained in a special issue on the 1984 election, "It was the conscious intent of [Reagan's] managers to run him as a kind of national icon."

"*Paint RR as the personification of all that is right with, or heroized by, America*," a Reagan campaign strategy memo advised. "Leave Mondale in a position where an attack on Reagan is tantamount to an attack on America's idealized image of itself—*where a vote against Reagan, is, in some subliminal sense, a vote against a mythic* 'AMERICA.' "[2] (Italics in original.)

The Reagan-as-icon strategy culminated in the landslide hype that swept the mass media. *Newsweek's* special issue led off with a piece titled "America: Reagan Country": "It was the night that Ronald Wilson Reagan became Mr. America. In a star-spangled blowout, the American people reaffirmed their identification with his can-do-confidence, his patriotic pride, and their vote transcended party and ideology: It was more than 52 million Americans roaring 'Thank you!' to a president who had made the country feel good about itself...

"Reagan claimed his mandate as he had won it, with a rippling sea of American flags before him and his wife, Nancy, at his side...her gaze as adoring and his message as rousing as ever. He harked back to the simple but evocative themes that had launched his political career nearly a generation ago. '...Here in America the *people* are in charge.' "[3]

Buried in the coverage of mythic America's mythic election was *Newsweek's* own observation that "the president remained, as he always had been, a polarizing figure dividing the nation by sex, class, race and ideological persuasion; *his* America was lopsidedly white, male, conservative and well-to-do."[4] What Reagan personifies, in other words, is the American logic of the minority.

Reagan's Mythical Mandate

The American people were barely engaged in the political process, much less in charge. The hidden key to the 1984 election was that many more eligible voters stayed away from the polls (76 million) than voted for Ronald Reagan (55 million). Reagan's landslide was the product of an essentially non-participatory democracy.

Only 55 percent of the eligible electorate voted for president, and those who voted were not a representative sample of the American public. The voting population is skewed toward higher-income brackets. In the 1980 election, for example, an estimated 70 percent of Americans earning more than $25,000 in annual income voted, compared with 25 percent of those earning less than $10,000.[5] Reagan won the votes of 27.6 percent of the eligible electorate in 1980, a smaller share than Wendell Willkie received in losing to Franklin Roosevelt in 1940. Reagan's 32.3 percent of the eligible electorate in 1984 was a smaller share than that of Eisenhower in both his elections, Kennedy or loser Nixon in 1960, Johnson in 1964 or Nixon in 1972.[6]

Reagan's legendary popularity is fiction masquerading as fact. As political analysts Thomas Ferguson and Joel Rogers observed, "Press claims that Reagan's first term marked him as the most popular President of the postwar period are simply false. Over all of that term, his approval rating averaged 50 percent, lower than the averages for Eisenhower (69%), Kennedy (71%), Johnson (52%), and Nixon (56%), and not far above that of Carter (47%). Reagan's high point was reached shortly after taking office, when in May 1981 he recorded a 68 percent approval rating. Four out of the five other elected postwar Presidents had higher peaks—Eisenhower (79%), Kennedy (83%), Johnson (80%), and Carter (75%)—while Nixon's 67 percent approval peak was not significantly lower. Reagan's low point of 35 percent, on the other hand, reached in January 1983, was significantly lower than those of Eisenhower and Kennedy, matched the level Johnson sank to just before he withdrew from national politics in 1968, and came close to the...approval rating that Nixon received in July and August 1974, just before he resigned the Presidency in disgrace."

What about the common view that Reagan has had a special bond with the American people—that they liked him personally, even while disapproving of his policies? As Ferguson and Rogers explain, "significant differentials between performance and personal approval ratings of Presidents are utterly routine...[and] in fact the differential Reagan enjoyed was proportionately smaller than those of most of his predecessors, not larger...[If] one controls for economic conditions, Reagan's popularity does not differ significantly from Jimmy Carter's."[7] The difference is that the press helped create and protect Reagan's so-called Teflon coating, while magnifying Carter's scratches.

Polls during the Reagan presidency have shown substantial majorities disapproving of many policies and priorities, such as cutbacks in education, health care, job training and aid to the poor.[8] By November 1984, polls on Central America had tracked a consistent record of opposition to policy in El Salvador and Nicaragua. "The public does not believe that the U.S. interests at stake in the region are as vital as the Administration has portrayed them," explained William LeoGrande in a study of polling data, "and they are fearful that U.S. involvement will lead to 'another Vietnam.' "[9] While a majority opposed intervention, most people were also uninformed. The percentage knowing which side the United States was backing in Nicaragua fluctuated from 22 percent in a March 1982 NBC poll, to 13 percent in a June 1983 CBS poll, to 29 percent in an August 1983 ABC poll.[10]

Administration disinformation has influenced public opinion, though not enough to command majority support for U.S. policy. A March 1982 *Los Angeles Times* poll asked people whether they believed administration charges that "Nicaragua is being used as a staging area by Cuba and Russia to send military supplies and men to the rebel forces in El Salvador." Only 11 percent disagreed, while 45 percent said they believed the claim and 44 percent said they didn't know. A CBS/*New York Times* poll that month found that 17 percent of the respondents thought there were Cuban or Soviet troops in El Salvador, 20 percent thought there were Cuban or Soviet advisers and 13 percent thought there were both advisers and troops; only 7 percent knew there were neither troops nor advisers. From March 1982 to August 1983, ABC/*Washington Post* polls found the public divided evenly between those who thought there would be no war in El Salvador without Cuban and Nicaraguan involvement and those who thought there would. On the other hand, "when people are explicitly asked whether the main cause of the turmoil in Central America is Cuban and Soviet subversion or the domestic conditions of poverty and human rights abuse, they overwhelmingly see the indigenous causes as more important."[11]

Anti-communism has been a strong force in public opinion, but not strong enough to shift the polls in favor of administration policy. For example, "public opinion is strongly opposed to the deployment of U.S. combat troops to El Salvador, but opposition is 25 to 30 points lower when the alternative is posed as a 'communist takeover' of the government there." When the Nicaraguan government is characterized as "Marxist" people are more likely to support aid to the contras.[12]

Between early 1983 (when pollsters began asking about U.S. involvement in the war against Nicaragua) and January 1984, opposition to administration policy ranged from a low of 48 percent (following the Grenada invasion) to a high of 78 percent, with most polls registering between the mid-50s and low-60s. Support for overthrowing the government of Nicaragua was generally in the low-20 percent range.[13] The trend of two-to-one opposition to contra aid continued after Reagan's reelection. So did widespread public confusion about which side the administration was on. For example, an April 1986 *New York Times*/CBS poll, showing that 62 percent were opposed to contra aid while 25 percent favored it, found that 38 percent knew the United States was supporting the contras; others didn't know or thought the United States was supporting the Nicaraguan government.

The 1986 poll found that "opposition to aid for the contras crossed all political, ethnic and regional and socio-economic lines. No demographic group favored it. But within that broad picture, some differences emerged. Aid was opposed by a lower percentage of men than women, whites than blacks, Republicans than Democrats and conservatives than liberals." The poll also found that "the higher the education and income, the less the opposition. Those earning more than $50,000 a year were against aid by a margin of 52 to 40 percent, while those earning less than $12,500 a year opposed it by 68 to 17 percent." When asked directly, 62 percent said they feared the United States would get involved in Nicaragua the way it did in Vietnam. When asked to volunteer reasons for opposing contra aid, "the most frequent reason given against the aid, and given most often by urban residents and those with lower incomes and less education, was that problems in the United States were more important." The funds should be spent on domestic problems.[14]

The Reagan administration clearly had no popular mandate to support the contras and overthrow the Nicaraguan government. That didn't stop the administration from pursuing its policy, or hypocritically accusing the Nicaraguan government of violating the will of its people.

Cruz Control

Two days before Reagan's reelection, Nicaraguans went to the polls to elect a president, vice president and legislative National Assembly. Months before the election occurred Reagan branded it a "Soviet-style sham." Months afterward he declared that the "Sandinista government is a government that seized power out of the barrel of a gun—it's never been chosen by the people."[15]

Later, a U.S. ambassador in Central America told me something quite different: "I worked hard to project the Nicaraguan election. There was no evidence of cheating. And the count came out pretty much as I called it—60 percent plus or minus for the FSLN. If Arturo Cruz would have stayed in he would have shaved three or four points off the Sandinistas, but most of his strength would have come from other opposition parties."[16]

Arturo Cruz was central to Washington's strategy to discredit the Nicaraguan election and portray the contras as a "democratic resistance": package Cruz as the major democratic opposition candidate; then, use his withdrawal from the election as the standard for denouncing the election as a sham. The ploy was exposed, but the press and Congress bought it anyway. Later, it was revealed that by spring 1984 Cruz was already receiving CIA funding.[17]

As early as August 1984, Mario Rappaccioli, a leader in the *Coordinadora* (Democratic Coordinating Committee), the rightwing alliance that nominated Cruz, told reporters that "Cruz does not intend to run and is interested only in discrediting the elections."[18]

Two weeks before the election, *New York Times* reporter Philip Taubman quoted a U.S. official: "The Administration never contemplated letting Cruz stay in the race, because then the Sandinistas could justifiably claim that the elections were legitimate, making it much harder for the United States to oppose the Nicaraguan Government."

Taubman reported that several administration officials familiar with activities in Nicaragua said the CIA "had worked with some of Mr. Cruz's supporters to insure that they would object to any potential agreement for his participation in the election." Officials specifically named COSEP, a major player in the Coordinadora. COSEP was "in frequent contact with the C.I.A. about the elections." COSEP president Enrique Bolaños and other leaders of the group "met during the spring and summer with C.I.A. officials in Washington and San Jose, Costa Rica." Bolaños claimed that he and COSEP "have nothing to do with the C.I.A." But U.S. intelligence officials said "that Mr. Bolaños and other Nicaraguan business leaders had had a close association with the agency since 1980," under the Carter administration's covert aid program."[19]

A closer look at Cruz and the Coordinadora shows why Cruz never had a chance of winning a free and fair election, which is precisely why he could only serve U.S. purposes by not running. Cruz appeared as a counterpart to Salvadoran President Jose Napoleon Duarte. Like Duarte, he was cultivated by Washington to present a "moderate" face for U.S.-backed forces. But unlike Duarte, Cruz was not a longtime political leader with a proven domestic base, nor a charismatic figure. Although he signed on to the Group of Twelve, opposing Somoza during the insurrection, Cruz chose to remain in Washington in his post at the Inter-American Development Bank when other members of the Twelve returned to Nicaragua in 1978, risking their lives as well as their careers. As Cruz himself acknowledged, "Due to the understandable personal limitations imposed by my career as an officer in an international institution, sometimes my contribution, of necessity, was somewhat marginal."[20] Cruz had lived in Washington since 1970, except for the July 1979-March 1981 period when he returned to Nicaragua to serve as head of the Central Bank and a member of the government junta. In April 1981, he went back to Washington to serve briefly as Nicaragua's ambassador to the United States. By the summer of 1983, Cruz had openly promoted Eden Pastora in an article in *Foreign Affairs*.

Nicaraguan Vice President Sergio Ramirez, a founding member of the Group of Twelve, made a prophetic observation when I asked him about Cruz in 1986: "We invited Mr. Cruz to be a member of the Group [of Twelve] after the second meeting of the Group in Cuernavaca in July 1977. And, he accepted...but in a very reluctant way. He never accepted to come to Nicaragua when the Group decided to come back here to confront the dictatorship...He said that it risked his process of retirement [with] the Inter-American Development Bank...I am very surprised that he participates now so openly with a political group, because I know him very well. He's a very shy man in politics. He's not a man of decisions. He prefers to be in the theory world...I have heard now about internal fighting in the cupola of the counter-revolutionary leadership. And he's now participating in these confrontations, trying to get...more power in the cupola. But I think...he's going to be discharged or he's going to resign, and he's going to go back to his desk in the bank where he prefers to be."[21]

The internal opposition group behind Cruz, the Coordinadora, was an alliance of COSEP; two small unions that had been tolerated by Somoza, the Social Christian CTN and the AIFLD-backed CUS; and the four most conservative political parties: the Social Christian Party (PSC), affiliated with the international Christian Democratic movement; the Nicaraguan Conservative Party (PCN), founded in June 1984; the Constitutionalist Liberal Party (PLC), a 1967 split from Somoza's Liberal Party; and the Social Democratic Party (PSD), founded in August 1979. Pedro Joaquin Chamorro Jr., the *La Prensa* codirector who went into exile in Costa Rica in December 1984 and became editor of the contra paper, *Hoy*, and later a member of the contra directorate, was a PSD leader.

"Internationally, the Reagan administration portrayed the Coordinadora as a giant," wrote one analyst of Nicaraguan politics, "but, in Nicaragua, this giant had clay feet."[22] The Coordinadora parties may have more supporters among Americans than Nicaraguans. PCN leader Mario Rappaccioli said of the other three parties, "They have so few people I could fit them all in a bus."[23] Actually, the Social Christian Party, not Rappaccioli's PCN, was considered the largest party (and the least reactionary of the bunch), but the PCN and COSEP dominated the Coordinadora.

Stripped of democratic rhetoric, the Coordinadora offered Nicaraguans the Somocismo without Somoza that the U.S. had tried and failed to create before. Rappaccioli's reactionary outlook is evident in a remark he made about the United States: "All the American media, especially the *Washington Post*, are communist."[24]

Contra leader Adolfo Calero described the Coordinadora as "my political wing." *La Prensa* codirector Jaime Chamorro has claimed, "Our fight is the same as the F.D.N.'s. It is like the difference between an infantry and an air force; two arms of the same thing...Editorially we do not support the contras' war; maybe we do personally, individually, but our official position is not pro-contra...but [the fight for democracy] can be won only by taking up arms. A government can be changed only by a conjunction of factors: the military, the international, the diplomatic, the church, the press."[25]

Before, during and after the election, *La Prensa* acted, not as the independent paper it is touted to be in the United States, but as a highly partisan supporter of the Coordinadora and U.S. policy. It would not even carry paid advertising by the other parties contesting the election. Clemente Guido, the presidential candidate of the Democratic Conservative Party (PCD)—a party that has historically represented land-owning interests, but has tried to broaden its base in the middle class—charged *La Prensa* with exercising its own brand of censorship during the electoral campaign; the only coverage it gave the PCD was hostile. "We Conservative Democrats," said Guido, "call it a 'dictatorship of paper.' " Guido found *Nuevo Diario* to be "more pluralistic," explaining that although he didn't like its editorial policy, the paper gave the opposition fair coverage.[26]

A large share of *La Prensa's* international coverage is devoted to the United States, often featuring the views of U.S. government officials. On March 16, 1984, for example, the day after the Council of State approved final legislation regulating the upcoming election, *La Prensa* carried only a small article on that while its top story was devoted to U.S. Ambassador Anthony Quainton. Its banner headline was "Quainton at breakfast with correspondents, says: Fears of Nicaragua, very exaggerated." The article quoted Quainton's remarks that tensions between Nicaragua and the United States "were due to Nicaragua's threatening attitudes toward El Salvador and Honduras." It ended with Quainton's assertion that the United States supported a peaceful solution in Central America through the Contadora process, but Nicaragua must stop helping the Salvadoran guerrillas and abandon its dependence on the Soviet Union and Cuba and its militaristic path. That same month, I heard Coordinadora leaders describe the U.S. military buildup in Central America as positive, saying it had "obliged the Sandinista government to soften its conduct of the revolution."[27]

La Prensa is anti-Sandinista, not independent. Some analysts have compared the role of *La Prensa* to Chile's *El Mercurio* and Jamaica's *The Daily Gleaner* in the destabilization of the Allende and Manley governments.[28] As far as Nicaraguan government leaders were concerned, it was better to risk condemnation in censoring *La Prensa* then to receive post-mortem sympathy like Allende.

La Prensa would be shut down for over a year by the government in June 1986 after the U.S. Congress approved $100 million in aid for the contras. By then *La Prensa* was being funded heavily by the U.S. National Endowment for Democracy; it received $100,000 in 1985 and over $250,000 in 1986 and 1987.[29] *La Prensa* editor Jaime Chamorro lobbied for the contra $100 million in an April 21, 1986 op ed. in the *Washington Post*. Imagine the *New York Times* being funded by and supportive of Japan or Germany during World War II, or the electability of the candidate they sponsored being a litmus test for the 1944 U.S. presidential election.

Campaigns

In December 1983, the Coordinadora issued a nine-point list of requirements for authentic elections. These included not only such conditions as the removal of state of emergency restrictions on press and assembly, but demanded major changes in government policy and direct negotiations with the contras as conditions for

Coordinadora participation in the election. A U.S. diplomat in Central America acknowledged, "the content of that [nine-point] statement showed that they had already decided not to participate. These were things that the Sandinistas would never accept."[30]

The Coordinadora named Arturo Cruz as its presidential candidate in July; Adan Fletes, previously nominated by the PSC as presidential candidate, became Cruz's running mate. When he arrived in Nicaragua on July 22, Cruz reiterated the nine points, emphasizing negotiations with the contras as a basic condition for participation.

The day before Cruz's arrival, contras kidnapped Noel Rivera, a successful coffee grower in Matiguas, Matagalpa who cooperated with the government. Rivera, a father of five, was beaten and bayoneted to death.

Cruz announced on July 25 that the Coordinadora would boycott the election, but that he would continue to campaign as if he was an official candidate. The next day "FDN contras murdered seven unarmed villagers in Tapasle, Matagalpa in an effort to discourage their neighbors from registering [to vote]. All of the victims were castrated and had their throats slit; some were dismembered and had their body parts scattered. One had the skin scraped off his face. Two other men were kidnapped."[31]

The Coordinadora boycott, the *Washington Post* reported, "effectively means that the domestic opposition is counting on the U.S.-financed covert guerrilla war and on other international pressure—rather than taking a primary role itself—to bring down the government or force it to further open the political process...Opposition leaders admitted in interviews that they never seriously considered running in the Nov. 4 election but debated only whether to campaign for two months and then withdraw from the race on grounds that the Sandinistas had stacked the electoral deck against them." The *Post* added, "It remains unclear how well the Democratic Coordinator would have fared in the election, as virtually all political observers predicted that the Sandinistas would win easily, even without the boycott."[32]

The government declared a four-day holiday, July 27-30, so that people could register to vote at over 4,000 polling stations throughout the country. More than 100 stations could not open because of the war.[33] On July 27, contras killed voter registration workers in Yali and Muelle de los Bueyes and wounded the secretary of a local voting precinct in an ambush in the Wilicon area. The next day, contras ambushed groups of people who were transporting voter registration documents in the Santa Cruz and La Vigia areas and stole the documents.[34]

Though voting was strictly voluntary, registration was required by law because the information generated through the registration process was to serve as a basis for a new nationwide census (there were no reported cases, however, in which penalties were imposed for nonregistration). A total of 1,560,580 persons were registered, representing 93.7 percent of the estimated voting age population.[35] Voting age was set at 16 years, a reflection of the country's relatively youthful population (Nicaragua's median age is about 16, compared to 32 in the United States) and the massive participation of youth in the overthrow of Somoza, defense and programs such as the literacy campaign.

The Coordinadora tried at first to boycott the registration and *La Prensa* refused to run paid promotional advertising by the Supreme Electoral Council (a fourth, autonomous branch of government that administers the electoral process, following the model in Costa Rica and other Latin American countries). But "the Coordinadora showed how weak its base of support is…In the first two days of the [registration] drive the turnout was so massive despite the boycott…that Cruz's supporters hastily changed their line and said they too favored registration."[36]

Most state of emergency restrictions were lifted at the start of the electoral campaign on August 1. Press censorship was eased. As Pedro Joaquin Chamorro Jr. put it, "Now they're allowing us to publish almost anything regarding politics."[37]

In late September, the FSLN asked the Supreme Electoral Council to extend the period for registering candidates and reopened negotiations with Cruz and the Coordinadora; Colombian President Betancur, Carlos Andres Perez and associates of former West German Chancellor Willy Brandt acted as mediators. A provisional agreement was reached on October 2 at talks in Rio de Janeiro, Brazil. The Coordinadora dropped its demand for direct negotiations with the contras and pre-election changes in government policy. According to Cruz's running mate Adan Fletes, the FSLN agreed to "all our conditions," including a large increase in free media time to compensate for the Coordinadora's late entry into the campaign. In a key provision of the draft, the FSLN agreed to postpone the election to January 1985 in return for a cease-fire with the contras to be negotiated by the Coordinadora.

A detailed report by election observers from the U.S. Latin American Studies Association (LASA) reviewed different explanations for the failure to reach a final agreement: "Adan Fletes told our delegation that the draft agreement was never signed because the FSLN's negotiator walked out of the talks. The FSLN claims that, once the draft accords had been initialed, Coordinadora leaders in Managua insisted on a delay of several days to reconsider the agreement, which the FSLN was unwilling to grant. Some independent journalistic reports corroborate this version. Others believe that negotiators for both sides may have exceeded their authority in Rio, and upon checking with their colleagues in Managua, they were urged to seek any pretext for getting out of the agreement. The Sandinistas clearly wanted and needed an agreement, to enlist the Coordinadora's participation and prevent the November 4 elections from being discredited internationally. Arturo Cruz, according to several key informants interviewed by our delegation, may also have wanted to run; but the more conservative elements of his Coordinadora coalition (especially the businessmen represented in COSEP), encouraged by hardliners within the Reagan Administration, vetoed any agreement."

The LASA report concluded: "The weight of the evidence available to us suggests that the Coordinadora group made a policy decision to pursue its political goals in 1984 outside of the electoral process. Its abstention from the elections was not the result of FSLN intransigence…Given the terms for campaigning and holding the elections to which the FSLN had agreed by October 2…it is evident that the FSLN *was* willing to 'take specific steps to create an environment conducive to genuine electoral competition,' as the Coordinadora and the U.S. State Department insisted that it do."[38]

As election day drew closer, Washington stepped up pressure on opposition parties outside the Coordinadora to join the abstentionist forces. "Within Nicaragua," observed the LASA report, "the behavior of U.S. diplomats was clearly interventionist. This behavior included repeated attempts to persuade key opposition party candidates to drop out of the election, and in at least one case, to bribe lower-level party officials to abandon the campaign of their presidential candidate, who insisted on staying in the race."[39]

According to Democratic Conservative Party candidate Clemente Guido, the U.S. embassy made large financial offers to several party leaders. "Two weeks before the election," said Guido, "a U.S. Embassy official visited my campaign manager and promised to help him with money to succeed me as party leader if he withdrew from my campaign. He did."[40]

Mauricio Diaz, the presidential candidate of the Popular Social Christian Party (PPSC), was visited by the U.S. Embassy political counselor on October 24. Created from a split in the Social Christian Party (PSC) in 1976, the PPSC characterizes itself as "Christian Democrats of the Left" and the PSC as "Christian Democrats of the Right." Diaz and the PPSC resisted U.S. pressure and remained in the race.[41]

Washington was more successful in disrupting the electoral campaign of the strongest opposition party, the Independent Liberal Party (PLI), whose base is among the middle class and professionals. Virgilio Godoy, the PLI's presidential candidate, had served as minister of labor until February 1984. Two weeks before the election, on October 20, Godoy was visited by U.S. Ambassador Harry Bergold and Embassy Political Counselor J. Michael Joyce (this was one of many PLI visits by U.S. officials during the campaign). The next day, Godoy announced his withdrawal from the election. When the LASA delegation asked Godoy what was discussed at the October 20 meeting, he replied, "The Ambassador wanted to express the point of view of his government regarding the elections; that this was not the best time to hold elections." An old friend of Godoy commented, "I can't explain his behavior. He would not just sell himself to the U.S. Embassy. I think he was subject to terrible pressure from the Embassy."

Under U.S. pressure the PLI split into abstentionist and nonabstentionist factions. Angry nonabstainers charged that Godoy was offered $300,000 not to run. The PLI's vice-presidential candidate and a number of PLI candidates for the National Assembly remained in the race after Godoy's withdrawal.[42]

"The PLI withdrawal from the elections has now left the Sandinistas holding a near-worthless hand," boasted a secret briefing paper for an October 30 National Security Council meeting on Central America. "An election held on November 4 will not give them the legitimacy they covet, although it will further consolidate Sandinista control over Nicaragua. Efforts continue to press the Sandinistas to postpone the elections and agree to Coordinadora demands."

The NSC document described the administration's domestic and international "public diplomacy strategy" on the Nicaraguan election. Domestic propaganda included distribution of the *Resource Book: The Sandinista Elections in Nicaragua*, "which documents the undemocratic nature of the election" and encouragement of experts outside the government "to make public statements, prepare articles, and appear on media programs, especially immediately prior to and following the November 4 elections, e.g., the morning TV shows on November 5." Plans for "the International Community" included encouragement of "public statements condemning the Nicaraguan elections" from "government officials, political party leaders...intellectuals, church, and labor leaders." In a nonchalant reference to U.S. government manipulation of the international press, the document noted, "Media contacts should be encouraged to write editorials questioning the validity of the elections."

"Congressional failure to fund the armed opposition [the contras] is a serious loss," the NSC document observed, "but our handling of the Nicaragua elections issue and Sandinista mistakes have shifted opinion against the sham elections." It stated confidently, "We have succeeded in returning the public and private diplomatic focus back on the Nicaraguan elections as the key stumbling block to prospects for national reconciliation and peace in the region."[43]

As former *New York Times* editor John Oakes put it, "The most fraudulent thing about the Nicaraguan election was the part the Reagan Administration played in it."[44]

The FSLN itself was the target of some U.S. dirty tricks. In one case, Washington tried to transform its wishful thinking of a split in the FSLN—between Borge "hardliners" and Ortega "pragmatists"—into reality. In August, full-page ads appeared in newspapers in Costa Rica, Venezuela and Panama signed by the "Friends of Tomas Borge." Their message was "Not Cruz, not Ortega. Borge for President." The ads described Borge as "the last true Sandinista revolutionary, the only one that can force through the promises of the 1979 revolution."[45]

Contra radio and leaflets advocated abstention, and electoral institutions and officials in the war zones were attacked. For example, Santos Jose Vilchez, president of the voter registration office at Pijibay was kidnapped along with four others on August 3. On August 7, 50 contras invaded El Morado and kidnapped ten campesinos. They removed voter registration cards and threatened to kill those who tried to vote. On September 14, contras kidnapped the president of the local voting precinct in the district of San Martin.[46]

The contras stepped up attacks in October as the election drew closer. Forty-three civilians were killed during the week of October 21.[47] On October 28, in El Dorado, contras kidnapped the president and secretary of the local electoral board. The next day, contras attacked the Santa Julia cooperative. A mortar landed in the cooperative's headquarters where three families were living.

"Maria Soza Valladares was sick in bed, but all her children were in the middle of the room 'as if they were waiting for the mortar' which killed Marta Azucena, 11 years old, Carmelita Azucena, five, and Ronaldo Miguel, three. Another child, Alexis, eight, was severely injured and died on the way to the hospital. Maria Soza, herself injured, tried to rescue her dead and dying children, but it was too late. Her daughter Maria, six, covered with blood, walked all the way to the health center in San Gregorio through the ensuing crossfire...Eventually, she and her mother spent almost a month in the hospital...Aurelia Ortiz, eight months pregnant, was also in the room with her children when the mortar exploded, killing Jose Rodolfo, five, and Maura de Jesus, seven. A month later, she gave birth to a stillborn child." The next day—the day the National Security Council was reviewing U.S. sabotage of the Nicaraguan election—eighteen campesinos were kidnapped in the Casa de Tabla area.[48]

Although the contras announced a cease-fire for election day, attacks continued. According to the Supreme Electoral Council, sixteen polling places could not function because of the war. Two polling places were attacked and an election official was killed. Near Wiwili, contras kidnapped 100 civilians.[49]

Nicaragua Votes

On election day, Nicaraguan voters had a clear choice of political platforms ranging from conservative to orthodox communist. If the Coordinadora had not boycotted, the most rightwing parties would have been represented as well.

In addition to the PCD, PLI and PPSC, positioned to the right of the FSLN in the Nicaraguan political spectrum, three parties on the ballot represented what could be considered Nicaragua's old left and far left. The Nicaraguan Socialist Party (PSN), founded in 1944, is the communist party recognized historically by the Soviet Union. The Nicaraguan Communist Party (PCdeN), a split from the PSN, regards the FSLN as a party of petty-bourgeois reformers. The Marxist-Leninist Popular Action Movement (MAP-ML) advocates the expropriation of all business property.

On November 4, Nicaraguans turned out in large numbers, with 75.4 percent of the registered voters casting ballots. The FSLN led the balloting with 67 percent of the vote, winning 61 seats in the National Assembly. The PCD, second with 14 percent, won 14 seats. The PLI, which was expected to finish second before the confused withdrawal of its presidential candidate, won 9.6 percent of the vote and 9 seats. The PPSC won 5.6 percent of the vote and 6 seats. The PCdeN, PSN and MAP-ML won, respectively, 1.5, 1.3 and 1 percent of the vote, and 2 seats each in the National Assembly. Of the total votes cast, 6.1 percent were invalid—including unmarked or defaced ballots and ballots with more than one party or presidential candidate marked—representing voter confusion (for many this was the first vote in their lifetimes) as well as protest votes.[50] Together, opposition parties (of the right and left) won a significant one-third of the popular vote and 35 seats (36.5 percent) in the 96-member National Assembly, including 6 seats designated for losing presidential candidates. Not surprisingly, abstentionist forces such as COSEP dismiss the Assembly as a "rubber stamp."[51]

Most international observers, such as the Latin American Studies Association, the International Human Rights Law Group and the British Parliamentary Human Rights Group, judged the election to be free and democratic. LASA's detailed analysis of Nicaraguan election procedure illustrates why most observers considered the election free and fair: "The election of the Assembly was based on a standard model of proportional representation...The choice of this kind of proportional representation system [common in Western Europe] is significant because it tilts the National Assembly toward political pluralism, by assuring the representation of a wider range of interests and opinions within the electorate than would be achieved under a U.S.-style single-member district system...Without it, the smallest opposition parties would have had virtually no chance of winning seats."[52]

The electoral law provided for public financing and free, uncensored air time. Each party, regardless of size, received an initial allotment of 9 million cordobas (about $900,000) and were permitted to receive additional funding from domestic and foreign sources. The Electoral Council also distributed donated materials such as paper and ink to the parties. During the campaign, each party had "access to a total of 22 hours (15 minutes per day) of free, uninterrupted television time, in prime early evening hours, on both channels; and 44 hours (30 minutes per day) of free radio time on all state-run radio stations."[53] As already noted, newspaper censorship was eased during the electoral period. There was no censorship of Nicaragua's 39 radio stations, with an audience far larger than the newspapers' combined readership, including two stations run by the Catholic hierarchy which was supportive of the Coordinadora. Also campaign billboards, posters and wall murals, as well as graffiti, widely promoted the different party messages.

Nicaraguans could also tune in regularly to the AM and FM broadcasts transmitted by contra-run radio stations and pro-contra radio broadcasting in neighboring countries. Over 70 foreign radio stations, including the familiar Voice of America, penetrated Nicaraguan territory, mostly from Costa Rica and Honduras. Honduran and Salvadoran television was received in northern Nicaragua, and in much of southern Nicaragua Costa Rican television was received more clearly than Nicaraguan.[54]

Nicaraguan electoral law "provided a broad array of protections and guarantees," the LASA report explained. The "law created a system of open scrutiny of all electoral proceedings (registration, campaigning, voting, vote tabulation) by party-nominated observers, at each level of electoral organization. Systems for receiving complaints and appeals for each step in the process were also established, as well as mechanisms for evaluation of complaints, reports to the interested parties, and correction of abuses of violations of the law." Nicaragua received material or technical election assistance from Sweden, Norway, Finland and France. And Nicaraguan delegations toured democracies in Latin America, Western Europe and the United States (after first being denied U.S. visas) to research electoral procedures.

"The actual voting process," stated the LASA report, "was meticulously designed to minimize the potential for abuses...In response to a request by opposition parties, all voter registration cards were retained by election judges so that there would be no possibility of them being used as an *ex post facto* way of checking on whether a person had voted (as allegedly happened in connection with the 1984 election in El Salvador)." Also, unlike in El Salvador where voters marked ballots that were transparent even when folded for deposit in *clear* plastic ballot boxes, Nicaraguan voters deposited their folded ballots, designed for confidentiality (with Swedish technical assistance) with dark-colored strips across the back, into non-transparent ballot boxes. By the end of the day on November 7, "not a single formal complaint about voting or vote count irregularities had been presented at the

Supreme Electoral Council, by any party. Spokesmen for several of the participating opposition parties attested to the cleanness of the elections."[55] (Months later, *La Prensa* presented a charge of voter fraud; it was thoroughly discredited.)[56]

The LASA report concluded that the charge of systematic intimidation and harassment of opposition candidates and supporters by Sandinista Defense Committees and gangs, known as *turbas,* was unfounded. The sporadic disruptions that did occur took place mainly in the pre- or early campaign period, and were not representative of the overall character of the campaign. The Electoral Council substantiated nine turba disruptions before and during a campaign with over 270 political rallies and demonstrations. In at least one case, Cruz supporters acted as turbas, attacking a group of women, including widows of men killed by the contras or by Guardia during Somoza's reign, carrying placards protesting the Coordinadora's call for direct talks with the contras. Not one person lost their life as a result of campaign violence (civilians did die at the hands of the contras), "a remarkable record in a country experiencing its first open electoral campaign in any Nicaraguan's lifetime, at a time of armed conflict and high emotions."[57] In El Salvador and the Philippines, in contrast, there were (and are) many political killings.

Regarding the charge that the FSLN abused its incumbency status, the LASA delegation found that "generally speaking...the FSLN did little more to take advantage of its incumbency than incumbent parties everywhere (including the United States) routinely do, and considerably *less* than ruling parties in other Latin American countries traditionally have done." (LASA's italics.) Sergio Ramirez observed, "We do have an advantage over our opposition. We are in power...It's certainly easier to run for President from the White House; but nobody accuses Ronald Reagan of anything illegal because he takes advantage of all that apparatus."[58]

The downside to incumbency was largely ignored: The party in power is generally blamed for poor economic conditions, however fairly or unfairly, and by 1984 Nicaragua was experiencing a worsening economic crisis.

The LASA report concluded that by Latin American standards, the Nicaraguan election "was a model of probity and fairness...we must conclude that there is *nothing* that the Sandinistas could have done to make the 1984 elections acceptable to the United States Government."[59] (LASA's italics.)

Democracies and Double Standards

When LASA observers asked a U.S. diplomat in Central America why the United States enthusiastically endorsed the 1984 Salvadoran elections, where all political groups to the left of the Christian Democrats were excluded, while condemning the more inclusionary electoral process in Nicaragua, he replied: "The United States is not obliged to apply the same standard of judgement to a country whose government is avowedly hostile to the U.S. as for a country, like El Salvador, where it is not."[60]

Using a single standard, Lord Chitnis of the British delegation favorably contrasted Nicaragua's election with El Salvador's 1984 presidential election: "in every relevant aspect, the situation in Nicaragua provided the necessary conditions for all political parties to participate freely. This was not the case in El Salvador. In Nicaragua …Arturo Cruz…was free to return to his country…and held public meetings without any perceptible fear for his life. In El Salvador, Guillermo Ungo, the leader of the FMLN-FDR, would not have been able to do this. As the British Government's official observers noted he 'would have run a very high risk of being assassinated…' " In Nicaragua, Chitnis found genuine political choice. "By comparing, for example, the party political platform of the Democratic Conservatives with that of the MAP on the extreme left, this seems to me indisputable. In El Salvador, such political choice did not exist. As the British Government's observers to the Salvadorean election said it was clear that in that country no political party from the centre to the left would have been able to contest the elections, and none did."

On the question of censorship, Chitnis criticized the Nicaraguan government as well as *La Prensa's* decision not to publish official Electoral Council notices or reports of deaths from contra attacks. "But, what of the anti-government journalist in El Salvador?" he asked. "Assuming he finds a paper or magazine willing to publish his articles—a huge assumption—he too will be in fear of his life. Not long ago, the mutilated, decapitated bodies of journalists were found on the roadside. Indeed, there is now no opposition paper to censor. They have been forced into silence."[61]

In the words of Americas Watch, "Any discussion of press freedom in El Salvador must begin by pointing out the elimination of the country's two main opposition newspapers. *La Cronica del Pueblo* was closed in 1980 when members of the security forces raided a San Salvador coffee shop where the paper's editor and one of its photographers were meeting. Editor Jaime Suarez, a 31-year-old prize-winning poet, and Cesar Najarro, 28, were disembowelled by machetes and then shot. In 1981 *El Independiente* was closed when Army tanks surrounded its offices. This was the culmination of a long series of attacks, which included the machinegunning of a 14-year-old newsboy, bombing attempts, and assassination attempts against editor Jorge Pinto." As for censorship of Salvadoran Church outlets, the "Archdiocese's radio station, WSAX, spent several years out of commission after its offices were repeatedly bombed."[62] According to the Committee to Protect Journalists, 65 reporters have been murdered in El Salvador and Guatemala. In short, the press in El Salvador and Guatemala have been "censored by death squads."[63]

The mainstream U.S. media applied the administration's double standard. One study found that at the time of El Salvador's 1982 election, "during a seven-day period centered on election day the three networks ran a total of twenty-two stories, the average length of which was just under five minutes, making it one of the most thoroughly covered foreign elections in television history. The Nicaraguan election was, by comparison, all but ignored, receiving a total of 18 minutes and 40 seconds of evening news coverage between August 1 and November 7."[64]

The coverage mirrored the administration line, playing up both Salvadoran elections as democratic triumphs, virtually ignoring the state of siege and the annihilation of independent and opposition press, and dismissing the absence of the major political opposition (the FDR-FMLN) as a factor in judging fairness. Coverage of Nicaragua, in contrast, highlighted the state of emergency, played up Cruz and the Coordinadora (who were not the major opposition) and dismissed the election as a sham.[65]

Ignoring or trivializing even their own reporting about manipulation by U. S. officials, the major media stuck to the administration's Cruz control setting. A *New York Times* editorial of November 7, 1984 was headed "Nobody Won in Nicaragua": "Only the naive believe that Sunday's election in Nicaragua was democratic or legitimizing proof of the Sandinistas' popularity...The Sandinistas made it easy to dismiss their election as a sham. Their decisive act was to break off negotiations with Arturo Cruz, an opposition democrat whose candidacy could have produced a more credible contest. He sought delay until January but was denied time to deliver a truce from the U.S.-armed 'contra' rebels." In the *Time's* distorted account, the Sandinistas scorned Cruz not only as a democrat but as a peacemaker.

A *Washington Post* editorial of November 26 was even more contemptuous: "The Sandinistas produced a big turnout—easy in Central America where the democratic tradition is weak and the power of official suggestion is strong. They also produced a big victory. That too was easy: the major opposition didn't run, and while the minor opposition had a fling in the media, the Sandinistas alone control mass organizations and used them to bring in a landslide—although it was not one of those 99.93 percent Soviet jobs." The *Post* added: "The main reason the major opposition did not run was that the Sandinistas cheated—with mob violence, logistical harassment and on-and-off censorship. It is true, as some have charged, that certain American officials quietly encouraged some in the Nicaraguan opposition not to take part, although it's not at all clear that this kept the Nicaraguan opposition from joining the elections. The Sandinistas are tough customers with a Marxist-Leninist streak, and the opposition had reason to doubt their good faith. Still, this American dabbling created a damaging suspicion of American maneuver which remains part of the post-election scene."

Making a meek call for a political solution, the editorial contrasted Nicaragua with El Salvador: "Politically underdeveloped countries consumed by externally fueled civil wars need to negotiate as well as vote. El Salvador's elected government is now talking with the armed left elements, which shunned the last elections. Managua is talking with its political opposition but has yet to match President Duarte and address its armed opposition."

The *Post* editorial is a lesson in double standards and double speak. Does anyone recall hearing that it was "easy in Central America" to produce a big turnout during the Salvadoran elections? To the contrary, the turnout (proportionately smaller than Nicaragua's) was taken as a triumph of ballots over bullets—not the bullets of the government and its death squad offspring responsible for most Salvadoran murders, but the bullets of the FMLN who "shunned" the elections. During the 1982 Salvadoran election, television news was bursting with pictures of long lines of voters (without the background information that the lines were a predictable result of an inadequate number of polling sites).

In the *Post* editorial, the Nicaraguan government is referred to simply as "Managua" while the Salvadoran is called "El Salvador's elected government"; the

FDR-FMLN is atomized into "armed left elements" while the contras are credentialed as the "armed opposition." The *Post* portrayed the Sandinistas as a kind of "Marxist-Leninist" Mafia—"tough customers" cheating with "mob violence." U.S. officials, on the other hand, "quietly encouraged"; the main result of their "dabbling" was to create a "damaging suspicion of American maneuver"—maneuver sounding much more benign than bribery and political extortion, not to mention contra kidnapping and killing.

In his report of the Nicaraguan election results, buried on page 12 of the *New York Times*, Stephen Kinzer presented a distorted assessment under the headline "Sandinistas Hold Their [sic] First Election." It was a sharp contrast to *New York Times* coverage of the 1982 Salvadoran election, with, for example, two March 29 front-page stories, headlined: "Salvadorans Jam Polling Stations; Rebels Close Some—Votes Cast Amid Gunfire" and "Rural Voters Hike for Miles To Be Heard," as well as an inside story titled, "For First Time Since '32 Crackdown, Democracy Is Trying for a Comeback."

Where El Salvador was made to seem like Beirut because of the FMLN, Nicaragua was made to appear temporarily at peace thanks to the contras. Kinzer wrote, "Although Nicaragua is torn by civil strife, there were no reprted [sic] clashes today. The Nicaraguan Democratic Force, the largest of the pro-American guerrilla groups fighting to depose the Sandinistas, had called a one-day cease-fire."

"The Government established nearly 4,000 voting places," observed Kinzer, "and lines were generally short. There was little visible enthusiasm, though in the capital there was a marked contrast between the poorer sections and the better areas. Although there was movement and interest in the voting in some slums, the large houses in comfortable neighborhoods were closed, and people who answered their doors said they considered the election not worth their participation."

This is a remarkable passage. The *Times* must assume the reader either doesn't realize that the overwhelming majority of Nicaraguans are poor or thinks the votes of wealthier Nicaraguans are more important. In contrast to the United States, where the largest party is the party of nonvoters and turnout is skewed toward those with higher incomes, in Nicaragua voter turnout was high, with abstentions skewed toward the wealthier minority of the population. The widespread enthusiasm found among Nicaragua's poor majority signified a marked redistribution of the political franchise to those historically most marginalized.

Kinzer quoted a disproportionate mix of Sandinista supporters and opponents. Supporter "Sebastian Guevara, 20, a health worker from Granada, said Mr. Cruz 'is a traitor because he wants us to negotiate with the killers who are murdering our people.' " That's in a passage headed "Some Support for Cruz," mostly quoting and reinforcing Cruz's views about the election being a "farce."

In an earlier section, we read that "Mr. Corea, like many older people who spoke in interviews, expressed nostalgia for the days when there were only two parties, the Liberals and the Conservatives, instead of the seven that appeared on the ballot today." The article neglected to mention that the Liberal Party was the Somozas' domain. Some voters "recalled previous elections, when candidates would slaughter animals and give steaks away to voters." Kinzer made a multi-party political system and an end to traditional vote buying sound sinister.

The insidious main message was nailed home in the article's ending—this election was like Somoza elections, minus the steaks, but not the fear: "In the dusty town square at Masatepe, 25 miles south of the capital, 84-year-old Andres Aguirre brushed aside offers of help as he deliberately made his way to the poll. His eyes seemed to twinkle as he stroked his full beard.

" 'I've always voted because it is always required,' he said. 'Of course, the law says one thing, but after a while one realizes that voting is part of patriotism, and patriotism leads to long life.' "[66] In the *New York Times* the death squad environment of El Salvador is projected onto Nicaragua.

A companion piece reported that the Nicaraguan election spelled heightened tensions between Washington and Managua and undermined efforts for regional peace. Eight paragraphs into the article is the news: "If the regional peace talks collapse and the negotiations between the United States and Nicaragua fail to make progress, Administration officials said, the chances of some kind of American military intervention in Nicaragua would increase if President Reagan is re-elected on Tuesday."

The article ended with an all-too-typical press contortion to achieve "objectivity" at the expense of truth regarding U.S. policy: "Some Administration officials have reported that the Administration, while publicly calling for free elections in Nicaragua, argued in private that major opposition candidates should not take part to insure that the elections would appear to be unrepresentative. This contention has been denied by other officials." Since the *New York Times* and other papers had already documented such manipulation, the passage was a big step backward into the shadows obscuring U.S. intervention.[67]

Pluralist Opposition Voices

A year and a half later, I asked some opposition leaders to comment on the election and the U.S. role in it. Mauricio Diaz, the presidential candidate and secretary general of the Popular Social Christian Party (PPSC), told me: "For us the 1984 elections represented a challenge. The challenge of democratization—that it was possible to initiate the construction of a Western-style, democratic electoral system within a revolutionary process...

"Obviously, the natural intermediaries of the United States received a mistaken slogan. The slogan of not participating in the elections was an erroneous measure, whose costs have been paid by the individual political organizations...[In] spite of the limitations of the electoral process, it was universally recognized as legitimate. Those countries who sought to delegitimize, to question, to stigmatize or to accuse it of fraud were isolated.

"The elections threw up a new political framework in the national political context...The elections demonstrated that the FSLN is not the vanguard of the whole Nicaraguan people, as they claimed...It is interesting that as a result of the electoral process, the FSLN was obliged to give a 'turn of the wheel'— a turn of the wheel that meant the recognition of a duly instituted pluralism, of a National Assembly as representation or expression of the Nicaraguan will. And that [Assembly] now has a mandate to make a constitution, which for us should be democratic or it won't be useful to the Sandinistas or the opposition. In this sense, the U.S. position of pressuring the organizations closest to its policies is an error that has forced President Reagan to assume ever more radical attitudes upon not finding duly legitimized interlocutors within the rules of the game of the revolutionary process...

"The Coordinadora's position was a simple one: all or nothing, the power or nothing.

"We believe that you can't, with integrity, ask that a recently installed government, which leaves behind almost a half century of dictatorship without any civil practice on the part of the people, with very little political culture—that suddenly, from night to morning, we should arrive at Costa Rican-style democracy. I think that's infantile. And that, in any case, the organizations that believe it's possible to create a democratic system in Nicaragua should also act to create the conditions for it. To nourish and enrich the public political debate. Not to assume a death house attitude, by locking oneself up in one's organization and waiting for the gringos to resolve matters...

"I've always maintained that in Nicaragua the true freedom fighters are the political parties that are trying to endow this country with a democratic political constitution and not those famous 'freedom fighters,' who, in the hypothetical case that they triumph, I don't believe it would be to restore democracy in Nicaragua. We have terrible experiences like Mr. Pinochet in Chile, where it was supposed that he would assume power transitionally while creating conditions for returning power to civilians."

I asked Diaz to elaborate further on the impact of U.S. policy on the development of pluralism in Nicaragua. He said, "It is illogical to think that a democratic regime in Nicaragua will be achieved through aggression. There's a wise saying that the peasants have: 'The *Yanquis* do it to the Sandinistas, they charge the Sandinistas and the people pay'. .What do they mean by this? That while the North American administration is taking drastic, aggressive measures against Nicaragua, the Sandinista government takes other measures [e.g. the state of emergency] whose fundamental effects are felt by the people...[The] United States would have done better by Nicaragua if the $100 million [in 1986] had gone for the municipal elections rather than the contras...Nicaragua is a bleeding country in which the quota of lives given in the defense of the nation's sovereignty is too high."[68]

Rafael Cordova Rivas of the Democratic Conservative Party (PCD) also believes "it was an error on the part of the United States and an error on the part of rightist groups and classes in Nicaragua not to have participated in the election...[The election] was an open trench...He who wanted to fill it could fill it. We filled it..We've proved through our positions taken in the Assembly that we still hold to conservative principles...

"We live under constant pressure from the U.S. Embassy to get the PCD to take a Reaganite position. Up to now they haven't achieved that, nor do I believe they'll achieve it."[69]

Eduardo Coronado, then vice president of the Independent Liberal Party,* noted two objections to a U.S. policy that "has sought a military solution to the Nicaraguan and Central American crisis. First, for a practical reason. The more aid the United States gives the contras, the more aid the Soviet Union gives to the FSLN. As the world powers put up the money and the arms, we put up the dead, which is no business for any country. Second, politically, in the sense that we are anti-interventionists, we believe that we should resolve our own problems. Any foreign inheritance, whether right or left, takes away our independence and creativity for driving forward or forging our own revolution."

In the view promoted by the United States, said Coronado, "our revolution is seen as polarized between two approaches. The approach of the counterrevolution supported by the United States and the approach of the FSLN and the other left [parties] supported by the Soviet Union or Cuba...We consider it an erroneous view because here within the political spectrum you must account for the civic opposition parties...As civic opposition parties we are placed outside the drama that Nicaragua is being submitted to. We're [made] marginal to the drama Nicaragua is living. In spite of that, we're the ones who, in the flesh, suffer the sudden attacks of the counterrevolution and the security measures taken by the FSLN to defend itself, which takes away space for our political development...

"We believe the military solution won't solve anything; besides being a long painful war it would lead to a dictatorship, or totalitarianism of the right or left. It would oblige a radicalization of this process...It would dash the hope of an original revolution for Latin America...

"We see that there must be reciprocal concessions...There can be no peaceful solution without eliminating factors that interrupt an internal understanding— elements such as the war and the state of emergency. These two disturbing elements should be eliminated at the same time. The war and the state of emergency, both sides must cease at the same time. Having eliminated those two interrupting factors, negotiations can take place for the total dismantling of the counterrevolution, for the democratization of Nicaragua under just terms for all parties without falling into the political hegemony of a single party. Rather, the formation of a system in which all political parties have an equal opportunity to direct the destiny of the country in accord with its political calling."[71]

The nonabstentionist opposition parties are neither a monolithic bloc nor a rubber stamp for the FSLN. They harshly criticized the FSLN during the election and they continue to do so today. They represent a broad spectrum of political, economic and social beliefs whether on church-state relations, agrarian reform, the roles of private and state enterprise, women's rights, or relations with the Soviet Union. The parties to the right of the FSLN, outside the Coordinadora, generally affirm the principles embraced by the Government of National Reconstruction in 1979 and institu-

---

* Later in 1986, Coronado and four other PLI delegates in the National Assembly broke ranks with PLI president Virgilio Godoy and voted with the Assembly majority to approve Nicaragua's new constitution. In November 1987, a majority of PLI members voted to elect Coronado party leader; the party is divided into factions led by Coronado and Godoy.[70]

tionalized by the constitution: political pluralism, a mixed economy and nonalignment. But they have different visions of how these principles should be carried out. They want the chance to test their principles, programs and popular appeal without the pressures of war.

The MIGs are Coming! The MIGs are Coming!

Nicaragua was in the news on election night in the United States, but the story was not Nicaragua's election. The story was Soviet MIGs. As reported by CBS Evening News on November 6, 1984, the Soviet freighter *Bakuriani* was on its way to Nicaragua with MIG 21 fighters aboard—according to administration officials citing satellite surveillance (Robert McFarlane was later identified as the lead leaker).

The "sham election" story was succeeded quickly by the security threat story. The CIA terrorist manuals were ancient history.

U.S. officials told Moscow that delivery of MIGs to Nicaragua would not be tolerated—portraying the vintage 1950s MIGs as if they were intended for use in a Soviet blitz. The administration warned that it would take military action to destroy MIGs and MIG facilities. Senator Christopher Dodd and other prominent liberal Democrats agreed. A U.S. warship appeared off the Nicaraguan port of Corinto where the Soviet freighter docked. This was no idle threat of gunboat diplomacy; Corinto had been rocketed and mined in the last year.

The Nicaraguan government reiterated its sovereign right to import jet fighter aircraft for defensive purposes, but insisted that no MIGs were being delivered. Three weeks earlier, Daniel Ortega had told *Newsweek,* "We have been making gestures to different countries, [including] Western countries, in a search for interceptor planes...Nicaragua is the only country [in the area] that doesn't possess this type of plane. And yet Nicaragua is the one country that needs it."

Referring to the Contadora peace proposal which Nicaragua agreed to sign in September only to have Washington pressure its allies into withdrawing their initial approval (discussed in chapter 13), Ortega noted, "The Contadora proposal contemplates a freeze on the introduction of armaments into Central America 29 days after [the plan] is signed. Thus that problem would be overcome, because then negotiations would address the issue of how to find a balance within the armed forces of the region...At the same time, the best thing would be that the Central American countries that have this type of airplane get rid of them, so that those of us that don't have them won't be forced into seeking them."[72]

As the State Department-sponsored Jacobsen report pointed out, "All-too-many US claims [about Soviet bloc military aid to Nicaragua] proved open to question. In May 1983 the White House announced that reconnaissance photos proved the Soviet ships Novovolynsk and Polotosk carried heavy military equipment; American reporters present at the unloading saw only field kitchens from East Germany, and 12000 tons of fertilizer...President Reagan later declared that the ship Ulyanov was 'loaded with weaponry'; yet a respected Conservative British observer saw 'no signs of offensive weaponry or armoured vehicles', only 200 transport vehicles, 80 jeeps, 5 ambulances, and assorted civilian equipment."[73]

By November 9, U.S. officials were acknowledging that they were almost certain no jet fighters were aboard the Soviet freighter. However, they continued to warn of military action in response to delivery of such aircraft. "Officials said they would not rule out air strikes, sabotage or other military action to disable Soviet MIG fighters if they were delivered to Nicaragua. They reiterated that the Administration had no plans to invade Nicaragua."[74]

Inside Nicaragua, there was widespread fear that the MIG scare was a pretext for imminent U.S. invasion. On the morning of November 3, the day before Nicaraguans went to the polls, a U.S. SR-71 Blackbird spy plane flew over the country, purposely creating a sonic boom to rattle nerves below. It was the first in a series of provocative self-announced spy flights.

The U.S. Air Force SR-71 is reportedly "the world's fastest, technically most advanced spy plane, capable of seeing more from a greater distance than any other aircraft." It "can survey 100,000 square miles from 15 miles up in only one hour. Difficult to detect by radar, it can also track SAM [surface-to-air] missiles at a distance of up to 100 miles. The Blackbird can reach speeds of up to Mach 4, or 2,600 miles per hour; no country has ever succeeded in shooting one down." It has "a pair of cameras that automatically produce 1,800 overlapping photos of up to 1,600 miles of terrain; and a camera that can produce pictures with a ground resolution of 12 inches."[75] Complementing the U.S. fleet of espionage satellites, the Blackbird, with its cloud-penetrating infrared sensors, can provide speedy battlefield intelligence.

Reporter Marc Cooper described the impact of Blackbird sonic booms over Nicaragua: "A few days after Ronald Reagan was reelected President...I was sitting at breakfast with a group of Nicaraguan and Argentine cultural workers...The discussion this morning was the same as every morning that week: Would there be an invasion? I was arguing that direct American military intervention would be 'politically difficult, illogical.' Others at the table rebutted that rationality had little to do with U.S. policy.

"And then at exactly 9:25 a.m., somewhere between the eggs and plantains, and the pros and cons, the sky bellowed, the windows rattled, and our table shook as a supersonic boom reverberated off the lush hills of the Nicaraguan countryside. For the third morning in a row, and for the fifth time in 10 days, at precisely the same hour, a U.S. SR-71 Blackbird spy plane had broken the sound barrier over Nicaraguan national air space. You could almost touch the tension and the indignation in the kitchen. The morning newspaper reports of State Department denials of invasion plans had been abruptly and rudely contradicted by the Pentagon's booming overflight.

"Twenty-five-year old [militia member] Maria Ester...was visibly shaken. 'I wish Reagan would just get it over with and send in the Marines. We are ready to fight them,' she pronounced in near-perfect English, a product...of an adolescence spent in San Francisco. 'This is the worst it has ever been. Worse even than last year after Grenada. Last night in my neighborhood we were making plans on where to hide our children.' "[76]

Imagine being forced into a duel in which the number of steps taken before turning to shoot are not predetermined and the rules are that your adversary will shoot first with vastly superior firepower. As you walk you're assaulted and wounded by the adversary's proxies with the expectation you will surrender or die, or at least be severely disabled before the final duel. Most of the time, you hope the ultimate duel, a full invasion, will never come. But there are moments when you feel that it's so inevitable, why not get it over with. You want the opportunity to win peace and recover. When the Blackbird flew over that morning, Maria Ester and her compatriots were four years into that cruel duel.

The MIG warnings and Blackbird spy flights were not the only post-election trumpets of war jarring Nicaragua. The Washington-based Center for Defense Information summarized other danger signs: units of the 82nd Airborne and the 101st Air Assault Division, "which would spearhead any U.S. invasion force," were involved in "Quick Thrust" combat exercises at Fort Stewart in Georgia. With Honduras and El Salvador, the United States was conducting the "King's Guard" naval exercise, moved up several weeks from its originally scheduled date, in the Gulf of Fonseca. The battleship *Iowa* and 24 other ships were on naval maneuvers in the Caribbean. Two Pacific-based aircraft carriers and two Atlantic-based carriers were apparently "close enough to reach Central America in a matter of days."[77]

U.S. officials denied plans for a military strike against Nicaragua. "A year ago," the *New York Times* reported, "just before the invasion of Grenada, spokesmen for the Reagan Administration said United States warships had been sent to the Caribbean as a precaution in case Americans on Grenada were endangered by the overthrow of the Government there. At the same time, they denied reports that an invasion of Grenada was imminent."[78]

Nicaragua wasn't taking any chances. The army and militia went on full alert. Tanks were again deployed defensively around Managua. Agriculture Minister Jaime Wheelock told 12,000 students about to leave as volunteers in the coffee harvest that they were needed more for defense of the capital. "It's better that the coffee falls instead of our country," Wheelock explained.

Foreign Minister Miguel D'Escoto told reporter Marc Cooper, "[If] you ask 'is a U.S. invasion possible,' I answer that it hardly seems possible that such a man as Reagan should be reelected, yet he has been. If we lived in a different country, we could sit back and ask if the invasion was *really* coming. But living in Nicaragua we don't have that luxury. We must prepare for the worst."[79]

As fall turned to winter, there was no direct U.S. invasion. The Nicaraguans did not pave the way with a coup, as in Grenada. They mobilized rapidly. Inside the United States, opponents of U.S. policy rang loud public alarm bells and promised nationwide nonviolent civil disobedience should the administration escalate. The Reagan administration knew it had four more years to try and overthrow the Nicaraguan government without U.S. ground troops, and to smooth the way for their possible deployment.

In the end, the MIG scare achieved much for the administration: It established a remarkable bipartisan pretext for future military action, giving the United States, the country waging war on Nicaragua, the right to limit how Nicaragua could defend itself and, if Nicaragua crossed that line, to escalate the war under the guise of protecting U.S. national security. Nicaragua continued to go without the jet fighters necessary to intercept contra aircraft and disrupt contra air supply, much less challenge U.S. spy flights or potential Honduran, Salvadoran or U.S. bombers. Washington was able to study Nicaraguan forces and the Nicaraguan people in a state of full alert, facilitating improvements in U.S. military strategy, including the psychological operations component. The Nicaraguan economy was damaged further by the disruption of the coffee harvest. The mass media-promoted impression of Nicaragua immediately following its election was one of militarization, not democratization. In the face of escalating U.S. aggression, election-period moves to ease the state of emergency were reversed, heightening political tensions within Nicaragua and providing an excuse for Arturo Cruz and other Coordinadora leaders to publicly embrace the contras.

Obscured by the MIG scare, was a reality acknowledged even by U.S. military and intelligence analysts. In the words of a classified CIA report, Nicaragua's "overall [military] buildup is primarily defense-oriented and much of the recent effort has been directed to improving counterinsurgency capabilities."[80] This included the newly-acquired Soviet-built MI-24 helicopter gunships, which Nicaragua used with great effect against the contras until the United States supplied them with Redeye ground-to-air missiles.

Cold War Ghosts

Once again, the administration proved that image was more important than reality in its campaign against Nicaragua. Nicaragua's military buildup was projected anew through Cold War lenses that filtered out the hot war with the contras and the threat of U.S. escalation.

"The Nicaraguans seem intent on militarizing their society and accumulating a level of weapons and armed capability that is entirely outside the standpoint of any conceivable defensive mission," asserted Secretary of State Shultz. "A senior White House official compared the flow of Soviet-bloc weapons to Nicaragua to the military buildup in Cuba that preceded the Cuban missile crisis in 1962," the *New York Times* reported. "He said that while there was no plan to block arms shipments to Nicaragua at sea, 'we're not going to rule out any contingency there.' "[81] "Any contingency" hardly narrows the scope of Nicaragua's "conceivable defensive mission."

The Reagan administration has published numerous reports on the alleged Soviet-Cuban military buildup in Nicaragua. Like the 1981 White Paper on El Salvador, they fail to make their case even when using the most distorted evidence, but they leave lasting threatening impressions. A 1984 State and Defense Department report warned, "A new military airfield at Punta Huete, when completed, will have the longest runway in Central America (3,200 meters), and will be capable of receiving any aircraft in the Soviet inventory." The report claimed, "a basis has been laid for the receipt of modern jet fighters and for accommodating large military planes, such as heavy transport planes and Soviet 'Backfire' bombers."[82]

A glossy 1985 State and Defense Department booklet, *The Soviet-Cuban Connection in Central America and the Caribbean*, devotes a whole page to grainy photos of President Daniel Ortega on official visits to the Soviet Union, East Germany and Poland. Photos of Ortega with Western leaders don't pass U.S. censorship. The booklet includes a chart with the Pentagon's estimates of "Soviet-Bloc Military Deliveries to Nicaragua."[83] The chart conveniently measures in tons, weighing heavily such unmighty weapons as the T-55 tank. Yet even the distorted picture cannot hide the fact that the first jump in Soviet aid came in 1982, after contra attacks intensified and the doors of Western arms suppliers slammed shut under U.S. pressure.

In 1986, administration officials claimed that Nicaragua had received more than $500 million in Soviet military aid since 1981. The interesting point about that figure is how small it is, when compared with U.S. military aid to other Central American countries in the same period and considering that, unlike U.S. allies, Nicaragua's armed forces had to be (in the Carter administration's words) "entirely rebuilt." In 1985, the United States provided $136.3 million in military assistance for El Salvador and $67.4 million for Honduras, not counting assistance provided through military maneuvers or the CIA. In addition, a large part of security assistance is provided through the more benign sounding "economic support funds," of which El Salvador was authorized $285 million and Honduras $147.5 million in 1985.[84] Between 1980 and 1984, the U.S. provided over $2.3 *billion* in security assistance to Central America, and the figure has since multiplied.[85] Using a formula that counted the costs of military construction, exercises, troops stationed in the area, and maintaining ground, air and naval forces assigned to the region, as well as military and economic support funds, analysts Joshua Cohen and Joel Rogers concluded that the actual cost of U.S. military programs in Central America and the Caribbean for 1985 was roughly $9.5 billion.[86]

As of early 1985, the Nicaraguan Air Force included no supersonic fighters or fighter bombers and a total of 31 less advanced fighters, trainers, transport and support craft, not including helicopters. By comparison, Honduras had 32 to 50 supersonic fighters and fighter bombers and 48 armed and unarmed trainers, transport and support craft; El Salvador had 53 supersonic fighters and fighter bombers and 64 other aircraft, not including helicopters.[87] Comparisons with U.S. airpower are ludicrous. Nicaragua has less aircraft than a single U.S. aircraft carrier such as the *America*, with its 85 jet fighters and other aircraft. And Nicaragua has virtually no navy.

As for the Punta Huete airfield, Washington is inventing a threat, just as it did with the Point Salinas airport in Grenada. Punta Huete was begun under Somoza, with U.S. technical assistance, in order to provide the Nicaraguan Air Force with a base apart from the civilian international airport in Managua. The need for such a project was underscored by the CIA-backed bombing of the Managua airport in 1983. U.S. officials raise the concern that Punta Huete would give Soviet "Bear" reconnaissance planes the kind of U.S. Pacific Coast surveillance capability they have for the East Coast by operating out of Cuba. Nicaragua has said repeatedly it has no intention of offering military bases to the Soviet Union. In any case, Soviet aircraft already patrol off the U.S. West Coast from bases within their own territory on the Kamchatka Peninsula across from Alaska.

Hypothetical Soviet submarines and "Backfire" bombers operating out of hypothetical Soviet bases in Nicaragua are presented as plausible threats to Central America, the Panama Canal, Caribbean sea lanes and the United States itself.[88] One scenario assumes Nicaraguan or Cuban-based attacks on U.S. shipping in the event of conventional war with the Soviet Union in Europe or the Middle East, for example.

"Weinberger is always saying 40 to 50 percent of NATO sealift goes out of Gulf ports," a U.S. ambassador in Central America told me. "It would take a lot of air wings to take Cuba out, maybe seven or eight; another five for Nicaragua." The Pentagon doesn't "want to waste air wings in our own backyard."[89]

Pentagon planners assume the Nicaraguans are ready to waste their population and country as a platform for Soviet weapons. They pretend to believe that prolonged World War II-style conventional war is plausible in the nuclear age, when, in fact, nuclear weapons are fully integrated into Pentagon war doctrine from battlefield backpack nuclear weapons on up the escalation ladder. If the Soviet Union was going to madly attempt a nuclear first strike against the United States, it would hardly advertise it by launching a fleet of bombers from Nicaragua, or from Cuba—where the largest foreign military base is the U.S. base at Guantanamo.

Talk of Nicaragua becoming "another Cuba" distorts reality in both countries. As former U.S. diplomat Wayne Smith points out, the "frightening Soviet military buildup" in Central America and the Caribbean "is mostly an illusion...There are no nuclear missile submarines operating out of Cuban bases...None. Nor has a single Backfire bomber ever even landed in Cuba. Several Soviet "Bear" long-range reconnaissance aircraft are deployed to Cuba. They do not, however, as Dr. [Jeane] Kirkpatrick stated, overfly American territory from Cuban bases. One can understand the indignation with which the North American Air Defense Command says that is not so."[90]

Former National Security Adviser McGeorge Bundy sees Central America more clearly than he did Vietnam: "the realities of relative strength make it totally clear that no one is going to make war on us from Central America. There is something genuinely zany in thinking about the area in those terms."[91]

The idea of a Nicaraguan invasion of its neighbors is also zany. In the wake of the MIG scare, Miguel D'Escoto wrote: "I am astonished that senior officials of the Reagan administration accuse Nicaragua of obtaining arms in order to attack Honduras and El Salvador. Besides all the bad things they say about us, do they think we are insane?

"For us to attack our neighbors would be to serve ourselves up to our enemies on a silver platter. It would give the Reagan administration precisely the pretext it has been looking for to try to intervene against us by direct military means."[92]

As the *New York Times* reported in March 1985, "Senior Administration officials in speeches and in public reports, have frequently said Nicaragua intends to attack its neighbors. But State and Defense Department officials say unofficially that they do not believe Nicaragua has any such intention."[93]

Nicaragua, D'Escoto wrote, "has to obtain defensive arms for one simple reason. The Reagan administration is trying to overthrow the government of Nicaragua. They have mined our ports. They have bombed our airport, attacked our oil storage facilities, blown up vital bridges and highways. They have recruited, trained and armed more than 10,000 mercenaries and directed them in an illegal 'covert war' against us.

"These CIA-supported mercenaries have been staging hit-and-run raids against us from Honduran territory for over three years. There have been more than 1,000 raids in that time period...We have exercised restraint because we do not want a war with Honduras or the United States...

"It is sheer hypocrisy for the Reagan administration to effectively close off Western sources of arms and then denounce us for obtaining them from other sources. What do they expect us to do, deny ourselves the means for self-defense at the same time they are waging war against us?"[94]

Wayne Smith states the all-too-often obscured obvious point: supporting the contras "is certainly no way to limit the size and nature of the Nicaraguan armed forces...The Sandinistas would hardly accept arms reductions at a time when their ports are being mined by the most powerful nation in the world and that nation is also supporting a force of guerrillas determined to overthrow them. The reaction of any sensible government to such circumstances would be to strengthen its military forces."[95]

Policy Tilts

The MIG scare came amid a post-election joust over Nicaragua policy between longer-term rollbackers (mainly in the State Department) and shorter-term rollbackers (mainly in the CIA and NSC staff). All wanted to prompt renewed congressional support for the contras. The State Department sought to keep Nicaragua policy on the two-track path of military assault with diplomatic maneuvers. Some CIA, NSC and Pentagon officials were ready to escalate, at least by breaking diplomatic relations with Nicaragua and providing the contras with more direct military support.

"Some of those who want us to adopt a harder line have long wished that MIG's [sic] would be delivered because they know that would tilt the policy in their direction," said one administration official. "The next best thing to the delivery of MIG's was the possibility that they might arrive any day."[96]

On November 28, 1984, Secretary of Defense Weinberger gave a much-publicized address to the National Press Club putting forth six tests for the commitment of U.S. military force (dubbed the six commandments): the United States should not commit forces to combat overseas unless it is vital to the national interest; "if we decide it is necessary to put combat troops into a given situation, we should do so wholeheartedly, and with the clear intention of winning"; political and military objectives should be clearly defined; the "relationship between our objectives and the forces we have committed, their size, composition and disposition, must be continually reassessed and adjusted if necessary"; before the United States "commits combat forces abroad, there must be some reasonable assurance we will have the support of the American people and their elected representatives in Congress"; the commitment of U.S. forces should be a last resort.[97]

Weinberger's concern about winning was not new. During his 1981 confirmation hearings, Weinberger reflected on the lessons of the Vietnam War and asserted that the United States should not commit troops to "a war that is not vital for our national security to enter and we should never enter a war that we do not intend to win or in which we do not expend every single effort of every weapon and every facility that we have to win...Once we entered it [Vietnam], it became a war that we should have won."[98]

The gist of Weinberger's message was that the political will to win must be strong and sustainable, and U.S. forces should avoid the danger of "a gradualist, incremental approach, which almost always means the use of insufficient force." In response to a question at the National Press Club, Weinberger refused to rule out an attack on Nicaragua, saying he would let his text speak for itself.

Clearly, the political will for a direct invasion of Nicaragua among the people and Congress was lacking. The administration would continue to support the contras, on and off the books, pursue its regional buildup and intensify the "public diplomacy" campaign to narrow the gap between the will for a military solution within the administration and among the people.

10

I'm A Contra Too!

I guess in a way they are counterrevolutionary, and God bless them for being that way. And I guess that makes them contras, and so it makes me a contra, too.

President Reagan, March 1986.

The idea is to slowly demonize the Sandinista government [in] order to turn it into a real enemy and threat in the minds of the American people, therby eroding their resistance to U.S. support for the contras and, perhaps, to a future U.S. military intervention in the region.

U.S. government official, 1985.[1]

Our assessment was that if there was not something done, beginning with the...[Boland] cutoff of funds in '84, and then the proscriptions later on in the year, that within six to ten months the Nicaraguan resistance would cease to be.

Oliver North, Iran-Contra hearings, July 9, 1987.

Before his metamorphosis from Coordinadora candidate to contra leader, Arturo Cruz painted a nightmarish portrait of FDN triumph. In June 1984, Cruz told Reggie Norton of the Washington Office on Latin America that "he had been talking with the 'Key Biscayne mafia,' the contra leadership, and they had threatened that when they returned to power they would hold a series of 'Nuremberg' trials and Cruz would be among the first to be tried...'the first persons they would hang from the trees' would be the 'Sandinista arrepentidos,' former Sandinistas who were now sorry for their temporary Sandinista association."[2] A year earlier, Cruz called Somocista FDN leaders "civic cadavers." He warned of the responsibility facing "people with good credentials" in the FDN's political directorate—he referred to Calero and Robelo—to control events and prevent revenge in the unlikely event of an FDN victory.

"Carrying perhaps an even greater responsibility," Cruz wrote in *Foreign Affairs,* "those who sustain the forces inimical to the Sandinistas must not ignore the fact that idealistic young boys and girls constitute the Revolution's rank and file. Therefore, those who aid insurrection in my country—whose disenchantment with the Revolution's course and concern for the security of their own country I do not dispute—should be aware of the risk they take of bearing a historical responsibility for contributing, albeit indirectly and unintentionally, to a possible mass execution of the flower of our youth."

Cruz urged that "a line of distinction should be drawn, now more than ever, between 'contras' and armed dissidents," notably Eden Pastora.[3] Pastora's promise was never realized and Cruz, ignoring his own warning, went to work with the FDN Guardia he once deplored.

Three days after the Nicaraguan election, Oliver North wrote a top secret memo to his boss Robert McFarlane. On November 6, 1984, North and Calero had "discussed longer-range planning for a Calero-Cruz coalition and the requirements for military cooperation with the MISURA in the seizure of Puerto Cabezas." With another person, whose name is deleted in the declassified memo, North "reviewed the prospects for a liberation government in which Cruz and Calero would share authority."[4]

Cruz publicly announced his support for U.S. aid to the contras on January 3, 1985. He spoke of a "commonality of purpose" with the FDN.[5] In March, Cruz endorsed the unity "Document of the Nicaraguan Resistance Concerning National Dialogue" issued in San Jose, Costa Rica; among the signatories were Adolfo Calero, Alfonso Robelo, Pedro Joaquin Chamorro Jr., Alfonso Callejas, Steadman Fagoth and Fernando "El Negro" Chamorro. The so-called San Jose Declaration was an ultimatum for the Nicaraguan government's surrender couched in the well-coached public relations rhetoric of free elections and democracy. North and several other Americans helped draft the document in a Miami hotel room. Eden Pastora and Alfredo Cesar refused to sign and, instead, launched the Opposition Bloc of the South (BOS).

In April, it was reported that Cruz, "an important figure in the Reagan administration's efforts to win congressional support for anti-Sandinista guerrillas, secretly received money from the Central Intelligence Agency, according to U.S. government officials."[6] (Cruz was receiving CIA funding by spring 1984.) Speaking at Harvard Law School, Cruz acknowledged receiving the money as "a retainer" for academic work from a foundation linked to the CIA. While admitting that the contras committed "damnable atrocities" against civilians, Cruz accused the Sandinistas of "dictatorial" rule. "I don't have to apologize for the contras," he asserted.[7]

The National Strategy Information Center (NSIC), an intelligence lobby and think tank cofounded by William Casey, paid Cruz $40,000 for six months as a "research fellow." The NSIC, which receives U.S. government money, funded Cruz at the behest of Oliver North and NSC official Vincent Cannistraro.[8]

In June 1985, Arturo Cruz became one of three directors, with Adolfo Calero and Alfonso Robelo (together known as the Triple A), of the new contra political front, the United Nicaraguan Opposition (UNO). Pedro Joaquin Chamorro Jr. served as information director. By August, Cruz and Robelo were frustrated with their figurehead roles.

In a "For Your Eyes Only" memo to North (alias BG for Blood and Guts), aide Robert Owen transmitted Robelo's views: "To quote Robelo, 'I'm tired of the lack of equivalency in the Triple A. Cruz and I were integrated into the FDN to clean their face.'...[Robelo] Is finding it extremely difficult to work with Calero as he believes Calero looks on him and Cruz as appendages, not equals...[Robelo] made it clear he was not threatening to quit, yet. But he also wanted the message conveyed that things must change and he expects Calero to be more accommodating, or at least to make a pretense of it."[9]

Cruz's threats to resign carried into the fall. Renewed talk of a serious split emerged in April and May 1986, but again U.S. officials were able to patch up UNO with the promise of reform. "More and more," declared Assistant Secretary of State for Inter-American Affairs Elliott Abrams, "the opposition today looks like what the Nicaraguan people want their government to look like tomorrow."[10]

At the time, Cruz, Robelo and Calero were all on the secret U.S. payroll managed by North. Cruz received $7,000 monthly, Robelo $10,000 and Calero about $12,500 a month. Some 40 UNO staff members and consultants reportedly earned upwards of $36,000 a year.[11]

On February 21, 1987, Cruz acknowledged at a sparsely attended lecture sponsored by CAUSA USA that the contra cause was "floundering because we haven't been perceived as politically legitimate." When I asked him what he thought the prospects were for achieving political legitimacy, he responded pessimistically: "The Bay of Pigs of Nicaragua would be a political Bay of Pigs, not a military Bay of Pigs...The real issue isn't personalities like Calero, but whether this is a genuine liberation movement or a vanguard-based conquest of power...[If] reforms are not carried out the prospects for success are very remote."[12]

Cruz quit the contra directorate on March 9. His highly public resignation letter said that UNO "has clearly defined itself not as a pluralist structure in the service of a goal equally pluralistic, but rather as an instrument of a small, exclusive circle." He dismissed contra political leaders as "right-wing hack politicians."[13] The "Key Biscayne mafia" had prevailed.

The Strongmen

Edgar Chamorro also thought that "moderates" could succeed when he joined the FDN. He too quit, with greater revulsion than Cruz at contra practices. Chamorro characterized Cruz as a respected moderate with a history of working for business and banking elites. But he could never control the Guardia. No moderate could. The administration saw Cruz "like a Duarte type," he told me. "They are just using people's different traits to sell the package to you Americans, to Congress. It's a very artificial thing. So Cruz is the same."

Chamorro is less kind in his view of the contras' other political leaders. Alfonso Robelo, the millionaire agro-industrialist who served on the first National Reconstruction Government Junta, "is an opportunist," Chamorro said. "He's now an opportunist with the contras...He's an ambitious guy. He just wants power."

"Calero is much more a Somoza-style guy," Chamorro told me. "He believes he has to be a dictator. I've had many conflicts with Calero because he's not a democratic individual, in the sense that he won't debate things; he's not interested in democratic process. He's interested in pleasing the United States...He sees himself as another Somoza, but this time a good one...

"They believe the country was good as it was, basically. That the labor laws were good, that the educational system was good. Everything was fine. The only thing was that there was too much corruption...Somoza, for them, was just a greedy real estate agent that loved land and wanted to corrupt; once in a while there was a little crime...I don't find Calero a moderate. He and Bermudez would make a strong Pinochet case or Guatemala kind of government."

Aristides Sanchez is "one of the fellows close to Calero," said Chamorro. "I know him very closely. He was the landlord of Leon—very rich. His father worked for Somoza for many years. He's a fellow who just sees this as going to get those Sandinistas out of Nicaragua, to get back all his property and his control. Men like him or Bermudez, they have no scruples, no remorse...If he's a communist, they say, then he deserves everything bad...

"They laugh at people who they have had to kill, or be cruel to. They make a joke of it. I can't find the word for you...You have to be cruel or hard. They'll celebrate it and even make it light. I have seen that in Americans also who are in wars. Their psychology is to come to the celebration of the use of force as a way to accept it. They have to glorify it. But in the contras I saw an element of even laughing with it. I have seen it with some other people. It's a defense with some of these criminal characters, to feel that they can do it." I asked Chamorro if he meant it was a self-defense mechanism. "Yes, but they have no doubts," he replied. "They haven't even the slightest. They have no remorse. It's a mixture of getting even and also 'this time we're going to give you [the Sandinistas] what you gave us.' "

A tough critic of the Sandinistas, Chamorro still noted an important difference between the Sandinistas and the Guardia: "The National Guard in Nicaragua don't relate...to people the same way. They are oppressors. They are used to looking down on people. To exploit people. To get things out of them. The Sandinistas came with a different philosophy, a different approach to people, much more humane...in the sense that they were going to give them what they had been working for. It's a different relationship. That for me is very fundamental...That doesn't mean that they couldn't ruin themselves if they become too autocratic."[14]

Since the beginning, the main contra army has been led by National Guardsmen. A March 1986 report by the congressional Arms Control and Foreign Policy Caucus found ex-Guard officers in twelve of thirteen positions of the FDN military high command. Colonel Enrique Bermudez is the supreme commander. At the time of the report, Lieutenant Walter "Toño" Calderon, who reportedly commanded troops in Somoza's palace guard, served as commander of tactical operations (or theater commander). Lieutenant Harley "Venado" (the Deer) Pichardo was commander of personnel (G-1). The commander of intelligence (G-2) was Lieutenant Rodolfo "Invisible" Ampie. Lieutenant Luis "Mike Lima" Moreno was commander of operations (G-3). Captain Armando "El Policia" Lopez, one of Bermudez's closest associates, was commander of logistics (G-4). His *nom de guerre*, "the Policeman," dates to the Somoza era when he commanded units of Managua's repressive Metropolitan Police, a branch of the National Guard. The commander of airdrops was Captain Juan Gomez, "a close personal associate of Somoza's and for years his personal pilot." Captain Justiniano "Tino" Perez, who served under Somoza's son in command of the Guardia's elite training school and was spirited out of Nicaragua by an American operative as the Sandinistas took power, was the liaison with Miskito forces.

Major Ricardo "Chino" Lau was in charge of special operations. The FDN claims that Lau left the FDN in 1983, but he continued to serve as commander of counterintelligence until 1985. He then reportedly commanded "a small unit that carries out special counter-intelligence missions in Honduras for Bermudez, such as execution of suspected Sandinista informers." Lau's unit was said to include Lieutenant "El Policita" Lopez, the son of Armando Lopez, also known as "El Bestia," the Beast. Lau's replacement as commander of counterintelligence was Major Donald "El Toro" (the Bull) Torres. The only FDN high command member reported not to have served in the Guard was Carlos "El Pajarito" (Little Bird) Guillen, commander of special operations for Nicaragua. According to the congressional caucus report, Guillen's father was a Guard officer but he himself was in Mexico studying medicine during the revolution. According to the Nicaraguan government, however, Guillen joined the National Guard as a private in 1976.[15]

Chamorro believes that the contra political leaders "will promise to control the National Guard. But they will keep killing people that are not like them, with death squads or the army. It's not a revolutionary group. It's a mercenary group.

"They're not interested in changing or in educating people [to control their own destinies]. I never remember Calero talking about education for poor people or the needy or building schools or hospitals. All they talk about is making the economy work again according to the American way of economic development— let's invest in this farm and get money out of it. Let's make money out of this country. Let's keep exploiting…They come from a background that sees life like an opportunity to make money…

"And they are also not independent. They are very subservient to the United States. This concept of servitude is very strong in people like Calero…like in the twenties…The independent guy becomes *persona non grata* for Washington."[16]

Chamorro's views are echoed partly in a candid, confidential memo to Oliver North from Robert Owen. In the March 17, 1986 memo, Owen described the "FDN/UNO Political Situation" this way:

> I put it as FDN/UNO because the FDN is now driving UNO, not the other way around. UNO is a creation of the USG [U.S. government] to garner support from Congress.

When it was founded a year ago, the hope was it would become a viable organization. In fact, almost everything it has accomplished is because the hand of the USG has been there directing and manipulating.

No doubt the hope was Cruz and Robelo would turn into strong leaders to somewhat [counter] balance the strength of Calero and the FDN. Both Cruz and Robelo have been disappointments. Calero, on the other hand, has used his strength and will and the FDN to further consolidate his hold on the resistance and to gain control of UNO. Perhaps UNO is the correct acronym, for there is only one leader in the Democratic Resistance, Adolfo Calero.

As long as the USG understands this, one must look at what the FDN political structure represents. Calero is the strong man and the only one who counts in the FDN; what he says is law. Under him is his strong man, or enforcer, Aristedes Sanchez. Bermudez is in the inner circle, but he is not 100% trusted, because he is seen as a potential rival for power. Also within the inner circle is Mario Calero [Adolfo's brother]. Off to the side, but still part of the group and acting more like temple guards are Bosco Matamoros (loyally devoted Washington rep) and Oscar Montes (the financial accountant). Both of these people are intensely loyal and will do whatever Adolfo says. The next ring down consists of the Tefel brothers, Hyme Morales, Statahen, etc. None of these people can stand Robelo or Cruz. At every turn they will undermine them and do all in their power to see they are not given any power, thus the strength remains with Calero.

Should USG officials think any different than the above, they are not looking at the facts. If members of the USG think they control Calero, they also have another thing coming. The question should be asked, can and does Calero manipulate the USG. On several occasions, the answer is yes. Two examples are Mario Calero and Bosco. For well over a year, USG officials have wanted to remove these two, yet they remain. Why, because Calero won't budge, they are part of his security; to threaten them is to threaten him.

I write the above only to point out the facts as I see them. Perhaps a strongman is the only thing Nicaraguans understand; perhaps Adolfo Calero is the man to lead Nicaragua back to democracy. He is a creation of the USG and so he is the horse we choose to ride. I have no problem with this, as long as we know and understand his shortcomings. The best way to point these out are to take a close look at who he keeps around him, only those who he intimately trusts. Unfortunately, they are not first rate people; in fact they are liars and greed and power motivated. They are not the people to rebuild a new Nicaragua. In fact, the FDN has done a good job of keeping competent people out of the organization. If it hasn't, then Nicaragua is lost forever with the type of leadership that has emerged...

UNO is a name only. There is more and more fluff being added, but there is no substance...The reality as I see it is there are few of the so called leaders of the movement who really care about the boys in the field. THIS HAS BECOME A BUSINESS TO MANY OF THEM; THERE IS STILL A BELIEF THE MARINES ARE GOING TO HAVE TO INVADE, SO LETS GET SET SO WE WILL AUTOMATICALLY BE THE ONES PUT INTO POWER.

If the $100 million is approved and things go on as they have these last five years, it will be like pouring money down a sink hole. The Agency has done a shitty job in the past, there is no evidence they are going to change, especially as they are going to have the same people running it as far as I know. State Department is no better...Without significant changes, things will not get better, they will get worse. The heavy hand of the gringo is needed...(Owen's caps.)[17]

Holding Body and Soul Together

The "heavy hand of the gringo" was not stayed by the Boland amendment. Reagan administration officials anticipated a possible cutoff of contra funding in the wake of the mining scandal, just as they had earlier anticipated a 1983-84 shortfall with Operation Elephant Herd. In a 1983 interview preceding the approval of $24 million for the contras, Adolfo Calero asserted that covert U.S. aid would not end even if Congress voted to halt it: "It would not be cut off. It would come from some other place. It would be washed some way or another."[18]

By the time Congress voted against new funds for the contras in May 1984, President Reagan had verbally approved a fall-back program to be run out of the National Security Council—with the guidance and cooperation of high officials in the CIA, Pentagon, State Department and Justice Department, as well as the White House. Oliver North became the chief action officer, charged with holding the contras "together in body and soul."

In North's words, "To keep them together as a viable political opposition, to keep them alive in the field, to bridge the time between the time when we would have no money and the time when the Congress would vote again, to keep the effort alive because the President committed publicly to go back, in his words, 'again, and again, and again' to support the Nicaraguan resistance."[19]

The stakes were high. If the contras were not assisted after the Boland cutoff, said North, "within six to ten months the Nicaraguan resistance would cease to be...They would be annihilated in the field."[20]

In February 1984, North drafted a National Security Decision Directive recommending "immediate efforts to obtain additional funding of $10-$15 million from foreign or domestic sources to make up for the fact that the current $24 million appropriation will sustain operations only through June 1984."[21] McFarlane struck that draft language from the document, but pursued a similar course with Reagan's verbal authorization. McFarlane also tried, without success, to have Israel take over management of the contra program in addition to providing weapons, advisers and funding.[22]

CIA Director Casey hand-carried a secret "Eyes Only" memorandum to McFarlane on March 27: "In view of possible difficulties in obtaining supplemental appropriations to carry out the Nicaraguan covert action project through the remainder of this year, I am in full agreement that you should explore funding alternatives with [Israel] and perhaps others [e.g. Saudi Arabia]. I believe your thought of putting one of your staff in touch with the appropriate [deleted] official should promptly be pursued. You will recall that the Nicaraguan project runs out of funds in mid-May. Although additional moneys are indeed required to continue the project in the current fiscal year, equipment and materiel made available from other sources might in part substitute for some funding. We are therefore currently exploring two such alternatives." One of these alternatives, which are blacked out in the declassified memorandum, refers to Israel. The other refers to South Africa, whose "officials already had been approached" and "the initial reaction had been favorable."

Casey added, "Finally, after examining legalities, you might consider finding an appropriate private US citizen to establish a foundation that [unreadable] be recipient of nongovernmental funds which could be disbursed to [deleted] and FDN."[23]

Casey had personally discussed support for the contras with a South African official in January. Since then he had received at least one affirmative cable from a CIA official in South Africa. According to CIA documents, the South Africa approach was widely discussed in the administration. An April 9 CIA cable noted, "SecState has been briefed on the initiative and approved." Shultz has denied this.

Between April 10 and 13, Dewey Clarridge traveled to South Africa to discuss Nicaragua and other still-classified Latin America-related topics, but after arriving he was told by CIA Deputy Director John McMahon to "hold off" on contra discussions because of the furor over the mining of Nicaragua's harbors. Administration officials were having second thoughts about the political risks of a South Africa-contra link (Shultz's first documented opposition to obtaining aid from South Africa is reportedly dated April 18).[24]

"Current furor over here over the Nicaraguan project urges that we postpone taking [South Africa] up on their offer of assistance," Clarridge wrote in a May 11 CIA cable. "Please express to [a South African official] my deep regret that we must do this, at least for the time being, and I fully realize that he cannot crank up assistance on a moment's notice, should we decide to go forward in the future."[25]

Clarridge, the CIA station chief and his deputies in Honduras, and other U.S. officials assured the contras (and their Honduran sponsors) they would not be abandoned. Edgar Chamorro recalled for the World Court a spring 1984 visit to Honduras by NSC aide Christopher Lehman who "told us that President Reagan was unable at that time to publicly express the full extent of his commitment to us because of the upcoming presidential elections in the United States. But, Mr. Lehman told us, as soon as the elections were over, President Reagan would publicly endorse our effort to remove the Sandinistas from power and see to it that we received all the support that was necessary for the purpose. We received a similar assurance of continued United States Government support, notwithstanding the refusal of the Congress to appropriate more funds, from Lt. Col. Oliver North."[26] Thus, the contras learned administration respect for democracy and civilian majority rule.

The *Washington Post* reported in June that FDN leaders, speaking privately, "insist they have received assurances the U.S. money will continue to flow despite reluctance in Congress." The *Post* added, "Some reports have said that the United States has requested that Israel and possibly Saudi Arabia contribute support to get around the congressional restriction, and rebel leaders said they already had set up a support channel through Israel."[27] The *Post* was on target then, as were numerous press accounts before and after, but Congress showed a dogged willingness to disbelieve the mounting evidence of Boland amendment contravention and to suspend disbelief when it came to administration denials.

Before the *Post* account, FDN commander Bermudez said on NBC News, "We have received some weapons from the weapons…that [the] Israeli government took from [the] PLO in Lebanon." According to NBC, Israel had armed a quarter of the contra army "at Washington's urging." Earlier reports of this arrangement had appeared in the press in 1983.[28] By the end of September 1984, Israel had reportedly given the contras nearly $5 million more in aid, including cash and Eastern bloc and Chinese-made weapons. In 1985, Israel supplied surface-to-air missiles along with rifles, grenades, ammunition and other weapons.

Israel also supplied military advisers. According to an NSC document, there were more than 30 Israeli advisers in Honduras by the end of 1983.[29] While their total number has remained a well-guarded secret over the years, the Israeli advisers were reportedly paid $6,500 to $10,000 a month. In 1985 and 1986, Israeli arms were shipped to El Salvador's Ilopango Air Base by the CIA proprietary Southern Air Transport for delivery to the contras.[30]

Partnership with Apartheid

South Africa's contra support also went forward. Several months after Clarridge's trip to South Africa, Safair Freighters (U.S.A.) Inc. was incorporated. The parent company, Safair Freighters of South Africa, transferred three Lockheed L-100 aircraft to the U.S.-based Safair, which in turn leased them to Southern Air Transport.[31]

According to Clarridge, the South Africans were reluctant to deal with the contras directly so he suggested they provide aid through a third country. David Duncan, a Miami-based arms dealer, said that South Africa sold arms to the contras, provided fifteen to twenty trainers stationed in Honduras and financed a $72 million military-owned industrial complex, port facility and hospital in Honduras. The funds were reportedly laundered through a Liechtenstein holding company.[32]

A February 1985 intelligence report stated that Pretoria shipped 200,000 pounds of weapons through Costa Rica to Eden Pastora. As North recorded it in his notes, Clarridge told him on January 5 there were "200 T [tons] of arms en route from South Africa to CR." After a meeting with CIA officials in Central America, North noted that the South African arms should be transferred to the FDN: "Move S/A delivery from ARDE to FDN."[33]

South African support for the contras appears to have been part of a larger deal involving U.S. military assistance to Saudi Arabia, Saudi oil deliveries to South Africa (in violation of an international boycott) and Saudi and South African assistance to the Angolan UNITA and the contras.[34]

Saudi Pipeline

A major source of third-country cash for the contras was the misogynist monarchy of Saudi Arabia. Since the early 1970s, the Saudi kingdom has secretly contributed billions of dollars to movements and governments in at least a dozen countries to further U.S. and Western objectives.

"It takes King Fahd about 10 seconds to sign a check," said William Quandt, a former NSC Middle East specialist. "It takes Congress weeks to debate the smallest issue of this sort. If you can get somebody else to pay for it, it's nice and convenient." A former diplomat explained, "They have been terrific in lots of places. Anytime we needed them to pay for something, we always turned to the Saudis. We viewed them as this great milk cow."[35]

The Saudis paid Morocco to train the South African-backed UNITA forces of Jonas Savimbi, trying to overthrow the government of Angola, while the Clark amendment banned such aid by the United States. This Boland-like amendment was in effect from 1976 until July 1985, when Congress repealed it and put the United States openly on the side of the apartheid regime.[36] In 1977, the Saudis financed an airlift of Moroccan troops to Zaire to prop up the Mobutu dictatorship. The Saudis also helped Washington fund the Afghan rebels at a joint cost of over $500 million a year. Other areas of U.S.-Saudi cooperation have included Yemen, Somalia, Pakistan and the Sudan. Saudi Arabia also leads the Middle East Council in the World Anti-Communist League.

The Saudis reportedly undertook three operations at Casey's personal request. In early 1985, Casey arranged with Saudi Arabia's ambassador to the United States, Prince Bandar, for the Saudis to deposit $3 million in a Swiss account to finance the assassination of Sheikh Fadlallah, leader of the Hizbollah (Party of God) in Beirut. The CIA fingered him for the bombings of U.S. facilities in Beirut. It wasn't assassination, argued CIA Legal Counsel Stanley Sporkin: it was "preemptive self-defense."

The Saudis contracted a veteran of the British Special Air Services to arrange the hit. On March 8, a car loaded with explosives blew up near Fadlallah's high rise residence, killing 80 and wounding 200 bystanders and neighbors. Fadlallah escaped injury. His followers hung a "Made in USA" banner in front of a blown-out building. To better cover their tracks, the Saudis led Fadlallah to some of the hired assassins (who didn't know the Saudis were the paymasters, much less of the U.S. role). At Casey's request, the Saudis also backed anti-Qadaffi forces in Chad and contributed $2 million to assist in a secret operation to block the Italian Communist Party's democratic ascent."[37]

For Washington, Saudi funding of covert action was a perfect use of petrodollars. For the Saudis, it nurtured an alliance that delivered billions of dollars in military supplies (also bought with petrodollars), including a 1981 purchase of AWACS radar planes. The key Pentagon official shepherding that controversial AWACS sale through Congress was General Richard Secord. By most accounts, including their own, North and Secord met during this AWACS sale, which North assisted as a low-level NSC staffer. (Some reports claim they actually met over a decade earlier, during covert operations in Laos.)[38]

In May 1984, McFarlane met with Prince Bandar after official and unofficial emissaries—including a Secord assistant, two chief executives of U.S. corporations and the CIA's Middle East division chief—received negative replies regarding contra support, thus creating a trail of deniability to cover administration tracks. (Secord himself became involved in a 1985 solicitation.)[39] McFarlane claimed that he did not technically solicit funds, but has acknowledged (in rather tortured language) that "it was unmistakable in his [Bandar's] own mind that my concern and my view of this impending loss would represent a significant setback for the President, and if anyone with any gumption could manage without being led or asked, then a contribution would have been welcome."[40]

At a White House meeting on June 22, McFarlane gave Bandar an index card with a contra account number. The Saudis agreed to contribute $8 million in monthly installments.

At a June 25 National Security Planning Group meeting attended by Reagan, Bush, Shultz, Weinberger, Casey, Meese and McFarlane, the Saudi contribution was apparently not discussed, but the general topic of third-country funding was. Shultz conveyed the view of White House Chief of Staff James Baker that for the United States to act as a conduit for third-country contra funding would constitute an "impeachable offense."

The next day, Casey and CIA Legal Council Stanley Sporkin discussed the legality of third-country funding with Attorney General William French Smith and Justice Department officials. Smith stated "that he saw no legal concern" if the U.S. government "discussed this matter with other nations so long as it was made clear that they would be using their own funds to support the Contras and no U.S. appropriated funds would be used for this purpose." Smith added that "any nation agreeing to supply aid could not look to the United States to repay that commitment in the future." Casey said he would inform the Intelligence Committees if third-country funding was pursued; he apparently did not.[41]

Soon after the June 22 meeting, McFarlane telephoned Bandar using a pre-arranged code, "My friend did not get his cigarettes, and he's a heavy smoker." On July 6, the first million was laundered through a Swiss Bank Corporation account and deposited in account 54148 at the Miami branch of the BAC International Bank of the Cayman Islands.[42]

McFarlane informed Reagan of the Saudi contribution by placing a notecard in his morning briefing book. "The President was pleased and grateful," said McFarlane.

McFarlane personally told Bush of the Saudi contribution and may have told Baker and Meese. Without naming Saudi Arabia, he told Shultz and Weinberger that the contra funding problem had been resolved.[43]

In February 1985, with the Boland cutoff in effect, McFarlane met Bandar to prepare for an upcoming visit from King Fahd, and they again discussed the contras. Reagan met privately with Fahd on February 11. The Saudis agreed to raise their contra tribute.

"My Friend," North wrote Calero, "Next week, a sum in excess of $20M will be deposited in the usual account...It should allow us to bridge the gap between now and when the vote is taken and the funds are turned on again." The money, North said, should be used to redeploy and hide contra forces from an expected Sandinista offensive; outfit and train "the forces and volunteers"; and develop a regular air resupply operation. "This new money," he continued, "will provide great flexibility we have not enjoyed to date. I would urge you to make use of some of it for my British friend [Special Air Services veteran David Walker] and his services for special operations. I can produce him at the end of this month...

"Please do *not* in any way make *anyone* aware of the deposit. Too much is becoming known by too many people. We need to make sure this new financing does *not* become known. The Congress must believe that there continues to be an urgent need for funding. Warm regards, Steelhammer."[44] (North's italics.)

McFarlane said he did not inform Shultz of the new Saudi funding, but Weinberger and Joint Chiefs of Staff Chairman John Vessey Jr. "learned of the contribution from other sources." In a March 15 meeting with Deputy CIA Director McMahon, Weinberger mentioned that Saudi Arabia "had earmarked $25 million for the contras."[45]

North reviewed contra funding and operations in a top secret April 11 memo to McFarlane. "From July 1984 through February 1985, the FDN received $1M [million] per month for a total of $8M. From February 22 to April 9, 1985, an additional $16.5M has been received for a grand total of $24.5M. Of this, $17,145,594 has been expended for arms, munitions, combat operations, and support activities." An itemized ledger of FDN expenditures and outlays for July 1984-February 1985 was attached.[46]

In the spring and summer of 1985, North tried to facilitate a contra donation from a "Saudi Prince." The Prince turned out to be an Iranian con man, later convicted of bank fraud in Philadelphia. The FBI questioned North about his fundraising with the Prince in July 1985. As the FBI agent left the interview with North on July 18, North introduced him to Adolfo Calero, the "George Washington of Nicaragua."[47]

North was contacted by Kevin Kattke, a maintenance engineer for Macy's department store in Bay Shore, New York and amateur spy. Kattke founded the Freeport, New York-based National Freedom Institute on North's advice and was in regular contact with North and Raymond Burghardt, NSC director for Latin American affairs.[48] According to the FBI report, Kattke said he represented a Saudi prince interested in giving $14 million to the contras from oil sale profits. "North advised Kattke that inasmuch as US public law forbid expenditures of government funds to aid Nicaraguan insurgents [sic], it was inadvisable for a member of the NSC (North) to meet with the Prince directly. North advised Kattke that Richard Miller would contact Kattke to meet the Prince." The FBI identified Miller as the president of International Business Communications who "has been doing confidential contract and consultant work for NSC and U.S. Department of State for the approximate past 3 years. Miller's work concerns the funnelling of private funds to Nicaraguan freedom fighters who oppose the Sandinista government."

According to the FBI report, "Information regarding the Prince's expressed interest in donating to the Nicaraguan freedom fighters was discussed by North personally with President Ronald Reagan and National Security Adviser Robert Mac Farlane [sic] as recently as June, 1985."[49] (The Prince also proposed assistance in freeing American hostages in Lebanon. North followed up on this with the help of a Drug Enforcement agent assigned to him for hostage-release efforts.)[50]

The FBI report was conveniently "lost" until Senate investigations in 1987.[51]

Dollars from Dictators

"U.S. Is Considering Having Asians Aid Nicaragua Rebels," stated the *New York Times* headline of March 6, 1985. A Democratic congressional aide was quoted: "I think they are convinced they are not going to get the $14 million, and they are trying to figure out some way of getting money to the contras. They are not going to get it through third countries or though humanitarian aid. Congress will see through that in a minute." Congress kept looking away.

By then the administration had already begun soliciting contraband from Asian dictators with the help of retired General John Singlaub. In November 1984, Singlaub met in Washington with representatives of Taiwan and South Korea, regimes he was close to through his military and World Anti-Communist League activities. "I was very specific," said Singlaub, "in stating that they [the contras] needed bullets and guns" and antiaircraft missiles. He suggested three options for providing the funds: 1) contributing directly to the contras' bank account; 2) giving money to Singlaub for arms purchases; and 3) colluding in a scheme whereby the proceeds from over-charges in purchases of U.S. weapons—in the United States or through a third country such as Israel—would be diverted to the contras.[52]

Singlaub made a follow-up visit to Taiwan and South Korea in January 1985. In a secret February 6 memo, North informed McFarlane that "the FDN is in urgent need of near-term financing—approximately $2M." Regarding this matter, he told McFarlane that "as a consequence of GEN Singlaub's recent trip, both the [Taiwan representative?] and the [South Korean representative?] indicated to [deleted] that they want to help in a 'big way.' [Deleted] (CIA) has withheld the dissemination of these offers and contacted me privately to insure that they will not become common knowledge. Singlaub will be here to see me tomorrow. With your permission, I will ask him to approach [deleted] at the [Taiwan] Interests Section and [deleted] at the [South Korean] Embassy urging that they proceed with their offer."[53]

The next day, Singlaub told North that the two countries wanted a signal of approval from a recognized administration spokesman.[54] The signals were arranged. In the summer of 1985, Gaston Sigur Jr., then an NSC aide and, since March 1986, assistant secretary of state for East Asian and Pacific Affairs, was asked by North to contact Taiwan's U.S. representative to facilitate a contra donation. In August, North met the Taiwanese official at the Hay Adams Hotel in Washington, resulting in a fall donation of $1 million. Later that fall, North directed Sigur to ask Taiwan for more money and they came through with another $1 million in early 1986. Sigur also arranged for North to meet an official of South Korea in the summer of 1985.

This wasn't Sigur's first involvement in contra solicitation. In November 1984, he had arranged a meeting between North and the senior military representative of the Peoples Republic of China at the Cosmos Club in Washington.[55] North informed the FBI beforehand and asked for surveillance so that there would be no misunderstanding about the meeting's purpose. "The Director of the FBI was aware of that meeting," said North. "This was not some deep, dark secret."

As North recounted it, he and the Chinese official "had a long philosophical discussion over lunch about Soviet hegemony, the kinds of things that I thought would be attractive and of concern to him…and I made him aware that there was a purchase under way [through Richard Secord], that these things [SA-7 surface-to-air missiles] were desperately needed. And he then facilitated that."[56]

The Sultan of Brunei was recommended as a likely contra donor in a December 1984 letter to North from Edie Fraser of the public relations firm, Miner and Fraser. Fraser said that the Sultan had donated $500,000 to Nancy Reagan's anti-drug campaign and "it has been recommended that he might kick in a million dollars…for the Refugees for Central America."[57]

The Sultan was tapped a year and a half later by the State Department. (State also asked Singapore for contra assistance, but Singapore didn't manufacture the desired long-range communications equipment.)[58] In December 1985, Congress had changed the law to permit solicitation of third countries for "humanitarian aid." As Shultz put it later at a May 16, 1986 National Security Planning Group meeting, "It would be easier to get money for the contras from a third country than it would from Congress."[59]

In August 1986, traveling under the alias "Mr. Kenilworth," Assistant Secretary of State Elliott Abrams solicited funds from a Brunei official while walking in a London park. He gave him a card with a bank account number provided by North. But an unplanned diversion occurred. North or his secretary, Fawn Hall, transposed two numbers for the Lake Resources account at Credit Suisse Bank in Geneva. Brunei transferred $10 million into the wrong account, and the mix-up wasn't resolved in time to redirect the money before the Iran-contra scandal broke.[60]

In the fantasy North spun for the Iran-contra committees, other countries were eager to contribute toward the fight for "democracy" when the U.S. Congress would not. In reality, as Adolfo Calero acknowledged, the FDN tried unsuccessfully to raise money from other countries when Congress cut off funds. "I realize," said Calero, "if the United States didn't wink an eye to other countries we wouldn't get anything. Officials from other countries told me this."[61]

North & Company

To outwit the gullible congressional watchdogs, President Reagan authorized the NSC staff to add extensive operational activities to its better-known planning and coordination role. In January 1983, the president had signed National Security Decision Directive No. 77, authorizing the NSC to coordinate the interagency program known as "Project Democracy." It combined "public diplomacy" with an extra secret covert operations arm. The post-Boland Nicaragua operation came under the "Project Democracy" rubric.[62] North took on functions normally performed by a CIA official and, in John Poindexter's words, became "the switching point that made the whole system work."[63]

The retooled contra support system depended upon the complicity of the National Security Council, composed of President Reagan, Vice President Bush,

Secretary of State George Shultz, Secretary of Defense Caspar Weinberger (statutory members) and CIA Director William Casey (a de facto member), as well as the complicity of numerous government officials outside the NSC staff, including Vice Presidential National Security Adviser Donald Gregg; Vice Presidential aide Colonel Sam Watson; CIA Deputy Director for Clandestine Operations Clair George; European Division and Counterterrorism Unit Chief Duane "Dewey" Clarridge; Clarridge's successor(s) as CIA Latin American Division chief (unidentified); CIA Central America Task Force Chief Alan Fiers, formerly station chief in Saudi Arabia; CIA station chiefs Joe Fernandez (alias Tomas Castillo) in Costa Rica and John Mallett (alias George) in Honduras; the late Joint Chiefs of Staff aide Admiral Arthur Moreau; Generals Paul Gorman and John Galvin of the Southern Command; Deputy Assistant Secretary of Defense Nestor Sanchez; various officials of the Special Operations Division and Intelligence Support Activity; U.S. Military Attache to El Salvador Colonel James Steele; Assistant Secretary of State for Inter-American Affairs Elliott Abrams; State Department Office of Public Diplomacy Directors Otto Reich and Robert Kagen and Assistant Director Jonathan Miller; Ambassadors Lewis Tambs in Costa Rica, Thomas Pickering and Edwin Corr in El Salvador, and John Negroponte and John Ferch in Honduras; White House Office of Public Liaison Directors Faith Whittlesey and Linda Chavez; FBI Director William Webster; FBI Executive Assistant Director Oliver "Buck" Revell; Attorney General Edwin Meese; Assistant Attorney General Lowell Jensen; and others.

In Marine Lt. Colonel Oliver North, the president found a player who could be trusted to carry the contra ball over, under and around congressional obstacles. As two associates heard him tell it, "If it weren't for those liberals in Congress, we wouldn't be doing half of what we do illegally."[64]

"I'm not in the habit of questioning my superiors," North told the Iran-contra committees. "I saluted smartly and charged up the hill. That's what lieutenant colonels are supposed to do."

Like his boss Admiral John Poindexter, North saw himself as a soldier serving his commander in chief, more like an aide to a military junta than to an elected president. "This Lieutenant Colonel," North said, "is not going to challenge a decision of the Commander in Chief...And if the Commander in Chief tells this Lieutenant Colonel to go stand in the corner and sit on his head, I will do so." Part of North's mission was to shield his superiors, especially the president. "That is the part of any subordinate," said North. "Every centurion had a group of shields out in front of him, a hundred of 'em."[65]

North epitomized the Reaganaut view that revolutions were Soviet-Cuban plots. Rep. Michael Barnes first met North in 1983 when North was White House liaison to the Kissinger Commission. "I remember him doing a briefing for the commission...in which he said, and I quote, 'Fidel Castro is responsible for 90% of the problems in Central America.' Well, anybody who knows anything about Central America knows that's laughable."[66]

NBC News anchor Tom Brokaw was briefed by North in April 1985. Pointing to the usual grainy surveillance photos, North called Nicaragua a "major asset of the Soviet bloc." Describing a military camp, North told Brokaw, " 'The interesting thing

here is the baseball diamond. Nicaraguans don't play baseball. Cubans play baseball.'
I looked to see if he were kidding. He was not," said Brokaw.[67]

North matched Kissinger as a sportsologist. In 1970, Kissinger rushed into
White House Chief of Staff Bob Haldeman's office with a file of classified reconnaissance photos. " 'It's a Cuban seaport, Haldeman, and these pictures show the Cubans
are building soccer fields...These soccer fields could mean war, Bob.' Haldeman
asked why. 'Cubans play *baseball.* Russians play *soccer,*' Kissinger replied."[68] In
reality, Nicaraguans and Cubans play both baseball and soccer.

The stories would be funny, if not for the fact that reporters protected North's
cover and used him as a major background source for news no less disinforming
than the baseball claim, and far more harmful. *Time* magazine reporter David Halevy
met with North an average of once a week: "Ollie tried, through me, to get the
American public informed, and he did a very good job in trying to do it."[69]

North was assigned in August 1981 to the NSC staff, then headed by Richard
Allen, to assist in the preparation of briefing materials on the sale of AWACS and
other military equipment to Saudi Arabia. He then became a member of the defense
policies group, specializing in counterterrorism. When foreign policy novice William Clark became national security adviser, North played an increasing role in crisis
management. North's three-year tour of duty with the NSC was extended at the request of McFarlane, who took over as national security adviser in October 1983, the
same month North was promoted to lieutenant colonel.

North was an increasingly trusted "can-do" officer, famous for his long hours
and red tape cutting. In June 1983, he became deputy director of political-military
affairs under Donald Fortier (Fortier died of cancer in August 1986) and then replaced
Roger Fontaine as the NSC principal on the Central America RIG chaired by Assistant Secretary of State Langhorne Motley (Elliott Abrams succeeded Motley in 1985).
Poindexter, who moved up from deputy national security adviser in December 1985,
would have recommended that North be promoted to the third-rank title of special
assistant to the president. But, he explained, there was "more flexibility" with the
lower title.[70] More deniability, in other words.

The Iran-contra affair was not North's first mystery. His official biography states
he served in Vietnam as an infantry platoon commander from December 3, 1968 to
August 21, 1969 and then in a G-3 operations billet at Headquarters Battalion, 3rd
Division, until November 23, 1969. According to the bio, First Lieutenant North was
then assigned to the Basic School, Quantico, Virginia from November 29, 1969 to
February 2, 1973. However, while testifying as a character witness at the New York
securities fraud trial of NSC aide Thomas Reed, North said he was on active duty in
Vietnam "from 1968 through the early part of 1970, and then again in 1971." He
said, "I was an infantry platoon and company commander in the Special Operations
Force, team commander." Marine records show no such outfit, but North reportedly performed covert missions under the joint CIA-Pentagon Special Operations
Group headed by General Singlaub.[71]

During December 1974 and January 1975, North, most recently a company
commander in Okinawa, Japan, was hospitalized voluntarily for three weeks at
Bethesda Naval Hospital for emotional problems. (Some sources claim he was hospi-

talized before that, in August.) North was reportedly found by a superior officer running around naked, babbling incoherently, waving a pistol and threatening suicide. After North was discharged from Bethesda and found fit for duty, the record of his hospitalization was removed from his medical and personnel files.[72]

Cut-Outs: Owen, Hull and Singlaub

Like previous covert operations, the Nicaragua operation relied upon a network of intermediaries, or "cut-outs," and nominally private commercial enterprises, known as "proprietaries," used to conceal U.S. government involvement.

Robert Owen was a key North cut-out. Owen and North first met in 1983 when Owen was working for Senator Dan Quayle (R-IN). Before that Owen had worked briefly for the U.S. program in Thailand for Cambodian, Vietnamese and Laotian refugees. An expatriate Indiana constituent living in Costa Rica, John Hull, visited Quayle's office along with two other Americans and "a Nicaraguan who had just come in from the jungles of Nicaragua [contra Luis Rivas]." North was one of the people Owen took them to see. In August, Owen went to Costa Rica on a round-trip ticket paid for by Hull, a longtime CIA asset.

Owen went to work for the public relations firm Gray & Company which, in April 1984, was asked to represent the contras. Assigned to pursue the matter, Owen went to see North and then worked with Senior Vice President Neil Livingstone to develop proposals for contra support. "The first proposal," Owen explained, "was one on setting up proprietary companies which could be used to purchase goods overseas and provide assistance to the Contras. Another one was using a nonprofit organization to provide assistance through raising funds here in the United States to provide humanitarian and non-lethal assistance."[73]

After further discussion with North, Owen traveled to Costa Rica and Honduras in late May and early June to assess contra needs. In a July 2 letter referring to weapons as toys and firecrackers, Owen told North that $1 million to $1.5 million a month was needed.[74] In August, Owen met with North, Singlaub and Calero while in Dallas for the Republican Convention. They discussed contra arms requirements. In late October, Owen arranged to leave Gray & Company and work for the FDN at $2,500 a month plus expenses. Gray & Company decided not to take on the contra account, but Neil Livingstone (who is affiliated with the American Security Council) put a nonprofit organization he started, called the Institute on Terrorism and Subnational Conflict, at the contras' disposal.[75]

Owen's code name was "the Courier" or "TC." North used a variety of code names, such as "Steelhammer," "B.G." (Blood and Guts), "Mr. Green" and "Mr. Goode." Calero was codenamed "Sparkplug." Secord was "Copp." Owen acted as North's liaison to the contras—passing letters and weapons lists, delivering maps and reconnaissance photos (North got them from the CIA and Pentagon), facilitating the development of an airstrip in Costa Rica and cashing travelers checks to pay contra salaries. When Owen got married on October 19, 1985, North gave him $1,000 in travelers checks as a present. The checks came from the slush fund North kept, upon Casey's advice, in his office safe to pay contra leaders and miscellaneous expenses.

According to CIA station chief in Costa Rica Joe Fernandez, CIA Central America Task Force chief Alan Fiers "at one time was so impressed with Mr. Owen that he was being considered as a possible applicant for the clandestine service. The man is—has all the attributes that we want in our officers."[76]

The ode to Ollie North that Owen read at the close of his Iran-contra testimony was penned by John Hull, a crucial U.S. cut-out before and after the Boland cutoff. In a letter to Owen in November 1983, Hull noted that B.G. (Blood and Guts) was going to have McFarlane as his new boss. He hoped this would make North "more powerful as we need more like him."[77]

Hull, the son of a military intelligence officer, moved to Costa Rica in the early 1960s and became the millionaire owner of extensive properties, including a 1,500 acre ranch in northern Costa Rica near the Nicaraguan border. On the ranch, where he raises cattle and grows oranges, Hull pays his workers 60 cents an hour and relishes his role as "El Patron."[78]

Congressional sources say Hull has worked for the CIA since at least the early 1970s. Hull has called himself a "coordinator" between the contras and the U.S. Government.[79] In 1982, he rented a contra safe house in San Jose at CIA request. Hull helped plan the 1983 bombing attack on Managua's international airport and assisted Pastora's forces until he and the CIA broke with Pastora in 1984. The United States used Hull's ranch, with its six landing strips, to deliver supplies to the contras before and after the Boland cutoff. Contra sources have said that station chief Joe Fernandez told them Hull was the CIA's representative in northern Costa Rica. Hull's property served as a contra base camp and a meeting ground for competing factions on the southern front.[80]

In another twist on contra diversions, Hull received a $375,000 loan in 1984 from the U.S. government's Overseas Private Investment Corporation (OPIC) to manufacture ax and wheelbarrow handles from local timber. OPIC did not follow normal procedure in evaluating the loan's collateral or assuring its use. The U.S. Embassy in Costa Rica, under Ambassador Curtin Winsor Jr., had strongly urged approval of the loan to "strengthen" U.S. relations with Costa Rica. In late 1985 and 1986, Owen sought without success to get another $400,000 loan from OPIC for Hull. In January 1986, an OPIC memorandum reported that "John Hull has done nothing to get the business started or pay off the OPIC loan."[81] OPIC referred the case to the Justice Department.

Hull and Owen tried to avoid media attention. Retired General John Singlaub did all he could to exploit it.

By his own account, Singlaub was in touch with North shortly after North joined the NSC staff, but their first substantive meeting was a 1984 Singlaub briefing on the findings of a Pentagon panel on Central America. The panel, which Singlaub chaired at the request of Undersecretary of Defense Fred Ikle, recommended an increased emphasis on small-unit operations and psychological warfare. As panel member Harry Aderholt put it, "The U.S. military is a firepower, high-tech outfit, and that's not what's needed. That's what our Army likes to do; they like to never see 'em, just shoot 'em."[82]

In January 1984, Singlaub offered to help Calero by raising money and providing retired military advisers. Singlaub's World Anti-Communist League chapter, the United States Council for World Freedom (discussed in chapter 4), established the Institute for Regional and International Studies (IRIS), a tax-exempt "educational" organization to recruit people with skills in intelligence and psychological warfare ready to train the contras and the Salvadoran police and military. IRIS Director Alexander M.S. McColl is a veteran of Singlaub's Vietnam-era Special Operations Group and the military affairs editor of *Soldier of Fortune*.[83]

Singlaub was optimistic about contra prospects. "Given the tools," he told the Iran-contra committees, "this band of brave warriors can seize and shut down the first Soviet base on continental American soil." The contras, he said, compared favorably with other U.S.-backed forces: they were better motivated and had geography on their side. What's more, Singlaub claimed, with no indictment of the other forces intended, they had a better record on human rights.[84] In August 1985, he was reported as favoring the use of more former Somoza guardsmen by the FDN.[85] Singlaub also worried that the Soviets wanted to build a canal through Nicaragua, threatening the U.S. with not just a second Cuba but a "second Canal."

Singlaub, like North and others in the administration, saw congressional opponents as communist fellow travelers: There "are some hard-core left wing [members of Congress] like Michael Barnes and Boland and Ron Dellums and quite a few others that have always supported the communist organizations around the world."[86] Singlaub believes that "Congress has a role in foreign policy," the role of advice and consent through appropriations, "unless it interferes with U.S. sovereignty and the ability of the President to carry out security." Then the president can act unilaterally.

Singlaub channelled $5.3 million worth of East-bloc weapons to the contras in 1985 through the Washington-based arms brokerage, GeoMilitech, for which he was a consultant. On at least two occasions between July and December 1985, Singlaub discussed GeoMilitech's contra arms shipments with Casey. As Singlaub recalled, these conversations were probably at a social event and not in Casey's office "because he and I agreed that I would not mention the subject of support for the Nicaraguan freedom fighters to him. He threatened to throw me out of his office if I did."[87] Thus, Casey's deniability was maintained. As Singlaub earlier told CBS's "60 Minutes," Casey "has indicated approval, and...has been encouraging. He introduces me to the people that need to have the detailed information. So, he's been cooperative and sees me when I come into town on short notice."[88]

In December 1985, Casey met with GeoMilitech President Barbara Studley, a contra supporter who formerly hosted a radio talk show in Miami. They discussed a three-way diversion proposal, which Singlaub had reviewed earlier, with the objective "to create a conduit for maintaining a continuous flow of Soviet weapons and technology, to be utilized by the United States in its support of Freedom Fighters in Nicaragua, Afghanistan, Angola, Cambodia, Ethiopia, etc." The problem: "With each passing year, Congress has become increasingly unpredictable and uncooperative regarding the President's desire to support the cause of the Freedom Fighters."

To meet the objective without needing "the consent or awareness of the Department of State or Congress," the proposal suggested a three-way trade. The United States would provide credit toward Israel's purchase of U.S. high technology; Israel would provide military equipment to China to upgrade China's armed forces; and China would provide Soviet-compatible arms which would be laundered through a foreign trading company and dispersed to insurgents "per U.S. instructions."[89]

Casey, Israel and China were said to be receptive to the proposal. In addition to Casey, the plan was reportedly briefed to Alexander Haig and Richard Allen (they deny it). The unsigned proposal was later found in North's safe. Singlaub told the Iran-contra committees that he didn't like that particular plan because "one of the countries involved [China] was one that I did not feel we ought to be enhancing their military capability."[90]

As Singlaub began to receive increasing notice in the news media, he and North discussed the pros and cons of heightened visibility. On the negative side, Singlaub's association with North could create problems. On the positive side, the visibility was useful for fundraising and also boosted contra morale. Moreover, said Singlaub, it served "as sort of a lightning rod if the press was following me and asking me questions about this aid, and I was working clearly within the Boland Amendment and every other law that I thought existed, then that would take the heat off of those who were trying to be more covert in their actions."[91]

This "lightning rod" role was no less important than Singlaub's role in brokering arms sales, soliciting third-country funding or raising donations through the World Anti-Communist League network. Before the Saudi contribution was known, Singlaub was credited along with Calero in raising $15 million to $25 million for the contras.[92] Behind that smokescreen, Singlaub had actually raised $279,612 in 1985 and $259,173 in 1986, according to figures reported by the Iran-contra committees.

Private Aid Auxiliary

Singlaub is the most visible leader of a rightwing network of retired military officers, mercenaries, missionaries, fundraisers and lobbyists. The network has not been a private substitute for government, but an auxiliary arm of the executive branch.

Congress partly sanctioned this auxiliary when, in October 1984, it passed the Denton amendment, named for Senator Jeremiah Denton (R-AL), authorizing the Pentagon to use ships and planes on a space-available basis to transport "nonlethal" private aid.

In February 1985, former Justice Department attorney John Loftus sent Congress a report detailing his suspicions that Casey and Singlaub, using the World Anti-Communist League, had resurrected an old private conduit system for laundering money to "freedom fighters." The old conduit was the Crusade for Freedom, a public charity established by retired General Lucius Clay that provided "private" support for the National Committee for a Free Europe (now Radio Free Europe) and the American Committee for Liberation (now Radio Liberty). The two committees— home to Nazis and Nazi collaborators who, as Loftus noted, migrated to WACL— were secretly laundering government money to Eastern European insurgents at the direction of the NSC and the State Department's clandestine Office of Policy Coordination. Private citizen Ronald Reagan was an apparently unwitting celebrity fundraiser for the Crusade for Freedom.[93] When in 1982, President Reagan first introduced the public version of "Project Democracy," now institutionalized in the National Endowment for Democracy, he called for a "crusade for freedom."[94]

According to a 1985 report of the congressional Arms Control and Foreign Policy Caucus, "close to 20 privately incorporated U.S. groups have reportedly sent (or plan soon to send) aid, supplies or cash contributions to Nicaraguan refugees in Honduras and to the contras themselves...[The] driving forces behind the major groups are a small group of about a half a dozen men, most of whom have military or paramilitary backgrounds or mercenary experience...While many of the groups work closely together, they have different stated purposes. Some openly admit their aid is for military purposes...Most groups call their aid 'humanitarian,' but either privately or publicly acknowledge that some of it (e.g. medical supplies and food) ends up at contra camps. These groups also have conceded that their 'humanitarian' aid to refugees (which include families of the contras) may indirectly aid the contras by freeing up the contra accounts to purchase weapons and pay combatants."[95]

The contra auxiliary includes the World Anti-Communist League and its U.S. Council for World Freedom, the American Security Council, Council for Inter-American Security and Western Goals discussed earlier (also see chapter 15). Among the other key groups in the auxiliary are the following:

The Florida-based Air Commandos Association, led by retired Brigadier General Harry "Heinie" Aderholt, is a group of approximately 1,600 past and present members of the U.S. Special Forces. Aderholt, *Soldier of Fortune's* unconventional warfare editor, coordinated the joint CIA-Pentagon-AID program to provide "humanitarian" relief to the Hmong secret army in Laos and served as chief of covert air operations in Singlaub's Special Operations Group. When established in 1968, the Air Commandos distributed supplies, donated primarily by World Medical Relief, to the Hmong and other paramilitary forces in Laos and Thailand. In addition to distributing aid to the Miskito Indians and contra families in Honduras, Air Commandos has assisted the Salvadoran Army and worked with the Guatemalan Army's counterinsurgency "civic action" program which has forcibly resettled Guatemalan Indians into so-called development poles (known as strategic hamlets during the Vietnam War).

Soldier of Fortune (circulation about 200,000) was founded in 1975 by the Colorado-based Omega Group headed by retired Lt. Col. Robert K. Brown, a veteran of the Phoenix program and special operations in Laos and ex-mercenary in white-ruled Rhodesia. Brown sports a T-Shirt boasting, "I Was Killing When Killing Wasn't Cool." *Soldier of Fortune (SOF)* runs articles on counterinsurgency warfare, glamorizes training and combat missions by *SOF* personnel, advertises weapons and mercenary services and encourages donations to its affiliated El Salvador/Nicaragua Defense Fund, which printed and distributed some 500 copies of the CIA contra manual, and Refugee Relief International, which provides medical training and supplies to El Salvador and the contras. Refugee Relief is led by Thomas Reisinger, the assistant director of *SOF* for special projects; board members include Singlaub, Aderholt and *SOF* Military Affairs Editor Alexander McColl. (In March 1988, a Texas jury ordered *Soldier of Fortune* to pay $9.4 million in damages to the family of a woman killed by a hit man her husband hired through a classified ad in the magazine; *SOF* is appealing the verdict.)

The CIA contra manual is mild compared to some of the murder and sabotage manuals *SOF* promotes, with such titles as *How to Kill* Vols. I-V, *Hit Man* ("Learn how a pro makes a living at this craft without landing behind bars"), *Techniques of Harassment* and *Elementary Field Interrogation*. The last manual includes explicit instructions for psychological and physical torture. Under a section titled, "the cook out," the manual advises:

> Ignite a piece of C-4 [explosive] in front of your subject and use it to boil water in a small pot...Pour a little of the boiling water on his genitals for effect, if you wish.
>
> Now, take a similar amount of the same explosive and tape it over the subject's eye, leaving one eye unobstructed to see that you are holding a lighted match within a few inches of the material on his eye. Begin your questions, if the subject panics or refuses to answer, hold the flame to his nipple to let him know you're serious. No one wants to be blinded by fire.[96]

Civilian Materiel Assistance (CMA, formerly Civilian Military Assistance), based in Memphis, Tennessee, was founded in 1983 by Tom Posey, a former Marine Corporal, John Bircher and Ku Klux Klansman, along with fellow members of the Alabama National Guard. Posey appeared in *Newsweek* in front of a banner with the slogan "Kill 'Em All: Let God Sort 'Em Out."[97] On an approved U.S. Treasury application to become a firearms dealer, Posey wrote, "I plan to buy weapons and ammo to send to El Salvador."[98] CMA has chapters in most states and recruits heavily through state National Guards and gun shows. It has provided men, training, arms and other supplies to the contras. "We like to think of ourselves as missionary-mercenaries," explained Posey.[99]

Two CMA mercenaries, Dana Parker and Jim Powell, were killed on September 1, 1984 when their CIA-supplied helicopter was shot down over Nicaragua. Parker and Powell—as well as two of the three Cessnas supplied by the Pentagon to the CIA for the contras under Operation Elephant Herd—were part of an air-ground attack on a northern Nicaraguan military school near Santa Clara. The bombing raid killed one woman and three children.[100]

CMA has also reportedly aided the United Lao National Liberation Front, a rightwing Laotian organization based in California and headed by Vang Pao, the exile leader of the CIA's secret army. According to a longtime associate of Vang Pao, CMA tried to recruit Lao pilots for the contra war.[101]

The Virginia-based National Defense Council was founded in 1978 by Andy Messing, a close friend of North's and member of Singlaub's Pentagon advisory panel, who has said "that going to war is his favorite pastime."[102] Singlaub, Aderholt and the late Edward Lansdale have served on the board. The Defense Council organizes "fact-finding" tours to Central America for members of Congress, and the Air Commandos Association distributes Defense Council aid to Guatemala's "civic action" program.

Brigade 2506, made up largely of Bay of Pigs veterans, has sent personnel and supplies to the contras in Central America and provided a warm sanctuary in Miami. Brigade 2506 has close ties to the Dade County Republican Party formerly headed by George Bush's son, Jeb. The kind of freedom fighting the Brigade supports is evident in its choice of Chilean dictator Pinochet for its first Freedom Award in 1975. Brigade members have undertaken terrorist attacks against Cuba and, in 1976, former Brigade leaders joined in creating a terrorist alliance called the Congress of United Revolutionary Organizations (CORU). CORU has worked with the Chilean military and European fascist movements in political assassinations around the world, including the 1976 Washington car bombing that killed Orlando Letelier, Chile's ambassador to the United States under Allende, and his Institute for Policy Studies colleague Ronni Karpen Moffitt.[103]

Brigade 2506 member Felipe Vidal, a reported CIA operative, hoped to provide a permanent paramilitary infrastructure for an "international anti-communist brigade," based first in Costa Rica where he worked closely with John Hull and CMA. As Vidal explained it, Nicaragua is "a strategic point from which to begin attacking Castro...During the 1970s, the form of [our] struggle was terrorism against Castro in Mexico, France, Barbados and the United States...Once Reagan got into power, there was no need for these organizations because the [U.S.] government's policy coincided with the Cuban community's."[104] Actually, Cuban exile terrorist organizations still operate. But many of their members found employment in the contra war, among them Luis Posada, Felix Rodriguez and Rafael Quintero (discussed later).

The Virginia-based Christian Broadcasting Network (CBN) was founded by the Reverend Pat Robertson, a 1988 Republican presidential candidate. CBN's 700 Club, a pillar of televangelism, reaches 30 million homes. Its relief organization, Operation Blessing, has supported the contras. In distributing aid to the contras and other Central America projects, CBN has worked with the Air Commandos, Refugee Relief International, World Medical Relief, Friends of the Americas, Knights of Malta and other groups.

The Sovereign Military Order of Malta (SMOM), known as the Knights of Malta, is an elite, international Vatican order dating back to the Crusades. SMOM has the unique status of a nation state with no territory, but with its own constitution, diplomats and passports, and the benefit of shipping internationally through diplomatic pouch without Customs inspection. Every year, in a Rome ritual on St. John's Day, Knights and Dames of Malta "dressed in scarlet uniforms and black capes, brandishing swords and waving flags emblazoned with the eight-pointed Maltese cross...swear allegiance to the defense of the Holy Mother Church."[105]

The late William Casey was a Knight, as was former CIA Director John McCone and the legendary chief of the pre-CIA Office of Strategic Services (OSS),

General William "Wild Bill" Donovan. In July 1944, Pope Pius XII decorated Donovan with the Grand Cross of the Order of Saint Sylvester, the oldest of papal knighthoods, an award "given to only 100 other men in history, who 'by feat of arms, or writings, or outstanding deeds, have spread the Faith, and have safeguarded and championed the Church.' " Donovan's Knighthood personifies the often close links between the Church and the CIA (OSS) in combating communism, real and imagined—from intervention in the 1948 Italian elections to contemporary Latin America. In 1948, the SMOM gave a high award of honor to General Reinhard Gehlen, Hitler's chief of intelligence for the Soviet front, who folded his operation into the Cold War crusades.[106]

The American Knights are led by J. Peter Grace (who once called food stamps "basically a Puerto Rican program"), chairman of the multinational W.R. Grace & Company and the American Institute for Free Labor Development (AIFLD) and appointed by Reagan to head the Private Sector Survey of Cost Control in the Federal Government. Peter Grace assisted the U.S. "Project Paperclip," which brought some 900 Nazi scientists to the United States, including war criminal Otto Ambros, a chemist, poison gas expert and director of the I.G. Farben Company which used Aushwitz concentration camp inmates as slave labor for the Nazi war machine.[107]

Other U.S. Knights and Dames include former Secretary of State Alexander Haig, former Treasury Secretary William Simon, former National Security Adviser William Clark, former Director of the U.S. Information Agency Frank Shakespeare, Senator Jeremiah Denton, Attorney Prescott Bush Jr. (brother of George Bush), William F. and James Buckley, the late Clare Boothe Luce, Chrysler Chairman Lee Iacocca and former Mayor of New York Robert Wagner, who served as a Carter emissary to the Vatican to discuss Nicaragua. The "Grand Protector and Spiritual Adviser" to the Knights has traditionally been the archbishop of New York, from the time of Francis Cardinal Spellman through John J. O'Connor.[108]

Active before in support of the U.S. war in Vietnam, the Knights distribute assistance to the contras and through military-run "civic action" programs in Honduras, Guatemala and El Salvador. Roberto Alejos, whose plantation was used to train forces for the Bay of Pigs invasion, is a leader of the Knights in Honduras and Guatemala.

Knights of Malta has distributed millions of dollars worth of medical and other supplies donated by Americares, an organization led by Robert Macauley, which also did "humanitarian" work in Vietnam. A June 1985 Americares fact sheet boasted of the Shoeshine Boys Foundation, "so named because resident children [in Americares' Saigon rescue mission] helped raise money for their welfare by shining the shoes of American G.I.s." Former National Security Adviser Zbigniew Brzezinski is Americares' honorary chairman; Peter Grace chairs the advisory commission, which includes William Simon, retired General Richard Stilwell and Prescott Bush.

PRODEMCA (Friends of the Democratic Center in Central America) is an administration-backed effort to win bipartisan support for its Central America policy, which has been funded by the National Endowment for Democracy (NED). PRODEMCA was a major conduit of NED funding for *La Prensa* and the so-called Nicaraguan Center for Democratic Studies, and has lobbied heavily for contra aid.

PRODEMCA's president is Penn Kemble, a leader in the neoconservative Coalition for a Democratic Majority, and members include Jeane Kirkpatrick, Peter Grace, William Simon, AIFLD Director William Doherty, Boston University President and Kissinger Commission member John Silber and Institute for Religion and Democracy founder Michael Novak. In March 1986, PRODEMCA ran an ad in the *New York Times* and other papers: "We Support Military Assistance to the Nicaraguans Fighting for Democracy." Among the signers were Carter officials Brzezinski, former Deputy National Security Adviser David Aaron and former Assistant Secretary of State Richard Holbrooke.

Citizens for America (CFA) was established in August 1983 by Rite Aid drugstore heir and Reagan friend Lew Lehrman. Donors include Nelson Bunker Hunt and Joseph Coors of Coors Beer and numerous rightwing causes. "We are the President's grass-roots lobby," said CFA's Tracee Howell.[109] CFA has lobbied heavily for contra aid. In June 1985, it sponsored the meeting between Adolfo Calero, UNITA's Jonas Savimbi and leaders of U.S.-backed forces in Afghanistan and Laos that led to the founding of "Democracy International."

The Reverend Sun Myung Moon's Unification Church has assisted the contras largely through its affiliates, CAUSA and the Nicaraguan Freedom Fund. Adolfo Calero, Steadman Fagoth, Pedro Chamorro and other contra leaders said that the Unification Church sometimes paid their bills for strategy meetings and fundraising events and helped them build state-level political support in the United States.[110] CAUSA (discussed in chapter 4), has aided the contras since at least 1981 with supplies, cash and propaganda. It cooperates closely with rightwing organizations such as WACL, Western Goals and the Council for Inter-American Security. Thomas Dowling, a member of CAUSA USA's board of advisers who posed as a Catholic priest in 1985 testimony defending the contras before Congress, received $2,500 in travelers checks from North's slush fund.[111] Another Unification Church affiliate, the Collegiate Association for the Research of Principles (CARP), is active on college campuses and has a record of physically harassing opponents of U.S. policy in Central America and providing surveillance information to the FBI.[112]

In 1985, the Unification Church-owned *Washington Times* established the Nicaraguan Freedom Fund to raise funds for the contras. Moon's deputy, Colonel Bo Hi Pak, pledged $100,000 to the fund which was headed up by William Simon and Michael Novak; board members included Charlton Heston and Midge Decter, head of the Committee for a Free World (Elliott Abrams is Decter's son-in-law; *Commentary's* Norman Podhoretz is her husband). Jeane Kirkpatrick pledged $20,000 to the fund and donated another $2,500 she received for her cat's appearance in the Ralston Purina calendar. The Nicaraguan Freedom Fund reported raising $350,000 in six months and distributed it through Americares.

Friends of the Americas (FOA) was founded in 1984 by Louisiana State Representative "Woody" Jenkins and his wife Diane Jenkins, a former assistant attorney general. The Baton Rouge-based FOA provides aid to Miskito Indians and contra families in Honduras, including "Shoe Boxes for Liberty" packed with personal supplies. FOA material was transported to Honduras by Air National Guard units in Louisiana and Mississippi even before the Denton amendment. In 1985,

President Reagan awarded Diane Jenkins the First Annual Ronald Reagan Humanitarian Award at the Nicaraguan Refugee Fund dinner in Washington.

The Nicaraguan Refugee Fund was founded in September 1984. Its chairman, True Davis, said he was recruited to that post by Somoza's longtime ambassador to the United States, Guillermo Sevilla Sacasa.[113] In April 1985, the Fund sponsored a $250 to $500-a-plate fundraising dinner at the Marriott Hotel Ballroom. The dinner committee included Joseph Coors, Jeane Kirkpatrick, Peter Grace, Penn Kemble, Ellen Garwood and Nelson Bunker Hunt. President Reagan addressed the nearly 700 guests: "While the world was turning away, you were helping. People like you are America at its best."[114] Pat Robertson gave the invocation.

The Nicaraguan Refugee Fund was the successor to a CIA-FDN front called the Human Development Foundation, a Panamanian corporation with a Miami address, which in July 1984 took out newspaper ads soliciting contributions: "The Victims of Communist Dominated Nicaragua Need Your Help." According to Edgar Chamorro, the ads brought in a few checks totaling $750 and an envelope full of dead cockroaches.[115] The following September, the *New York Times* reported contra claims that millions of dollars from private individuals, corporations and foreign governments "including Israel, Argentina, Venezuela, Guatemala and Taiwan" had been channelled through the foundation.[116]

The Nicaraguan Refugee Fund dinner, keynoted by Reagan, raised $219,525. After expenses were deducted, however, the contra "refugees" received only $3,000. Various consultants reaped the bulk of the money. The public relations firm Miner and Fraser, employer of former Somoza diplomat Alvaro Rizo, was paid $50,000.[117] Carl "Spitz" Channell was another consultant (discussed later).

"Public Diplomacy"

"The whole treatment of Nicaragua in the U.S. is a public relations opportunity, an ad man's treatment." That's what a U.S. ambassador in Central America told me in April 1986.[118]

The administration's domestic propaganda-lobby operation transgressed laws regulating the activities of tax-exempt organizations and prohibiting unauthorized government propaganda and political lobbying, CIA influence in domestic politics and the participation of active duty military officers in partisan political activities (Hatch Act). Reagan's own 1981 Executive Order 12333 prohibited the CIA from undertaking operations intended to "influence United States political processes, public opinion, politics, or media." Nonetheless, the CIA regularly instructed contra leaders in all of the above, including how to tailor their lobby pitch to sway specific congresspeople.

As Edgar Chamorro told the World Court, "I attended meetings at which C.I.A. officials told us that we could change the votes of many members of the Congress if we knew how to 'sell' our case and place them in a position of 'looking soft on Communism.' They told us exactly what to say and which members to say it to.

They also instructed us to contact certain prominent individuals in the home districts of various members of Congress as a means of bringing pressure on these members to change their votes."[119]

Chamorro recalled for me how CIA personnel would contact the contras before politicians came through Honduras "and tell us who was coming, who was who, what to say, what not to say, how to treat them…They would brief us if he was a liberal or non-liberal. That kind of thing. Make distinctions…Sometimes they would try not to mix liberals with conservatives. Be careful when you are in a group of liberals…you talk to them like you talk to a reporter. You know how far you can go. So there was some manipulation of how much you would talk."[120]

An April 1982 National Security document (discussed earlier) had warned: "We continue to have serious difficulties with U.S. public and Congressional opinion, which jeopardizes our ability to stay the course." It recommended a "concerted public information effort." Following the January 1983 National Security Directive No. 77, the "public diplomacy" effort would be overseen by a special planning group including the national security adviser, secretaries of state and defense, and directors of AID and the U.S. Information Agency (USIA).

The CIA retained a Miami-based public relations firm, Woody Kepner Associates, with a six-month contract beginning in February 1983 and extended through mid-1985 for a total of $1.8 million. Kepner rented the FDN an office suite at the David William Hotel in Coral Gables, Florida, produced slick promotional materials and arranged speaking tours and media appearances for contra representatives.[121] To Edgar Chamorro, the contract typified CIA-FDN relations: "Although I signed the contract as FDN public relations director, it was nearly impossible for me to evaluate Kepner's work…or to get him to respond to our demands…He responded only to the C.I.A.'s suggestions. Of course, I must admit, it was not my money."[122]

According to Chamorro, Woody Kepner helped edit and publish a CIA-sponsored book by former *La Prensa* editorial page editor Humberto Belli, *Nicaragua: Christians Under Fire*, published by the ostensibly independent Puebla Institute. "The Puebla Institute grew and took on other projects. One was 'human rights' work which is neither thorough nor accurate, but which is used alongside the work of more established and reputable human rights organizations in order to counter their criticisms of the *contras'* human rights abuses."[123]

One of the charges slapped on Nicaragua was anti-Semitism although it was discredited by many sources, including U.S. Ambassador Tony Quainton who cabled Washington in July 1983: "the evidence fails to demonstrate that the Sandinistas have followed a policy of anti-Semitism or have persecuted Jews because of their religion." Undeterred by the evidence, the administration pretended that Somoza associates who happened to be Jewish sought exile because of anti-Semitism.[124]

Edgar Chamorro recalled a meeting with three CIA officers in the spring of 1983 to discuss ways of promoting the contras inside the United States. One propaganda idea was to target American Jews by portraying the Sandinistas as anti-Semitic. According to Chamorro, the CIA officers "said that the media was controlled by Jews, and if we could show that Jews were being persecuted it would help a lot."[125] The real anti-Semitism emanated from Washington.

In 1985, Congress asked the General Accounting Office (GAO) to determine whether the CIA had violated the prohibition against political activity in the United States. On September 16, when investigators interviewed the FDN's Washington spokesperson, Bosco Matamoros, he stated that "he is not engaged in any lobbying activities, and that his salary and expenses are paid from private funds." Eight days later, Matamoros registered under the Foreign Agents Registration Act, declaring that he was a lobbyist and had "received aid from the U.S. government." He cited payments of $2,500 per month dating back as far as June 1981.[126]

The "public diplomacy" effort involved a network of rightwing donors, organizations, lobbyists and public relations (PR) specialists working in conjunction with the National Endowment for Democracy, NSC, CIA and two special offices: the White House Office of Public Liaison and the State Department Office of Public Diplomacy. In May 1983, the White House Office of Public Liaison, headed by Faith Ryan Whittlesey (the former ambassador to Switzerland), established the Outreach Working Group on Central America.

The Outreach Group was a vehicle for packaging PR themes, networking and briefing administration supporters, and encouraging them to rally their constituencies behind administration policy. A rare article on the public diplomacy effort noted, "White House officials scoffed when a reporter asked whether they might be running a ministry of propaganda."[127]

On May 20, 1983, NSC official Walter Raymond Jr., a propaganda expert and former senior CIA officer, informed National Security Adviser William Clark that the "Faith Whittlesey effort" was "off to a good start" and discussed the establishment of a "Coalition for a Democratic Central America." In a section headed "Private Funding Effort," Raymond wrote, "I have provided Jeff Davis with a list of funding programs that require private sector support...Roy Godson reported that he met early this week with a group of private donors that Charlie Wick [chief of the USIA and top fundraiser for the 1980 Reagan campaign] brought to the sitroom two months ago. The group made their first commitment of $400,000 which includes support to Freedom House, a pro-INF [Intermediate-Range Nuclear Forces] group in Holland, Accuracy in Media, and a European based labor program. These are useful steps forward. More to follow."[128]

On August 9, Raymond further informed Clark about "Private Sector Support for Central American Program." The objective was to "move out into the middle sector of the American public and draw them into the 'support' column." A number of proposals to "market the issue"—all endorsing the creation of a "bipartisan coalition"—were under discussion among government officials such as Casey, Whittlesey, Wick and Kirkpatrick, and conservative public relations specialists, lobbyists and donors (e.g. the Richard Mellon Scaife group). Raymond and Godson "recommended funding via Freedom House or some other structure that has credibility in the political center. Wick, via [publisher Rupert] Murdoch, may be able to draw down added funds for this effort."[129]

Roy Godson, a Georgetown University professor, was a member of the 1980 CIA transition team and has been a paid consultant to the USIA, the NSC and the

President's Foreign Intelligence Advisory Board. He is Washington director of the National Strategy Information Center, which provided funding to Arturo Cruz. Godson has also been a paid adviser to the CIA-connected U.S. Youth Council, the parent of the International Youth Year Commission, which is assumed to be the "Intl. Youth Comm." named on the flow chart of North-supervised contra support entities published in the *Tower Board Report*.[130] Godson solicited donations for North and the Nicaragua operation, at least once using the Heritage Foundation as a conduit.[131]

Whittlesey returned to Switzerland as ambassador in May 1985 (she served there from 1981 to 1983) and turned the embassy into a contra propaganda outpost. Journalist Diana Johnstone described the Whittlesey embassy as "a *de facto* branch office of the World Anti-Communist League and its protegees the contras."[132]

Psywar at Home

Complementing and then superseding the Outreach Group was the State Department Office of Public Diplomacy for Latin America and the Caribbean (S/LPD), directed by the Cuban-born Otto Reich, a former AID official and instructor at the U.S. Army School of the Americas. Though based at State, the Office of Public Diplomacy was an interagency office, including personnel from Defense, AID and USIA, operating under the direction of the NSC (Raymond and North).

"If you look at it as a whole," said a senior U.S. official, "the Office of Public Diplomacy was carrying out a huge psychological operation of the kind the military conducts to influence a population in denied or enemy territory."[133]

The Office of Public Diplomacy worked to destroy positive images of Nicaragua, cultivate negative images, discredit administration critics and reverse public and congressional opposition. In Reich's words "attacking the President was no longer cost free."[134]

Part of the strategy was for administration officials to refuse to appear in public forums with well-versed opponents. In a noted case in May 1986, Harvard University's John F. Kennedy School of Government buckled to administration pressure and withdrew an invitation to Robert White, the former U.S. ambassador to El Salvador now with the International Center for Development Policy, to respond to a speech on "Democracy in Central America" by Assistant Secretary of State Elliott Abrams. Abrams' press secretary explained that "Secretary Abrams doesn't object to sharing a platform with critics, and even suggested to Harvard officials which members of the faculty could serve in that capacity." But White was not a "serious critic," the press secretary said; "he's become something of a crank."[135] In the administration version of democratic pluralism, White, a liberal with years of experience in the foreign service, was outside the bounds of debate—not to mention leftist critics.

Reich acted as a quasi-government censor, monitoring and pressuring the news media to toe the administration line and accusing critical reporters of being agents of Nicaraguan disinformation. Following a November 1984 National Public Radio (NPR) report about the slaughter of civilians in a farming cooperative by contras,

Reich protested the "biased" coverage to top editors and producers of NPR, which he called "little Havana on the Potomac"—a label that by Reich's standard would apply to anyone left of the *New York Times*. As NPR foreign affairs correspondent Bill Buzenberg recounted, "Reich bragged that he had made similar visits to other unnamed newspapers and major television networks...Reich said he had gotten others to change some of their reporters in the field because of a perceived bias, and that their coverage was much better as a result."[136] Whatever the direct impact of Reich's visit, NPR later made Linda Chavez, Whittlesey's successor as director of the White House Office of Public Liaison and before that the reactionary staff director of the United States Commission on Civil Rights, a regular commentator—another victory for rightwing propaganda masquerading as editorial "balance."

The Office of Public Diplomacy also romanced the press by selectively leaking classified information all too often accepted as fact by reporters. It produced reams of disinformation in the form of publications (such as the *Soviet-Cuban Connection in Central America and the Caribbean*), sometimes produced jointly with the Defense Department, spiced with declassified information and surveillance photos. In its first year alone, S/LPD took credit for sending material to 239 editorial writers in 150 cities and arranging 1,500 speaking engagements.[137]

The congressional *Iran-Contra Report* said "public diplomacy" meant "public-relations lobbying, all at taxpayers' expense."[138] Beginning in 1983, the Office of Public Diplomacy worked closely with the pro-contra lobby, Citizens for America (CFA). S/LPD also issued contracts to private firms and individuals, including a small, secret contract with Arturo Cruz Jr.[139]

The most important contractual relationship was with Richard Miller, Frank Gomez and International Business Communications (IBC). Richard Miller, director of broadcast services for the 1980 Reagan campaign, formed the public relations firm IBC upon leaving his post as AID director of public affairs in 1984. Miller began working with Frank Gomez, formerly deputy assistant secretary of state for public affairs and director of USIA's foreign press centers. Gomez received a contract to assist S/LPD immediately upon leaving his government post in February 1984. The contract was renewed in May and assumed within a few months by IBC, functioning by then as a Miller-Gomez partnership. These sole-source Gomez/IBC contracts totaled more than $441,000 through September 1986.[140]

IBC prepared briefing books, newspaper op eds. and other materials; arranged interviews, press conferences and speaking tours for contra leaders and pro-contra Nicaraguan exiles; and prepared a computerized mailing list of some 3,300 groups and individuals in a position to influence the debate over Central America. The October 1984 contract also required IBC to analyze guerrilla documents captured in El Salvador and identify "support groups in the United States."[141] In September 1984, IBC was hired to represent the FDN front group, the Nicaraguan Development Council, a secret sponsor of the Nicaraguan Refugee Fund dinner.[142]

The Office of Public Diplomacy engaged in so-called white propaganda. S/LPD Deputy Director Jonathan Miller (no relation to Richard) described "white propaganda" operations in a confidential "eyes only" memorandum to White House Communications Director Patrick Buchanan. Among the examples given were: a March

1985 *Wall Street Journal* op ed. piece written with the secret assistance of S/LPD staff; op ed. pieces for the *New York Times* and *Washington Post* secretly written by an S/LPD consultant "for the signatures of opposition leaders Alphonso Rubello [*sic*], Adolpho Callero [*sic*] and Arturo Cruz"; and a series of meetings and interviews with print and broadcast media for "Alphonso Rubello" arranged through an S/LPD "cut-out."

"I will not attempt in the future to keep you posted on all activities," Miller told Buchanan, "since we have too many balls in the air at any one time and since the work of our operation is ensured by our office's keeping a low profile." Miller asked that "as you formulate ideas and plans of attack, you give us a heads-up since our office has been crafted to handle the concerns that you have in getting the President's program for the freedom fighters enacted."[143]

In 1986, Reich became ambassador to Venezuela and was replaced by Robert Kagen. Walter Raymond prepared a secret memorandum for Poindexter to send to Casey, assuring him that "the departure of Otto Reich has not resulted in any reduction of effort...Although the independent office was folded into Elliott Abrams' bureau, the White House has sent a clear tasker to the community that this limited reorganization in no way reflected a dimunition [*sic*] of activities. On the contrary, the same interagency responsibilities are being exercised, and the group reports directly to the NSC...In reality, the reorganization also means that Elliott Abrams plays a strong public diplomacy role, and in this way we have harnessed one of the best public diplomacy assets that we have in the government."

Raymond noted that he chaired a weekly Central American public diplomacy meeting with participants from the NSC, the CIA's Central American Task Force, State, USIA, AID, Defense and the White House Press and Public Liaison Offices: "This group takes its policy guidance from the Central American RIG and pursues an energetic political and informational agenda."[144] (In mid 1987, Raymond became an assistant director of the USIA.)

A 1987 GAO investigation of the Office of Public Diplomacy concluded that it "engaged in prohibited, covert propaganda activities designed to influence the media and the public to support the Administration's Latin American policies. The use of appropriated funds for these activities constitutes a violation of a restriction on the State Department annual appropriations prohibiting the use of federal funds for publicity or propaganda purposes not authorized by the Congress."[145]

By then the propaganda-lobby operation had scored dramatic success in winning renewed congressional support for the contras. It had also merged with the underground NSC program of contra military support through the fundraising partnership of Richard Miller and Carl Channell.

Channelling Contrabutions

Carl "Spitz" Channell made his first mark in rightwing fundraising as finance director for the National Conservative Political Action Committee (NCPAC). In 1982, he formed a succession of entities, including the lobby organization, Sentinel; the tax-exempt "educational" National Endowment for the Preservation of Liberty (NEPL); the American Conservative Trust (ACT), a political action committee (PAC); the tax-exempt American Conservative Foundation; and another PAC, the Anti-Terrorism American Committee. In 1986, Channell took over the McCarthyite Western Goals Foundation.

Channell's direct involvement in the contra cause began in January 1985 when PR consultant Edie Fraser asked him to help organize the Nicaraguan Refugee Fund Dinner. Channell recruited San Francisco fundraising consultant Daniel Conrad, who later became the number two person in Channell's lobby-fundraising empire. On March 4, following a conversation with Channell and Conrad, Fraser provided material on the dinner to Oliver North with a handwritten note: "Ollie, Very Imp., Two people want to give major contribs i.e. 300,000 and up if they might have one 'quiet' minute with the President."[146]

The two-part pitch by North and Channell became a key source of money for the contras. On June 27, Channell and Miller organized their first White House briefing for a group of donors, with North as principal speaker. Similar group briefings took place on October 17 and November 21, 1985 and January 30 and March 27, 1986. As described in the *Iran-Contra Report*, "the White House briefings were meticulously planned by NEPL, IBC, North, and White House personnel. Internal White House memorandums…show that North was the switching point for arranging and coordinating the briefings with White House liaison, White House Counsel, and White House security." Among those participating in the briefings, besides North, were Pat Buchanan, Elliott Abrams, Political Assistant to the President Mitch Daniels and Deputy Assistant to the President and Director of the Office of Public Liaison Linda Chavez.[147]

After the briefings, donors would be taken across the street to the Hay-Adams Hotel for a reception and dinner often attended by government officials and contra leaders, where donors were directly solicited by the "private" fundraisers. The January 30 briefing included a presidential "drop-by" arranged by NEPL/IBC consultant David Fischer. Fischer was Reagan's top personal assistant on the campaign trail and then in the White House from January 1981 until April 1985. Between December 1985 and February 1987, Fischer and his partner Martin Artiano were paid $662,400 by NEPL/IBC for consulting services, including arranging donor meetings with the president.[148]

An account of a typical North "briefing" was provided by donor William O'Boyle: North "described the military and political situation in Nicaragua. He had photographs of an airport in Nicaragua that had been recently built…One of the uses for which the airport was intended was to recover the Russian Backfire bombers after they made a nuclear attack on the United States…

"He described the refugee problem…We could look forward in the next few years to millions of refugees flooding across our borders…

"He showed photographs which indicated that the Nicaraguan government officials were indicated [*sic*] in smuggling dope…He also told an anecdote about some Nicaraguan agents that were recently caught with dope and money and so forth and disguised as American agents."[149]

North's dramatic fairy tales helped raise millions of dollars for the contras. Conrad described the North pitch as preparation for "the call to the alter." North met privately with Channell, Miller and star donors such as Ellen Garwood and Nelson Bunker Hunt. He even took his family in the spring of 1986 on a plane chartered by NEPL to spend the weekend at donor Barbara Newington's estate in Connecticut; Channell and Miller were also there. Newington merited two private meetings with President Reagan.[150]

NEPL's funds-for-guns program was called the "Toys Project." Donor E. Thomas Claggett contributed $20,000 after a personal meeting with Channell and North. "I wasn't interested in it going for chocolate bars or soda pops," he said. "I wanted something to kill the commies—direct military support for the troops—guns and ammunition...Certainly nobody ever told me it was going to buy toys."[151]

Twelve contributors accounted for just over 90 percent of NEPL's 1985 and 1986 contributions. Garwood was the largest donor, with $2,518,135 in 1986, nearly $2 million of which went to "Toys." During 1985-86, Newington gave $2,866,025 and Hunt gave $484,500.[152]

"The President obviously knows why he has been meeting with several select people to thank them for their 'support for Democracy' in [Central America]," North told Poindexter in May 1986.[153]

Reagan claimed to have thought the donations were for political advertising. But Poindexter has testified, "There wasn't any question in my mind" that the President was aware that he was thanking contra contributors. "In the White House during this period of time that we were encouraging private support, we really didn't distinguish between how the money was going to be spent."[154] David Fischer arranged presidential photo opportunities or meetings with at least seven major contributors in 1986. At least five of the six contributors who donated more than $300,000 to NEPL were invited to meet with Reagan.[155]

NEPL raised over $10 million on behalf of the contras, of which more than $1.2 million went for political advertising and lobbying; over $1.7 million was laundered through IBC and I.C. Inc. to the contra-related Lake Resources account (I.C. Inc. was a Cayman Islands corporation established by Miller and Gomez to receive profits expected from marketing the oil of the Prince who turned out to be a con artist; in May 1986, I.C.'s name was changed to Intel Co-Operation Inc.); about $1 million was laundered through IBC and I.C. Inc. into accounts controlled by Calero; and nearly $500,000 was distributed at North's request to other persons and entities engaged in contra-related activities. The rest went to NEPL/IBC fees, salaries, commissions and expenses. Miller and Gomez took a 10 percent commission on payments funnelled to the contras through their companies.[156]

In a November 1985 notebook entry, North wrote under the heading "R Miller": "On hand & acted on: [Deleted.] 180K moved to Copp for [deleted.] 100K for Calero—sent. [Deleted] 48K [illegible] to Copp. IBC—10%."[157] Copp was code for Richard Secord, manager of the pro-contra "Enterprise."

11

The Enterprise
and Other Fronts

We were in some measure trying to recreate [the CIA's Air America], on a smaller scale, of course.

Richard Secord, Iran-Contra Hearings, May 8, 1987.[1]

I felt that this [Nicaragua] was a very important issue—that is, showing the Russians that we can deal with this phenomenon—but we didn't choose the right instrument to do it. Succinctly put, where I went wrong was not having the guts to stand up and tell the President that. To tell you the truth, probably the reason I didn't is because if I had done that, Bill Casey, Jeane Kirkpatrick and Cap Weinberger would have said I was some kind of commie.

Robert McFarlane, Iran-Contra Hearings, May 14, 1987.[2]

The core of the pseudo-private "Project Democracy" contra support operation was the Enterprise, a conglomerate of proprietary corporations run by Richard Secord and Albert Hakim. The Enterprise (Secord's term) was shielded by the more visible private auxiliaries and fueled by laundered donations and diversions.

At CIA Director Casey's direction, the Enterprise was to be an "off-the-shelf, self-sustaining, stand-alone entity" that could carry out operations in Nicaragua, Iran or anywhere in the world independent of congressional appropriations. As North recounted, Casey wanted "something you can pull off the shelf and use on a moment's notice."[3] The formal CIA apparatus was subject to congressional review (however inadequate); the Enterprise was not.

In Hakim's words, "whoever designed this structure, had a situation that they could have their cake and eat it too. Whichever [sic] they wanted to have, a private organization, it was private; when they didn't want it to be a private organization, it wasn't."[4]

Using the discreet financial services of former IRS lawyer Willard Zucker's Compagnie de Services Fiduciaries (CFS), Hakim established a network of collecting, treasury and operating companies. A portion of the funds went to a "reserves" account for building up the Enterprise as a self-sustaining entity. Between April and September 1985, the Enterprise expanded rapidly with the establishment of Lake Resources, which took over from Energy Resources as the main collecting company; Gulf Marketing; Udall Research; Dolmy Inc.; and Albon Values. Toyco was established in April 1986. The treasury companies held funds for specialized operating companies for different regions: Latin America, Africa and the Middle East. Albon Values was the Central American treasury company, channelling funds into two operating companies: Toyco, which, in the now-familiar vernacular, purchased contra arms and made payments to contra leaders, and Udall, which brought and operated aircraft and built an airstrip in Costa Rica.

"The idea," explained Hakim, "was that each collecting company would serve as the sole receiver of funds for the Enterprise for a period of time. When the first collecting company became too visible it could be cast aside and the next company would be taken off the 'shelf' and brought into use."[5] Exposure of any one company would not bring down the compartmentalized network.

Yellow Fruit Seeds

The Enterprise pursued activities similar to those described in a draft plan delivered in late July 1983 to Business Security International (BSI)—the cover company for the Pentagon Special Operations Division's "Yellow Fruit" unit (discussed in chapter 7)—by Colonel James Longhofer and Rudy Enders, head of the CIA's Office of Special Activities in the International Activities Division. Retired Army Intelligence Officer William Golden told congressional investigators that he last saw the plan in BSI's safe. Golden, currently a civilian employee at the Fort Huachuca, Arizona Army intelligence base, was assistant Army attache in Managua from December 1981 until July 1983, where he provided military intelligence to the CIA and Defense Intelligence Agency and helped coordinate activities with the Honduran military and the contras. In July 1983, Golden became the operations officer and financial manager for BSI and ended up as a whistleblower in the Yellow Fruit scandal.

In his deposition for the Iran-contra committees, Golden said the document he saw at BSI was "a contingency plan that would be implemented in the event that funding for the contras was cut off for any reason." He believes that a draft presidential finding was included. The plan, he said, didn't mention the Boland amendment per se, "but that is what was talked about in the office...Everybody was worried about the Boland Amendment. It was going to cut off funds for the contras and we would all be out of a job and how are we going to get around this thing."

According to Golden and journalist Steven Emerson, the contra support plan had three key components: (1) contra weapons were to be funnelled through inflated sales of equipment to other countries, including Honduras, Guatemala, Brazil and Argentina; (2) offshore bank accounts would be established; (3) Yellow Fruit agents would assist in building airstrips in Costa Rica on John Hull's ranch and other sites.

Golden said he believes "implementation [of the plan] was attempted. At least the mechanisms were being put in place to do that, because they started surveying the airfield. I believe that [a bank account] was established or was in the process of being established when I left there to support that operation." Several weeks after seeing the plan, Golden signed a dozen bank signature cards related to Yellow Fruit projects. He assumed that the bank accounts were never established because of BSI's demise, until CBS News contacted him regarding their report (first confirmed by the Pentagon and later retracted) that he was a signator to a Credit Suisse account along with Richard Secord and Oliver North. Golden verified he was a signator to an account with a bank official.

According to news reports, $2.5 million was withdrawn from the account on a single day in 1985; of that, $75,000 was reportedly used to charter the Danish freighter *Erria* to deliver arms to the contras.[6]

The Enterprisers: Secord-Wilson Orbits

According to North, Casey recommended Secord "as the person to assist us outside the government to comply [sic] with the Boland proscriptions." Secord, said Casey, was "a person who had a background in covert operations, a man of integrity, a West Point graduate...a man who...got things done, and who had been poorly treated."[7]

Air Force Major General Richard Secord was on the fast track in 1981 as deputy assistant secretary of defense for the Near East, Africa and South Asia when he was linked to Edwin Wilson, the ex-CIA operative later convicted of selling arms to Libya. Secord was introduced to Wilson in 1974 by CIA officers Theodore Shackley and Thomas Clines. At the time, Secord was an Air Force colonel serving as the Pentagon's desk officer for Laos, Thailand and Vietnam, then as executive assistant to the head of the Defense Security Assistance Agency; Shackley was chief of the CIA's Far East division (before that he was head of the Western Hemisphere division); and Clines was in the CIA's International Communism branch.

Their paths had crisscrossed since the 1960s, when Secord was directing air operations for the secret war in Laos and Shackley was CIA station chief and Clines his deputy, first in Laos and then South Vietnam. Before going to Laos, Clines was Wilson's case officer in Special Operations. Wilson was assigned to the CIA's Special Operations division in 1964, after CIA work as an undercover labor organizer whose main job was to fight leftwing unions in Europe, Latin America and Vietnam; at one point, he carried payoffs to Corsican mobsters hired by the CIA to oust communist dockworkers from the port at Marseilles, France.

Special Operations set Wilson up as head of a new CIA proprietary, Maritime Consulting. As author Peter Maas explained, Wilson's "job was to bring in cargoes wherever the CIA wanted its participation untraceable…He sent incendiary, crowd-dispersion and harassment devices to Chile, Brazil and Venezuela. Arms to the Dominican Republic…Advanced communications gear to Morocco. Weapons of all kinds to Angola. A whole range of high-tech electronics equipment to Iran. More arms for a CIA-backed coup in Indonesia. Military parts and supplies to Taiwan and the Philippines. Logistical support for the so-called secret war the CIA began to wage in Laos. He also arranged for boats—flotillas of them, if required—such as the ones used in continuing raids against Cuba."[8]

Clines and Shackley served during the early 1960s as chief and deputy chief of the Miami station, which under the code name JM/WAVE ran Operation Mongoose against Cuba. Operation Mongoose included sabotage raids and plots to assassinate Fidel Castro employing Cuban exiles and Mafia gangsters. Among the Mongoose saboteurs and would-be assassins were future contra operatives Felix Rodriguez, Luis Posada and Rafael "Chi Chi" Quintero.

Wilson added other business to the CIA assignments, making money for himself and enhancing his cover. Wilson delivered; the CIA did minimal auditing. In 1971, Wilson left the CIA to join Task Force 157, a supersecret arm of the Office of Naval Intelligence with a need for proprietaries. In 1976, Wilson's contract was terminated and Task Force 157 was disbanded under a cloud of impropriety.

An ex-CIA operative named Frank Terpil interested Wilson in Libya. Terpil's sales company, Intercontinental Technology, had been purchased in 1975 by Stanford Technology Corporation, a California-based electronics and security firm founded in 1974 by the Iranian-born Albert Hakim to sell surveillance equipment to the Shah. Terpil and Wilson used Stanford Technology as a base for Libyan transactions, at least through 1976, reportedly without Hakim's knowledge.[9]

Hakim and Secord met in Teheran when Secord was chief of the Air Force Military Assistance Group (1975-1978). According to the *Iran-Contra Report*, "CIA files disclose that in August of 1976, CIA officer Ted Shackley tried to arrange for Secord to assist Hakim in his efforts to obtain security contracts with the Iranian government in return for Hakim providing intelligence for the CIA. Under Shackley's proposal, Clines was supposed to introduce Hakim to Secord. Shackley's proposal was rebuffed by a CIA official, in part because Hakim had taken advantage of the Iranians by selling them 'unneeded over sophisticated equipment at exorbitant price[s]'…Hakim testified that Wilson introduced him to Clines and Shackley and that Wilson set up this arrangement on the understanding that he, Wilson, would receive a share of any profits made by Hakim."[10]

By 1980, if not before, Hakim was a CIA asset. Secord said he gave Hakim's name "to the U.S. intelligence people for…vetting and possible use in the operation to rescue the American hostages being held in Iran. He was contacted by the intelligence people, was vetted, and did volunteer his services as did several others."[11] Hakim procured jeeps, vans and other vehicles. Major Oliver North, then based at Camp Lejeune, North Carolina, reportedly led a secret group of Marines to the mountains of eastern Turkey in April 1980 to back up the hostage rescue mission.[12] Secord served as deputy task force commander and air commander of a second hostage rescue mission in April-November 1980 that was never carried out.

In 1976, Wilson contacted Rafael Quintero, a former colleague from Task Force 157, to arrange the assassination of a Qadaffi enemy. Before hearing the actual assignment, Quintero checked Wilson out with Clines, who said Wilson "still pulled a hundred percent." Assuming the job "was an authorized hit," Quintero recruited two Cubans, Rafael and Raoul Villaverde.[13] They backed out after hearing more about the Wilson-Terpil Libyan operation; as far as they were concerned, Qadaffi was in the communist camp and they didn't kill *for* communists.

Clines and Shackley tried at first to shield Wilson as his Libyan activities came under investigation, but in the end they couldn't protect even their own careers under George Bush's successor as CIA director, Admiral Stansfield Turner. Shackley, who was widely expected to be appointed CIA director in a second Ford administration, was demoted from his post as associate deputy director of Operations and made deputy head of the National Intelligence Tasking Center. Clines was removed as head of the CIA's Office of Training, but end-runned Turner to become the CIA's Pentagon liaison. In 1978, Clines made plans to quit the CIA and Wilson, who had been lending Clines money for many years, helped him set up an oil-drilling equipment company. Clines brought in Quintero for whom he arranged a $135,000 loan from Wilson. Clines also set up a security firm, Systems Services International. Shackley quit the CIA in 1979 and became a consultant to Clines' companies, and later, Hakim's Stanford Technology.[14] As noted earlier, Somoza was one of Clines' security clients.

Secord stayed friendly with Wilson while serving as head of the Air Force International Programs Office (1978-1981), which directed all Air Force security assistance programs and foreign military sales. Wilson bought Secord out of a bad real estate investment and gave him regular use of his private plane. In 1979, Wilson loaned Clines $500,000 to set up a company to exploit the billions of dollars in arms sales destined for Egypt after the Camp David accords. Clines reportedly had three silent American partners: Secord, Shackley and Erich von Marbod, then deputy director of the Defense Security Assistance Agency.[15]

Clines' Egyptian American Transport Services Company (EATSCO) cashed in on U.S. arms sales to Egypt, with von Marbod's authorization. Clines cut off contact with Wilson when his indictment became public in April 1980. In 1981, "as the press coverage on Wilson intensified, Tom Clines suddenly appeared in the office of Wilson's Geneva lawyer, Edward Coughlin, to pay back the $500,000 that had been advanced to him and three other unnamed 'U.S. citizens,' and to sever on paper any business connection he had with Wilson."[16] As the net tightened around Wilson, von Marbod resigned abruptly from the Air Force in December 1981. EATSCO, meanwhile, was investigated for massive abuse in billing the Pentagon. Secord was removed from his Pentagon post as deputy assistant secretary of defense, pending a polygraph test. But he was summarily reinstated by Deputy Secretary of Defense

Frank Carlucci, a former deputy director of the CIA.

In February 1982, Wilson prosecutor Larry Barcella was visited by Michael Ledeen, then a State Department expert on terrorism. "Ledeen [said] that he had heard disquieting rumors about an investigation of Shackley and von Marbod. Especially von Marbod. He was a man of impeccable honor, practically his idol...Any billing abuses that were being questioned might have gone for a covert operation."[17] Ledeen later became involved in the covert sale of U.S. arms to Iran, an operation that some suspect was arranged by the Reagan transition team even before Reagan's inauguration (discussed in chapter 15). Erich von Marbod became a consultant for Sears World Trade, a subsidiary of Sears Roebuck, that brokered aerospace technology, electronics, helicopters and other equipment for foreign customers. The president of Sears World Trade was Frank Carlucci, who would later replace Poindexter as national security adviser and then succeed Weinberger as secretary of defense.

In June 1982, Barcella lured Wilson with ironic bait from his refuge in Tripoli to the Dominican Republic, where he was put on a plane to the United States: William Clark's NSC, Wilson was told, "had decided to take up [his] recommendation that he set up fronts to mount covert military actions against Communist guerrillas in Central America." Wilson's briefcase was later "found to contain a comprehensive forty-page proposal for the covert Central American operation, featuring a 1,500-man Special Mobile Airborne Reaction Force called SMARF."[18] After the Iran-contra scandal broke, Wilson, then serving a 52-year sentence at the federal prison in Marion, Illinois, told *Newsweek*, "If I wasn't in jail, I'd have headed up this operation."[19]

Clines claimed that the three unnamed American partners in EATSCO didn't really exist.[20] On January 16, 1984, he pleaded guilty to EATSCO's bilking the Pentagon of some $8 million. Under a plea-bargain, Clines paid a corporate fine of $10,000 on behalf of his company, Systems Services International (part owner of EATSCO), and was ordered to pay another $100,000 within 30 days to settle civil claims.[21] The Iran-contra committees turned up a mysterious receipt, dated February 16, 1984, for a $33,000 check payable to Clines from Secord. Secord associate Glenn Robinette delivered the check to Clines' bank. Secord claimed it was a loan, and not a partner's share of the $100,000 fine.

Although Secord's ties to Wilson and EATSCO never led to an indictment, his reputation suffered and he retired from the Air Force in May 1983. That was what Casey meant when he said Secord was "poorly treated." (The Justice Department closed the conflict of interest and bribery investigation of Secord and Clines in January 1986.)[22]

Secord went into the international security business with Albert Hakim. He became president of the Stanford Technology Trading Group International, a Virginia-based company owned 50/50 with Hakim. In July 1983, Secord also began working for his old Pentagon office as a $242-a-day consultant.[23] From January 1984 to August 1986, he was a member of the Special Operations Policy Advisory Group (SOPAG).

Air Central America

North enlisted Secord to help run the contra program in the summer of 1984. It was not Secord's first involvement with contra supply nor his first covert assignment since retiring from the Air Force. Secord reportedly managed a 1982 operation in which Israel shipped weapons captured in the Lebanon invasion to a CIA arms depot in San Antonio, Texas for shipment to the contras.[24] In April 1984, Secord was tapped to head a new antiterrorism task force established by a national security directive signed by Reagan. The task force was responsible for helping to plan a commando rescue mission to free hostages being held in Beirut.[25] A possibly related, unexplained entry in North's notebooks, dated April 27, 1984 reads: "Team to Israel $54 million worth of arms...McFarlane talked to [Israeli official] can't produce $; similar to Secord arrangement; 65 lift vans; $750K."[26]

Sometime after meeting with North about the Nicaragua operation, Secord met with Adolfo Calero in North's office. At a follow-up meeting with Calero, Secord, who was inexperienced in Latin America, brought along Rafael Quintero as an adviser. Quintero, said Secord, is "a man for whom I have a lot of respect...trust." He met Quintero years earlier through Tom Clines, "another very close associate...from CIA days."[27]

By late 1984, the Enterprise had arranged the first of four contra arms deals (through July 1985), totaling nearly $9 million plus a $2 million profit, financed by the Saudi money in Calero's account.[28] During 1984 and 1985, the contras were also supplied via Honduras with $2 million worth of rifles, grenades and ammunition through R.M. Equipment, a firm led by Ronald Martin and retired Lt. Col. James McCoy. McCoy was the last U.S. military attache during the Somoza regime and a friend of Calero.[29] The first two Enterprise deals involved a Canadian arms dealer, Transworld Armament. Then Tom Clines was brought in. Clines used Defex, a Portuguese arms dealer, to buy arms from Poland and Western Europe. Guatemala provided false end-user certificates to mask the contra shipments. Quintero coordinated the arms deliveries and liaison with the contras in Central America.

To arrange air shipment for the arms, the Enterprise hired retired Air Force Lt. Col. Richard Gadd, former liaison between the Joint Chiefs of Staff and the Special Operations Command at Fort Bragg, North Carolina. Gadd retired in fall 1982 to set up a private air transport system available for clandestine U.S. government operations including Nicaragua. He was contracted by the Special Operations Division, which was used, along with the Army's Intelligence Support Activity (ISA), to aid the contras both before and after the Boland cutoff. (See chapter 7.) Gadd provided on-demand transport service to Yellow Fruit, ISA and Seaspray, including operations such as the Queens Hunter reconnaissance project.[30]

Gadd set up several interlinked proprietaries: Eagle Aviation Services and Technology (EAST), American National Management Corporation (ANMC), AIRMACH and a short-lived company called Sumairco that flew logistical operations for the Grenada invasion. ANMC and EAST received millions of dollars in government air transport contracts, including a December 1983 contract from the Special Operations Command to "provide air logistics services in the Caribbean"; a February 1984 contract from a Special Forces unit to "plan and provide special services to transport personnel and special equipment during training exercises" and "plan special mobilization procedures for rapid response low visibility operations"; and a 1984 contract to provide transportation and logistical support for the Army Delta Force during the Los Angeles Olympics. Gadd was also contracted to keep flight crews and three types of aircraft available for sensitive short-notice missions, including the Lockheed Hercules L-100, a large cargo plane that can land on short runways.[31]

In the clandestine world of air transit, Gadd worked closely with the CIA-sponsored Southern Air Transport. Southern Air is a spinoff of Air America, the best known of the CIA airlines that secretly supported wars from China, Burma and Tibet to the Bay of Pigs and the Dominican Republic to Indonesia, Laos and Vietnam. Air America's motto was "Anything, Anywhere, Anytime." As Air America chronicler Christopher Robbins put it: "Its civilian status allowed it to operate without the bureaucracy and red tape that surrounded the military, cross international borders with a minimum of fuss, and break the rules whenever a mission demanded it."[32]

In the early days, before its workforce grew into the thousands, Air America relied on Air Force pilots. The pilots would "disappear from the military in a complex process known as 'sheep-dipping' after seeming to go through all the legal and official motions of resigning from the services. The pilot's records would be pulled from the Air Force personnel files and transferred to a special AF intelligence file...The man would become, to all outward appearances, a civilian. At the same time his ghostly paper existence within the intelligence file would continue to pursue his Air Force career: When his contemporaries were promoted, he would be promoted, and so on."[33] Whether or not Lt. Col. Richard Gadd actually had a clandestine file still with the Air Force, he was following the path of sheep-dipped personnel who had gone before him into "civilian" covert operations.

Southern Air Transport was a small Miami-based company when the CIA bought it in 1960 and transformed it into its Caribbean and Latin American air arm. Another proprietary, Intermountain Aviation, was formed in 1961 to provide specialized support for guerrilla operations. Intermountain was used in 1965 to secretly violate Washington's stated embargo policy and sell B-26 bombers to Portugal for use against independence movements in Angola, Mozambique and Guinea Bissau.[34]

Like the Enterprise would later, the CIA's proprietary network turned a profit—padded by hundreds of millions of dollars in contracts with the U.S. Air Force and AID. The CIA general counsel had ruled in 1958 that "income of proprietaries, including profits, need not be considered miscellaneous receipts to be covered into the Treasury but may be used for proper corporate or company purposes." Critics warned about a "back door" process where "profits were being used to provide secret funding for covert operations."[35]

The CIA air empire was franchised in the 1970s as it came under increasing scrutiny. Southern Air was sold on December 31, 1973 to the man who had fronted for the CIA as nominal company owner. The current chairman of Southern Air is James Bastian, the longtime attorney for Air America. Intermountain's assets were eventually acquired by the Oregon-based Evergreen Helicopters in March 1975. A former Intermountain officer managed the Investair Leasing Corporation whose plane was used in the 1983 bombing of the Managua airport.[36]

Southern Air flew military supplies to the contras when the CIA was still officially running the operation. In 1985, Gadd arranged for Southern Air to transport the Enterprise arms shipments from Portugal to Central America. Gadd and Southern Air established Amalgamated Commercial Enterprises (ACE), a front company registered in Panama, to hold title to aircraft acquired by the Enterprise and serviced by Southern Air.

Aircraft were among the "big-ticket" items that "private benefactors" were asked to pay for. On June 18, 1985, for example, Reagan "Kitchen Cabinet" member Joseph Coors met with Casey in the Old Executive Office Building to ask him how he could help the contras. Casey told Coors he couldn't answer, but arranged an immediate meeting with North. North told Coors that the contras needed a Maule aircraft, costing $65,000, and gave him the Lake Resources account number at Credit Suisse. Later, North showed Coors a picture of the plane said to be bought with Coors' money.[37]

In May 1986, Secord felt the airlift operation was not functioning well, especially on the southern front. Gadd was phased out and replaced as operational manager by Air Force Colonel Robert Dutton. Dutton, another heir to the sheep-dipping tradition, began working for Secord right after his retirement on May 1, 1986 as assistant director of the Air Force Office of Special Plans. Dutton brought twenty years experience in Air Force special operations to the Enterprise. He had served under Secord in the Air Force Military Assistance Group in Iran and in the second Iran hostage rescue mission.

Dutton later told the Iran-contra committees that based upon his past experience with special operations, he assumed the Nicaragua operation was authorized by the president. He didn't see how they could have done what they did without presidential authority. When Dutton insisted that the Nicaragua operation was like other government-run operations he had participated in, chief Senate Counsel Arthur Liman asked him to acknowledge that the others didn't involve private people. Dutton rightly replied that the others did involve private people. Pressed, he would only say that the others may not have involved private individuals to the extent this one did.[38]

The others may not have used "private" personnel as extensively because (with the exception of the Clark amendment for Angola) they weren't operating under a Boland-type prohibition. In any case, virtually all the key "private" people were ostensibly retired military and CIA officers such as Secord, Dutton, Gadd, Clines, Quintero, Rodriguez and Singlaub, or CIA agents and assets like Hull and Hakim. In a case about which less is known, one of Casey's two special assistants, Ben Wickham Jr., reportedly told associates in early 1985 that he was resigning to raise money for the private network supervised by North. Wickham served as CIA station chief in Nicaragua from 1982 to 1984. In 1987, he was reported back at work at the CIA.[39]

Just Say Uncle

A mere six months after the Boland cutoff, Congress reenlisted in the war on Nicaragua under the fraudulent banner of "humanitarian aid." The administration's propaganda-lobby operation paid off, with dividends to the Enterprise.

North told Poindexter in January 1985 that "with adequate support the resistance could be in Managua by the end of 1985."[40] Psychological warfare escalated as the administration requested $14 million in new military aid for the contras who Reagan called "our brothers."[41]

Meanwhile, Washington tightened the economic vise on Nicaragua. Secretary Shultz sent the president of the Inter-American Development Bank (IDB) a January 30 letter warning that the United States might curtail contributions to the bank if it looked favorably upon a proposed $58 million agricultural loan to provide credits to small and medium-sized farmers in Nicaragua. Acknowledging that the loan "would be used to support and expand the production of coffee, cotton, grain, sugar and other crops," Shultz wrote IDB President Antonio Ortiz Mena: "As you are aware, money is fungible; monies received from the Bank would relieve financial pressures on the GON [Government of Nicaragua] and free up other monies that could be used to help consolidate the Marxist regime and finance Nicaragua's aggression against its neighbors."

An IDB official said, "we read" Shultz's letter "as a threat...Even during the time of Allende [when Washington blockaded Chile economically], there was never such a communication from the secretary of state." Dropping the pretense that U.S. opposition to the Nicaragua loan was based on non-political economic criteria as stipulated in the IDB charter, a U.S. official said that it "shouldn't come as a great surprise to anybody that we favor loans to friendly countries and discourage them to unfriendly countries."[42] Nicaraguan farmers lost out as Washington blocked the IDB loan.

In a February 21 news conference, Reagan acknowledged that his objective was to "remove" the Sandinista government "in the sense of its present structure, in which it is a Communist totalitarian state and it is not a Government chosen by the people—so you wonder sometimes about those who make such claims as to its legitimacy." Asked if that was not advocating overthrow, Reagan dissembled: "Not if the present Government would turn around and say—all right—if they'd say uncle, or all right, and [say to the "freedom fighters"] come back into the revolutionary Government and let's straighten this out and institute the goals"—the goals the Sandinistas supposedly betrayed.[43]

Some reporters helped Reagan maintain the illusion that "remove" did not mean overthrow. Said Connie Chung of NBC News, "Reagan wants to remove the Sandinistas in Nicaragua, not oust them."[44] *Business Week*, on the other hand, acknowledged that Reagan had "stripped the camouflage from U.S. support" for the contras and called on Congress to reject renewed aid "as equivalent to a declaration of war against Nicaragua."[45]

The day after Reagan's remarks about removing the Nicaraguan government, Shultz told the Commonwealth Club of San Francisco: "Those who would cut off these freedom fighters from the rest of the democratic world are, in effect, consigning Nicaragua to the endless darkness of Communist tyranny. And they are leading the United States down a path of greater danger...We may find later, when we can no longer avoid acting, that the stakes will be higher and the costs greater." A senior State Department official (perhaps Shultz himself speaking on background) remarked, "He is saying that the United States should follow a middle ground between passivity and invasion, and this can be done by aiding the contras."[46]

General Paul Gorman, the retiring head of the Southern Command (May 1983 to February 1985), claimed before the Senate Armed Services Committee that Central American countries, while publicly calling for diplomatic measures, had unofficially said the Nicaraguan government "must change" and "if that means they must be removed, then so be it." Yet Gorman acknowledged, "I don't see any immediate prospect that these guys in blue [camouflage] suits in the hills are going to march into Managua. It seems to me that the whole resistance movement has got another year or more of slogging to go before that were ever in prospect."[47]

Reagan's rhetoric reached new heights on March 1. He said the contras "are the moral equal of our Founding Fathers and the brave men and women of the French Resistance."

Later that month, reporter Joel Brinkley spelled out administration intentions on the front page of the *New York Times*. Renewed aid to the contras would bring additional measures such as trade sanctions, economic boycotts and reduced diplomatic relations. Moreover, administration officials were making a point of telling members of Congress that the first Boland amendment had expired and, with renewal of aid, there would be no legal prohibition to seeking the overthrow of the Nicaraguan government.

A senior intelligence official said the White House "is bent on overthrowing them" and "that's why they're making such a point of saying they are not constrained by law." Another senior administration official was more coy: "The President has spoken on this very clearly, but I wouldn't say a military overthrow is the best possible way of changing the Government. It would be better if Daniel Ortega packed his bags and moved to Havana."

Apparently unworried that Congress might start behaving less willingly gullible, a senior State Department official "said the idea that the rebels had been armed and equipped initially so they could intercept arms shipments was ludicrous." As for the current rationale of "pressuring" the Sandinistas to negotiate, administration officials explained that "the ultimate aim of the pressure, and the only acceptable outcome in Nicaragua, is a change of Government in Managua." The "only Contadora agreement that would be acceptable in Washington...is one in which the Sandinista Government renounced its Marxist ideals, invalidated the recent elections and turned the country into a 'pluralistic democracy' with leaders acceptable to the Reagan Administration." Officials expressed a next best hope that the "pressure," with the war's rising economic and political costs, would cause the Nicaraguan government to "disintegrate."[48]

Trojan Horses

North and Donald Fortier, the NSC director of political-military affairs, wrote a secret March 22 memorandum to McFarlane with the inter-agency/private auxiliary plan for winning the requested $14 million in military aid. A sample of items on the lengthy, confidential "Chronological Event Checklist" illustrates the scope of the propaganda-lobby effort:

- Assign U.S. intelligence agencies to research, report, and clear for public release Sandinista military actions violating Geneva Convention/civilized standards of warfare. Responsibility: NSC (North, Raymond).

- Nicaraguan internal opposition and resistance announce unity on goals and principals [sic] (March 2, San Jose) (completed). Responsibility: State/LPD (Miller), NSC (North).

- Request that Zbigniew Brzezinski write a geopolitical paper which points out geopolitical consequences of Communist domination of Nicaragua (paper due March 20). Responsibility: NSC (Menges).

- Brief presidential meeting with Lew Lehrman and other leaders of the influence groups working on MX and resistance funding. Responsibility: NSC (Raymond, North).

- Brief OAS members in Washington and abroad on second term goals in Central America. Explore possible OAS action against Nicaragua. Responsibility: OAS (Middendorf), NSC (Menges), State/LPD (Reich).

- Prepare a "Dear Colleagues" [letter] for signature by a responsible Democrat which counsels against "negotiating" with the FSLN. Responsibility: NSC (Lehman).

- Results due on public opinion survey to see what turns Americans against Sandinistas (March 20). Responsibility: NSC (Hinckley).

- Joachim Maitre [currently dean of the Boston University College of Communications]—Congressional meetings, speeches, and op-ed pieces. Responsibility: State/LPD (Kuykendall).

- Prepare document on Nicaraguan narcotics involvement. Responsibility: Justice (Mullen).

- VP [Vice President Bush] in Honduras; meeting with Pres Suazo (March 16). Responsibility: VP (Hughes).

- Production and distribution of *La Prensa* chronology of FSLN harassment. Responsibility: State/LPD (Reich).

- Pedro Juaquin [sic] Chamorro (Editor *La Prensa*) U.S. media/speaking tour (March 25-April 3). Responsibility: State/LPD (Miller/Gomez).

- Request Bernard Nietschmann to update prior paper on suppression of Indians by FSLN (to be published and distributed by April 1). Responsibility: State/LPD (Blacken).

- 25 Central American spokesmen arrive in Miami for briefing before departing to visit

Congressional districts. Along with national television commercial campaign in 45 media markets. Responsibility: CFA [Citizens for America] (Abramoff).

- Targeted telephone campaign begins in 120 Congressional districts...Responsibility: CFA (Abramoff).

- Nicaraguan Refugee Fund (NRF) dinner, Washington, DC; President as Guest of Honor (April 15). Responsibility: State/LPD (Miller), NSC (Raymond).

- AAA [Calero, Cruz, Robelo] available to Washington press. Responsibility: State/LPD (Gomez).

North and Fortier informed McFarlane of "military operations and political action...timed to influence the vote," including "special operations against highly visible military targets in Nicaragua" and "various efforts designed to support significantly increased military operations immediately after the vote."

On the Spitz Channell front, North and Fortier told McFarlane: "Next week the networks auction their air time for 15, 30, and 60 second commercials during prime viewing hours...[U.S. interest groups are prepared to] commit nearly $2M for commercial air time and the production of various advertising media."[49]

In early April, with the congressional votes still lacking to win a straight-out vote on military aid, the administration concocted a peace plan ploy, following up on the contra ultimatum issued in San Jose. "Humanitarian" aid would go to the contras during a 60-day ceasefire period. If at the end of 60 days (June 1), the Nicaraguan government had not reached a peace settlement with the contras, the assistance would revert to military aid. Nicaragua rightly called the proposal a "public relations" maneuver. Less diplomatically, House Speaker Tip O'Neill called it a "dirty trick."[50] The administration claimed Latin American support for the plan, but that too was trickery. Colombian President Belisario Betancur explained that when he called the proposal for a ceasefire and negotiations a positive step, he wasn't informed it was linked to the renewal of contra funding, which he and other Contadora leaders opposed. Betancur said the contra aid linkage made it "no longer a peace proposal, but a preparation for war."[51]

Meanwhile, the administration was secretly sabotaging actual peace talks between Miskito leader Brooklyn Rivera and the Nicaraguan government. As North later wrote in a secret May 31 memo to McFarlane, "After nearly two months of careful coordination with Rivera, he agreed on Saturday to break-off his discussions with the Sandinistas and announced the end of the Indian/FSLN dialogue from Bogota."[52]

Congress was essentially told to go along with Reagan on contra funding, or the administration would go around Congress. As Reagan put it, "We're not going to quit and walk away from them, no matter what happens."

North wrote up a "Fallback Plan for the Nicaraguan Resistance." He told McFarlane in March 1985, "Secrecy for the plan is paramount." It required that "present donors [chiefly Saudi Arabia] continue their relationship with the resistance beyond the current funding figure...The current funding relationship...is sufficient to purchase arms and munitions between now and October—if additional monies are provided for non-military supplies (e.g. food, clothing, medical items, etc.)."

The fall-back plan envisioned the administration bypassing Congress with a presidential appeal to the public for "humanitarian" aid: "Send your check or money order to the Nicaraguan Freedom Fighters, Box 1776, Gettysburg, PA." McFarlane rejected the presidential speech idea, but he approved the already-initiated creation of a tax-exempt "Nicaraguan Freedom Fund, Inc."[53] The Nicaraguan Freedom Fund was subsequently launched by the *Washington Times* and endorsed by Reagan (described in chapter 10).

Casey met with McFarlane on March 22 and, according to a CIA record of the meeting, "expressed some concern, based on his conversation with Poindexter earlier in the day, that the Administration was going to be content to seek authorization for non-lethal aid to the contras, relying on third countries to supply either arms or funds for arms." Casey worried that continuing this way would leave Congress "off the hook" and congressional opponents would attempt to discover and punish third countries supporting the contras. McFarlane "noted that was a good point and he felt that rather than have another meeting on this subject he would take the issue to the President and let him decide."[54] The president apparently decided to go with public "humanitarian" aid and secret arms funding. Later that year, Congress allowed third-country support for "humanitarian" aid.

Word leaked in mid April that the administration had sent congressional appropriations committees a top secret document revealing plans to expand the contra force to put more "pressure" on Nicaragua. This was presented as the only alternative to an expensive "containment" strategy which could raise the cost of U.S. military and economic aid programs in Central America from $1.2 billion to $4-5 billion a year (administration figures). The document said the administration had, for the present, ruled out "direct application of U.S. military force," but warned that this course "must realistically be recognized as an eventual option, given our stakes in the region, if other policy alternatives fail."[55]

Leading Democratic supporters of contra aid, such as Senator Sam Nunn (D-GA) and House Foreign Affairs Committee Chairman Dante Fascell (D-FL), promoted the plan to launder contra funds through a "humanitarian" aid account.[56] Amid this congressional brokering, the *New York Times* illustrated how "humanitarian assistance can indirectly support guerrilla fighters" with an account of a $7.5 million AID program approved by Congress in June 1984 to provide medical and food aid for Miskito refugees in Honduras near the contra base camp at Rus Rus, as well as road building and other construction.[57] Auxiliary groups like Friends of the Americas were also active in the area.

Representatives Barnes and Hamilton proposed an alternative aid package, with $10 million for Nicaraguan refugees to be distributed through the International Red Cross or UN High Commissioner for Refugees and $4 million to defray peacekeeping costs in the event of a successful Contadora peace plan. Reagan attacked the aid proposal in his April 20 radio address as a "shameful surrender" that would "hasten the consolidation of Nicaragua as a Communist-terrorist arsenal."[58]

On April 23, the Senate approved $14 million in military and paramilitary aid linked to a non-binding Reagan pledge to use the funds for non-military purposes; the House voted it down. The next day, the House voted down other aid alternatives as liberals and conservatives unexpectedly combined to kill the Barnes-Hamilton compromise. As William LeoGrande observed: "The press headlined the votes as a total defeat for Reagan's Nicaragua policy because all the aid proposals had failed. In fact, the votes indicated that the administration's position was stronger than anyone had anticipated."[59]

Red Herring

The House votes left a vacuum, not a policy decision. A group led by conservative Democrat Dave McCurdy of Oklahoma began meeting to draft a new bill. Opportunity quickly knocked in the form of Ortega's trip to Moscow. Ortega had traveled to Moscow before so the Nicaraguans were shocked by the unprecedented outcry in the United States. Nicaragua's ambassador to the United States, Carlos Tunnermann, recalled how the trip was presented as "a mortal sin. President Ortega, the foreign minister, myself and others have explained to dozens of congresspeople what produced the trip…how it wasn't scheduled [to coincide with the vote]…The trip was not exclusively to Moscow. It encompassed five socialist countries and seven Western European countries. It was a trip that could not have been changed simply because of a congressional vote. It was vital to us because we had a shortage of oil."[60] Nicaragua could no longer count on Mexico to supply oil and it was anticipating U.S. sanctions that would require immediate alternative outlets for Nicaraguan imports and exports.

U.S. politicians and commentators screamed insult and outrage over the "Moscow trip" and pretended that if Ortega hadn't taken such an "ill-timed" trip the House "No" votes on contra aid would have stood.

On May 1, Reagan cited the trip as one reason for declaring a "national emergency" because of Nicaragua's "unusual and extraordinary threat to the national security and foreign policy of the United States" and slapping Nicaragua with the economic embargo that had been waiting in the wings. Although the embargo hurt Nicaragua economically and "disrupted a natural trading partner relationship," Alejandro Martinez Cuenca, the minister of foreign trade and commerce, believes it backfired against the United States. No country joined in the embargo, it was condemned in international forums and Nicaragua was able to shift its primary export market to Western Europe and build upon its policy of diversifying international economic relations—a policy of "not putting all your eggs in one single basket."[61]

The embargo had wide support in Congress. Neoliberal Rep. Stephen Solarz (D-NY) called it "an appropriate approach" and opportunistically equated Nicaragua with South Africa. "I don't see how you can support sanctions against Nicaragua and not against South Africa," said Solarz. "In both instances, you have Governments deeply committed to policies we are opposed to. In South Africa it is apartheid and in Nicaragua it is repression at home and revolution abroad."[62]

"There's a movement on our side to accommodate the lust members feel to strike out against Communism," said Rep. Bill Alexander (D-AR), the chief deputy whip.[63] Shultz played to the mix of anti-communist lust and fear of "another Vietnam," claiming on May 23 that without contra aid "we will be faced with an agonizing choice about the use of American combat troops."[64]

Brinkmanship

The option of U.S. combat troops was the subject of two *New York Times* articles in early June: "U.S. Military Is Termed Prepared for Any Move Against Nicaragua" and "An Invasion Is Openly Discussed." The first stage of the U.S. military buildup in Central America had been completed with "a vigorous tempo of war games, construction of staging areas and listening posts, the creation of an elaborate intelligence network and a major effort to fortify allied armies"; the Southern Command had even stored 100 percent of its estimated oil requirements. As part of a continuing effort to draw Costa Rica deeper into the war, Green Berets were training the Costa Rican civil guard in counterinsurgency skills at a new camp near the Nicaraguan border.

Talk of the invasion option had "become commonplace in official circles," the *New York Times* reported. The apparent consensus was that the United States "could quickly and easily rout the Sandinistas." As one intelligence official put it, an invasion of Nicaragua was undesirable "from a propaganda point of view" but, if necessary, it would be "like falling off a log."

Intelligence sources said "major Nicaraguan installations are lightly defended... With minimal risk, American pilots could destroy the small Nicaraguan Air Force, radar, artillery, tanks, supply depots and command centers." Colonel William Comee Jr., then Southcom director of operations and later commander of the Joint Task Force in Honduras, reportedly estimated "it would take the United States two weeks to gain control of 60 percent of the Nicaraguan population."

In the most likely scenario, the United States would install a contra government and army. "The Sandinistas would be up in the hills, but that would be a problem for the new Nicaraguan government," explained one U.S. officer. "It wouldn't be our problem. We'd probably have a program like El Salvador, advisers and assistance, but no Americans involved in the fighting." The officer downplayed the threat of prolonged guerrilla war, asserting that the Sandinistas have "lost the support of people in the mountains. They'll get their heads chopped off up there."[65]

Senator Richard Lugar (R-IN), then chairman of the Senate Foreign Relations Committee, said he thought the United States would break diplomatic relations with Nicaragua, "But I don't know how soon...We might recognize a government in exile." With "a second Cuba," he said, "we might be invited" by Nicaragua's neighbors to invade "as we were invited in the East Caribbean" to invade Grenada.[66]

Contrary to the impression left by the *Times* articles, there was no consensus behind the "falling off a log" rhetoric. The administration had, as suspected, secretly studied what it would take to invade Nicaragua. As was reported a year later, however, the Joint Chiefs urged caution, "arguing that it would take 125,000 U.S. troops and that casualties would number between 3,000 and 4,000 in the first few days—and sharply questioning whether American public opinion would back such an effort." Unlike Grenada, Nicaragua would not be a "quick hit victory." The administration remained divided over the invasion option.[67]

One 1984 study, drawing on scenarios developed by military analysts and consultants, estimated that after more than four months of "relatively high intensity warfare" an occupation force of U.S. and CONDECA troops would be needed to confront sabotage and insurgency for the remainder of a five-year period. Assuming "perhaps unrealistically, that the opposition to the American occupation diminishes dramatically over time, and that the internal resistance is effectively prevented from receiving support from outside the country" and that contra and CONDECA troops "carry the burden of pacification" after the initial occupation, U.S. casualties would total "between 2,392 and 4,783 dead with 9,300 to 18,600 wounded." Nicaraguan casualties would be far higher. The total economic cost to the United States would be nearly $10.7 billion, including equipment losses, operating costs and economic assistance.[68]

While some officials were cautious, others were itching for an opportunity to invade. "There were these guys in the White House who were just dying for an excuse to send in the 82nd Airborne," said a former senior official. "The line they had was that with 125,000 troops and 4,000 to 5,000 casualties, we could occupy the country in four to six weeks."[69]

In a 1984 dinner discussion with reporters, McFarlane had "railed against the Pentagon's unwillingness to use power in Central America. They want the weapons, he declared in substance, 'but they don't want to use them.' " For example, McFarlane and other officials from various departments had urged a naval blockade of Nicaragua, a subject of constant study since early in the administration. But the Pentagon brass consistently argued that a blockade would tie down too many assets needed elsewhere. In the words of former Army Chief of Staff General Edward Meyer, "The civilians in the State Department have always been more willing to employ force than the military. Military men know that once a war starts it's hard to stop. They are not sure that the civilians who ordered it are going to be around when the chips are picked up."

According to past and present policymakers, "the Reagan administration has been on the brink of war [i.e. direct invasion] in Central America from its first year in office...They say the question of whether U.S. combat troops will be sent remains to be settled."[70]

"Humanitarian" Aid

On June 12, 1985, the House reinvigorated the war on Nicaragua by approving $27 million in "humanitarian" aid. The Senate had approved $38 million on June 7. Ortega's trip to Moscow became the convenient excuse for the pro-contra compromise promised weeks in advance. "Ortega's visit was a red herring," Rep. McCurdy acknowledged. "I'm trying to go to Moscow in October myself."[71]

By 1985, the Reaganaut propaganda-lobby operation had succeeded in demonizing Nicaragua to the extent that even most policy critics mouthed the administration's deluded rhetoric. Senator Mark Hatfield (R-OR) chided his colleagues, "In the debate in April we had a hate-in—everybody said, 'I hate the Sandinistas more than you do; I just hate them differently.' "[72]

Six weeks before Congress voted to renew aid to the contras, *Newsweek* ran a gruesome series of photos titled "Execution in the Jungle": "The victim dug his own grave, scooping the dirt out with his hands...He crossed himself. Then a contra executioner knelt and rammed a k-bar knife into his throat. A second enforcer stabbed at his jugular, then his abdomen. When the corpse was finally still, the contras threw dirt over the shallow grave—and walked away." The photos were taken by Frank Wohl, a conservative student sympathizer traveling with the contras.[73]

House Speaker Tip O'Neill advised Reagan to look at the *Newsweek* photographs if he wanted a good reason to vote against contra aid. "I saw that picture," Reagan replied, "and I'm told that after it was taken, the so-called victim got up and walked away."[74]

The "Execution in the Jungle" fit the continued pattern of contra terror. Publicly, the administration covered up the contra trail of blood, but internal documents acknowledged the human rights problem, as illustrated by a secret briefing paper for Elliott Abrams to use for the September 1985 chiefs of mission conference attended by key U.S. officials involved in Central America: "The armed Nicaraguan resistance is a potent force but still a long way from success. Public support is growing but is still tenuous. They must understand the absolute necessity of fighting a 'clean' war."[75] Considering the training provided in the CIA contra manual, for example, it's no wonder the contras didn't fight a "clean" war.

The Boland prohibition against using funds to support military or paramilitary activities in Nicaragua remained in effect through October 18, 1986, when the $100 million aid legislation supplanted it. Funds of $27 million were authorized only for "humanitarian" aid: "food, clothing, medicine and other humanitarian assistance, and it does not include the provision of weapons, weapons systems, ammunition, or other equipment, vehicles or material which can be used to inflict serious bodily harm or death." There was also a loophole allowing the exchange of intelligence information with the contras.[76]

"Humanitarian" aid was Orwellian double-speak and everyone knew it. In the words of *Congressional Quarterly*, "It was difficult for members to oppose something labeled 'humanitarian' aid for the contras, even though everyone understood that the money would be used to keep a military force fighting in the field."[77]

In adopting the humanitarian aid label, the U.S. government debased a term well established in international law and practice. Eleven nongovernmental voluntary organizations, including Lutheran World Relief, American Friends Service Committee and OxFam America, issued a statement explaining that under the Geneva Conventions combatants have no claim to "humanitarian" aid. Governmental or nongovernmental providers of genuine humanitarian assistance must be recognized as neutral parties to the conflict. Humanitarian aid must be offered impartially and provided strictly to noncombatants on the basis of need. Providing "humanitarian assistance to a military force is a contradiction in terms."[78]

On August 29, 1985, President Reagan signed an executive order creating the Nicaraguan Humanitarian Assistance Office (NHAO) for the purpose of disbursing the $27 million to UNO. Ambassador Robert Duemling was named director. Abrams was responsible for day to day policy guidance. After a conversation with North in September, Duemling wrote in his notes: "War costs $2 mil/mo. North thinks that $1.25 mil. can come from NHAO."[79]

In October, UNO leaders Calero, Cruz and Robelo signed a letter to Duemling requesting that he retain Robert Owen's Institute for Democracy, Education and Assistance (IDEA). IDEA was a nonprofit front group established by Owen in January 1985. Duemling agreed to the Owen contract in November after additional pressure from North. The IDEA-NHAO contract for $50,675 stipulated that "Owen shall not during the term of this Grant perform any service which is related to the acquisition, transportation, repair, storage or use of weapons, weapons systems, ammunition or other equipment, vehicles or material which can be used to inflict serious bodily harm or death."[80] Owen not only facilitated lethal aid for the contras during this period, he did so employing NHAO planes at North's direction. Duemling himself acknowledged twice ordering planes to shuttle weapons in "mixed loads" for the contras in early 1986 at the direction of Elliott Abrams.[81]

Enterprise airlift operative Richard Gadd also enjoyed NHAO largesse. His AIRMACH corporation received at least $487,000 in classified NHAO contracts to deliver "nonlethal" aid after the reported intervention of Abrams.[82] AIRMACH subcontracted with Southern Air Transport to deliver "humanitarian" supplies to Ilopango Air Base in El Salvador where the planes were reloaded with arms and ammunition for drops to the contras before returning to the United States.

A June 1986 GAO report revealed that millions of dollars in "humanitarian" aid had been traced to offshore bank accounts (e.g. Cayman Islands, Bahamas) and to the Honduran Armed Forces, raising questions about illegal diversion of funds and payoffs.[83] Later that month, several alienated contra military officers described corruption among the top contra leaders. "They have clean boots and dirty hands," was a common complaint.

"I think the entire leadership is corrupt," said Gerardo "Chaco" Martinez, former commander of the Jeane Kirkpatrick Task Force. Former task force commander Marion "Gorrion" Blandon said he was carried on the contra payroll at $400 a month for two years during which he wasn't paid. A former contra intelligence officer, Alberto Suhr, recalled seeing a receipt for 5,000 rifles at $600 a piece; the rifles were actually purchased for $160 each. He described other methods of fraud, such as billing for higher-cost grades of rice, beans and corn, while actually buying lower-cost grades. Currency exchange was another profit maker. As Suhr explained it, dollars were changed to Honduran *lempiras* at the black market rate (then about 2.60-2.65 to the dollar) while accounting was done at the official rate (then about 2 to the dollar) at which Washington was billed for supplies, creating a 30 percent profit on each transaction—amounting to nearly $1 million graft for every $3 million in U.S. aid.[84]

The GAO reported that as of September 4, 1986, NHAO disbursed $26.8 million. According to receipts, about $9.8 million was paid to U.S. suppliers and $17 million was spent in Central America. The GAO could not verify the bulk of the expenditures. Regarding payments to Central American brokers, it found, for example, that "of the total amount of about $3 million deposited to one broker account as of May 10, 1986, only $150,000 could be traced to Central America, none of which was paid to suppliers shown on the invoices and receipts received by NHAO. Instead, most of the funds were transferred from the account to other bank accounts in the United States and other countries. Thus, from the broker's bank records, we could not determine whether the funds reached the intended suppliers in the region." The GAO confirmed that "currency was exchanged at rates higher than the in-country official exchange rate—up to 31 percent higher."[85]

Among the known "humanitarian" expenses were color televisions, volleyball uniforms and living room sets.[86]

Enterprise Liftoff

On April 1, 1985, Owen wrote a memo to North (alias "The Hammer") filling him in on discussions concerning the development of a new southern front. Owen described a meeting arranged by Arturo Cruz Jr. with contra leaders Leonel Poveda, Guillermo Mendieta and Alejandro Martinez: "They say they represent El Negro Chamorro's camp, which now consists of some 43 men under the command of Jose Robelo (Chepon), and another camp which is under the command of the Cubans and Calero's people." They would be a southern front alternative to Eden Pastora. Owen reported that "some of Pastora's field commanders are ready to join any side which will provide them with food and medicines. They have not been resupplied in at least 8 months."

In an April 9 update to the memo, Owen added, "Sparkplug [Calero] has decided to go with El Negro Chamorro as the military commander of the South. There will be a political/military council which will have supervisory capacity over Chamorro," made up of Chamorro, Donald Lacayo, Indalacio Pastora, Picasso, "who is married to Calero's wife's sister," Poveda and possibly others.

"The concern about Chamorro," continued Owen, "is that he drinks a fair amount and may surround himself with people who are in the war not only to fight, but to make money. People who are questionable because of past indiscrestions [sic] include: Jose Robelo (Chepon): potential involvement with drug running and the sales of goods provided by USG [U.S. government]. Carlos Coronel: Talks with all sides, potentially too much with the Sandinistas and is making $ on the side. Leonel Poveda: Rumored to have been involved with the sale of goods and pocketing certain 'commissions.' Sebastian Gonzalez (Wachan): Now involved in drug running out of Panama…

"Whatever structure is established for the South, tight control must be kept on the money and resources. In the past it has been too easy to sell goods and too many people have learned how to make a good living off the war."[87]

On July 1, North, Calero, Bermudez, Secord, Clines and Quintero met all night in the Miami Airport Hotel. "The meeting," Secord recalled, "commenced on a pretty hard note, with Colonel North being worried about and critical of the Contras, because he had been receiving reports that the limited funds they had might be getting wasted, squandered, or even worse, some people might be lining their pockets." North specifically mentioned Adolfo Calero's brother, Mario, who handled contra purchasing out of New Orleans.

The meeting then turned to a review of military problems. It was agreed that airlift was the most urgent concern. The contras had a few old aircraft operating out of Honduras, but when the CIA pulled back under Boland there were few people trained in logistics, maintenance and communications—what Secord called the "sinews of war." The contra task forces inside Nicaragua were dependent on the resupply of consumables—beans and bullets—from air. "You either had to develop an air drop capability or they were going to be forced from the field," said Secord. It was tacit admission of the lack of a real popular base.

The second major problem was the need for a new and successful southern front, based in Costa Rica, to divert Sandinista forces from the Honduras-based northern front. The third problem was the contras' "lack of access to their urban areas and the need for them to get into some of the urban areas."

North asked Secord to take over contra procurement and organize an airlift operation for supplying existing FDN forces and the new southern front. Secord asked Gadd to organize the airlift. Quintero went to El Salvador and, with the assistance of his friend Felix Rodriguez, arranged for the airlift operation to be run out of Ilopango Air Base. "That," said Secord, "was the key. Without that we had nothing."[88]

Felix Rodriguez (alias Max Gomez) is an old CIA hand. He came to the United States from Cuba in 1954 to go to high school and moved here permanently in 1958, a year before the triumph of the revolution. In 1959, Rodriguez went to the Dominican Republic with the Anti-Communist Legion. He returned to the United States and in late 1960 began training for the Bay of Pigs operation. When the April 1961 invasion of Cuba failed, Rodriguez, who had infiltrated into Cuba in advance, sought refuge for over five months in the Venezuelan Embassy in Havana. He then returned to the United States, trained at Fort Benning, Georgia, and joined the anti-Cuba operations being run by Theodore Shackley and Tom Clines from Miami. In 1967, Rodriguez was sent to Bolivia to help track Che Guevara. After Che was captured, interrogated and executed, Rodriguez took his watch; he still wears it. Rodriguez then went to train a special intelligence unit in Ecuador and police counterintelligence in Peru.

Rodriguez served in Vietnam from 1970 to 1972 as a provincial reconnaissance unit trainer under the Saigon area command of Donald Gregg. There Rodriguez helped develop the concept of using low-level helicopter reconnaissance and small, mobile paramilitary teams for search and destroy missions against guerrilla units. According to Edwin Wilson, Rodriguez worked in the Phoenix program: "He was the kind of guy who really impressed gung-ho people...They'd take three Vietnamese up in a helicopter, throw two overboard and the other guy talked."[89]

Rodriguez went on to CIA operations in South America and the Caribbean before taking disability retirement in 1976. He reportedly served as an adviser to the Argentine military for two years in the early 1980s.[90] This was during the period he was, as mentioned earlier, reportedly working with Tom Clines to support the contras.

Rodriguez became a business partner of Gerard Latchinian, a Miami-based arms broker. In February 1986, Latchinian was convicted of conspiring to assassinate Honduran President Roberto Suazo and received a 30-year sentence. The 1984 conspiracy, which involved smuggling $10.3 million of cocaine into the United States to finance a hit squad and coup, also included General Jose Bueso, the chief of the Honduran Armed Forces Joint Command who was ousted along with General Alvarez in March 1984. In the fall of 1986, North, Clarridge and General Paul Gorman urged the Justice Department to grant Bueso leniency as "a friend of the United States," i.e. of the contras and the U.S. military.

They wanted to ensure, as North put it in computer notes to Poindexter, that Bueso didn't "break his longstanding silence about the Nic[araguan] Resistance and other sensitive operations" and "start singing songs nobody wants to hear." Poindexter told North, "You may advise all concerned that the President will want to be as helpful as possible to settle this matter." Abrams also supported the leniency request at an early October meeting. Although Bueso was not pardoned, he was allowed to serve a five-year prison sentence at a minimum security prison at Eglin Air Force Base in Florida.[91]

In March 1982, Rodriguez drew on his Vietnam experience and wrote a five-page proposal for the creation of an elite mobile strike force, called the Tactical Task Force (TTF), that would "be ideal for the pacification effort in El Salvador and Guatemala" (reminiscent of the SMARF proposal discovered upon Ed Wilson's arrest). Rodriguez dubbed the search and destroy units "Pink Teams" and advocated using napalm and cluster bombs to give them "more destructive power." Rodriguez's proposal included a map of Central America which indicated that Nicaragua would be a target of Pink Team operations (based in El Salvador and Honduras).

Rodriguez met with his old friend Donald Gregg, national security adviser to George Bush, and Richard Stone, special envoy for Central America, in early March 1983. Gregg, a CIA officer from 1951 to 1979, served as head of the NSC Intelligence Directorate before moving to Bush's office in August 1982. On March 17, Gregg sent Rodriguez's Pink Team plan to then Deputy National Security Adviser McFarlane along with a secret one-page memo on "anti-guerrilla operations in Central America." Gregg indicated his support for Rodriguez's plan, as well as that of Stone and CIA official Rudy Enders. McFarlane forwarded the documents to Oliver North.

On March 21, McFarlane sent National Security Adviser William Clark the Rodriguez proposal, Gregg's memo and a description of Israeli paramilitary support for the contras. McFarlane noted: "This is representative of the kind of things we can do with Israel if we work quietly behind the scenes. I set this in motion with my Israeli counter-part, David Kimche, over a year ago. We could do a lot together if we would work at it."

Clark approved and wrote "Great" on McFarlane's cover memo.[92] Rodriguez went on to advise the Salvadoran military along the lines of the Pink Team strategy as well as help manage the contra supply operation.

In January 1985, Rodriguez met twice with Vice President Bush. At the second meeting before Rodriguez left for Central America, he showed Bush a picture taken with Che Guevara. Rodriguez arrived in El Salvador on March 15.[93] Before that he had contra business to attend to.

According to Central American intelligence sources, Rodriguez met with Guatemala's General Mejia to discuss "a plan, first broached by Rodriguez during a previous visit, whereby Guatemala would provide cover for U.S. arms shipments to the contras in exchange for increased U.S. aid."[94] On March 5, North informed McFarlane that the Guatemalans would falsely certify that the Guatemalan Army was the final destination for "nearly $8M worth of munitions to be delivered to the FDN," beginning on or about March 10. North told McFarlane that the end-user certificates, which he attached to the memo, "are a direct consequence of the informal liaison we have established with GEN [Mejia] and your meeting with he and President [deleted]." North recommended an increase in U.S. aid to Guatemala as compensation for "the extraordinary assistance they are providing to the Nicaragua freedom fighters."[95] U.S. aid to Guatemala jumped from $18.6 million in 1984 to over $98 million in 1985 to $114.2 million in 1986.

On February 14, 1985, General Gorman sent a confidential "eyes only" cable to Ambassador to El Salvador Thomas Pickering and Colonel James Steele, the commander of the U.S. Military Group in El Salvador: "I have just met here with Felix Rodriguez...He is operating as a private citizen, but his acquaintanceship with the VP [Vice President] is real enough, going back to latter's days as DCI [Director of Central Intelligence]. Rodriguez' primary commitment to the region is in [deleted] where he wants to assist the FDN. I told him that the FDN deserved his priority." Gorman earlier told Pickering that Rodriguez "has been put into play by Ollie North." Pickering forwarded that cable to Craig Johnstone at the State Department.[96]

Gregg met with Rodriguez on February 19, supposedly only to discuss El Salvador. North recorded a February 19 conversation with General Gorman in his notebook: "F.R. [Rodriguez] told his priority should be FDN. Told him in delicate stage of transition from CIA run op to Southern Command run op with LRPs [Long Range Reconnaissance Patrols] and PROWL"—two classified operations in El Salvador. CIA operatives trained the small Salvadoran Long Range Reconnaissance Patrols and accompanied them in their mission of tracking guerrillas in rebel-held territory and calling in air strikes. This was one way the administration secretly exceeded the public limit of 55 U.S. military advisers in El Salvador. Gorman, fearing a higher risk of exposure, did not want "volunteers" like Rodriguez involved in the Southern Command-run program. Nonetheless, with Ambassador Pickering's approval, Rodriguez did assist the search and destroy missions.[97]

On September 10, North met with Gregg and Steele. In his notebook, North listed the following among the discussion topics: "Calero/Bermudez visit to [Ilopango Air Base] to estab[lish] log[istical] support/maint[enance]," as well as other possible locations for the resupply base. (Gregg has denied knowledge of the contra supply operation prior to summer 1986.)[98] On September 20, North wrote Rodriguez, asking him to arrange space at Ilopango for the contra supply operation; Quintero followed up. Rodriguez became the logistical coordinator for the airlift at the base and liaison with base commander Juan Rafael Bustillo and other Salvadoran officers, as well as with Colonel Steele.

Rodriguez recruited a friend from U.S. operations against Cuba, Luis Posada (alias Ramon Medina), to assist the airlift as "support director" at Ilopango. Posada handled finances, housing and transportation and coordinated aircraft landing, refueling and takeoff. Eventually, Posada also became responsible for receiving, refueling and relaunching NHAO flights.[99]

The CIA-trained Posada is a fugitive terrorist. On October 6, 1976, a bomb destroyed a Cubana Airlines DC 8 en route from Barbados to Havana, killing all 73 people aboard. Posada and three other Cuban exiles living in Venezuela, including CORU chief Orlando Bosch, were jailed (Posada went to Venezuela in 1967, where he worked for DISIP, Venezuelan secret intelligence). In August 1985, Posada bribed a prison supervisor and escaped. Months later, reportedly disguised by plastic surgery as well as an alias, Posada was at Ilopango working for the airlift and protected by his old contacts in the CIA and the Salvadoran military.[100]

Congress granted additional money to the CIA in December 1985 to provide communications equipment to the contras and allowed the State Department to solicit third countries for "humanitarian" assistance. On January 9, 1986, Reagan signed a new finding on Nicaragua which consolidated prior findings and authorized the CIA to provide intelligence advice, training and communications equipment to the contras; $13 million was allocated. In the copy of the finding published by the Iran-contra committees, there is only one line not blacked out after the phrase "the CIA is directed to": "Provide assistance and non-lethal material support to the armed Resistance forces of the Nicaraguan democratic opposition."[101]

The CIA also spent "several million dollars" in "political funds" from the CIA budget to support and influence contra activity from September 1985 through 1986. The congressional Intelligence Committees were reportedly notified. CIA funding went to Sandinista opponents inside Nicaragua; to support UNO and FDN operations; to contra propaganda; and, in the words of one U.S. official, to "create the aura that they are an actual political entity among our allies in Europe."[102] In summer 1986, the CIA used "political funds" to transport FDN and Kisan (Miskito) representatives around Honduras in an effort to settle factional differences and consolidate the contras for an offensive against Nicaragua pending congressional approval of military aid. The CIA used Honduran Air Force helicopters with U.S. pilots for the flights.[103]

Meanwhile, on January 15, 1986, North took new steps on the recommendation of Casey and Poindexter to ensure secure communications for the Enterprise contra operation. He distributed fifteen classified KL-43 encryption devices provided by the National Security Agency to Secord, Gadd, Steele, Rodriguez, Quintero, Southern Air Transport President William Langton, Fernandez and others. Costa Rica station chief Joe Fernandez met with the new CIA Latin America Division chief while he was on an orientation trip to the region in April and told him North had provided a KL-43. Fernandez said he didn't have time to participate in the resupply operation. The new chief told Fernandez he'd "look into it" back in Washington.[104]

Fernandez ended up playing a pivotal role in the resupply, relaying when and where to make air drops. He said they "were able to obtain information about areas where they [the contras] were and that they had under temporary control. I would say temporary control means 48 hours and no more, because of the pressure of the Sandinista military operations."[105] About the material dropped, Fernandez said, "This was all lethal. Benefactors only sent lethal stuff."[106]

On January 16, 1986, North wrote in his notebook that General John Galvin (Gorman's successor as Southcom commander) was "cognizant of the activities under way in both Costa Rica and at [Ilopango Air Base] in support of the DRF [Democratic Resistance Force, FDN]." North added, "Gen. Galvin is enthusiastic about both endeavors." North, Poindexter, Galvin and others met on January 16 to discuss, among other things, "covert strategy/training/planning/support" for the contras. Galvin testified later that he knew of the resupply operation, but claimed to have believed it was financed and run by private individuals.[107]

By April, the airlift was operating almost daily supply missions for the FDN's northern front. According to the *Iran-Contra Report*, "Most missions delivered supplies from the main FDN base [Aguacate, in Honduras] to the FDN's forward-operating positions. Other flights dropped lethal cargo to units operating inside Nicaragua. Many of these flights were helped informally by CIA field officers on the ground, who prepared flight plans for aerial resupply missions, briefed the air crews on Nicaraguan antiaircraft installations, and provided minor shop supplies to the mechanics. On one occasion, the CIA operations officer at an FDN base flew Ian Crawford, a loadmaster for the resupply operation, in a CIA helicopter with lethal supplies on board over the border area so Crawford could see where he and his crew were airdropping cargo three to four times daily."[108]

The operation still had problems, including poor maintenance and coordination between the FDN and the southern front. On April 20, North and Secord flew to Ilopango for a meeting with Steele, Rodriguez, Bustillo and Bermudez and other FDN military leaders. On May 1, Gadd was replaced by Dutton as operational manager. At that point, the operation had approximately nineteen pilots, loadmasters (kickers) and maintenance operators at Ilopango, with one Maule and two C-7 aircraft and one C-123 cargo plane. Pilots earned $3,000 per month, plus a $700 bonus for every flight inside Nicaragua.[109] The crews lived in three safe houses in San Salvador. The Enterprise warehouse at the base was stocked with machine guns, grenades, C-4 explosive, ammunition, uniforms and other military gear.

As an Air America veteran once noted, "Every time there's a war the same damned people always show up."[110] That was certainly the case with the war on Nicaragua. Eugene Hasenfus was an Air America kicker in Laos. William Cooper, the managing pilot, was a former Air America pilot who worked for Southern Air along with pilot Wallace "Buzz" Sawyer; Sawyer also flew for Seaspray. Cooper's deputy John McRainey was an Air America veteran, as were pilots Frank Hines, Jerry Stemwedel and Jake Wehrell.[111]

It was Secord's desire "to try to slowly replace the American crews with foreigners," assuming Congress didn't give the CIA another green light. In Secord's view, the problem wasn't a legal one, but an "appearance problem. If we were to have one or more of these people captured, as ultimately occurred, it becomes a real problem when it is American citizens."[112]

The Enterprise contracted David Walker, the retired commander of the British 22nd Special Air Services regiment, an elite commando unit, to provide two pilots and a loadmaster, but they didn't have the right experience.[113] At least two South African pilots were employed, as indicated on airlift payroll records, but the Americans remained the mainstay of the operation.

David Walker was also contracted to resolve the urban access problem by arranging military actions. As North explained, "Walker was involved—his organization, as I understand it—in support of the Nicaraguan resistance, with internal operations in Managua and elsewhere, in an effort to improve the perception that the Nicaraguan resistance could operate anywhere that it so desired." Another unnamed contract agent was apparently responsible for "so-called policies of intimidation" which have not been explained.[114]

On December 4, 1984, North wrote a top secret memorandum to McFarlane, informing him that "This weekend, at the request of [Navy] Sec. John Lehman, I met with Mr. David Walker, a former British SAS officer who now heads two companies (KMS and SALADIN) which provide professional security services to foreign governments. Walker had been approached several months ago...In addition to the security services provided by KMS, this offshore (Jersey Islands) company also has professional military 'trainers' available. Walker suggested that he would be interested in establishing an arrangement with the FDN for certain special operations expertise aimed particularly at destroying HIND helicopters. Walker quite accurately points out that the helicopters are more easily destroyed on the ground than in the air."[115]

In an April 11, 1985 memo to McFarlane on FDN military operations, North referred to two operations probably involving Walker. The first involved an expenditure of $50,000 "for the operation conducted in Managua against the ammunition depot at the EPS [Nicaraguan Army] military headquarters." The second, listed under future operations, was "a major special operations attack against Sandino airport [in Managua] with the purpose of destroying the MI-24 helicopters and the Sandinista Air Force maintenance capability."[116] Walker never succeeded in destroying helicopters on the ground.

Southern Front

In July 1985, Lewis Tambs prepared to take up his new post as ambassador to Costa Rica. "Colonel North asked me to go down and open up the southern front," he said. Tambs never questioned whether his instructions were legal under the Boland amendment: "There's a saying in the foreign service: 'When you take the King's shilling, you do the King's bidding.' "[117] Everyone knew where King Ron stood on supporting the contras.

Tambs shared his southern front mandate with CIA Station Chief Joe Fernandez (whose cover was first secretary of the U.S. embassy), Deputy Chief of Mission George Jones and Defense Attache Colonel John Lent. On August 10, North met with Fernandez and Tambs in Costa Rica and discussed the establishment of a secret air base. Tambs informed Fernandez on August 12 that he had received permission from the Costa Rican government to build an airstrip to resupply the southern front. The next day, Fernandez cabled CIA headquarters with the news. "Headquarters was pleased."[118]

Robert Owen arrived in Costa Rica on August 20 to pursue arrangements for the airstrip. He surveyed the proposed site along with Fernandez and a Costa Rican official and informed North of the plans: "The area decided on is on the west coast, bordered by a National Park on the north, the ocean to the west, the Pan American Highway to the east, and mountains and hills to the south. The property is owned by an American living in New York. It is managed by a Colonel in the [Costa Rican] Civil Guard who will be glad to turn it over to [deleted] who has been designated by [deleted] to be an administrator for the project...

"The cover for the operation is a company, owned by a few 'crazy' gringos, wanting to lease the land for agricultural experimentation and for running cattle...The Colonel will provide a cook, the peones [sic] to work the farm, and security...Once the new strip is completed, it will be designated a military zone and will be guarded by the Colonel's people."[119] The airstrip, known as Santa Elena or Point West, was built by the Enterprise subsidiary, Udall Corporation, and completed in May 1986.

On December 12, 1985, North and Poindexter, who had just replaced McFarlane as national security adviser, took a one-day trip to Central America. In recommending the trip to Poindexter, North said that one of its real purposes was to deliver to Central American officials the message that "we [the United States] intend to pursue a victory and that [a Central American country, probably Honduras] will not be forced to seek a political accommodation with the Sandinistas."[120]

Poindexter briefed Reagan on December 13, "including informing the President of the efforts to secure the land necessary for the airstrip" in Costa Rica. Poindexter's notes refer to this as the "private airstrip."[121] In March 1986, just before Oscar Arias was inaugurated president of Costa Rica, Reagan attended a photo session that wasn't listed on his daily schedule. The unusual guest was Costa Rican Minister of Public Security Benjamin Piza; North and Fernandez accompanied him. Afterwards, Piza met with Secord to discuss the airstrip.

By March 1986, the resupply to FDN forces operating from Honduras was well underway, but the southern front airlift was not. In a March 28 memo to North, Owen wrote that he, Steele, Rodriguez, Posada and Quintero had decided to stockpile lethal and nonlethal supplies at Ilopango and merge the air drops to southern front forces. "The Caribou, or better yet a C-123, can be loaded at Cinci [Cincinnati, code for Ilopango], takeoff for points south, deliver and refuel at Point West on the way back to Cinci." Until Point West was ready, the airlift could use the L-100 aircraft employed by NHAO. "According to Max Gomez [Rodriguez], the Salvos [Salvadorans] are being very helpful and were even willing to provide an A-37 to fly support for the L-100."[122]

The Enterprise stepped up efforts to supply the southern front with a C-123 and second C-7 Caribou acquired by Gadd in early April. North coordinated virtually every aspect of the first air drop of southern front lethal supplies into Nicaragua. As explained in the *Iran-Contra Report*, "KL-43 messages among the planners show both the level of detail in which North was concerned and the coordination among various U.S. Government agencies to ensure that the drop succeeded." The first message from North to Secord read:

> The unit to which we wanted to drop in the southern quadrant of Nicaragua is in desperate need of ordnance resupply...Have therefore developed an alternative plan which [CIA Task Force Chief for Central America Alan Fiers] has been briefed on and in which he concurs. The L-100 which flies from MSY to [an FDN base, presumably Aguacate] on Wednesday should terminate it's [sic] NHAO mission on arrival at [the FDN base]. At that point it should load the supplies...which—theoretically [the CIA station chief in Honduras] is assembling today at [the FDN base]—and take them to [Ilopango]. These items should then be transloaded to the C-123...On any night between Wednesday, Apr 9, and Friday, Apr 11 these supplies should be dropped by the C-123 in the vicinity of [drop zone inside Nicaragua]. The A/C [aircraft] shd [should] penetrate Nicaragua across the Atlantic Coast...If we are ever going to take the pressure off the northern front we have got to get this drop in—quickly. Please make sure that this is retransmitted via this channel to [Fernandez], Ralph [Quintero], Sat [Southern Air Transport] and Steele. Owen already briefed and prepared to go w/ the L-100 out of MSY if this will help. Please advise soonest.

Secord and Gadd leased the L-100 from Southern Air Transport and, on April 8, Secord transmitted the following instructions to Quintero:

> CIA and Goode [North] report Blackys [presumably El Negro Chamorro] troops in south in desperate fix. Therefore, [the CIA station chief in Honduras] is supposed to arrange for a load to come from [the FDN base] to [Ilopango] via L100 tomorrow afternoon...Notify Steele we intend to drop tomorrow nite or more like Thurs nite...Meanwhile contact [Fernandez] via this machine and get latest on DZ [drop zone] coordinates and the other data I gave you the format for...CIA wants the aircraft to enter the DZ area from the Atlantic...

By April 9, arrangements were nearly complete. Fernandez sent a cable to CIA Task Force Chief Fiers "requesting flight path information, vectors based on the coordinates of the drop zone, and hostile risk evaluation to be passed to the crew. CIA headquarters provided the information, as it did on three other occasions that spring," according to the *Iran-Contra Report*. Fernandez provided the drop zone location to Quintero and "Steele told the Southern Air Transport crew how to avoid Sandinista radar." However, on April 10, the L-100 was unable to locate the contra forces. It tried again the next day and was able to drop more than 20,000 pounds of lethal supplies to contras inside Nicaragua. "This was the first successful drop to the southern forces. Before the plane left, Steele checked the loading of the cargo, including whether the assault rifles were properly padded."

Fernandez reported to North: "Per UNO South Force, drop successfully completed in 15 minutes...Our plans during next 2-3 weeks include air drop at sea for UNO/KISAN indigenous force...maritime deliveries NHAO supplies to same, NHAO air drop to UNO South...lethal drop to UNO South...

"My objective is creation of 2,500 man force which can strike northwest and link-up with quiche to form solid southern force. Likewise, envisage formidable opposition on Atlantic Coast resupplied at or by sea. Realize this may be overly ambitious planning but with your help, believe we can pull it off."[123]

In May, Fernandez met with Eden Pastora's field commanders in a San Jose safe house. He told them they would only get more U.S. aid if they transferred their allegiance to "El Negro" Chamorro. According to several contra officials, Fernandez provided $5,000 cash rewards to the six Pastora commanders who defected.[124]

North asked Dutton to acquire another C-123 (the first had been damaged in flight) and arranged, with Tambs' assistance, for the C-7 Caribou to refuel at the San Jose International Airport after dropping supplies. On June 16, North told Fernandez that in order to facilitate future southern front air drops, he had "asked Ralph [Quintero] to proceed immediately to your location. I do not think we ought to contemplate these operations without him being on scene. Too many things go wrong that then directly involve you and me in what should be deniable for both of us."[125]

12

Hits, Guns and Drugs

[Senators Kerry, et al.] are traitors to our country. If I had the power—believe me I'm not an assassin, I never participated in any assassination, my work here has been humanitarian—but if it were within my power people like [Senators] Kennedy and Kerry would be lined up against a wall and shot tomorrow at sunrise.

John Hull, CIA contra liaison in Costa Rica.[1]

Everything I know from human intelligence [deleted] would suggest that anybody that was in the game of subversion down there was in one way or another involved with drugs...If you have an intention, whether you are on the right or on the left down there, to be involved in violent activities, the easy way to get into them, to fund them, to get the information, the people, the guns, the people who are willing to commit murder, you deal in drugs because that's just a convenient way to put yourself in touch with unscrupulous and violent people.

General Paul Gorman, former chief of U.S. Southern Command, commenting on the contra leadership's involvement in drug trafficking, July 1987.[2]

Eden Pastora was not only out as the star of the southern front, he was lucky to be alive. In the spring of 1984, the CIA gave Pastora's ARDE forces a 30-day ultimatum: unite with the FDN or get cut off. ARDE began to splinter. Chief political spokesman Alfonso Robelo favored the merger while Pastora remained opposed. "There are strong pressures by the CIA," said Pastora in a May 23 interview with Costa Rica's Radio Monumental, "and they have blocked all help to us. For the last two months, we have not received a bullet or a pair of boots, we have not received anything." Pastora declared on Costa Rican TV that the CIA was pressuring ARDE to join the FDN, "but the CIA will have to kill me first."[3]

The majority of ARDE's leaders broke with Pastora at the end of May and voted to unite with the FDN. Pastora called a news conference for May 30; Costa Rican authorities insisted it be held at an ARDE camp in Nicaraguan territory.

La Penca

About two dozen journalists made the trip from San Jose (a four-hour drive followed by two hours in outboard-powered canoes) to the La Penca camp on the Nicaraguan side of the San Juan river. They did not all make it back alive.

Reporters Martha Honey and Tony Avirgan described what happened: a supposed Danish freelance photographer known as "Per Anker Hansen" placed a metal camera box "containing the bomb on the floor by a counter where Pastora, surrounded by journalists, was standing. Then he snapped a few pictures and, muttering loudly that his camera was malfunctioning, backed away from the crowd...

"At 7:20 p.m., the bomb exploded, killing Rosita [a contra radio operator] instantly and ripping [huge] holes in the ceiling and floor. Most of the journalists and guerrillas in the room were wounded, some fatally."

Pastora was rushed from the scene with shrapnel wounds, burns and broken ribs in the only available speedboat. Linda Frazier, an American working for Costa Rica's English-language *Tico Times*, and Jorge Quiros Piedra of Costa Rica's Channel 6 TV died at La Penca from their wounds; Evelio Sequeira, also of Channel 6, died a week later. Tony Avirgan, an ABC cameraman, was one of eighteen journalists injured. (Martha Honey was not at La Penca.)

According to Avirgan and Honey (Avirgan's wife and colleague), "Shortly after the blast, *La Nacion* reporter Edgar Fonseca contacted his newspaper with his two-way radio, begging for speedboats and helicopters to evacuate the wounded...but neither Costa Rican officials nor the U.S. Embassy [whose citizens were among the dying and injured] seriously attempted to arrange helicopters...The U.S. Embassy's response to the bombing was, essentially, to do nothing."[4] *Tico Times* publisher Richard Dyer was shocked at the embassy's uncharacteristic refusal of assistance.[5] Though within hours Costa Rican investigators were given a description of "Hansen," the borders were not closed for 48 hours.

Pastora immediately blamed the CIA for the bombing. U.S. and Costa Rican officials blamed the Nicaraguan government. Reporters generally followed Washington's "leads" away from the CIA. U.S. officials and contra supporters such as Robert Leiken of the Georgetown University Center for Strategic and International Studies spread the story, carried in the U.S. and Costa Rican press, that the Basque separatist group, ETA, had carried out the bombing for the Sandinistas. Arturo Cruz Jr. added a vicious twist, telling reporters, "The perpetrator of the bombing may have been a newswoman (Linda Frazier) who herself was blown up by the explosion." Avirgan was also named as a prime suspect. U.S. Ambassador Curtin Winsor Jr. commented, "other diplomats, not myself of course, are saying that Tony has ties to ETA."

The ETA was set up as a scapegoat by the CIA at least a year earlier. Edgar Chamorro recalled that in mid 1983 a CIA agent working with the FDN in Honduras asked him to distribute a stack of posters showing a hand holding a gun superimposed over a map of Central America, with text claiming the ETA was planning terrorist activities in the region.[6]

Honey and Avirgan began assembling evidence that the La Penca bombing was carried out by a terrorist group made up of Cuban exiles, North Americans and FDN members—including John Hull, Felipe Vidal, Rene Corvo and Adolfo Calero, among others. Costa Rican intelligence officials and John Hull reportedly facilitated "Hansen's" movements in Costa Rica before the bombing. A source told Honey and Avirgan that the plotters planned to make FARN leader Fernando "El Negro" Chamorro commander of the southern front. As discussed in the previous chapter, El Negro became military commander of the new southern front in 1985.

Eden Pastora believes John Hull is a probable conspirator in the assassination attempt. He calls him "the most untouchable man in Costa Rica." Two senior CIA officials have said that the CIA investigation of the bombing led to Miami and was then dropped.[7]

Honey and Avirgan identified "Hansen" as a Libyan terrorist named Amac Galil who was recruited in Chile. The plotters reportedly reasoned that if Hansen were identified, it would be assumed—mistakenly—that he was working for Qaddafi.

Robert Owen was in Costa Rica meeting with Hull and CIA Station Chief Joe Fernandez when the bombing took place. He told the Iran-contra committees, "I was down there on a survey for Colonel North. The evening actually that it happened, I was in San Jose. As a matter of fact, Senator, if I can just say, I have been named in a lawsuit in this case [by Honey and Avirgan, discussed later], which is absolutely scurrilous, and there is no truth to it…

"We [Owen, Hull and Fernandez] discussed what was going on. And I was just shocked as everyone else when we learned, about 3:30 in the morning, when some of the Nicaraguans came to the apartment and talked with us, and told us what had happened."

Owen was asked by a sympathetic Senator Orrin Hatch about his knowledge of the bombing incident. "One [theory] is the United States was behind it," Owen replied. "I don't give that any credence whatsoever. Eden Pastora received from my understanding, over $3 million from Colonel Qadhafi. Before the bombing, he received a message Colonel Qadhafi wanted him to come and meet with him…Some people believe Colonel Qadhafi was sending him a message."[8] Owen's disinformation went unchallenged.

Pieces of Puzzles

In early May 1985, about a year after the attempted assassination of Pastora, Leslie Cockburn of the CBS News program "West 57th" was in Tegucigalpa, where she encountered a U.S. military delegation whose apparent mission was to scout locations for additional airfields and work on contingency planning for an invasion of Nicaragua. The invasion talk, she recounted, took parochial turns: "The air force representatives sipped their beers and lobbied passionately for a strategy based on precision bombing strikes on various key targets around Managua. The army men argued with equal force for a graduated invasion, to commence with a landing on the Atlantic coast of Nicaragua and the establishment of a base at Bluefields...The navy was no less heated in pleading the wisdom of using the fleet to blockade the country while Seal teams sabotaged coastal installations."

Cockburn met privately with a worried Army Special Forces officer who "had been down in Costa Rica, ostensibly overseeing the military training of the Civil Guard, but he had also gone on missions inside Nicaragua." He said a group of Cuban exiles and U.S. mercenaries were training on American-owned land near Los Chiles, close to the Nicaraguan border. It was a flashpoint where a Nicaraguan "incursion" against the mercenary forces could trigger a confrontation between the U.S. military and the Nicaraguan Army.[9]

Shortly before that conversation, Costa Rican authorities arrested a group of Civilian Military Assistance (CMA)-Brigade 2506-backed mercenaries on John Hull's land and charged them with violation of Costa Rican neutrality and possession of explosives. This was a rare exception to the Monge government's pattern of complicity with contra activity. The five mercenaries arrested that April 25 were Steven Carr and Robert Thompson of Florida, Claude Chaffard of France and John Davies and Peter Glibbery of Britain. Glibbery and Davies were soldiers of fortune in South Africa when they heard about jobs in Central America.

Steven Carr and Peter Glibbery came to feel abandoned in jail and betrayed, and then threatened, by Hull and company. They began to talk to the few reporters who cared then to listen about John Hull, the CIA-contra liaison in Costa Rica, and Robert Owen, the messenger from Washington. Glibbery recalled meeting with Frank Camper, who ran the Recondo mercenary training school in Alabama, and of hearing about Camper's ties to the FBI, CIA and Defense Intelligence Agency (DIA). Through Camper, he and John Davies met CMA leader Tom Posey and Sam Hall, the mercenary who would later be arrested in Nicaragua while scouting a military base. Glibbery and Davies met John Hull and Felipe Vidal in Miami before heading to Costa Rica where they received VIP treatment at the San José airport.

Carr said he had traveled to Hull's ranch in March via a charter aircraft flying from Fort Lauderdale to Ilopango Air Base in El Salvador, where six tons of contra weapons were unloaded in the presence of U.S. military personnel. He talked of collecting those weapons from safe houses in Miami, and seeing three kilos of cocaine in a house belonging to Francisco "Paco" Chanes, a Brigade 2506 supporter in the "shrimp importing" business. Carr said Rene Corvo was in charge of the operation.

Glibbery talked about incursions into Nicaragua to a contra camp about fifteen kilometers east of the Los Chiles border crossing. And Carr described an attack on La Esperanza in Nicaragua, led by Corvo over Hull's objection: "Hull told him not to do it because of an upcoming vote in Congress. He told him the publicity would be bad [should any Americans get killed] and [would] blow the chances" for millions of dollars in new contra funding.[10]

Shortly after Carr, Glibbery and the other mercenaries were arrested, Honey and Avirgan came in contact with Carlos Rojas Chinchilla, a Costa Rican with a strange and scary story. Carlos said a contra named David had appealed to him for help in defecting from a dirty tricks unit based at John Hull's ranch. According to David, members of the group behind the La Penca bombing planned to place a bomb outside the U.S. Embassy in Costa Rica, assassinate the new ambassador, Lewis Tambs, and blame it on the Sandinistas to provoke Costa Rican and U.S. retaliation. Honey and Avirgan warned the U.S. Embassy of what they had heard.

On July 18, the Reagan administration issued a warning of its own—to Nicaragua. It asserted that hard intelligence indicated Nicaragua was supporting planned terrorist attacks against U.S. personnel in Honduras. There would be "serious consequences," U.S. Ambassador Harry Bergold warned, if Nicaragua carried out such actions anywhere in Central America.[11]

The administration claimed that Nicaragua had provided support to the Salvadoran guerrillas who killed four U.S. marines and two other U.S. citizens in San Salvador on June 19. According to senior officials, the United States had seriously considered attacking a base in Nicaragua where Salvadoran guerrillas were allegedly trained. With the July 18 warning, the administration had, in the words of a senior U.S. official, "laid down the gauntlet"; another attack blamed on Nicaragua would warrant a "limited" U.S. military strike. It would be "another situation like acquiring MIG's."[12]

David and Carlos were captured during a subsequent meeting and reportedly taken to John Hull's ranch. They managed to escape, but sources told Honey and Avirgan that David was recaptured and murdered. Honey and Avirgan continued their investigation in the face of death threats.[13]

The alleged subplot to assassinate Ambassador Tambs has been tied to the contra drug connection. By this account, Tambs had earned the wrath of Colombian cocaine tycoons such as Pablo Escobar and the Ochoa brothers when he was ambassador to Colombia between 1983 and 1985; there was said to be a $1 million bounty on Tambs' head. There is another, perhaps more plausible, explanation: the plotters may have planned to place the bomb outside the embassy, killing mainly passersby, and accuse the Nicaraguan government of attempting to assassinate Tambs, without ever intending that Tambs be harmed.[14] Subordinates may have thought there was a real intent to assassinate Tambs; the Colombian drug lords may have been told that to encourage them to donate funds and other support. At this writing, a definitive account is not possible.

Jesus Garcia, a Miami Cuban, was working as the booker at the Dade County jail—where drug traffickers and gun smugglers who contributed to the anti-Castro and contra causes reportedly received special treatment—when Tom Posey was arrested in January 1985 on the charge of carrying a concealed weapon at the Miami airport. After Posey was bailed out by Jose Coutin, CMA's Miami representative, and Jack Terrell, a CMA field commander, he and Garcia kept in contact. In February, Posey, Rene Corvo, Bruce Jones (a former CIA liaison to the contras in Costa Rica), and others brought Garcia into the plan to hit the U.S. Embassy in Costa Rica and allegedly assassinate Ambassador Tambs.

Although Garcia was alienated by the embassy plot, he helped Rene Corvo, Steven Carr and Robert Thompson with an arms shipment leaving Fort Lauderdale airport on March 6. Within a few months, Garcia was apparently set up by a Posey associate and arrested on August 13 for selling a machine gun and silencer. He was assigned a Miami public defender by the name of John Mattes who unexpectedly found himself with a complex and controversial case. Garcia was convicted in December and federal prosecutor Jeffrey Feldman tried to deter Mattes from pursuing the larger potential federal case—arms and drug trafficking, criminal conspiracies—in which Garcia was a bit player.[15]

The continued investigations by Mattes and Honey and Avirgan compiled a growing list of sources, among them Alabaman Jack Terrell. Terrell, known as "Colonel Flaco" (the Thin One), knew about assassination plots. He worked with CMA for a short period, beginning in September 1984, and kept a diary of his activities. One entry described a December 1984 meeting in Adolfo Calero's Miami home, where a second assassination attempt against Pastora was plotted; John Hull, Robert Owen, Felipe Vidal, Enrique Bermudez and Aristides Sanchez were said to be present:

> The termination of Zero [Pastora] discussed with Adolpho [sic], Aristedes, John Hull, Donald Lacy and a man not identified but told [he is with] 'company' [CIA]. Many people involved. Some look like Cubans, some Nicaraguans, some Argentinian.—A.C. Adolfo Calero very upset with statements made by Pastora. Says he too Sandinista. Must die. Big problem. Asks me to put it together and not tell them how it will be done, just do it. Will have complete cooperation of all Costa Rican officials. Have several safe houses in C.R. [Costa Rica] under control of John Hull and Bruce Jones. Seems Rob Owen in on most of this. Am told he is private consultant and liaison man for U.S. (Company)...
>
> Must appear that Sandinistas did it. Discussion on capturing Zero and having men dress in captured uniforms. Am told this must be very visible hit and people must believe the Sandinistas did it. Am told to let Hull know when ready to move...A.C. open to anything. He desperate. Wants and needs southern front.[16]

According to Terrell, Vidal remarked, "We put a bomb under him [Pastora] the first time, but it didn't work because of bad timing."[17]

Pumping Smoke

Joseph "Shooter" Adams, a former U.S. Marine intelligence officer, was Calero's security chief and personal bodyguard from fall 1984 to spring 1986. Adams also told reporter Allan Nairn of a December 1984 meeting to plot Pastora's assassination and said that both Posey and Terrell were present.

For two months, from January to March 1985, Adams was on special assignment, leading a team—including eight U.S. mercenaries and a man named Paul Douglas Johnson, who described himself as a DIA agent—on an Operation Pegasus mission inside Nicaragua's Mosquitia. Adams said he first heard of Operation

Pegasus, which was under Terrell's command, in December 1984 from Tom Posey in a series of meetings at Calero's house. Posey "said Pegasus's goal was to be pumping smoke in Managua when the F-15s came over."

Adams also said he helped maintain a list of Managua civilians, including a nun and priests, and political leaders such as Daniel Ortega, who would be marked for assassination when FDN forces entered Managua. Contra Commander Enrique Bermudez was involved in preparing the list in January 1985. "If the FDN would occupy the city, we would go in and pull these people out and exterminate them," explained Adams. "The average soldier in the FDN wouldn't know who these people were from anybody, whereas we would be able to profile them and know where they were working and living."

Adams said he had access to the list "because my specialty was close-in urban tactics. They wanted me to train an elite urban team for house-clearing techniques." Adams claimed he learned about house-clearing while training with the U.S. Delta Force in 1983. "In DELTA, we were trained for hostage situations. You simply go in and kill all the bad guys and get the good guys out."[18]

Terrell described Operation Pegasus as a plan to train an elite corps of 30 Americans and 210 contra special forces to raid Managua, destroy electric utilities, blow up dams and assassinate Sandinista leaders, including Tomas Borge, Miguel D'Escoto and Nora Astorga (who died of cancer in February 1988). "We wanted to send a message to the Sandinistas that they could be struck at their heart at will and there would be personal consequences," said Terrell.

According to Terrell, the Managua operation was timed for March 1985 to influence the upcoming vote on contra aid. This fits the scenario of actions, including "special operations against highly visible military targets in Nicaragua," outlined in North and Fortier's March 22 memo to McFarlane (discussed in the previous chapter). Terrell said the operation was cancelled when CMA activities at the Las Vegas contra base camp in Honduras were disrupted after the visit of a reporter. By January 1985, Terrell had begun to distance himself from CMA and work directly with the MISURA forces whom he considered poorly treated by FDN leaders.[19]

On January 31, Owen wrote to North with concern about Terrell's increasingly independent activities:

> Flacko [sic] is back in Miami. On Tuesday he met with Steadman Faggoth [sic] to work out an arrangement. In essence, Flacko is to assume the responsibility of training the Indians at Rus Rus. Supposedly the Council of Elders will agree to this...
>
> Flacko has been working on getting the support of some of the Cuban community, including: the Cuban legion and Joe Contine (sp?) [sic]; the Brigade; the Cuban Independent Movement, which is Monto's group; and Alpha 66. He hopes this support will be both financial and manpower.
>
> Flacko's long term goal is to build up the Miskito and train them to the point where they can start taking land. The area he wants them to concentrate on is where there is a port and where one of the operating gold mines is. The ultimate plan is to open the port and take the gold mine. Once the port is open a boat would sail from Miami directly to the port with men and supplies, drop them off and take out the gold which is captured.
>
> Flacko is also setting himself up to be the one who handles all financial support to the Miskitos. Thus everything going to them in terms of support from groups in the U.S.

goes through him. He and his buddy Tieador then have an opportunity to make a little on the side...

All this is being done under the guise of CMA...Flacko met with the Honduran consul in Miami today and he is supposed to be going back to Honduras in the next day or so to ensure Flacko and his people can get in on Monday.

Owen went on to discuss possible ways of getting Terrell out of the picture, including having him arrested:

Would seem a good idea to deal with Flacko as soon as possible. Probably will not be scared off as he believes he has done nothing to violate the neutrality act. If he is held probably will still move forward after he is let out, unless he can be locked up for a good long time. Best bet might be to dry up his funds, have someone talk to him about National Security and put the word out that he is not to be touched. But, if possible it might be wise to do this in some way that doesn't ruin whatever pr potential CMA has for the good of the cause.

Posey has been doing the best he can to either sit on Flacko or deal him out, but that is not possible because right now Flacko knows too much and it would do no one any good if he went to the press. He has got to be finessed out.[20]

Terrell and Owen shared the view that many contra leaders saw the war as a business. Terrell complained of Indian families going without while the families of FDN commanders came "from their leased houses in Tegoose [Tegucigalpa]" to pick up canned goods donated by Miami Cubans "like they were shopping at Safeway." Terrell's assessment of the contra leadership was cutting: "Whatever you want to call this operation in Honduras, Costa Rica, and Nicaragua, the closest thing that the [contra] leadership have to a combat situation is when they put on their pinstripe uniforms and come to Washington to do combat for money...You've got estimates ranging between five thousand and thirty thousand tough contra soldiers on this border, yet they hold not an inch of dirt. The only progress they've made is in purchasing condominiums...Bottom line it's business."[21]

The plan to seize the mines and the port of Puerto Cabezas was not a Terrell rogue action, but a plan advocated by North. On April 11, 1985, North informed McFarlane of future operations, including: "a major ground operation against the mines complex in the vicinity of Siuna, Bonanza, and La Rosita (Nicaragua)—the purpose of the operation is to secure the principal lines of communication in and out of Puerto Cabezas."[22]

North repeatedly advocated plans to seize Puerto Cabezas, declare a provisional government and divide Nicaragua as a prelude to conquering it. He impressed contra donor William O'Boyle in March 1986 by telling him of a "secret plan" to overthrow the Nicaraguan government that would involve a U.S. naval blockade and contra seizure of territory for a provisional government. North said that if Congress did not approve new contra funding the plan would proceed quickly as a "last ditch" effort. With funding, it would proceed "on a slower time schedule, giving the contras more time to consolidate their position."[23]

On May 2, 1986, North informed Poindexter that the contras were preparing to launch a major offensive to capture a "principal coastal population center" (Puerto Cabezas) and proclaim independence. If so, said North, "the rest of the world will wait to see what we do—recognize the new territory—and UNO as the govt—or evacuate them as in a Bay of Pigs."

Not surprisingly, North advocated that the United States back the contras. According to Elliott Abrams, the plan was discussed in the RIG, but rejected. Abrams acknowledged he might have indicated to North that he supported the plan, but claimed he never took the idea seriously: "It was totally implausible and not doable."[24] In December 1987, contra forces would try and fail to capture Siuna, Bonanza and La Rosita.

Bluffs and Suits

Terrell was "dealt out" in March 1985. He was picked up by Honduran authorities on March 15 and put on a plane for Miami. Since then, he has told his story to government and nongovernment investigators and been a critic of continued U.S. aid to the contras. Whatever the limits to Terrell's credibility, he knew enough to concern Owen and North.

North tried to muzzle Terrell in 1986 using the FBI and Enterprise security man Glenn Robinette, a retired CIA technical services employee working as a security consultant. Robinette posed as an attorney interested in collaborating with Terrell on a book, movie and television project. In mid 1986, the FBI received (dis)information from a "classified source" that pro-Sandinista individuals might be contemplating the assassination of President Reagan. Terrell was set up as an FBI suspect in the alleged threat.

At North's suggestion, Robinette became an FBI informer. Robinette briefed FBI Associate Director Oliver "Buck" Revell, who discussed Terrell with the White House Sub-Group of the Terrorist Incident Working Group (OSG/TIWG). North prepared a memo for Poindexter to send Reagan titled "Terrorist Threat: Terrell."[25] North himself was interviewed by the FBI and said he had heard that Terrell tried to import guns from Miami into a Central American country. At the same time, "North stated that neither he nor his staff are responsible for funding, arming, or administrating Contra programs" and denied he was "involved with any covert operations being run in the United States." The FBI reportedly dropped its investigation of Terrell after agents surveilled him and concluded he was not a threat.[26]

Meanwhile, the investigation by Martha Honey and Tony Avirgan was progressing, much to the dismay of contra supporters. In October 1985, after Honey and Avirgan published the results of their initial investigation, John Hull sued them for libel in Costa Rica, denying that he worked with the CIA. In May 1986, a Costa Rican judge threw out Hull's complaint after two days of testimony that did more to substantiate the Honey and Avirgan case than discredit it. Hull appealed and lost again.

On May 29, 1986, the Christic Institute, a Washington-based public interest law firm, filed a civil law suit, brought under the Racketeer Influenced and Corrupt Organizations (RICO) Act, on behalf of Honey and Avirgan in U.S. District Court in

Miami. The suit, amended in December 1986, named 29 defendants as conspiring in a broad racketeering enterprise to assassinate Pastora and smuggle guns and drugs in illegal pursuit of the contra war. The defendants are John Hull, Adolfo Calero, Robert Owen, Richard Secord, Albert Hakim, Thomas Clines, Theodore Shackley, Rafael Quintero, John Singlaub, Tom Posey, Bruce Jones, Rene Corbo [Corvo], Felipe Vidal, Francisco Chanes, Pablo Escobar, Jorge Ochoa, Moises Dagoberto Nunez, Ramon Cecilio Palacio, Ricardo Gris, William Gris, Roger Lee Pallais, Hector Cornillot, Jorge Gonzales, Alvaro Cruz, Frederico Saenz, Mario Delamico, James McCoy, Ronald Martin and Amac Galil. (While the lawsuit is valuable, the Christic Institute's concept of a rogue "Secret Team" conspiracy driving U.S. foreign policy is mistaken.)

At the time the suit was filed, few Americans had heard of most of the defendants and few observers took the suit seriously. Richard Secord, however, had hired Glenn Robinette in late March 1986 to investigate Honey and Avirgan. He directed Robinette to find out any "dirt." Robinette was paid $4,000 a month plus expenses from April to December 1986; he received additional payment in March 1987 and continued investigating into April. Thousands of dollars in expense money was used for bribes in Costa Rica. "I spread it out down there," said Robinette, paying people "for what I wanted to know."[27]

Although Robinette acknowledged discussing the Honey and Avirgan suit with Owen and Quintero as well as Secord, he has denied knowledge of the contra supply operation under the NSC-run "Project Democracy." In a July 26, 1986 memo to Poindexter, however, North referred to Robinette as a Project Democracy security officer. In April 1986, Secord asked Robinette to install a security system at North's residence. The installation, contracted out to former CIA colleagues in Vatech and another company called Autodoor, was completed in July. Later, North and Robinette tried unsuccessfully to cover up the illegal gift with phony bills.

With the Iran-contra scandal some of the Christic suit defendants became household names. Still, much information was being suppressed, notably in the area of drug smuggling.

Drug Propaganda

The only Nicaragua drug connection the administration wanted publicized, was the one it invented about Sandinista cocaine. Seeded with leaks from anonymous U.S. officials and intelligence sources, that story broke in the *Washington Times* on July 17, 1984 and was embellished in the major media.[28]

Drugs became a staple in the administration's anti-Sandinista propaganda diet, pushed yet again by President Reagan in his March 1986 nationally-televised address to win $100 million for the contras: "I know every American parent concerned about the drug problem will be outraged to learn that top Nicaraguan government officials are deeply involved in drug trafficking." Reagan displayed a blurry photo: "This picture, secretly taken at a military airfield outside Managua, shows Federico Vaughan, a top aide to one of the nine Comandantes who rule Nicaragua, loading an aircraft with illegal narcotics bound for the United States…No, there seems to be no crime to which the Sandinistas will not stoop—this is an outlaw regime."[29]

The White House source for the Sandinista connection was a millionaire drug smuggler named Adler Berriman (Barry) Seal. In March 1984, facing a lengthy jail term for a narcotics conviction, Seal made a final effort to turn informer with an appeal to Vice President Bush's anti-drug task force (prosecutors in Florida and Louisiana had turned him down). Through the Bush task force's intervention, Seal went undercover for the DEA's operation against Jorge Ochoa and the Colombian cartel.

Seal told a Miami grand jury in July 1984 that he had learned Nicaragua was a transit point for drug shipments and the site of a proposed cocaine processing lab. He claimed to have flown 1,500 kilos of cocaine from Colombia to Managua, where Ochoa had instructed him to refuel on the way to the United States. According to Seal, the plane was mistakenly hit shortly after takeoff by Nicaraguan antiaircraft fire so a Nicaraguan official stashed the coke for later pick up. The CIA put a hidden camera in the C-123 cargo plane Seal used to transport the cocaine on June 24. The photos allegedly show Vaughan, Colombian drug smuggler Pablo Escobar and men dressed in civilian clothes, said to be Sandinista soldiers, loading duffel bags packed with cocaine onto the C-123 at a military airstrip outside Managua. Seal completed the sting mission when he landed the C-123 at Homestead Air Force Base in Florida.

U.S. officials called Vaughan an aide to Interior Minister Tomas Borge and implicated Defense Minister Humberto Ortega by claiming Seal landed at the "military airfield" at Los Brasiles. The Nicaraguan government identified Vaughan as the deputy manager of a state-run export-import company during 1982-1983 who had left well before the Seal operation; he was not an aide to Borge.

Miami-based DEA agent Robert Joura said the DEA was disappointed when the story leaked, as it threatened the larger operation against the Colombian cartel. "When the C.I.A. asked if they could put a camera in the plane, it didn't seem like a big deal. But whoever ended up with the photo felt what they were doing with the *contras* was more important than our work. Maybe certain people weren't being forthright with us from the beginning."[30]

Jonathan Kwitny reviewed the Nicaragua drug story in April 1987 for the *Wall Street Journal*: the DEA "says the cocaine on Mr. Seal's C-123 is the only drug shipment by way of Nicaragua that it knows of—and Mr. Seal said he had brought it there to begin with. The Nicaragua 'military airfield' that officials said Mr. Seal flew from is in fact a civilian field used chiefly for crop-dusting flights, the State Department now concedes." Richard Gregorie, the chief assistant U.S. attorney in Miami, who supervised Seal's work as an informer, "says he could find no information beyond Mr. Seal's word tying any Nicaraguan official to the drug shipment. As for Federico Vaughan…federal prosecutors and drug officials now say they aren't sure who he is."[31]

Thanks to his CIA-DEA work, Seal got off on his prior drug charges with six months probation. But the probation stipulated that he spend nights—unarmed—in a Baton Rouge, Louisiana Salvation Army shelter. Seal was machinegunned to death as he parked his car there on February 19, 1986, allegedly to keep him from testifying against Jorge Ochoa. In May 1987, three Colombians were convicted of Seal's murder in a U.S. court.[32]

Associates of Seal have said he assisted the contra supply program. One said he flew DC-6s from Ilopango Air Base in El Salvador to the Aguacate contra base in Honduras. Others are vague as to whether Seal flew himself "or simply assisted in connecting planes with pilots for the secret flights."[33]

There's less mystery about the C-123 Seal used in the Nicaragua sting. Southern Air Transport became the C-123's owner in March 1986. In October, it was shot down over Nicaragua while making a supply run for the contras. Eugene Hasenfus was the sole survivor.

The Contra Connection

Stories on the contra drug connection were few and far between. A groundbreaking piece by Brian Barger and Robert Parry ran on December 17, 1985 over the Associated Press Spanish wire, apparently by mistake. An editor there called up the latest draft of the story on computer and ran it without checking if it was cleared for publication; it was not. Barger and Parry were still struggling with their editors who were engaged in the kind of self-censorship that goes on regularly in the American press. The Spanish version referred to Brigade 2506 and John Hull in its discussion of contra cocaine smuggling through Costa Rica and carried a denial from Hull, who called the charges "communist disinformation." The English-language version, which ran on December 20, dropped Hull from the story.

Barger, as reported in the *Columbia Journalism Review*, recalled hearing about contra drug smuggling the previous March. "His sources, he says, were concerned that if the drug trafficking was discovered, the Reagan administration would be set back in its efforts to obtain more military funding for the rebels...'Later, Bob [Parry] and I found that officials from several [U.S.] law enforcement agencies were looking into the charges, and there was a feeling that their reports were going into a vacuum. Eventually, they began talking with us.' "[34]

Unfortunately, the major media created a contra drug vacuum almost as effective as the administration's. The *New York Times* did not pick up the December 1985 Associated Press story; the *Washington Post*, after some delay, buried it inside.

Another story broke in March 1986, this time in the *San Francisco Examiner*. Seth Rosenfeld reported that "a major Bay Area cocaine ring helped to finance the contra rebels." Julio Zavala and Carlos Cabezas, convicted in connection with a 1983 cocaine seizure considered the biggest in West Coast history, testified to financing contra groups with cocaine profits. Prosecutors actually returned $36,020 seized as drug money after two contra leaders claimed it was given to Zavala to do political work in the United States. A letter signed by Francisco Aviles and Vicente Rappaccioli of the Conservative Party of Nicaraguans in Exile stated that Zavala "is a member of the Conservative party as assistant treasurer and is located in the United States of North America promoting the reinstatement of democracy in Nicaragua, for which mission he received forty-five thousand dollars in cash, on the last week of January 1983, in San Jose, Costa Rica." Another letter stated that Zavala was a longtime member of the UDN-FARN.

Zavala told the *San Francisco Examiner* that Aviles handled funds for FARN leader Fernando "El Negro" Chamorro and "that he delivered to Aviles a total of about $500,000, mostly from cocaine profits. Much of this was collected from other cocaine smugglers in Miami, New Orleans and the Bay Area." He explained "some were idealistic, but others only wanted to curry favor with contra forces that had power in the region and might one day rule Nicaragua." Zavala also said that in fall 1982 he arranged a Bay Area deal for grenades and machine guns for El Negro's forces. As for Carlos Cabezas, an attorney, he said he worked with the UDN-FARN and ARDE.[35]

William Walker, deputy assistant secretary of state for Inter-American affairs, acknowledged that "one or two" mid-level contras may have "succumbed to temptation" and engaged in drug smuggling. He said, "Those people have essentially been told to knock it off by their commanders."[36]

The *New York Times* carried an Associated Press story on April 11 describing a federal investigation into gunrunning and drug trafficking by contras and supporters. The investigation, run out of the U.S. Attorney's office for southern Florida, had undertaken FBI interviews with Jack Terrell, Steven Carr and others. It was stalled by a Justice Department-White House coverup (described in chapter 14).

On May 7, the *New York Times* ran a piece titled "Contras Cleared on Gunrunning." As happens all too often, the *Times* acted as a platform for administration disinformation, in this case designed to help with passage of the $100 million in requested contra aid. Referring to the Florida investigation into gunrunning and drug trafficking, a senior Justice Department official was quoted, "There just ain't any evidence…We ran down all the allegations and didn't find anything"—except "a single individual who may have been involved with maybe a dozen guns."

The next month, the *San Francisco Examiner* reported another contra drug connection, this one involving Norwin Meneses (reportedly the brother of Somoza's chief of police for Managua),[37] described in a confidential 1984 DEA report as "the apparent head of a criminal organization responsible for smuggling kilogram quantities of cocaine into the United States." Meneses, who met several times with Adolfo Calero and Enrique Bermudez in Honduras, hosted FDN fundraisers in California. He also employed FDN members in his drug business, among them Renato Pena-Cabrera, the FDN's San Francisco spokesperson, convicted of cocaine possession in 1985.[38]

In late August, after the $100 million had been approved by both chambers of Congress, the administration released a report, *Allegations of Drug Trafficking and the Nicaraguan Democratic Resistance.* It acknowledged some evidence of drug trafficking by Pastora associates while covering up for the favored FDN-UNO: There "has been no evidence that organizations associated with the major resistance umbrella group [UNO] have participated in or benefited from drug trafficking."[39]

CBS' "West 57th" ran two segments on contra drug connections in April and

July 1987, interviewing drug smugglers George Morales, Gary Betzner and Mike Tolliver, and money launderer Ramon Milian Rodriguez, all convicted on charges unrelated to their contra activities. Milian Rodriguez laundered $200 million a month through his Panama-based operation for a clientele including Pablo Escobar and Jorge Ochoa. His mentor in the money-laundering business was Manuel Artime, a Bay of Pigs political leader. Milian Rodriguez arranged $200,000 payments for each of the Cuban burglars jailed for their part in the "Plumbers" unit caught in the 1972 Watergate break-in.[40] One of those burglars, Eugenio Rolando Martinez, reportedly a close friend of Felix Rodriguez and Luis Posada, was pardoned by President Reagan in 1981.[41]

Milian Rodriguez said that in the mid 1970s he arranged for the covert delivery of $30 million to $40 million from the CIA to Somoza.[42] Somoza's 1980 assassination in Paraguay may have been linked to drug smuggling. According to historian Thomas Walker, "though the government of Paraguayan dictator Alfredo Stroessner subsequently captured or killed several Argentine 'terrorists' who it claimed responsible for the killing, circumstantial evidence points to the involvement of high-ranking officers in Stroessner's own military who may have been upset at Somoza's alleged effort to elbow his way into the lucrative drug smuggling business previously dominated by these officers."[43]

Milian Rodriguez said he laundered $10 million from the Colombian cartel to the contras from late 1982 through 1985. In secret, sworn testimony to the Senate Foreign Relations Subcommittee on Terrorism, Narcotics and International Operations, Milian Rodriguez claimed that he had been solicited by his old friend Felix Rodriguez and that Adolfo Calero was one of the cash recipients: "Felix would call me with instructions on where to send the money." (Felix Rodriguez has acknowledged that Milian Rodriguez was an old friend, but denied asking for drug money.)

According to Milian Rodriguez, Felix Rodriguez called in late 1984 for help in laundering cash from about a dozen Miami companies to the contras. For one of the companies, Ocean Hunter, he moved about $200,000 a month in cash through a designated courier. Ocean Hunter shipped frozen shrimp from Costa Rica to Florida and reportedly smuggled cocaine in the shrimp containers. It was at the house of Ocean Hunter partner Paco Chanes that Steven Carr saw three kilos of cocaine—allegedly part of a larger 350 kilo shipment—along with contra weapons.[44]

Ocean Hunter is affiliated with a Costa Rican shrimp firm called Frigorificos de Puntarenas which received a contract from NHAO. As Leslie Cockburn summarized it, "The NHAO account, established at the Consolidated Bank in Miami, had three signatories, Chanes himself, Luis Rodriguez, and a Costa Rican partner, Moises Dagoberto Nunez. 'Dago' Nunez is a Cuban American and friend of John Hull's. Between January and May of 1986 this trio received no less than $231,587 of U.S. taxpayers' money. Some of the money was in turn paid out to accounts in Israel and South Korea...at a time when the two countries were reportedly supplying arms to the contras."[45]

Robert Owen was selected by NHAO to oversee the Frigorificos contract, which was designated for nonlethal aid to the Kisan Atlantic Coast forces. Owen reportedly picked up a fraudulent receipt for uniforms and boots from the Creaciones Fancy

Store in San Jose. Instead, $15,000 in NHAO/Frigorificos money was spent on guns and ammunition.[46]

Owen, as mentioned in the previous chapter, reported to North on suspected drug smuggling by southern front leaders at least as early as April 1, 1985. After talking with Owen on August 9, 1985, North wrote in his notebook: "DC-6 which is being used for [contra supply] runs out of New Orleans is probably being used for drug runs into U.S."[47] On February 10, 1986, Owen wrote a memo to North that appears particularly ironic in light of his own apparently informed ties to Paco Chanes and other operatives in the contra drug connection: "No doubt you know the DC-4 Foley got was used at one time to run drugs, and part of the crew had criminal records. Nice group the Boys [CIA] choose. The company is also one that Mario [Calero] has been involved with using in the past, only they had a quick name change. Incompetence reins [sic]."[48] Foley refers to Patrick Foley, a former CIA operative working for Summit Aviation, the CIA-affiliated company involved in supplying planes to the contras.[49]

George Morales is a powerboat racing champion and cocaine smuggler jailed in June 1986. According to Morales, in spring 1984, contra-CIA operative Octaviano Cesar offered to stall his indictment or get it dropped if he would donate $250,000 every three months to the contras, train pilots and put his planes at the contras' disposal. Prior to that Morales had bought and leased contra safe houses in Miami. Morales said he donated a total of $3 million in cash—$400,000 of it picked up with Cesar at a Bahamas bank in October 1984. Cesar switched his allegiance from Pastora to the FDN and, by August 1984, Morales' pilots were reportedly ferrying guns to John Hull's ranch and bringing out drugs on the return trip. Hull was allegedly paid $300,000 per flight.[50]

A Morales pilot, Gary Betzner, claimed to have taken "two loads—small aircraft loads—of weapons to John Hull's ranch in Costa Rica and returned to Florida with approximately a thousand kilos of cocaine, five hundred each trip." It was Betzner's understanding "that it wasn't the private guns that went down that were that important; it was what was coming back. That could buy much larger and better and more sophisticated weapons, and it was unaccounted-for cash."[51] According to at least two pilots—Geraldo Duran and "Tosh"—the Enterprise's Santa Elena airstrip was also used for drug running.[52]

Pilot Michael Tolliver had many years of experience flying guns and drugs when he received a call in August 1985 from Barry Seal. Through Seal's contacts, Tolliver said he met a Mr. "Hernandez," who introduced him to Rafael Quintero in December 1985 to discuss flight arrangements (Quintero told Tolliver to cut off contact with Seal in January 1986). In March 1986, Tolliver flew a DC-6 loaded with guns and ammunition from Butler Aviation at the Miami Airport down to Aguacate Air Base in Honduras, where contras unloaded the plane. Tolliver said he was paid $70,000 to $75,000 for flying the arms by "Hernandez," who Tolliver believes to be Felix Rodriguez.

After a three-day layover, Tolliver said he flew the aircraft, reloaded with over 25,000 pounds of marijuana, as a "nonscheduled military flight" into Homestead Air Force Base near Miami. "We landed about one-thirty, two o'clock in the morning," said Tolliver, "and a little blue truck came out and met us. [It] had a little white sign on it that said 'Follow Me' with flashing lights. We followed it."

"I was a little taken aback," Tolliver recalled for "West 57th." "I figured it was a setup, or it was a DEA bust or a sting or something like that." It wasn't. Tolliver said he left the marijuana and took a taxi from the base.[53]

"West 57th" traced the DC-6 to a company called Vortex, which had received an NHAO contract in February 1986 for $96,961 to ship "humanitarian" supplies to the contras. The contract was signed by Vortex Vice President Mike Palmer who, in 1985, had been jailed in Colombia for drug smuggling. In June 1986, Palmer was charged with conspiracy and drug possession in Detroit. By then he was a Customs and DEA informant. In September 1987, he participated in a sting operation netting the "biggest drug bust in Michigan's history"—piloting a DC-6 from Colombia with $44 million worth of cocaine and marijuana seized by narcotics agents outside Detroit.[54]

In April 1987, a Customs Service official told the *Boston Globe* that Tolliver's story had "credibility. We think he did land at Homestead." But the official described Tolliver as a "free-lancer," who "bluffed his way" through the system whereby CIA-arranged contra flights were able to fly in and out of U.S. airports free of Customs inspections. It was not explained how Tolliver bluffed his way into an *Air Force* base, leaving behind over 25,000 pounds of marijuana that apparently bluffed their way out.

Customs said that 50 to 100 flights had gone through without inspection in the two years prior to April 1987. That is an interesting admission, given the various restrictions on CIA contra assistance before fall 1986. The Customs official tried to squeeze the flights through the loophole for CIA communications exchange: "We presumed the agency was shipping radio equipment and the like down there and it was best not to have inspectors going through the cargo."[55]

By early fall 1986, the DEA office in Guatemala had uncovered "convincing evidence" that American contra supply crews were involved in smuggling cocaine and marijuana. A crew member used North's name and warned he had White House protection when DEA agents searched his house in San Salvador. After the contra supply operation collapsed in the wake of the Hasenfus crash, the drug investigation was not actively pursued.[56]

In July 1987, Nicaraguan exile Leticia Thomas-Altamirano was convicted in Milwaukee as a member of a cocaine trafficking conspiracy that allegedly supported the contras. Her fugitive brother Detlaf Thomas had earlier told an undercover federal narcotics agent that he was working for the contras, providing them 75 percent of his cocaine profits.[57]

These are just some of the links—some more substantiated at present than others—in the contra drug connection.[58] Investigations are proceeding at this writing in the House Judiciary Subcommittee on Crime, chaired by William Hughes (D-NJ), and the Senate Foreign Relations Subcommittee on Terrorism, Narcotics and International Operations, chaired by Senator John Kerry (D-MA), which is looking into drug involvement by the Honduran and Panamanian military as well as the contras. "We don't know the extent of the Honduran military's involvement in drugs," said a State Department official. "But our educated guess is that all of the senior officers have knowledge, many are involved...and they are all reaping the profits."[59]

The Iran-contra committees chose to short-circuit the contra connection. There is a potentially explosive Bush connection to the contra drug network (beyond Felix Rodriguez) that will be reviewed in chapter 15.

Stranger than Fiction

The contra drug connection fits a historical pattern of collaboration between covert warriors and gangsters—from the southeast Asian "Golden Triangle" opium-heroin trade; to anti-Castro operations involving Mafia gangsters angered at the loss of their Cuban gambling and prostitution paradise; to the Miami cocaine trade with its Bay of Pigs veterans; to the laundering of drug money through the Nugan Hand Bank, with its old-boy network of spooks and military men; to the heroin-subsidized Afghan resistance.[60]

In his book on the Nugan Hand Bank—another scandal involving Secord, Clines and many others inside and outside the contra network—Jonathan Kwitny recounted a Vietnam War-era event that reveals just how sordid the interlocking drugs and war trade can get: Investigators from the Army's Criminal Investigation Division "were investigating corruption in the sale of supplies to commissioned- and noncommissioned-officers' clubs. The corrupt U.S. and Vietnamese officers they caught tried to bargain away jail terms by describing the heroin traffic involving Vietnamese politicians and senior U.S. officers." The reports checked out.

As one investigator told it, they "filed reports to the Pentagon revealing that G.I. corpses being flown back to the United States were cut open, gutted, and filled with heroin. Witnesses were prepared to testify that the heroin-stuffed soldiers bore coded body numbers, allowing conspiring officers on the other end, at Norton Air Force Base in California, to remove the booty—up to fifty pounds of heroin per dead G.I."

According to the former investigator, the Army "acted on these reports—not by coming down on the dope traffickers, but by disbanding the investigative team and sending them to combat duty." Other reports corroborated the use of G.I. corpses for heroin smuggling via military channels.[61]

As Robert Owen told the Iran-contra committees, regarding his role as an NSC courier and bagman, "we used to joke that truth is always stranger than fiction. In this case, it is true."[62]

13

Contadora, Contradora

The Central American area down to and including the isthmus of Panama constitutes a legitimate sphere of influence for the United States…Our ministers accredited to the five little republics stretching from the Mexican border to Panama…have been advisers whose advice has been accepted virtually as law in the capitals where they respectively reside…

We do control the destinies of Central America, and we do so for the simple reason that the national interest absolutely dictates such a course…Until now Central America has always understood that governments which we recognize and support stay in power, while those which we do not recognize and support fall. Nicaragua has become a test case.

Undersecretary of State Robert Olds,
"Confidential Memorandum on the Nicaragua Situation," 1927.

Sixty years after Sandino battled the U.S. marines, Nicaragua is again a test case of U.S. control. It is also a test case for a new era of Latin American independence. In Foreign Minister Miguel D'Escoto's words, "Unless and until the United States embarks on a serious process of reevaluation of what constitutes its vital interests and unless in a new listing of its vital interests it excludes the controlling of the political, social and economic destiny of each country in Latin America, we are going to continue with difficulties."[1]

About two decades ago, Chile's Foreign Minister Gabriel Valdes, a Christian Democrat, gave an unwelcome lesson in North-South inequities to President Richard Nixon. Valdes explained that for every dollar in U.S. aid, Latin America was exporting $3.80 in return. Valdes remembered National Security Adviser Henry Kissinger "looking at me as if I were a strange animal." At a meeting the next day, Kissinger

rebuked Valdes, "You come here speaking of Latin America, but this is not important. Nothing important can come from the South. History has never been produced
in the South."[2]

U.S. officials still see Nicaragua as "an appendix to North American history,"
Vice President Sergio Ramirez told me. The United States, he said, wants "to isolate
Nicaragua, to make us appear as a political project that has nothing to do with the
interests of Latin American countries," as a "very strange" thing linked with Soviet
interests. But "the situation is very different from the one we had in the sixties, when,
for the United States, it was very easy to get Latin American countries to isolate
Cuba...Now we have a real opportunity to confront the United States with the Latin
American position."[3] Contadora embodies that opportunity.

In January 1983, the foreign ministers of Mexico, Colombia, Panama and
Venezuela launched their quest for Central American peace from the Panamanian
island of Contadora. It was an appropriate site because the Panama Canal treaty had
been a symbol of Latin American solidarity in the seventies. As D'Escoto explained,
Panamanian leader Omar Torrijos (killed in a suspicious plane crash in 1981) made
the struggle for sovereignty over the Canal "a Latin American cause" and all Latin
American governments felt a "certain pride because they had managed to get something as a result of this unity."[4] President Carlos Andres Perez of Venezuela called
the treaty, "the most significant advance in political affairs in the Western Hemisphere in this century."[5]

The Canal treaty holds a key to understanding the U.S. response to Contadora.
The so-called DeConcini Condition to the treaty states that "if the Canal is closed,
or its operations are interfered with, [the United States and Panama shall each] have
the right to take such steps as each deems necessary...including the use of military
force in the Republic of Panama."[6] The treaty thus preserved perpetual U.S. authority
to intervene unilaterally in the Americas.

U.S. control of Latin American destiny was challenged successfully at the June
1979 OAS meeting when members rejected the Carter administration proposal to intervene militarily in Nicaragua. Contadora would institutionalize that unprecedented
constraint. Three years after that historic OAS meeting, came a more profound shock
to the Inter-American system. In the spring of 1982, when Argentina attempted to
assert its sovereignty over the Malvinas Islands (Falklands), the United States outraged Latin Americans by siding with Britain, an "extra-hemispheric" power, in the
ensuing war. It taught Latin America a lesson on the limits of cooperation with the
United States given Argentina's support of the contras.

Latin America was ready for new initiatives in regional cooperation outside
the parameters of the traditional U.S.-dominated Inter-American system. In the words
of Guadalupe Gonzales, director of the International Affairs program of the Mexican
Center for Economic Investigation and Training (CIDE), Contadora was the "first
historical pilot program" of a new style of regional coordination.[7]

An Urgent Appeal

At their January 1983 peace summit, the Contadora foreign ministers expressed "their deep concern regarding foreign intervention—direct or indirect—in Central American conflicts" and advised against classifying "such conflicts in the context of an East-West confrontation." They made "an urgent appeal to all Central American countries to reduce tensions and establish a framework for a permanent atmosphere of peaceful existence and mutual respect between nations through dialogue and negotiation." And they "warned all nations to abstain from actions which could worsen the situation and create the danger of a general conflict which could extend throughout the region."[8]

Washington quickly rebuffed Contadora by carrying out the first Big Pine military maneuvers with Honduras, less than ten miles from the Nicaraguan border. By May, President Reagan had publicly embraced the contras as "freedom fighters" and, in a speech to Cuban exiles in Miami, he praised Teddy Roosevelt's Big Stick credo.[9] Secretary of Defense Weinberger freshly staked the U.S. claim to the region, redrawing the map to assert that El Salvador is "on the mainland of the United States" and "we do have responsibility for the defense of the continental United States, over and above all other priorities."[10]

Meeting in Cancun, Mexico the next month, the presidents of the Contadora countries expressed their deep concern for the rapid deterioration of the situation in Central America and stated: "Peace in Central America can become a reality only in so far as respect is shown for the basic principles of coexistence among nations: non-intervention; self-determination; sovereign equality of states; cooperation for economic and social development; peaceful settlement of disputes; and free and authentic expression of the popular will."[11]

Contadora cooperation could be mutually beneficial. Panama sought support from other Latin American countries to protect the transfer of the Canal under President Reagan who had campaigned against the treaty. For Venezuela, an OPEC member, the practice of political bargaining was "seen as an important means for protecting its petroleum, resolving border disputes with Colombia and Guyana, and keeping the United States at bay."[12] Mexico worried about the threat of regional war as well as closer U.S. military ties with Guatemala. As one analyst observed, "The militarization of Central America has deeply exacerbated the Mexican regime's sense of threat to its own sovereignty…While few policymakers openly discuss the possibility of a U.S. intervention in Mexico itself, the thought of U.S. troops on the country's southern flank and close to the oil fields—for whatever purpose—is hardly comforting. As one high official of the Institutional Revolutionary Party (PRI) explained: 'We already share one border with the United States. We do not want to share two.' "[13]

Daniel Ortega backed the Contadora initiative with a six-point peace proposal during a July 19, 1983 speech commemorating the fourth anniversary of the Nicaraguan revolution: 1) sign immediately a nonaggression pact between Nicaragua and Honduras; 2) cut off all arms supplies to El Salvador from any country; 3) stop all military aid to forces opposed to any Central American government; 4) guarantee respect for the right of self-determination of Central American countries and nonintervention in domestic affairs of each country; 5) stop economic discrimination or hostility against any Central American country; 6) prohibit foreign military bases in Central America and suspend all military maneuvers that involve foreign armies.[14]

When Nicaragua first entered the Contadora process it desired a series of bilateral nonaggression pacts with the United States and other Central American countries, following up on Mexico's 1982 initiatives. Honduras, in contrast, adopted the Reagan administration position opposing bilateral negotiations and proposing that all regional issues be negotiated multilaterally and simultaneously, "a negotiating process in which the United States could exercise an effective veto (albeit by proxy)."[15] To prevent the Contadora process from collapsing over procedural issues, Nicaragua made a major concession and accepted the multilateral negotiating framework.

The United States, meanwhile, proceeded with plans to hold naval maneuvers just off Nicaragua's Caribbean coast as well as Big Pine II maneuvers with Honduras. "We've virtually slapped the Contadora group across the head," protested Senator Christopher Dodd. Ambassador Quainton refused to rule out a possible naval "quarantine" of Nicaragua.[16]

On September 9, 1983, the Contadora Group and five Central American countries—Nicaragua, El Salvador, Honduras, Costa Rica and Guatemala—endorsed a "Document of Objectives" with 21 Basic Points for Peace in Central America covering political, security and economic issues. Three days later, Undersecretary of Defense Fred Ikle endorsed a military solution: "We do not seek a military defeat for our friends. We do not seek a military stalemate. We seek victory for the forces of democracy...We must prevent consolidation of a Sandinista regime in Nicaragua...If we cannot prevent that, we have to anticipate the partition of Central America. Such a development would then force us to man a new military front-line of the East-West conflict, right here on our continent."[17]

Washington encouraged the military leaders of Honduras, Guatemala and El Salvador to reactivate CONDECA, the Central American Defense Council. On October 25, the United States invaded Grenada, coating the Big Stick with a veneer of collective defense. A majority of OAS members voted to censure the United States. The Contadora process became more urgent.

"Drop Dead or We'll Kill You"

All versions of the Contadora treaty have addressed stated U.S. security concerns with detailed provisions for withdrawal of foreign military advisers and elimination of foreign military bases; prohibition of aid to irregular forces or armed bands seeking to overthrow or destabilize other governments; restriction of military maneuvers; and limits on military personnel and armaments. Treaty compliance mechanisms have been strengthened systematically to include an International Corps of Inspectors and a Verification and Control Commission. The treaty also commits the signers to undertake measures for national reconciliation, including genuine amnesties, and to establish or enhance democratic political systems with free elections, civil liberties and respect for human rights.

The Contadora system of collective security contrasts starkly with the U.S. concept of "collective self-defense" rejected by the World Court. Contadora would hold the United States accountable, not only to international law, but to an autonomous treaty system.

Aiming to sabotage Contadora at the least political cost to the United States and the greatest cost to Nicaragua, the Reagan administration employed a three-part strategy: paying public tribute to the Contadora process in order to coopt Congress and paint Nicaragua as the intransigent party; pressuring Contadora countries to realign their policies with U.S. objectives; and pressuring Central American allies to oppose restrictions on U.S. actions and isolate Nicaragua—vetoing treaty drafts when Nicaragua approved and professing support when Nicaragua required changes.

An April 1983 NSC Summary Paper secretly stated the U.S. position of "co-opting cut-and-run negotiating strategies by demonstrating a reasonable but firm approach to negotiations and compromise on our terms." Compromise *on our terms* means capitulation by Nicaragua. Washington's position was, in D'Escoto's words, "Drop dead or we'll kill you." If Nicaragua would not negotiate surrender, then the United States would force concessions in the Contadora process while blocking a final treaty from being enacted. Said one State Department official, "The U.S. would like to go on supporting Contadora as long as nothing happens."[18]

The administration agreed in May 1984 to open talks with Nicaragua at the behest of Mexican President Miguel de la Madrid. In return, de la Madrid agreed to upgrade relations with El Salvador under newly elected President Jose Napoleon Duarte. The Nicaragua negotiations also served important domestic political purposes: mollifying Congress in the wake of the mining scandal, easing public fears of "another Vietnam" and undercutting the Democrats during the 1984 presidential campaign.

Mexico was the focus of a behind-the-scenes dispute leading to the resignation of the CIA's senior national intelligence officer for Latin America, John Horton. Casey had insisted that Horton revise an intelligence report on Mexico to portray its economic and political problems as a threat to Mexican stability and an indirect danger to Central American and U.S. security. When Horton refused, contending that intelligence data did not support that alarmist conclusion, Casey had another analyst rewrite it. As Horton put it later, there was "pressure from Casey on subjects that are politically sensitive to jigger [intelligence] estimates to conform with policy."

According to administration officials, Casey wanted a tougher report "to help persuade the White House to approve a program of covert and economic American pressures on Mexico to induce its support for United States policies in Central America." President Reagan reportedly rejected such a program at that time because Mexico appeared to be lessening its support for Nicaragua and the Salvadoran revolutionaries.[19] Mexico was nonetheless subject to various forms of pressure to pull back from Contadora, stop supplying Nicaragua with oil and otherwise ally itself with U.S. policy in Central America. As one administration official explained, "It is not usually done in a direct manner. We deal more effectively with Mexico indirectly." In one concrete case, "the U.S. Agriculture Department passed word to its counterpart in Mexico City that the State Department was blocking an agreement for exporting Mexican fruits and vegetables because of Nicaragua."[20]

Trumping Nicaragua

Fall 1984 should have been a turning point toward peace, capped by the Boland amendment and the Contadora treaty. Instead, the Reagan administration wrought more war and lawlessness.

Nicaragua agreed to sign the Contadora treaty on September 7, 1984. El Salvador, Costa Rica and Honduras had all indicated their preliminary approval. Washington coached its proxies to backpedal from the treaty summit as if it were the edge of a cliff.

"It is important to note," wrote analysts Jim Morrell and William Goodfellow, "that Secretary Shultz, while stating reservations about verification and timing procedures, had called the treaty 'an important step forward,' one that 'presents many positive elements.' Only after Nicaragua accepted it did it become 'unsatisfactory' and 'one-sided.' "[21] And only after Nicaragua agreed to sign was the treaty downplayed as a draft. Diplomats from the four Contadora countries insisted that "everyone has treated it as a final document," including U.S. officials.[22] Senior U.S. officials discussed denying Ortega a visa to visit Los Angeles, following that year's UN General Assembly meeting, partly to "punish Mr. Ortega and the Sandinistas for accepting the Contadora peace proposal."[23]

A secret NSC background paper of October 30, 1984 proclaimed: "We have trumped the latest Nicaraguan/Mexican efforts to rush signature of an unsatisfactory Contadora agreement...Following intensive U.S. consultations with El Salvador, Honduras, and Costa Rica," this so-called Tegucigalpa bloc submitted a counterdraft on October 20 that "reflects many of our concerns and shifts the focus within Contadora to a document broadly consistent with U.S. interests." Washington sought to isolate Nicaragua from the so-called Core Four: El Salvador, Honduras, Costa Rica and Guatemala, whose position was less reliable. As the NSC document noted, "The uncertain support of Guatemala for the Core Four is a continuing problem...We will continue to exert strong pressure on Guatemala to support the basic Core Four position."[24]

The Tegucigalpa draft deleted the ban on foreign military exercises in the region as well as the requirement for removal of foreign bases within six months. Only the United States (among foreign countries) actually had bases and conducted military maneuvers in the region. The new draft also weighted the verification commission against Nicaragua by adding the five Central American countries (mostly U.S. dependencies); four impartial outside countries would be chosen by the Contadora Group. And it dropped the final protocol, open to signature by all countries "desiring to contribute to peace and cooperation in Central America" by agreeing not to "thwart the aims and purpose of the act." The State Department objected to the protocol on the grounds that it admitted a political role in Central America for the Soviet Union and Cuba, who would presumably be expected to sign.[25] More importantly, the United States did not want to sign such a protocol itself, in support of a treaty it wanted to avoid.

Reflecting on the changes being sought in the treaty, a Mexican foreign policy analyst observed, "Contadora is not strong enough to impose its will on the United States."[26] In January 1985, the United States broke off negotiations with Nicaragua, claiming that Nicaragua was using them to undermine Contadora. By then, however, a U.S. official had acknowledged "that the Administration doesn't really want a settlement with the Sandinistas." In another official's words, "No one knows whether the United States should invade Nicaragua, but people don't want to foreclose that option by signing some kind of agreement."[27]

Foreigners in "Our Own Backyard"

The September 1985 version of the treaty, drawn up under concerted U.S. pressure, was unacceptable to Nicaragua without revision. Nicaragua accepted 100 of 117 provisions of the new draft; on 17 it called for a return to the 1984 treaty.[28] For example, the new draft replaced the prohibition of international military maneuvers with regulation of allowable maneuvers—maneuvers used by the United States to train for future military action against Nicaragua, supply the contras, strengthen military infrastructure and preposition equipment and troops in the region. Prohibition of military maneuvers and foreign bases, the State Department acknowledged in objecting to the September 1984 treaty, would "reduce our presence and our pressure on Nicaragua."[29] A freeze or moratorium on arms acquisition was unacceptable to Nicaragua without a simultaneous prohibition of foreign military maneuvers.

Nicaragua also demanded that the U.S. role be confronted directly by insisting that a Contadora treaty could not be signed unless the United States showed it was prepared to abide by it. Nicaragua wanted "a halt to the US aggression against Nicaragua in all its forms, including covert assistance delivered through private organizations and individuals to the mercenary forces as well as official aid, and the solemn commitment of the US government to refrain from promoting or permitting similar acts in the future." Nicaragua contended, "As long as the US government does not assume, in a public, clear and responsible manner, an international commitment to not militarily invade Nicaragua, directly or indirectly, the Nicaraguan people have the right to guarantee a level of armaments and of military and paramilitary forces capable of putting them in a position to defend their sovereignty with dignity."[30]

At the December OAS meeting in Cartagena, a Nicaraguan official summarized Nicaragua's position: "We are being asked to disarm without any promise that the war against us will end. If we accept it [the revised treaty], we would be committing suicide."[31] Nicaraguans have a deeply etched historical example of disarming in the face of an armed enemy: the 1934 assassination of Sandino and the slaughter of his followers by the National Guard.

Analysts Morrell and Goodfellow wrote: "Nicaragua's earlier concessions have now limited its room for maneuver. Carried out in the face of an extremely hostile US administration, they would clearly jeopardize Nicaragua's safety. If Nicaragua is now being called intransigent, it is paying the price for going the extra mile earlier in the negotiations."[32]

Nicaragua's objections to asymmetry in the Contadora treaty were the flip side of U.S. objections to symmetry—symmetry between support of the FMLN and the contras, between Nicaragua and its neighbors, and between the U.S. and other foreign countries, principally Cuba and the Soviet Union. As D'Escoto told me, the United States "considers it a terrible affront to be regarded as a foreigner in its own 'backyard.' "[33] (Latin Americans who emigrate to the United States, on the other hand, are characterized as illegal or legal *aliens.*)

A Contadora treaty that compromised on U.S. terms would prohibit *extra-hemispheric* military involvement (prohibiting Cuba as a Soviet ally). It would be a Contadora Corollary to the Monroe Doctrine, preserving perpetual U.S. authority to intervene militarily, perhaps under the guise of "collective self-defense."

"Who Negotiates with a Cancer?"

En route to the December 1985 OAS meeting, Secretary Shultz told reporters, "Our commitment" to the contras "is indefinite." At the meeting he cavalierly rejected the possibility of resuming bilateral talks with Nicaragua, claiming past talks had resulted in a Nicaraguan effort "to undermine" Contadora, "so we don't intend to go back to that."[34]

Lunching with the four Contadora ministers on December 2, Shultz reportedly said that Nicaragua was a "cancer" in Central America requiring a "surgical solution." Moreover, he told them that Soviet leader Mikhail Gorbachev "indicated to President Reagan during last month's summit in Geneva that the Soviet Union would not move to stop a US attack against Nicaragua."[35] As *New York Times* columnist Tom Wicker noted later, "who negotiates with a cancer?"[36]

Shocked by Shultz's remarks, the Contadora nations reunited behind a joint resolution for submittal to the UN General Assembly, calling for new talks between the United States and Nicaragua. The United States had earlier pressured Colombia, Venezuela and Panama to temporarily withdraw their support for the resolution.

There was growing evidence of fatigue among the Contadora countries. Mexico was pulling back from a leading role to concentrate on its domestic economic crisis and work with the United States in debt renegotiations. Colombia had also sought support from the Reagan administration in its negotiations with the International Monetary Fund.[37] On December 7, the Contadora mediation effort was suspended temporarily in response to a Nicaraguan request noting the upcoming transitions of government in Guatemala, Honduras and Costa Rica. Voicing the conventional wisdom, a Western diplomat in Central America said, Contadora is going "into a coma, it's all but dead."[38]

Marco Vinicio Cerezo, the newly elected president of Guatemala, resuscitated Contadora when he toured Central America in December and committed Guatemala to a policy of "active neutrality." Cerezo would not support the U.S. policy of isolating Nicaragua.

On January 12, 1986, the Contadora Group and Support Group of Argentina, Peru, Brazil and Uruguay rebounded with the Carabelleda Message. Together, the Contadora and Support Group countries represent about 90 percent of the population and economic resources of Latin America. Luis Herrera Lassa, director of the Mexican-based Latin American Center for Strategic Studies, described the Support Group, formed in July 1985, as a very significant development. "The Uruguay-Argentina-Brazil rapprochement, starting with the democratization of all three, is something more than a momentary historical identification between these countries…This democratic nucleus of the Southern Cone could be a balancing factor in the hemisphere vis-a-vis the United States," at least on some levels.[39]

Washington saw the Support Group's formation as a threat. In a September 1985 meeting of U.S. officials, Elliott Abrams stated, "it's necessary that we develop an active diplomacy in order to hinder the attempts at Latin American solidarity that could be directed against the U.S. and its allies whether these efforts are initiated by the Support Group, Cuba or Nicaragua."[40]

In his message to the Contadora ministers meeting in Carabelleda in January 1986, host Venezuelan President Jaime Lusinchi rejected the view that Contadora had died: "Contadora has neither died nor can die, because it is more than an ideal for peace: it is a will, a conviction."[41]

According to the Central American Historical Institute, Contadora "had come to a fork in the road: either abandon negotiations or take into account the Nicaraguan thesis, i.e., recognizing that the presence of the US is an essential element in a real solution."[42] The Carabelleda Message called for steps "to establish an atmosphere of mutual trust that will restore the spirit of negotiation," including an end to external support to irregular forces operating in the region, suspension of international military maneuvers and freezing of arms purchases. It offered Contadora's assistance to foster negotiations between the governments of the United States and Nicaragua, asserting that "respectful negotiation between them, with mutual and equitable concessions, is a condition for regional detente."[43]

The Carabelleda principles were reaffirmed at the Central American presidents summit in Guatemala on January 15, on the occasion of Cerezo's inauguration, and again at the Contadora ministers meeting in Punta del Este, Uruguay, in late February. U.S. officials gave rhetorical support for revival of the Contadora process, but insisted the United States would continue to support the contras and refrain from talks with the Nicaraguan government, advocating instead that Nicaragua talk with the contras.

On February 10, the eight Contadora foreign ministers undertook an unprecedented joint mission to Washington. Meeting with Shultz, they urged the administration to halt aid to the contras, back a negotiated settlement and resume direct talks with Nicaragua. Shultz repeated the U.S. position that a resumption of bilateral talks would "undermine Contadora." President Reagan snubbed the Contadora ministers, choosing instead to meet that week with contra leaders.

Shortly after, White House spokesman Larry Speakes was asked if the administration aim was to overthrow the Sandinistas. He replied, "Yes, to be absolutely frank."[44]

In his February 25 request to Congress for $100 million in new contra funding, Reagan claimed, "Our persistent efforts to achieve a peaceful solution have failed to resolve the conflict because Nicaragua has continued to reject meaningful negotiations. Communist attempts to circumvent and subvert Contadora, apparent from the beginning of the negotiating process, have left a clear trail of lost opportunities for peaceful reconciliation. In most recent months, Nicaragua has repeatedly frustrated negotiations aimed at producing a final, comprehensive Contadora treaty."

In March, the administration intensified pressure on Latin American nations to recognize the contras as a legitimate political force and endorse the Reagan demand for "democratization," beginning with direct negotiations between Nicaragua and the contras. Mexico, caught up in negotiations with the United States for an economic aid package, was under the greatest pressure. In Colombia, Washington was urging "the army and political right to pressure the government to take a more anti-Sandinista stance."[45]

President-elect Oscar Arias of Costa Rica had declared his opposition to contra aid on February 20, asserting, "the U.S. has forgotten the lessons of Vietnam."[46] A Western diplomat acknowledged that Reagan's newly appointed special envoy for Central America, Philip Habib, was rebuking Arias as well as Honduran President Jose Azcona for questioning the pro-contra policy. "They have been told they have been embarrassing the President and that this could cost them."[47]

Borderline

White House Communications Director Patrick Buchanan led the $100 million charge on Capitol Hill: "By cutting arms shipments to Nicaragua's freedom fighters, by tying the president's hands with the Boland amendment, the national Democratic Party has now become, with Moscow, co-guarantor of the Brezhnev doctrine in Central America...With the vote on contra aid, the Democratic Party will reveal whether it stands with Ronald Reagan and the resistance—or Daniel Ortega and the communists."[48]

Reagan compared the contras to Winston Churchill and likened the contra aid package to Lend-Lease during World War II.[49] On March 20, the House voted down the aid request. Although the McCarthyite rhetoric backfired in the short run,

Nicaragua was further demonized and the political stakes were raised for the next round.

The House vote, as in 1985, was not the final word. As the *New York Times* reported the day after, leaders in both parties agreed "that a majority of Congress supports military aid for the rebels in some form." Once again, a Nicaraguan action served as an excuse for the predicted House reversal. Ortega did not go to Moscow, but Nicaraguan troops attacked the contras in their border base camps. Though it wasn't the first time the Nicaraguan Army had denied the contras safe sanctuary, it was the first time the administration had hyped one of the cross-border raids as an invasion of Honduras. Nicaragua timed the counteroffensive to the battlefield and seasonal calendar (March offers prime dry season conditions), not the Washington political calendar. The CIA Intelligence Directorate considered it a routine raid, prompting Casey to press for a politically biased reassessment. The "invasion" was news to the Honduran government, who knew the Nicaraguan targets were the contras who Honduras publicly denied were in Honduran territory. Turning up the heat on Congress, on March 25, Reagan ordered $20 million in emergency military aid for Honduras and U.S. helicopters ferried Honduran troops to the border area. By then the Nicaraguan counteroffensive was over.[50]

Congressional Democrats joined the White House melodrama. House Speaker Tip O'Neill, who had argued passionately against military aid to the contras, accused Nicaragua of aggression against Honduras and denounced Ortega as "a bumbling, incompetent Marxist-Leninite communist." House leaders again portrayed Nicaragua's action as a slap in the face and said it greatly enhanced the chances of congressional approval of new aid, as if aid would not otherwise have passed.[51]

While Washington pretended that Honduras was being invaded, President Azcona left for Easter vacation at the beach and the Honduran military refrained from transforming the cross-border action into a war with Nicaragua. Within days, a senior Honduran official told reporters that the Reagan administration had pressured Honduras and manipulated the event to influence Congress and derail Honduran efforts to improve relations with Nicaragua. "Obviously they [U.S. officials] were interested that the incident have the connotations of an international confrontation," he said, "but we had no interest in that." He acknowledged that the contras' border presence had brought "a de facto occupation of our territory." He said, "We couldn't bring our country to the brink of war because of a battle between the counter-revolutionaries and the Sandinistas."[52]

The "emergency" U.S. military aid provided another channel to launder assistance to the contras. On March 27, the Senate approved $100 million in military and "nonlethal" contra support.

In April, the United States bombed the Libyan capital of Tripoli on a mission to kill Muamar Qaddafi and his family. At least 17 persons died, including Qaddafi's fifteen-month old adopted daughter, and over 100 were injured in the veiled assassination mission widely applauded in the United States as a blow against "international terrorism."[53] Reagan continued lobbying for aid to the contras to prevent the Nicaraguan government from building "a Libya on our doorstep." A U.S. ambassador in Central America told me, "It's irresistible that if you get the American people hating Libya, not to hitch on Nicaragua."[54]

Peace is War

The Contadora countries did not buckle to U.S. pressure and recognize the contras, but at the April ministers meeting in Panama they backed away from the Carabelleda principle of simultaneity. Nicaragua was pressed to be more "realistic" and sign the September 1985 version of the treaty without insisting that the United States simultaneously halt its aggression against Nicaragua and renew bilateral negotiations. Negotiators argued that by signing the treaty, Nicaragua would make it more difficult for the United States to continue support for the contras since Congress would likely reject the requested funding. A June 6 deadline was set for signing. The other Central American countries, including Guatemala, stated their readiness to sign.[55]

The Support Group presidents, however, did not abandon Carabelleda. President Alan Garcia of Peru had taken a particularly strong stand, declaring on March 16 that if the United States invaded Nicaragua, Peru would break diplomatic relations with Washington: "We would consider whatever act of aggression against a Latin American country an act of aggression against Peru."[56] Garcia and Uruguayan President Julio Sanguinetti reaffirmed their support for Carabelleda, and specifically the principle of simultaneity, in an April 11 letter to President Ortega. "What is at stake," they wrote, "is the possibility for the Central American countries to consolidate their own peace, and for Latin America to freely determine its own destiny." Argentine President Raul Alfonsin declared, "the US should recognize that the democratic ethical-philosophical foundation which it proclaims for its internal national life must be honored also in relations between the different nations of the hemisphere. After all, Latin America has been shortchanged in terms of democratic treatment."[57]

On April 12, President Ortega reasserted Nicaragua's willingness to sign the treaty in June, but only "if the United States has ceased its aggression against Nicaragua by that date and if agreement has been reached on the pending issues of the modified act, all within the framework of the concept of 'simultaneity' explicitly set forth in the Carabelleda Message." Ortega also reiterated Nicaragua's desire to form border commissions with Honduras and Costa Rica. A *Boston Globe* editorial of April 14 expressed understanding of Nicaragua's reluctance to sign under the circumstances: "Some might argue that the Sandinistas would have been politically wise to sign a Contadora peace treaty—even a hollow document—to prove that they are not intransigent.

"From Managua's point of view, there was little sense in giving the administration a license to continue the war and—when Nicaraguan demobilization is delayed, as it will be if the war continues—yet another opportunity to accuse the Sandinistas of bad faith."

Controversy erupted in the United States when Special Envoy Philip Habib seemingly misread his assignment as negotiations rather than public relations. In an April 11 letter to Rep. Jim Slattery (D-KS), which the State Department projected as an official statement of U.S. policy, Habib interpreted Contadora "provisions as requiring a cessation of support to irregular forces and/or insurrectional movements from the date of signature." Attention was focused on this point, but Habib went on to say: "Although the United States is not a party to the Contadora negotiations and *would not be legally bound* by signature of a Contadora treaty, we will as a matter of policy support and abide by a comprehensive, verifiable and *simultaneous implementation* of the Contadora Document of Objectives of September 1983, *as long as such an agreement is being fully respected* by all the parties. We would not feel politically bound to respect an agreement that Nicaragua was violating." (Italics added.)

Democrats portrayed the letter as a welcome shift in administration thinking. Rightwingers saw red. The administration quickly corrected a one-word mistake: instead of "from the date of signature" it should have read "from the date of implementation." Nicaragua would have to disarm under the gun and meet U.S. demands for contra democracy before the treaty was considered implemented. The position remained, commit suicide or we'll kill you.

As the Contadora process neared the June deadline, the Department of Defense released a report, "Prospects for Containment of Nicaragua's Communist Government." A prize May 20 *New York Times* headline summarized the report: "Pentagon Predicts Big War If Latins Sign Peace Accord."

The Pentagon report assumed that if a treaty were signed, Nicaragua would violate it. The United States and its allies, meanwhile, would comply diligently for two to three years—closing down U.S. military bases and on-site advisory and training efforts; ceasing U.S. military assistance to El Salvador, Honduras, Costa Rica and Guatemala; reducing U.S. military exercises with Honduras; cutting off aid to the contras; and disbanding contra forces in Honduras and Costa Rica. Then, to contain communist expansionism, the United States could be forced to commit 100,000 troops and several carrier groups, and spend over $9 billion a year.

The often absurd report clearly expressed the well-entrenched administration view, summarized by Sergio Ramirez: any "solution to the Central American problem must start with the disappearance of the Sandinista government."[58]

The State Department immediately challenged the brazen Pentagon report, leading some to believe there was a serious dispute over the content of administration policy rather than its form. In August 1985, however, Elliott Abrams had remarked, foreshadowing the Pentagon report, "It is preposterous to think we can sign a deal with the Sandinistas to meet our foreign policy concerns and expect it to be kept."[59] Around the time of the Habib furor, an unnamed high-ranking State Department official (perhaps Abrams) said that the Reagan administration was "hoping for the overthrow of the Sandinistas" and he "saw little benefit to be gained from talking about a negotiated accord."[60]

In April 1986, I asked a U.S. ambassador in Central America why there could not be a tripartite agreement involving the United States, Nicaragua and Contadora that accommodated the security concerns of all parties. He said there had been some possibility for this in 1984, at Manzanillo. Nicaragua would have agreed, provided internal structures were not addressed. But, said the ambassador, "the U.S. was never interested in that sort of deal." Later, he observed, "It's geography, as Henry Kissinger said during his commission, 'the U.S. could not accept even a Yugoslavia in Central America.' "[61]

"Democratization"

"As a first-hand witness," said Gerardo Trejos Salas, Costa Rica's vice minister for foreign affairs from 1985 until May 1986, "I can affirm that...Washington tried by all means available to block the signing of the Contadora Peace Act."[62]

Washington attempted to further Nicaragua's regional isolation by prompting U.S. allies to challenge Nicaragua's political legitimacy and demand "democratization." In stark contrast to the positive nature of the Central American presidents' summit during Cerezo's inauguration, President-elect Oscar Arias discouraged Ortega from attending his May 8 inauguration, claiming that Costa Rica could not guarantee Ortega's safety.

The isolation strategy backfired. As described by the Central American Historical Institute, the San Jose meeting became Arias' "first foreign policy failure." Arias "brought to the meeting a prepared document reflecting Reagan administration positions, titled 'For Democracy in Central America'; a document which also found its way to the press. Nicaragua, according to this proposal, would have to 'democratize' within the next two years, by holding new elections, dissolving its legislative assembly, dialoging with the contras and introducing changes in the Constitution that it is at this moment in the process of drafting. The idea was that Arias' document would be signed by all the presidents, but the plan was short-circuited by the Contadora and Support Group presidents present in the meeting. Instead Argentina, Uruguay, Peru, Colombia and Panama (Mexico and Venezuela did not attend) signed a document which exhorted 'an extra-regional country' with interests in the area to give signals in favor of peace. President Arias did not hold back from publicly expressing his disgust at this clear allusion to the United States."[63]

With its new constitution, said Nicaraguan Ambassador Carlos Tunnermann, "Nicaragua will comply with the whole process of internal democratization of which Contadora speaks," institutionalizing guarantees for political pluralism and human rights. "We don't believe Contadora to be incompatible with the continuation of the revolutionary process," he told me. It is the United States that has problems because Contadora "allows the survival of the revolution" and rejects the "option of force" represented by the Reagan Doctrine.[64]

As the June deadline neared, U.S. officials worried that Nicaragua would sign the treaty. Nicaragua went to the May Contadora meeting in Panama with what it termed a position of "utmost flexibility." It urged adoption of the concept of a "reasonable balance of forces," i.e. "the magnitude of military force of a defensive nature each state needs to defend its national territory against an external attack."[65]

Honduras again played the role of U.S. proxy by countering with a proposal for equal weapons restrictions on the Central American nations, notwithstanding their particular defense requirements.

The Central American presidents, including Ortega, met in Esquipulas, Guatemala in late May. President Cerezo described the summit's purpose as "not to back the U.S. or Nicaragua, but to back Central America." Latin Americans, he said, "must become the protagonists of our own history."[66] The presidents offered their support of Contadora and agreed to establish a Central American Parliament to strengthen Central American "dialogue, joint development, democracy and pluralism as basic factors for peace in the area and for Central American integration."[67]

The Esquipulas summit deflated tensions as the June 6 deadline came and went. On May 27, with the aim of breaking the deadlock over arms control, Nicaragua announced a proposed list of military matters and materiel that it "is willing to reduce, limit, regulate or and do without in the framework of the current Contadora negotiations to achieve peace." The list included "all type of military aircraft [and] helicopters," military airports, tanks, heavy mortars, foreign military advisers, etc. Meeting in Panama in early June, Contadora ministers agreed to a compromise treaty draft for further discussion.

On June 20, Nicaragua announced it would accept the revised treaty. Abrams rejected it as "inadequate" and Reagan dismissed Nicaragua's actions as "propagandistic."[68] Two days before Nicaragua's announcement, the *New York Times* reported that "administration officials interviewed uniformly spoke in the past tense when discussing the idea of negotiation."

Swing Shift: Congress Contravenes World Court

The House of Representatives swung behind the administration on June 25. The vote was 221 to 209, with 51 Democrats voting for the aid and only 11 Republicans voting against it. Among the eleven members who had opposed contra aid in March and voted for it in June were six Democrats, including Armed Services Committee Chairman Les Aspin (D-WI). "For Aspin, the motive was largely ideological," explained William LeoGrande. "Privately he had favored contra aid for over a year, but he hesitated to break ranks for fear of further complicating his already difficult relations with the party leadership and the liberals, relations strained by his championing the MX missile."[69]

The aid package provided $70 million in military aid and $30 million in so-called non-military aid for the contras, plus $300 million in economic assistance to El Salvador, Honduras, Guatemala and Costa Rica. The CIA was expected to provide another $400 million to the contras from its secret contingency funds.

Rep. Gerry Studds responded to the aid passage with a ringing indictment: "I fear that this body has made a mistake of truly monumental and historic proportions, a mistake which will come back to haunt us and our successors for many years to come. I think it may well be the historic equivalent of the Gulf of Tonkin

Resolution and I fear there may be blood on the hands of this body…Such aid would support a policy that is illegal, brutal, ineffective, historically ignorant, domestically and internationally unpopular and it will deepen direct U.S. involvement in a war in which we cannot with honor participate and which we cannot win."

Two days after the House vote, the World Court issued its expected verdict citing the United States for violating international law. Specifically, the Court rejected the U.S. justification of "collective self-defense" and decided that the United States "by training, arming, equipping, financing and supplying the *contra* forces or otherwise encouraging, supporting and aiding military and paramilitary activities in and against Nicaragua, has acted, against the Republic of Nicaragua, in breach of its obligation under customary international law not to intervene in the affairs of another State." The Court also specifically condemned the overflights of Nicaraguan territory, attacks on port facilities, mining of the harbors, production of the "psychological warfare" manual and the trade embargo.

The World Court ruled not only that the United States "is under a duty immediately to cease and to refrain from all such acts," but that it "is under an obligation to make reparation to the Republic of Nicaragua for all injury carried to Nicaragua by the breaches of obligations under customary international law."[70]

On August 2, President Ortega announced new peace initiatives in an address to the Chicago-based Operation PUSH founded by Reverend Jesse Jackson. Ortega called on the United States to comply with the World Court verdict and negotiate a Peace and Friendship Treaty with Nicaragua; proposed joint border patrols with Honduras and Costa Rica; called for signing the Contadora treaty on September 15, the anniversary of Central American independence; and invited President Reagan to visit Nicaragua, with the opportunity to meet all sectors of Nicaraguan society and deliver a televised address to the Nicaraguan people.[71]

Not surprisingly, the Reagan administration was not interested in pursuing bilateral negotiations or a Contadora agreement. Elliott Abrams asserted, "No one knows how long it will take either to get the Sandinistas to modify their behavior [sic] or for the people of Nicaragua to essentially throw them out. It could be sooner than a lot of people think."[72]

On August 14, the Senate voted 53 to 47 to approve a contra aid package identical to that passed in the House. Among the eleven Democrats voting in favor of aid, were Senators Lloyd Bentsen of Texas, Sam Nunn of Georgia and Bill Bradley of New Jersey.

That same day, fundraiser Spitz Channell met in Washington with representatives of Mexico's conservative opposition, the National Action Party. According to notes taken by Jane McLaughlin, then an employee of Channell's National Endowment for the Preservation of Liberty, Channell told the Mexicans that President Reagan would help their cause at election time if they would support the contra program. A Channell spokesperson later said they had only discussed a possible advertising campaign to pressure the Mexican government into supporting U.S. Central America policy.[73]

Intensive Care

The congressional swing shift drove more nails into Contadora's coffin. But the Latin Americans kept Contadora alive in the hope of a dramatic breakthrough. In the words of Argentine Foreign Minister Dante Caputo, "Every time they try to bury us, we resurrect ourselves."[74]

The Contadora and Support Group ministers met in New York on October 1 and issued a statement titled "Peace is still Possible in Central America": "Our demand as Latin Americans is for room to act. Room to offer each other a peaceful, fair and lasting solution." There was no room for peace in Washington. The Reagan administration moved quickly with its congressional mandate for war. U.S. officials reportedly prepared to press Central American allies to freeze or break relations with Nicaragua.[75]

In November, Honduras and Costa Rica conditioned their future Contadora participation on Nicaragua dropping its suit against them in the World Court. Following the favorable World Court ruling in its case against the United States, Nicaragua had filed suit on July 28 against Honduras and Costa Rica for harboring contra base camps. Nicaragua's Deputy Foreign Minister Victor Hugo Tinoco observed that Nicaragua too could impose conditions on its participation in Contadora, such as the removal of contra camps in Honduras and Costa Rica, but that "would lead us nowhere."[76]

Contadora diplomats grimly assessed the situation in an internal strategy paper citing intensification of the war along the Nicaraguan-Honduran border, the threat of direct U.S. military involvement and the impasse in talks among the Central American countries. They observed, "The false impression that this stagnation is caused by Nicaragua rather than by these other nations has been allowed to prevail."[77]

UN Secretary General Javier Perez de Cuellar and OAS Secretary General Joao Clemente Baena Soares joined together to revive Contadora. On November 18, they offered the services of their organizations in monitoring border incidents and supervising the disbanding or relocating of irregular forces, the reduction of armed forces, the dismantling of military bases and the expulsion of foreign military advisers. Later that month, the administration escalated the regional arms race with its offer to upgrade Honduran airpower with more advanced F-5E fighter bombers.

Tensions rose with a cross-border clash between Nicaragua and Honduras in early December, as Nicaragua attempted to keep the contras bottled up in their base camps in the Las Vegas salient jutting into Nicaragua. U.S. helicopters again ferried Honduran troops to the border area (utilizing the airstrip at Jamastran), violating congressional legislation that prohibited U.S. troops from being within twenty miles of the Nicaraguan border. General John Galvin, head of the Southern Command, traveled to Honduras to supervise the operation. Under heavy pressure from Washington, Honduran jet fighters crossed the border and conducted air strikes against a Nicaraguan outpost in Murra and an airstrip in Wiwili, killing seven Nicaraguan soldiers and wounding twelve soldiers and four civilians, including two children.[78] Nicaragua blamed the United States for the air attacks to avoid escalating hostilities with Honduras.

The Contadora and Support Group ministers met in Rio de Janeiro in mid December and expressed deep concern for recent developments. In a reference to the World Court judgement, they pointed to "exacerbation of interventionist policies and actions by countries from outside the Central American area, which are clearly in violation of international law." They called for the creation of conditions that would allow the implementation of actions proposed by the Carabelleda Message and the Contadora Act. They also announced a new initiative for peace: an "urgent visit" to Central America by the Contadora and Support Group ministers and the UN and OAS secretaries general.

Alarmed by these peace initiatives, the U.S. ambassador to the OAS, Richard McCormack, questioned the OAS secretary general's authorization for the trip and UN Ambassador Vernon Walters criticized Perez de Cuellar. The initiative went forward in spite of U.S. pressure. Before the regional tour got underway, however, Elliott Abrams and Philip Habib met in Miami on January 7, 1987 with Costa Rican Foreign Minister Rodrigo Madrigal, launching a more brazen effort to undercut Contadora with an alternative Costa Rican "peace plan."

The January Contadora mission was unsuccessful in reviving negotiations. Costa Rica, Honduras and El Salvador all singled out Nicaragua as the problem. At a news conference following a frosty meeting with Contadora mediators, President Azcona declared, "While there are no free elections [in Nicaragua], meetings and agreements serve no useful purpose." He added, "We don't want a war with Nicaragua, nor do we want civil wars. But we want it to remain clear that we will not permit any aggressions against our territory, nor are we going to assign economic resources to watching our border to prevent the contras from passing through our territory."[79] Azcona was not interested in Nicaragua's offer to drop the World Court cases if Honduras and Costa Rica agreed to bilateral talks and the establishment of demilitarized zones monitored by international peacekeeping forces.

Central American and Contadora representatives met with delegates from the European Economic Community (EEC) on February 9 and 10. Three European representatives expressed their governments' concern about a recent visit to Europe by Ambassador Habib, during which "they said he strongly suggested the possibility of an American attack on Nicaragua and asked for reduced European support for the Nicaraguan government."[80]

Avoiding Regional War

"The importance of Contadora," said Sergio Ramirez, "should be measured in what it has avoided rather than in what it has accomplished."[81] Mexican analyst Luis Herrera Lasso observed, "In the sense of a neutral peace, Contadora will never succeed, because a neutral peace will never be achieved in Central America...The U.S. presence, the external variable, will be determinant...We can say Contadora is destined to fail. But that doesn't mean Contadora isn't justified."[82]

Even gravely ill, Contadora has served as Latin America's alternative to U.S. intervention, an antidote to Nicaraguan isolation, a crucial forum for communication and a support for Hondurans and Costa Ricans resisting the proxy roles assigned their countries by the United States. On numerous occasions, Nicaragua, Honduras and Costa Rica have pulled back from the brink of war to which the United States was steering them. At the risk of an oversimplified analogy, Honduras and Costa Rica are not resigned to going the way of Laos and Cambodia in a regional war.

A Western diplomat (generally code for a U.S. diplomat) in Tegucigalpa observed, "Honduras has always been a means to an end."[83] Many Hondurans and Costa Ricans chafe at their U.S.-assigned roles of platform and pretext for U.S. intervention. Honduras' most recent wartime enemy was not Nicaragua, but El Salvador, with whom Washington expects Honduras to have a cozy alliance. Under U.S. pressure, noted Tom Farer, former president of the Inter-American Commission on Human Rights, "power within the military tilted toward General Gustavo Alvarez Martinez and his colleagues, who composed the faction that was most belligerent, most authoritarian, most closely tied to extremist business leaders (this faction also had connections with the Reverend Sun Myung Moon), and most eager to convert the country into an American subsidiary."[84] When General Alvarez was sacked in March 1984 by fellow military officers, it was not only because he was too greedy and autocratic, but because he was too eager to please Washington in forging an alliance with El Salvador. (Alvarez was rewarded with $50,000 as a Pentagon consultant in 1986 and an undisclosed sum by the Rand Corporation in 1985 for a paper on U.S. policy in Central America.)[85]

The Honduran Association of Coffee Producers, representing some 33,000 Hondurans, has called for expulsion of the contras. The contras have occupied a 450-square kilometer area in the eastern province of El Paraiso (Paradise). Dubbed Nueva Nicaragua (New Nicaragua; old Nicaragua would be more appropriate), the area is complete with a Ciudad Reagan (Reagan City). The contra occupation has brought killings, disappearances, rapes, robberies and the dislocation of some 20,000 Hondurans. Hondurans have also protested prostitution and child abuse by U.S. troops stationed at Palmerola Air Base.

Honduran Vice President Jaime Rosenthal said bluntly, "Public opinion is against the contras. The government will not be able to resist that for long." About contra leaders, he said, "They are living a very good life [off U.S. aid]. Calero lives better than I do."[86]

"There is pressure" against the contra presence, acknowledged a U.S. ambassador in Central America, "even among businesspeople who hate the Sandinistas. They're tired of having the contras inhabiting part of the country. Their reputation is shady—drug dealing, etc. If the contras fail, they'll all fall on Honduras."[87]

Threats against Honduran contra critics have multiplied. The president of the conservative opposition National Party, Nicolas Cruz Torres, and the head of the Committee for the Defense of Human Rights in Honduras (CODEH), Dr. Ramon Custodio, have both received death threats for opposing the contra presence.

Custodio's home and office were bombed. On August 4, 1986, terrorists blew up the car of contra critic Rodrigo Wong Arevalo, news director of Radio America, who escaped death only because he was running behind schedule.[88]

Hondurans have increasingly described their homeland as an "occupied country"—occupied by the United States and the contras. Edmond Bogran, a congressman from Azcona's own Liberal Party, said, "The truth is, we are a satellite state, a client state of the United States. Our government can have no policy of its own toward Nicaragua because of its total dependence." He expressed shame that Honduras had to do "Washington's dirty work" in helping stall Contadora.[89]

Costa Ricans complain of the "Hondurization" of their country. Social stability is being undermined by U.S. pressures to convert from a welfare state to a warfare state and by the rightwing forces feeding on U.S. intervention. In December 1985, members of Costa Rica Libre, headed by World Anti-Communist League chapter leader Bernal Urbina Pinto, stoned and teargassed participants in the international March for Peace in Central America which included members of parliament from Denmark and Norway. The year before, Bruce Jones, then a CIA contra liaison and later an associate of Singlaub's U.S. Council for World Freedom, told a reporter, "We're compiling a list of all the communists in northern Costa Rica, in case we ever have to do an Operation Phoenix here."[90]

Even anti-Sandinista Costa Ricans have become convinced the contras can't succeed. They are skeptical of the prospects for a U.S. invasion and fearful of the consequences for their own country. "If you could guarantee to me," said one Costa Rican official, "that the US 82nd airborne would land in Managua, liquidate the Sandinista comandantes and form a coalition government that would stand up, then a lot of people would be for it. But, that couldn't happen. They wouldn't be able to liquidate the Sandinistas. In the long term, they might democratize Nicaragua, but de-democratize Costa Rica."[91]

As Tom Farer observed, "the capitalist and military elites of Central America are divided between those who lost their hearts to Miami and those with a passion for an autonomous, national existence. And the latter know they are at a historic crossroads. U.S. intervention can guarantee the status quo for another generation. All that will be lost is national dignity. For some soldiers and politicians in Central America that price now seems too high. Perhaps the real contribution of the Contadora states has been to underline the price and to reinforce the belief that it need not be paid."[92]

History Made in the South

Contadora is supported by the OAS, the UN General Assembly, the European Economic Community, the Nonaligned Movement, the Socialist International and the International Christian Democratic Movement. A U.S. ambassador in Central America acknowledged "there's widespread dislike of the American position." But, he said, "This is a strong, self-confident administration that welcomes support, but doesn't worry if it's not there. This administration has showed its willingness to go for unilateralism over and over again. Together with the enormous dependence of Latin American countries on the U.S. banks, with the debt crisis, the dislike couldn't affect U.S. policy. There are no real costs...Maybe in historical terms there's a real cost, but not within the Reagan administration world view."[93]

The consequences of U.S. *compliance* with Contadora would be far-reaching, threatening the very structure of neocolonialism. With removal of U.S. military support for the contras and Salvadoran regime, the contras would surely be defeated and the Salvadoran revolutionaries would achieve recognition as a legitimate political force under a peace settlement or prevail militarily. Washington's fears go beyond the immediate impact of a Contadora treaty. "Contadora is not an isolated effort," explained Venezuelan President Lusinchi in his January 1986 address at Carabelleda. "Those who see or judge it as something out of touch with the new reality in Latin America are mistaken. Ours is a reality marked by a renewed willingness to deal with a number of adversities jointly, as one." He specifically mentioned the Consensus of Cartagena initiated by Latin debtor countries in 1984.[94]

Contadora must be seen "within the context of growing Latin American unity," reflected in the December 1986 agreement by the eight Latin American Contadora sponsors to establish a permanent forum to discuss such regional issues as Central America, foreign debt and "independent development."[95] A Brazilian diplomat observed, "We're aiming at something like the Group of Seven," the annual Western summit.[96] The achievement of a Contadora treaty would sanction Nicaragua's right to reshape its economy and could galvanize collective action around the debt crisis— the economic Big Stick. That could, in turn, rekindle the Third World movement for a New International Economic Order.

"Deep down," observed Ambassador Tunnermann, "Contadora signifies the end of the Monroe Doctrine." Solutions to Latin American problems will no longer be "based on what is compatible with U.S. interests," but rather on "that which is compatible with Latin America's criteria." This doesn't mean "Contadora is incompatible with legitimate U.S. interests," but if the United States wishes to maintain supremacy in the region, said Tunnermann, "then, yes, Contadora implies a limitation to that illegitimate presence."[97]

Contadora also challenges the Cold War order by rejecting the superpowers' right to police their respective spheres of influence. In exercising its right of might, the United States draws upon a vastly superior global bases network. A Contadora treaty would give a boost to demilitarization efforts around the world—notably anti-bases campaigns in Panama, Puerto Rico, the Philippines and England—and establish a precedent for autonomous systems of regional collective security. In short, Contadora can be seen as a building block for Nonalignment and a New International Economic Order, twin pillars of history made in the South.

14

Under the Coverups

Legality was viewed as an obstacle that had to be gotten around. That was the spirit of the program.

Reagan administration official who helped supervise the war on Nicaragua.[1]

By the time Congress voted $100 million more for contra war in the summer of 1986, the public rationales of arms interdiction, freedom fighting and pressuring Nicaragua to negotiate had all been shredded. The $100 million was a de facto pardon for administration deceit, contra atrocities, terrorist manuals, the mining of harbors, sabotage of the Contadora treaty and widespread lawlessness condemned by the World Court. Congress voted knowing that most Americans were opposed to the policy of overthrowing the Nicaraguan government and that only U.S. combat troops could install the contras in power.

With Congress back on board, the administration made plans to phase out the Enterprise's involvement in Nicaragua. NSC aide Oliver North, National Security Adviser John Poindexter, CIA Director William Casey and Enterprise manager Richard Secord discussed selling the Enterprise's Nicaragua-related assets to the CIA, as a means of financing interim contra support operations and enhancing the Enterprise's self-financing capacity for covert activity elsewhere.

North sent Poindexter a secret computer message (known as a PROF note) on July 24, 1986: "We are rapidly approaching the point where the PROJECT DEMOCRACY [PRODEM] assets in CentAm need to be turned over to CIA for use in the new program. The total value of the assets (six aircraft, warehouses, supplies, maintenance facilities, ships, boats, leased houses, vehicles, ordnance, munitions, communications equipment, and a 6520-[foot] runway on property owned by a PRODEM proprietary) is over $4.5M."[2]

CIA Deputy Director for Operations Clair George opposed using assets that would link the CIA to the "private" resupply operation. The issue was still not resolved when the Enterprise lost one of its assets: the Santa Elena airstrip.

Removing Fingerprints

After becoming president of Costa Rica in May 1986, Oscar Arias took action on a campaign promise to uphold his country's military neutrality. The contras' Santa Elena airstrip was no longer welcome. The U.S. Embassy assured Arias it would be shut down. It was not.

On September 5, CIA Station Chief Joe Fernandez informed North that the Costa Rican government was planning a press conference to announce the discovery and closure of the airstrip. North jotted in his notebook: "0005—call from [Fernandez]—Security Minister plans to make public Udall role w/Base West [Santa Elena] and allege violation of [Costa Rican] law by Udall, Bacon, North, Secord, et al."

North held a conference call with Assistant Secretary of State Elliott Abrams and Ambassador Lewis Tambs, and recorded in his notes: "Tell Arias: Never set foot in W.H. [White House]. Never get 5 [cents] of $80M promised by [AID Director] McPherson." North informed Poindexter that he called Arias with the threats and that, as a precaution, "Project Democracy" aircraft and personnel were removed from the site. "Thanks, Ollie," Poindexter replied in a PROF message. "You did the right thing, but let's try to keep it quiet."[3]

Abrams and Tambs later testified that Tambs was the one to call Arias. Abrams said he instructed Tambs to tell Arias that disclosure of the airstrip would jeopardize Arias' upcoming meeting with Reagan. He reported this to Secretary of State Shultz and also told Ambassador Habib to follow up on a visit to Costa Rica. North later claimed he had not really called Arias, but only said that to cover Abrams.[4] Whatever actually happened, the Costa Rican government cancelled the news conference. Although Arias has denied receiving threats, other Costa Rican officials "say a long delay in releasing $40 million of American economic aid" in 1986 "may have been an attempt to pressure Costa Rica."[5]

After a three-week lapse, the press conference occurred on September 26. Costa Rica's interior minister told reporters the government had shut down an airstrip that had been used for supplying the contras, smuggling drugs or both. Udall corporation was named, as was Robert Olmstead (an alias for William Haskell, who purchased the land), but Secord and North went unmentioned.

North assured Poindexter that "all appropriate damage control measures" had been undertaken to "keep USG [U.S. government] fingerprints off this...Udall Resources, Inc., S.A., is a proprietary of Project Democracy. It will cease to exist by noon today. There are no USG fingerprints on any of the operation and Olmstead is not the name of the agent—Olmstead does not exist. We have removed all Udall Resources...to another account in Panama, where Udall maintained an answering service and cover office. The office is now gone as are all files and paperwork."[6]

Administration press guidance, prepared by North, Abrams and CIA Central America Task Force Chief Fiers among others, and approved by Poindexter, lied: "No U.S. Government funds were allocated or used in connection with this site nor were any U.S. Government personnel involved in its construction. Any further inquiries should be referred to the Government of Costa Rica." In response to the expected question, "Was the airstrip intended for use by the Contras?" the press guidance suggested the answer: "The Government of Costa Rica has made clear its position that it will not permit the use of its territory for military action against neighboring states. The U.S. Government respects that position." North, meanwhile, suggested to Poindexter that steps be taken to "punish" Costa Rica for the disclosure.[7]

Exposure of the airstrip was just the kind of event Albert Hakim had planned for. It did not blow the cover off the Enterprise.

Throughout September, the airlift based at Ilogango in El Salvador picked up momentum. On September 9, airlift manager Robert Dutton flew with a C-123 crew into southern Nicaragua in an attempt to drop military supplies. They were unable to locate the contras and Dutton proposed to North that future missions use two aircraft to increase delivery potential and protect against increased Nicaraguan antiaircraft fire. North approved the use of two aircraft, but cautioned Dutton not to fly personally inside Nicaragua again. The operation couldn't risk the fallout from Colonel Dutton being shot down over Nicaragua.

By late September, the airlift was successful enough for pilot Bill Cooper to write Dutton, "Ho-Hum, just another day at the office." Now it was Dutton who warned Cooper to be careful.[8]

Smoking Plane

On October 2, Secretary Shultz had occasion to quote Winston Churchill: "In time of war, the truth is so precious, it must be attended by a bodyguard of lies."[9] Shultz was responding to the outcry following exposure of an administration disinformation campaign against Libya which had hoodwinked the American press (the novelty was not in the disinformation campaign, but in the unusually vigorous press reaction). Shultz may as well have been speaking about Nicaragua. A few days later, the bodyguard of lies attending that war came under fire.

On the morning of October 5, a C-123 cargo plane took off from Ilopango Air Base loaded with about 10,000 pounds of ammunition, rifles, grenade launchers and other materiel for the northern front contras inside Nicaragua. The crew included an FDN radio operator and three Americans, all veterans of the secret air war in southeast Asia: pilot Bill Cooper, copilot Wallace "Buzz" Sawyer and cargo kicker Eugene Hasenfus. Contra supply planes regularly overflew Nicaragua with impunity. Nicaragua's air defenses were inadequate; it had no jet fighters to send up in pursuit.

The C-123 flew a southern route to avoid Nicaraguan antiaircraft guns, heading south over the Pacific, then northeast from the Costa Rican border. At 12:30 P.M., the C-123 was detected by a Nicaraguan post near San Carlos along the San Juan River. Five minutes later the Light Hunter Battalion Third Company had the plane in its sights.

Nineteen-year-old Jose Fernando Corales raised his shoulder-mounted ground-to-air missile launcher and fired. The plane spewed smoke and veered toward earth as the soldiers cheered. Corales would later have the honor of throwing out the opening ball for Nicaragua's baseball championships.

Eugene Hasenfus was the sole survivor, having bailed out with a parachute borrowed from his brother. (Parachutes weren't standard issue for the airlift crews.) About twenty hours later, Hasenfus surrendered to Nicaraguan troops who tracked him to an abandoned hut in the jungle. He was the first American POW in the war on Nicaragua.[10]

Fernandez, meanwhile, had sent southern front forces to look for the missing C-123. Felix Rodriguez called Vice President Bush's deputy national security adviser, Colonel Sam Watson, to inform him the plane had disappeared.[11] North's associate, Colonel Robert Earl, reported to Poindexter on October 6: "one of the Democracy Inc aircraft apparently went down on a resupply mission to FDN forces in the north...It is currently unknown where or why the aircraft went down, but [country deleted] assets are discreetly organizing a SAR [search and rescue] effort over international waters & friendly territory portions of the route. Three Americans and one Nicaraguan national aboard. I will keep you advised of details as I get them."[12]

Hasenfus spoke briefly at a news conference in Managua on the evening of October 7: "My name is Gene Hasenfus. I come from Marinette, Wisconsin. Yes, and I was captured yesterday in southern Nicaragua. Thank you." Hasenfus' good fortune in surviving was bad luck for the Reagan administration.

In late July, U.S. Military Group Commander James Steele had met with members of the resupply crew in El Salvador to address logistical and security problems. He warned them to "leave your billfold at home when you go out" to avoid the risk of identification.[13] The downed C-123 crew carried identification.

The Nicaraguan government displayed ID cards and other documents taken from the wreckage, indicating that Cooper and Sawyer were attached to the U.S. Military Group in El Salvador and that Cooper was an employee of Southern Air Transport. There were business cards for the Nicaraguan Humanitarian Assistance Office and Robert Owen. The Nicaraguans said the C-123 was one of five aircraft operating from El Salvador.

On ABC's "Nightline," Ted Koppel argued with Alejandro Bendaña, the secretary general of the Nicaraguan Foreign Ministry; Bendaña insisted that the U.S. government was behind the operation. The administration's line, voiced by the president and top officials, was this was a private flight with no U.S. government connections.

"There's no question," Koppel told Bendaña, "that the Reagan administration is not crazy about you folks and would like to see the Sandinista government collapse. There is also no question that it wants to see aid for the Contras. But if private citizens want to donate money, and if some private Americans want to get aboard some Korean-vintage airliner or cargo plane and try and drop supplies over your country, that's not quite the same thing as a new Vietnam, is it?"

"It's not happening behind the back of the U.S. government," Bendaña responded, "and, in fact, your own press has reported amply how many of these operations were, in fact, directly run from the White House, from the office of a Mr. North, I believe."[14]

Like other news media, "Nightline" followed administration leads and pointed to John Singlaub as the master of the "private" supply operation. Coincidentally, the day the C-123 was shot down—before it was known in the United States—CBS' "60 Minutes" aired a story on Singlaub. "During the 15 months that the Congress refused to give President Reagan the $100-million he asked for to aid Nicaragua's contra rebels," Mike Wallace declared, "retired General John Singlaub defied the will of Congress by taking over for the CIA as virtual director of that war." Singlaub was quoted: "I made a point of getting word to the White House and to the agency [CIA]. They saw what we were doing, and from time to time I would get a 'Good job, Jack; appreciate what you're doing.' "[15]

Singlaub, who was in the Philippines at the time organizing death squads under the guise of hunting treasure, wasn't prepared to take the heat for the Hasenfus flight with its potentially serious legal ramifications.

Hasenfus appeared again at a news conference on October 9, this time with a lot more to say. He explained that William Cooper had recruited him five months earlier. They had worked together in Air America flying CIA supplies in Laos, Cambodia, Thailand and Vietnam from 1965 to 1973; before that Hasenfus served five years in the Marine Corps. Hasenfus told reporters about "two Cuban naturalized Americans" named "Max Gomez" (Felix Rodriguez) and "Ramon Medina" (Luis Posada) who "did most of the coordination for the flights and oversaw all of our housing, transportation, also refueling and some flight plans"; he assumed they worked for the CIA. Hasenfus described "working out of the El Salvador Air Force base at Ilopango" and "flying into Honduras to an air base called Aguacate" where "we would load up small arms and ammunition and fly into Nicaragua."

Hasenfus was a witness to the events long denied by the U.S. government. The DEA, meanwhile, identified the C-123 as the aircraft used in the Barry Seal drug sting operation.[16]

The Nicaraguan government released flight logs and a code book taken from the wreckage. The U.S. government code was "Playboy" and those of El Salvador, Honduras and Costa Rica were "New Look," "Hammerhold" and "Timex." Felix Rodriguez was "Condor." The U.S. Palmerola Air Base in Honduras was "fruit stand"; guns and explosives were "apples" and "pears." Buzz Sawyer's log books recorded flights to Aguacate and Mocoron airfields in Honduras and Costa Rica's international airport in San Jose. They revealed still-unexplained May and June 1985 flights to Robbins Air Force Base in Georgia and U.S. air bases in Puerto Rico, Panama and Cuba, and a February 6, 1986 flight to McClellan Air Force Base in Sacramento, California. Sawyer also made frequent flights in Angola during 1985 while employed by Southern Air Transport.[17] Though Southern Air has had a contract with diamond mine operators in Angola, it is suspected of channelling U.S. aid to the antigovernment UNITA forces.

"RR was Briefed"

Nicaragua announced that Hasenfus would go on trial. North sent an October 12 PROF message to Robert McFarlane (who maintained secure communications with North and Poindexter after leaving the national security adviser post) that clearly implicates Reagan in the contragate coverup:

> We urgently need to find a high powered lawyer and benefactor who can raise a legal defense for Hassenfus [sic] in Managua. If we can find such persons we can not only hold Gene and Sally Hassenfus together (i.e., on our side, not pawns of the Sandinista propaganda machine) but can make some significant headway of our own in counter-attacking in the media. Obviously, there is the added benefit of being able to do something substantive in the legal system to defend this young man [Hasenfus, 45, was two years older than North]…By Tuesday, a Swiss lawyer, retained by Corporate Air Services [a front corporation employing contra supply crew members], should be in Managua. We should not rely on this person to represent the whole case since he is supported by covert means. We would be far better off if we had an overt mechanism here in the States which represented USG/Hassenfus' interests, and who would not have to respond to questions regarding the origins of Corporate Air Services, Inc. (CASI), or its other ongoing activities. The CASI lawyer is being instructed to cooperate fully w/ this U.S. Attorney, whoever he/she may be. Have also located approx. $100K from a donor who does not care if this contribution becomes known (although the donor has done things in the past to keep CASI in operation—a fact which need not become known). Can you help? If need be, I can meet w/ you/others tomorrow or Tues. Believe this to be a matter of great urgency to hold things together. *Unfortunately RR was briefed that this plan was being contemplated before he left for Iceland [Summit] and am concerned that along about Wednesday when people begin to think of things other than meetings in cold places, he will remember this and nothing will have been done.* Any thoughts wd be much appreciated. Elliott Abrams willing to sit-in any time after Yom Kippur fast is finished tomorrow night. Pls Advise.[18] (Italics added.)

The congressional *Iran-Contra Report* avoided this note (which was published in a footnote to the *Tower Board Report*) and concluded "there is no evidence the President knew of U.S. involvement in the Hasenfus flight."[19]

Contra spokesman Bosco Matamoros said the contras took full responsibility for the flight. "There was no United States Government connection," he claimed. But even government officials acknowledged this was, as with Singlaub, "just an effort to deflect attention from the White House."[20] Matamoros was following orders originating at a RIG meeting attended by Abrams and Fiers. As reported to Poindexter by NSC aide Vincent Cannistraro, "UNO to be asked to assume responsibility for flights and to assist families of Americans involved."[21]

Meanwhile, the administration staged a photo opportunity over the caskets of Sawyer and Cooper. After telling the Nicaraguans bearing the caskets to the U.S. Embassy in Managua that they could not enter the compound, the administration accused Nicaragua of "ghoulish behavior" when the caskets were left at the embassy gate. In Vietnam, the corpses of combatants were used to transport heroin to the United States. In Nicaragua, they were used as props in the "public diplomacy" campaign.

"60 Minutes" correspondent Mike Wallace interviewed Hasenfus in Managua on October 19. "What would you like to say to the American people? What would you like to say to President Reagan? What would you like to say to Bill Casey, the head of the CIA?"

Referring to Casey, Hasenfus replied, "I'd like to be—have him sitting where I'm at and see what he'd say."[22]

U.S. officials lied to Congress and the people in an effort to maintain deniability in the face of growing evidence of U.S. government involvement.[23] Primed by Hasenfus' revelations, reporters, meanwhile, used Salvadoran telephone records to trace frequent calls from airlift safe houses to Richard Secord and Oliver North.

Hasenfus was convicted on November 15 on charges of terrorism and other crimes. He received the maximum sentence of 30 years. A month later, on December 17, he was pardoned and freed by the Nicaraguan government. "This is a Christmas and New Year message to the American people," said President Ortega. "It is a very concrete message of peace."[24]

By then the administration was caught up in the widening Iran-contra scandal. Yet, the contra $100 million continued to flow.

Gullible's Troubles

By the summer of 1985, long before the Hasenfus revelations, reporters such as Robert Parry of the Associated Press (now with *Newsweek*) and Alfonso Chardy of the *Miami Herald* were zeroing in on Oliver North and the White House's continuing role in running the contra war.

For North and company, freedom of *La Prensa* in Nicaragua was one thing; freedom of the U.S. press was another. North singled out Chardy in a June 3, 1985 memo to Poindexter: "For several weeks now there have been rumors of stories being prepared which allege an NSC connection to private funding and other support to the Nicaraguan resistance. The rumors originally surfaced with a reporter Alfonso Chardi [*sic*]...At my request [deleted] went to Chardi...and told Chardi that if he (Chardi) printed any derogatory comments about the FDN or its funding sources that Chardi would never again be allowed to visit FDN bases or travel with their units."[25]

Reacting to the press reports and concerned about possible violation of the Boland amendment, House Western Affairs Subcommittee Chairman Michael Barnes, House Intelligence Committee Chairman Lee Hamilton and, later, Senators David Durenberger and Patrick Leahy, chairman and vice chairman of the Senate Intelligence Committee, wrote McFarlane seeking information about NSC contact with the contras. McFarlane issued his now-famous categorical response that "at no time did I or any member of the National Security Council staff violate the letter or spirit" of congressional restrictions. In answering specific questions put to him by the elected officials, McFarlane covered up the NSC role, including his own part in arranging the Saudi contribution.[26] As North later testified about McFarlane's responses, they were "erroneous, misleading, evasive, and wrong."

Barnes made a series of attempts to review relevant NSC documents, prompting McFarlane and North to prepare particularly revealing documents for alteration. But the Barnes effort fizzled in the face of purposefully bothersome NSC conditions.[27] Barnes later said that if he had asked the Foreign Relations or Intelligence Committees for subpoenas, he "would not have had sufficient support to get them." North "was a very respected guy back then," Barnes said. "There was just not a mood at that time to support an aggressive investigation."[28]

The following summer, amid new press accounts of the White House contra program, Rep. Ron Coleman (D-TX) introduced a Resolution of Inquiry on June 4, 1986, directing the president to provide documents and information about NSC support for the contras, including the provision of funds and supplies through private individuals and foreign governments; contacts with the contras related to military activities; and contacts with persons such as John Singlaub, Robert Owen and John Hull. Coleman explained that "disturbing new reports that our own government officials may have deliberately violated the law that prohibited any open or hidden U.S. assistance for military operations inside Nicaragua [suggest that there] may have been an intentional disregard for our own democratic process."

The resolution was referred to the House Committees on Intelligence, Foreign Affairs and Armed Services. Poindexter wrote Chairmen Lee Hamilton, Dante Fascell and Les Aspin that information provided in fall 1985 by McFarlane had already "made it clear that the actions of the National Security Council staff were in compliance with both the spirit and letter of the law regarding support of the Nicaraguan resistance." Poindexter later told the Iran-contra committees that he "felt that the Boland Amendment did not apply to the NSC staff and I felt that indeed we were complying with the letter and spirit of the Boland Amendment. Now, it doesn't say that we are not helping the Contras. We were."[29]

North met with House Intelligence Committee members on August 6 at their request. He misled them in his opening presentation and lied in response to specific questions. NSC staffer Bob Pearson attended the meeting and prepared a summary for Poindexter:

> Session was success—Hamilton will entertain motion soonest to report unfavorably on Resolution of Inquiry and made clear believes [Intelligence Committee] can turn aside future offers of similar resolutions. North's remarks were thorough and convincing—Hamilton underlined his appreciation to Admiral [Poindexter] and to [unclear] for full cooperation offered by NSC...
> In response to specific questions, Ollie covered following points:
> —contact with FDN and UNO aimed to foster viable, democratic political strategy for Nicaraguan opposition, gave no military advice, knew of no specific military operations.
> —Singlaub—gave no advice, has had no contact in 20 months: Owen—never worked from OLN [North] office, OLN had casual contact, never provided Owen guidance.[30]

Poindexter forwarded Pearson's note to North with the message, "Well done." It was well done indeed. Hamilton told Coleman on August 12 that the Intelligence

Committee would not move forward with the Resolution of Inquiry: "Based on our discussions and review of the evidence provided, it is my belief that the published press allegations cannot be proven."[31]

Ed Meese could hardly have conducted a less inspired inquiry. It took a smoking plane to shake Congress from its oversight stupor.

Damage Control

The Hasenfus shootdown triggered new inquiries by Congress and investigations of Southern Air Transport by the FBI and Customs Service. On October 5, Fernandez sent a KL-43 message to Dutton telling him that the "situation requires we do necessary damage control."[32]

While Reagan and his top officials denied U.S. government involvement in the contra support operation, North and Poindexter worked behind the scenes to derail or at least delay investigations into the activities of Southern Air Transport. North and Poindexter later said they wanted to prevent disclosure of Southern Air's involvement in U.S. arms shipments to Iran and protect the hostage negotiations. But covering up the NSC-Southern Air contra operation was a chief concern.

As FBI agents began interviewing Southern Air employees, North called FBI Executive Assistant Director Oliver "Buck" Revell on October 8. North assured Revell that Southern Air was not involved in illegal activities and that he had no knowledge of the plane that crashed. North said Southern Air was still flying arms shipments to Iran, which Revell already knew about as a member of the Operations Sub Group, and expressed his concern about the inquiry. Nonetheless, Revell obtained authority from Deputy Assistant Attorney General Mark Richard to begin an official investigation of Southern Air on October 10.

The day before, North had called William Rosenblatt, the Customs Service Assistant Commissioner for Enforcement, and told him he was concerned about the broad subpoena Customs had served on Southern Air. North said the Southern Air people were "good guys" who had committed no crimes, and denied that the C-123 contained arms when it left the United States (the same C-123 North had denied knowledge of to Revell). Rosenblatt narrowed the focus of the investigation to the aircraft itself and to the question of whether arms or ammunition were being exported without a license.

Poindexter called Attorney General Meese and asked him to delay both the Customs and FBI investigations.[33] Meese called Treasury Secretary James Baker about the Customs investigation (under Baker's jurisdiction) and told Associate Attorney General Steven Trott (now a federal appeals court judge) to ask FBI Director William Webster to delay the Southern Air investigation for ten days. Trott called Webster on October 30, telling him that without a delay the investigation could compromise "sensitive hostage negotiations."

Hostage David Jacobsen was released on November 2, just before the 1986 mid-term elections. North and Secord traveled to Beirut to coordinate his release.[34]

The next day, the Lebanese magazine *Al-Shiraa* exposed the U.S.-Iran project which most U.S. media had neglected for so long. Still, Meese waited more than ten days before giving Trott the go-ahead for the FBI investigation.[35] The FBI investigation did not resume until November 26, the day after the Iran-contra diversion announcement (discussed in the next chapter).[36]

Those post-Hasenfus maneuvers fit a pattern of interference with criminal investigations that threatened to expose the contra support operation. In August 1986, North had contacted Customs Service Commissioner William von Raab to complain that Customs agents in Georgia were giving the Maule Aircraft Corporation a hard time. Months before, Customs had held up a helicopter allegedly to be used only to evacuate contra wounded from the war zones. It was purchased by Singlaub's U.S. Council for World Freedom with donations from Ellen Garwood. Singlaub called von Raab and suggested he discuss the matter with North. When von Raab called North, North told him the people involved with the helicopter were "good guys." Customs ended up issuing a license and releasing the helicopter known as the "Lady Ellen."[37]

In the Maule matter, Customs was following up on a July 1986 CBS News report that showed a Maule aircraft on the airstrip at Aguacate and a registration form signed by Secord for a Maule "dated July 26, 1984, one month after funds for CIA aid to the contras had run out." A Maule executive told CBS that Secord had bought "over a period of a couple years, probably three or four" Maules. CBS reporter David Martin added, "Two days after that interview Maule Air received a phone call from someone—they won't say who—warning them they could be forced out of business if they did not retract everything they had told CBS News."

Martin continued: "These documents show that another of the planes Maule says Secord bought was sold to a Panamanian corporation and exported to Honduras in September 1985...This battle plan, written by some of the contra commanders, calls for using short-take-off-and-landing planes in an assault on the Nicaraguan capital of Managua to 'capture, eliminate or neutralize the Sandinista leaders.' "

Martin reported that one of the checks used to pay for the Maules was drawn on the account of the Geneva-based CSF Investment Ltd. and "sources close to the contras claim the money for the planes originally came from Saudi Arabia." Martin also reported, "A well-informed source said North has used Secord on several secret projects since Secord retired in 1983."[38]

This was some of the evidence reported in the press when House Intelligence Committee Chairman Lee Hamilton rejected the Coleman Resolution of Inquiry.

The Customs Service began investigating allegations that Maule Air had shipped four planes to Central America to support the contras—a possible violation of U.S. export control laws. North told Commissioner von Raab that Maule Air shipped "Piper Cubs" down south and that Maule was "a close friend of the President." Von Raab told North he would look into the investigation and assigned the matter to William Rosenblatt. When Rosenblatt contacted North he was told that the Maule people were "good guys" and that the four "super Piper Cubs" were used to supply the contras with medical and humanitarian supplies.

Rosenblatt agreed to postpone issuing subpoenas in exchange for North's promise to produce documentation on the aircraft. After six weeks of stalling, North produced some documents on November 17. They were insufficient and Rosenblatt resumed the investigation, apparently informing North.[39]

Rosenblatt was involved in another incident with North, this one related to drug smuggling. Sometime in 1986, Joseph Kelso, who was on probation after being convicted for illegally exporting arms to Iraq, approached Customs under an alias and offered to work as an informer. Kelso and another informer traveled to Costa Rica to gather information on a counterfeiting and drug ring. In August, two Customs agents went to Costa Rica to debrief them and were told that DEA agents in Costa Rica had been paid to conceal their knowledge of narcotics supplies and laboratories.

The Customs agents revealed what they had heard to DEA agents in Costa Rica. That night, Kelso and the other informer were arrested by local police accompanied by a DEA agent. After interrogation they were driven to John Hull's ranch by Costa Rican security personnel, where Hull questioned Kelso. When Hull tried to have Kelso arrested by Costa Rican intelligence officers, Kelso escaped. Hull informed North and Owen of the incident.

After returning to the United States, Kelso faced charges of parole violation and negotiated through his lawyer with U.S. authorities. To demonstrate that Kelso was working not only with Customs, but intelligence agencies, his lawyer provided an assistant U.S. attorney with tape recordings Kelso made while working undercover. According to a report by Representatives Peter Rodino, Dante Fascell, Jack Brooks and Louis Stokes, included with the *Iran-Contra Report*, "These tapes were provided only under the express condition they not be sent to Washington, D.C. where, Kelso feared, they could get into the 'wrong hands.' "

Ambassador Tambs, meanwhile, sent a complaint to Customs, which reached Rosenblatt, about sending informers to Costa Rica without notifying the embassy. Rosenblatt insisted on getting the tapes from the local Customs agent, notwithstanding the restriction against sending them to Washington.

"In or about" September, Rosenblatt called North to find out if Kelso was working for U.S. intelligence. North suggested that Rosenblatt allow Robert Owen to listen to the tapes to verify the claims. According to the *Iran-Contra Report*, "Rosenblatt agreed on the assumption that Owen was part of the NSC staff, or otherwise assisting North." Owen himself, however, told Rosenblatt he worked for a private organization. In October, Rosenblatt gave Owen his only copy of the tapes. Representatives Rodino, Fascell, Brooks and Stokes observed: "Not surprisingly, Owen never returned the tape recordings. Instead he made two trips to Costa Rica to meet with the DEA agents. When asked about the incident during his deposition, Owen refused to answer questions, claiming a questionable 'attorney work-product' privilege. Owen claimed that all of his activities during the Kelso incident were attempts to investigate allegations made against him in the Avirgan-Honey lawsuit."[40]

Miami Stall

More is known about an NSC-Justice Department coverup involving the investigation conducted by Assistant U.S. Attorney Jeffrey Feldman in the Miami office headed by U.S. Attorney Leon Kellner. In January 1985, the same month that CMA leader Tom Posey was arrested for carrying a concealed weapon at the Miami airport, a rightwing film producer named Larry Spivey placed a call from a Miami motel to FBI Special Agent Michael Boone in Los Angeles. Spivey had just met with Jack Terrell, Tom Posey and others who were planning an assault into southern Nicaragua.

According to Rodino, et al., Spivey met previously with North and North "also called Boone to warn him that Adolfo Calero believed that Terrell was dangerous and his invasion plot was untenable. Boone asked the FBI in Miami to interview Spivey and Posey.

"FBI Agent George Kiszynski interviewed Posey and Spivey at the FBI office in Miami. During the interview of Posey, Kiszynski called North from the FBI office. Spivey told Kiszynski that North was relieved that the FBI was now involved and in control of Posey, who had agreed to cooperate with the FBI. Kiszynski's report of the interview was sent to North, with the approval of FBI headquarters. Therefore, the FBI knew as early as January 1985 of North's connection to their investigation of the CMA and Posey.

"Two weeks later, Posey complained to Spivey that the FBI was not giving him any guidance regarding what to do. Spivey called the Alabama FBI agent assigned to Posey and also called FBI Executive Assistant Director Oliver 'Buck' Revell. Spivey told them that they should not view Posey as a 'target.' He said that North had earlier told him that during a meeting with Attorney General Smith and Robert McFarlane, President Reagan told them that Posey and men like him should never be prosecuted and called Posey a 'national treasure.' This statement was included in the FBI report that was filed."

Spivey also testified "that, in early 1985, North admitted he could go to jail for violating the Boland Amendment, so he was going to 'lay low' until Ed Meese was confirmed as Attorney General. Time did not permit the [Iran-contra] Committees to investigate Spivey's claim."[41] As discussed in chapter 12, North was using the FBI in an attempt to sideline Terrell without hurting Posey's CMA.

On July 21, 1985, the *Miami Herald* ran an article by Martha Honey and Tony Avirgan with Steven Carr's allegations of a contra arms shipment from Fort Lauderdale; it caught the attention of the southern Florida FBI. Carr's allegations were corroborated in January 1986 by Jesus Garcia, who offered, as discussed earlier, to provide information to federal authorities following his arrest in December 1985.

The FBI gathered documentary evidence such as flight plans and records and interviewed additional sources who pointed to the involvement of North, Owen and Hull. On March 14, 1986, Assistant U.S. Attorney Jeffrey Feldman and an FBI agent met with Executive Assistant U.S. Attorney Ana Barnett. U.S. Attorney Leon Kellner informed them that he had received a call from a Justice Department official wanting information about the investigation. That same day, Feldman and two FBI agents asked to meet with Garcia's lawyer John Mattes and Mattes' investigator Ralph Maestri. "I thought, this is great; they're finally going to take this thing seriously," Mattes told the *Village Voice.* "We brought all our notes on Tom Posey, John Hull, and Rob Owen." Instead, Feldman warned them to end their investigation and accused them of obstructing justice and tampering with witnesses.[42]

The House of Representatives opened debate on contra aid on March 17. That same day, a Justice Department official called Kellner's office and requested a delay in the Garcia sentencing hearing, scheduled for March 19, at which Garcia planned to tell the court what he knew about the contra arms network and its White House connection. Feldman filed a motion for a 30-day continuance on March 18. Garcia wasn't sentenced until six months later on September 15, at which time he did mention North and Owen.[43]

On March 20, FBI agent Kevin Currier responded to an urgent message from headquarters to provide an immediate summary of the Florida investigation by sending a 38-page memorandum. Revell needed the update for Deputy Attorney General D. Lowell Jensen (now a federal judge). Jensen discussed the case with Meese, and Poindexter was briefed. Jensen forwarded a copy of Revell's memo to Associate Attorney General Steven Trott, who, in turn, forwarded it to Deputy Assistant Attorney General Mark Richard, with the message: "Please get on top of this. [Jensen] is giving a heads up to the N.S.C. He would like us to watch over it. Call Kellner, find out what is up, and advise him that decisions should be run by you."[44]

According to Jensen, Revell's memorandum, which remains classified, indicated that the CIA and State Department were also being briefed. Jensen, Trott and Richard "all contend that the sensitive nature of the investigation, its international overtones, and the possible danger to Ambassador Tambs [the alleged assassination plot] made an NSC briefing advisable."[45]

That "heads up" to the NSC was no exception. North was regularly sent FBI files on the contra support network, "in effect, letting him monitor the investigation of his own activities." He wasn't cut out of the loop until October 31, when FBI Director William Webster received a memo—weeks before Meese announced the Iran-contra diversion—warning that North himself might be prosecuted for his Central America activities; Webster told the Senate Intelligence Committee in April 1987 that, although he had initialed the memo, he did not remember it.[46] North also received confidential information from Republican aides on the Senate Foreign Relations Committee regarding the investigation led by Senator John Kerry.[47]

On March 31, 1986, Feldman and FBI agents Currier and Kiszynski traveled to Costa Rica to investigate the allegations of gunrunning and the Tambs assassination plot. (North recorded their visit in his notes the same day.) Feldman briefed Ambassador Tambs at the embassy, showing him a chart illustrating the alleged conspiracy with North's name above Hull and Owen. According to Feldman, Tambs "turned white...The only thing he said when I pulled out the chart was 'Get Fernandez in here.' "[48] Fernandez spoke warmly of North as "the person who introduced me to the President of the United States last week."

During the next two days, Feldman and the FBI agents interviewed Steven

Carr and other imprisoned mercenaries. Hull cancelled his interview, declining to meet without counsel on the advice of Kirk Kotula, the U.S. consul general in San Jose.[49] Fernandez, State Department Security Officer James Nagel and others at the embassy had tried to discourage Feldman from seeing Hull and said the investigation should be discontinued. In his deposition to the Iran-contra committees, Feldman said, "I was told that the National Security Council had been in touch with Mr. Hull...that Ronald Reagan knows who John Hull is...that certain agencies have their operational requirement and it's not fair for other agencies to interfere."[50]

Owen wrote to North (alias "William") about the investigation on April 7, 1986: "Feldman...had with him a Special Agent from Panama and two from Miami. They are Kevin Currier and George Kiszynski, who is with the Anti-Terrorist Task Force. In the past he has followed and been assigned to watch Felipe Vidal.

"According to [Fernandez], Feldman looks to be wanting to build a career on this case. He even showed [Fernandez] and the Ambassador a diagram with your name at the top, mine underneath and John's [Hull] underneath mine, then a line connecting the various resistance groups in C.R. [Costa Rica].

"Feldman stated they were looking at the 'big picture' and not only looking at a possible violation of the neutrality act, but at possible unauthorized use of government funds...

"If and when I am contacted by the FBI, I will not answer any questions without an attorney present. Even then, I will not answer any questions. It is the only way I can see to stem the tide." Owen added, "Perhaps, it is time I retire from this line of work and focus on another part of the world and against another group of Godless communists."[51] Owen's fears proved premature.

Feldman met with Kellner, Barnett and others on April 4 to discuss the results of the Costa Rica trip. Feldman explained that while the assassination plot had not been substantiated to date, the charges of gunrunning and Neutrality Act violations warranted a grand jury. According to Assistant U.S. Attorney David Liewant, Kellner spoke by phone with a high Justice Department official in Washington, and reported that "Washington wanted him to go very slow on the case, since it could affect the upcoming vote on contra aid in Congress." (Kellner, Barnett and Feldman have denied Liewant's account.)[52]

Kellner asked Feldman to draft a memorandum on the investigation explaining his approach to possible prosecution. On May 7, the *New York Times* ran a story (mentioned earlier) quoting a "senior Justice Department official" that Kellner's office had found no evidence to support allegations of gunrunning and drug trafficking. On May 14, Feldman produced a detailed redraft of his memorandum which concluded it was time to issue grand jury subpoenas for documents and witnesses. A few days later, Kellner returned it with the notation, "I concur, we have sufficient evidence to institute a grand jury investigation into the activities described herein."[53]

Feldman's memo contained detailed information about the contra supply network, including arms shipments and mercenary recruitment by Posey, CMA and Rene Corvo, and evidence of U.S. government involvement. Feldman stated, "Fernandez...told me that prior to March 1984 the U.S. military used Hull's Costa Rica ranch to deliver equipment to the contras. Fernandez also said that since March

1984, Hull has assisted the contras by providing them with food, medical supplies, and other nonlethal necessities." Feldman noted, "It is unclear whether John Hull has had an official role in U.S. sponsored contra operations since March 1984. Fernandez denied that Hull had been an operative for the CIA or [any] other agency since that time. Hull, however, has allegedly made remarks that suggest otherwise."[54]

Kellner held further staff discussions on May 20 and reversed the decision to convene a grand jury as premature. Feldman rewrote the memorandum, stating that a grand jury would be in order after he completed further "background work" on the case. But a special counsel in Kellner's office rewrote it to conclude that a grand jury investigation "would represent a fishing expedition with little prospect that it would bear fruit."[55] The memorandum was then submitted to the Justice Department on June 3 (it retained Feldman's original May 14 date although it included a reference to the May 30 filing of the Christic Institute suit). On July 31, the FBI agents completed additional investigation and Currier gave Feldman a "prosecution memorandum" which was forwarded to Kellner on or about August 14. Kellner continued the stall.

On October 6, the day after the Hasenfus shootdown, Chief Assistant U.S. Attorney Richard Gregorie told Kellner he felt the case was ready to go to the grand jury. After further delay, Kellner gave the go-ahead to Feldman in early November—"six months after Feldman had first suggested the need for a grand jury."[56]

A few weeks later, an important witness was dead. In May, Steven Carr had jumped bail and returned to the United States with the surreptitious aid of the U.S. Embassy. Though concerned about threats from Hull's group to keep his mouth shut, he still talked to the press and investigators. On December 13, Carr collapsed in a driveway in Van Nuys, California and was pronounced dead at 4 A.M. He was 27 years old. The Los Angeles coroner's office concluded that Carr died of an accidental cocaine overdose, but uncertainty remains. Another autopsy, commissioned by Carr's family, determined that marks behind Carr's left elbow were not scratches, but needle marks from an injection. "No one ever explained," wrote Leslie Cockburn, "why Carr should have been injecting himself behind his left elbow. (He was not a habitual needle u᷿ er.)"[57]

In April 1987, after the Carr case was closed, public defender John Mattes received a call from mercenary Peter Glibbery who was still imprisoned in Costa Rica. Glibbery told Mattes that Hull had just threatened him, saying he would wind up dead like Steven Carr if he refused to sign an affidavit discrediting Senator Kerry, Mattes and Honey and Avirgan, and recanting his earlier statements. The CIA killed Carr, Hull reportedly said. Hull acknowledged visiting Glibbery with an affidavit on March 29, but denied threatening him.[58] If Glibbery's account is correct, Hull's reference to the CIA killing Carr may have been bluster. Or, perhaps Hull knew Carr *was* murdered, though not necessarily through the CIA.

The congressional *Iran-Contra Report* reviewed interference in seven investigations (discussed here or in earlier chapters) and concluded incredibly that only NSC staff members were at fault: "We do not mean to impugn the integrity of the law enforcement officials involved. Suggestions that national security could be compromised, coming from NSC aides, inevitably were given weight by law enforcement officials and led them on occasion to provide information to the NSC staff and to delay investigations."[59]

Reps. Rodino, Fascell, Brooks and Stokes diverged from the myopic majority: "law enforcement agencies in these cases are not entirely without responsibility...[Media and investigative] leads [about North's involvement] were never pursued until after the Hasenfus crash when members of the House Judiciary Committee requested that these allegations be investigated and that an independent counsel be appointed. Furthermore, officials from the FBI, Customs, and the Department of Justice went out of their way to provide North with information regarding criminal investigations...North used this information to conceal and divert attention away from his unlawful operations.

"Our nation has painfully learned from past experience that a democracy cannot exist when those responsible for enforcing the law can be manipulated for political purposes."[60]

Reagan's Contradictions

The President was fully aware of the extent of the relationship between N.S.C. members and members of the democratic resistance group and he has been aware of it all along.

> Presidential spokeman Larry Speakes, August 1985,
> quoted in Joel Brinkley, *New York Times*, February 15, 1987.

The President told the [Tower] Board on January 26, 1987, that he did not know that the NSC staff was engaged in helping the Contras.

> *Tower Board Report*, February 26, 1987.

Now the contra situation...There's no question about my being informed. I've known what's going on there, as a matter of fact, for quite a long time now, a matter of years...And to suggest that I am just finding out or that things are being exposed that I didn't know about—no. Yes, he—I was kept briefed on that...As a matter of fact, I was very definitely involved in the decisions about support to the freedom fighters— my idea to begin with.

> President Reagan, meeting with editors, May 15, 1987.

The President told the truth about everything to everybody he talked to.

> Presidential spokesman Marlin Fitzwater, November 19, 1987.

He just pleaded guilty to not telling Congress everything it wanted to know. I've done that myself.

> President Reagan, commenting on former National Security Adviser Robert McFarlane's
> plea-bargain with Independent Counsel Lawrence Walsh on charges of
> withholding information from Congress, March 1988.

I still think Ollie North is a hero. And, on the other hand, in any talk about what I do on pardons [for North and Poindexter], I think with the case now before the courts, that's just something I can't discuss now. But I just have to believe that they are going to be found innocent because I don't think they are guilty of any lawbreaking.

> President Reagan, March 25, 1988, regarding the March 16 indictment of North,
> Poindexter, Secord and Hakim on charges including conspiracy to defraud the
> government, false statements, falsification, destruction and removal of documents and
> obstruction of justice. Carl "Spitz" Channell and Richard Miller pleaded guilty
> to conspiracy to defraud the government in 1987.

15

Diversions

Well, when the President does it, that means that it is not illegal.

Richard Nixon, television interview, May 19, 1977.

When the Commander-in-Chief of a nation finds it necessary to order employees of the government or agencies of the government to do things that would technically break the law, he has to be able to declare it legal for them to do that.

Ronald Reagan, agreeing with Nixon.[1]

Your work will make a great movie one day.

President Reagan to Oliver North, November 25, 1986.[2]

The bombshell dropped in a Reagan-Meese press conference on November 25, 1986. Funds from the now widely exposed U.S. arms sales to Iran were diverted to the contras. North was fingered as the culprit and fired. Poindexter, his allegedly unwitting accomplice, was allowed to resign.

The mid-term election had given Democrats control of the Senate and put the administration on the political defensive. Behind the now torn Teflon curtain, Wizard Reagan's White House was trading guns for hostages. The "freedom fighters' " yellow brick road was paved with slush funds.

The policy of selling arms to Iran may have originated in 1980 with a Reagan campaign effort to deny Carter the opportunity to benefit from release of the American hostages before the presidential election. According to former Iranian President Bani-Sadr and others, Reagan advisers such as Richard Allen and Robert McFarlane negotiated an October deal to trade weapons to Iran after Reagan took office in exchange for Iranian stalling in the hostage negotiations with Carter. The hostages were not released until the day Reagan was inaugurated—the ultimate photo opportunity. Israel began sending weapons to Iran in the first half of 1981. While these events are beyond the scope of this book, they should not be beyond the scope of the Iran-contra investigations.[3]

Cleansing

The televised diversion confession illustrated the principle that the best defense is a good offense. The White House wanted to preempt the Watergate-style charges of coverup that would have ensued if investigators and reporters successfully followed the money in the seemingly separate Iran and contra scandals to their intersection at North and Secord. In the days preceding the diversion announcement, investigators at the International Center for Development Policy suspected a diversion of funds and were urging reporters to pursue the story.

Weeks earlier on October 7, CIA Director William Casey heard from a former law client, Roy Furmark, that Saudi billionaire Adnan Khashoggi and two Canadian investors were complaining of not being repaid monies advanced in the Iran arms sales, and were threatening to expose the deal. Furmark also said that Iranian businessman Manucher Ghorbanifar, the initial channel to Iran, was upset at being cut out, and (by most accounts) told Casey that Ghorbanifar suspected funds had been diverted to the contras.[4]

North later tried to pin the idea for the diversion on Ghorbanifar, with an apparently phony story about a bathroom conversation in late January 1986. It was only one of many North flights of fancy at the Iran-contra hearings. The first diversion was authorized in late November 1985 when Israel was still the arms conduit. On December 6, North told Israeli Ministry of Defense officials that he intended to divert profits from future arms sales to Nicaragua operations. He recommended to Poindexter that the United States take over the actual arms sales using Secord as a conduit—an arrangement adopted in Reagan's January 17, 1986 finding on Iran.[5]

By the time of the diversion announcement on November 25, much of the paper trail had been shredded, burned or altered. "I started shredding documents in earnest," North testified, "after a discussion with Director Casey in early October when he told me that Mr. Furmark had come to him and talked to him about the use of Iran arms sales money to support the resistance. That…was preceded shortly—by the crash or shootdown of the aircraft Mr. Hasenfus was on. And Director Casey and I had a lengthy discussion about the fact that this whole thing was coming unraveled and that things ought to be 'cleaned up' and I started cleaning things up."[6]

The "cleanup" accelerated when Attorney General Meese began his conveniently sloppy inquiry on November 21. In North's office, Meese's men quickly found a smoking memo that had somehow escaped the shredders and burn bags. In the so-called "diversion memo," North described a planned arms sale to Iran and stated:

The residual funds from this transaction are allocated as follows:

— $2 million will be used to purchase replacement TOWs for the original 508 sold by Israel to Iran for the release of Benjamin Weir. This is the only way that we have found to meet our commitment to replenish these stocks.

— $12 million will be used to purchase critically needed supplies for the Nicaraguan Democratic Resistance Forces. This materiel is essential to cover shortages in resistance inventories resulting from their current offensives and Sandinista counter-attacks and to "bridge" the period between now and when Congressionally approved lethal assistance (beyond the $25 million in "defensive" arms) can be delivered.

The memo recommended to Poindexter "that the President approve the structure depicted above under 'Current Situation' and the Terms of Reference at Tab A, dated April 4, 1986." The recovered memo's spaces for a presidential "Approve" or "Disapprove" were blank.[7]

Fall Guys

Whether accidental or contrived, the discovery and revelation of the diversion memo allowed the administration to shape the Iran-contragate agenda around a decoy question: What did the president know *of the diversion* and when did he know it? If the *Iran-Contra Report* is correct, the diversion itself was not that significant financially: at least $3.8 million of the total $16.1 million in arms sales profits were used by the Enterprise for contra assistance.[8] That is far less than the tribute solicited from third countries; donated by patrons of the American right; or diverted through "humanitarian" assistance, military exercises, aid to Honduras and CIA-Pentagon programs such as Operation Elephant Herd. And it is less than alleged revenues from drug contraband, the subject that dared not speak its name at the hearings.

Two Baltimore antiwar activists who tried to unfurl a banner at the hearings— "Ask About Cocaine"—were promptly thrown out and arrested. The only citizen voices not considered a disruption in the hearing room were those represented by the stack of telegrams displayed by Oliver and Betsy North. Some of those supposedly all sympathetic telegrams were actually protesting North's behavior. Instead of exposing the orchestrated telegram campaign designed to intimidate Congress, the media played up "Olliemania."

Newsweek's cover for July 20, 1987 featured Oliver and Betsy North under the headline: "The Fall Guy Becomes a Folk Hero: Ollie Takes The Hill." Never mind that *Newsweek's* own poll presented later in the story indicated that more people disagreed than agreed with the statement "He is a patriot and hero." The lead raved about North as "a new national folk hero who somehow embodied Jimmy Stewart, Gary Cooper and John Wayne in one bemedaled uniform. He touched off a tidal wave of telegrams, flowers and letters." The networks gave North's testimony star treatment.

Watergate veteran Carl Bernstein commented that "the decision by the networks not to offer gavel-to-gavel coverage of the hearings…said, in effect, that the issues weren't important or dramatic enough to justify keeping people away from their soaps. When the networks got back on the air, they sent us a pack of theater critics, not reporters, who assured us that Ollie was playing boffo."[9] North was crowned a "winner." Democracy was the loser.

To avoid the issue of impeachment, Congress conditioned it on the implausible discovery of a diversion smoking gun covered with Ronald Reagan's fingerprints. The larger violations of law and constitutional responsibility to see that the laws are "faithfully executed," which were outlined in Rep. Henry Gonzalez's (D-TX) lonely resolution calling for Reagan's impeachment, were ignored or underrated.[10] In the words of Sam Dash, chief counsel to the Watergate committee, "There is no reason why the House Judiciary Committee could not define what President Reagan did as an impeachable offense."[11]

Congress still trembled before the false idol of Reagan's popularity and accepted the symbolic sacrifice of North and Poindexter. When Poindexter testified that Reagan did not know of the diversion, it was, for most politicians and commentators, time to "put the Iran-contra affair behind us." Ronald Reagan would not go the way of Richard Nixon. This time, the "fall-guy" plan worked.

The fall-guy plan, as described by North, was a scenario developed with Casey as early as spring 1984 for someone to take the political rap for the president if the contra support program was exposed. On the volatile Iran-contra diversion, Poindexter would have to take the fall with North if their "top boss," Reagan, was to be protected. The fall-guy plan worked even though North said he rebelled when he learned on November 25 that he might be a criminal as well as political scapegoat.[12] And it worked although Poindexter winked that the buck stopped with Reagan, even as he claimed it stopped with himself.

Poindexter testified that Reagan would have approved of the diversion as an "implementation" of his policies, but he chose to "insulate" him "from the decision and provide some future deniability for the President if it ever leaked out." When questioned about a White House statement contradicting his testimony and stating that Reagan would not have authorized the diversion, Poindexter replied, "I understand that he [the President] said that, and I would have expected him to say that. That is the whole idea of deniability."[13]

While most Iran-contra committee members understood that Reagan was responsible, whether he explicitly authorized the diversion or not, Congress did not hold him accountable. Deniability worked because Congress let it work, for the diversion and larger crimes. Senate committee Chairman Daniel Inouye (D-HI) was relieved. He had hoped from the start "we never come across a smoking gun" linking Reagan to the diversion because "these are dangerous times to be going through that type of exercise [impeachment]." He said the congressional report would avoid critical assessment of Reagan's role because "whenever our president is weakened and our country divided, our adversary takes advantage."[14]

The Reagan administration sacrificed democracy in the name of "dangerous times." Congress did the same.

Beating Around the Bush

While Poindexter protected the president's deniability, Bush's national security adviser, Donald Gregg, covered up for the vice president. Bush was spared political discomfort during the Iran-contra hearings when his aides testified out of public sight. He was treated again with kid gloves in the *Iran-Contra Report*. The news media, meanwhile, gave more urgent attention to former Senator Gary Hart's extramarital relations than Bush's extra-legal relations with the contras; at this writing, Donna Rice is a household name, Donald Gregg is not.

George Bush's potential smoking gun was Felix Rodriguez. As discussed in chapter 11, Rodriguez met twice with Bush in January 1985 before traveling to Central America. Though Gregg denies that he or the vice president knew of Rodriguez's work with the contras, the evidence suggests otherwise. Rodriguez met in February with General Paul Gorman of the Southern Command who reported Rodriguez's work with the contras to both Colonel James Steele and the U.S. ambassador to El Salvador, Thomas Pickering. Gorman highlighted Rodriguez's "acquaintanceship" with the vice president dating back to Bush's days as CIA director. Rodriguez also met that month with Gregg, a longtime friend. On September 10, North met with Gregg and Steele and, according to North's notes, discussed establishing contra airlift operations at Ilopango Air Base. Ten days later, North asked Rodriguez to make the arrangements.

In November, Bush sent a handwritten note to North: "As I head off to Maine for Thanksgiving I just want to wish you a Happy one with the hope you get some well deserved rest...Your dedication and tireless work with the hostage thing and with Central America realy gives me cause for great pride in you and *Thanks*." In his deposition to the Iran-contra committees, Gregg claimed to believe that Bush was thanking North for help with Bush's Central America trip, two years earlier, in 1983.[15]

On January 9, 1986, North wrote in his notebook: "Felix talking too much about VP connection."[16]

Gregg arranged for Bush and Rodriguez to meet again on May 1, 1986. The scheduling memo for the May 1 meeting states: "To brief the Vice President on the status of the war in El Salvador and resupply of the Contras."

Phyllis Byrne, the secretary who typed the memo, testified that Colonel Sam Watson, Gregg's deputy, gave her that information. Watson, who met with Rodriguez on April 30 and again in June, testified that he did not provide that description. It seems obvious that Byrne would not have made up the business of the meeting or accidentally slipped in "resupply of the Contras," a subject supposedly unknown to Bush and his staff at that time. The phrase "resupply of the contras" was retained in Gregg's briefing memorandum for Bush.[17]

Gregg denied knowing of Rodriguez's contra connection, although he met with him periodically and was in frequent phone contact. And Watson denies it, although he spent three days in Central America, January 19 to 21, 1986, largely in the company of Rodriguez and Col. James Steele. During the trip, ostensibly to "dis-

cuss counterinsurgency operations" in El Salvador, Watson made two visits to contra camps in Honduras.[18]

According to Rodriguez, at the May 1 meeting he was planning to tell Bush
that he was leaving Central America, without telling him the reason—which he later
explained as disgust with the Secord group and its Ed Wilson connections. Before
Rodriguez's announcement, North and Ambassador to El Salvador Edwin Corr came
in and told Bush what a good job Rodriguez was doing. Rodriguez testified he was
then embarrassed to tell Bush he was leaving, and ended up staying on. Rodriguez
said at "no point in any of this conversation did I ever mention doing anything that
was remotely connected to Nicaragua and the contras."[19] Former Senator Nicholas
Brady, who was also present at least for part of the meeting, testified that the resupply operation was not discussed. If true, Brady's presence may explain why the meeting did not cover the topic listed on the scheduling memo—if indeed it did not.

Rodriguez had a heated dispute with Rafael Quintero in August over whether
the Enterprise or the FDN, as Rodriguez believed, owned the supply planes. He
decided to take his complaints to Donald Gregg. Gregg claims that's when he first
learned Rodriguez was working with the contras.

According to Gregg's notes of their August 8 meeting, Rodriguez made the fol-
lowing points: "Using Ed Wilson group for supplies…'Mr. Green' = Rafael
Quintero…A swap of weapons for $ was arranged to get aid for Contras. Clines and
General Secord tied in. Hand grenades bought for $3—sold for $9 [to Calero]…DICK
GADD purchases things got 1st Caribou—big profit. Clines is getting $ from [name
deleted] or whatever: buying things at great profit. He hired pilots for Qadhafi with
Wilson. BOB DUTTON brought in as mgr for project after a flap…"[20]

Gregg convened a meeting on August 12 to discuss Rodriguez's allegations
with Watson, Steele, Corr, Fiers, North's NSC associate Robert Earl (formerly with
Bush's task force on terrorism), NSC Director of Latin American Affairs Raymond
Burghardt and Deputy Assistant Secretary of State William Walker. Gregg reportedly emphasized that he considered Clines unreliable, but had faith in Rodriguez. It
was reported in December 1986 that Gregg couldn't remember whether he informed
Bush of the meeting.[21] But Gregg testified to the Iran-contra committees that he did
not pass on information about or from the meeting to Bush, because "it was a very
murky business…We had never discussed the contras. We had no responsibility for
it. We had no expertise in it. I wasn't at all certain what this amounted to.

"I had the names of four or five Americans on an obscure air base in Central
America who apparently were ripping off donated funds and making unseemly
profits. I felt I had passed along that material to the organizations who could do
something about it, and I frankly did not think it was Vice Presidential level."[22]

On its face, the explanation is absurd. Bush was a member of the National
Security Council, for which the contras were a primary concern. Bush's involvement
is evident in the pre-Boland II paper trail on the contras. A November 1983 memo
from North and Constantine Menges (Burghardt's predecessor) to McFarlane states
that the "President and Vice President have been asked to concur on these increases
[in the number of weapons supplied to the contras] in each previous case."[23] Mc-
Farlane, as noted earlier, personally told Bush of the Saudi money to finance the

contras. On April 15, 1985, Bush and McFarlane gave a White House briefing on Central America to donors attending the Nicaraguan Refugee Fund Dinner that Reagan keynoted.

Gregg, a longtime CIA officer, headed the NSC Intelligence Directorate in charge of covert operations, including the contras, until mid 1982. Bush seems a logical person to talk with if Gregg were really concerned about Clines' involvement since Bush was director of the CIA when the Wilson scandal surfaced.

Watson's notes on the meeting state: "Felix—Tom Clines, Secord—Ripping off Contras—Fraud, a crime to profit."[24] Conspicuously absent from Gregg's list of people representing "organizations who could do something about it" were officials of the Justice Department. Gregg said he had no idea then that the resupply missions were illegal. "The only illegality or the only unpleasant smell about what Felix had was that there were corrupt, inept guys who were ripping off whatever operation it was they were involved in."[25]

About Gregg's note that "a swap of weapons for $ was arranged to get aid for Contras, Clines and General Secord tied in"—which sounds like the Iran-contra diversion—Rodriguez professed ignorance and Gregg claimed it referred to the use of "proceeds which were coming from the public donations, et cetera."[26] It remains unexplained in the *Iran-Contra Report*. So does a reference to North talking with the "VP" about Rodriguez in an August KL-43 message from Richard Secord to Robert Earl.

According to reporter Allan Nairn, citing "former intelligence agents who collaborated with the Vice President's office, Bush's principal involvement with the contras dates to a series of 1983 conversations between Bush and Casey concerning Congressional plans to restrict contra operations…[and] the prospects for alternative contra aid channels. The conversations at times included President Reagan and…Edwin Meese."[27]

Gregg wrote a secret September 18, 1984 memo to Bush, titled "Funding for the Contras," reporting: "In response to your question, Dewey Clarridge supplied the following information." The memo discussed political and military aspects of the contra war as well as private fundraising.[28]

In 1983, Gregg provided a letter of recommendation to Gustavo Villoldo, a former CIA agent and Bay of Pigs veteran, to work as a contra combat adviser in Honduras. As described by Miskito leader Steadman Fagoth, who worked closely with Villoldo, his strategy featured "small-group battle tactics, economic and commercial sabotage, and a program of political kidnappings, aimed at the wives and children of Sandinista officials." Villoldo worked in Honduras until late 1984; by then his relations with FDN leaders and CIA officials had deteriorated.

Nairn wrote that "Villoldo was part of an old-boy network of former CIA agents known to Gregg from his own career at the agency. According to intelligence sources who dealt with Bush's office, Gregg provided these men with contacts and introductions, gave them directions on how to tap into sources of clandestine funds, and encouraged them to recruit contra advisers in the United States and Latin America. Deniability was said to be a prime consideration, and none is known to have had written contractual relationships with Bush's office or the White House staff."[29]

Richard Brenneke, an Oregon-based arms dealer and former CIA agent, said his notes reflect conversations with Gregg about contra supply during 1985 and 1986. Brenneke said he checked the credentials of potential buyers with Gregg and that Gregg and his staff provided guidance on buyers, suppliers and logistics.[30]

Gregg's old-boy network reportedly said Yes to drug smuggling. Felix Rodriguez's alleged involvement in funneling millions of dollars of cocaine money to the contras was discussed in chapter 12. Other allegations implicate Gregg and Bush.

As Robert Parry reported in *Newsweek*, Brenneke claims that he was recruited by the Israeli Mossad station chief in Guatemala, Pesakh Ben-Or, to participate in the contra supply network run by former Mossad officer Michael Harari, an adviser to Panamanian General Manuel Noreiga. According to Brenneke, Gregg was the Washington contact for the supply operation, which was financed by the Medellin cocaine cartel. The cartel provided planes to fly arms to the contras; the same planes flew drugs to the United States. Noriega, who is under indictment for unrelated drug charges in the United States, allegedly took a cut of the profits for drug traffic through Panama.

Brenneke claims that he was aboard a plane flying drugs to Amarillo, Texas in mid 1985. When he tried to discuss the drug connection with Gregg, he was told: "You do what you were assigned to do. Don't question the decision of your betters." Gregg denies ever speaking with Brenneke. Staff members of the Kerry narcotics subcommittee say they have corroborated part of Brenneke's account with another ex-Mossad agent and with former Panamanian Consul Jose Blandon. Blandon testified to Kerry's committee that Noriega—who was on the CIA payroll at $200,000 a year, the same salary as the president of the United States—told him that he knew things that "could affect the elections of the United States."[31]

In late August 1986, Barbara Studley, the Miami arms dealer who worked with John Singlaub in supplying the contras, wrote a memo to North warning that the disclosure of "covert black money" flowing into Honduras "could damage Vice President Bush." Studley wrote the memo after meeting with David Duncan, a Miami arms dealer knowledgeable about South African support and other schemes to supply the contras (see chapter 10).

One of the potentially damaging Honduras-contra connections is the so-called Arms Supermarket run by Mario Delamico, a friend of Felix Rodriguez; Ronald Martin; and James McCoy, the former U.S. military attache to the Somoza regime and friend of Adolfo Calero. According to Brenneke, the Arms Supermarket was stocked by a network run by Mossad's Honduras station chief, David Marcus Katz, which was different from the network run by Harari in Panama.[32]

North's notebooks contain frequent references to the Arms Supermarket, which North knew to be financed by drug money. A July 12, 1985 entry reads: "[deletion] plans to seize all...when Supermarket comes to a bad end. $14M to finance came from drugs." North's entry for September 10, 1985 (mentioned earlier), refers to a meeting with Colonel Steele and Don Gregg and states: "Approached by Mario delAmico. Claims to be close to [deleted]. Claims to be close to the FDN." In June 1986,

North noted a need to "pay off" Supermarket partners Martin and McCoy.[33]

Another Bush-contra connection is his son, Jeb. In February 1985, John Ellis "Jeb" Bush, then the Dade County Republican chairman and now Florida's secretary of commerce, gave his father a letter from Doctor Mario Castejon, a Guatemalan politician seeking support for an international medical brigade to treat contra combatants in the field. In a March 3 letter responding to Castejon, the vice president suggested that he meet with North.[34] This was at a time when the U.S. government was prohibited from supplying the contras directly or indirectly with any aid, lethal or nonlethal.

Jeb Bush has been a key White House emissary to the Miami Nicaraguan community and a champion of the contra cause. He has appeared at numerous contra fundraising events.[35] According to Nairn, U.S. Customs agents from Miami reportedly told Independent Counsel Lawrence Walsh that Jeb Bush may have been linked to contra arms shipments. Jeb Bush has acknowledged helping to raise funds for "humanitarian" aid, but strongly denies any involvement in arms shipments. "Sure, there's a pretty good chance that arms were shipped," he told Nairn, "but does that break any law? I'm not sure it's illegal. The Neutrality Act is a completely untested notion, established in the 1800s."[36]

As for George Bush, he agrees with Reagan that Oliver North is a hero. He told "60 Minutes" correspondent Diane Sawyer, "Don't put me down as feeling anything is definitely wrong with what Ollie North has done in support of the Contras, 'cause I'm for support for the Contras...And I keep repeating that. I want to get that into every single question so it won't end up on the cutting room floor...I support strongly the Contras. I really feel viscerally on this."[37]

Watchdogs With Blinders

In a study of the 1975 Church Committee inquiry on the CIA, (led by the late Senator Frank Church of Idaho) former committee investigator Loch Johnson observed, "The most conspicuous figure in the tapestry woven by the committee reports was a blind and toothless congressional watchdog."[38] During the May 1976 debate over new intelligence oversight legislation, Senator Lowell Weicker (R-CT) lamented, "We have had weak sight, we have had blind sight, we have had hindsight, we have had short sight, but we have not had oversight."

Years later, little has changed, and not all of the changes are positive. As Rep. Norman Mineta (D-CA), a charter member of the House Intelligence Committee, quipped in 1983, "We are like mushrooms. They [the CIA] keep us in the dark and feed us a lot of manure."[39]

When the klieg lights turned on, the memories of government officials and their intermediaries often turned off. "A mass epidemic of amnesia...seemed to sweep Washington in the summer of 1975," wrote Johnson. "Witnesses with vaunted reputations for clear minds mysteriously could no longer remember essential details of operations in which they had been intimately involved."[40]

So it went in 1987. Poindexter and Meese held the convenient amnesia records, but witness after witness said "I don't recall," "I can't recollect," on matters large and small. A joke made the rounds during the Reagan-appointed Tower Board (composed of former Senators John Tower and Ed Muskie and former National Security Adviser Brent Scowcroft): "What did the president forget and when did he forget it?"

There was another problem. What did Congress want to know and when did it want to know it? As columnist Mary McGrory remarked during the Church Committee hearings, if the CIA preferred cloaks and daggers, Congress had a "penchant for earmuffs and blinders."[41] The Iran-contra hearings made the Church Committee hearings look like the Inquisition.

Regarding Nicaragua, the Iran-contra hearings actually did more damage than good: they served as a national soap box for contra disinformation. As Adolfo Calero put it, "We came out of the hearings smelling like a flower."[42] It often appeared that the chief crime of the diversion was that the Enterprisers pocketed hefty profits while the poor contras went without.

The hearings often degenerated into a one-sided contra aid debate. A two-sided debate would have been stacked in favor of the contras; 17 out of 26 committee members voted for the $100 million: Senators San Nunn (D-GA), David Boren (D-OK), Howell Heflin (D-AL), William Cohen (R-ME), Warren Rudman (R-NH), Orrin Hatch (R-UT), James McClure (R-ID) and Paul Trible (R-VA) and Representatives Dante Fascell (D-FL), Les Aspin (D-WI), Ed Jenkins (D-GA), Dick Cheney (R-WY), William Broomfield (R-MI), Henry Hyde (R-IL), Bill McCollum (R-FL), Michael DeWine (R-OH) and James Courter (R-NJ). Opposed were Senators Daniel Inouye (D-HI), George Mitchell (D-ME) and Paul Sarbanes (D-MD) and Representatives Lee Hamilton (D-IN), Thomas Foley (D-WA), Peter Rodino (D-NJ), Jack Brooks (D-TX), Edward Boland (D-MA) and Louis Stokes (D-OH). Informed and vocal contra critics, such as Senators John Kerry (D-MA) and Christopher Dodd (D-CT) and Representatives Pat Schroeder (D-CO), Ronald Dellums (D-CA), Gerry Studds (D-MA), George Miller (D-CA), Les AuCoin (D-OR) and Barbara Boxer (D-CA), weren't there to counter the diatribes of Hatch and Hyde.

To make matters worse, the contra supporters won not by advantage, but by default. Contra opponents complied unilaterally with a prior committee agreement to focus on process, not policy. They shared in the pretense that the objective of the contra program was the "noble" cause of democracy in Nicaragua.[43] They preached platitudes such as "the ends don't justify the means"—belied by their own records, for example, in supporting the bombing of Libyan civilians to "combat terrorism." Contra supporters argued passionately that the ends sometimes justified the means, and they used an unchallenged, distorted version of reality to insist that national security was at stake.

Even with contra critics such as Kerry on the committees, slander of the Nicaraguan government would probably have gone unchallenged. As *Boston Globe* editorial writer Randolph Ryan noted, "The general rule that governs all American politicians and all American journalists who aspire to be taken seriously is that you never, ever, give the Sandinista government a fair shake, at least not in public."

Senator Kerry, who John Hull (quoted in chapter 12) would like to see shot for treason, has prefaced his comments about contra aid with the "serious" politician's disclaimer: "I agree with the president about the Sandinista problems, and yes, they have been increasingly repressive within that regime. I don't think there's anybody in the U.S. Congress who is saying anything positive about the Sandinistas. But that's not the issue." As Ryan put it, "What the world sees when it looks at Washington is a quavering Congress which is allowing President Reagan to shift the terms of debate steadily to the right, steadily toward war, although the facts do not justify it."[44]

The combination of one-sided debate and Ollie-media-mania had an instant impact on public opinion. During the hearings, someone asked me what had changed in Nicaragua. Had the Nicaraguan government taken a sharp turn for the worse? She assumed it had, having heard only bad things about Nicaragua and praise aplenty for the contras. She wasn't alone. Public opinion polls registered a significant increase in the percentage of Americans favoring contra aid. Though the polls reverted to large majorities opposing contra assistance, there were important lingering effects. The pro-contra grassroots base was rejuvenated. The Big Lies repeated during the hearings have resonated loudly in subsequent pro-contra campaigns. And senators and congressmen (they were all men) showed that even upon their loftiest perch they could be cowed by an anti-communist stampede.

The $100 million flowed throughout the hearings and more was to follow. In May 1987, the House rejected Rep. Barbara Boxer's amendment requiring the president to certify that no roads, airports or other facilities improved as part of U.S. military maneuvers in Honduras would be used to support the contras. In June, it passed Rep. Robert Walker's (R-PA) ambiguous amendment that found "that travel by United States citizens to Central America for the purpose of performing services or providing other assistance for the Government of Nicaragua or for Communist or Communist-supported guerrilla groups causes serious damage to the national security and foreign policy of the United States" and called for the State Department to restrict travel by American citizens "if the purpose…is to perform services or provide other assistance to the military operations of the Government of Nicaragua." Conservatives hoped the language would apply to volunteers working on development projects in Nicaragua's war zones or Witness for Peace and Veterans for Peace activists living in and visiting areas of likely attack.

With the public phase of hearings behind it, Congress authorized in September the first $3.5 million in new installments on contra aid. That same month, the contra support organization CMA held its national convention. Bumper stickers read: "Give Aid to the Contras, Give AIDS to the Sandinistas." CMA leader Tom Posey told a reporter, "A lot of people in Congress, were it up to me, would be in prison by sundown today." (John Hull would shoot them at sunrise.) Adolfo Calero's brother Mario, the contra supplier who has lived in the United States since age ten, derided the hearings as "Congress-gate." He cited a flaw in the otherwise optimum American political system: "There is a very good word in Spanish—you don't have it in English—and it's *libertinaje*. It means 'excessive liberty.' "[45]

Assaulting Civil Liberties

A trail of abuse was excavated during the 1975 Church (Senate) and Pike (House) investigations. As summarized by Church Committee investigator Loch Johnson:

> The CIA program to open mail from or to selected American citizens produced a secret computer bank of 1.5 million names; the FBI intelligence unit developed files on well over a million Americans, and carried out 500,000 investigations of "subversives" from 1960 to 1974 without a single court conviction; the NSA computers were fed every single cable sent overseas by Americans from 1974 until 1975; Army intelligence units conducted investigations against 100,000 American citizens during the Vietnam War.
>
> The tactics sometimes used were alien to the principles embraced by the Bill of Rights and the body of statutes that have evolved to protect civil liberties...They were, in fact, more reminiscent of the means resorted to by Hitler's SS and Beria's secret police under the Stalin regime: drug experiments conducted by the CIA on unsuspecting subjects; assassination plots attempted against foreign leaders in peacetime; murder and other violence incited among blacks by anonymous FBI letters; the families and friendships of dissidents disrupted by concealed bureau harassment; burglaries carried out in the homes and offices of suspected subversives; elections manipulated in democratic countries; tax information misused for political purposes; academic and religious groups infiltrated.[46]

Many such activities occurred in the 1980s. None received serious attention at the Iran-contra hearings. The alleged U.S. role in the 1984 bombing of Pastora's press conference was treated as if it were baseless slander. There was no inquiry into assassination programs against Sandinista officials and community leaders. There was no investigation of government and rightwing surveillance, infiltration and harassment of groups and individuals opposed to U.S. policy in Central America.

In November 1980, W. Mark Felt, former acting associate director of the FBI, and Edward Miller, chief of the FBI Intelligence Division, were convicted of authorizing break-ins into the homes of citizens without a warrant or probable cause. A few months later, on April 15, 1981, President Reagan granted them an unconditional pardon. Felt commented, "This is going to be the biggest shot in the arm of the intelligence community for a long time."[47]

In his book on political spying, Frank Donner observed, "The White House, it is clear, viewed the two [FBI] men as heroes who were entitled not merely to forgiveness but to commendation; according to President Reagan, they 'acted on high principle to bring an end to terrorism that was threatening our nation.' "[48] The "terrorism that was threatening our nation," which for Reagan justified massive violation of civil liberties, was not an invasion but the Weather Underground.

In December 1981, Reagan signed Executive Order 12333. It threw open the floodgates on domestic spying that had been tightened somewhat after exposure of the FBI COINTELPRO operations against the American Indian Movement, the Black liberation movement, the antiwar movement and others. As summarized by the New York-based Center for Constitutional Rights (CCR), "Under the labels of 'foreign intelligence,' 'counter-intelligence' and 'terrorism,' the FBI and the CIA are permitted to surveil Americans, even if they are not suspected of breaking the law or acting on behalf of a foreign power...Warrantless searches are permitted on probable cause to believe that the target of the investigation, if not the target of the search, is 'an agent of a foreign power.' The meaning of 'agent of a foreign power' is not even defined...The Order also allows for the infiltration of lawful political organizations not only for the purpose of gathering intelligence, but also for the purpose of control."[49]

Reagan administration action recalled the Nixon-era Huston Plan that recommended giving the FBI, CIA and National Security Agency (NSA) wide authority to monitor Americans' international cables, telegrams and mail; intensify electronic surveillance of domestic dissidents; break into offices and homes; and expand surveillance of college students. Former Nixon aide Tom Huston, author of the plan, later came to see the approach as dangerous. Huston testified in 1975: "The risk was that you would get people who would be susceptible to political considerations as opposed to national security considerations, or would construe political considerations to be national security considerations—to move from the kid with a bomb to the kid with a picket sign, and from the kid with a picket sign to the kid with the bumper sticker of the opposing candidate. And you just keep going down the line."[50] The Reagan administration kept going down the line.

On November 6, 1984, election day in the United States, an Ohio political science professor was returning from a trip to observe the Nicaraguan election. U.S. Customs agents seized and photocopied Nicaraguan campaign materials (along with a copy of the CIA's contra manual). The photocopies were disseminated to a Customs intelligence division and the following information was entered under the professor's name in the Customs computer: "INTELLIGENCE: SUBJECT IN POSSESSION OF MATERIALS PERTAINING TO ELECTIONS IN NICARAGUA—ALLEGED." That's only one of many such Orwellian welcomes greeting American travelers returning from Nicaragua. Others have had their personal address books, diaries and notebooks seized and copied.[51]

Break-ins are another sign of the resurgent thought police. As of January 1988, the Movement Support Network of the Center for Constitutional Rights had recorded over 90 burglaries and break-ins with apparent Central America-related political motives since 1983 when it first began tracking them. As described by the Center for Constitutional Rights in congressional testimony, the "burglaries fit a pattern. The targets are similar in that they are individuals or organizations engaged in dissent from administration Central American policies. Many of the groups or individuals targeted are the subjects of FBI investigations, or are at least referenced and indexed in FBI files. Most significant is the fact that the burglaries appear not to be motivated by any pecuniary interest. Only in a few instances is anything of monetary value taken, although valuables, including cash, have been readily available...The intruders...appear to know their victims' schedules. They also appear to know the general or precise location of the documents. In all cases files are rifled, in most cases papers (most often membership or donor lists, or other important files, such as those containing the names of persons [Central American refugees] being given sanctuary) are strewn about the premises or left lying atop desks and filing cabinets. In a few instances important documents have been stolen."

For example, on November 30, 1986, days after the diversion announcement, a break-in occurred at the Washington offices of the International Center for Development Policy. Files were ransacked and one stolen document concerned a Southern Air Transport contra arms flight.

On July 12, 1986, intruders ransacked the apartment of a Michigan woman active in the Central America Solidarity Committee. "They rifled her files and threw papers and books on the floor. However, her T.V., stereo, and rent money were ignored. Two weeks earlier, the woman's name appeared in a Detroit newspaper, in a story about the arrest of 12 persons (including herself) for an act of civil disobedience."

From November 1984 through June 1986, the offices sharing space in the basement of the Old Cambridge Baptist Church in Cambridge, Massachusetts, were broken into eight times. The targets included: the New England Central American Network (NECAN), Central American Solidarity Association, Central American Information Office, Educators in Support of ANDES (the Salvadoran teachers union) and New Institute of Central America (NICA). The Church itself had become a sanctuary for Central American refugees the week before the first break-in. On May 15, 1987, the NICA office experienced another break-in. Intruders poured muriatic acid on some computer disks. NECAN was broken into again on May 3, 1988.

Among the other organizations and sanctuary churches that have experienced break-ins are: the Central American Historical Institute, located on the campus of Georgetown University in Washington, DC; MADRE, a New York-based national friendship association with women in Central America and the Caribbean; Calvery United Methodist Church in Washington, DC; Veterans Fast for Life, World Peacemakers and Washington Pledge of Resistance, all housed in the Church of the Saviour in Washington, DC; North American Congress on Latin America, publishers of the *NACLA Report on the Americas*; three offices at the Wheadon United Church in Evanston, Illinois; United Church of Sante Fe, New Mexico; St. Williams Catholic Church, Louisville, Kentucky; University Baptist Church, Seattle, Washington; Michigan Interfaith Committee on Central American Rights.[52]

There are different theories regarding the break-ins which are not mutually exclusive: They may be carried out by FBI agents with headquarters' authorization or by members of rightwing groups at the behest of local FBI agents. Or they may be the work of rightwing organizations working independently or in concert with government agencies.

Following the long and sordid tradition of government-nongovernment collaboration to counter the varied menaces of "radicalism," the FBI has relied on a network of so-called private intelligence informants to provide information on critics of Central America policy, including background data on activists and donors and reports on organizational activities. A central figure in this rightwing thought police auxiliary is former Western Goals "subversive" tracker John Rees. Rees and his wife S. Louise Rees have infiltrated left organizations (using pseudonyms) and worked as informers for the Washington, DC police and the FBI. They publish the *Information Digest*, a newsletter focused primarily on left and liberal groups and individuals that is circulated to the FBI and other federal security and intelligence agencies, local police units, rightwing organizations, corporate security offices, private detective agencies and selected media such as *Reader's Digest*. The Rees *Digest* also receives information from local police and police informants. Among the other ideological-ly-biased sources of FBI "intelligence" are the John Birch Society; Young Americas Foundation (founded by older, former members of Young Americans for Freedom); the Council for Inter-American Security; Unification Church members, working, for example, through their college-based affiliate, CARP; and rightwing Central Americans inside the United States.[53]

An ex-FBI operative, Frank Varelli, has testified to infiltrating the Dallas chapter of CISPES (Committee in Solidarity with the People of El Salvador) and compiling a "terrorist photo album," with reports on such "subversives" as former Ambassador to El Salvador Robert White, Rep. Michael Barnes and Senators Christopher Dodd and Claiborne Pell, now chairman of the Foreign Relations Committee. The "terrorist photo album," reportedly includes photos and reports on 690 individuals opposed to the administration's Central America policies. According to Varelli, the FBI provided him with John Rees' material to prepare entries in the "terrorist" album.[54]

Varelli (born Franklin Agustin Martinez Varela) posed as a Salvadoran refugee named Gilberto Mendoza whose family had been killed by death squads. In reality, Varelli's father was the ex-commander of the Salvadoran National Police. Varelli infiltrated Dallas CISPES from 1981 to 1984. He said the FBI wanted to "break" CISPES and conducted break-ins at the homes of CISPES members over a six-month period, taking or photographing documents. He said an agent he worked with used to go regularly to the Southern Methodist University campus "to pay the Moonies"; the Moonies would start fights whenever CISPES held demonstrations. Varelli provided the FBI with reports on CISPES activities and prepared false literature to be distributed under CISPES' name. He said he did not follow suggestions that he plant guns on CISPES members to make the peaceful organization appear to match the FBI's subversive image. Nor did he carry out an FBI plan to seduce a nun who was a CISPES activist and blackmail her with hoped-for secret bedroom photos.[55]

Varelli testified in hearings before the House Judiciary Subcommittee on Civil and Constitutional Liberties, chaired by Rep. Don Edwards (D-CA), in February 1987. So did the Center for Constitutional Rights and other concerned organizations. Unfortunately, Congress and the media paid scant attention. Dan Noyes and Angus MacKenzie of the San Francisco-based Center for Investigative Reporting were on the FBI story before then and KRON television aired a report in February 1987; Project Censored awarded Noyes, MacKenzie and KRON producer Jonathan Dann the top honors in their list of the ten most underreported stories of 1986. Not until a year later, when CCR obtained and released a portion of the relevant FBI files (heavily censored) under the Freedom of Information Act, did the sweeping FBI surveillance receive wide exposure, however fleeting.

The FBI began investigating CISPES in 1981 for alleged violations of the Foreign Agents Registration Act. Among the material the FBI submitted to the Justice Department in its request to investigate CISPES was an article by John Rees in the *Review of the News*, a John Birch Society publication; FBI Assistant Director Revell cited it later to defend the investigation. When no evidence of illegality was found, the FBI renewed the nationwide investigation in 1983 under the wide counter-terrorism authority described above. In the nationwide probe, coordinated from Dallas and later from Washington, the FBI used wiretaps, undercover agents, informers and photographic surveillance not only of CISPES but of hundreds of organizations whose work brought them in touch with CISPES or its members. The FBI treated other organizations as potential "front groups" of CISPES.

Among the groups included in the FBI CISPES files were Amnesty International, the American Federation of Teachers, the American Civil Liberties Union, Clergy and Laity Concerned, First Run Features film distributors, Friends Peace Committee, Maryknoll Sisters, Mobilization for Survival, National Association of Women Religious, New Jewish Agenda, North American Congress on Latin America, Oxfam-America, Peace Links, Progressive Student Network, SANE, Southern Christian Leadership Conference, United Auto Workers, U.S. Catholic Conference, Washington Office on Latin America and Witness for Peace.

As CCR Freedom of Information Act Coordinator Ann Marie Buitrago explained, "failure to turn up evidence of illegality increased the pressure to expand the hunt for 'fronts' and intensify the search for covert activities" supposedly covered by peaceful, legal activity.[56]

The "Intelligence" section of the Heritage Foundation report, *Mandate for Leadership,* much embraced by the Reagan administration, states that "internal security files cannot be restricted to actual or imminent threats...Clergymen, students, businessmen, entertainers, labor officials, journalists, and government workers may engage in subversive activities without being fully aware of the extent, purpose or control of their activities...An adequate internal security program...must proceed on the understanding that many conventional and legalistic distinctions are serious impediments when imported into intelligence and internal security work." The report suggests: "One solution would be to contract with one or several of the many private corporations that have specialized in providing and analyzing such information, that can collect and disseminate relevant information without legal complications and that can respond to a crisis without transgression of administrative jurisdictions."[57] This is a mandate for destroying the already battered heritage of civil liberties.

The CISPES investigation, which was carried out under former FBI Director William Webster, now director of Central Intelligence, and Executive Assistant Director Oliver Revell, led to no indictments or arrests and found that CISPES was not engaged in "international terrorism," a result not at all surprising to those familiar with the work of CISPES or other organizations opposed to U.S. policy in Central America.

"This investigation has an odor of harassment about it," said Rep. Don Edwards, whose committee oversees the FBI. "The FBI is supposed to catch criminals—not political activists. [The late FBI Director J. Edgar] Hoover investigated long-haired young people and Dr. Martin Luther King. This looks like sort of a repeat."[58]

Heavily censored documents being released by the FBI at this writing show that the CISPES investigation was one of at least five probes concerning Central

America policy dissidents. Eighteen FBI field offices hold files under the caption "Nicaraguan Proposed Demonstrations in the US" and fifteen offices hold files under the caption "Nicaraguan Terrorist." One document headed "Nicaraguan Terrorist Matters: International Terrorism—Nicaragua," a teletype from the Chicago FBI office to FBI headquarters, deals with a 1986 demonstration by the Chicago Pledge of Resistance. The Pledge of Resistance is explicitly committed to nonviolent protest. As David Lerner of the Center for Constitutional Rights put it, "The FBI's surveillance of opponents of all of Reagan Central America policies is pervasive."[59]

Home-Grown Terror

Opponents of contemporary U.S. policy toward Central America have not only been surveilled, harassed and burglarized, they have been arrested, fined, imprisoned and assaulted for using nonviolent civil disobedience to rouse the nation's conscience. On September 1, 1987, Vietnam veteran Brian Willson was struck by a military munitions train during a demonstration outside the Concord Naval Weapons Station, a shipping point for weapons for Central America. A few days later, Tom Posey remarked, "I was rather delighted."[60]

Willson had put his body on the line before, first in war and then for peace. He and three other veterans—Duncan Murphy, George Mizo and Charles Liteky, a recipient of the Congressional Medal of Honor—conducted a 47-day fast on the Capitol steps in the fall of 1986 to galvanize public action to stop the war in Nicaragua. At the end of November 1986, Chicago FBI Special Agent John C. Ryan was ordered to conduct a "terrorism" probe of Veterans Fast for Life after vandalism at military recruiting offices. Ryan protested against applying the terrorism label to investigation of a nonviolent organization and refused to proceed on that basis. In August 1987, Ryan—who had received commendations for investigating organized crime—was fired after 21 years with the FBI.[61]

Willson and the other participants in the "Nuremberg actions" outside the Concord Naval Base had informed the police and military of their planned protest, and expected to be removed and arrested as they had been before. This time the train came barreling through and Willson was struck as he tried to jump clear.

Willson lost both his legs, but not his spirit. "I feel like standing on those tracks was like what we have often said the Germans didn't do," he explained. "Why weren't the Germans stopping the death trains going through Germany?...The life of a Nicaraguan or an El Salvadoran or an Angolan is worth no less than my life and we kill them every day with our policies. Therefore, the question I like to pose is 'How do we begin to stand in the way of that train?'"[62]

Those trying to reroute U.S. policy in Central America are facing a rising number of death threats and personal attacks. It is reminiscent of the FBI-protected San Diego-based Secret Army Organization terrorism against antiwar activists during 1967-1972 and of the CIA-nurtured terrorism of the Central American death squads.[63]

On July 7, 1987, a 24-year-old Salvadoran refugee support worker named

Yanira Corea was abducted outside the Los Angeles CISPES office. She was tortured and raped by three men. They interrogated her about the activities of coworkers, burnt her with cigarettes and carved the initials EM into her hands, which stand for *escuadron de la muerte*, death squad. They raped her with a wooden stick. One man said they should kill her. Another said, "No, this way we are going to let them know that we are here."

Before releasing Corea, they cut her tongue and wrapped her underwear around her mouth, and they threatened to harm her three-year-old son if she didn't give up her work. A few days before her abduction, Corea had received a letter with a stolen photo of her son. It contained petals of dried flowers with the note, "Flowers in the desert die," a Salvadoran death squad warning. In El Salvador, Corea's father received a letter warning that he would be punished if she persisted in her political activities. In November, when Corea was in the New York office of MADRE while on a speaking tour, a paper was slipped under the door. It was the torn half of a poster announcing Corea's appearance. There was a handwritten threat: "Do you know where your son is?" A crude drawing showed the torso of a decapitated child with a head lying nearby.[64]

On July 17, armed men abducted Ana Maria Lopez, a 31-year old Guatemalan woman also working with refugees in Los Angeles. They warned her to stop criticizing the Salvadoran government before releasing her 25 miles east of the city. In July alone, 24 people reported death threats to the Los Angeles police. Father Luis Olivares' church received an anonymous letter signed with the chillingly familiar initials EM.[65]

At this writing, the most extensive treatment given these death squad activities in the mainstream media was the February 4, 1988 episode of the television series "Simon and Simon." Unfortunately, many viewers had no idea it was based upon a true story. (A later episode of "Cagney and Lacey" also addressed the death squads.)

The Center for Constitutional Rights compiled 43 incidents of Central America-related death squad activity and rightwing threats (e.g. from the Cuban exile terrorist group, Omega 7) in nineteen U.S. cities between January 1984 and October 1987—not including many acts of vandalism and threats left behind during break-ins. Among the groups active on Nicaragua who have received threats are Pledge of Resistance in Washington and the development assistance group, TecNica, in Berkeley. A freelance journalist in Missouri, active on Central America issues, received a death threat over the phone on May 1, 1987. The caller said, "We will make one, two, many Benjamin Linders and you will be next."[66]

Benjamin Linder is not a household name in the United States, but he should be. Linder was an American engineer working in Nicaragua where, on April 28, 1987, he was ambushed and killed by contras along with two Nicaraguan colleagues. They were surveying a stream for possible use in bringing hydroelectric power to the village of San Jose de Bocay in northern Nicaragua. Linder had previously directed installation of a small hydroelectric plant bringing the first electricity and light to El Cua.

Doctor David Linder, a pathologist, analyzed his son's autopsy. Ben Linder was injured in the arm and legs and then executed. "They blew his brains out at point-blank range as he lay wounded," his father said.[67] Pablo Rosales, one of the Nicaraguans killed with Linder, was stabbed to death.

At Linder's funeral in Nicaragua, President Ortega paid him tribute: "He didn't arrive on a flight loaded down with arms, or with millions of dollars. He arrived on a flight full of dreams."

Ortega invoked Hemingway in his eulogy for Ben Linder and those killed before him. "So, for whom do the bells toll here in Nicaragua? For Pierre Grosjean, 33 years old, French doctor assassinated in Rancho Grande...Ambrosio Mogorron, 34 year old Spanish nurse, assassinated in San Jose de Bocay...For Albrecht Pflaum, 32 years old, West German doctor, assassinated in Zompopera...For Maurice Demierre, 29 years old, Swiss agronomist assassinated in Somotillo...For Paul Dessers, 39 years old, civil engineer from Belgium, assassinated in Guapotal...For Joel Fieux, 28 years old, radio technician from France, assassinated in Zompopera...For Bernhard Erick Kobersteyn, 30 year old West German civil engineer, assassinated in Zompopera...For Ivan Claude Leyraz, 32 years old, Swiss construction engineer, assassinated in Zompopera...For Benjamin Linder, 27 years old, North American engineer, assassinated in La Camaleona, Nicaragua...For more than ten Cuban teachers, technicians and volunteers, assassinated during these last few years...For the 40,000 victims that the US aggression has claimed from the Nicaraguan population in these six years of war." Ortega ended with an appeal for a negotiated peace.[68]

Contra spokesman Frank Arana announced in May 1986 that "any foreigner who voluntarily aids in development and reconstruction projects is considered an enemy."[69] In April 1987, FBI agents in five cities visited employers of twelve volunteers working with TecNica. The FBI agents had the employers call the volunteers into their offices and then the agents criticized them for "helping the communists" and warned them not to return to Nicaragua.[70] About 1,500 Americans are working in Nicaragua—teachers, engineers, computer technicians, agronomists, nurses, midwives and so on—forming an unprecedented grassroots peace corps.

It Can Happen Here

On Monday afternoon, July 13, Iran-contra committee member Jack Brooks was questioning Oliver North when he hit a sensitive nerve. Rep. Brooks asked, "Colonel North, in your work at the NSC, were you not assigned at one time to work on plans for the continuity of government in the event of a major disaster?"

North's lawyer, Brendan Sullivan, objected. Chairman Inouye told Brooks, "I believe the question touches upon a highly sensitive and classified area. So may I request that you not touch upon that, sir?"

"I was particularly concerned," Brooks responded, "because I read in Miami papers and several others that there had been a plan developed by that same agency, a contingency plan in the event of emergency that would suspend the American Constitution, and I was deeply concerned about it and wondered if that was the area in which he had worked." Inouye insisted that any discussion on the matter be reserved for executive session.

The following day, Senate Intelligence Committee Chairman David Boren addressed the issue: "Colonel North, during the discussion earlier and under questioning from Congressman Brooks, the question of the so-called Martial Law Plan had come up. We had some discussion about this in the Executive Session...And the White House counsel's office has indicated it would be appropriate [to ask questions]...as long as I refer to matter that's been printed in the media and is in the public domain."

Boren asked North about a June 5, 1987 article in the *Miami Herald*: "Let me just quote one paragraph...It says, 'Lieutenant Colonel Oliver North, for example, helped draw up a controversial plan to suspend the Constitution in the event of national crisis such as nuclear war, violent and widespread internal dissent, or national opposition to a US military invasion abroad.' And I would ask you, did you participate in or advocate any such plan to suspend the Constitution...?"

"Absolutely not."

"To your knowledge, has the government of the United States adopted any such plan, or does it have in place—in being, any such plan?"

"No sir. None."

Boren mentioned that the Intelligence Committee would be briefed on the matter.[71] End of discussion. But North was lying and Boren should have known it.

From 1982 to 1984, as Alfonso Chardy reported in the *Miami Herald*, North was the NSC liaison to the Federal Emergency Management Agency (FEMA), then headed by Louis Giuffrida. As described by a government official, FEMA developed a secret contingency plan that "was written as part of an executive order or legislative package that Reagan would sign and hold within the NSC until a severe crisis arose." The plan called for suspension of the Constitution, appointment of military commanders to run state and local governments and declaration of martial law during a national crisis of the kind cited by Boren, including domestic opposition to a U.S. military invasion abroad.

The *Herald* obtained a June 30, 1982 memo, written by John Brinkerhoff, Giuffrida's deputy for national preparedness programs, that outlined the martial law portions of the plan. The scenario "resembled somewhat a paper Giuffrida had written in 1970 at the Army War College in [Carlisle, PA], in which he advocated martial law in case of a national uprising by black militants. The paper also advocated the roundup and transfer to 'assembly centers or relocation camps' of at least 21 million 'American Negroes.' "

Attorney General William French Smith was reportedly alarmed by the FEMA plans and wrote National Security Adviser McFarlane on August 2, 1984 with his objections: "I believe that the role assigned to [FEMA] in the revised Executive Order exceeds its proper function as a coordinating agency for emergency preparedness." The *Herald* did not know whether the executive order was signed and, if so, whether it contained the martial law plan developed by FEMA.[72]

There are other reports of an April 1984 National Security Decision Directive No. 52 authorizing FEMA to undertake a secret nationwide readiness exercise code named REX 84. REX 84 was reportedly designed to test the readiness of FEMA to supervise Department of Defense and National Guard personnel, as well as new "State Defense Force" units, in the event the president declared a "State of Domestic National Emergency" concurrent with the launching of a direct invasion in Central America (code named "Operation Night Train"). In the event of such a "national emergency," some 400,000 undocumented Central American "aliens would reportedly be held in detention camps throughout the United States.[73]

Rep. Henry Gonzalez claimed that FBI dossiers on American citizens considered security threats were forwarded to FEMA; the list was known as ADEX (Administrative Index). According to the *Austin American-Statesman*, internal administration documents reveal a power struggle over an index with 12,000 names between then FBI Director Webster, who wanted the FBI to retain control, and Meese and McFarlane, who demanded that FEMA be given the list.[74]

The ADEX list follows in a long line of military intelligence and FBI surveillance and "custodial detention" lists known as "Security Index," "Communist Index," "Reserve Index," "Agitator Index" and so on. Despite Congress' 1971 repeal of the emergency detention provisions of the Internal Security Act of 1950, the FBI continued compiling the lists. The ADEX list contains data on individuals considered "subversives" or members of "subversive" organizations as well as potential financial contributors, teachers, lawyers, writers and intellectuals who the FBI thought would influence others.[75] Mass detention happened here during World War II and it could happen again.

FEMA (established in 1979) has responsibility for planning for "continuity of government" during a period of national crisis—everything from earthquakes and other natural disasters to nuclear war. "Whenever you start talking about martial law, you get a lot of dark smoke at the Pentagon and FEMA," said Joseph Gould of the Center for Defense Information. "The planning is all done in the name of providing for 'continuity of government' in a crisis."

FEMA official Bill McAda has acknowledged that procedures for providing "continuity of government" during an emergency would be authorized in executive orders veiled in secrecy for "national security" reasons. And FEMA director Julius Becton, a former Army general, has observed, "There is no congressional oversight on executive orders."[76]

When Reagan was governor of California, a state with a historically extensive private-public political surveillance and harassment network, Giuffrida played a key role with Edwin Meese, then Reagan's executive secretary, in developing a martial law plan embodied in Operation Cable Splicer (related to national Nixon-era plans called Operation Garden Plot and Lantern Spike). Then Colonel Giuffrida was head of Reagan's California Specialized Training Institute (CSTI), a National Guard school. Operation Cable Splicer (I, II and III) involved a series of martial "war games" during 1968-1972 involving state and local police, the National Guard and elements of the U.S. Sixth Army. The targets of the exercises were activists on college campuses and in the Black community.

Governor Reagan ordered mass arrests and advocated violent repression to put down student protest he portrayed as communist-inspired insurrection. Speaking to California growers, Reagan said that student militants want to "prove this system of ours, faced with a crisis, will not work. If there's going to be a bloodbath, let's get it over with." Meese expressed similar sentiment during the 1980 campaign when staffers brought up the name of James Rector, a student killed in 1969 when Reagan ordered highway patrolmen and National Guard troops to clear out demonstrators in Berkeley's People's Park. Said Meese, "James Rector deserved to die."[77]

In a training manual titled "Legal Aspects of Managing Civil Disorders," Giuffrida wrote: "There are severe statutory limitations and procedural requirements imposed by the Government Code which are not present in a Martial Rule situation. As stated above, Martial Rule is limited only by the principle of necessary force."

A decade later, a 1981 Defense Department directive issued by then Deputy Secretary of Defense Frank Carlucci stated: "In those areas in which martial law have been proclaimed, military resources may be used for local law enforcement. Normally a state of martial law will be proclaimed by the President. However, in the absence of such action by the President, a senior military commander may impose martial law in an area of his command where there has been a complete breakdown in the exercise of government functions by local civilian authorities."

Constitutional protections have been lost before in the name of national security. In the words of Harvard Law Professor Derek Bell, "When the factual situation is perceived to be dangerous, either by the general public or by people in power, then you could have here the kind of thing we've seen happen in the Third World. It happened with Lincoln's shocking suspension of habeas corpus by executive order, it happened with martial law after Pearl Harbor, it happened with the interning of Japanese Americans in World War II. The fact is, if you look at the things this government has been doing in Central America, the mining of harbors, the illegal arms shipments to the contras, there is good cause to worry about the possibility of martial law here."[78]

An important safeguard against martial law in the future is to guard against manifestations of police-state behavior in the present. The surveillance and harassment of opponents of U.S. policy in Central America is an intolerable abuse of civil liberties today and a potential stepping stone toward greater repression tomorrow.

The Myopic Majority

Unfortunately, the Iran-contra hearings covered up the record of abuse discussed above. The congressional inquirers insulated the CIA, FBI, Pentagon, Justice and other departments from serious investigation and accountability. They put a handful of men under a microscope and wore blinders to avoid looking at the institutions they served. They treated the Enterprise as an aberration rather than the latest mutation of covert warfare. And, in the end, their recommendations were, to borrow Senator Rudman's term for the Republican minority report, pathetic.

The committees opted to fine-tune the instruments of covert action while reaffirming its legitimacy. One of their specific recommendations for the NSC, "that Presidents adopt as a matter of policy the principle that the National Security Adviser...should not be an active military officer" was quickly ignored with the appointment of Lt. General Colin Powell. His deputy is none other than John Negroponte, the former ambassador to Honduras and chief proconsul of the contra war.

CIA Director William Webster, who headed the FBI when it undertook a massive spying campaign against critics of Central America policy, was embraced as Casey's "clean" successor. "If you can't trust an agency like ours," says Webster, "you're in trouble, because we are going to do a lot of things that we can't tell you about."[79]

In 1975, James Angleton, the late former chief of CIA Counterintelligence, said the task of the counterintelligence officer was to construct a "wilderness of mirrors" in which the opponent would be forever lost and confused.[80] Not accommodating enough, Congress was treated as an opponent and a decade later it is even more timid. Congress exhibits an occasional desire to tame that artificial wilderness and a strong tendency to preserve it as a supposed barrier against perceived enemies abroad. Meanwhile, the domestic dangers to democracy flourish.

The Iran-contra committees' recommendations follow from their assumptions and conclusions. "Covert operations are a necessary component of our Nation's foreign policy," states the *Iran-Contra Report*.[81] The records of the House and Senate Intelligence Committees testify to that.

As Chairman Hamilton said at the conclusion of North's testimony, "During my six years on the Intelligence Committee, over 90 percent of the covert actions that were recommended to us by the President were supported and approved. And only the large-scale paramilitary operations, which really could not be kept secret, were challenged."[82]

"Covert operations," the *Iran-Contra Report* concludes, "are compatible with democratic government if they are conducted in an accountable manner and in accordance with law. Laws mandate reporting and prior notice to Congress. Covert action Findings are not a license to violate the statutes of the United States." They are, as Congress knows, a license to violate international law to which the United States is legally bound.

The *Iran-Contra Report* defines covert action as "an attempt by a government to influence political behavior and events in other countries in ways that are concealed." If exposed, covert actions are expected to provide the U.S. government with a cushion of "plausible denial." As defined in President Truman's 1948 National Security Council Directive, NSC 10/2, covert actions are: "propaganda; economic warfare; preventive direct action, including sabotage, anti-sabotage, demolition and evacuation measures; subversion against hostile states, including assistance to underground resistance movements, guerrillas and refugee liberation groups, and support of indigenous anti-communist elements."

The *Iran-Contra Report* perpetuates the myth that such covert actions as "subversion against hostile states" do not constitute war: "Paramilitary covert actions are in the 'twilight area' between war, which only Congress can declare, and diplomacy, which the President must manage. This type of activity is especially troublesome as a constitutional separation of powers issue."[83]

Covert action is apparently not troublesome as a violation of national sovereignty and international law. International law gives no state the right to "influence political behavior and events in other countries in ways that are concealed." Quite the contrary, as the World Court reaffirmed. For example, the United Nations charter, to which the United States is a signatory, states that "All Members shall refrain in their international relations from the threat or use of force against the territorial integrity or political independence of any state." The only exception to the principle of nonintervention is the right of self-defense, which is limited to acts of self-defense against an armed attack. The United States has no legal right, much less a moral one, to take military, paramilitary or any other covert action to "influence political behavior and events" it doesn't like. Indeed, it is obligated not to do so.

At the close of North's testimony before the Iran-contra hearings, Senator Inouye, a highly decorated World War II veteran, began to speak of North's "obligation to disobey unlawful orders" under the Uniform Code of Military Justice. "This principle was considered so important that we...the government of the United States proposed that it be internationally applied, in the Nuremberg trials. And so, in the Nuremberg trials, we said that the fact that the defendant—"

At that point, North's lawyer interrupted, objecting vehemently to the Nuremberg reference. Inouye never completed the passage upon resuming his remarks.

In closing, Inouye gave the hearing's sole explanation of opposition to contra aid. His reasoning is instructive: "Throughout the past 10 days, many of my colleagues on this panel, in opening their questions to the colonel, prefaced their remarks by saying, 'Colonel, I'm certain you know that I voted for aid to the contras.' Ladies and gentlemen and Colonel North, I voted against aid to the contras. I did so not as a communist. I did so not as an agent of the KGB. I did so upon information that I gathered as a member of the bipartisan commission on Central America...as chairman of the Foreign Operations Committee...as a senior member of the Defense subcommittee, and...as chairman and member of the Senate Intelligence Committee...

"I voted against aid to the contras. It wasn't easy to vote against your commander-in-chief. It's not easy to stand before my colleagues and find yourself in disagreement, but that is the nature of democracy. I did so because I was firmly convinced that to follow the path or the course that was laid down by the Reagan proposal was—would certainly and inevitably lead to a point where young men and women of the United States would have to be sent into the conflict...

"I know that the path of...diplomacy is frustrating—at times angering. But I would think that we should give it a chance, if it means that, with some patience, we could save even one life. So that is why I wish my colleagues to know that I voted against aid to the Nicaraguan freedom fighters."[84]

You would not know from Inouye's defensive remarks that a majority of Americans opposed aid to the contras or that the contras were not freedom fighters. There were no words for the Nicaraguan dead.

The mainstream media provided precious little commentary on the link between Nuremberg and Nicaragua, which went far beyond Colonel North. As senior *Atlantic* Editor Jack Beatty wrote: "The Iran-contra affair is not, however, the most serious abuse of power for which the president has yet to answer. That distinction belongs to the spree of political killings that Reagan has unleashed on the Nicaraguan people...

"In 1946, at the Tokyo Tribunals, we hanged a former Japanese foreign minister because, to quote from the charge against him, 'he was derelict in his duty in not insisting before the cabinet that immediate action must be taken to put an end to atrocities and was content to rely on assurances which he knew were not being implemented.' In other words, in regards to the atrocities being committed by Japanese troops in Manchuria, he was in the same relation as Mr. Reagan and Elliott Abrams & Company have been in regard to the atrocities committed by the contras in Nicaragua. Every year the administration has given its assurances that the atrocities would stop; and every year they have continued...

"I remember one atrocity from 1985: a squad of contras raped a teen-aged bride repeatedly, over several hours, and forced her husband to watch. And I remember what a State Department man, commenting on such incidents, said at the time. The contras, he said, have 'a thing' with young girls."[85]

In the warped value system that rules Congress, it is the diversion of a few million dollars from Iran to the contras and lying to Congress that are the real crimes, not the war crimes committed against Nicaragua. The foreign policy problem we face is not one of oversight. It is one of vision.

16

Crosscurrents

Nicaragua does not pose a military threat to the United States. It is a few hours' exercise for the armed forces of the United States to remove the tanks and the HINDS [helicopters] and all the rest of the stuff.

General Paul Gorman, National Defense University, November 14, 1986.[1]

The next chapter of history has yet to be written. We must write it ourselves.

President Oscar Arias, September 1987.[2]

Events did not stand still in Central America while scandal unfolded in Washington. As 1986 turned to 1987, the outlook for Central America was war and more war. The question was whether war would take the form of deepening "Lebanonization," with the contras indefinitely in search of a country, or "Vietnamization," with a direct U.S. invasion.

"Someday," said President Azcona, "someone is going to make a map of Central America in which Honduras will appear as nothing more than the country where the contras were."[3]

Regarding Nicaragua, President Reagan's 1987 State of the Union message was as uncompromising and distorted as ever: "Our commitment to a Western Hemisphere safe from aggression...began with the Monroe Doctrine in 1823...Some in this Congress may choose to depart from this historic commitment, but I will not...Nicaraguan freedom fighters have never asked us to wage their battle, but I will fight any effort to shut off their lifeblood and consign them to death, defeat or a life without freedom. There must be no Soviet beachhead in Central America."

Nicaragua had become the litmus test of Reagan's Rollback Doctrine. "In Nicaragua, we are talking about a place extremely far from the Soviet Union and extremely close to our borders, and with a Western culture," explained Elliott Abrams. "If you can't make it here, you're not going to make it."[4]

Inside and outside government, most analysts thought the contras could not make it, at least not during Reagan's tenure. Perennial optimist Elliott Abrams predicted a "political-military victory" for the contras in two to four years. General John Galvin of the Southern Command claimed that "with sustained support, there is no doubt that the contras can win." He predicted, though, that victory could take more than seven years. Galvin's predecessor, General Paul Gorman, was more disparaging; he called the contras a "cross-border raiding force."[5]

Gorman told a National Defense University audience of his "very deep doubts about the present course of action" in Nicaragua. "I do not believe that the Central Intelligence Agency is capable of mounting a successful insurgency, or supporting it for that matter. And I do not see in the Nicaraguan rebels a likely alternative to the present Sandinista regime."[6]

"The rebels have never looked so isolated, nor more dependent on Washington for their survival," the New York Times reported in late 1986. "We've done this thing badly," a U.S. official in Honduras remarked, "and a lot of people who have helped us are going to get hurt."[7]

Would Washington abandon the failing contra war, as Truman did in 1952 with the Burma-based Chinese nationalists, or Nixon did in 1973 with the Hmong in Laos? Or would the war escalate under the dual slogan: no second Cuba, no second Bay of Pigs?

Signs of Escalation

"Obviously, if the contras don't do the job for him," a U.S. ambassador in Central America told me, "Reagan's gonna ask himself if I'm going to leave office with these guys still in power."[8]

Looking toward 1987, there appeared to be a strong possibility of rapid escalation—before the 1988 presidential election campaign. The contras could not do the job and, as Poindexter put it, "the President does not want to leave this problem to his successor. He wants to get rid of the Sandinistas now." Options for escalation included the U.S.-backed installation of contra forces in Puerto Cabezas and/or Bluefields on the Atlantic Coast, naval blockade, air strikes and full-scale invasion.[9]

Domestic opposition had sometimes sidetracked Washington's war on Nicaragua, but it had not derailed it. Congress acted less concerned about ongoing public opposition than a future charge of "losing Nicaragua." Given the right pretexts (e.g. portraying a Nicaraguan counteroffensive against border-area contra base camps as an invasion threatening Honduras; staging a "Sandinista terrorist attack" in Costa Rica or elsewhere; Nicaraguan acquisition of MIGs), congressional support for U.S. action might be strong and opposition weak. Congressional opposition would be even weaker if public opinion followed historical precedent and "rallied round the flag"—albeit temporarily—with the introduction of U.S. troops.

Many military analysts believed that the United States could consolidate control over Nicaragua, install the contra heir to the National Guard and begin withdrawing U.S. troops in three to six months. Compared with Vietnam, U.S. casualties would be relatively low and, instead of a protest-fueling draft, the Pentagon would rely on reserve forces.

According to a December 1986 report by Jay Levin of the *Los Angeles Weekly*, relying on a high-ranking Green Beret officer and other sources, preparations were so far along that, prior to the Iran-contra scandal, a U.S. invasion of Nicaragua would likely have occurred by April 1987. "I went down there and said, 'Anybody who thinks there is going to be an invasion is crazy,' " the Green Beret officer recalled. "I thought that until the exercises in June [1986]. When I saw what the 75th Rangers, which were the lead forces into Grenada were doing, it began to dawn on me that perhaps I ought to take a closer look at this operation, take a look at Central Command and check the order of battle and various unit trainings and officer positionings. And I became convinced we're going in."

"Except maybe at the very top," the Green Beret Officer said, "there is no longer a Vietnam syndrome"—reluctance by the Pentagon to fight another war without solid congressional and public support. "Among the officer corps in Central America," the officer said, it was "taken for granted" that the United States would invade Nicaragua. "In the regular Army, it's seen as a rebound from Vietnam. The officers who are now in charge of planning *lost* in Vietnam; it's a chance for them to cap off their careers with a victory. I don't think we give a shit about the Central Americans." Other active-duty and reserve officers agreed that the "general belief" in the military was that an invasion would occur.

When asked how he thought the United States might justify an invasion, the Green Beret officer said, "The excuse is not the problem. Look how flimsy an excuse they had to start Vietnam—a torpedo on the horizon. If they want to do it, they're going to do it. With anything. Contras dressed in Sandinista uniforms could attack U.S. Reserve units, for example. I don't think it's going to be particularly well-crafted or disguised."

In the weeks before the Iran-contra scandal broke, there were unusual troop movements, including the sudden transfer to Honduras of 1,000 troops of the Army First Infantry Division (mechanized) and First Aviation Battalion units from Fort Riley, Kansas, and over 200 troops in the First Air Cavalry's 19th Aviation Support Unit from Fort Hood, Texas, along with 21 UH-1 heavy-duty airlift helicopters and 3 UH-1 Medivac helicopters.[10]

At the beginning of November, the 82nd Airborne, the Army's chief invasion unit, completed a massive exercise code named Market Square, based at Fort Bragg, to train 14,000 paratroopers for Central American combat. The 82nd Airborne was supported by logistical elements from the 18th Airborne, Air Force transport and attack planes, Navy jet fighters, Marine Corps attack planes and simulated gunfire from the battleship *New Jersey.*

Their mission was to defend the nation of "San Lorenzo" (Honduras) from aggression by "Macapa" (Nicaragua) and "La Palmera" (Cuba). The 82nd Airborne made a parachute assault against Macapa and Air Force F-16s bombed the ground forces of Macapa and La Palmera. In the exercise, Macapa shifted to guerrilla warfare and Airborne Infantry units practiced raiding guerrilla positions.[11]

During April and May 1987, the United States carried out a month-long exercise code named Solid Shield 87, involving 50,000 U.S. troops. Like the earlier Market Square maneuvers, Solid Shield was designed to simulate operations against Nicaragua and Cuba. It tested the ability of the Army, Navy, Air Force, Marines and Coast Guard to mobilize and coordinate operations. It included a simulated evacuation of the U.S. naval base at Guantanamo on the assumption (ill-founded in precedent or stated policy) that Cuba would retaliate for an attack on Nicaragua.

The purpose of the exercise, said U.S. officers, was "to wave a big stick at Nicaragua."[12] It was also a shield for the spring contra offensive, designed to inhibit Nicaragua from destroying the contras in their border sanctuaries. Among the other maneuvers that year was Lempira 87, in which the 237th Airborne demonstrated it could be deployed from California to Central America within 48 hours.

There was talk of Honduras becoming another South Korea, with a permanent U.S. military presence. "Our presence in Honduras...is temporary, and yet it's indefinite," Assistant Secretary of Defense Richard Armitage told Congress, justifying another $65 million in construction funds to upgrade U.S. military facilities over the next five years.[13]

An Invasion Scenario

Believing that public airing of the costs in lives and dollars could help deter invasion, the Center for Defense Information (CDI) published a "plausible" invasion plan based on unclassified information and "structured to meet worst case conditions and insure early victory"; it was prepared by retired Army Lt. Col. John Buchanan. According to the CDI scenario, an invasion of Nicaragua would likely involve 50,000 U.S. troops supported by another 100,000 to 150,000 military and civilian personnel outside of Nicaragua. Invasion forces would begin assembling to move into assault positions 35 days before D-Day under the guise of maneuvers.[14]

Three days before invasion, carrier-based electronic warfare aircraft would begin jamming Nicaraguan communications and air strikes would destroy Nicaragua's small air force, radar sites and most antiaircraft guns. In the next two days, U.S. aircraft flying from Honduras would destroy most tanks and other mechanized forces and take out resistance at the Punta Huete Air Base. A powerful new radio station would begin broadcasting from a U.S. Navy ship calling on Nicaraguans to support the friendly forces coming to "restore" the revolution.

On D-Day, U.S. Army Delta Force squads would carry out assassinations and kidnappings of Nicaraguan leaders. Army Ranger battalions would spearhead an assault on Punta Huete where Army Airborne troops would land and begin a drive toward Managua. An Army air assault brigade would invade Nicaragua from a dozen points across the Honduran border and an Army mechanized infantry brigade and light infantry division would strike from Honduras to destroy Nicaragua's forces along the Pan American highway. U.S. Marines would seize seaports and coastal airports and, over the next five days, would seize the Rama riverport and move on Managua from the southeast. Marine, light infantry and mechanized forces would seize the port of Corinto and assault the main cities on the Pacific side such as Leon and Esteli.

Air and water transport would be blocked and with oil supplies in U.S. hands ground transportation would grind to a halt. U.S. forces would lay siege to Managua, blocking food supplies and controlling the city's water supply. According to the CDI scenario, the capital would fall without the need for extensive urban warfare.

Two weeks after D-Day, U.S. troops would occupy all cities and Nicaraguan forces would have shifted to guerrilla warfare and sabotage. Over the next two weeks, U.S. troops would search out and destroy guerrilla forces and the first elements of the U.S. assault forces would begin withdrawing.

All forms of communication would be controlled by the U.S. military commander. "Just as they did in Grenada," the CDI report observed, "U.S. Army civil affairs and psychological operations (psyop) specialists will play a big role in the invasion." The United States would conduct a massive propaganda campaign on radio and television and in the press. "Walls throughout Nicaragua will be plastered with propaganda posters, leaflets will be dropped from helicopters on small villages, and specially equipped jeeps will broadcast anti-Sandinista messages. Pro-U.S. graffiti, seemingly put there by friendly Nicaraguans, will be everywhere."

During the next three months, Washington would install a new government, shift the primary burden of military operations to the contras and continue withdrawing U.S. forces according to counterinsurgency requirements. Over the next two years, the United States would construct a new Nicaraguan Army and reduce U.S. military forces to approximately 14,000 for a minimum training and anti-guerrilla presence. Four and a half years after D-Day, U.S. forces would be reduced to perhaps 8,000.

CDI estimates U.S. casualties at 410 killed in action and 2,650 wounded in the first two weeks of fighting, plus about 50 non-battle fatalities. Nicaraguan military casualties are estimated at 5,350 dead and 10,550 wounded. Total U.S. casualties would number about 1,100 dead and 6,000 wounded at the end of four and a half years. The Nicaraguan Army, militia and guerrillas would suffer 9,000 dead and 17,000 wounded. (A composite of Pentagon simulations suggests that the United States would use 50,000 to 70,000 troops for two to four weeks of heavy fighting, resulting in 5,000 to 10,000 casualties including 2,000 to 4,000 American dead and wounded.)[15] Civilian casualties would likely be very high, perhaps five times as high as military casualties, according to CDI. Using that formula, there would be 45,000 civilian dead, making an invasion at least as bloody as the overthrow of Somoza.

According to the CDI scenario, the Nicaraguan Army and militia would be unable to mount an effective resistance after two weeks of heavy combat followed by small-scale attacks and low-level sabotage. "Due to its peculiar geographical position, with oceans on two sides and U.S. allies on the other two, Nicaragua will be relatively easy for American forces to police. Some weapons will get to the Sandinistas but not enough to permit an intense level of guerrilla warfare." The CDI scenario assumes that "the initial assault will be executed with great speed, heavy firepower and overwhelming numbers so as to destroy as many Nicaraguan units as possible before they can retreat to redoubts. And the assault will promptly be followed by aggressive action to dislodge those who do escape before they can regroup and rearm." Compared with Vietnam, U.S. forces would have an improved counterinsurgency capability because of technological advances, such as sophisticated electronic sensors providing for greater detection over wider areas.

The CDI scenario also assumes that Nicaraguan opposition would diminish dramatically in the final two years. Contra ranks would be purged of Somocistas to make the pro-U.S. government more legitimate. The United States would effectively rebuild the Nicaraguan economy and buy Nicaraguans' support with plentiful consumer goods, education, medical care, public works and widespread prosperity, at a cost of approximately $6 billion over four to five years—in addition to the $6 billion to $7 billion cost of prosecuting the war.

While the CDI scenario is instructive as a guide to potential U.S. plans, key assumptions range from rosy to incredible (assumptions Pentagon planners may share). Throughout the contra war, Washington has favored the most rightwing elements represented by Adolfo Calero and Enrique Bermudez at the expense of so-called moderates such as Arturo Cruz. The Somocistas would wield power in "liberated" Nicaragua, with or without a Duarte-type figurehead.

Prosperity did not follow the U.S. invasion of Grenada; instead, social programs were dismantled in a country whose population is less than one-thirtieth that of Nicaragua. The economic system Washington seeks to restore in Nicaragua is one fueled by cheap labor, emphasizing production for export at the expense of domestic consumption. For ideological as well as practical reasons, U.S. aid will not subsidize living standards to foster widespread prosperity in a system that reproduces mass impoverishment. The United States is already paying El Salvador's annual operating budget, with no end to the war there in sight. So-called civic action programs have proved more conducive to elite corruption than mass cooptation. Contra leaders have already demonstrated their skill at diverting U.S. aid to personal coffers. And what about Honduras? Would this loyal proxy, poorer than Nicaragua, be left to fall further behind or would some of the supposed U.S. beneficence flow to Honduras?

On the military front, other analysts credit the Nicaraguans with being able to impose far heavier casualties in the initial fighting and wage effective rural and urban guerrilla warfare denying the United States victory—as in El Salvador—and ultimately leading to a U.S. withdrawal in the face of widespread public protest.[16] Nicaragua has an armed and war-hardened population—unlike in Grenada—with tens of thousands of experienced troops, reservists, militia, guerrilla fighters and Sandinista supporters experienced in urban insurrection. Moreover, during the Nicaraguan revolution about 30 percent of the guerrilla forces were women. In a new guerrilla war that figure might even be higher since thousands of women have undergone militia training and women have much to lose under a rightwing government.

The CDI's quick-occupation scenario also discounts the possibility of intensification of the guerrilla wars in El Salvador and Guatemala and anti-U.S. action in

Honduras and Panama, requiring an increased and more dispersed commitment of U.S. forces. There could also be Spanish Civil War-type military brigades coming to Nicaragua's defense from Latin America and Europe, and even a Lincoln Brigade from the United States. In the event of regionalized war, guerrillas could find northern sanctuary in Mexico and southern sanctuary in Colombia.

In the words of Mexican novelist and former diplomat Carlos Fuentes, "throughout Latin America, an invasion of Nicaragua could be the detonator the explosive continent is awaiting. Yet another gringo invasion would be an intolerable humiliation, a moral and political trigger to ignite issues of inflation, unemployment, debt, fragile democracies and disillusioned middle classes. Latin America is waiting for a reason to blow up. It has many negative reasons for doing so. Reagan could give it a positive reason: self-defense against the United States on a scale, and with consequences, that no one in Washington seems capable of imagining."[17]

An invasion of Nicaragua would also trigger mass protest in the United States like nothing this country has seen since the civil rights and Vietnam War-era peace movements. About two thousand people were arrested in Pledge of Resistance protests following the imposition of the U.S. *embargo* on Nicaragua in May 1985. Colleges and universities have experienced rising protest against U.S. intervention in Central America and CIA recruiting on campus. An estimated 100,000 people demonstrated in Washington in the April 1987 National Mobilization for Peace and Justice in Central America and Southern Africa. In a related action, more than 500 people were arrested while attempting to block the gates at CIA headquarters.

Tens of thousands of Americans demonstrated across the country in response to the March 1988 deployment of U.S. troops to Honduras, providing only a glimmer of the protest that would meet a direct invasion of Nicaragua. Would the Reagan administration or its successor resort to the authoritarian plans discussed earlier, including mass detention? How much democracy would be sacrificed at home in the false name of democracy in Nicaragua?

New Contra Fronts

As the Iran-contra scandal deepened in 1987, the political feasibility of rapid escalation lessened. Still, the war intensified.

Washington escalated the war on Nicaragua's military and economic infrastructure. It provided the contras with portable Redeye ground-to-air missiles to neutralize Nicaragua's counterinsurgency helicopters. In addition to information on defense facilities such as radar, antiaircraft weapons and helicopters, the CIA provided the contras with detailed descriptions of dams, bridges, port facilities, electrical substations, oil facilities, telephone relay stations and other targets. Because many of these facilities were built by the Army Corps of Engineers during the U.S. military occupation of the 1920s and under the Somoza regime, the CIA was able to give the contras copies of blueprints as well as maps and other data.[18]

As the *Boston Globe* editorialized, "Those in Congress who have trouble deciding where they stand on the contra war might consider the message being sent to all developing countries: If you let US officials into your country to help with development projects and then someday change your government in ways of which they disapprove, they may return and blow them up." The editorial continued: "If ever a case was being constructed, bridge after dynamited bridge, for eventual US war-reparations payments, it is being made this season in Nicaragua."[19]

The sabotage missions are the specialty of contra commandos—who may include mercenaries and CIA Unilaterally Controlled Latin Assets (UCLAs)—parachuted into Nicaragua from aircraft reportedly piloted by Americans, Nicaraguans, Belgians and expatriates of white-ruled Rhodesia (now Zimbabwe) working under contract for the CIA. Because congressional legislation prohibited U.S. military and intelligence personnel from operating inside Nicaragua, the CIA hired a private contractor (perhaps a CIA proprietary or someone like Colonel Robert Dutton or British specialist David Walker) to handle the airdrops. Congressional oversight committees were informed.[20]

The infrastructure assault was part of a new spring offensive. It was designed to test the equipment and training provided under the $100 million and impress Congress into voting more dollars for the supposedly improved contra forces.

General John Galvin, head of the Southern Command, assured Congress that the contras had a better chance of winning than they did just a few months earlier. The reason for his optimism? "Lots of victories. They're going after soft targets. They're not trying to duke it out with the Sandinistas directly."[21] Soft targets are generally civilian targets.

Continued contra terrorism was evident in a headline in the *Washington Post*, which has supported contra aid editorially: "The Contras Have Learned to Hit Where It Hurts—Village health clinics increasingly have become victims of the rebels' struggle." The article described an attack—the contras called it one of the month's "most important operations"—in which a Baptist Church-sponsored health clinic, "the pride of the community," was burned down.[22]

In April, Washington replaced UNO with a new contra front, the "Nicaraguan Resistance." Its directors included Adolfo Calero, Alfonso Robelo, Pedro Joaquin Chamorro Jr., Aristides Sanchez, Alfredo Cesar (representing the Costa Rica-based Southern Opposition Bloc) and Maria Azucena Ferrey, a Christian Democrat (formerly vice president of the Social Christian Party). Robelo has since resigned.

The CIA allowed selected reporters to accompany contra forces inside Nicaragua as part of their new "public diplomacy" campaign. One in-depth account was not what the CIA intended. After nearly a month with contra forces in Jinotega, Northern Zelaya and Matagalpa provinces, *Newsweek* reporter Rod Norland and photographer Bill Gentile produced a piece titled "The New Contras? Back in battle, but losing the war for the people's hearts and minds."

The 150-man taskforce accompanied by Norland and Gentile was led by Attila, who boasted of victory in 1987. Along the way they ran into Toño. "His prognosis was more reserved. 'If we can do our best this year, we can win the war in Washington for more aid...If aid is renewed, we can win by next year.' " They met a contra with the *nom de guerre,* "Ronald Reagan." He chose it after hearing Reagan declare himself "a contra, too." An unhappy fourteen-year old "contra" gave himself the name "Lonesome." He had been abducted along with twenty other campesinos picking coffee in Matagalpa three months earlier.

Norland said the contras' technology and intelligence data was impressive: a portable Datotek computer to decode radio messages, U.S. aerial reconnaissance maps showing Nicaraguan military "positions in such detail that the location of every latrine was noted." They received supplies by helicopter, disguised illegally with a red cross.

Norland was not impressed with the contras' performance: "We were more like rabble on the loose than a guerrilla army in enemy country." Contra discipline quickly eroded. "The quest for food outweighed any hunger for combat. Every campesino hut became a target." Peasants were often cleaned out before Norland's unit arrived. The contras "made a show of paying" for food, but that didn't help peasants when the nearest road was many miles away. As the contras grew hungrier, "fewer bothered with the nicety of payment—especially after they lost wads of their food money gambling. 'Why not make me a gift of this chicken?' one would ask. No one ever refused."

"Frightened peasants become instant, if temporary, 'collaborators' when scores of heavily armed, hungry men drop in for breakfast," wrote Norland. "There is no overt coercion; the physical appearance of the contras is usually sufficient. Many of the men have skulls and crossbones tattooed on their arms or painted on their shirts, or boast names like 'Exterminator' and 'Dragon.' "

Norland described another form of "collaboration." Campesinos were made to scout for the contras "and, worse, to walk on their point (the first man in the column) to make sure we weren't falling into a trap. They bragged that these men were their collaborators, but when we talked to them privately it was clear they felt more like human mine detectors." One of those forced to walk point was a 60-year old peasant limping from arthritis in his knee. The contras' so-called human rights delegate dubbed him a volunteer "in the service of liberty and democracy."

After leaving the contra taskforce, Norland and Gentile followed Sandinista soldiers in a successful counteroffensive in the Bocay region. "The two fire fights we experienced in all our time with the contras were both defensive maneuvers. By contrast, the Sandinista unit we accompanied, the Simon Bolivar Battalion, found contras and fought after only two days," Norland recounted. "The conduct of the Sandinistas made a striking contrast with the contras. Their discipline held firm after many months in the Isabelia Mountains—even though the Simon Bolivar Battalion was made up mostly of draftees on two-year tours of duty. Many told us they hadn't seen a paved road or had a cold drink in 15 months of steady action."

"We never saw the Sandinistas impress campesinos as guides or make them walk in front of the troops," wrote Norland. "Peasants we talked to from both sides all agreed that only contras do that." Norland concluded, "In the battle for hearts and minds, the contras are still the losers."[23]

On July 17, the *New York Times* reported from Washington that the contras had "claimed their biggest victory in the six-year war against the Sandinista government." They supposedly overran the Nicaraguan military garrison and airfield at San Jose de Bocay, 25 miles south of the border with Honduras.[24] Two days later, Stephen Kinzer reported from San Jose de Bocay that "United States backed Nicaraguan guerrillas killed nine Sandinista soldiers, three children and a pregnant woman but failed to capture their target here Thursday." Eighteen civilians were wounded and most of the 50 homes in a nearby grain cooperative were destroyed. There was no evidence, Kinzer reported, of damage to either the dirt airstrip or "the small collection of shacks that serves as local headquarters for the Nicaraguan Army."

Elvira Arauz was among those whose home was burned to the ground. She "was especially distraught at the loss of the cow she said provided milk for her seven children. 'We came down here from the mountains to escape the contras,' she said as she examined charred food sacks to see if they could be made into clothing. 'We can't go back because they'll kill us.' "[25]

In a rare juxtaposition, the Kinzer article was followed by a short piece titled "President Says Support For Contras Is on Rise." "Some tell me that the people in this country just don't care about the freedom fighters," said Reagan in his weekly radio address. "But I don't think that's true. The more people know about the Sandinista Communists, the more they support the freedom fighters. That's why the closer you get to Nicaragua, the stronger the support grows."

The Closer You Get: Peace Summit

Just as the White House was repairing Iran-contra quake damage in Washington, an aftershock rolled through Central America. What began early in 1987 as a U.S.-Costa Rican initiative to supplant Contadora and isolate Nicaragua became a Central American peace plan that isolated the Reagan administration. Working on the assumption that the contra cause was doomed in Central America, if not in Washington, Costa Rican President Oscar Arias pressed his neighbors to write their own ending to the region's conflicts.

Washington's original plan was simple enough. The presidents of Costa Rica, Honduras, El Salvador and Guatemala would meet in San Jose on February 14-15 and sign an accord focused on Nicaraguan negotiations with the contras and the restoration of "democracy," code for the establishment of a pro-U.S. government. Nicaragua would have fifteen days to take it or leave it. Then, in the words of Salvadoran Foreign Minister Acevedo, the other governments would recommend political and diplomatic sanctions against Nicaragua for "rejecting the peace plan, not complying with the Contadora document" and showing it is a regime "with which one cannot exist."[26]

As it turned out, it was El Salvador and Honduras (and the Reagan administration) who would not accept the modified Arias plan which demanded concessions of all sides, including the United States, in all the regional conflicts. At the San Jose Summit, the Central American presidents issued a joint declaration, "A Time for Peace." There was no consensus, however, over the Arias proposal that stipulated amnesty and cease-fires in all countries with armed struggles, a cutoff of outside aid to insurgent forces, political dialogue with peaceful *internal* opposition forces and free elections according to existing national timetables, a provision recognizing the legitimacy of current governments including Nicaragua.

After initial anger at being excluded from the meeting, Nicaragua agreed to participate in a follow-up summit in Guatemala. The Contadora and Support Group countries gave the Arias plan their blessing as a complement to the Contadora effort.

The Reagan administration sought to hammer the pentagonal peg of contra war into the round peace proposal—in a repetition of its Contadora sabotage. Special Envoy Philip Habib toured the region (excluding Nicaragua) and urged Arias to drop the notion of simultaneity and, instead, require Nicaragua to make political concessions before a cease-fire and suspension of aid to the contras. The meeting "went badly," a Costa Rican official said. "We could face a terrible moment when we find Costa Rica and Guatemala in greater agreement with Nicaragua than with Honduras and El Salvador," a U.S. official commented.[27] Responding to U.S. pressure, President Duarte urged postponement of the summit then scheduled for June 25.

The full-court press came on June 17. Arias went to meet Reagan at the White House and found him flanked by Vice President Bush, National Security Adviser Frank Carlucci, Chief of Staff Howard Baker, Deputy Secretary of State John Whitehead, Assistant Secretary of State Elliott Abrams and Special Envoy Philip Habib.

"It was very scary stuff," recalled Arias adviser John Biehl. "The Oval Office was filled with all the big boys, and Oscar appeared like Spartacus going before the Roman generals."[28]

A White House statement quoted Reagan as telling Arias, "The greatest concern is the need for the Sandinistas to act on genuine democratization before pressure on the regime is removed in any way."[29]

Arias reiterated his position: "I don't think the contras are the answer. I think the contras are the main excuse by the Sandinistas to abolish individual liberties. I propose to get rid of the contras so they have no excuses. It is true they cannot become a pluralistic society if there is a war."[30]

Appearing before the House Foreign Affairs Committee on July 9, Habib was asked what the administration would do if the Central Americans approved the Arias proposal without the (pro-contra) changes wanted by the United States. "It can't happen," Habib responded. But it was happening.

Having failed to sabotage the peace plan with de facto killer amendments, the administration tried to preempt it with the so-called Reagan-Wright plan presented with House Speaker Jim Wright on August 5. It rejected simultaneity and called for a cease-fire to precede the suspension of military aid to the contras; "humanitarian" aid could continue beyond a cease-fire. As interpreted by the White House in an addendum, the plan mandated a gradual reduction of contra aid "as the resistance forces are integrated into Nicaraguan society" and required Nicaragua to hold new elections "well in advance of the currently scheduled 1990 national elections."

"If the White House had thought the plan was acceptable" to Nicaragua, said one administration official, "they would have changed it."[31]

Like earlier ploys, the Reagan-Wright plan had a negotiations deadline timed for war, not peace: September 30, the end of fiscal 1987 contra funding. Assuming the plan failed, the administration would then ask Congress for a major increase in contra support. The contras weren't informed of the peace ploy until just before it was announced. Though relieved to find out the Reagan administration wasn't seriously proposing to abandon them, they were angry at not being consulted. As one contra source put it, "They treated us worse than puppets."[32]

On August 7, the Central Americans sidestepped the Reagan ploy and signed a historic peace accord based on the Arias proposal and rooted in the sovereign spirit of Contadora. As Arias explained later, "We had a chance to choose between rationality and madness."[33]

The Central American peace accord requires *simultaneous* steps to halt outside assistance to insurgent forces (except for repatriation or relocation aid), prohibit the use of one's territory for aggression against other states and implement ceasefires, amnesty, dialogue with "all unarmed political groups of internal opposition and with those who have availed themselves of the amnesty" and democratization, meaning not only concrete steps such as lifting state of emergency restrictions, but "an authentic democratic, pluralist and participatory process that includes the promotion of social justice, respect for human rights, [state] sovereignty, the territorial integrity of states and the right of all nations to freely determine, without outside interference of any kind, its economic, political, and social model." A verification commission was composed of the foreign ministers of Central America, the Contadora and Support Groups, and the secretaries general of the United Nations and Organization of American States. The Central American presidents agreed to meet in five months to evaluate the progress of the accord they signed in Esquipulas, Guatemala. (See appendix B.)

Peace Panic

House Speaker Jim Wright made a quick escape from the trap the administration was springing and embraced the Central American peace plan, much to the relief of congressional contra aid opponents.

Reagan officials went into a peace panic before settling on a new gimmick: contra aid was "an insurance policy" to see that Nicaragua carried out all the provisions of the peace plan—as defined and imagined by the administration. Contra aid would be an insurance policy of sorts: the kind of insurance policy someone takes out before they torch their property or murder their spouse. More contra aid would insure the demise of the peace plan; the administration would reap the benefits.

The administration floated a contra aid figure of $270 million to last the eighteen months through the end of Reagan's term. Philip Habib resigned as special envoy on August 14, when it became clear that the administration would not pursue negotiations with Nicaragua. He was replaced by a relatively unknown official named Morris Busby, who told the House Subcommittee on Western Hemisphere Affairs that he would talk with all the Central American governments but Nicaragua. Reagan called the peace plan "fatally flawed" and said there "should be no uncertainty of our unswerving commitment to the contras."[34]

In the United States, the plan was widely interpreted to conform to the interventionist agenda. The plan described the cessation of aid to irregular forces as "an indispensable element for achieving a stable and lasting peace." In the United States, however, the requirement to cut off U.S. aid to the contras and close contra base camps in Honduras was ignored or treated as something optional. Nicaragua, meanwhile, was seen through special bifocals. Whatever it did to comply with the plan appeared small and fuzzy. Whatever was left incomplete, pending the required simultaneous halt to contra assistance, overshadowed everything else.

In the dissenting words of a *Boston Globe* editorial: "The Reagan plan is premised on an Alice-in-Wonderland fiction: the US attack on Nicaragua does not exist; yet, for peace to arrive, the contra pressure must continue. As Managua moves to comply with the Arias plan, the White House steadily escalates its demands. This creates, in the words of Sen. Christopher Dodd, a 'self-fulfilling process of noncompliance.' "[35]

On August 25, Nicaragua became the first country to establish the national reconciliation commission stipulated by the peace plan. To head the commission, the government appointed a staunch critic, Cardinal Obando y Bravo. The other three members are Vice President Sergio Ramirez, Popular Social Christian Party leader Mauricio Diaz and Dr. Gustavo Parajon, a physician who heads the Evangelical (Protestant) Committee for Development Aid (CEPAD). Washington immediately accused Nicaragua of stacking the commission in its favor, playing down the significance of Cardinal Obando's appointment and erroneously portraying Diaz and Parajon as "unlikely to deviate from the Sandinista line."[36]

In contrast, El Salvador's commission was headed by Alvaro Magaña, a conservative banker endorsed by the military as president of El Salvador in 1982. Other members include Salvadoran Vice President Rodolfo Castillo; Marco Rene Revelo, the conservative Bishop of Santa Ana; and Alfredo Cristiani, head of the ultra-right Arena party. "They're all sympathizers of the right and the military," a Latin American ambassador observed. "With this panel Duarte has closed the political spaces for dialogue."[37] The Reagan administration made no such complaints.

In September, Nicaragua rescinded a law permitting the government to confiscate the property of absentee landlords residing outside the country for six consecutive months. It began pardoning contra prisoners and agreed to the reopening of *La Prensa* without censorship. "We are not encouraged," said State Department spokeswoman Phyllis Oakley, "by what appear to be cosmetic gestures of compliance."[38]

Nicaragua moved forward on amnesty by setting up peace commissions throughout the war zones under the auspices of the regional and national reconciliation commissions and with the cooperation of the Red Cross and the Church. It has had an Atlantic Coast amnesty in effect since 1983 and a general amnesty since 1985, as described in earlier chapters. According to the Interior Ministry, from December 1983 through July 1987, 3,494 contras laid down their arms under the amnesty provisions predating the Central American peace accord. An additional 6,120 refugees, primarily Miskito and Sumu Indians, were repatriated in that period. After the signing of the accord, the number of amnestied contras and refugees returning each month doubled—from about 329 per month for the first seven months of 1987 to 656 per month from August to November 1987. Among the over 600 contras receiving amnesty following the signing were southern front commander Fernando "El Negro" Chamorro, who has rejoined the Conservative Party; Denis Loaisiga, second-in-command of the Jorge Salazar command; former ARDE director Carlos Colonel; and former FDN intelligence officer Lester Ponce. Former FDN spokesman Edgar Chamorro also accepted amnesty.

The peace and reconciliation process has progressed most on the Atlantic Coast, where autonomy is now law. In April 1987, over 200 elected delegates from communities on the Atlantic Coast, meeting in Puerto Cabezas, debated and approved the Autonomy Statute; on September 2, it was ratified by the Nicaraguan National Assembly. The Autonomy Statute guarantees the election of regional councils to govern coastal affairs and specifies political, economic, social and cultural rights, including the right to traditional forms of communal land ownership.[39]

Washington continued to obstruct the Atlantic Coast peace and autonomy process. In June, the administration attempted to fashion a more viable Indian front. For the last five years, said top Indian leaders and diplomats in Honduras, "the C.I.A. has relied on bribes, threats and the exile of selected Indian officials to prevent the Indians from choosing their own leaders, because it feared losing control of the Miskitos and also feared they might choose not to fight."[40]

Yatama, the new group, supposedly under more Indian and less CIA direction, quickly splintered. At a meeting following the signing of the Central American peace accord, a U.S. official based in Tegucigalpa, Richard Chidester, offered to pay fourteen Miskito leaders $3,000 a month to join the Nicaraguan Resistance front. Four reportedly accepted the payments which came from the CIA's general account for political projects.[41] Modesto Watson, one of the ten who rejected the offer, said he proposed an Indian assembly to decide if Yatama should join. "He said Chidester responded that there was no time 'for this bullshit' because we need to take you all to Washington to talk with Congress and have your photos taken with Reagan in order to win new *contra* aid.' "[42]

Despite U.S. efforts to disrupt it, the peace and autonomy process moved forward. In October, Yatama lost a major portion of its troops when Miskito commander Uriel Vanegas led his 400-strong force in a peace accord with the government. Vanegas is bitter about those Indian leaders who "have sold the Indian cause 'for a few dollars, a few guns…They talk Miskito but they don't think like Miskitos…They live in the cities. They go from Tegucigalpa to the United States. From San Jose to the United States."[43]

On November 3, as Brooklyn Rivera, a Yatama leader, was moving toward peace talks with the Nicaraguan government, seven of his field commanders quit and joined the Nicaraguan Resistance after being encouraged to do so by Charles Harrington, a U.S. Embassy political officer in Costa Rica. The commanders were apparently promised $3,000.

Martha Honey and Tony Avirgan reported that "according to several Indian sources, a plot was hatched [in November] to kidnap, in San Jose, the 3-year-old daughter of John Paul Lederach, a U.S. missionary [with the Menonite Central Committee] who has been one of the two main Moravian Church mediators shuttling between Sandinista and Yatama officials. The plot, which involved a Cuban-American C.I.A. contract operative and several *contras* aligned with the Nicaraguan Resistance, was aimed at getting Lederach...out of the process. But Lederach was tipped off about the plot and his child and pregnant wife quickly moved out of Costa Rica. He decided to continue to act, along with Andy Shogreen, the superintendent of the Moravian Church in Nicaragua, as the main intermediary in the peace talks.

"In early December, rebel sources say, they uncovered a second plot, this one to assassinate Lederach, Lutheran Pastor Ulrich Epperlein and Moravian Pastor Higgins Miller, all of whom were working with Atlantic Coast exiles in Costa Rica. These sources say the assassin was to be paid $50,000 for the three murders. A source familiar with both plots says the aim was 'to get [the mediators] out of the process.' "[44] In late January 1988, Brooklyn Rivera led a nine-member Indian delegation to Nicaragua to conduct peace talks, the first since Washington scuttled negotiations in 1985.

Contratortions

On September 21, 1987, President Reagan addressed the United Nations General Assembly and declared: "To the Sandinista delegation here today I say: your people know the true nature of your regime...Understand this: we will not, and the world community will not, accept phony 'democratization' designed to mask the perpetuation of dictatorship."[45]

The next day, in an address to the U.S. Congress, President Arias appealed to the United States to "restore faith in dialogue and give peace a chance." And in his address to the United Nations on September 23, Arias called "on any powers intervening in the region to suspend military aid." He declared, "We want to take the fate of our region into our own hands."[46]

Reagan made clear that the United States would not let go. He told the OAS on October 7: "I make a solemn vow: as long as there is breath in this body, I will speak and work, strive and struggle for the cause of the Nicaraguan freedom fighters."

Reagan reiterated the "insurance policy" pretext: renewed assistance to the contras, which the administration planned to seek in Congress, "will continue until the Sandinistas, negotiating with the freedom fighters, conclude an agreement for a cease-fire and full democracy is established in Nicaragua. Once a cease-fire is fully in effect, only that support necessary to maintain the freedom fighters as a viable force will be delivered. Then we—and they—will be watching to see how genuine the democratic reforms in Nicaragua are.

"The best indicator will be when the freedom fighters are allowed to contest power politically without retribution, rather than through force of arms. As that happens our support levels to the resistance forces will decrease proportionately. And the assistance money will then be redirected to strengthening the democratic process underway in Nicaragua."[47]

The next day, President Ortega addressed the United Nations. As he was criticizing the United States for violating the Central American peace accord and continuing its efforts to overthrow the Nicaraguan government, the six-member U.S. delegation, led by Ambassador Vernon Walters, walked out. "Some people find their ears hurt when the truth is spoken," Ortega commented. "They have committed aggression against us and they have killed our people, but now they are upset when the truth is told to them." He called on the United States to agree to "an unconditional bilateral dialogue with a view to signing agreements providing security for both States and making possible the normalization" of relations.

"I hope the President of the United States will not act as his delegation acted today," said Ortega. "When President Reagan addressed the Assembly, the delegation of Nicaragua listened to him. We are not afraid of words; we are not afraid of political and ideological debate. A year ago I myself sat in this Hall and listened to President Reagan...President Reagan should not hasten to say no. Before consulting those who give him hot-headed ideas, such as military options, including outright invasion, let him remember that Rambo exists only in the movies."[48]

Ambassador Walters dismissed Ortega's speech as "typical revolutionary babble" and declared, "I find it intolerable to see the platform of the U.N. used to hurl invective against my country and our President."[49]

The United States, meanwhile, continued using Honduras as a platform from which to hurl the contras against Nicaragua. According to the Nicaraguan Defense Ministry's monthly summary, September 5-October 5, the armed forces engaged in 481 confrontations with the contras—150 more than the previous period. The report cited 55 contra actions against the civilian population, including eleven attacks on cooperatives, communities or resettlements, ten ambushes of civilian vehicles and sixteen sabotage actions against electric or telephone lines, leaving a total of 22 civilians dead, 40 wounded and 34 kidnapped. During the same period, U.S. aircraft flew at least 14 surveillance flights over Nicaraguan territory and more than 58 flights, most originating in Honduras, dropped supplies to the contras, including in the four zones where the Nicaraguan government had declared a unilateral cease-fire in the hope of advancing the amnesty process and a general cease-fire.[50]

Nicaragua continued its open-door policy for U.S. citizens and officials, even those most supportive of the contras. Jeane Kirkpatrick, whose name was adopted by the contras for one of their military task forces, gave a pro-contra speech in Managua on October 11 to hundreds of Nicaraguans invited by the U.S. Embassy. The United States has no such open-door policy for Nicaraguans. Noting that the United States refused a visa to Nicaraguan Interior Minister Tomas Borge, a

Democratic senatorial aide remarked, "Which country is supposed to be the democracy?"[51]

U.S. assistance to the contras violated the peace accord every day. Administration officials acknowledged they were only paying the accord lip service so Congress would shell out more aid, sharing in the pretense that the peace plan and contra aid were compatible. The U.S. media, which had already stuffed most of the Iran-contra scandal down the memory hole, followed the lead of the self-fulfilling prophets of failure in the White House. The dominant theme in mainstream commentary was "Can Nicaragua be trusted?" Though the Reagan administration had recently showed it could not be trusted to tell the truth to Congress, much less adhere to the Boland amendment, few asked whether the administration could be trusted to comply with the Central American accord.

Trust, though, is not the coin of the diplomatic realm, as Reagan finally realized in negotiations with the Soviet Union. "In diplomacy," observed former Ambassador to El Salvador Robert White, "only amateurs rely on trust when dealing with adversaries. Yet lack of trust does not justify refusal to negotiate. Our goal should be to achieve agreements that work to the advantage of each party and that hold signatories accountable for violations.

"Why has such an approach not worked with Nicaragua? Because it has never been tried. The Reagan doctrine asserts the right to overthrow the Sandinista Government or, at a minimum, to dictate its overall restructuring. Diplomacy can find no common ground when the aim of one side is to eliminate the other side; that condition is called war."[52]

In October, President Arias was awarded the Nobel Peace prize in the hope that the seeds of peace would bear fruit. November 5 was the original 90-day deadline for simultaneous compliance with the accord. It became instead a checkpoint since the United States was in complete noncompliance. In the words of a report by the Center for International Policy, "The continued [contra] aid flow from the United States not only violated the text of the plan, but defeated its central purpose: to encourage fighters to make the transition to peaceful political competition."[53] Despite the rhetoric about the peace plan ending any chance for congressional approval of more contra aid, November 5 was also the date the House approved $3.2 million more in contra funding through mid December.

Nicaragua announced on November 5 that it would agree to negotiate a cease-fire with contra leaders through an intermediary, dropping its long-standing demand that cease-fire talks should be part of negotiations with the United States, the top adversary. Nicaragua also announced that it would shortly release over 980 political prisoners and reiterated that it would release all those jailed for violating security laws during the contra war and lift the state of emergency when other countries complied with the provisions requiring an end to support for the contras. The fifteen-member Verification Commission accepted Nicaragua's adherence to the principle of simultaneity.

Later that month, Nicaragua freed 985 prisoners, most of them contras and contra collaborators. The Reagan administration dismissed the release as insignificant, insisting there were up to 10,000 political prisoners in Nicaraguan jails. As

Americas Watch reported, the State Department's "figures are so high that they would include the entire prison population of Nicaragua within the category of 'political prisoners.' " Americas Watch determined that as of May 1986 (before the prison releases beginning in the fall), there was a total of 8,000 prisoners in the penitentiary system of whom 3,700—including 2,200 former National Guardsmen and 1,500 people accused of security-related crimes—could be considered "political prisoners" in the broad Latin American sense of the term, which encompasses captured combatants. In addition, there were about 3,700 common-crime offenders and about 600 members of the army or police serving sentences (a reflection of Nicaragua's commitment to hold uniformed personnel accountable to law).[54]

El Salvador used the peace plan amnesty provision not only to release the few hundred political prisoners still alive in Salvadoran jails, but as an excuse to legalize the de facto immunity from prosecution enjoyed by military and paramilitary killers and torturers, including those responsible for wholesale massacres of civilians. As for Guatemala, it also drafted an amnesty law, but, as even the New York Times pointed out, "it will have little practical effect since the Guatemalan Army killed virtually every suspected rebel it captured in the last eight years."[55] Not to mention tens of thousands of alleged civilian rebel sympathizers. As in El Salvador, the Guatemalan military has enjoyed immunity from prosecution.

On November 13, Nicaragua presented a detailed cease-fire plan to serve as its opening proposal in negotiations to be mediated by Cardinal Obando. The plan called for the contras to assemble in cease-fire zones where the Nicaraguan Army would suspend operations and, at the end of one month, to surrender their weapons, accept amnesty and participate freely in the national dialogue and political process.[56]

The contras announced a counter-proposal on December 1 that claimed contra control over more than half Nicaragua's national territory. It proposed the right to keep arms after a cease-fire took effect, pending full "democratization," including such measures as the abolition of collective farms.[57] In reality, the contras controlled no territory—whether in the sense of a liberated zone (such as the FMLN controlled in El Salvador) or a zone where the Nicaraguan Army could not operate.

The Nicaraguan proposal reflected the peace plan's provision for cease-fire, amnesty and "a dialogue with all unarmed internal political opposition groups and with those who have availed themselves of the amnesty." The contra plan reflected the Reagan administration's effort to transform the cease-fire talks into a Nicaraguan surrender, or sabotage them. Not surprisingly, the first round of talks taking place in the Dominican Republic on December 3 broke up in failure.

On December 12, the Democratic-controlled Senate voted about $16 million in ostensibly non-military aid to take the contras through February 1988. The aid "is clearly not acceptable," declared House Speaker Jim Wright.[58] It was time for the administration to play its ace: Nicaraguan defector Roger Miranda.

Mirandized

The Miranda affair gave a convenient name to a rule long employed by the administration in its dealings with Congress: You have the right to vote for contra aid. If not, everything we say the Nicaraguans do can and will be used against you. Congress generally pleaded guilty and bargained for a lower contra aid sentence, which the Nicaraguans had to serve.

Miranda's carefully-timed charges served, as did Ortega's "Moscow" trip in 1985, to cover a congressional retreat that was already underway. The Central Americans had led the Democrats safely through the Reagan ambush to the higher ground of peace. The Democrats began retreating even before the administration regrouped, and kept running after it became clear the administration was firing blanks.

Major Roger Miranda was a top aide to Nicaraguan Defense Minister Humberto Ortega. When he left Nicaragua on October 25, he was, reported Alfonso Chardy, apparently "a CIA mole." According to administration sources, "Miranda was not a walk-in defector, but was already known to the CIA because he had sporadically passed information to the United States as far back as a year ago." According to the Nicaraguan government, Miranda fled because Defense Ministry auditors were closing in on his financial irregularities.[59]

The Miranda affair was handled by Congress and the major media as if the Iran-contra scandal had never happened, though Miranda was shepherded around Washington by confirmed liar Elliott Abrams and psywar specialist Robert Kagen of the Office of Public Diplomacy. Following the usual disinformation pattern, Miranda's charges were trumpeted in headline stories and then rebutted piecemeal on the less attention-grabbing inside pages. The revelations began on December 13 with a *Washington Post* story by William Branigin, misrepresenting a speech given by Defense Minister Humberto Ortega in anticipation of disclosures from Miranda's then-secret debut with journalists. Branigin's lead was misleading: "The Sandinista government is engaged in a massive, long-term military buildup aimed at putting up to 600,000 Nicaraguans under arms by 1995 and equipping the Sandinista armed forces with advanced Soviet-made MiG fighter planes, missiles and artillery, Defense Minister Humberto Ortega confirmed today."[60]

The first and lasting impression was that Nicaragua was building a standing army of up to 600,000 and engaging in an offensive, pro-Soviet military buildup violating the spirit, if not the letter, of the Central American peace accord. Miranda's contention that Nicaragua's reserves and civilian militias would grow to 500,000 while the regular army *shrinks* from 80,000 to 70,000 was buried in the seventeenth paragraph of Branigin's article. The ominous-sounding missiles in Branigin's lead don't refer to nuclear missiles or conventional offensive missiles, but defensive antiaircraft missiles. The MIGs remained on the wish list.

Branigin cited a Nicaraguan government document stolen by Miranda, titled "Preliminary Guidelines for 1991-95." It assumed that contra forces would be defeated during 1988-90, so the longer-term objective is to consolidate the armed forces "to avert the possibility of a direct invasion by American troops and assure their defeat, should the invasion occur." As Defense Minister Ortega put it in his speech, the Nicaraguans wanted to "let the gringos know that this is not Grenada." Going unreported was Humberto Ortega's affirmation of Contadora and Nicaragua's willingness to negotiate limits on weapons.[61]

Stephen Kinzer's front-page December 14 article in the *New York Times* led with the claim that "the Soviet Union is preparing to send large quantities of new weapons to Nicaragua, despite provisions of the new regional peace accord that called for limiting the size of national armies in Central America." As the *New York Times* acknowledged days later in its corrections box, "There is no explicit statement in the accord calling for nations to limit their armies."[62] The *Times* did not explain that the accord calls for negotiations in this area under the Contadora process, nor that Nicaragua had previously accepted limits on weapons and personnel when it agreed to sign the Contadora treaty in 1984—a treaty scuttled by the United States.

Midway through Kinzer's article, off the front page, readers were told Miranda's explanation for an arms buildup lasting into 1995. Soviet aid to Nicaragua was based upon five-year plans: "At the beginning of this year, Mr. Miranda said, the Nicaraguan conflict had become so intense that the Sandinistas consumed their entire 1985-1990 allotment of Soviet-bloc weapons and ammunition. 'In three years, they used up everything that was supposed to last for five years'…It was this crisis, Mr. Miranda said, that led to the recent approval of new secret agreements committing the Soviet bloc to continue arming the Sandinistas until 1995."

James LeMoyne's front-page December 16 article reported President Ortega's explanation that Nicaragua would maintain a Swiss-like reserve system because it was "not defended by any military pact" and could not rely on trust in U.S. intentions, along with his statement that "we are willing to discuss limits on weapons and men in the armed forces" if the United States "stops its aggression" against Nicaragua. Yet the article was titled "Nicaragua to Keep Big Military Force, Its Leader Declares."[63]

Newsday's Jim Mulvaney got right to the point about the military proposal: the document "calls for the arming of massive numbers of relatively unsupervised civilians—the same people the Reagan administration has repeatedly claimed would rise up against the Marxist regime [sic] if only they had rifles."[64] It was a point that generally escaped the mainstream press.

Richard Halloran's December 20 *New York Times* article deflating the Nicaraguan document that supposedly provided the basis for Miranda's charges was relegated to page 20: "A Nicaraguan military plan made public by the Defense Department here portrays a haphazardly organized and equipped Sandinista armed force that is short of not only weapons and ammunition but also basics like food, clothing and medicine." It indicated, wrote Halloran, "that the Russians have been erratic and unreliable suppliers."

According to Halloran, the plan (translated by the U.S. government as "Primary Guidelines for Functionally Improving, Strengthening and Equipping the Sandinista People's Army for the Period 1988-1990 and Preliminary Guidelines for the Five-Year Period 1991-1995") contradicts the administration assessment of "the Sandinista

Government as bent on offensive military operations intended to expand Nicaraguan power over neighbors." The weapons mentioned in the plan are mainly defensive and the reserve units, a major portion of the expanded forces, "would be armed almost solely with rifles." The plan calls for gradually converting the armed forces, after the expected defeat of the contras by 1990, into "a more conventional force intended to deter or defeat an invader." The military supplies requested of the Soviet Union would replace losses in operations against the contras and provide "the necessary quantity of munitions units in the event of a possible invasion and prior blockade" of Nicaragua.[65] Since Washington has repeatedly considered the option of blockading Nicaragua, with or without a direct U.S. invasion, it is only logical that Nicaragua would plan its defensive needs accordingly.

The same day as Halloran's buried piece, the *New York Times* ran a front page story headlined "Arias Criticizes Nicaraguan Plan For More Troops." The article could also have been titled "Arias Criticizes US Plan To Aid Contras." Arias is quoted saying: "External aid to all rebel forces must be discontinued. Irregular forces are an obstacle in the road to democracy. They cannot be regarded as vultures of war, remaining intact, while they wait for peace efforts to fail." Those blunt words appear near the end of the article jump on page 20.[66]

Miranda's credibility was doubted even within the administration. As *Newsweek* put it, "One intelligence source said the results of an early polygraph exam were not entirely convincing, and there were gaps in his knowledge of the inside workings of the Sandinista front."[67]

The increasingly transparent disinformation campaign still served its purpose. The Big Lie of Nicaragua as a conniving Soviet military proxy was reinforced yet again in the headlines. And Jim Wright pinned the Democratic retreat on the Nicaraguans: "The Sandinistas have had a history of snatching defeat from the jaws of victory."[68]

On December 20, Congress agreed with the White House on a 1988 catch-all appropriations measure that included $8.1 million in funding for the contras and quiet provisions worth up to $8.8 million more. Reagan had threatened to veto the budget resolution if contra aid was absent. The supposedly non-military package included $3.6 million for contra food, clothing, shelter and medical supplies and $4.5 million for transportation; the transportation money could be used for mixed deliveries of previously purchased arms and ammunition. There was more: the Defense Department would provide the CIA with sophisticated electronic equipment free of charge for contra supply planes to jam Nicaraguan radar and combat antiaircraft missiles, an estimated value of $3 to $6 million. Pentagon insurance of about $2.8 million would cover contra supply planes against loss or damage.[69]

The day before the congressional deal, it was reported that television stations in El Salvador and Honduras had aired a CIA-produced videotape of Miranda embracing the contra cause.[70] Later, it was revealed that Miranda was rewarded about $800,000 for his timely defection—twice the usual CIA rate for high-ranking defectors.[71]

When Miranda first briefed selected reporters, Ortega wasn't in Moscow, but Gorbachev was in Washington. According to the Soviets, Gorbachev had suggested a reciprocal agreement whereby the Soviets would curtail arms shipments to Nicaragua and the United States cut off aid to the contras in the context of the regional peace plan. Reagan neither pursued that idea nor discussed Miranda's charges of a peace-plan-busting military buildup.

As the *New York Times* reported three days before Congress approved new contra aid, when asked why Reagan had not confronted Gorbachev with the alleged Nicaraguan buildup, a State Department official replied, "You don't understand. Miranda was for the press and Congress, not for Gorbachev."[72]

Airborne Diplomacy

The year 1988 opened with fresh reports that President Reagan had told his top advisers he wanted the Sandinistas out by the time he left office.[73] The contras were directed to step up military attacks (e.g. a late December 1987 assault on the Atlantic Coast mining towns of Bonanza, Siuna and Rosita killed 16 civilians and wounded 75) while seeking political legitimacy through cease-fire charades.

Washington increased the pressure on the fragile Central American presidents. January 15 was the date of the Central American Presidents' Summit to follow up the peace accord. Elliott Abrams and National Security Adviser Colin Powell were dispatched to the region to threaten dependent Central American governments that U.S. aid would be jeopardized if they dared judge Nicaragua fairly and hold the United States accountable to the accord. The effect of U.S. blackmail was evident when, over Ortega's objections, the other presidents decided to abolish the International Verification and Follow-Up Commission. Charged with monitoring compliance with the accord, the Verification Commission angered Washington by finding too much fault with El Salvador and Honduras and too little fault with Nicaragua.

The Verification Commission noted that "in spite of the wartime suffering [Nicaragua] has made concrete steps" toward democratization. It explicitly faulted the United States: "In spite of the exhortation of the Central American presidents the government of the United States of America maintains its policy and practice of providing assistance, military in particular, to the irregular forces operating against the government of Nicaragua. The definitive cessation of this assistance continues to be an indispensable requirement for the success of the peace efforts and of this Procedure as a whole."[74]

Washington reacted to the judgement of the Verification Commission as it had to the World Court, accusing it of bias. Given that the commission was composed of Central and South American governments representing over 90 percent of the people of Latin America, as well as the OAS and UN secretaries general, the accusation of favoritism toward Nicaragua was an implicit indictment of U.S. policy.

Nicaragua prevented a collapse of the peace process by making two dramatic unilateral concessions: lifting the state of emergency and agreeing to direct cease-fire talks with the contras. Honduras, meanwhile, continued to host the contra base camps and the resupply operation on Swan Island. On January 15, during the Central

American summit, the northern regional director for the Committee to Defend Human Rights in Honduras (CODEH) was machinegunned to death along with a teachers' union official. The two were witnesses in CODEH's unprecedented suit against Honduras—for carrying out disappearances—before the Inter-American Court on Human Rights of the OAS. A third witness, a member of the Honduran secret police, had been assassinated ten days earlier.[75]

The administration asked Congress for over $36 million in contra assistance, including $32.65 million in so-called nonlethal aid which, by Washington's elastic definition, included jeeps and helicopters; $3.6 million in military aid was to be held in "escrow" until the end of March, at which time it would be released if the president certified that Nicaragua was to blame for failed cease-fire negotiations. It was insurance that the contras would avoid a truce. There was more to the package: up to $7 million in air defense equipment for contra supply planes and $20 million in indemnity funds to replace lost contra aircraft.[76] The real total then was about $60 million to cover four months, March 1 through June 30, equivalent to the administration's initial aid proposal of $270 million for eighteen months.

On February 3, the House of Representatives narrowly voted down the aid request (219 to 211). The next day, the Senate approved it (51 to 48) in a vote that was symbolic because under the rules governing this particular legislation, the aid was killed if voted down in the House.

The House Democratic leadership had won swing votes against the package among so-called moderate Democrats by promising to develop a "non-military" aid package. History began repeating itself. On March 3, the House unexpectedly defeated the Democrats' moderately lethal aid. Posing as aid in compliance with the peace accord, it would have sustained the contras as a fighting force and provided incentive for them to avoid a truce. The package provided nearly $31 million in aid, including $14.56 million in food, shelter, medical aid and clothing for the contras over four months, to be delivered by the Department of Defense (a supposed advance over the CIA); $1.44 million in aid to the Miskitos; and $14.56 million for child victims of the war to be distributed by the Red Cross, half of it within Nicaragua. The booby trap was that at the end of four months there would be an expedited vote on military aid if failure in the cease-fire talks was pinned on Nicaragua.

This "compromise" in state-sponsored terrorism was narrowly defeated because most Republicans held out for explicit military aid and a handful of principled Democrats, such as Reps. Ron Dellums, Barbara Boxer and Pat Schroeder, refused to endorse the "lesser evil" approach embraced by many of their liberal colleagues.

As in 1985, the congressional cutoff was not expected to last. As in 1986, a Nicaraguan "invasion" of Honduras (an operation to drive the contras out of Nicaragua's Bocay region in Jinotega province) was the ready cover for an expected congressional cave-in to some form of contra aid. This time the administration upped the ante by deploying 3,500 U.S. troops (82nd Airborne and 7th Infantry) to Honduras.

Airborne Diplomacy was designed to swing votes in Congress; short-circuit Nicaragua's counteroffensive against the contras; keep Honduras in line behind Washington and in violation of the Central American peace plan; divert military sup-

plies to the contras; and compete in the headlines with the March 16 Independent
Counsel indictments of fall-guys North, Poindexter, Secord and Hakim. The deployment prompted immediate protest as tens of thousands of Americans demonstrated
in towns and cities across the country. Then events took a dramatic turn.

Cease-Fire?

Close to midnight on March 23, the Nicaraguan government and the contras
signed a cease-fire accord. The agreement, hammered out in three days of talks in
Sapoa, a small town near the Costa Rican border, stipulated a 60-day truce, phased
amnesty, and press and electoral freedom. It was witnessed and would be verified
by Cardinal Obando and OAS Secretary General Joao Clemente Baena Soares. The
first round of negotiations for a permanent cease-fire began in Managua on April
16. The contra proposals were designed to transform the cease-fire into a Trojan
Horse for the counterrevolution.

The Sapoa accord was the unexpected product of uncertainty in Washington,
contra discouragement, mounting casualties on both sides, Nicaraguan economic
crisis, Sandinista military momentum and regional peace initiatives. U.S. officials had
urged the contras to hold out for new military aid and invoke the "invasion" as an
excuse to cancel the Sapoa talks. But contra leaders were angry over the Republicans'
refusal to support the lesser-evil democratic alternative in February and distrusted
the administration's ability to deliver the aid that fueled the war. "We did not like
the Democrats' package," said one contra leader. "But if we had to pick between
that and zero, we take the package. The Republicans put their own partisan interests over ours. That was a bitter lesson."[77]

With a military solution appearing more hopeless, many contras feared they
would have even less to bring to the negotiating table if they waited for an administration green light which might never come. Administration officials were taken
aback at the contras' unusual self-initiative. Rhetoric about pressuring the Sandinistas to negotiate came back to haunt. "Our cover story has become reality," said a
top U.S. official with bitterness. "We talked about wanting peace. Well, here it is."[78]

There was no guarantee the cease-fire would lead to a lasting military peace,
rather than serve as an intermission before renewed fighting. As contra leader Alfredo
Cesar put it, "Our troops get a two-month rest with supplies while we test the
Sandinistas' willingness to comply."[79]

Supplies flowed again, thanks to the 82nd Airborne express and the U.S. Congress, which passed bipartisan aid bills on March 30 and 31. The Senate followed
the House in approving a $48 million-plus package including: $17.7 million over six
months for contra food, clothing, shelter and medical supplies, $2.19 million for
Yatama and $1.5 million in communications equipment; $2.5 million to cover administrative expenses for AID which was to arrange delivery to the contras through
a "neutral" third-party; unspecified transportation costs; $10 million for the Sapoa
Verification Commission headed by Cardinal Obando and OAS Secretary General

Baena Soares; and $17.7 million for a children's survival fund to be administered through neutral private voluntary organizations, at least half in Nicaragua.

Nicaragua received the 1982 World Health Organization award for the greatest achievement in health by a Third World nation. The $17.7 million was small reparation for the war wrought on Nicaragua's children since then. And it carried the taxing and politically loaded stipulation that the aid could not be delivered through the national health care system or any government-sponsored programs.

Republicans agreed to the package when House Speaker Jim Wright promised prompt action on a White House request for military aid if the cease-fire talks broke down. While less of a booby trap than an expedited procedure, the promise relieved some of the pressure on the contras to forge a negotiated settlement. The administration could take some comfort from the fact that the Democratic floor leader for the aid bill, liberal Rep. David Bonior of Michigan, referred to the contras as the "democratic resistance."

The contra war survived sustained public opposition, battlefield failure, World Court condemnation and explosive scandals. It survived the Iran-contra morass. The administration wants to ensure that it survives any cease-fire. At this writing, the administration is pursuing two basic strategies: sabotaging peace negotiations and mining the political battleground inside Nicaragua.

The United States has delivered aid to the contras in Honduras in violation of the cease-fire and the Central American peace accord which allow only humanitarian aid to be delivered through neutral parties to ceasefire zones or for resettlement. In addition, the rightwing auxiliaries of Singlaub, Moon, Channell and company remain in the contra aid business. The administration is working to secure continuing contra aid from Congress.

Contra fighters and supporters are divided over the prospect of a true accord with the Nicaraguan government. There is jockeying for power among those who envision returning to Nicaragua under a peace settlement and among those who want the war to continue. Under heavy administration pressure, the contras broke up negotiations in early June and momentum shifted again toward the forces of war.

But what if the White House was forced into a fall-back position of claiming that contra "pressure" worked and sanctioning a negotiated settlement. Under a peace facade, Washington could carry out a retooled destabilization campaign involving terrorism, sabotage and diverse forms of economic, psychological and political warfare in which the contra-infused internal opposition becomes the main counterrevolutionary vehicle. The objective could be to provoke a Nicaraguan government crackdown that could be used to justify rejuvenation of the contra war, further economic and diplomatic sanctions and/or a direct U.S. invasion. Or the aim could be Sandinista electoral defeat in the national elections scheduled for 1990.

Come Back to Jamaica

Unlike in Chile, Washington cannot count on a military coup in Nicaragua because the Sandinistas control the army. The contras and their political allies are trying to change this under the guise of depoliticizing the armed forces. But the Sandinistas know that without control over the army, the United States could invade Nicaragua from outside and inside. There is another important difference between Nicaragua and Chile: the Nicaraguan population is armed. Washington may try instead for an "electoral coup."

The model for an "electoral coup" strategy is the Nixon-Ford-Carter destabilization of the social democratic Manley government in Jamaica. There a combination of economic boycott, decapitalization, austerity (in which the International Monetary Fund played a critical role), media manipulation, sabotage, murder, bombings and other violence rolled back the Manley government's social programs, eroded its credibility and popular support and resulted in its 1980 electoral loss to the U.S.-backed party of Edward Seaga.

In his book, *Jamaica: Struggle in the Periphery*, Michael Manley reflected on the events leading up to electoral defeat: "The economic crisis and the IMF programme created the conditions in which the credibility of the government began to erode. The opposition accelerated the process by collaborating in the tactics of destabilisation. In the end the communist bogey wearing Cuban robes became the focus of a hysteria." The impact of world economic crisis "placed unprecedented strain on Jamaican management" of the economy, management already strained by the demands of new government programs. "Not for one instant did the JLP [Seaga's party] and the *Gleaner* [Jamaica's largest daily] ever relax in the charge that our economic difficulties were solely and exclusively the fault of our bad management. The level of crime and violence seemed to suggest that we were unable to manage security either."

"Jamaicans were psychologically exhausted by violence by the time the election came," writes Manley. "It was as if the collective, psychological landscape had been laid waste. People were tired, scared, distrustful and uncertain."[80]

Manley cites a section from *The Field Manual of the Department of the [U.S.] Army, Psychological Operations*, as reading "like a description of Jamaica between January 1976 and October 1980":

Psychological activities [*sic*] are those carried out in peace time or in places other than war theaters, planned and carried out to influence the feelings, attitudes, behavior of foreign groups in a manner favorable to the achievement of the policies of the United States. The climate for psychological warfare can only be developed successfully if the daily life of the nation is kept in a state of commotion...

STRATEGY
i) Create discouragement, demoralization, apathy;
ii) Discredit the ideology of the popular movement;
iii) Promote disorganized and confused behavior;

iv) Encourage divisive and anti-social actions to undermine the political structure of the country;

v) Promote and support movements of resistance against the authorities.

"The local exponents of these techniques," writes Manley, "had been good students. It is not altogether surprising that we were no longer a credible choice for so many people."

Manley outlined similarities in the destabilization of Jamaica and Chile, citing this description of Chile on the eve of the 1973 military coup: "Consequently what developed was a rampant crisis, insidious, intangible and invisible, responsibility for which could never be laid at the proper door. The enemy advanced in disguise. From without it took the form of processions of 'housewives,' and from within it wore the mask of 'natural catastrophe'—of inflation, poverty, the transport strike, locked petrol pumps, and rationing. Anonymous and faceless, parliamentary obstruction, by preventing tax reform and refusing to finance the social sector of the economy, forced more and more currency to be issued; omnipresent but fleeting; generalised and consequently depersonalised, there was stockpiling by shops, hoarding by customers, smuggling of goods out of the country, and a black market among the well-to-do; ramifying and secret, strike funds were supplied to the owners' associations by the CIA. Nowhere were there any identifiable enemies or targets."[81]

Mining the Internal Front

Rampant crisis may be the future Washington has in store for Nicaragua—under Republicans or Democrats claiming support of "democracy." Rampant crisis nurtured by open and covert financing of opposition institutions and politicians, using the so-called National Endowment for Democracy and secret CIA political funds, and by constant disinformation through *La Prensa* (following the examples of *El Mercurio* in Chile and *The Daily Gleaner* in Jamaica) and other pro-U.S. media. Rampant crisis to keep the economy screaming. Rampant crisis to deny the Nicaraguan government the benefits of peace and allow the U.S.-backed opposition to say, "See, it wasn't the war, it's Sandinista mismanagement that's responsible for the mess." Rampant crisis in the form of continued decapitalization; CIA-orchestrated strikes; sabotage of energy, food, health care, transport, communication and military facilities by Pentagon and CIA operatives such as those known as Unilaterally Controlled Latin Assets; increased robbery and other crimes fueled by high unemployment; assassinations and terrorist violence.

In fostering rampant crisis, Washington would exploit the release and repatriation of thousands of former National Guardsmen and contras trained in the skills of the CIA manuals. On top of this, there may be continued cross-border raids by contra factions relying on support from rightwing donors, if not from the U.S. government.

Destabilization sealed by electoral defeat would be far more difficult to orchestrate in Nicaragua where more people recognize the tactics of counterrevolution. The Manley government and its supporters were not defending a revolution (indeed, Manley, seen as more moderate now, may be reelected in Jamaica without a repeat destabilization). In Nicaragua the opposition is more divided and the Sandinistas more united. Under a peace accord, contra chiefs—already competing among themselves—would return to Nicaragua expecting to be crowned leaders of a unified internal opposition. They will find an array of parties and leaders with vested interests and varying politics and personal loyalties. Even the contras' ideological allies may not be willing to abdicate.

The CIA has not been able to create a unified internal front to date. It will have difficulty creating unity in the future, much less majority support.

Nicaraguans have learned from the experiences of Chile and Jamaica, as they have learned from Cuba, Vietnam and Grenada. In surviving a new wave of destabilization, however, Nicaraguans will be forced to sacrifice more lives, more resources, more progress. It's a price they should not have to pay.

17

Openings

In July 1987, the Santa Elena airfield once used for the contras became part of Costa Rica's Guanacaste National Park. Hundreds of school children planted trees in the dirt of the airstrip. It was a gesture of peace in a region withered by war.

Nicaraguans have been held hostage, tortured and murdered for the ultimate ransom: the surrender of their national sovereignty. Between the start of the contra war and June 1987, over 43,000 Nicaraguans were killed, wounded or kidnapped. There were nearly 22,500 dead on both sides of the war. Civilian casualties totaled 10,473 including 3,218 dead, 1,579 wounded and 5,676 kidnapped. Among the dead were at least 331 children under age fifteen. By March 1988, the death toll was above 25,500 and still rising.[1]

The war's toll may be clearer to Americans in comparative terms. If the Nicaraguan population (3.4 million) were the size of the United States (242 million), the total killed would be over 1.8 million—more than the populations of Houston, Philadelphia or Nebraska.

Nicaraguan deaths are proportionately higher than total U.S. deaths, on and off the battlefield, in the Revolutionary War, the War of 1812, the Civil War, World War I, World War II, the Korean War and the Vietnam War. Civilian deaths in equivalent terms would be over 229,000 (as of June 1987), more than twice the U.S. death toll in Korea and Vietnam. What about the 331 known children killed as of June 1987? The U.S. equivalent would be 23,559.

Imagine more than one out of three names on the Vietnam War memorial representing children. That's the reality behind words like "pressure" and "freedom fighting" and "low intensity conflict," all euphemisms for war fought in a smaller nation's territory to recast its government in a U.S.-approved mold. All such euphemisms should be exposed and rejected.*

Self-Righteous Intervention

The United States has long maintained the right to define Latin American destiny, to make and un-make governments according to prevailing U.S. interests. President Reagan told his aides in 1987 that "when I leave office the Sandinistas will be gone."[2] The only way that could happen is with a direct U.S. invasion, and then the Sandinistas would be gone from office, but not Nicaragua. Invasion will remain a real prospect even after Reagan leaves office, however remote it appears at any particular moment, because invasion is considered by virtually all U.S. policy and opinion makers to be a legitimate tool of "defense" against supposed threats to U.S. security.

Liberals and conservatives alike claim for the United States the unilateral, self-ordained right to intervene. During the Iran-contra hearings, Rep. Lee Hamilton coauthored a revealing op ed., "A Strategy for Handling Nicaragua," with Viron Vaky, former assistant secretary of state for Inter-American affairs in the Carter administration. They wrote, "If our interests require the overthrow of the Sandinistas, then we should overthrow them; if they do not, then we need a better policy to advance our interests."

"In our view," they opined, "only United States military force can remove the Sandinistas from power. But there is no convincing evidence that the threat they pose to American interests is so serious as to warrant the costs and consequences of such intervention.

"Rather, the Sandinista threat can be contained by a negotiated settlement enforced by United States power, including diplomatic and economic pressure. This is a more sustainable approach than a strategy that relies on the contras."[3]

As I wrote earlier, the fundamental policy problem we face is not flawed oversight, but faulty vision.

---

* For my views on so-called low intensity conflict, a euphemism for counterinsurgency, counterrevolution and state terrorism, whose increasingly common usage contributes to Pentagon disinformation and furthers the goal of lulling the American people into accepting undeclared war as a state of peace, see "Born-Again War: The Low-Intensity Mystique," *NACLA Report on the Americas,* March-April 1987. Also see William LeoGrande's article in the January-February issue.

Self-Determination

We must have the wisdom to see that self-righteous intervention is not a shield, but a threat—a threat to democracy at home and a threat to self-determination abroad. The only safeguard for national security for all countries, large and small, is mutual security under the rule of international law, with strengthened mechanisms for peaceful conflict-resolution and negotiated settlements to armed conflicts. That is the promise of the Central American peace plan and Contadora: mutual security and self-determination.

In the words of economist Xabier Gorostiaga, "Historically," the Central American and Caribbean "region has always been considered 'America's backyard'...any threat to the status quo has always triggered an immediate response. US military intervention in the region has been more frequent than in any other part of the world...The underlying assumption of US policy towards the region appears to be that its own geopolitical interests are incompatible with the emergence of genuinely independent nation states...Today, as the nationalist struggle acquires wider economic and social dimensions, any process of transformation must necessarily call this 'informal empire' into question, implying a decisive break with a neocolonial mode of domination first challenged in the 19th century by the rise of Central American liberalism and later, in the inter-war period, by nationalist leaders such as Augusto Sandino and Farabundo Marti.

"It is precisely because of the incompatibility between Caribbean Basin aspirations for genuine independence and the US perception of its own security interests that the Reagan Administration must depict the Central American conflict as an extension of the Cold War. The real question is what scope for defining new foreign policy alternatives exists in the United States itself...Liberal critics may disagree with the Reagan Administration over tactics and rhetoric but appear unwilling to challenge the underlying geopolitical concept of 'informal empire.' Few politicians in the US appear willing to support the view that the goal of regional political stability will best be served in the long term by recognising the sovereignty of the region, a sovereignty which must include the region's right to determine its own foreign policy."

Gorostiaga notes that "regional instability is not the result of US 'weakness'; if anything, it is the extension of US power in the region which gives rise to instability. The National Security Doctrine is, today, a recipe for national insecurity, and it is increasingly clear that the majority of the region's population is unwilling to accept politically authoritarian and economically exploitative regimes in the name of perceived North American geopolitical interests. In this sense, economic and social change in the Caribbean Basin must entail a revolution in the geopolitics of the area."[4]

In November 1987, the presidents of the Contadora and Support Group countries (Mexico, Colombia, Panama, Venezuela, Brazil, Uruguay, Peru and Argentina) met in Acapulco, Mexico for their second annual political and economic summit. The "Group of Eight" identified their principal challenges as "Maintaining peace and security in the region; Consolidating democracy and respect for human rights; Recovering our societies' capacity to generate sustained, autonomous development; Solving the foreign-debt problem; Establishing a fair, open international trade system free from protectionism; Encouraging the process of integration among our countries and with the whole of Latin America and the Caribbean; Ensuring more effective participation by our countries in the international economy; Promoting the autonomous and rapid development of science and technology; Strengthening the capacity for negotiation of the eight governments and of the region as a whole; and Reaffirming the region's cultural identity and promoting exchanges of educational experiences."

The presidents noted that "peace in our region is closely linked to respect for the principles of self-determination of peoples, nonintervention in the internal affairs of States, peaceful settlement of controversies, a ban on the threat or actual use of force, equality of States before the law and international cooperation for development."[5]

In a shock to Washington, an Uruguayan proposal that Cuba be reintegrated into regional organizations (such as the OAS and Inter-American Development Bank) was endorsed by the summit. "There is a consensus among the presidents," said conservative President Jose Sarney of Brazil, "that we ought to struggle for the total integration of Cuba into the inter-American system."[6]

With Cuba, as with Nicaragua, the Latin Americans realize that opening doors, not closing them, is the way to invite mutually beneficial relations in the region. Latin America is saying, in essence, that it cannot become a peaceful and prosperous neighborhood and remain Uncle Sam's "backyard."

Building Bridges

We can have a decent, lawful and viable alternative policy toward Nicaragua and Central America generally that rejects self-righteous intervention and respects self-determination. It can be summarized as follows:

1. Stop all military, economic, political and "psychological warfare" efforts to manipulate, destabilize or overthrow the Nicaraguan government.

2. Comply with the World Court judgement, including the provision for reparations, and lift all economic sanctions against Nicaragua, including the trade embargo and the blockade of loans to Nicaragua from international financial institutions.

3. Reopen bilateral talks between the United States and Nicaragua, sign a nonaggression pact and normalize relations.

4. Comply with Central American peace agreements and support the Contadora process, including the objective of removing Central America as an arena of East-West conflict.

5. Halt military maneuvers in the region; cease efforts to militarize Costa Rica; cut off all war-related aid to Honduras, El Salvador and Guatemala; and support

negotiated solutions to the wars in El Salvador and Guatemala. Grant extended voluntary departure status to Central American refugees.

6. Tie U.S. aid to compliance with internationally-recognized standards of human, political, labor and economic rights (as recognized in the United Nations' Universal Declaration of Human Rights) and respect for indigenous culture. Restore the meaning of humanitarian aid, directing such aid through programs run by reputable nonpartisan private and international organizations.

7. Target development assistance to programs that increase self-sufficiency in food and other basic needs; encourage economic diversity and environmental protection; raise the living standards of the majority through agrarian reform and expanded health care, literacy, education, housing, public works, employment, etc.; and demonstrate grassroots participation and empowerment. Support a rejuvenated Central American Common Market enhancing regional cooperation and self-reliance.

8. Encourage people-to-people contact between the United States and Central America through cultural and educational interchanges, "sister city" arrangements and other programs designed to exchange skills and promote mutual understanding. End the political censorship manifest in U.S. visa denials and eliminate U.S. government restrictions on travel by American citizens.

9. End surveillance and harassment of individuals and groups trying to change U.S. policy toward Central America; fully respect civil liberties; and encourage political pluralism in the United States.

10. Outlaw covert action as a tool of U.S. policy which is incompatible with democracy at home or abroad; eliminate the government's ability to wage undeclared war; and strengthen U.S. compliance with and support for international law.[7]

Around the world millions of people are struggling to improve their lives and control their own destinies. We should not see that as a threat, but as a common bond. Surely American farmers facing foreclosure can understand the Central American struggle for agrarian reform. Surely American workers can identify with Central Americans who want to be able to organize for better wages and working conditions without threat of imprisonment or death. One out of five American children now lives in poverty; surely we can understand the desire of Central Americans to see that their children survive and prosper.

Self-determination is a two-way street. The same propaganda system that keeps us from seeing the realities of Central America keeps us from seeing the realities of our own inequities, and our own need for democratization.

In 1984, Dora Maria Tellez, the medical student turned guerrilla leader who became Nicaragua's minister of health, was asked how she compared the revolutionary struggle with running the government. "It's an absolute difference," she replied. "If they gave you the task of demolishing this house, you would knock down the walls and then the windows, etc. But if later they tell you 'now build the house,' you must first become a stonemason, then learn the proportions of cement to stone, and so on. You must take out the old foundation, put down the new foundation, and when you've put up columns, walls and a roof, you still have to fix up the interior of the house, put in furniture. It's the same difference."

She was then asked to describe the impact of U.S. intervention: "First, we knocked down the house. We ripped out the foundation and began to set a new foundation, to install the pilings and erect the walls. While we're erecting one wall, Reagan comes along and knocks down the one we put up on the other side. So, we leave this one to go rebuild the fallen wall...Meanwhile, he knocks down a different one. What would we do if they weren't doing this to us? We would get the walls up and even put the roof on!"[8]

We cannot know what the new house of Nicaragua would look like today if the United States had not tried to destroy it. When the United States stops laying siege to Nicaragua it may take years for Nicaraguans to take down the physical and emotional barricades no longer necessary for survival, reverse the war-hardened political polarization, reconstruct the economy, raise living standards and renew progress in social programs.

Americans won't all have the same opinion of the new Nicaragua. We don't all agree now. When we view the new house of Nicaragua, however, we should do so as neighbors, not landlords.

APPENDIX A

The CIA's Blueprint
for Nicaragua

Philip Agee, October 1979

Destabilization Revisited

During the months ahead the CIA will have to prepare contingency plans for clandestine intervention for consideration by the National Security Council. If the revolutionary leadership in Nicaragua embarks on radical programs deemed inconsistent with perceived U.S. interests, the options are likely to include elements of the destabilization programs already applied in the 1970's in Chile, Angola, Portugal and Jamaica.

The immediate political goal would be to split the Sandinista leadership, create an emotive international "cause," and isolate leading radicals, falsely painting them as allied with Cuban and Soviet interests while against traditional Western, liberal values. Money and propaganda support for "moderates" and others responsive to American wishes would serve to enhance the local and international stature of leaders opposed to radical policies. Propaganda through local and international media, falsified documents and other provocations, and exploitation of historical differences within the Sandinista movement can contribute to splitting the political leadership. The goal would be to weaken the revolution by fomenting new disagreements or a return to the divisions of the past. With a sharp line drawn between radicals, communists, etc., and "moderates," efforts can be made to align international groups and other countries against the one and in favor of the other.

Strikes in key unions promoted through CIA-backed local and international unions can impede reconstruction and create a climate of tension. Tensions and disagreements can also be fostered between the Nicaraguan government and those that supported the revolution against Somoza.

As the "cause" is established, mainly through propaganda promoting simplistic, black-and-white impressions, efforts can be made to foment popular disillusion with the revolution and radical policies. One obvious lever is restriction of relief and reconstruction aid, but conservative elements in the Catholic Church have been effective political weapons in other countries. Here also, association of radicals with Cuba and the Soviet Union through media operations can contribute.

Possible key issues in the "cause" would be an international clamoring for "free" elections and opposition political organizing. "Return to barracks" is another, as is "betrayal of the revolution" through the "substitution of one dictatorship for another." The neighborhood defense committees would be denounced as a political apparatus. In any election campaign, the CIA could make huge sums available to its favored candidates and parties.

A climate of tension, fear and uncertainty can also contribute to capital flight, worsened economic conditions, and an exodus of professionals and others of a frightened middle class. Operations can be undertaken to induce defectors and create refugees who can then be exploited through international media operations. Acts of violence such as bombings and assassinations would also contribute to the desired psychological climate. Perhaps the military forces of El Salvador, Honduras and Guatemala—probably the CIA's closest allies in the region—could be strengthened in order to provoke border incidents and additional tension.

Eventually, if the scenario continued, the CIA could seek to provoke "moderates" in the political and military leadership to oust radicals from positions of power. If this were unrealistic, impossible or failed, U.S. diplomatic efforts could seek joint intervention through reviving the Inter-American Peace Force proposal rejected by the Organization of American States on the eve of the Sandinista victory in July.

A Team Effort

The CIA would not be the only U.S. government agency involved in intervention in Nicaragua, and participation by non-governmental organizations would be needed. U.S. representatives on international and commercial lending institutions, as well as the Export-Import Bank, would have instructions to impede credits. U.S. diplomats and military officers, in addition to the CIA, would try to influence leaders of other countries. U.S. businessmen engaged in Nicaragua would delay investments and other job-producing operations. And American media organizations would be important participants in propaganda campaigns...

From a distance, one cannot know whether the CIA could find or create the "moderate" opposition that will serve the U.S. government's interests. But the CIA surely knows that in its pursuit of American ploicy goals, it has many potential allies in Nicaragua besides supporters of the old regime. As traditional, non-Somoza interests are affected by revolutionary programs, the CIA may discover a fertile field in which to plant the seeds of counter-revolution.

Source: Excerpted from (former CIA agent) Philip Agee, "The CIA's Blueprint for Nicaragua," *Covert-Action Information Bulletin,* October 1979.

APPENDIX B

Central America Peace Accord

NATIONAL RECONCILIATION

Dialogue

To urgently carry out, in those cases where deep divisions have resulted within society, steps for national reconciliation which would allow for popular participation with full guarantees in authentic political processes of a democratic nature based on justice, freedom and democracy...For this purpose, the corresponding Governments will initiate a dialogue with all unarmed internal political opposition groups and with those who have availed themselves of the amnesty.

Amnesty

In each Central American country, except those where the International Commission of Verification and Follow-Up determined that such a measure is not necessary, an Amnesty decree will be issued containing all the provisions for the guarantee of the inviolability of life; as well as freedom in all its forms, property and the security of the persons to whom these decrees apply. Simultaneous with the issuing of the amnesty decree by the Government, the irregular forces of the respective country will place in freedom all persons in their power.

National Reconciliation Commission

In order to verify the compliance with the commitments...concerning amnesty, cease-fire, democratization and free elections, a National Reconciliation Commission will be established whose duties will be to verify the actual carrying out in practice of the national reconciliation process, as well as the full exercise of all civil and political rights of Central American citizens guaranteed in this document. The National Reconciliation Commission will be comprised of a delegate and an alternate delegate from the executive branch; a bishop delegate and an alternate bishop delegate recommended by the Episcopal Conference, and chosen by the Government from a list of three candidates...The same procedure will be used to select a delegate and alternate delegate from the legally registered political opposition parties...

In addition, each Central American Government will choose an outstanding citizen, outside of public office and not pertaining to the party in power, and his respective alternate, to be part of this commission...

Exhortation for the Cessation of Hostilities

...The Government of [those states currently fighting irregular or insurgent groups] commit themselves to undertake all the necessary steps for achieving an effective cease-fire within the constitutional framework.

Democratization

The Governments commit themselves to promote an authentic democratic, pluralist and participatory process that includes the promotion of social justice, respect for human rights, [state] sovereignty, the territorial integrity of states and the right of all nations to freely determine, without outside interference of any kind, its economic, political, and social model; and to carry out in a verifiable manner those measures leading to the establishment, or in their instances, the improvement of representative and pluralist democratic systems which would provide guarantees for the organization of political parties, effective popular participation in the decision making process, and to ensure free access to different currents of opinion, to honest electoral processes and newspapers based on the full exercise of citizens' rights...

Complete political pluralism should be manifest. In this regard, political groupings shall have broad access to communications media, full exercise of the right of association and the right to manifest publicly the exercise of their right to free speech, be it oral, written or televised, as well as freedom of movement by members of political parties in order to proseltyze. Likewise, those Governments...which have in effect a state of exception, siege, or emergency [law], shall terminate that state and re-establish the full exercise of all constitutional guarantees.

Free Elections

Once the conditions inherent to every democracy are established, free, pluralist and honest elections shall be held as a joint expression of the Central American states to seek reconciliation and lasting peace for its peoples. Elections will be held for a Central American parliament, whose founding was proposed in the Esquipulas Declaration of May 25, 1986...

These elections will take place simultaneously in all the countries throughout Central America in the first half of 1988, on a date mutually agreed to by the Presidents of the Central American states...

After the elections for the Central American parliament have been held, equally free and democratic elections shall be held with international observers and the same guarantees in each country, to name popular representatives to municipalities, congresses and legislative assemblies and the presidencies of the republics. These elections will be held according to the proposed calendars and within the period established in the current political Constitutions.

Cessation of Assistance to Irregular Forces or Insurrectionist Movements

The Governments of the five Central American states shall request the Governments of the region, and the extra-regional governments which openly or covertly provide military, logistical, financial, propagandistic aid in [the form of] manpower, armaments, munitions and equipment to irregular forces or insurrectionist movements to cease this aid, as an indispensable element for achieving a stable and lasting peace in the region.

The above does not include assistance for repatriation, or in lieu thereof, the reassigning of assistance necessary for those persons having belonged to these groups or forces to become reintegrated into normal life. Likewise, the irregular forces or insurgent groups who operate in Central America will be asked to abstain, in yearnings for a true Latin American spirit, from receiving such assistance…

The Non-Use of Territory to Invade Other States

The five countries…reaffirm their commitment to prevent the use of their own territory and neither render or permit military or logistical support to persons, organizations, or groups attempting to destabilize the governments of the Central American countries.

Negotiations on Matters Relating to Security, Verification, Control and Limitation of Armaments

The Governments of the Central American states, with the participation of the Contadora group in exercise of its role as mediator, will continue negotiations on the points still pending in the Contadora Treaty Proposal for Peace and Cooperation in Central America concerning security, verification and control.

In addition, these negotiations will entail measures for the disarmament of the irregular forces who are willing to accept the amnesty decrees.

Refugees and Displaced Persons

The Governments…commit themselves to give urgent attention to the groups of refugees and displaced persons brought about through the regional crisis, through protection and assistance, particularly in areas of education, health, work and security, and whenever voluntary and individually expressed, to facilitate in the repatriation, resettlement and relocation [of these persons]. They also commit themselves to request assistance for Central American refugees and displaced persons from the international community…

Cooperation, Democracy and Freedom for Peace and Development

In the climate of freedom guaranteed by democracy, the Central American countries will adopt agreements permitting for the intensification of development in order to achieve more egalitarian and poverty-free societies. Consolidation of democracy presupposes the creation of a system of economic and social justice and well-being. To achieve these objectives the Governments will jointly seek special economic support from the international community.

INTERNATIONAL VERIFICATION AND FOLLOW-UP

International Verification and Follow-Up Commission

An international verification and follow-up commission will be established comprised of the Secretary Generals of the Organization of American States and the United Nations or their representatives, as well as the Foreign Ministers of Central America, of the Contadora Group and the Support Group...

Calendar for the Implementation of Agreements

Within a period of 15 days from the signing of this document, the Foreign Ministers of Central America will meet as the Executive Committee to regulate, promote and make feasible compliance with the agreements contained herein...Ninety days from the signing of this document, the commitments pertaining to Amnesty, Cease-Fire, Democratization, Cessation of Assistance to Irregular Forces or Insurrectionist Movements, and the Non-Use of Territory to Invade Other States, will enter into force simultaneously and publicly as defined herein.

One-hundred-twenty days from the signing of this document, the International Commission for Verification and Follow-Up will analyze the progress [made] in the compliance with the agreements provided for herein.

After 150 days, the five Central American Presidents will meet and receive a report from the International Commission of Verification and Follow-Up and they will make the pertinent decisions.

Final Provisions

The points included in this document form part of a harmonious and indivisible whole. The signing of [the document] incurs an obligation, accepted in good faith, to simultaneously comply with the agreement in the established periods...

Source: translation provided by the Nicaraguan Foreign Ministry, August 1987.

Bibliography

Anderson, Scott and Anderson, Jon Lee. *Inside the League.* New York: Dodd, Meade & Company, 1986.

Arce, Bayardo. *Sandinismo y política imperialista.* Managua: Editorial Nueva Nicaragua, 1985.

Bagley, Bruce M., ed. *Contadora and the Diplomacy of Peace in Central America.* Boulder, CO: Westview Press/Johns Hopkins University School of Advanced International Studies (SAIS), 1987.

Bagley, Bruce M.; Alvarez, Roberto; Hagedorn, Katherine J., eds. *Contadora and the Central American Peace Process: Selected Documents.* Boulder, CO: Westview Press/SAIS, 1985.

Barnett, Frank R.; Tovar, Hugh B.; Shultz, Richard H., eds. *Special Operations in US Strategy.* Washington, DC: National Defense University Press/National Strategy Information Center, 1984.

Barry, Tom and Preusch, Deb. *The Central America Fact Book.* New York: Grove Press, 1986.

Bermann, Karl. *Under the Big Stick: Nicaragua and the United States Since 1848.* Boston: South End Press, 1986.

Blachman, Morris J.; LeoGrande, William M.; Sharpe, Kenneth, eds. *Confronting Revolution: Security Through Diplomacy in Central America.* New York: Pantheon, 1986.

Black, George. *Triumph of the People: The Sandinista Revolution in Nicaragua.* London: Zed Press, 1981.

Blum, William. *The CIA: A Forgotten History.* Atlantic Highlands, New Jersey: Zed Books, 1986.

Bonner, Raymond. *Weakness and Deceit: U.S. Policy and El Salvador.* New York: Times Books, 1984.

Booth, John. *The End and the Beginning: The Nicaraguan Revolution.* Boulder, CO: Westview Press, 2nd ed. 1985.

Borge, Tomas, *El Axioma De La Esperanza.* Bilbao, Spain: Desclee de Brouwer, 1984.

____ et al.. *Sandinistas Speak.* New York: Pathfinder Press, 1982.

Bradlee, Ben Jr. *Guts and Glory: The Rise and Fall of Oliver North.* New York: Donald I. Fine, 1988.

Brody, Reed. *Contra Terror in Nicaragua.* Boston: South End Press, 1985.

Brown, Cynthia, ed. *With Friends Like These: The Americas Watch Report on Human Rights and U.S. Policy in Latin America.* New York: Pantheon, 1985.

Brzezinski, Zbigniew. *Power and Principle: Memoirs of the National Security Adviser 1977-1981.* New York: Farrar, Straus and Giroux, 1983.

Burbach, Roger and Flynn, Patricia. *The Politics of Intervention: The United States in Central America.* New York: Monthly Review Press/Center for the Study of the Americas, 1984.

Burns, E. Bradford. *At War in Nicaragua: The Reagan Doctrine and the Politics of Nostalgia.* New York: Harper & Row, 1987.

Cabestrero, Teofilo. *Blood of the Innocent: Victims of the Contras' War in Nicaragua.* Maryknoll, NY: Orbis Books, 1985.

____. *Ministers of God, Ministers of the People.* Maryknoll, NY: Orbis Books, 1983.

Carter, Jimmy. *Keeping Faith: Memoirs of a President.* New York: Bantam Books, 1982.

405

Chamorro, Edgar. *Packaging the Contras: A Case of CIA Disinformation.* New York: Institute for Media Analysis, 1987.

Chomsky, Noam. *Turning the Tide: U.S. Intervention in Central America and the Struggle for Peace.* Boston: South End Press, 1985.

____. *The Culture of Terrorism.* Boston: South End Press, 1988.

____ and Herman, Edward S. *The Washington Connection and Third World Fascism.* Boston: South End Press, 1979.

Christian, Shirley. *Nicaragua: Revolution in the Family.* New York: Vintage Books, 1986.

Cockburn, Leslie. *Out of Control.* New York: Atlantic Monthly Press, 1987.

Cohen, Joshua and Rogers, Joel. *Rules of the Game: American Politics and the Central America Movement.* Boston: South End Press/PACCA, 1986.

____. *Inequity and Intervention: The Federal Budget and Central America.* Boston: South End Press/PACCA, 1986.

Collins, Joseph with Frances Moore Lappe, Nick Allen and Paul Rice. *Nicaragua: What Difference Could a Revolution Make?* San Francisco: Food First/Institute for Food and Development Policy, revised ed. 1985.

Commission on United States-Latin American Relations. *The United States and Latin America: Next Steps.* New York: Center for Inter-American Relations, 1976.

Committee of Santa Fe. *A New Inter-American Policy for the Eighties.* Washington, DC: Council for Inter-American Security, 1980.

Congressional Quarterly. *The Iran-Contra Puzzle.* Washington, DC, 1987.

Coraggio, Jose Luis. *Nicaragua: Revolution and Democracy.* Boston: Allen & Unwin, 1986.

Danaher, Kevin; Berryman, Phillip; Benjamin, Medea. *Help or Hindrance? United States Economic Aid in Central America.* San Francisco: Institute for Food and Development Policy, 1987.

Davis, Peter. *Where is Nicaragua?* New York: Simon and Schuster, 1987.

Dickey, Christopher. *With the Contras: A Reporter in the Wilds of Nicaragua.* New York: Simon and Schuster, 1985.

Dinges, John and Landau, Saul. *Assassination on Embassy Row.* New York: Pantheon, 1980.

Diskin, Martin, ed. *Trouble in Our Backyard.* New York: Pantheon, 1983.

Donner, Frank J. *The Age of Surveillance: The Aims and Methods of America's Political Intelligence System.* New York: Vintage Books, 1981.

Dugger, Ronnie. *On Reagan: The Man and His Presidency.* New York: McGraw-Hill, 1983.

Eich, Dieter and Rincon, Carlos. *The Contras: Interviews with Anti-Sandinistas.* San Francisco: Synthesis Publications, 1984.

Emerson, Steven. *Secret Warriors: Inside the Covert Military Operations of the Reagan Era.* New York: G. P. Putnam's Sons, 1988.

Everett, Melissa. *Bearing Witness, Building Bridges: Interviews with North Americans Living and Working in Nicaragua.* Philadelphia: New Society Publishers, 1986.

Fagen, Richard. *Forging Peace: The Challenge of Central America.* New York: Basil Blackwell/PACCA, 1987.

Gabriel, Richard. *Military Incompetence: Why the American Military Doesn't Win.* New York: Hill and Wang, 1985.

Grossman, Karl. *Nicaragua: America's New Vietnam?* Sag Harbor, New York: The Permanent Press, 1984.

Hackel, Joy and Siegel, Daniel, eds. *In Contempt of Congress: The Reagan Record on Central America.* Washington, DC: Institute for Policy Studies, 1987.

Haig, Alexander. *Caveat: Realism, Reagan, and Foreign Policy.* New York: Macmillan, 1984.

Hamilton, Nora; Frieden, Jeffry A.; Fuller, Linda; Pastor, Manuel Jr., eds. *Crisis in Central America: Regional Dynamics and U.S. Policy in the 1980s.* Boulder, CO: Westview Press/PACCA, 1988.

Harris, Richard L. and Vilas, Carlos M., eds. *Nicaragua: A Revolution Under Siege.* London: Zed Books, 1985.

Herman, Edward S. *The Real Terror Network: Terrorism in Fact and Propaganda.* Boston: South End Press, 1982.

Hersh, Seymour M. *The Price of Power: Kissinger in the Nixon White House.* New York: Summit Books, 1983.

Honey, Martha and Avirgan, Tony. *La Penca: Report of an Investigation.* Washington, DC: Christic Institute.

Hunter, Jane. *Israeli Foreign Policy.* Boston: South End Press, 1987.

Instituto de Estudio del Sandinismo. *El Sandinismo: documentos basicos.* Managua: Editorial Nueva Nicaragua, 1983.

Inter-American Dialogue. *The Americas at a Crossroads.* Washington, DC: Woodrow Wilson International Center for Scholars, 1983.

____. *The Americas in 1984: A Year for Decisions.* Washington, DC: Aspen Institute, 1984.

____. *Rebuilding Cooperation in the Americas.* Washington, DC: Aspen Institute, 1986.

Irvin, George and Gorostiaga, Xabier. *Towards an Alternative for Central America and the Caribbean.* Boston: Allen & Unwin, 1985.

Johnson, Loch K. *A Season of Inquiry: The Senate Intelligence Investigation.* Lexington, KY: University Press of Kentucky, 1985.

Kirkpatrick, Jeane J. *Dictatorships and Double Standards: Rationalism and Reason in Politics.* New York: Simon and Schuster, 1982.

Klare, Michael T. and Kornbluh, Peter, eds. *Low Intensity Warfare: Counterinsurgency, Proinsurgency, and Antiterrorism in the Eighties.* New York: Pantheon, 1988.

Kornbluh, Peter. *The Price of Intervention: Reagan's War Against the Sandinistas.* Washington, DC: Institute for Policy Studies, 1987.

Kruger, Henrik. *The Great Heroin Coup: Drugs, Intelligence, and International Fascism.* Boston: South End Press, 1980.

Kwitny, Jonathan. *Endless Enemies: The Making of an Unfriendly World.* New York: Penguin, 1984.

____. *The Crimes of Patriots: A True Tale of Dope, Dirty Money, and the CIA.* New York: W.W. Norton, 1987.

Lamperti, John. *What are We Afraid Of? An Assessment of the "Communist Threat" in Central America.* Boston: South End Press/NARMIC, 1988.

Landau, Saul. *The Dangerous Doctrine: National Security and U.S. Foreign Policy.* Boulder, CO: Westview Press/PACCA, 1988.

Latin American Studies Association (LASA). Delegation to Observe the Nicaraguan General Election of November 4, 1984. *The Electoral Process in Nicaragua: Domestic and International Influences.* LASA, 1984.

LeFeber, Walter. *Inevitable Revolutions: The United States in Central America.* New York: W.W. Norton & Co., 1984.

Leiken, Robert S., ed. *Central America: Anatomy of Conflict.* New York: Pergamon Press, 1984.

Lernoux, Penny. *Cry of the People.* New York: Doubleday, 1980.

____. *In Banks We Trust.* New York: Anchor Press/Doubleday, 1984.

Maas, Peter. *Manhunt: The Incredible Pursuit of a C.I.A. Agent Turned Terrorist.* New York: Random House/Jove Books, 1986.

Marchetti, Victor and Marks, John D. *The CIA and the Cult of Intelligence.* New York: Laurel/Dell, 1980.

Marcus, Bruce, ed. *Nicaragua: The Sandinista People's Revolution.* New York: Pathfinder Press, 1985.

Marshall, Jonathan; Scott, Peter Dale; Hunter, Jane. *The Iran-Contra Connection.* Boston: South End Press, 1987.

McGinnis, James. *Solidarity with the People of Nicaragua.* Maryknoll, NY: Orbis Books, 1985.

Melrose, Dianna. *Nicaragua: The Threat of a Good Example?* Oxford: Oxfam, 1985.

Morley, Morris and Petras, James. *The Reagan Administration and Nicaragua: How Washington Constructs Its Case for Counterrevolution in Central America.* New York: Institute for Media Analysis, 1987.

Moyers, Bill. *The Secret Government: The Constitution in Crisis.* Washington, DC: Seven Locks Press, 1988.

National Security Archive. *The Chronology: The Documented Day-by-Day Account of the Secret Military Assistance to Iran and the Contras.* New York: Warner Books, 1987.

_____. *Secret Military Assistance to Iran and the Contras: A Chronology of Events and Individuals.* Washington, DC, 1987.

Pastor, Robert A. *Condemned to Repetition: The United States and Nicaragua.* Princeton, NJ: Princeton University Press, 1987.

Pearce, Jenny. *Under the Eagle: U.S. Intervention in Central America and the Caribbean.* Boston: South End Press, 1982.

Pierre, Andrew J., ed. *Third World Instability: Central America as a European-American Issue.* New York: New York University Press/Council on Foreign Relations, 1985.

Poelchau, Walter, ed. *White Paper Whitewash: Interviews with Philip Agee on the CIA and El Salvador.* New York: Deep Cover Books, 1981.

Policy Alternatives for the Caribbean and Central America (PACCA). *Changing Course: Blueprint for Peace in Central America and the Caribbean.* Washington, DC: Institute for Policy Studies, 1984.

Prados, John. *Presidents' Secret Wars.* New York: William Morrow, 1986.

Randall, Margaret. *Sandino's Daughters: Testimonies of Nicaraguan Women in Struggle.* Vancouver: New Star Books, 1981.

_____. *Christians in the Nicaraguan Revolution.* Vancouver: New Star Books, 1983.

Ranelagh, John. *The Agency: The Rise and Decline of the CIA.* New York: Simon and Schuster, revised ed. 1987.

Robbins, Christopher. *Air America.* New York: Avon Books, 1979.

_____. *The Ravens: The Men Who Flew in America's Secret War in Laos.* New York: Crown Publishers, 1987.

Robinson, William I. and Norsworthy, Kent. *David and Goliath: The U.S. War Against Nicaragua.* New York: Monthly Review Press, 1987.

Rosset, Peter and Vandermeer, John, eds. *The Nicaragua Reader: Documents of a Revolution Under Fire.* New York: Grove Press, revised ed. 1983.

_____. *Nicaragua: Unfinished Revolution: The New Nicaragua Reader.* New York: Grove Press, 1986.

Sklar, Holly. *Trilateralism: The Trilateral Commission and Elite Planning for World Management.* Boston: South End Press, 1980.

_____. *Reagan, Trilateralism and the Neoliberals: Containment and Intervention in the 1980s.* Boston: South End Press, 1986.

Somoza, Anastasio as told to Jack Cox. *Nicaragua Betrayed.* Boston: Western Islands, 1980.

The Report of the President's National Bipartisan Commission on Central America. New York: MacMillan Publishing Company, 1984.

The Testimony of Lieutenant Colonel Oliver L. North. *Taking the Stand.* New York: Pocket Books, 1987.

Turner, Stansfield. *Secrecy and Democracy: The CIA in Transition.* New York: Harper & Row, 1985.

U.S. Central Intelligence Agency. *Psychological Operations in Guerrilla Warfare.* New York: Vintage, 1985.

Vance, Cyrus. *Hard Choices: Critical Years in America's Foreign Policy.* New York: Simon and Schuster, 1983.

Vanderlaan, Mary B. *Revolution and Foreign Policy in Nicaragua.* Boulder, CO: Westview Press, 1986.

Varas, Augusto, ed. *Soviet-Latin American Relations in the 1980s.* Boulder, CO: Westview Press, 1987.

Vergara Meneses, Raul; Vargas Cullell, Jorge; Castro, Rodolfo; Barry, Deborah; Leis, Raul. *Centroamerica: La Guerra de Baja Intensidad.* San Jose, Costa Rica: Editorial Departamento Ecumenico de Investigaciones, 1987.

Vilas, Carlos M. *The Sandinista Revolution: National Liberation and Social Transformation in Central America.* New York: Monthly Review Press, 1986.

Walker, Thomas W., ed. *Nicaragua: The First Five Years.* New York: Praeger, 1985.

_____. *Reagan versus the Sandinistas.* Boulder, CO: Westview Press, 1987.

Wheelock Roman, Jaime. *Nicaragua: The Great Challenge.* Managua: Alternative Views, 1984.

Woodward, Bob. *Veil.* New York: Simon and Schuster, 1987.

Zwerling, Philip and Martin, Connie. *Nicaragua: A New Kind of Revolution: Forty-Five Key Spokespeople Interviewed.* Westport, CT: Lawrence Hill and Co., 1985.

U.S. Government Publications

Departments of State and Defense. *Background Paper: Nicaragua's Military Build-up and Support for Central American Subversion.* July 1984.

____. *The Soviet-Cuban Connection in Central America and the Caribbean.* March 1985.

Jacobsen, Carl. *Soviet Attitudes Towards, Aid To, and Contacts With Central American Revolutionaries.* U.S. State Department, 1984.

Joint Low-Intensity Conflict Project Final Report. *Analytical Review of Low-Intensity Conflict.* Vol. 1. Fort Monroe, VA: U.S. Army Training and Doctrine Command, August, 1986.

Muskie, Edmund S.; Tower, John; Scowcroft, Brent, *Report of the President's Special Review Board.* February 1987.

U.S. Congress. *Human Rights in Nicaragua, Guatemala, and El Salvador: Implications for U.S. Policy.* Hearings before the House Committee on International Relations, Subcommittee on International Organizations. June 1976.

____. *Human Rights and U.S. Foreign Policy.* Hearings before the House Committee on International Relations, Subcommittee on International Organizations. May-August, 1979.

____. *United States Policy Toward Nicaragua.* Hearings before the House Foreign Affairs Committee, Subcommittee on Inter-American Affairs. 1979.

____. *Central America at the Crossroads.* Hearings before the House Foreign Affairs Committee, Subcommittee on Inter-American Affairs. September 1979.

____. *Review of the Presidential Certification of Nicaragua's Connection to Terrorism.* Hearing before the House Committee on Foreign Affairs, Subcommittee on Inter-American Affairs. September 1980.

____. *U.S. Intelligence Performance on Central America: Achievements and Selected Instances of Concern.* Staff report of the House Permanent Select Committee on Intelligence, Subcommittee on Oversight and Evaluation. September 1982.

____. *U.S. Support for the Contras.* Hearing before the House Committee on Foreign Affairs, Subcommittee on Western Hemisphere Affairs. April 1985.

____. *Review of the President's Report on Assistance to the Nicaraguan Opposition.* Hearing before the House Committee on Foreign Affairs, Subcommittee on Western Hemisphere Affairs. December 1985.

____. *Adverse Report on the Joint Resolution Relating to the Additional Authority and Assistance for the Nicaraguan Democratic Resistance Requested by the President.* House Permanent Select Committee on Intelligence. March 1986.

____. *Investigation of United States Assistance to the Nicaraguan Contras.* Vol. 1. Hearings and Markup before the House Committee on Foreign Affairs, Subcommittee on Western Hemisphere Affairs. March 1986.

____. *Investigation of United States Assistance to the Nicaraguan Contras.* Vol. 2. Hearings and Markup before the House Committee on Foreign Affairs, Subcommittee on Western Hemisphere Affairs. April-June 1986.

____. *The Downing of a United States Plane in Nicaragua and United States Involvement in the Contra War.* Hearing before the House Foreign Affairs Committee, Subcommittee on Western Hemisphere Affairs. October 1986.

____. *Report by the House Permanent Select Committee on Intelligence.* December 31, 1986.

____. *United States Policy Options with Respect to Nicaragua and Aid to the Contras.* Hearings before the Senate Committee on Foreign Relations, January-February 1987.

____. *Preliminary Inquiry into the Sale of Arms to Iran and Possible Diversion of Funds to the Nicaraguan Resistance.* Report of the Senate Select Committee on Intelligence. February 1987.

____. *Report of the Congressional Committees Investigating the Iran-Contra Affair, With Supplemental, Minority, and Additional Views.* U.S. Senate Select Committee on Secret Military Assistance to Iran and the Nicaraguan Opposition and U.S. House of Representatives Select Committee to Investigate Covert Arms Transactions with Iran. November 1987.

_____. *Report of the Congressional Committees Investigating the Iran-Contra Affair, Appendix A, Source Documents.* Senate Select Committee on Secret Military Assistance to Iran and the Nicaraguan Opposition and House Select Committee to Investigate Covert Arms Transactions with Iran. 1988.

_____. *Report of the Congressional Committees Investigating the Iran-Contra Affair, Appendix B, Depositions.* Senate Select Committee on Secret Military Assistance to Iran and the Nicaraguan Opposition and House Select Committee to Investigate Covert Arms Transactions with Iran. 1988.

_____. *Testimony of Richard V. Secord.* Joint Hearings before the House Select Committee to Investigate Covert Arms Transactions with Iran and Senate Select Committee on Secret Military Assistance to Iran and the Nicaraguan Opposition. May 1987.

_____. *Testimony of Robert C. McFarlane, Gaston J. Sigur, Jr., and Robert W. Owen.* Joint Hearings before the House Select Committee to Investigate Covert Arms Transactions with Iran and Senate Select Committee on Secret Military Assistance to Iran and the Nicaraguan Opposition. May 1987.*

U.S. Congress Arms Control and Foreign Policy Caucus. *Who Are the Contras? An Analysis of the Makeup of the Military Leadership of the Rebel Forces and of the Nature of the Private American Groups Providing Them Financial and Material Support.* April 1985.

_____. *The Contra High Command: An Independent Analysis of the Military Leadership of the FDN.* March 1986.

U.S. General Accounting Office. *Central America: Problems in Controlling Funds for the Nicaraguan Democratic Resistance.* December 1986.

---

* No other volumes of testimony were published at the time this bibliography was compiled.

Notes

Introduction

1. Jules Archer, *The Plot To Seize The White House* (New York: Hawthorn Books, 1973), p. 209.
2. Major General Smedley D. Butler, "America's Armed Forces," Part 1, "Military Boondoggling," *Common Sense*, October 1935, pp. 6, 7, 10.
3. Butler, Part 2, " 'In Time of Peace': The Army," p. 8.
4. See Karl Bermann, *Under the Big Stick: Nicaragua and the United States Since 1848* (Boston: South End Press, 1986).
5. Ibid., pp. 145-49.
6. Butler, Part 3, "'Happy Days Are Here Again': The Navy," pp. 13-14. Also see Bermann, *Under the Big Stick*, p. 149.
7. Bermann, *Under the Big Stick*, pp. 163-64.
8. A.C. Sandino, *Manifesto a los pueblos de la tierra y en especial al de Nicaragua* (Managua: Tipografia La Prensa, 1933), cited in Gregorio Selser, *Sandino* (New York: Monthly Review Press, 1981), p. 206.
9. William Howard Taft, Message to Congress, December 3, 1912, excerpted in *The Annals of America: 1905-1915: The Progressive Era*, Vol. 13 (Chicago: Encyclopedia Britannica, 1968), pp. 371-72. Also see Bermann, *Under the Big Stick*, p. 153.
10. Archer, *The Plot To Seize The White House*, pp. 57-58.
11. Quoted in Bermann, *Under the Big Stick*, pp. 187-88.
12. Ibid., pp. 188-90.
13. Butler, Part 1, pp. 7-8.
14. Butler, Part 2, pp. 10, 12.
15. See Bermann, *Under the Big Stick*, pp. 219-26.
16. Alejandro Bendaña, "Crisis in Nicaragua," *NACLA Report on the Americas*, November-December 1978, p. 2, citing *Time*, October 8, 1956.
17. Selser, *Sandino*, pp. 170-79; Bermann, *Under the Big Stick*, p. 217.
18. John Booth, *The End and the Beginning: The Nicaraguan Revolution* (Boulder, CO: Westview Press, 1985, 2nd ed.), p. 72, citing Pedro Joaquin Chamorro C., *Los Somoza: Una estirpe sangrienta* (Buenos Aires: El Cid Editores, 1979), p. 77.

Chapter 1: Carter Strikes Out

1. Quoted in Booth, *The End and the Beginning*, p. 162.

2. Anastasio Somoza as told to Jack Cox, *Nicaragua Betrayed* (Boston: Western Islands, 1980), p. 262.

3. Zbigniew Brzezinski, *Power and Principle: Memoirs of the National Security Adviser 1977-1981* (New York: Farrar, Straus and Giroux, 1983), p. 49.

4. See Holly Sklar, *Reagan, Trilateralism and the Neoliberals: Containment and Intervention in the 1980s* (Boston: South End Press, 1986) and *Trilateralism: The Trilateral Commission and Elite Planning for World Management* (Boston: South End Press, 1980).

5. *New York Times,* November 1, 1979.

6. A Second Report by the Commission on United States-Latin American Relations, *The United States and Latin America: Next Steps* (New York: Center for Inter-American Relations, December 20, 1976).

7. Richard Cooper, Karl Kaiser and Masataka Kosaka, *Towards a Renovated International System* (New York: Trilateral Commission, Triangle Paper #14, 1977), p. 10.

8. Robert A. Pastor, *Condemned to Repetition: The United States and Nicaragua* (Princeton, NJ: Princeton University Press, 1987), p. 37, citing Bernard Diederich, *Somoza and the Legacy of U.S. Involvement in Central America* (New York: E.P. Dutton, 1981), p. 24.

9. John Huey, *Wall Street Journal,* February 23, 1978.

10. Walter LeFeber, *Inevitable Revolutions: The United States in Central America* (New York: W.W. Norton & Co., 1984), p. 226, citing Diederich, *Somoza,* pp. 88-89.

11. See Jim Hougan, *Spooks* (New York: William Morrow, 1978), pp. 383-88.

12. Author's interview with Sister Mary Hartman, Managua, April 15, 1986.

13. Penny Lernoux, *Cry of the People* (New York: Doubleday, 1980), p. 81.

14. Cited by Noam Chomsky and Edward S. Herman, *The Washington Connection and Third World Fascism* (Boston: South End Press, 1979), pp. 283-84.

15. Dianna Melrose, *Nicaragua: The Threat of a Good Example?* (Oxford: Oxfam, 1985), p. 11; Tom Barry and Deb Preusch, *The Central America Fact Book* (New York: Grove Press, 1986), pp. ix, 129; *World Bank Atlas, 1978.*

16. Lernoux, *Cry of the People,* p. 85.

17. Interview with Humberto Ortega by Marta Harnecker, "Nicaragua: The Strategy of Victory," in Tomas Borge et al., *Sandinistas Speak* (New York: Pathfinder Press, 1982), p. 57.

18. Pastor, *Condemned to Repetition,* p. 54.

19. Ibid., p. 56.

20. Shirley Christian, *Nicaragua: Revolution in the Family* (New York: Vintage Books, 1986), p. 52.

21. George Black, *Triumph of the People: The Sandinista Revolution in Nicaragua* (London: Zed Press, 1981), p. 103.

22. Central American Historical Institute (hereafter CAHI), "The Group of Twelve Then and Now," *Up date* 4:24, August 1, 1985.

23. Quoted in Christian, *Nicaragua,* p. 49.

24. Ibid., p. 51.

25. For a critique of Christian's book and her earlier reporting on Nicaragua, see George Black, "Christian: Nicaragua: Revolution in the Family," *The Nation,* September 7, 1985.

26. Dan Morgan, *Washington Post,* April 21, 1987.

27. Christian, *Nicaragua,* p. 57.

28. John M. Goshko, *Washington Post,* February 17, 1978; Bermann, *Under the Big Stick,* pp. 264-65, citing Hearings Before the House Subcommittee on International Organizations, *Foreign Assistance Legislation for Fiscal Year 1979* (1978), pp. 126-27.

29. Black, *Triumph of the People,* p. 114.

30. H. Ortega, "Nicaragua," p. 64.

31. Pastor, *Condemned to Repetition,* p. 66. Also see John M. Goshko, *Washington Post,* May 16, 1978.

32. Carl Jacobsen, *Soviet Attitudes Towards, Aid To, and Contacts With Central American Revolutionaries* (hereafter *Jacobsen Report*), U.S. State Department, June 1984, p. 6.

33. MPU Program reprinted in *NACLA Report on the Americas,* November-December 1978, pp. 36-37.

34. John M. Goshko, *Washington Post,* August 1, 1978.

35. Somoza, *Nicaragua Betrayed,* pp. 136, 143-44, 147.

36. Pastor, *Condemned to Repetition,* pp. 70, 76-81.

37. Ward Churchill, "Soldier of Fortune's Robert K. Brown," *CovertAction Information Bulletin,* Fall 1984, p. 13.

38. H. Ortega, "Nicaragua," p. 67.

39. Ibid., p. 69; Booth, *The End and the Beginning,* p. 165.

40. Bendaña, "Crisis," p. 2.

41. Philip Wheaton and Yvonne Dilling, *Nicaragua: A People's Revolution* (Washington, DC: EPICA Task Force, 1980), pp. 42-43, citing OAS Inter-American Commission on Human Rights, "Report on the Situation of Human Rights in Nicaragua," October 1978. Refugee quoted in Bendaña, "Crisis," p. 26.

42. "Nicaragua: Executions and Disappearances," *Amnesty International Newsletter,* November 1978 and *Newsweek,* cited in Lernoux, *Cry of the People,* p. 99.

43. H. Ortega, "Nicaragua," p. 70.

44. Pastor, *Condemned to Repetition,* pp. 79, 82-86, 97-98.

45. Quoted in Somoza, *Nicaragua Betrayed,* pp. 313-24. Somoza incorrectly dated the Jorden transcript November. I have not reproduced Somoza's use of italics.

46. Bermann, *Under the Big Stick,* p. 268, citing Diederich, *Somoza,* p. 207.

47. Pastor, *Condemned to Repetition,* p. 93.

48. Author's interview with Sergio Ramirez, Managua, April 26, 1986.

49. Marlise Simons, *Washington Post,* November 3, 1978.

50. Anonymous source quoted by Robert B. Cullen, *Miami Herald,* November 18, 1978.

51. Pastor, *Condemned to Repetition,* pp. 106-07.

52. Alan Riding, *New York Times,* December 17, 1978.

53. Quoted in Somoza, *Nicaragua Betrayed,* pp. 324-33.

54. Pastor, *Condemned to Repetition,* pp. 115-16.

55. See, for example, Cynthia Arnson, "Arms Race in Central America," *The Nation,* March 10, 1979.

56. Bermann, *Under the Big Stick,* p. 269.

57. Christian, *Nicaragua,* pp. 99-100; Pastor, *Condemned to Repetition,* p. 126.

58. Pastor, *Condemned to Repetition,* p. 127.

59. Peter Maas, *Manhunt* (New York: Jove/Random House, 1987), pp. 138, 231-32.

60. James Ridgeway, "The Ex-Spy and the Old Boys," *Village Voice,* February 24, 1987.

61. Peter Cary with Miguel Acoca, "The old boys' role in the Iran-Contra affair," *U.S. News & World Report,* August 10, 1987.

62. Ben Bradlee Jr., *Boston Globe,* January 25, 1987.

63. Affidavit of Daniel P. Sheehan, General Counsel, From Plaintiffs' "Opposition to Motions to Dismiss RICO Claims," Christic Institute, Washington, DC, pp. 39-40. Also see *Declaration of Plaintiffs' Counsel,* Christic Institute, 1988, pp. 62-66.

64. Philip Taubman, *New York Times,* December 9, 1981.

65. Helga Silva and Richard Morin, *Miami Herald,* June 25, 1979.

66. "Nicaragua: The Beginning of the End" and "Mike the Merc: Soldier of Misfortune," *Latin America Political Report,* September 22, 1978, cited in Lernoux, *Cry of the People,* pp. 100-101.

67. Black, *Triumph of the People,* p. 140.

68. Wheaton and Dilling, *Nicaragua,* pp. 45-46.

69. See Black, *Triumph of the People,* p. 147.

70. Author's interview with Sergio Ramirez, April 26, 1986.

71. Black, *Triumph of the People,* p. 151.

72. Carter, *Keeping Faith: Memoirs of a President* (New York: Bantam Books, 1982), pp. 155, 181.

73. Graham Hovey, *New York Times,* January 24, 1979.

74. Christopher Dickey, *With the Contras: A Reporter in the Wilds of Nicaragua* (New York: Simon and Schuster, 1985), p. 45.

75. Pastor, *Condemned to Repetition,* pp. 332-33, fn. 10.

76. Carter, *Keeping Faith,* pp. 182-83.

77. John M. Goshko, *Washington Post,* June 13, 1979. According to Pastor, Carter refused Panama Canal-Nicaragua linkage; see *Condemned to Repetition,* pp. 114-15 and p. 341, fn. 19.

78. H. Ortega, "Nicaragua," pp. 71, 74.

79. Christian, *Nicaragua,* p. 110.

80. Pastor, *Condemned to Repetition,* pp. 130, 132.

81. Ibid., pp. 132-33.

82. Ibid., p. 135.

83. Ibid., p. 137.

84. Christian, *Nicaragua,* p. 119.

85. Pastor, *Condemned to Repetition,* p. 144.

86. Pastor, Ibid., pp. 142-45, 190.

87. "Excerpts From Vance's Speech to O.A.S. Ministers," *New York Times,* June 22, 1979; Jack Anderson, *Miami Herald,* July 25, 1979; Richard Burt, *New York Times,* June 23, 1979; Testimony of Viron Vaky, *United States Policy Toward Nicaragua,* Hearings before the House Subcommittee on Inter-American Affairs, 96th Congress, 1979, pp. 33-34, cited by Bermann, *Under the Big Stick,* pp. 270-71.

88. Quoted in Bermann, *Under the Big Stick,* p. 270, citing *New York Times,* June 22, 1979; John M. Goshko, *Washington Post,* June 23, 1979.

89. LeFeber, *Inevitable Revolutions,* p. 234.

90. Pastor, *Condemned to Repetition,* pp. 147-48, citing Brzezinski's diary.

91. Ibid., p. 148.

92. Ibid., p. 149.

93. Brzezinski, *Power and Principle,* pp. 139, 503.

94. Richard Burt, *New York Times,* March 4, 1980.

95. Zbigniew Brzezinski, *Between Two Ages: America's Role in the Technetronic Era* (New York: Viking, 1970), pp. 279, 288-89.

96. Brzezinski, *Power and Principle,* p. 49.

97. Black, *Triumph of the People,* p. 167.

98. Pastor, *Condemned to Repetition,* p. 152.

99. Somoza, *Nicaragua Betrayed,* pp. 240-41.

100. Christian, *Nicaragua,* p. 123.

101. Quoted in Somoza, *Nicaragua Betrayed,* pp. 333-56.

102. Pastor, *Condemned to Repetition,* p. 155, citing a declassified cable from Secretary of State to the U.S. Embassy, Managua, June 29, 1979.

103. Quoted in Somoza, *Nicaragua Betrayed,* pp. 363-66.

104. Peter Kornbluh, *The Price of Intervention: Reagan's War Against the Sandinistas* (Washington, DC: Institute for Policy Studies, 1987), p. 16, citing Pezzullo cable.

105. Author's interview with Miguel D'Escoto, Managua, May 9, 1986.

106. Alan Riding, *New York Times,* June 30, 1979. Also see Warren Hoge, *New York Times,* June 30, 1979.

107. Vaky cable, June 30, 1979, cited in Kornbluh, *Price of Intervention,* p. 16.

108. Pastor, *Condemned to Repetition,* pp. 159-63.

109. Karen DeYoung, *Washington Post,* July 7, 1979.

110. Pezzullo cable, July 6, 1979, cited in Kornbluh, *Price of Intervention,* p. 16.

111. Alan Riding, *New York Times,* July 10, 1979.

112. Pezzullo cable, July 6, 1979, cited in Kornbluh, *Price of Intervention,* pp. 17-18.
113. Author's interview with Sergio Ramirez, April 26, 1986.
114. Karen DeYoung, *Washington Post,* July 10, 1979, cited in Bermann, *Under the Big Stick,* p. 272.
115. Pastor, *Condemned to Repetition,* pp. 170-71.
116. Quoted in *Washington Post,* July 18, 1979.
117. Pastor, *Condemned to Repetition,* pp. 173-74.
118. Christian, *Nicaragua,* p. 131.
119. Pastor, *Condemned to Repetition,* p. 181.
120. Alan Riding, *New York Times,* July 18, 1979.
121. Pastor, *Condemned to Repetition,* pp. 184-85.
122. *Los Angeles Times,* July 17, 1979.
123. Dickey, *With the Contras,* pp. 51, 55.

Chapter 2: Fleeting Coexistence

1. Pastor, *Condemned to Repetition,* p. 203.
2. Bayardo Arce, *Sandinismo y politica imperialista* (Managua: Editorial Nueva Nicaragua, 1985), pp. 15-16.
3. Michael E. Conroy, "Economic Legacy and Policies," in Thomas Walker, ed., *Nicaragua: The First Five Years* (New York: Praeger, 1985), p. 233.
4. Wayne King, *New York Times,* July 22, 1979.
5. ECLA, *The Crisis in Central America: Its Origins, Scope and Consequences* (Santiago, Chile: CEPAL, September 15, 1983), p. 13, cited in Conroy, "Economic Legacy," p. 229.
6. Melrose, *Nicaragua,* p. 11.
7. World Bank, *Nicaragua: The Challenge of Reconstruction* (Washington, DC: October 9, 1981), p. 11, cited in Conroy, "Economic Legacy," pp. 232-33.
8. Quoted in Roger Burbach and Tim Draimin, "Nicaragua's Revolution," *NACLA Report on the Americas,* May-June 1980, p. 13.
9. MADRE delegation interview in which the author participated with Dora Maria Tellez, Managua, March 1984.
10. Alan Riding, "Nicaragua: A Delicate Balance," *New York Times Magazine,* December 2, 1979, p. 80.
11. Christian, *Nicaragua,* p. 288.
12. Quoted in Riding, "Nicaragua," p. 90.
13. Arce, *Sandinismo,* p. 39.
14. Sergio Ramirez, "Our Promises Were Made to the Poorest of Our Country," July 14, 1983 speech, in Bruce Marcus, ed., *Nicaragua: The Sandinista People's Revolution* (New York: Pathfinder Press, 1985), p. 189.
15. Author's interview with a U.S. ambassador in Central America, April 29, 1986.
16. MADRE delegation interview in which the author participated, Santa Maria, Nicaragua, March 1984.
17. Carter, *Keeping Faith,* p. 585. Also see Pastor, *Condemned to Repetition,* pp. 192-95.
18. Author's interview with Miguel D'Escoto, May 9, 1986.
19. Quoted in Karen Elliott House and Beth Nissen, *Wall Street Journal,* April 29, 1980.
20. Testimony of Lawrence Pezzullo, in *Central America at the Crossroads,* Hearings before the Subcommittee on Inter-American Affairs of the House Committee on Foreign Relations, 96th Congress, 1st Session, September 11, 1979, pp. 29-30.
21. William M. LeoGrande, et al., "Grappling with Central America: From Carter to Reagan," in Morris J. Blachman, William M. LeoGrande, Kenneth Sharpe, eds., *Confronting Revolution: Security Through Diplomacy in Central America* (New York: Pantheon, 1986), p. 301.

22. John M. Goshko, *Washington Post,* July 25, 1979.

23. Leslie Gelb, op ed., *New York Times,* August 29, 1979.

24. See Americas Watch, *On Human Rights in Nicaragua* (New York: May 1982), pp. 28-30.

25. Testimony of Viron Vaky, September 11, 1979, *Central America at the Crossroads,* pp. 3-4.

26. Charles A. Krause, *Washington Post,* July 30, 1979.

27. Terri Shaw, *Washington Post,* August 12, 1979.

28. Richard J. Meislin, *New York Times,* August 13, 1979.

29. Charles A. Krause, *Washington Post,* September 1, 1979.

30. State Department and Pentagon, *Congressional Presentation Document, Security Assistance Programs FY 1981,* p. 419, cited in Robert Matthews, "The Limits of Friendship: Nicaragua and the West," *NACLA Report on the Americas,* May-June 1985, p. 25.

31. *Miami Herald,* August 17, 1979.

32. Matthews, "Limits of Friendship," p. 26.

33. Graham Hovey, *New York Times,* August 30, 1979.

34. Pastor, *Condemned to Repetition,* p. 207.

35. Bermann, *Under the Big Stick,* p. 276.

36. Congressional Quarterly, *Congress and the Nation Vol. V, 1977-1980* (Washington, DC: 1981), p. 87.

37. William M. LeoGrande, "The United States and Nicaragua," in Walker, ed., *Nicaragua,* p. 427, citing *Newsweek,* July 20, 1980.

38. See *Review of the Presidential Certification of Nicaragua's Connection to Terrorism,* Hearing before the House Subcommittee on Inter-American Affairs, 96th Congress, 2nd Session, September 30, 1980.

39. Sheryl Hirshon with Judy Butler, *And Also Teach Them to Read* (Westport, CT: Lawrence Hill, 1983), p. 161, citing Valerie Miller, "The Nicaraguan Literacy Campaign," in Thomas W. Walker, *Nicaragua in Revolution* (New York: Praeger, 1982).

40. Deborah Barndt, "Popular Education," in Walker, ed., *Nicaragua,* p. 335.

41. Cited in ibid., p. 323.

42. Author's interview with Carlos Fernando Chamorro, Managua, April 1, 1986.

43. Christian, *Nicaragua,* p. 172.

44. Hirshon, *Teach Them to Read,* p. 118.

45. Black, *Triumph of the People,* p. 350.

46. Richard L. Harris, "The Economic Transformation and Industrial Development of Nicaragua," in Richard L. Harris and Carlos M. Vilas, eds., *Nicaragua: A Revolution Under Siege* (London: Zed Books, 1985), pp. 46-48.

47. William I. Robinson and Kent Norsworthy, *David and Goliath: The U.S. War Against Nicaragua* (New York: Monthly Review, 1987), p. 201.

48. Author's interview with Lucio Jimenez, Managua, May 6, 1986.

49. For trade union and mass organization statistics see CAHI, "Nicaragua's Trade Unions," *Update* 3:30, September 6, 1984 and Luis Hector Serra, "The Grass-Roots Organizations," in Walker, ed., *Nicaragua,* pp. 66-67.

50. Christian, *Nicaragua,* pp. 184-86.

51. Quoted in Black, *Triumph of the People,* p. 343.

52. Ministerio de Planificacion, *Plan de Reactivacion Economica en Beneficio del Pueblo* (Managua: 1980), p. 31.

53. Joseph Collins, *Nicaragua: What Difference Could a Revolution Make?* (San Francisco: Food First/Institute for Food and Development Policy, 1985), pp. 38, 42, 48.

54. Quoted in Alan Riding, *New York Times,* August 16, 1981.

55. See Michael Dodson and Laura Nizzi O'Shaughnessy, "Religion and Politics," in Walker, ed., *Nicaragua,* pp. 132-33.

56. MADRE delegation interview in which the author participated with Sister Luz Beatriz Arellano, Managua, March 1984.

57. NACLA delegation interview in which the author participated with Moises Hassan, Managua, December 25, 1980.

58. Stephen M. Gorman and Thomas W. Walker, "The Armed Forces," in Walker, ed., *Nicaragua*, p. 104.

59. Dickey, *With the Contras*, p. 78.

60. Ellen Ray, William Schaap and Louis Wolf, "The CIA Chooses a New Contra Leader," *CovertAction Information Bulletin*, Summer 1986, pp. 25-26.

61. Christian, *Nicaragua*, pp. 203-206.

62. Dickey, *With the Contras*, p. 80.

63. Pastor, *Condemned to Repetition*, pp. 221-22.

64. Ray et al., "The CIA Chooses a New Contra Leader," pp. 25-26.

65. Tomas Borge, *El Axioma De La Esperanza* (Bilbao, Spain: Desclee de Brouwer, 1984), p. 93.

66. Raymond Bonner, *Weakness and Deceit: U.S. Policy and El Salvador* (New York: Times Books, 1984), p. 24.

67. Quoted in Charles Clements, *Witness to War* (New York: Bantam Books, 1984), pp. 259-60.

68. Quoted in Bonner, *Weakness and Deceit*, p. 23.

69. Jeane Kirkpatrick, "The Hobbes Problem," American Enterprise Institute *Public Policy Papers* 1981, pp. 133-36, excerpted in Robert S. Leiken and Barry Rubin, eds., *The Central American Crisis Reader* (New York: Summit Books, 1987), p. 506. The passage also appears in her revised version of "U.S. Security and Latin America," in Jeane J. Kirkpatrick, *Dictatorships and Double Standards* (New York: American Enterprise Institute/Simon and Schuster, 1982), p. 82.

70. Sergio Ramirez, "Our Promises Were Made," pp. 185-86.

71. *New York Times*, October 2, 1979. For Brzezinski's perspective on the brigade issue, see *Power and Principle*, pp. 346-52.

72. Bonner, *Weakness and Deceit*, p. 160.

73. Ibid., pp. 168, 174.

74. Ibid., p. 176.

75. Robert Armstrong and Janet Shenk, *El Salvador: The Face of Revolution* (Boston: South End Press, 1982), p. 139.

76. James LeMoyne, *New York Times*, November 24, 1987 and December 2, 1987.

77. Dickey, *With the Contras*, p. 88.

78. Don Oberdorfer, *Washington Post*, and Joel Brinkley, *New York Times*, March 22, 1985.

79. Bonner, *Weakness and Deceit*, p. 214.

80. Allan Nairn, "Behind the Death Squads," *The Progressive*, May 1984. Also see Kai Bird and Max Holland, "CIA Police Training," *The Nation*, June 7, 1986.

81. Bob Woodward, *Veil* (New York: Simon and Schuster, 1987), p. 262, citing Philip Taubman, *New York Times*, March 22, 1984.

82. James LeMoyne, *New York Times*, December 2, 1987.

83. Bonner, *Weakness and Deceit*, p. 216.

84. Carter, *Keeping Faith*, p. 586.

85. Bonner, *Weakness and Deceit*, p. 221.

86. Ibid., p. 222.

87. Ibid., pp. 225-26.

88. Ibid., p. 227.

89. Ibid., p. 228.

90. Pastor, *Condemned to Repetition*, pp. 210-11, 218-19.

91. International Court of Justice, *Case Concerning Military and Paramilitary Activities In and Against Nicaragua (Nicaragua v. United States of America)*, June 27, 1986, p. 75, par. 160. Also see Djuka Julius, interview with Daniel Ortega, *Excelsior* (Mexico City), June 24, 1987; quoted in the U.S. press by Philip Bennett, *Boston Globe*, June 25, 1987 and *Miami Herald*, June 26, 1987.

92. For Pastor's account of arms supply evidence and the decision to suspend aid, see *Condemned to Repetition*, pp. 225-28.

93. Paul E. Sigmund, "Latin America: Change or Continuity?" *Foreign Affairs: America and the World 1981*, p. 638; Juan de Onis, *New York Times*, January 23, 1981; *Miami Herald*, February 17, 1981.

94. Philip Geyelin, *Washington Post*, October 13, 1980, citing NBC White Paper, "The Castro Connection."

95. *Newsweek*, November 8, 1982, p. 44.

96. Author's interview with Miguel D'Escoto, May 9, 1986.

97. Viron P. Vaky, "Hemispheric Relations: 'Everything is Part of Everything Else,'" *Foreign Affairs: America and the World 1980*, p. 622.

Chapter 3: Reagan Strikes Back

1. Quoted in Alexander Cockburn, *The Nation*, November 10, 1984.

2. Ronnie Dugger, *On Reagan: The Man and His Presidency* (New York: McGraw-Hill, 1983), p. 518.

3. Committee of Santa Fe, *A New Inter-American Policy for the Eighties* (Washington, DC: Council for Inter-American Security, 1980), pp. ii, 1-2.

4. Ibid., pp. 20, 45, 53.

5. "Soviet Geopolitical Momentum: Myth or Menace?" *The Defense Monitor* XV:5, 1986, Center for Defense Information, Washington, DC.

6. Quoted in ibid., p. 8.

7. Ibid.

8. Ibid., p. 31.

9. Author's interview with a U.S. ambassador in Central America, April 29, 1986.

10. Alexander Cockburn, *The Nation*, February 15, 1986, citing John Simpson and Jane Bennett, *The Disappeared*.

11. Jeane Kirkpatrick, "Dictatorships and Double Standards," *Commentary*, November 1979, p. 34. Also see "U.S. Security and Latin America," *Commentary*, January 1981.

12. Tom Farer, "Reagan's Latin America," *New York Review of Books*, March 19, 1981, p. 10.

13. Kirkpatrick, "Dictatorships and Double Standards," p. 44.

14. Dugger, *On Reagan*, p. 521.

15. Reagan quote and Amnesty International statistics cited in ibid., p. 383.

16. "Nicaragua," Latin American Forecasting Study, Business International Corporation, August 1980.

17. Seymour M. Hersh, *The Price of Power: Kissinger in the Nixon White House* (New York: Summit Books, 1983), pp. 274, 294-95 on Chile.

18. C. DiGiovanni Jr., "U.S. Policy and the Marxist Threat to Central America," Heritage Foundation *Backgrounder*, October 15, 1980.

19. Alan Riding, *New York Times*, November 14, 1980.

20. Alexander Haig, *Caveat: Realism, Reagan, and Foreign Policy* (New York: Macmillan, 1984), pp. 99-100.

21. Author's interview with Rita Delia Casco, Managua, May 9, 1986.

22. Haig, *Caveat*, pp. 108-09, 145.

23. Steven Emerson, *Secret Warriors* (New York: G. P. Putnam's Sons, 1988), p. 122.

24. Alan Riding, *New York Times*, February 12, 1981; quoting Cruz; UPI, March 25, 1981, quoting Bush nell.

25. Tom Barry, *The Destabilization of Nicaragua* (Albuquerque, NM: The Resource Center, 1986), p. 11; Don Oberdorfer, *Washington Post*, August 4, 1982.

26. Jeff McConnell, "Counterrevolution in Nicaragua: the US Connection," in Peter Rosset and John Vandermeer, eds., *The Nicaragua Reader: Documents of a Revolution Under Fire* (New York: Grove Press, revised ed. 1983), p. 183.

27. George Black and Judy Butler, "Target Nicaragua," *NACLA Report on the Americas,* January-February 1982, p. 21.

28. Pastor, *Condemned to Repetition,* pp. 232-33.

29. Edward Walsh, *Washington Post,* April 2, 1981.

30. Juan de Onis, *New York Times,* February 20, 1981.

31. *Boston Globe,* February 23, 1981; Juan de Onis, *New York Times,* February 23, 1981.

32. Dan Hallin, "The Media Go to War—From Vietnam to Central America," *NACLA Report on the Americas,* July-August, 1983, pp. 3-4.

33. Juan de Onis, *New York Times,* February 24, 1981.

34. Mark Hertsgaard, "How Reagan Seduced Us," *Village Voice,* September 18, 1984, p. 17.

35. Quoted in *New York Times,* October 19, 1984.

36. For an unveiled look at Henry Kissinger, see Hersh, *The Price of Power.*

37. Quoted in Noam Chomsky, "Introduction" to Morris Morley and James Petras, *The Reagan Administration and Nicaragua: How Washington Constructs Its Case for Counterrevolution in Central America* (New York: Institute for Media Analysis/Monograph Series No. 1, 1987), pp. 3-4.

38. James Petras, "White Paper on the White Paper," *The Nation,* March 28, 1981.

39. Jonathan Kwitny, *Wall Street Journal,* June 8, 1981. Also see John Dinges, *Los Angeles Times,* March 17, 1981 and *In These Times,* April 1-7, 1981; Ralph McGehee, *The Nation,* April 11, 1981; Robert Kaiser, *Washington Post,* June 9, 1981.

40. Juan de Onis, *New York Times,* June 10, 1981.

41. Jonathan Kwitny, *Endless Enemies: The Making of an Unfriendly World* (New York: Penguin, 1984), p. 369.

42. Warner Poelchau, ed., *White Paper Whitewash: Interviews with Philip Agee on the CIA and El Salvador* (New York: Deep Cover Books, 1981), p. 101.

43. Bonner, *Weakness and Deceit,* p. 258, citing journalists Craig Pyes and Laurie Becklund on the D'Aubuisson connection.

44. Scott Anderson and Jon Lee Anderson, *Inside the League* (New York: Dodd, Meade & Company, 1986), p. 307, fn. 20, quoting Craig Pyes.

45. Haig, *Caveat,* pp. 138-39.

46. Ibid, p. 19.

47. Tomas Borge, "The Second Anniversary of the Nicaraguan Revolution," in *Sandinistas Speak,* p. 132.

48. "Did Nicaragua Say What the U.S. Says It Said?" *New York Times,* March 30, 1985.

49. Eldon Kenworthy, "Selling the Policy," in Thomas W. Walker, ed., *Reagan versus the Sandinistas* (Boulder, CO: Westview Press, 1987), galleys, p. 154, citing *Washington Post,* October 4, 1983.

50. Don Oberdorfer and Patrick E. Tyler, *Washington Post,* May 8, 1983. A censored copy of the signed finding appears in Report of the Congressional Committees Investigating the *Iran-Contra Affair, Appendix A,* Vol. 2 (Source Documents), p. 1156.

51. Bernard Gwertzman, *New York Times,* March 19, 1981.

52. Haig, *Caveat,* pp. 128-31.

53. Richard Halloran, *New York Times,* March 15, 1981.

54. Haig, *Caveat,* pp. 123-31.

55. Joanne Omang, *Washington Post,* January 1, 1987.

56. *Newsweek,* November 8, 1982, p. 44.

57. Quoted in Allan Nairn, "Endgame: A Special Report on U.S. Military Strategy in Central America," *NACLA Report on the Americas,* May-June 1984, p. 29.

Chapter 4: The Avengers

1. NACLA delegation interview in which the author participated with Moises Hassan, December 25, 1980.

2. Martha Honey, "Contra coverage—Paid for by the CIA," *Columbia Journalism Review,* March-April 1987, p. 32.

3. Eddie Adams, "Exiles Rehearse For The Day They Hope Will Come," *Parade,* March 15, 1981.

4. Jo Thomas, *New York Times,* March 17, 1981.

5. National Security Archive, *The Chronology* (New York: Warner Books, 1987), p. 8., citing *Wall Street Journal,* January 15, 1987.

6. Peter Cary, "The Old boys' role in the Iran-Contra affair," *U.S. News and World Report,* August 10, 1987.

7. Art Harris, *Washington Post,* August 16, 1981.

8. Dickey, *With the Contras,* p. 82. Also see Congressional Arms Control and Foreign Policy Caucus, *The Contra High Command,* March 1986, p. 7.

9. Dickey, *With the Contras,* p. 83.

10. Christian, *Nicaragua,* p. 204.

11. Allan Nairn, "The Guatemalan Connection," *Central America Update* Special Report, December 1980, p. 28.

12. Anderson and Anderson, *Inside the League,* frontpiece.

13. Ibid., p. 35.

14. Ibid., p. 24.

15. Quoted in Joe Conason and Murray Waas, "The Old Right's New Crusade," *Village Voice,* October 22, 1985.

16. Anderson and Anderson, *Inside the League,* pp. 48-49, 54-58.

17. Ibid., pp. 75, 111.

18. Lernoux, *Cry of the People,* pp. 75-76, 143-44.

19. See ibid., pp. 463-670.

20. Anderson and Anderson, *Inside the League,* p. 93.

21. Ibid., p. 101.

22. Ibid., pp. 92-93.

23. Ibid., p. 65.

24. Ibid., p. 60; Fred Clarkson, "Moon's Law: 'God Is Phasing Out Democracy,'" *CovertAction Information Bulletin,* Spring 1987, p. 36.

25. Anderson and Anderson, pp. 125-29, 279.

26. Clarkson, "Moon's Law," p. 44; CAUSA USA brochure.

27. Frank Greve, *Philadelphia Inquirer,* December 20, 1987.

28. Eric Alterman, "In Moon's Orbit," *The New Republic,* October 27, 1986, p. 13.

29. Quoted in Mark Jenkins, "Rebels Outside of CAUSA," *City Paper* (Washington), December 11-17, 1987. Also see James Ridgeway, "Moonrise over Washington," *Village Voice,* January 19, 1988.

30. Anderson and Anderson, *Inside the League,* p. 130.

31. Ibid., p. 152.

32. Diana Johnstone, "Contriving support for contra forces," *In These Times,* November 12-18, 1986.

33. See Ramsey Clark, et al. *Report of a U.S.-Philippine Fact-Finding Mission,* May 20-30, 1987.

34. Victor Marchetti and John D. Marks, *The CIA and the Cult of Intelligence* (New York: Laurel/Dell, 1980), p. 207.

35. Anderson and Anderson, p. 150.

36. Conversation with Chip Berlet, Political Research Associates, Cambridge, MA, April 13, 1988.

37. Chip Berlet, "The Hunt for Red Menace: Covert McCarthyism, the FBI and the Political Right," unpublished mss., March 1988; Anderson and Anderson, *Inside the League,* pp. 155-56.

38. Russ Bellant, *Old Nazis, The New Right and the Reagan Administration* (Cambridge, MA: Political Research Associates, forthcoming 1988) and Frank J. Donner, *The Age of Surveillance* (New York: Vintage Books, 1981), pp. 417, 422-24.

39. Allan Nairn, "Reagan Administration Links With Guatemala's Terrorist Government," *CovertAction Information Bulletin,* April 1981, pp. 19, 21.

40. Cited in Americas Watch, *Guatemala Revised: How the Reagan Administration Finds "Improvements" in Human Rights in Guatemala* (New York: September 1985), p. 6.

41. Nairn, "Reagan Administration Links," p. 21.

42. Anderson and Anderson, *Inside the League*, p. 141.

43. Ibid., p. 148.

44. Ibid., pp. 254-61; Letter from Reagan to WACL, August 31, 1984.

45. Anderson and Anderson, *Inside the League*, p. 184.

46. Ibid., p. 270.

47. Conason and Waas, "The Old Right's New Crusade," p. 19.

48. Author's interview with Edgar Chamorro, Boston, November 24, 1986.

49. Cited by Anderson and Anderson, *Inside the League*, p. 120.

50. See The Report of the Argentine National Commission, *Nunca Mas* [Never Again] (New York: Farrar Straus Giroux, 1986).

51. For U.S. military course descriptions see Lernoux, *Cry of the People*, pp. 180-81.

52. See Aldo C. Vacs, "From Hostility to Partnership: The New Character of Argentine-Soviet Relations," in Augusto Varas, ed., *Soviet-Latin American Relations in the 1980s* (Boulder, CO: Westview Press, 1987) and Marc Edelman, "The Other Superpower: The USSR and Latin America: 1917-1987," *NACLA Report on the Americas*, January-February 1987.

53. Anderson and Anderson, p. 143.

54. Henrik Kruger, *The Great Heroin Coup: Drugs, Intelligence, and International Fascism* (Boston: South End Press, 1980), p. 217, fn. 19.

55. Anderson and Anderson, *Inside the League*, p. 147; Kai Hermann, "Klaus Barbie: A Killer's Career," *CovertAction Information Bulletin*, Winter 1986. Also see Erhard Dabringhaus, *Klaus Barbie* (Washington, DC: Acropolis Books, 1984), pp. 179-80.

56. Hermann, "Klaus Barbie." On Bolivia's cocaine coup, see Gregorio Selser, *Bolivia: El Cuartelazo de Los Cocadolares* (Coyoacan, Mexico: MEX-SUR, 1982).

57. Anderson and Anderson, *Inside the League*, pp. 148, 224.

58. Transcript of Hector Frances' videotaped testimony, December 1, 1982, Mexico City. Also see Christopher Dickey, *Washington Post*, December 2, 1982.

59. Bermudez is cited by John Prados, *Presidents' Secret Wars* (New York: William Morrow, 1986), p. 381.

60. Transcript of Hector Frances.

61. Anderson and Anderson, *Inside the League*, pp. 247-48.

62. Ellen Ray and William Schaap, "Vernon Walters: Crypto-diplomat and Terrorist," *CovertAction Information Bulletin*, Summer 1986.

63. See Paul Horowitz and Holly Sklar, "South Atlantic Triangle," *NACLA Report on the Americas*, May-June 1982, pp. 3-5.

64. Affidavit of Edgar Chamorro, Washington, DC, September 5, 1985, for the International Court of Justice, Case Concerning Military and Paramilitary Activities In and Against Nicaragua.

65. Dickey, *With the Contras*, p. 119.

66. National Security Archive, *The Chronology*, p. 9.

67. Dickey, *With the Contras*, p. 108.

68. Christopher Dickey, "The Proconsuls," *Rolling Stone*, August 18, 1983.

69. William Shawcross, *Sideshow: Kissinger, Nixon and the Destruction of Cambodia* (New York: Pock et Books, 1979), pp. 268-69.

70. Ibid., pp. 270-72.

71. Dickey, "The Proconsuls."

72. Shawcross, *Sideshow*, p. 269.

73. Dickey, *With the Contras*, p. 103.

74. Roy Gutman, "Nicaragua: America's Diplomatic Charade," *Foreign Policy*, Fall 1984, p. 5. Also see Dial Torgerson, *Los Angeles Times*, August 13, 1981.

75. Gutman, "Nicaragua," pp. 4-5.

76. Quoted in Joanne Omang, *Washington Post,* January 1, 1987.

77. Author's interview with Miguel D'Escoto, May 9, 1986.

78. See *New York Times,* June 11, 1984.

79. Author's interview with Miguel D'Escoto, May 9, 1986.

80. Gutman, "Nicaragua," pp. 7-8.

81. Bernard Gwertzman, *New York Times,* August 29, 1981.

82. Gutman, "Nicaragua," p. 9. Also see Don Oberdorfer, *New York Times,* December 10, 1981.

83. Gutman, "Nicaragua," p. 10.

84. Dickey, *With the Contras,* p. 111; see pp. 109-11 for Enders' account of the talks.

85. Alan Riding, *New York Times,* August 24, 1981.

86. Emerson, *Secret Warriors,* p. 122.

87. Jackson Diehl, *Washington Post,* November 6, 1981.

88. Leslie H. Gelb, *New York Times,* November 5, 1981; Hedrick Smith, *New York Times,* November 6, 1981.

89. UPI, *New York Times,* November 16, 1981; *Christian Science Monitor,* November 24, 1981.

90. Dickey, *With the Contras,* pp. 104, 107.

91. Peter Goldman, et al., "Campaign '84: The Inside Story," *Newsweek* Election Extra, November-De cem ber, 1984, p. 32.

92. James McCartney, *Miami Herald,* November 13, 1981; John M. Goshko, *Washington Post,* November 13, 1981.

Chapter 5: Semi-Secret War

1. Quoted in Robert Matthews, "Sowing Dragon's Teeth: The U.S. War Against Nicaragua," *NACLA Report on the Americas,* July-August 1986, p. 23.

2. Washington Office on Latin America (WOLA) *Update,* February 1982.

3. Cited in William LeoGrande, "The United States and Nicaragua," in Walker, ed., *Nicaragua,* p. 435.

4. See Craig Nelson, "Why Reagan Likes the Leaks," *In These Times,* May 5-11, 1982.

5. Don Oberdorfer and Patrick E. Tyler, *Washington Post,* February 14, 1982.

6. Patrick E. Tyler and Bob Woodward, *Washington Post,* March 10, 1982.

7. Leslie H. Gelb, *New York Times,* March 14, 1982.

8. Saul Landau and Craig Nelson, "The C.I.A. Rides Again," *The Nation,* March 6, 1982.

9. Testimony of David MacMichael, International Court of Justice, Verbatim Record, September 13, 1985, pp. 42-44.

10. James LeMoyne, "Can the Contras Go On?" *New York Times Magazine,* October 4, 1987, p. 66.

11. See Louis Wolf, "The 'Cyclone' Moves in at Langley," *CovertAction Information Bulletin,* April 1981.

12. Murray Waas and Jeff Chester, *The Nation,* August 8-15, 1981.

13. *U.S. News & World Report,* November 5, 1984.

14. Don Oberdorfer and Patrick E. Tyler, *Washington Post,* May 8, 1983.

15. Joanne Omang, *Washington Post,* January 1, 1987.

16. Oberdorfer and Tyler, *Washington Post,* May 8, 1983; Presidential finding, December 1, 1981, *Iran-Contra Affair, Appendix A,* Vol. 2, p. 1024.

17. Ibid.

18. Juan O. Tamayo, *Miami Herald,* December 19, 1982.

19. "The Fire Next Door," *Newsweek,* March 1, 1982, p. 20.

20. See Prados, *Presidents' Secret Wars,* pp. 261-96.

21. See Christopher Robbins, *Air America* (New York: Avon Books, 1979) and *The Ravens* (New York: Crown Publishers, 1987).

22. Robbins, *Air America,* pp. 127-28; 225-43.

23. Jim Naureckas and Richard Ryan, "The Lessons of Laos," *In These Times,* April 15-21, 1987.

24. Robbins, *Air America,* pp. 100-101, 111.

25. Quoted in Philippe Bourgois, "Ethnic Minorities," in Walker, ed., *Nicaragua,* p. 211.

26. Ibid., pp. 203-04.

27. Americas Watch, *The Miskitos in Nicaragua 1981-1984,* November 1984.

28. Reed Brody, *Contra Terror in Nicaragua* (Boston: South End Press, 1985), pp. 121-23.

29. Transcript of "D'Escoto/Kirkpatrick," The MacNeil-Lehrer Report, WNET/Thirteen, February 4, 1982, p. 5.

30. Americas Watch, *Miskitos in Nicaragua,* p. 17.

31. Cynthia Brown, ed., *With Friends Like These: The Americas Watch Report on Human Rights and U.S. Policy in Latin America* (New York: Pantheon Books, 1985), galleys, p. 146.

32. Bourgois, "Ethnic Minorities," p. 205.

33. Senate floor debate, April 20, 1988.

34. Americas Watch, *Miskitos in Nicaragua,* pp. 19-23.

35. Brown, ed., *With Friends Like These,* galleys, pp. 145-53.

36. Americas Watch, *Guatemala Revised, pp. 10-13.*

37. Alan Riding, *New York Times,* December 13, 1981; *New York Times,* December 5, 1981.

38. Jo Thomas, *New York Times,* December 23, 1981.

39. Frank J. Prial, *New York Times,* January 9, 1982.

40. *New York Times,* January 8, 1982; Judith Miller, *New York Times,* January 9, 1982.

41. Matthews, "Limits of Friendship," p. 30.

42. *Washington Post,* July 10, 1982.

43. Matthews, "Limits of Friendship," p. 30.

44. *Jacobsen Report,* p. 19.

45. Robinson and Norsworthy, *David and Goliath,* pp. 48-49; Black and Butler, "Target Nicaragua," p. 35.

46. Black and Butler, "Target Nicaragua," p. 27.

47. Jim Morrell and William Jesse Biddle, "Central America: The Financial War," *International Policy Report,* March 1983; World Bank News Release No. 82/41, January 14, 1982.

48. Quoted in Bernard Gwertzman, *New York Times,* February 3, 1982.

49. Alan Riding, *New York Times,* February 5, 1982.

50. Bonner, *Weakness and Deceit,* pp. 262-64.

51. Quoted in *New York Times,* February 8, 1982.

52. Alan Riding, *New York Times,* February 22, 1982.

53. Alan Riding, *New York Times,* March 12, 1982.

54. LeoGrande, "The United States and Nicaragua," p. 438.

55. Gutman, "Nicaragua," p. 11.

56. LeoGrande, "The United States and Nicaragua," p. 439. Also see John Goshko, *Washington Post,* July 8, 1982.

57. Philip Taubman, *New York Times,* March 10, 1982.

58. Warren Hoge, *New York Times,* March 10, 1982.

59. Black and Butler, "Target Nicaragua," p. 41. Also see Don Oberdorfer, *Washington Post,* March 11, 1982.

60. Testimony of Lt. Col. John H. Buchanan, USMC (ret.), before the Subcommittee on Inter-American Affairs of the House Committee on Foreign Affairs, September 21, 1982, reprinted in *NACLA Report on the Americas,* September-October, 1982.

61. Nairn, "Endgame," p. 49.

62. Buchanan testimony.

63. Marc Edelman, "Lifelines: Nicaragua and the Socialist Countries," *NACLA Report on the Americas,* May-June 1985, pp. 49-50; *Wall Street Journal,* April 3, 1985.

64. *U.S. Intelligence Performance on Central America: Achievements and Selected Instances of Concern,* Staff report, Subcommittee on Oversight and Evaluation, House Permanent Select Committee on Intelligence, September 22, 1982, p. 21.

65. Nairn, "Endgame," p. 49, citing *Miami Herald,* September 24, 1982.

66. Philip Taubman, *New York Times,* March 13 and March 14, 1982.

67. "Taking Aim at Nicaragua," *Newsweek,* March 22, 1982.

68. Robinson and Norsworthy, *David and Goliath,* p. 48.

69. *New York Times,* March 17, 1982.

70. Oberdorfer and Tyler, *Washington Post,* May 8, 1983.

71. *New York Times,* March 26, 1982.

72. Jeane J. Kirkpatrick, Statement in the UN Security Council on the complaint by Nicaragua, March 25, 1982, in *The Reagan Phenomenon—and Other Speeches on Foreign Policy* (Washington, DC: American Enterprise Institute, 1983), pp. 184-85.

73. National Security Council, "U.S. Policy in Central America and Cuba Through F.Y. '84, Summary Paper," April 1982, excerpted in *New York Times,* April 7, 1983. Also see Raymond Bonner, *New York Times,* April 7, 1983.

74. Robert H. Holden, "Corporate Officials Embrace Latin Dictators at Private Chamber of Commerce Session," *Multinational Monitor,* June 1982.

75. Defense Intelligence Agency, *Weekly Intelligence Summary,* July 16, 1982, released by *CounterSpy,* July 28, 1983. Also see Robert Parry, Associated Press wireservice, August 19, 1983.

76. Affidavit of Edgar Chamorro.

77. Author's interview with Edgar Chamorro, November 24, 1986.

78. Honduran Federation of Unemployed, Foreign Broadcast Information Service (FBIS), May 23, 1985, cited in Kornbluh, *Price of Intervention,* p. 229, fn. 95.

79. Horowitz and Sklar, "South Atlantic Triangle," p. 35.

80. Ibid., p. 37.

81. Alan Riding, *New York Times,* May 16, 1982.

82. Charles Roberts, " 'Commander Zero' Resurfaces," in Rosset and Vandermeer, eds., *Nicaragua Reader,* pp. 220-23.

83. Christopher Dickey, *Washington Post,* April 16, 1982.

84. FSLN Communique to the Heroic People of Nicaragua and to the World, April 16, 1982.

85. Alan Riding, *New York Times,* July 2, 1982.

86. Bourgois, "Ethnic Minorities," pp. 204, 206.

87. Remarks made to Jon Lee Anderson, quoted in Jack Anderson, *Washington Post,* September 30, 1984, cited in Americas Watch, *Human Rights in Nicaragua: Reagan, Rhetoric and Reality,* July 1985, p. 71.

88. Bourgois, "Ethnic Minorities," p. 206.

89. Dickey, *With the Contras,* pp. 148-49.

90. Report of the Congressional Committees Investigating the *Iran-Contra Affair,* November 1987 (hereafter *Iran-Contra Report)* p. 32; Memorandum from Donald Gregg to William Clark, July 12, 1982, *Iran-Contra Affair, Appendix A,* Vol. 2, pp. 1019-22.

91. Dickey, *With the Contras,* p. 151.

Chapter 6: Fire, Smoke and Mirrors

1. Kornbluh, *Price of Intervention,* pp. 174, 259, fn. 63, citing *Boston Globe,* April 20, 1982.

2. Quoted in Dickey, *With the Contras,* p. 115.

3. Teofilo Cabestrero, *Blood of the Innocent* (Maryknoll, New York: Orbis Books, 1985), galleys, pp. 93-94.

4. Brody, *Contra Terror,* p. 63.

5. Quoted in Marlise Simons, *New York Times,* December 14, 1982.

6. Brody, *Contra Terror,* pp. 51-52; Alexander Cockburn and James Ridgeway, "Eyewitness to Terror," *Village Voice,* July 12, 1983.

7. Brody, *Contra Terror,* pp. 52-53.

8. *New York Times,* April 2, 1982.

9. CAHI, *From Banana Cases to Contra Bases: A Chronology of U.S.-Honduran Relations January 1977 to July 1986,* Washington, DC, 1986, p. 19.

10. Philip Taubman, *New York Times,* December 4, 1982.

11. *Boston Globe,* August 12, 1982.

12. CAHI, *Banana Cases to Contra Bases,* p. 13.

13. Philip Taubman and Raymond Bonner, *New York Times,* April 3, 1983.

14. "America's Secret War," *Newsweek,* November 8, 1982, pp. 42-55.

15. Kevin Danaher, Phillip Berryman and Medea Benjamin, *Help or Hindrance? United States Economic Aid in Central America* (San Francisco: Institute for Food and Development Policy, 1987), p. 86.

16. Karl Grossman, *Nicaragua: America's New Vietnam?* (Sag Harbor, New York: The Permanent Press, 1984), pp. 12-13.

17. Anderson and Anderson, *Inside the League,* pp. 224-27.

18. Grossman, *Nicaragua,* pp. 8, 15.

19. Affidavit of Edgar Chamorro.

20. Edgar Chamorro with Jefferson Morley, "Confessions of a 'Contra,' " *New Republic,* August 5, 1985, pp. 18-21.

21. Edgar Chamorro, *Packaging the Contras: A Case of CIA Disinformation* (New York: Institute for Media Analysis, Monograph Series No. 2, 1987) p. 13.

22. Chamorro, "Confessions of a 'Contra,' " pp. 18-21.

23. Ibid., pp. 20-21.

24. Affidavit of Edgar Chamorro.

25. Chamorro, *Packaging the Contras,* p. 14.

26. Oberdorfer and Tyler, *Washington Post,* May 8, 1983.

27. Quoted in Omang, *Washington Post,* January 1, 1987.

28. Oberdorfer and Tyler, *Washington Post,* May 8, 1983.

29. Omang, *Washington Post,* January 1, 1987.

30. Quoted in CAHI, *U.S.-Nicaraguan Relations: Chronology of Policy and Impact January 1981-January 1984* (Expanded Edition), p. 12.

31. Matthews, "Sowing Dragon's Teeth," p. 23, citing *Washington Post,* February 24, 1985.

32. Letter from William H. Taft IV, General Counsel of the Department of Defense, to Henry R. Wray, As sistant General Counsel of the U.S. General Accounting Office, February 2, 1984.

33. Affidavit of Edgar Chamorro.

34. Robinson and Norsworthy, *David and Goliath,* p. 61.

35. Taubman and Bonner, *New York Times,* April 3, 1983.

36. Affidavit of Edgar Chamorro.

37. Martha Honey, "Contra coverage—paid for by the CIA," *Columbia Journalism Review,* March-April 1987.

38. Affidavit of Edgar Chamorro.

39. Alfonso Chardy, *Miami Herald,* April 17, 1983.

40. Affidavit of Edgar Chamorro.

41. Brody, *Contra Terror,* pp. 160-61, 163.

42. Cabestrero, *Blood of the Innocent,* galleys, pp. 94-97.

43. CAHI, *U.S.-Nicaraguan Relations,* p. 14.

44. Leslie H. Gelb, *New York Times,* April 7, 1983.

45. James LeMoyne, "The Secret War Boils Over," *Newsweek,* April 11, 1983, p. 50.

46. CAHI, *Update* 2:7, April 21, 1983.

47. "The Contras—Chronicle of a Defeat Foretold," *Envío,* February 1987, pp. 22-25.

48. Author's interview with Flor de Maria Monterrey, Managua, April 28, 1986.

49. Gorman and Walker, "The Armed Forces," p. 112.

50. See Maxine Molyneux, "Women," in Walker, ed., *Nicaragua,* pp. 149-50.

51. Leslie H. Gelb, *New York Times,* April 22, 1983.

52. Nicaraguan Memorial, International Court of Justice, pp. 86-87.

53. *Business Week* editorial, May 23, 1983, p. 212.

54. "Central America: Why the Crisis Will Deepen," *Business Week,* May 23, 1983, pp. 62-70.

55. Americas Watch, *Human Rights in Nicaragua,* April 1984, pp. 20-21, 23, 40-41, 44-47; Brown, ed., *With Friends Like These,* galleys, p. 115.

56. CAHI, *Update* 2:17, August 3, 1983 and 3:16, May 24, 1984.

57. Alfonso Chardy, *Miami Herald,* April 20, 1983.

58. *Business Week,* May 23, 1983.

59. Robert J. McCartney, *Washington Post,* July 1, 1983.

60. Direccion General de Divulgacion y Prensa de la JGRN, *Conspiracion de la C.I.A. en Nicaragua,* June 1983.

61. *Latin America Weekly Report,* June 17, 1983.

62. Gutman, "Nicaragua," p. 14.

63. Author's interview with Miguel D'Escoto, May 9, 1986.

64. Philip Taubman, *New York Times,* May 23, 1983.

65. David Rogers and David Ignatius, *Wall Street Journal,* March 6, 1985.

66. *New York Times,* May 24, 1983.

67. Frank McNeil, "Stuck on the Contras," *Washington Post,* March 1, 1987; John M. Goshko, *Washington Post,* February 11, 1987; Frontline, "War on Nicaragua," WGBH/Boston, April 21, 1987.

68. Nicaraguan Memorial, International Court of Justice, p. 29.

69. *Sojourners,* March 1983, p. 19.

70. Interview with David MacMichael by John Lamperti, November 22, 1985. See Lamperti, *What Are We Afraid Of?* (Boston: South End Press, 1988).

71. Juan O. Tamayo, *Miami Herald,* June 5, 1983.

72. Bernard Gwertzman, *New York Times,* May 29, 1983.

73. *Time,* August 8, 1983, p. 20.

74. Leslie H. Gelb, *New York Times,* June 14, 1983; Rogers and Ignatius, *Wall Street Journal,* March 6, 1985.

75. National Security Council, "Strategy for Central America," July 6, 1983.

76. Philip Taubman, *New York Times,* July 17, 1983.

77. Philip Taubman, *New York Times,* July 23, 1983.

78. "Pressure in Paramaribo," *CovertAction Information Bulletin,* Winter 1984, p. 6.

79. Marlise Simons, *New York Times,* July 24, 1983.

80. Steven V. Roberts, *New York Times,* July 29, 1983.

81. Fred Kaplan, *Boston Globe,* January 3, 1987. Also see National Security Afchive, *The Chronology,* pp. 45-46, citing Kaplan's article and CBS News, December 8, 1986.

82. "Into the Fray: Facts on the US Military in Central America," *The Defense Monitor* XIII:3, 1984,

83. *Newsweek,* August 1, 1983; *Time,* August 8, 1983.

84. Charles Mohr, *New York Times,* July 31, 1983.

85. *Atlanta Constitution,* August 4, 1983.

Chapter 7: Shockwaves

1. *El Nuevo Diario,* September 9, 1983.

2. Jeff Gerth, *New York Times,* October 6, 1983.

3. *Report of the President's Special Review Board* (hereafter *Tower Board Report*), February 26, 1987, p. C-1; Presidential finding, September 19, 1983, *Iran-Contra Affair, Appendix A,* Vol. 1, pp. 252-54.

4. Dickey, *With the Contras,* p. 258.

5. Alexander Cockburn and James Ridgeway, "Reaganism Unchallenged," *Village Voice,* October 25, 1983. Also see Woodward, *Veil,* pp. 230-31, on Doty.

6. Chamorro, "Confessions of a Contra," p. 22.

7. Affidavit of Edgar Chamorro.

8. Cited in Brody, *Contra Terror,* p. 168.

9. Dickey, *With the Contras,* p. 258.

10. Affidavit of Edgar Chamorro.

11. Kornbluh, *Price of Intervention,* p. 47.

12. Embassy of Nicaragua, Washington, DC, Press Release, October 12, 1983.

13. Woodward, *Veil,* p. 281.

14. Transcript, *New York Times,* October 20, 1983.

15. Kornbluh, *Price of Intervention,* pp. 144-45, citing *New York Times,* June 8, 1984.

16. Seymour M. Hersh, "Who's in Charge Here?" *New York Times Magazine,* November 22, 1987, pp. 35, 62.

17. Emerson, *Secret Warriors,* pp. 45-47, 235.

18. Hersh, "Who's in Charge," p. 67.

19. Emerson, *Secret Warriors,* pp. 92-93.

20. Hersh, "Who's in Charge," pp. 69, 71.

21. Frank Greve and Ellen Warren, *Miami Herald,* December 16, 1984; another version appeared in the *Philadelphia Inquirer,* December 16, 1984. Also see "Fort Huachuca Buildup: War Technology in the Desert," *CovertAction Information Bulletin,* Winter 1984, pp. 31-33.

22. Richard Gabriel, *Military Incompetence: Why the American Military Doesn't Win* (New York: Hill and Wang, 1985), pp. 150, 182-83.

23. *Washington Post,* December 18 and 20, 1984.

24. Jay Peterzell, *Reagan's Secret Wars* (Washington, DC: Center for National Security Studies, 1984), p. 77.

25. Clarence Lusane, "Reagan's Big Lie," *CovertAction Information Bulletin,* Spring-Summer 1983, p. 31.

26. W. Frick Curry, "Grenada: Force as First Resort," *International Policy Report,* January 1984, p. 2.

27. Ibid.

28. Quoted in Seymour Hersh, "Operation Urgent Fury," Frontline, WGBH/Boston, February 2, 1988.

29. Ellen Ray and Bill Schaap, "U.S. Crushes Caribbean Jewel," *CovertAction Information Bulletin,* Winter 1984, p. 4.

30. Ibid., p. 5.

31. Woodward, *Veil,* p. 290.

32. Ray and Schaap, "U.S. Crushes Caribbean Jewel," p. 13, citing *Cleveland Plain-Dealer,* November 3, 1983.

33. Fitzroy Ambursley and James Dunkerley, *Grenada Whose Freedom?* (London: Latin America Bureau, 1984), pp. 85-86, citing *Los Angeles Times,* November 6, 1983.

34. *New York Times,* October 28, 1983.

35. Ray and Schaap, "U.S. Crushes Caribbean Jewel," p. 19, citing *Washington Post,* November 21, 1983.

36. Gabriel, *Military Incompetence,* pp. 182-85.

37. *Newsweek,* July 27, 1987, p. 38.

38. Quoted in Philip Taubman, *New York Times,* February 8, 1984.

39. Joseph B. Treaster, *New York Times,* July 25, 1984.

40. Woodward, *Veil,* p. 300.

41. Tom Wicker, *New York Times,* January 25, 1985.

42. Martin Burcharth, *The Nation,* March 1, 1986.

43. Gerald M. Boyd, *New York Times,* February 21, 1986.

44. Gabriel, *Military Incompetence,* p. 150.

45. Bernard Gwertzman, *New York Times,* October 30, 1983.

46. Gabriel, *Military Incompetence,* p. 177.

47. Linda Drucker, *Christian Science Monitor,* November 1, 1983; Jeff Gerth, *New York Times,* November 11, 1983; Patrick E. Tyler, *Washington Post,* November 12, 1983.

48. Jack Anderson, *Washington Post,* November 16, 1983.

49. Council on Hemispheric Affairs, Washington, DC, Press Release, November 18, 1983, cited in Norsworthy and Robinson, *David and Goliath,* p. 77.

50. Dickey, *With the Contras,* pp. 259-60.

51. Nicaragua Memorial, International Court of Justice, pp. 41-42, citing *Congressional Record* H 8394, October 20, 1983.

52. Edward Cody, *Washington Post,* January 31, 1984.

53. CAHI, *Update* 2:31, December 15, 1983.

54. Hedrick Smith, *New York Times,* December 1, 1983.

55. *Iran-Contra Report,* p. 36.

56. Ibid.

57. Nicaragua Memorial, International Court of Justice, pp. 47-48; *Time,* April 23, 1984, p. 24; David Ig natius and David Rogers, *Wall Street Journal,* March 5, 1985.

58. *Washington Post,* January 29, 1984.

59. Kornbluh, *Price of Intervention,* p. 252, fn. 68, citing Pacific New Service, March 29, 1984.

60. Ellen Ray and Bill Schaap, "The War Widens," *CovertAction Information Bulletin,* Spring 1984, pp. 4-5. Also see Joel Brinkley, *New York Times,* April 22, 1984.

61. National Security Archive, *Secret Military Assistance to Iran and the Contras: A Chronology of Events and Individuals,* (hereafter *Chronology II*) (Washington, DC: 1987), pp. 62, 70-71, citing *Newsday,* May 24, 1987.

62. David Rogers and David Ignatius, *Wall Street Journal,* March 6, 1985.

63. *Iran-Contra Report,* p. 36; Memorandum from Oliver North and Constantine Menges to McFarlane, November 4, 1983 and Memorandum from McFarlane to Reagan, November 7, 1983, in *Iran-Contra Affair, Appendix A,* Vol. 1, pp. 197-98.

64. Affidavit of Edgar Chamorro.

65. *Time,* April 23, 1984, p. 20.

66. CAHI, *Update* 3:13, April 5, 1984.

67. Peter Kornbluh, "The Covert War," in Walker, ed., *Reagan vs. the Sandinistas,* galleys, p. 26.

68. Stephen Kinzer, *New York Times,* March 14, 1984.

69. Philip Taubman, *New York Times,* April 9, 1984.

70. "Explosion Over Nicaragua," *Time,* April 23, 1984, p. 20.

71. MADRE delegation interview in which the author participated with Tomas Borge, Managua, March 1984.

72. *New York Times,* April 11, 1984.

73. *Time,* April 23, 1984, pp. 22-23.

74. Martin Tolchin, *New York Times,* April 11, 1984.

75. *New York Times* editorial, April 11, 1984.

76. Nicaragua Memorial, International Court of Justice, p. 44; *New York Times*, May 9, 1984.

77. Author's interview with Miguel D'Escoto, May 9, 1986.

78. CAHI, *Update* 4:27, September 10, 1985.

79. Stuart Taylor Jr., *New York Times*, April 13, 1984.

80. *Time,* April 23, 1984, p. 18.

81. John Vincour, *New York Times*, May 11, 1984.

82. *New York Times,* January 19, 1985.

83. *Nicaragua Informacion,* "Nicaragua's Case at the Hague," 1986.

84. Peter W. Rodino, "International Law," *Christian Science Monitor,* February 27, 1985.

85. Bernard Gwertzman, *New York Times,* July 19, 1983.

86. *The Report of the President's National Bipartisan Commission on Central America* (New York: Mac Millan Publishing Company, 1984), pp. 111, 135, 138, 153-55.

87. Robert J. McCartney, *Washington Post,* October 16, 1983.

88. MADRE delegation interview in which the author participated with Nora Astorga, Managua, March 1984.

89. *New York Times,* December 31, 1983.

90. MADRE delegation interview in which the author participated with Ambassador Anthony Quainton, Managua, March 1984.

91. Eugene Stockwell, *Christianity and Crisis,* January 23, 1984.

92. Carlos Fuentes, "Force Won't Work in Nicaragua," *New York Times,* July 24, 1983; also see Fuentes, "Are You Listening, Henry Kissinger," *Harpers,* January 1984.

93. Interview with William Casey, *U.S. News & World Report,* April 23, 1984.

94. NARMIC, *Invasion: A Guide to the U.S. Military Presence in Central America* (Philadelphia: American Friends Service Committee, 1985), p. 13.

95. Richard Halloran, *New York Times,* April 8, 1984; Hedrick Smith, *New York Times,* April 23, 1984.

96. Leslie H. Gelb, *New York Times,* April 29, 1984.

97. Transcript, *New York Times,* May 10, 1984.

98. Gordon Mott, *New York Times Magazine,* October 14, 1984, p. 86.

99. James Ridgeway, *Village Voice,* June 19, 1984, p. 25.

100. Brody, *Contra Terror,* pp. 55-58, 175.

101. Nicaragua Memorial, International Court of Justice, p. 58, citing *Congressional Record* S 12865, Oc tober 3, 1984.

Chapter 8: Terrorist Manuals

1. Affidavit of Edgar Chamorro.

2. National Security Archive, *Chronology II,* p. 93.

3. See Philip Taubman, *New York Times,* October 29, 1984.

4. Quoted in Kornbluh, *Price of Intervention,* p. 43.

5. Tayacan, *Psychological Operations in Guerrilla Warfare,* English translation by Library of Congress Congressional Research Service, Languages Service, October 15, 1984, pp. 14-15.

6. Ibid., p. 10.

7. Ibid., pp. 11-12.

8. Ibid., pp 14-15.

9. Ibid., p. 24.

10. Ibid., pp. 26-28.

11. Ibid., pp. 31-32.

12. Ibid., p. 33.

13. Ibid., pp. 33-35.

14. Affidavit of Edgar Chamorro.

15. Author's interview with Edgar Chamorro, November 24, 1986.

16. *Freedom Fighter's Manual,* translated and distributed by the Central American Historical Institute, Washington, DC.

17. Robert Parry, Associated Press, *The Hartford Courant,* June 30, 1984.

18. Reporter Brian Barger analyzed it as early as July 26, 1984 for Pacific News Service.

19. See Joel Brinkley, *New York Times,* October 20 and 23, 1984.

20. Transcript, *New York Times,* October 22, 1984.

21. Transcript, November 3, 1984, cited in Nicaragua Memorial, International Court of Justice, p. 32; also see *New York Times,* November 4, 1984.

22. Joel Brinkley, *New York Times,* October 22 and December 6, 1984.

23. Dickey, *With the Contras,* p. 262.

24. Cited in Judgement, *Case Concerning Military and Paramilitary Activities in and Against Nicaragua,* International Court of Justice, June 27, 1986, pp. 56-57; also see Brinkley, *New York Times,* December 6, 1984.

25. Dickey, *With the Contras,* p. 257.

26. Ibid., p. 262; National Security Archive, *Chronology II,* p. 99; Bob Woodward, et al., "Players in the Game," *Washington Post Weekly,* December 22, 1986; Alfonso Chardy, Sam Dillon and Tim Golden, *Miami Herald,* March 1, 1987.

27. Judgement, International Court of Justice, pp. 120, 139.

28. Americas Watch, *Violations of the Laws of War by Both Sides in Nicaragua 1981-1985* (New York: March 1985), pp. 4, 6.

29. *Violations of the Laws of War by Both Sides in Nicaragua 1981-1985: First Supplement* (New York: June 1985), p. 4.

30. William Greider, "U.S.-Sponsored Terrorism: The CIA has its own Good Book for Christian soldiers," *Rolling Stone,* December 6, 1984.

Chapter 9: Ballots, Bullets and MIGs

1. Quoted in Hersh, *Price of Power,* p. 265.

2. *Newsweek* Election Extra, November-December 1984, p. 88.

3. Ibid., p. 4.

4. Ibid., p. 36.

5. Joshua Cohen and Joel Rogers, *Rules of the Game: American Politics and the Central America Movement* (Boston: South End Press, 1986), p. 24.

6. Thomas Ferguson and Joel Rogers, *Right Turn* (New York: Hill and Wang, 1986), p. 29. Also see Walter Dean Burnham, "The 1980 Earthquake: Realignment, Reaction or What?" in Thomas Ferguson and Joel Rogers, *The Hidden Election* (New York: Pantheon, 1981).

7. Ferguson and Rogers, *Right Turn,* pp. 24-26.

8. See, for example, ibid., pp. 12-24.

9. William LeoGrande, *Central America and the Polls* (Washington Office on Latin America, May 1984), p. 40.

10. Ibid., Appendix, Table 26.

11. Ibid., pp. 18-19.

12. Ibid., pp. 36-37.

13. Ibid., p. 23 and Appendix, Table 21.

14. David K. Shipler, *New York Times,* April 15, 1986. Also see Louis Harris, *Inside America* (New York: Vintage Books, 1987), pp. 316-21.

15. Reagan interview of February 11, *New York Times,* February 12, 1985.

16. Author's interview with a U.S. ambassador in Central America, April 29, 1986.

17. Roy Gutman, "How the 1984 Vote was Sabotaged," *The Nation,* May 7, 1988.

18. Mark Cook, "The Reluctant Candidate," *The Nation,* October 13, 1984.

19. Philip Taubman, *New York Times,* October 21, 1984.

20. Arturo J. Cruz, "Nicaragua's Imperiled Revolution," *Foreign Affairs,* Summer 1983, p. 1033.

21. Author's interview with Sergio Ramirez, April 26, 1986.

22. Jose Luis Coraggio, *Nicaragua: Revolution and Democracy* (Boston: Allen & Unwin, 1986), p. 88.

23. Tony Jenkins, "Nicaragua's Disloyal Opposition," *The Nation,* August 12, 1986.

24. Ibid.

25. Ibid.

26. Karl Bermann and Glenn Fiscella, "Nicaragua Votes," A Special Report by the Tidewater Nicaragua Project Foundation (Hampton, VA: 1984).

27. MADRE delegation interview in which the author participated with Coordinadora President Luis Rivas Leiva (who later joined the contras) and Enrique Meneses of the Liberal Constitutionalist Party, Managua, March 1984.

28. See, for example, Fred Landis, "CIA Media Operations in Chile, Jamaica, and Nicaragua," *CovertAction Information Bulletin,* March 1982. Also see Centro de Comunicacion Internacional, *The Closing of La Prensa: A Case of Freedom of the Press or of National Defense,* Managua, July 1986.

29. Jacqueline Sharkey, *Common Cause Magazine,* September-October 1986, p. 36; Newsday, *Miami Herald,* October 13, 1987.

30. Report of the Latin American Studies Association Delegation to Observe the Nicaraguan General Election of November 4, 1984, *The Electoral Process in Nicaragua: Domestic and International Influences,* November 19, 1984, p. 19. Hereafter referred to as *LASA Report.*

31. Brody, *Contra Terror,* p. 178.

32. Robert J. McCartney, *Washington Post,* July 30, 1984.

33. CAHI, *Update* 3:27, August 13, 1984.

34. Brody, *Contra Terror,* pp. 178-79.

35. *LASA Report,* p. 14.

36. Cook, "The Reluctant Candidate."

37. McCartney, *Washington Post,* July 30, 1984.

38. *LASA Report,* p. 20.

39. Ibid., p. 30.

40. John B. Oakes, *New York Times,* November 15, 1984; *LASA Report,* p. 31. Also see Alexander Cockburn, *The Nation,* March 15 and May 10, 1986, for an account of U.S. bribery by PCD Youth President Marvin Jose Corrales, and related *New York Review of Books* letters exchange on May 8, 1986.

41. *LASA Report,* pp. 8-9, 31.

42. Ibid., pp. 30-31.

43. Background paper for NSC meeting on Central America, October 30, 1984. See Alma Guillermoprieto and David Hoffman, *Washington Post,* November 6, 1984, for a contemporaneous news report.

44. John Oakes, op ed., *New York Times,* November 15, 1984.

45. Robinson and Norsworthy, *David and Goliath,* p. 172.

46. Brody, *Contra Terror,* pp. 178-79.

47. *LASA Report,* p. 26, fn. 41.

48. Ibid., pp. 65, 79, 182.

49. Coraggio, *Nicaragua,* p. 86; Brody, *Contra Terror,* p. 182.

50. *LASA Report,* p. 17.

51. Author's interview with Jaime Benguechea, COSEP board member and president of the Chamber of Industry, Managua, April 23, 1986.

52. *LASA Report,* p. 12.

53. Ibid., pp. 15, 23.

54. See Howard H. Frederick, "Electronic Penetration," in Walker, ed., *Reagan versus the Sandinistas.*

55. *LASA Report,* pp. 14-15, 18.

56. CAHI, *Update* 4:13, May 10, 1985.

57. *LASA Report,* pp. 22-27.

58. Ibid., p. 23.

59. Ibid., p. 32.

60. Ibid.

61. Lord Chitnis, *The Election in Nicaragua: 4 November 1984,* pp. 20-21.

62. Americas Watch, *The Continuing Terror: Seventh Supplement to the Report on Human Rights in El Salvador* (New York, September 1985), pp. 151-52.

63. Cited in FAIR (Fairness & Accuracy in Reporting), *Extra!,* October/November 1987, p. 6.

64. "Double-standard reporting: Nicaragua and the networks," *Columbia Journalism Review,* January-February 1985, p. 17.

65. See, for example, Edward S. Herman, "The New York Times on the 1984 Salvadoran and Nicaraguan Elections," *CovertAction Information Bulletin,* Spring 1984; Jack Spence, "Second time around: how to cover an election," *Columbia Journalism Review,* March-April, 1984. Also see Edward S. Herman and Frank Brodhead, *Demonstration Elections* (Boston: South End Press, 1984).

66. Stephen Kinzer, *New York Times,* November 5, 1984.

67. Philip Taubman, *New York Times,* November 5, 1984.

68. Author's interview with Mauricio Diaz, Managua, May 7, 1986.

69. Author's interview with Rafael Cordova Rivas, April 30, 1986.

70. CAHI, *Update* 6:34, October 28, 1987; 6:43, December 30, 1987. Also see *Excelsior,* December 30, 1986.

71. Author's interview with Eduardo Coronado, Managua, May 7, 1986.

72. "Ortega Speaks Out," *Newsweek,* October 15, 1984.

73. *Jacobsen Report,* p. 15.

74. Philip Taubman, *New York Times,* November 10, 1984.

75. Charlie Cole, "Our Spy on High: The Air Force's SR-71 shows an eye for detail," *New York Times Magazine,* May 10, 1987. Also see James Bamford, *The Puzzle Palace: Inside the National Security Agency* (New York: Penguin Books, 1983), pp. 241-42.

76. Marc Cooper, "Nicaragua: Waiting for Uncle Sam," *Village Voice,* November 27, 1984, p. 25.

77. Center for Defense Information Fact Sheet, November 9, 1984.

78. *New York Times,* November 9, 1984.

79. Cooper, "Nicaragua," p. 25.

80. *Wall Street Journal,* April 3, 1985; Richard Halloran, *New York Times,* November 10, 1984.

81. Philip Taubman, *New York Times,* November 14, 1984.

82. Departments of State and Defense, *Background Paper: Nicaragua's Military Build-up and Support for Central American Subversion* (Washington, DC: July 18, 1984), p. 10.

83. Departments of State and Defense, *The Soviet-Cuban Connection in Central America and the Caribbean* (Washington, DC: March 1985), p. 25.

84. Danaher, et al., *Help or Hindrance,* pp. 86-87.

85. Caribbean Basin Information Project Press Kit, *On a Short Fuse: Militarization in Central America,* Washington, DC, 1985.

86. Joshua Cohen and Joel Rogers, *Inequity and Intervention: The Federal Budget and Central America* (Boston: South End Press, 1986), pp. 42-48.

87. Caribbean Basin Information Project, *On a Short Fuse.*

88. See, for example, Alfonso Chardy, *Miami Herald,* November 9, 1987, on U.S. contingency planning for hypothetical Soviet bases in Nicaragua.

89. Author's interview with a U.S. ambassador, April 29, 1986.

90. Wayne S. Smith, "Bringing Diplomacy Back In: A Critique of U.S. Policy in Central America," in Bruce M. Bagley, ed., *Contadora and the Diplomacy of Peace in Central America,* Vol. 1 (Boulder, CO: Westview Press/Johns Hopkins University School of Advanced International Studies, Papers in Latin American Studies, 1987), p. 71.

91. McGeorge Bundy, op ed., *New York Times,* January 6, 1984.

92. Miguel D'Escoto Brockmann, "Nicaragua: Arms are Defensive," *Miami Herald,* December 2, 1984.

93. Joel Brinkley, *New York Times,* March 30, 1985.

94. D'Escoto, "Nicaragua: Arms are Defensive."

95. Smith, "Bringing Diplomacy Back In," p. 73.

96. Philip Taubman, *New York Times,* November 11, 1984.

97. Richard Halloran, *New York Times,* November 29, 1984.

98. *Hearings on the Nomination of Caspar W. Weinberger to be Secretary of Defense,* Senate Committee on Armed Services, January 6, 1981, pp. 38-39.

Chapter 10: I'm A Contra Too!

1. *Miami Herald,* November 20, 1985, cited in Kornbluh, *Price of Intervention,* p. 166.

2. Reggie Norton, "Introduction" to Brody, *Contra Terror,* p. 15.

3. Cruz, "Nicaragua's Imperiled Revolution," p. 1044.

4. Memorandum from North to McFarlane, November 7, 1984, *Iran-Contra Hearings,* Vol. 2, Appendix, pp. 463-65.

5. "Statement by Arturo Cruz at a Press Conference," International Club, Washington, DC, January 3, 1985. Also see Joanne Omang, *Washington Post,* January 4, 1985.

6. *Wall Street Journal,* April 23, 1985.

7. Associated Press, *Washington Post,* April 25, 1985.

8. Deposition of Roy Godson, September 10, 1987, *Iran-Contra Affair, Appendix B,* Vol. 12, pp. 301-05. A portion of the deposition regarding Cruz and the NSIC is classified.

9. Memorandum from Owen to North, August 25, 1985, *Iran-Contra Hearings,* Vol. 2, Appendix, p. 809.

10. "United Nicaraguan Opposition: Democratic Reforms and Support for a Peaceful Solution to the Conflict in Nicaragua," U.S. Department of State, June 1986, p. 2. Also see Congressional Arms Control and Foreign Policy Caucus, "Contra 'Reforms': Are the Miami Agreements Significant?" June 18, 1986.

11. See, for example, Secord's financial notes listing Cruz's salary in *Iran-Contra Hearings,* Vol. 1, Appendix, pp. 454-58. Also see Robert Parry and David L. Gonzalez, *Newsweek,* May 4, 1987, p. 25.

12. Arturo Cruz, address sponsored by CAUSA USA, Embassy Suites Hotel, Boston, February 21, 1987.

13. See James LeMoyne, *New York Times,* March 10, 1987; Lloyd Grove, *Washington Post,* February 19, 1987; Betsy Cohn, Charles Roberts and Jim Lobe, CAHI, *Update,* "Arguments and Evidence: Ten Talking Points Against Contra Aid," October 1987, citing *Christian Science Monitor,* March 11, 1987.

14. Author's interview with Edgar Chamorro, November 24, 1986.

15. Congressional Arms Control and Foreign Policy Caucus, *The Contra High Command: An Independent Analysis of the Military Leadership of the FDN,* March 1986 and *Who are the Contras?,* April 1985; Nicaraguan Government, "The 'Freedom Fighters': The Return of Somoza's National Guard," 1986.

16. Author's interview with Edgar Chamorro, November 24, 1986.

17. Memorandum From Owen to North, March 17, 1986, *Iran-Contra Hearings,* Vol. 2, Appendix, pp. 820-24.

18. Quoted in Joanne Omang, *Washington Post,* October 19, 1983.

19. The Testimony of Lieutenant Colonel Oliver L. North, *Taking the Stand* (New York: Pocket Books, 1987), p. 373; McFarlane Testimony, *Iran-Contra Hearings,* Vol. 2, p. 21.

20. North, *Taking the Stand,* p. 275.

21. *Iran-Contra Report,* p. 38.

22. McFarlane Testimony, *Iran-Contra Hearings,* Vol. 2, pp. 14-15.

23. Memorandum from Casey to McFarlane, March 27, 1984, *Iran-Contra Hearings,* Vol. 2, Appendix, pp. 456-57; for the South Africa reference see (Country 6) *Iran-Contra Report,* p. 38 and p. 54, fn. 120.

24. Stephen Engelberg, *New York Times,* August 20 and 21, 1987.

25. *Iran-Contra Report,* p. 38.

26. Affidavit of Edgar Chamorro; Christopher Lehman is misidentified as Ronald Lehman II, another U.S. official.

27. Edward Cody, *Washington Post,* June 5, 1984.

28. NBC News Transcript, April 23, 1984. Also see, for example, Philip Taubman, *New York Times,* July 21, 1983.

29. Emerson, *Secret Warriors,* p. 123.

30. Jane Hunter, "Israel: The Contras' Secret Benefactor," *NACLA Report on the Americas,* March-April, 1987, pp. 22-23.

31. National Security Archive, *The Chronology,* p. 31, citing ABC World News Tonight, February 25, 1987.

32. Robert Parry, "From Pretoria to the Contras?" *Newsweek,* February 15, 1988, p. 36. Also see Stephen Engelberg with Elaine Sciolino, *New York Times,* February 4, 1988.

33. Emerson, *Secret Warriors,* p. 222.

34. See, for example, Michael Kranish, *Boston Globe,* March 22, 1987; David Corn, "South Africa Link," *The Nation,* September 12, 1987.

35. Steven V. Roberts, Stephen Engelberg and Jeff Gerth, *New York Times,* June 21, 1987.

36. See John Stockwell, *In Search of Enemies: A CIA Story* (New York: W. W. Norton & Co., 1978) and Cherri Waters, "Destabilizing Angola: South Africa's War and U.S. Policy," *Special Joint Report* of the Washington Office on Africa Educational Fund and the Center for International Policy, December 1986.

37. Woodward, *Veil,* pp. 394-98.

38. See, for example, Jonathan Marshall, Peter Dale Scott and Jane Hunter, *Iran-Contra Connection,* (Boston, South End Press, 1987), p. 200; Robb Deigh, *Insight,* January 12, 1987.

39. *Iran-Contra Report,* p. 45.

40. McFarlane Testimony, *Iran-Contra Hearings,* Vol. 2, pp. 17, 130; Woodward, *Veil,* p. 354.

41. *Iran-Contra Report,* pp. 39-40.

42. Woodward, *Veil,* p. 354-55; National Security Archive, *Chronology II,* p. 80.

43. McFarlane Testimony, *Iran-Contra Hearings,* Vol. 2, pp. 16-18, 131-32.

44. Letter from North (not Owen) to Calero, *Iran-Contra Hearings,* Vol. 2, Appendix, pp. 780-82.

45. *Iran-Contra Report,* p. 45 and p. 57, fn. 262; *Tower Board Report,* p. C-5.

46. Memorandum from North to McFarlane, April 11, 1985, *Iran-Contra Hearings,* Vol. 2, Appendix, pp. 520-25.

47. *Iran-Contra Report,* p. 111.

48. Nita M. Renfrew and Peter Blauner, "Ollie's Army," *New York,* December 7, 1987; James Ridgeway, "L.I. Spy," *Village Voice,* December 29, 1987.

49. Cable to FBI director, July 18, 1985, *Iran-Contra Hearings,* Vol. 2, Appendix, pp. 681-85.

50. *Iran-Contra Report,* pp. 90-91, 100-101.

51. Fox Butterfield, *New York Times,* May 1, 1987; David B. Ottaway and Walter Pincus, *Boston Globe,* May 1, 1987.

52. Testimony of John Singlaub, Iran-Contra Hearings, May 21, 1987; Benjamin Weiser, *Washington Post,* March 20, 1987.

53. Memorandum from North to McFarlane, February 6, 1985. Differently censored versions of this memorandum are found in National Security Archive, *Chronology II,* following p. 125; *Iran-Contra Hearings,* Vol. 2, Appendix, p. 479; and *Tower Board Report,* p. C-4.

54. Singlaub Testimony, Iran-Contra Hearings, May 20, 1987.

55. Testimony of Gaston Sigur Jr., *Iran-Contra Hearings,* Vol. 2, pp. 294-95.

56. North, *Taking the Stand,* pp. 117-19; also see *Iran-Contra Report,* p. 42.

57. Letter from Edie Fraser to North, December 28, 1984, *Iran-Contra Affair, Appendix A,* Vol. 1, p. 591; *Iran-Contra Report,* p. 88.

58. Bernard Gwertzman, *New York Times,* January 23, 1987.

59. Testimony of Elliott Abrams, Iran-Contra Hearings, June 2, 1987, quoted in National Security Archive, *Chronology II,* pp. 522-23.

60. See *Iran-Contra Report,* pp. 71, 352-53.

61. Testimony of Adolfo Calero, Iran-Contra Hearings, May 20, 1987. For North's version, see North, *Taking the Stand,* pp. 109-10.

62. Joel Brinkley, *New York Times,* February 15, 1987.

63. *Iran-Contra Report,* p. 42; Poindexter Testimony, July 15, 1987.

64. Robert Parry and Brian Barger, "Reagan's Shadow CIA," *The New Republic,* November 24, 1986.

65. North, *Taking the Stand,* pp. 342, 384.

66. "Lt. Col. Oliver North," MacNeil/Lehrer News Hour, Transcript, December 11, 1986.

67. Tom Brokaw, op ed., *New York Times,* July 7, 1987.

68. Hersh, *Price of Power,* p. 250, citing Haldeman's memoirs.

69. Quoted in Ben Bradlee Jr., *Guts and Glory: The Rise and Fall of Oliver North* (New York: Donald I. Fine, Inc., 1988), p. 533.

70. Testimony of John Poindexter, Iran-Contra Hearings, July 15, 1987.

71. Art Harris, *Washington Post Weekly,* March 9, 1987.

72. Eric Alterman, "Inside Ollie's Mind," *New Republic,* February 16, 1987; *Time,* January 5, 1987; Keith Schneider, *New York Times,* December 24, 1987; Bradlee, *Guts and Glory,* pp. 107-10.

73. Testimony of Robert Owen, *Iran-Contra Hearings,* Vol. 2, pp. 325-26.

74. Letter from Owen to North, July 2, 1984, *Iran-Contra Hearings,* Vol. 2, Appendix, pp. 776-77.

75. Owen Testimony, *Iran-Contra Hearings,* Vol. 2, p. 412; Bellant, *Old Nazis, the New Right and the Reagan Administration,* pp. 126-27.

76. Testimony of Joe Fernandez (Tomas Castillo), Iran-Contra Hearings, May 29, 1987, National Security Archive, *Chronology II,* p. 230.

77. Letter from Hull to Owen, November 7, 1983, *Iran-Contra Report,* p. 36; *Iran-Contra Affair, Appendix A,* Vol. 1, p. 108.

78. "The Misadventures of el patron," *Time,* November 16, 1987.

79. Frontline, "Murder on the Rio San Juan," PBS/WGBH/Boston, April 19, 1988.

80. See Jonathan Kwitny, *Wall Street Journal,* May 21, 1987.

81. Martin Tolchin, *New York Times,* October 31, 1987; Stephen Kurkjian, *Boston Globe,* October 28, 1987.

82. Fred Hiatt, *Washington Post Weekly,* December 24, 1984.

83. Peter Stone, *Boston Globe,* December 30, 1984.

84. Singlaub Testimony, Iran-Contra Hearings, May 20-21, 1987.

85. Shirley Christian, *New York Times,* August 13, 1985.

86. Quoted in *Common Cause Magazine,* September-October 1985, p. 27.

87. Singlaub Testimony, Iran-Contra Hearings, May 20, 1987.

88. "Singlaub," CBS News 60 Minutes, Transcript, October 5, 1986, p. 3.

89. National Security Archive, *Chronology II,* pp. 293-95 and appended proposal; *Iran-Contra Report,* pp 269-70.

90. Singlaub Testimony, Iran-Contra Hearings, May 20, 1987.

91. Ibid., May 21, 1987.

92. See, for example, Shirley Christian, *New York Times,* August 13, 1985; Peter H. Stone, *Washington Post,* May 3, 1985.

93. John Loftus, *Boston Globe,* July 5, 1987; also see Loftus, *The Belarus Secret* (New York: Alfred A. Knopf, 1982).

94. See Dugger, *On Reagan,* pp. 384-85.

95. Congressional Arms Control and Foreign Policy Caucus, *Who Are The Contras? An Analysis Of The Makeup Of The Military Leadership Of The Rebel Forces And Of The Nature Of The Private American Groups Providing Them Financial And Material Support,* April 18, 1985, pp. 13-14.

96. Cited in Ken Lawrence, "Nazis and Klansmen: Soldier of Fortune's Seamy Side," *CovertAction Information Bulletin,* Fall 1984, p. 23.

97. *Newsweek,* September 17, 1984.

98. Howard Kurtz, *Washington Post,* September 7, 1984.

99. Quoted in Kornbluh, *Price of Intervention,* p. 82.

100. For North's version of these events see memorandum from North to McFarlane, September 2, 1984, *Iran-Contra Hearings,* Vol. 2, Appendix, pp. 461-62.

101. James Ridgeway, *Village Voice,* September 16, 1986.

102. John Dillon and John Lee Anderson, "Who's Behind Aid to the Contras," *The Nation,* October 6, 1984.

103. John Dinges and Saul Landau, *Assassination on Embassy Row* (New York: Pantheon, 1980); Marshall, et al., *Iran-Contra Connection,* pp. 43-49.

104. Anderson and Anderson, *Inside the League,* pp. 248-49.

105. Martin A. Lee, "Their Will Be Done," *Mother Jones,* July 1983.

106. Ibid.; also see Martin A. Lee, *National Catholic Reporter,* October 14, 1983.

107. ABC News Closeup, "Escape from Justice: Nazi War Criminals in America," January 16, 1980, cited in Francoise Hervet, "The Sovereign Military Order of Malta," *CovertAction Information Bulletin,* Winter 1986, p. 28; Charles Higham, *American Swastika* (New York: Doubleday, 1985), p. 203. On the slur against Puerto Ricans see, for example, Joseph B. Treaster, *New York Times,* May 29, 1982 and Ann Hughey, *Wall Street Journal,* June 1, 1982.

108. On Cardinal O'Connor, see Wayne Barrett, *Village Voice,* December 25, 1984.

109. Quoted in *Washington Report on the Hemisphere,* December 10, 1986.

110. Frank Greve, *Philadelphia Inquirer,* December 20, 1987; Anderson and Anderson, *Inside the League,* pp. 233-34.

111. CAUSA USA brochure; Elaine Sciolino, *New York Times,* June 4, 1987.

112. Ross Gelbspan, *Boston Gobe,* April 20, 1988.

113. Kornbluh, *Price of Intervention,* p. 239, fn. 242.

114. "Text of Remarks by the President at the Nicaraguan Refugee Fund Dinner," Office of the Press Secretary, The White House, April 15, 1985.

115. Kornbluh, *Price of Intervention,* pp. 66-68.

116. Philip Taubman, *New York Times,* September 9, 1984.

117. Robert Parry, Associated Press, *Washington Post,* September 3, 1985.

118. Author's interview with a U.S. ambassador in Central America, April 29, 1986.

119. Affidavit of Edgar Chamorro.

120. Author's interview with Edgar Chamorro, November 24, 1986.

121. Kornbluh, *Price of Intervention,* pp. 35-37.

122. Chamorro, *Packaging the Contras,* pp. 14-15; Kepner contract, pp. 70-71.

123. Ibid., pp. 51-52.

124. See, for example, Jane Hunter, *Israeli Foreign Policy* (Boston: South End Press, 1987), pp. 169-78; Franz Schneiderman, "Bending Swords Into Plowshares: An Investigation of the Tensions Between Israel and Nicaragua," Council on Hemispheric Affairs, November 26, 1985.

125. Jeff McConnell, *Boston Globe,* January 18, 1987.

126. Peter Kornbluh, "The Selling of the F.D.N.," *The Nation,* January 17, 1987; Kornbluh, *Price of Intervention,* pp. 228-29, fn. 91.

127. Francis X. Clines, *New York Times,* June 15, 1984. Also see Lou Cannon, *Washington Post,* June 17, 1983; Christopher Hitchens, "The Selling of Military Intervention," *The Nation,* August 20-27, 1983.

128. Memorandum from Raymond to Clark, May 20, 1983, Iran-Contra Hearings, Exhibit OLN-219.

129. Memorandum from Raymond to Clark, August 9, 1983, Iran-Contra Hearings.

130. James Ridgeway, "The Professor of Conspire," *Village Voice,* August 4, 1987; *Tower Board Report,* p. C-17.

131. *Iran-Contra Report,* pp. 97-98; also see Godson deposition.

132. Diana Johnstone, "A U.S. ambassador's crusade for the contras," *In These Times,* April 8-14, 1987. Also see Joe Conason and Murray Waas, "Meese's Swiss Miss," *Village Voice,* January 27, 1987.

133. Alfonso Chardy, *Miami Herald,* July 19, 1987; also see Chardy, *Miami Herald,* October 13, 1986.

134. Memorandum from Reich to Raymond, March 1, 1986, *Iran-Contra Report,* p. 34.

135. Richard Higgins, *Boston Globe,* May 13, 1986.

136. Kornbluh, *Price of Intervention,* p. 164, citing speech by Bill Buzenberg, September 9, 1985, Seattle, Washington.

137. *Iran-Contra Report,* p. 52, fn. 42.

138. Ibid., p. 34.

139. Michael Kranish, *Boston Globe,* March 19, 1987.

140. *Iran-Contra Report,* p. 87. Also see Peter Kornbluh, "The Contra Lobby," *Village Voice,* October 13, 1987.

141. State Department-IBC Contract, October 1, 1984-December 31, 1984, Iran-Contra Hearings, Exhibit OLN-223.

142. *Iran-Contra Report,* p. 87.

143. Memorandum from Miller to Buchanan, March 13, 1985, attached to the Letter from the Comptroller General of the United States to Representatives Jack Brooks and Dante Fascell, September 30, 1987.

144. Memorandum for Casey prepared by Walter Raymond, August 1986, Iran-Contra Hearings.

145. Letter from the Comptroller General of September 30, 1987.

146. *Iran-Contra Report,* p. 88.

147. Ibid., p. 92.

148. Ibid., pp. 92, 96-97.

149. Ibid., p. 92.

150. Ibid., p. 94.

151. Kornbluh, *Price of Intervention,* p. 208.

152. *Iran-Contra Report,* p. 93.

153. PROF Note from North to Poindexter, May 19, 1986, *Iran-Contra Report,* p. 96.

154. Poindexter Deposition, May 2, 1987, *Iran-Contra Report,* p. 96.

155. *Iran-Contra Report,* p. 96.

156. Ibid., p. 98.

157. North Notebook, November 19, 1985, Iran-Contra Hearings.

Chapter 11: The Enterprise and Other Fronts

1. Secord Testimony, *Iran-Contra Hearings,* Vol. 1, pp. 343-44.

2. McFarlane Testimony, *Iran-Contra Hearings,* Vol. 2, p. 270.

3. North, *Taking the Stand,* pp. 174, 442-43, 479.

4. *Iran-Contra Report,* p. 335.

5. Ibid., p. 333.

6. Deposition of William T. Golden, May 6, 1987, *Iran-Contra Affair, Appendix B,* Vol. 12, pp. 402-25; Emerson, *Secret Warriors,* pp. 151-52, 155-56, 217; National Security Archive, *Chronology II,* pp. 111, 904.

7. North, *Taking the Stand,* pp. 162, 167.

8. Peter Maas, *Manhunt: The Incredible Pursuit of a C.I.A. Agent Turned Terrorist* (New York: Random House/Jove Books, 1986), pp. 25-26; 54.

9. *Ibid.,* p. 59; Philip Taubman and Jeff Gerth, *New York Times,* October 13, 1981.

10. *Iran-Contra Report,* p. 329, fn. 23.

11. Secord Testimony, *Iran-Contra Hearings,* Vol. 1, p. 47.

12. Marshall, et al., *Iran-Contra Connection,* pp. 165-66.

13. Maas, *Manhunt,* pp. 65-66.

14. Ibid., pp. 108, 138, 276.

15. Ibid., pp. 138-39.

16. Ibid., pp. 140-41, 222.

17. Ibid., p. 247.

18. Ibid., pp. 253, 267.

19. "Ollie North's Secret Network," *Newsweek,* March 9, 1987, p. 33.

20. Mass, *Manhunt,* p. 279.

21. Secord Testimony, *Iran-Contra Hearings,* Vol. 1, p. 215.

22. *Iran-Contra Report,* p. 328.

23. *Washington Post,* December 22, 1986.

24. *U.S. News and World Report,* December 15, 1986, cited in Marshall, et al. *Iran-Contra Connection,* p. 14. Also see Emerson, *Secret Warriors,* p. 123.

25. National Security Archive, *Chronology II,* pp. 64-65, citing *Miami Herald,* March 8, 1987.

26. *Iran-Contra Report,* p. 55, fn. 157.

27. Secord Testimony, *Iran-Contra Hearings,* Vol. 1, pp. 49-50.

28. *Iran-Contra Report,* pp. 337-38.

29. Kornbluh, *Price of Intervention,* p. 69.

30. Hersh, "Who's In Charge Here?", p. 68; Emerson, *Secret Warriors,* pp. 144-45.

31. Murray Waas and Joe Conason, with John Kelly, "The Gadd Factor," *Village Voice,* May 5, 1987; National Security Archive, *Chronology II,* p. 60; Thomas Palmer, *Boston Globe,* April 5, 1987.

32. Robbins, *Air America,* p. 7.

33. Ibid., pp. 9-10.

34. Ibid., pp. 64-65. Also see, Marchetti and Marks, *The Cult of Intelligence,* pp. 126-28.

35. Robbins, *Air America,* p. 67.

36. Ibid., pp. 62, 297.

37. Testimony of Joseph Coors, May 21, 1987, Iran-Contra Hearings.

38. Secord Testimony, *Iran-Contra Hearings,* Vol. 1, p. 64; Testimony of Robert Dutton, Iran-Contra Hearings, May 27, 1987.

39. Dan Morgan and Walter Pincus, *Washington Post,* April 5, 1987. Wickham's name appears in North's notebook, June 10, 1986, in *Iran-Contra Affair, Appendix A,* Vol. 1, p. 449.

40. Memorandum from North to Poindexter, January 28, 1985, *Iran-Contra Report,* p. 46; *Iran-Contra Affair, Appendix A,* Vol. 1, pp. 308-09.

41. Quoted in Bernard Weinraub, *New York Times,* February 17, 1985.

42. Karen DeYoung, *Washington Post,* March 8, 1985; Dana Priest, *Washington Post,* January 20, 1985; Jim Morrell, "Redlining Nicaragua: How the U.S. Politicized the Inter-American Bank," *International Policy Report,* December 1985 and "Nicaragua's War Economy," *International Policy Report,* November 1985.

43. Quoted in *New York Times,* February 22, 1985.

44. Quoted in Alexander Cockburn, "Beat the Devil," *The Nation,* March 9, 1985.

45. *Business Week* editorial, March 11, 1985, p. 128.

46. Bernard Gwertzman, *New York Times,* February 23, 1985.

47. Bill Keller, *New York Times,* February 28, 1985. Also see *Iran-Contra Report,* p. 49.

48. Joel Brinkley, *New York Times,* March 17, 1985.

49. Memorandum from North and Fortier to McFarlane, March 22, 1985, with Chronology, March 20, 1985, March 22, 1985, *Iran-Contra Affair, Appendix A,* Vol. 1, pp. 325-40. Also see "Public Relations Campaign for the Freedom Fighters," February 19, 1985 and "Public Relations Paper #2 for the Freedom Fighters," March 11, 1985, *Iran-Contra Hearings,* Vol. 2, pp. 783-95.

50. Bernard Weinraub and Gerald M. Boyd, *New York Times,* April 5, 1985.

51. Joel Brinkley, *New York Times,* April 16, 1985.

52. Memorandum from North to McFarlane, May 31, 1985, *Iran-Contra Hearings,* Vol. 2, Appendix, pp. 530-32.

53. Memorandum from North to McFarlane, March 16, 1985, *Iran-Contra Hearings,* Vol. 2, Appendix, pp. 511-13.

54. Memorandum for the Record prepared by John McMahon, March 22, 1985, *Iran-Contra Hearings,* Vol. 2, Appendix, p. 518.

55. Hedrick Smith, *New York Times,* April 17, 1985.

56. See Hedrick Smith, *New York Times,* April 18, 1985.

57. James LeMoyne, *New York Times,* April 19, 1985.

58. Gerald M. Boyd, *New York Times,* April 21, 1985.

59. William M. LeoGrande, "The Contras and Congress," in Walker, ed., *Reagan vs. the Sandinistas,* p. 187.

60. Author's interview with Ambassador Carlos Tunnermann, Washington, DC, September 10, 1986.

61. Author's interview with Alejandro Martinez Cuenca, Managua, April 28, 1986. Also see Martinez C., "The Failed Policy of the U.S. in Nicaragua," Speech to the World Affairs Council, Boston, March 10, 1986.

62. Bernard Gwertzman, *New York Times,* May 3, 1985.

63. Steven B. Roberts, *New York Times,* May 5, 1985.

64. Quoted in *New York Times,* May 24, 1985.

65. Bill Keller and Joel Brinkley, *New York Times,* June 4, 1985.

66. Joel Brinkley and Bill Keller, *New York Times,* June 5, 1985.

67. James McCartney, *Philadelphia Inquirer,* April 13, 1986.

68. Theodore Moran, "The Cost of Alternative U.S. Policies Toward El Salvador 1984-1989," in Robert S. Leiken, ed., *Central America: Anatomy of Conflict* (New York: Pergamon Press, 1984), pp. 166-68.

69. Stephen Engelberg, *New York Times,* May 3, 1987.

70. James McCartney, *Philadelphia Inquirer,* April 13, 1986.

71. Michael Lewin Ross, *In These Times,* June 26-July 9, 1985.

72. Quoted by Christopher Hitchens, *The Nation,* June 22, 1985.

73. "Execution in the Jungle," *Newsweek,* April 29, 1985, p. 43.

74. Thomas P. O'Neill Jr. with William Novak, *Man of the House: The Life and Political Memoirs of Speaker Tip O'Neill* (New York: Random House, 1987).

75. "The View From Washington," briefing paper for Chiefs of Mission Conference, September 8-10, 1985, p. 4.

76. *Report by the House Permanent Select Committee on Intelligence,* December 31, 1986, pp. 25, 29-30.

77. *Congressional Quarterly,* June 15, 1985, pp. 1139-1140.

78. "A Statement on the Nature of Humanitarian Assistance by U.S. Private and Voluntary Organizations," Church World Service, Washington, DC; also see CAHI, *Update* 7:7, February 28, 1988.

79. Duemling note, September 24, 1985, *Iran-Contra Affair, Appendix A,* Vol. 1, p. 402.

80. Letter from Calero, Cruz and Robelo to Ambassador Duemling, October 3, 1985, *Iran-Contra Hearings,* Vol. 2, Appendix, p. 829; Owen Contract, *Iran-Contra Hearings,* Vol. 2, Appendix, p. 835.

81. Associated Press, *New York Times,* August 15, 1987.

82. Waas, et al., *Village Voice,* May 5, 1987.

83. Statement of Frank C. Conahan before the House Subcommittee on Western Hemisphere Affairs, U.S. General Accounting Office, June 11, 1986.

84. David K. Shipler, *New York Times,* June 21, 1986. Also see Robert Parry, Associated Press, *Washington Post,* June 12, 1986.

85. U.S. General Accounting Office, *Central America: Problems in Controlling Funds for the Nicaraguan Democratic Resistance,* December 1986, pp. 9-11.

86. Letter from Robert Duemling, NHAO, to contra liaison Salvador E. Stadthagen, March 18, 1986, obtained by Peter Kornbluh, National Security Archive, *Harpers,* May 1988.

87. Memorandum from Owen to North, April 1/9, 1985, *Iran-Contra Hearings,* Vol. 2, Appendix, pp. 799-802.

88. Secord Testimony, *Iran-Contra Hearings,* Vol. 1, pp. 58-61.

89. Joe Conason and James Ridgeway, "Edwin Wilson Speaks," *Village Voice,* June 23, 1987.

90. Joseph B. Treaster, *New York Times,* December 10, 1986.

91. *Iran-Contra Report,* pp. 109-10; Susan F. Rasky, *New York Times,* February 23, 1987; National Security Archive, *Chronology II,* pp. 63, 95.

92. On Rodriguez, Gregg and the Pink Team strategy see Emerson, *Secret Warriors,* pp. 126-28. For Gregg's CIA background also see R. W. Apple Jr. *New York Times,* December 13, 1986.

93. Testimony of Felix Rodriguez, May 27, 1987, Iran-Contra Hearings.

94. Allan Nairn, "The Bush Connection," *The Progressive,* May 1987.

95. Memorandum from North to McFarlane, March 5, 1985, *Iran-Contra Hearings,* Vol. 2., Appendix, pp. 494-95; *Tower Board Report,* p. C-4.

96. Cable from Gorman to Pickering and Steele, February 14, 1985 and cable from Gorman to Pickering, February 8, 1985, *Iran-Contra Affair, Appendix B,* Vol. 12, pp. 941-42.

97. North, *Taking the Stand,* pp. 228-29; Doyle McManus, *Los Angeles Times, Miami Herald,* July 9, 1987; Deposition of Paul Gorman, *Iran-Contra Affair, Appendix B,* Vol. 12, pp. 871-73, 938, and back channel cable from Pickering to Gorman, Motley and Johnstone, pp. 943-44.

98. *Iran-Contra Report,* p. 62.

99. Alfonso Chardy, *Miami Herald,* August 26, 1987.

100. See John Dinges, "And Now, Posadagate," *The Nation,* November 15, 1986; Julia Preston and Joe Pichirallo, *Washington Post,* October 26, 1986.

101. Presidential Finding, January 9, 1986, *Iran-Contra Affair, Appendix A,* Vol. 2, pp. 1161-62; *Iran-Contra Report,* p. 64; National Security Archive, *Chronology II,* pp. 359-60.

102. Robert Parry and Brian Barger, Associated Press, *Boston Globe,* April 14, 1986.

103. Reuters, *Boston Globe,* August 9, 1986.

104. Fernandez (Castillo) Testimony, Iran-Contra Hearings, May 29, 1987 in National Security Archive, *Chronology II,* p. 478.

105. Ibid., pp. 336-37.

106. *Tower Board Report,* p. III-23.

107. *Iran-Contra Report,* p. 65.

108. Ibid., p. 67.

109. Rodriguez Testimony, Iran-Contra Hearings, May 28, 1987.

110. Robbins, *Air America,* p. 9.

111. See National Security Archive, *Chronology II,* pp. 459, 501; Erik Calonius with Tom Morganthau, "The Secret Warriors Tell Their Story," *Newsweek,* February 9, 1987; Emerson, *Secret Warriors,* p. 145.

112. Secord Testimony, *Iran-Contra Hearings,* Vol. 1, pp. 68-69.

113. Ibid. Also see Dan Morgan and Walter Pincus, *Boston Globe,* May 17, 1987.

114. North, *Taking the Stand,* p. 593.

115. Memorandum from North to McFarlane, December 4, 1984, *Iran-Contra Hearings,* Vol. 2, Appendix, p. 470.

116. Memorandum from North to McFarlane, April 11, 1985, *Iran-Contra Hearings,* Vol. 2, Appendix, pp. 520-21.

117. Testimony of Lewis Tambs, Iran-Contra Hearings, May 28, 1987.

118. Fernandez (Castillo) Testimony, Iran-Contra Hearings, May 29, 1987, in National Security Archive, *Chronology II,* p. 204.

119. Memorandum from Owen to North, August 25, 1985, *Iran-Contra Hearings,* Vol. 2, Appendix, p. 806. Also see Owen Testimony, *Iran-Contra Hearings,* Vol. 2, pp. 349-51.

120. PROF Note from North to Poindexter, December 5, 1985 and Memorandum from North to Poindexter, December 10, 1985, *Iran-Contra Report,* p. 64, and *Iran-Contra Affair, Appendix A,* Vol. 1, pp. 403-07.

121. *Iran-Contra Report,* p. 64.

122. Memorandum from Owen to North, March 28, 1986, *Iran-Contra Hearings,* Vol. 2, Appendix, p. 825.

123. *Iran-Contra Report,* pp. 66-67.

124. Alfonso Chardy, Sam Dillon and Tim Golden, *Miami Herald,* March 1, 1987.

125. *Iran-Contra Report,* p. 69.

Chapter 12: Hits, Guns and Drugs

1. Quoted in Frontline, "Murder on the Rio San Juan," WGBH/Boston, April 19, 1988.

2. Deposition of Paul Gorman, July 22, 1987, *Iran-Contra Affair, Appendix B,* Vol. 12, pp. 10-12.

3. Martha Honey and Tony Avirgan, *La Penca: Report of an Investigation* (Washington, DC: Christic In stitute), p. 3.

4. Ibid., pp. 6-8.

5. Frontline, "Murder on the Rio San Juan."

6. Honey and Avirgan, *La Penca,* pp. 17-19.

7. Frontline, "Murder on the Rio San Juan."

8. Owen Testimony, *Iran-Contra Hearings,* Vol. 2, p. 402.

9. Leslie Cockburn, *Out of Control* (New York: Atlantic Monthly Press, 1987), pp. 19-20.

10. Ibid., p. 43.

11. Charles Mohr, *New York Times,* July 19, 1985.

12. Joel Brinkley, *New York Times,* July 24, 1985; Alfonso Chardy, Knight-Ridder News Service/Bergen, New Jersey *Record,* July 17, 1985; Owen Ullmann and James McCartney, *Philadelphia Inquirer,* July 25, 1985.

13. *Affidavit of Daniel Sheehan,* pp. 26-27.

14. Author's conversation with David MacMichael, December 4, 1987.

15. Cockburn, *Out of Control,* pp. 55-68; also see Murray Waas and Joe Conason, "Did Meese Stall a Second Probe?" *Village Voice,* December 30, 1986.

16. Cockburn, *Out of Control,* p. 75; Honey and Avirgan, *La Penca,* p. 33.

17. Cockburn, *Out of Control,* p. 76.

18. Allan Nairn, "The Contras' Little List," *The Progressive,* March 1987.

19. James Ridgeway, "Contra-gate?" *Village Voice,* May 20, 1986.

20. Memorandum from Owen to North, January 31, 1985, *Iran-Contra Hearings,* Vol. 2, Appendix, pp. 778-79.

21. Cockburn, *Out of Control,* pp. 71-72.

22. Memorandum from North to McFarlane, April 11, 1985, *Iran-Contra Hearings,* Vol. 2, Appendix, p. 521.

23. Testimony of William O'Boyle, Iran-Contra Hearings, May 21, 1987, in Congressional Quarterly, *The Iran-Contra Puzzle*, p. C-38.

24. *Tower Board Report,* p. C-9.

25. Memorandum from Poindexter to Reagan, "Terrorist Threat: Terrell," July 28, 1986, *Iran-Contra Affair, Appendix A,* Vol. 2, Source Documents, pp. 1323-1324.

26. FBI report, July 22, 1986, *Iran-Contra Affair, Appendix A,* Vol. 1, pp. 855-59; *Iran-Contra Report,* pp. 112-13.

27. Testimony of Glenn Robinette, Iran-Contra Hearings, June 23, 1987.

28. For an overview see Joel Millman, "Narco-terrorism: A Tale of two stories," *Columbia Journalism Review,* September-October 1986.

29. Address by President Reagan, March 16, 1986, White House Office of the Press Secretary.

30. Martin A. Lee, "How the Drug Czar Got Away," *The Nation,* September 5, 1987.

31. Jonathan Kwitny, *Wall Street Journal,* April 22, 1987.

32. *New York Times,* May 14, 1987.

33. Joel Millman, "Who Killed Barry Seal?" *Village Voice,* July 1, 1986.

34. Millman, "Narco-terrorism," p. 50.

35. Seth Rosenfeld, *San Francisco Examiner,* March 16, 1986. Also see Rosenfeld articles of March 17-19.

36. Rosenfeld, *San Francisco Examiner,* March 18, 1986.

37. Christic Institute, "The Contra-Drug Connection," Washington, DC, November 1987, p. 4.

38. Kornbluh, *Price of Intervention,* p. 203, citing Seth Rosenfeld, *San Francisco Examiner,* June 23, 1986.

39. Robert Parry, Associated Press, *Washington Post,* August 27, 1986.

40. Cockburn, *Out of Control,* pp. 152-54.

41. Marshall, et al., *The Iran-Contra Connection,* p. 45.

42. Cockburn, *Out of Control,* p. 154.

43. Thomas W. Walker, *Nicaragua: The Land of Sandino* (Boulder, Colorado: Westview Press, 1986), p. 120, fn. 2.

44. Cockburn, *Out of Control,* pp. 152-67.

45. Ibid., p. 160. Also see Associated Press, *New York Times,* October 25, 1986.

46. Cockburn, *Out of Control,* p. 161. Also see Alfonso Chardy, *Miami Herald,* October 24, 1986.

47. "The Misadventures of el patron," *Time,* November 16, 1987.

48. Memorandum from Owen to North, *Iran-Contra Hearings,* Vol. 2, Appendix, p. 816.

49. "Drugs and Contras," *The Nation,* June 13, 1987.

50. Cockburn, *Out of Control,* pp. 168-72.

51. Ibid., pp. 172, 174.

52. Ibid., pp. 177-78.

53. Ibid., pp. 179-83.

54. Ibid., pp. 185-87; Knut Royce, *Newsday,* April 6, 1987; James Ridgeway, "Inside Vortex," *Village Voice,* October 20, 1987, p. 20; Testimony of Michael Palmer, Senate Foreign Relations Subcommittee on Terrorism, Narcotics and International Operations, April 6, 1988.

55. Stephen Kurkjian and Mark Hosenball, *Boston Globe,* April 26, 1987.

56. National Security Archive, *Chronology II,* p. 693, citing *New York Times,* January 20, 1987.

57. David E. Umhoefer, *Milwaukee Journal,* July 12, 1987.

58. On the question of substantiation, see, for example, Jonathan Kwitny, "Money, Drugs and the Contras," *The Nation,* August 29, 1987 and responses by Christic Institute counsel Daniel Sheehan and journalist Leslie Cockburn in *The Nation,* September 19, 1987.

59. Los Angeles Times, *Boston Globe,* February 13, 1988.

60. See Alfred McCoy, *The Politics of Heroin in Southeast Asia* (New York: Harper & Row, 1972); Kruger, *The Great Heroin Coup*; Robbins, *Air America*; Penny Lernoux, *In Banks We Trust* (New York: Anchor/Doubleday, 1984); Marshall, et al., *Iran-Contra Connection*; William Vornberger, "Afghan Rebels and Drugs," and other articles in *CovertAction Information Bulletin,* Summer 1987; Frontline,

"Guns, Drugs and the CIA," produced by Leslie Cockburn and Andrew Cockburn, WGBH/Boston, May 17, 1988.

61. Jonathan Kwitny, *The Crimes of Patriots: A True Tale of Dope, Dirty Money, and the CIA* (New York: W.W. Norton, 1987), p. 52.

62. Owen Testimony, *Iran-Contra Hearings*, Vol. 2, p. 388.

Chapter 13: Contadora, Contradora

1. Author's interview with Miguel D'Escoto, May 9, 1986.

2. Hersh, *Price of Power*, p. 263.

3. Author's interview with Sergio Ramirez, April 26, 1986.

4. Author's interview with Miguel D'Escoto, May 9, 1986.

5. Quoted in Carter, *Keeping Faith*, p. 184.

6. Barry and Preusch, *Central America Fact Book*, p. 302.

7. Interview with Guadalupe Gonzales by David Brooks for the author, Mexico City, November 4, 1986.

8. Information Bulletin, Contadora Island, Panama, January 9, 1983.

9. *Presidential Documents* 19:18, May 9, 1983 and No. 21, May 30, 1983, cited in *CAHI, U.S.-Nicaragua Relations*, pp. 21-22.

10. Quoted in *Washington Post*, June 15, 1983, cited in *CAHI, U.S.-Nicaragua Relations*, p. 24.

11. "Cancun Declaration of the Contadora Group of July 19, 1983," in Bruce Michael Bagley, et al., eds., *Contadora and the Central American Peace Process: Selected Documents*, SAIS Papers in International Affairs, No. 8 (Boulder, CO: Westview Press, 1985), p. 171.

12. Terry Karl, "Mexico, Venezuela, and the Contadora Initiative," in Blachman, *et. al.* eds., *Confronting Revolution*, p. 278.

13. Ibid., p. 274.

14. CAHI, *Update* 2:16, July 22, 1983.

15. William LeoGrande, "Rollback or Containment? The United States, Nicaragua, and the Search for Peace in Central America," *International Security*, Fall 1986, p. 99.

16. *Washington Post*, July 22 and July 25, 1983.

17. Fred Ikle, Speech to the Baltimore Council on Foreign Affairs, September 12, 1983.

18. Carla Anne Robbins, *Business Week*, May 21, 1984.

19. Philip Taubman, *New York Times*, September 28, 1984.

20. Kornbluh, *Price of Intervention*, pp. 246-47, fn. 65, citing Roy Gutman, *Newsday*, September 2, 1985.

21. Jim Morrell and William Goodfellow, "Contadora: Under the Gun," *International Policy Report*, May 1986, p. 3.

22. Bruce M. Bagley, "The Failure of Diplomacy," in Bagley, ed., *Contadora*, Vol. 1, pp. 191-92, citing United Press International, *Washington Post*, October 3, 1984.

23. Philip Taubman, *New York Times*, September 24, 1984.

24. "Background Paper for NSC Meeting on Central America, October 30, 1984." Also see Alma Guillermoprieto and David Hoffman, *Washington Post*, November 6, 1984.

25. "Contadora: A Text for Peace," *International Policy Report*, November 1984, p. 7.

26. Quoted in Richard J. Meislin, *New York Times*, November 16, 1984.

27. *New York Times*, November 2, 1984, cited in Kornbluh, *Price of Intervention*, p. 183.

28. Morrell and Goodfellow, "Contadora: Under the Gun," p. 5.

29. Jim Morrell, "Contadora: The Treaty on Balance," *International Policy Report*, June 1985.

30. *Posicion del Gobierno de Nicaragua*, in *Envio* 4:54, December 1985, p. 5a.

31. Alan Riding, *New York Times*, December 3, 1985.

32. Morrell and Goodfellow, "Contadora: Under the Gun," p. 6.

33. Author's interview with Miguel D'Escoto, May 9, 1986.

34. *Envio,* December 1985, p. 10a; *New York Times,* December 3, 1985.

35. Julia Preston, *Boston Globe,* December 15, 1985.

36. Tom Wicker, *New York Times,* February 11, 1986.

37. Bagley, "Failure of Diplomacy," p. 195.

38. Quoted in *Boston Globe,* December 15, 1985.

39. Interview with Luis Herrera Lasso by David Brooks for the author, Mexico City, November 4, 1986.

40. Bagley, "Failure of Diplomacy," p. 194, citing "The View from Washington," quoted in Charles R. Babcock, *Washington Post,* September 8, 1985.

41. OAS Document, January 14, 1986.

42. *Envio* 5:57, March 1986, p. 2.

43. "The Carabelleda Message for Peace, Security and Democracy in Central America," January 12, 1986, Document of the General Secretariat of the Organization of American States, Washington, DC, January 14, 1986.

44. Eleanor Clift, *Los Angeles Times,* February 19, 1986.

45. Dennis Volman, *Christian Science Monitor,* March 20, 1986.

46. Nelson Valdes, Pacific News Service, March 28, 1986.

47. William R. Long, *Los Angeles Times,* March 21, 1986.

48. Patrick J. Buchanan, "The Contras Need Our Help," op ed., *Washington Post Weekly,* March 17, 1986.

49. "I'm a Contra, Too,' " *Newsweek,* March 24, 1986.

50. See *Iran-Contra Report,* pp. 382-83.

51. See, for example, Adam Pertman, *Boston Globe,* March 26, 1986.

52. Sam Dillon and Tim Golden, *Miami Herald,* April 3, 1986.

53. See Seymour M. Hersh, "Target Qaddafi," *New York Times Magazine,* February 22, 1987.

54. Author's interview with a U.S. ambassador in Central America, April 29, 1986.

55. *Envio* 5:59, May 1986, p. 3.

56. Pacific News Service, March 19, 1986.

57. *Envio,* May 1986, p. 10.

58. Author's interview with Sergio Ramirez, April 26, 1986.

59. Shirley Christian, *New York Times,* August 18, 1985.

60. Bagley, "Failure of Diplomacy," citing Bernard Gwertzman, *New York Times,* July 17, 1986.

61. Author's interview with a U.S. Ambassador in Central America, April 29, 1986.

62. Jose Melendez, *Excelsior* (Mexico City), April 8, 1987, Central America NewsPak.

63. *Envio* 5:60, June 1986, pp. 2-3.

64. Author's interview with Carlos Tunnermann, September 10, 1986.

65. "Official Proposal Of The Government Of Nicaragua For A Prompt Conclusion Of The Process Of Negotiations And The Signature Of The Contadora Agreement," May 15, 1986, Unofficial Translation, Embassy of Nicaragua, Washington, DC.

66. *Excelsior,* May 16-17, 1986,.

67. "Declaration of Esquipulas," May 25, 1986, OAS Document, May 29, 1986.

68. Bagley, "Failure of Diplomacy," pp. 200-201.

69. William M. LeoGrande, "The Contras and Congress," in Walker, ed., *Reagan versus the Sandinistas,* galleys, p. 195.

70. International Court of Justice, *Case Concerning Military and Paramilitary Activities In and Against Nicaragua,* June 27, 1986, pp. 137-41.

71. "The Chicago Proposals for Peace," Embassy of Nicaragua, Washington, DC, August 2, 1986.

72. Quoted in George D. Moffett III, *Christian Science Monitor,* August 7, 1986.

73. National Security Archive, *Chronology II,* p. 651, citing *Miami Herald,* March 27, 1987.

74. Jim Morrell, "Contadora Vows to Continue," *International Policy Report,* August 1986.

75. Julia Preston, *Washington Post,* November 8, 1986.

76. *Washington Report on the Hemisphere,* December 10, 1986, p. 6.

77. Jim Morrell, "Contadora Eludes U.S.," *International Policy Report,* January-February 1987, p. 1.

78. See, for example, Steven Donziger, *Christian Science Monitor,* December 10, 1986; Stephen Kinzer, *New York Times,* December 9, 1986.

79. William Stockton, *New York Times,* January 22, 1987.

80. James LeMoyne, *New York Times,* February 11, 1987.

81. *Envío* 4:54, December 1985, p. 4c.

82. Interview with Luis Herrera Lasso by David Brooks, November 4, 1986.

83. Quoted in *Time,* April 25, 1988, p. 35.

84. Tom Farer, "Contadora: The Hidden Agenda," *Foreign Policy,* Summer 1985, p. 63.

85. George Black, "The Many Killers of Father Carney," *The Nation,* January 23, 1988.

86. Clifford Krauss, *Wall Street Journal,* December 5, 1986.

87. Author's interview with a U.S. Ambassador in Central America, April 29, 1986.

88. CAHI, *Update* 5:44, December 12, 1986.

89. Pamela Constable, *Boston Globe,* April 1986.

90. Anderson and Anderson, *Inside the League,* pp. 244, 249-50, 268.

91. Quoted in *Boston Globe,* November 23, 1986.

92. Farer, "Contadora," p. 72.

93. Author's interview with a U.S. ambassador in Central America, April 29, 1986.

94. Address by Mr. Jaime Lusinchi, President of Venezuela at the Opening of the Meeting of Foreign Affairs of Contadora, Carabelleda, January 11, 1986, OAS document, Washington, DC, January 14, 1986.

95. Rio de Janeiro Declaration, December 18, 1986, Embássy of Mexico press release, Washington, DC.

96. Alan Riding, *New York Times,* December 22, 1986.

97. Author's interview with Carlos Tunnermann, September 10, 1986.

Chapter 14: Under the Coverups

1. Quoted in David Ignatius, *Washington Post,* December 7, 1986.

2. PROF note from North to Poindexter, *Iran-Contra Report,* pp. 72-73.

3. North notebook entry, September 6, 1986, and Poindexter note, *Iran-Contra Affair, Appendix A,* Vol. 1, pp. 922-23; *Iran-Contra Report,* p. 142.

4. *Iran-Contra Report,* p. 143; Abrams Testimony, Iran-Contra Hearings, June 2, 1987.

5. James LeMoyne, *New York Times,* March 9, 1987.

6. PROF note from North to Poindexter, September 25, 1986, *Iran-Contra Report,* p. 76; also see pp. 143-44.

7. *Iran-Contra Report,* p. 76.

8. Ibid., pp. 75-77.

9. Quoted in Bernard Gwertzman, *New York Times,* October 3, 1986.

10. *Barricada Internacional,* October 16, 1986.

11. *Iran-Contra Report,* p. 77.

12. PROF note from Earl to Poindexter, October 6, 1986, *Tower Board Report,* p. B-166, fn. 93.

13. National Security Archive, *Chronology II,* pp. 625-26, citing *Philadelphia Inquirer,* January 18, 1987.

14. "Downed Plane in Nicaragua: Questions," ABC News Nightline, October 7, 1986, transcript, p. 2.

15. CBS News 60 Minutes, October 5, 1986, transcript, pp. 2, 7.

16. James LeMoyne, *New York Times,* October 10, 1986.

17. Philip Bennett and Stephen Kurkjian, *Boston Globe*, October 18, 1986; David Ottaway, *Washington Post Weekly*, January 5, 1987.

18. PROF note from North to McFarlane, October 12, 1986, *Tower Board Report*, p. B-166, fn. 93.

19. *Iran-Contra Report*, p.145.

20. Joel Brinkley, *New York Times*, October 14, 1986.

21. PROF note from Cannistraro to Poindexter, *Iran-Contra Report*, p. 144.

22. CBS News 60 Minutes, October 19, 1986, transcript, p. 7.

23. See, for example, Elliott Abrams' testimony in *The Downing Of A United States Plane In Nicaragua And United States Involvement In The Contra War*, Hearing before the House Foreign Affairs Subcommittee on Western Hemisphere Affairs, October 15, 1986.

24. Quoted in Stephen Kinzer, *New York Times*, December 18, 1986.

25. Quoted in Christopher Hitchens, "Minority Report," *The Nation*, April 1/8, 1987.

26. See McFarlane's exchanges with Barnes, Hamilton, Durenberger and Leahy in *Iran-Contra Hearings*, Vol. 2., Appendix, pp. 546-86.

27. See *Iran-Contra Report*, pp. 121-33.

28. David Corn and Jefferson Morley, *The Nation*, December 12, 1987.

29. *Iran-Contra Report*, pp. 140-41.

30. *Iran-Contra Hearings*, Vol. 2, p. 751.

31. *Iran-Contra Report*, pp. 141-42.

32. Ibid., p. 287.

33. Ibid., pp. 287-88.

34. Secord Testimony, *Iran-Contra Hearings*, Vol. 1, p. 124.

35. *Iran-Contra Report*, p. 288.

36. Murray Waas and Joe Conason, "Closing In On Meese," *Village Voice*, April 21, 1987.

37. *Iran-Contra Report*, p. 114, fn. 2; also see Bernard Gwertzman, *New York Times*, April 30, 1986.

38. CBS Evening News, transcript, July 14, 1986.

39. *Iran-Contra Report*, pp. 105-106.

40. On the Kelso affair, see "Additional Views" of Rodino, Fascell, Brooks and Stokes, *Iran-Contra Report*, p. 648, as well as main report, p. 106.

41. Ibid., pp. 648-49.

42. Murray Waas and Joe Conason, "Obstruction At Justice," *Village Voice*, March 31, 1987.

43. Ibid.; Joe Pichirallo, *Washington Post*, April 7, 1987; *Iran-Contra Report*, p. 114, fn. 30.

44. *Iran-Contra Report*, p. 107; Stephen Kurkjian and Murray Waas, *Boston Globe*, February 14, 1988.

45. *Iran-Contra Report*, p. 114, fn. 34.

46. Larry Martz and Robert Parry, *Newsweek*, April 20, 1987; *Iran-Contra Puzzle*, p. A-28.

47. Kurkjian and Waas, *Boston Globe*, February 14, 1988.

48. Ibid.; North notebook entry, March 31, 1986, *Iran-Contra Affair, Appendix A*, Vol. 1, p. 732.

49. *Iran-Contra Report*, pp. 107-108.

50. Murray Waas, *Boston Globe*, December 20, 1987.

51. Memorandum from Owen to North, April 7, 1986, *Iran-Contra Hearings*, Vol. 2, Appendix, p. 827.

52. Joe Conason and Murray Waas, "Finally, Meese Under Oath," *Village Voice*, July 28, 1987, citing a memo from Rep. William Hughes to members of the Judiciary Crime Subcommittee; Waas and Conason, "Closing In On Meese"; *Iran-Contra Report*, p. 108.

53. *Iran-Contra Report*, p. 108; excerpt from Feldman memo, *Iran-Contra Affair, Appendix A*, Vol. 1, pp. 773-74.

54. Quoted in Murray Waas and Joe Conason, "Contra Cover-Up Confirmed," *Village Voice*, April 14, 1987. Also see Stephen J. Hedges, *Miami Herald*, April 23, 1987.

55. Kurkjian and Waas, *Boston Globe*, February 14, 1988.

56. *Iran-Contra Report*, p. 109.

57. Cockburn, *Out of Control,* p. 238.

58. Dennis Bernstein and Vince Bielski, *In These Times,* April 15-21, 1987.

59. *Iran-Contra Report,* p. 113.

60. "Additional Views" of Rodino, et al., *Iran-Contra Report,* pp. 647-48.

Chapter 15: Diversions

1. Quoted in Dugger, *On Reagan,* p. 245.

2. Quoted in David E. Rosenbaum, *New York Times,* May 7, 1987.

3. See Christopher Hitchens, "Minority Report," *The Nation,* June 20 and July 4/11, 1987; Barbara Honegger with Jim Naureckas, "Did Reagan Steal the 1980 Election?" *In These Times,* June 24-July 7, 1987.

4. See *Iran-Contra Report,* pp. 288-89.

5. Ibid., pp. 197, 270-71.

6. North, *Taking the Stand,* pp. 26-27.

7. Undated Memorandum, "Release of American Hostages in Beirut" and Attached Terms of Reference dated April 4, 1986, *Iran-Contra Hearings,* Vol. 1, Appendix, p. 537.

8. *Iran-Contra Report,* p. 274.

9. Carl Bernstein, "TV Anchormen Are Missing the Big Story of the Hearings," *New York Times,* op ed., July 14, 1987.

10. House Resolution 111 submitted by Henry Gonzalez, March 5, 1987.

11. "Hearing Nothing, Saying Nothing: The Iran-Contra Investigation That Never Was," *Harpers,* February 1988, p. 55.

12. North, *Taking the Stand,* pp. 207, 329, 337, 530-31.

13. *Iran-Contra Report,* p. 271.

14. Quoted in David S. Broder, *Washington Post Weekly,* August 3, 1987.

15. Gregg Deposition, May 18, 1987, pp. 110-11; Bush note to North, November 27, 1985, *Iran-Contra Affair, Appendix B,* Vol. 12, p. 1143.

16. Hackel and Siegel, eds., *In Contempt of Congress,* p. 28.

17. *Iran-Contra Report,* pp. 71-72; Watson Deposition, *Iran-Contra Puzzle,* pp. C-145-46; Memorandum from Gregg to Bush, April 30, 1986, in Hackel and Siegel, eds., *In Contempt of Congress,* p. 28.

18. Allan Nairn, "The Bush Connection," *The Progressive,* May 1987; Office of Vice President Bush, Chronology of Contacts with Felix Rodriguez, December 15, 1986, revised May 14, 1987.

19. *Iran-Contra Report,* p. 72; Office of Vice President, Chronology, December 15, 1986.

20. Gregg notes, August 8, 1986, *Iran-Contra Affair, Appendix B,* Vol. 12, p. 1135; *Iran-Contra Report,* p. 74.

21. National Security Archive, *Chronology II,* p. 650, citing *Washington Post,* December 14, 1986.

22. Gregg Deposition, *Iran-Contra Affair, Appendix B,* Vol. 12, pp. 1076-77; *Iran-Contra Report,* p. 74.

23. Memorandum from North and Menges to McFarlane, November 4, 1983, *Iran-Contra Affair, Appendix A,* Vol. 1, p. 197.

24. *Iran-Contra Report,* p. 84, fn. 166.

25. David Hoffman, *Washington Post,* April 26, 1987.

26. Gregg Deposition, p. 1062.

27. Nairn, "The Bush Connection."

28. Allan Nairn, "George Bush's Secret War," *The Progressive,* March 1988.

29. Nairn, "The Bush Connection."

30. Nairn, "George Bush's Secret War" and "A Profile of Richard J. Brenneke," *The Progressive,* March 1988.

31. Rober Parry, with Rod Norland, "Guns for Drugs," *Newsweek,* May 23, 1988.

32. Jim Naureckas and Richard Ryan, "Bush's network," *In These Times,* June 8-21, 1988; David Corn, "Black Money, the *Pia Vesta* and Bush," *In These Times,* June 22-July 5, 1988.

33. North notes, September 10, 1985, *Iran-Contra Affair, Appendix A,* Vol. 1, p. 390; Parry, "Guns for Drugs."

34. The letter was reported in the *Miami Herald,* March 15, 1987.

35. Pamela Constable, *Boston Globe,* January 14. 1987.

36. Nairn, "The Bush Connection."

37. Diane Sawyer interview with George Bush, CBS News 60 Minutes, March 15, 1987.

38. Loch K. Johnson, *A Season of Inquiry* (Lexington, Kentucky: The University Press of Kentucky, 1985), p. 232.

39. Ibid., p. 263, citing *Newsweek,* October 10, 1983.

40. Ibid., p. 47.

41. Ibid., p. 203.

42. National Public Radio, August 4, 1987.

43. See, for example, remarks to North by Senator George Mitchell in North, *Taking the Stand,* pp. 535-36.

44. Randolph Ryan, *Boston Globe,* April 7 and December 20, 1986.

45. Lloyd Grove, *Washington Post,* September 8, 1987.

46. Johnson, *Season of Inquiry,* pp. 222-23.

47. "Testimony of the Center for Constitutional Rights (CCR)," before the House Committee on the Judiciary, Subcommittee on Civil and Constitutional Rights, February 20, 1987, pp. 4-5. Hereafter CCR Testimony.

48. Donner, *Age of Surveillance,* p. xiv.

49. CCR Testimony, p. 4.

50. Johnson, *Season of Inquiry,* p. 82.

51. CCR Testimony, pp. 12-16. Also see Margaret E. Leahy, "The Harassment of Nicaraguanists and Fellow Travelers," in Walker, ed., *Reagan versus the Sandinistas.*

52. CCR Testimony, pp. 21-26; Movement Support Network, Center for Constitutional Rights, "Incidents of Intelligence Gathering and Harassment," Revised Monthly; Paul Hirshon, *Boston Globe,* May 4, 1988.

53. Ross Gelbspan, *Boston Globe,* March 15 and April 20, 1988.

54. See CCR Testimony, p. 21; E. Bruce Berman Jr., "Project Terror," *The Phoenix* (Boston), March 3, 1987; Gelbspan, *Boston Globe,* March 15, 1988.

55. CCR Testimony, pp. 19-21; Diana R. Gordon, "Varelli: In from the Cold," *The Nation,* March 7, 1987; Gelbspan, *Boston Globe,* April 20, l988.

56. Dr. Ann Mari Buitrago, "Report on CISPES Files Maintained by FBI Headquarters and Released Under the Freedom of Information Act," Center for Constitutional Rights/Fund for Open Information and Accountability, January 1988.

57. Samuel T. Francis, editor, "The Intelligence Community" in Charles L. Heatherly, ed., *Mandate for Leadership* (Washington, DC: Heritage Foundation, 1981), pp. 940-41.

58. Quoted in Ross Gelbspan, *Boston Globe,* January 27, 1988.

59. Ross Gelbspan, *Boston Globe,* June 18, 1988.

60. Quoted in Lloyd Grove, *Washington Post,* September 8, 1987.

61. Angus MacKenzie, "Conversion," *National Catholic Reporter,* November 27, 1987; Stephen Kurkjian, *Boston Globe,* September 21, 1987.

62. Garry Abrams, *Los Angeles Times,* September 20, 1987. Also see James Ridgeway, "Blood on the Tracks," *Village Voice,* September 15, 1987.

63. On the Secret Army Organization, see Donner, *Age of Surveillance,* pp. 440-46.

64. Dennis Bernstein and Connie Blitt, *In These Times,* July 22-August 4, 1987; Ross Gelbspan, *Boston Globe,* July 12, 1987 and November 7, 1987.

65. "Death Squads Invade California," *Time,* August 3, 1987.

66. "Death Squad Activity and Right-Wing Threats," Movement Support Network, Center for Constitution al Rights, October 1987.

67. CAHI, *Update* 6:12, May 11, 1987.

68. Remarks by President Daniel Ortega during the funeral service for Benjamin Linder, Matagalpa, Nicaragua, April 30, 1987, *Envio,* May 1987, pp. 34-36.

69. Daniel Lazare and Jim Naureckas, *In These Times,* May 27-June 9, 1987.

70. Ross Gelbspan, *Boston Globe,* June 18, 1988; Seth Rosenfeld, *San Francisco Examiner,* April 12, 1987.

71. North, *Taking the Stand,* pp. 643, 732-33.

72. Alfonso Chardy, *Miami Herald,* July 5, 1987.

73. Affidavit of Daniel Sheehan, pp. 5-7.

74. Louis Dubose, "The Next Round-Up," *The Texas Observer,* May 15, 1987.

75. Donner, *Age of Surveillance,* pp. 162-67.

76. Dave Lindorff, "Oliver's Martial Plan," *Village Voice,* July 21, 1987.

77. Dugger, *On Reagan,* pp. 242-43.

78. Lindorff, "Oliver's Martial Plan."

79. Stephen Engelberg, *New York Times,* January 3, 1988.

80. Johnson, *Season of Inquiry,* p. 83.

81. *Iran-Contra Report,* p. 383.

82. North, *Taking the Stand,* p. 740.

83. *Iran-Contra Report,* pp. 375-76.

84. Senator Daniel Inouye, *Taking the Stand,* pp.752-53.

85. Jack Beatty, op ed., *Boston Globe,* January 15, 1988.

Chapter 16: Crosscurrents

1. General Paul Gorman, Symposium on "Inter-American Security Policy: Political-Economic Dimensions," sponsored by the National Defense University, Fort McNair, Washington, DC, November 14, 1986.

2. Quoted in Kate Doyle and Mark Statman, *In These Times,* September 30-October 6, 1987.

3. Quoted by Julia Preston, *Washington Post,* November 17, 1986.

4. Quoted in Doyle McManus, *Los Angeles Times,* December 14, 1986.

5. See Joanne Omang, *Washington Post,* February 6, 1987; Elaine Sciolino, *New York Times,* March 15, 1987; Molly Moore, *Washington Post,* February 25, 1987.

6. Gorman, Symposium on "Inter-American Security Policy."

7. James LeMoyne, *New York Times,* December 15, 1986.

8. Author's interview with U.S. ambassador, April 29, 1986.

9. Holly Sklar, "Scenarios for Escalation," September 1986, revised version published in Pledge of Resistance Newsletter, Winter 1987, and *The National Reporter,* Spring 1987; Alfonso Chardy, *Miami Herald,* November 4, 1986; Doyle McManus, *Los Angeles Times,* December 14, 1986.

10. Jay Levin, "The U.S. Invasion of Nicaragua," *San Francisco Bay Guardian,* December 10, 1986.

11. Richard Halloran, *New York Times,* November 3, 1986.

12. Richard Halloran, *New York Times,* March 22, 1987; James LeMoyne, *New York Times,* May 15, 1987.

13. Joanne Omang, *Washington Post,* April 7, 1987.

14. Center for Defense Information, "U.S. Invasion of Nicaragua: Appraising the Option," *The Defense Monitor* XVI: 5, 1987; author's interview with retired Lt. Colonel John Buchanan, Center for Defense Information, Washington, DC, November 20, 1986.

15. Alfonso Chardy, *Miami Herald,* September 20, 1987.

16. See, for example, retired Lt. Colonel Edward L. King, "A U.S. Invasion of Nicaragua," *F.A.S. Public In terest Report* (Federation of American Scientists), October 1985.

17. Carlos Fuentes, "The Hemisphere's Best Hope is in Contadora, Not Contras," *Los Angeles Times,* March 10, 1985.

18. Joel Brinkley, *New York Times,* March 19, 1987.

19. *Boston Globe* editorial, March 24, 1987.

20. See Alfonso Chardy and Sam Dillon, *Miami Herald,* April 1, 1987.

21. Fred Kaplan, *Boston Globe,* May 20, 1987.

22. Julia Preston, *Washington Post,* March 23, 1987.

23. Rod Norland, "The New Contras?" *Newsweek,* June 1, 1987, pp. 32-38.

24. Bernard E. Trainor, *New York Times,* July 17, 1987.

25. Stephen Kinzer, *New York Times,* July 19, 1987.

26. "Fear of Signing: The Maneuvering Around the Arias Peace Plan," *International Policy Report,* July 1987, p. 4, citing *El Tiempo* (Bogota), February 4, 1987. Also see CAHI, *Update* 6:9, March 13, 1987 and 6:22, July 31, 1987.

27. James LeMoyne, *New York Times,* June 16, 1987. Also see "Fear of Signing," pp. 4-5.

28. Quoted in "Nobel Winner Oscar Arias Makes Costa Rica The Mouse That Roars For Peace In Costa Rica," *People,* November 9, 1987, pp. 57-58.

29. Elaine Sciolino, *New York Times,* June 18, 1987.

30. Roy Gutman, *Newsday,* June 19, 1987.

31. Joel Brinkley, *New York Times,* August 6 and 15, 1987.

32. Alfonso Chardy, *Miami Herald,* August 11, 1987.

33. James Chace, "The End of the Affair?" *New York Review of Books,* October 8, 1987, p. 26.

34. Neil A. Lewis, *New York Times,* September 13, 1987; Robert Healy, *Boston Globe,* September 24, 1987.

35. *Boston Globe* editorial, October 13, 1987.

36. Reuters, *New York Times,* August 27, 1987.

37. Chris Norton, *Christian Science Monitor,* September 15, 1987.

38. Neil A. Lewis, *New York Times,* September 24, 1987.

39. See, for example, CAHI, *Update* 6:28, September 14, 1987 and "The Atlantic Coast: Testing Ground for Peace," *Envio,* November 1987.

40. James LeMoyne, *New York Times,* June 7, 1987.

41. "CIA Offered Nicaraguan Rebels Financing to Continue Struggle," UPI, *Excelsior* (Mexico City), October 22, 1987.

42. Martha Honey and Tony Avirgan, "The C.I.A.'s War," *The Nation,* February 6, 1988.

43. Ana Carrigan, "Ending the Other War in Nicaragua," *The Nation,* February 6, 1988; "The Atlantic Coast: Testing Ground for Peace," p. 21.

44. Honey and Avirgan, "The C.I.A.'s War." Also see, Menonite Central Committee, *Washington Memo,* January-February 1988.

45. Address by President Reagan to the United Nations General Assembly, September 21, 1987, U.S. State Department Bureau of Public Affairs, *Current Policy* No. 1001.

46. Neil A. Lewis, *New York Times,* September 23, 1987; Associated Press, *Boston Globe,* September 24, 1987.

47. "Central America at a Critical Juncture," Address by President Reagan to the Organization of American States, Washington, DC, October 7, 1987, U.S. State Department Bureau of Public Affairs, *Current Policy* No. 1007.

48. Address of President Ortega to the General Assembly of the United Nations, New York, October 8, 1987, English translation, Nicaraguan Mission to the United Nations.

49. Paul Lewis, *New York Times,* October 9, 1987.

50. CAHI, *Update* 6:36, October 30, 1987.

51. "The Nobel Difference," *Newsweek,* October 26, 1987, p. 46. Also see Stephen Kinzer, *New York Times,* October 13, 1987.

52. Robert E. White, op ed., *New York Times,* September 21, 1987.

53. Center for International Policy, "Compliance? The Central American Peace Accord," *International Policy Report,* November 5, 1987.

54. Americas Watch, *Human Rights in Nicaragua 1986,* February 1987, pp. 155-56, 166. Also see, CAHI, *Update* 6:38, November 25, 1987.

55. James LeMoyne, *New York Times,* November 5, 1987.

56. "Cease-Fire Proposal," *Barricada Internacional,* November 19, 1987, p. 3; Neil A. Lewis, *New York Times,* November 14, 1987.

57. See George Volsky, *New York Times,* December 2, 1987.

58. Quoted in Jonathan Fuerbringer, *New York Times,* December 13, 1987.

59. Alfonso Chardy, *Miami Herald,* November 4, 1987.

60. William Branigin, *Washington Post,* December 13, 1987.

61. Center for International Policy, "The Miranda Propaganda Coup," January 1988, p. 3.

62. Stephen Kinzer, *New York Times,* December 14, 1987; *New York Times,* December 18, 1987.

63. James LeMoyne, *New York Times,* December 16, 1987.

64. Jim Mulvaney, *Newsday,* December 17, 1987.

65. Richard Halloran, *New York Times,* December 20, 1987.

66. David E. Pitt, *New York Times,* December 20, 1987.

67. *Newsweek,* December 21, 1987.

68. Quoted in Neil A. Lewis, *New York Times,* December 15, 1987.

69. Neil A. Lewis, *New York Times,* December 22, 1987; Jennifer Spevacek, *Washington Times,* December 31, 1987.

70. Pamela Constable, *Boston Globe,* December 19, 1987.

71. Washington Post, *Boston Globe,* February 4, 1988.

72. R.W. Apple, *New York Times,* December 17, 1987. Also see Neil A. Lewis, *New York Times,* December 22, 1987; Joel Brinkley, *New York Times,* December 16, 1987; Reuters, *Boston Globe,* December 17, 1987; Wire Services, *Boston Globe,* December 18, 1987.

73. *Newsweek,* January 25, 1988.

74. International Commission on Verification and Follow-Up, "Agreement on Procedure to Achieve a Firm and Lasting Peace in Central America: Report on Compliance," Unofficial translation, January 14, 1988.

75. See Committee for the Defense of Human Rights in Honduras, *The Situation of Human Rights in Honduras 1987* (Somerville, MA: Honduras Information Center).

76. See, for example, Joel Brinkley, *New York Times,* January 27, 1988 and Neil A. Lewis, *New York Times,* February 1, 1988.

77. Quoted in "Is Peace at Hand?" *Time,* April 4, 1988, p. 27.

78. Ibid., p. 28.

79. Quoted in James LeMoyne, *New York Times,* March 26, 1988.

80. Michael Manley, *Jamaica: Struggle in the Periphery* (London: Third World Media Limited/Writers and Readers Publishing Cooperative Society, 1982), pp. 208-09. Also see William Blum, *The CIA: A Forgotten History* (Atlantic Highlands, NJ: Zed Press, 1986), pp. 299-304; James Phillips, "Renovation of the International Economic Order: Trilateralism, the IMF, and Jamaica," in Sklar, ed., *Trilateralism,* pp. 468-91.

81. Manley, *Jamaica: Struggle in the Periphery,* pp. 210-11.

Chapter 17: Openings

1. CAHI, *Update* 6:32, October 26, 1987 and Ambassador Carlos Tunnermann, March 22, 1988.

2. Alfonso Chardy, *Miami Herald,* September 20, 1987.

3. Viron Vaky and Lee H. Hamilton, op ed., *New York Times,* July 31, 1987.

4. Xabier Gorostiaga, "Towards Alternative Policies for the Region," in George Irvin and Xabier Goros-tiaga, *Towards an Alternative for Central America and the Caribbean* (Boston: Allen and Unwin, 1985), pp. 17-18.

5. "Acapulco Commitment to Peace, Development and Democracy," November 29, 1987, English trans-lation, pp. 10-11.

6. Larry Rohter, *New York Times,* November 29, 1987.

7. For related progressive policy programs see Richard Fagen, *Forging Peace: The Challenge of Central America* (New York: A PACCA Book/Basil Blackwell, 1987), pp. 129-31 and Danaher et. al., *Help or Hindrance?* pp. 79-82.

8. MADRE delegation interview with Dora Maria Tellez in which the author participated, Managua, March 1984.

Index